OREGON BLUE BOOK
2005–2006

compiled and published by

Bill Bradbury
Secretary of State

Julie Yamaka, Managing Editor
Phil Wiebe, Copy Editor
Gary Halvorson, Photo and Web Editor

Archives Division
Office of the Secretary of State
Salem, Oregon 97310

Acknowledgements: Special thanks to Dick Peckham, Proofreader; Roy Turnbaugh, section development; Steve Mabry, marketing; Sarah Radley, section formatting; Stephanie Evans, Mary Beth Herkert, Layne Sawyer, Todd Shaffer and Dave Wendell, fact gathering and checking, all of the Archives Division, Secretary of State; Kim Blanding, Office of State Court Administrator; Daniel Russell, Legislative Administration; Dave Yamaka, Oregon Employment Department; Brenda Bayes and Tami Dettwyler, Elections Division, Secretary of State; Linda Crawford and Jeff Morgan, Business Services Division, Secretary of State.

www.bluebook.state.or.us

Orders:
Bill Bradbury, Secretary of State
Oregon Blue Book
255 Capitol St. NE, Suite 180
Salem, OR 97310

TABLE OF CONTENTS

Color section following page 218.

BILL BRADBURY
SECRETARY OF STATE

STATE OF OREGON
SECRETARY OF STATE
136 STATE CAPITOL
SALEM, OREGON 97310-0722

Dear Oregonian,

I'm excited to provide you with the 2005–2006 edition of the *Oregon Blue Book*! This is our 94th year publishing the *Oregon Blue Book*, and, as always, it is the most complete source of information about state history, economy, government and culture.

This year's color insert is a celebration of the centennial of the Lewis and Clark Exposition fair held in Portland in 1905. We drew information and illustrations from the exhibits of numerous historical societies throughout the state, and Governor Vic Atiyeh generously allowed us to take photographs of his private collection for this special commemoration.

In addition to updating all of the Oregon facts and figures, we've rewritten the Economy section so that it is clearer and easier to read. We always strive to make the *Oregon Blue Book* as informative and user-friendly as possible, and some of the best suggestions for improvements have come from our readers. If you have ideas on how to make the *Oregon Blue Book* better, please let me know.

The *Oregon Blue Book* is also available online. Updated each day and containing links to more information than could fit into a printed book, the online version of the *Oregon Blue Book* is a valuable resource for anyone with access to a computer. Visit www.bluebook.state.or.us.

I hope you enjoy the 2005–2006 edition of the *Oregon Blue Book* as much as I do!

Best,

Bill Bradbury
Secretary of State

Dedication

The 2005–2006 *Oregon Blue Book* is dedicated to Oregon's mentors: people who invest their time in making a positive difference in a young person's life.

Mentoring is a powerful tool to help people, young and old, reach their full potential. Mentors are trusted friends, guides, listeners, coaches, tutors and confidantes. Mentors provide stable, positive, supportive relationships between generations to improve responsibility, achievement, and chances for lifelong success.

Effective mentoring takes time, but each individual's time results in a significantly positive return to our whole community. Youth who have a mentor are less likely to skip school, use drugs or alcohol, or use violence, and are more likely to participate in community service projects, improve school performance and improve personal relationships. Adults who mentor have an improved sense of community, diversity, responsibility, communication and cooperation, as well as the positive feelings that accompany a shared achievement.

People involved in mentoring report that the impact on their lives has been truly inspirational.

To become a mentor yourself, or to find out more about mentoring, visit Oregon Mentors at www.ormentors.org.

Thank you to all of the Oregonians who have invested in our community and built positive relationships with Oregon's youth. Your time spent mentoring helps us all to build a better Oregon.

TED KULONGOSKI
Governor

To the Citizens of Oregon:

As Oregon's governor, I am honored to serve this state, with its rich history and promising future. I'm proud of Oregon. We're blessed with such abundance. Our diverse cultural heritage encompasses Native Americans, Basques, African Americans, Latinos, Asians, Russians, and more. Our ecology stretches from Hell's Canyon to the Pacific Ocean and from the mighty Columbia to the Klamath Basin.

The *Oregon Blue Book* provides information about our culture, our ecology, and our government. Oregon's tradition of citizen participation in its government processes means that we each take part in preserving our history and creating a promising future. This book gives each Oregonian the power to be a participant.

The *Blue Book* provides information about our state and about our government. Here you'll find information on state, county, and local government, government officials, boards and commissions, and our judiciary. This is the information you need to contact your government with your ideas and your commitment to Oregon's future.

Please use this resource. It's here so that you can make sure that Oregon continues to be the best place for you and your children, a place we're proud to call home.

Sincerely,

Ted Kulongoski

Native American mother holds child in papoose—Oregon State Archives Photograph, OHD-G280

Facts, like maps, provide information that helps complete a picture of Oregon. This section contains the Oregon Almanac, Oregon Olympic medal winners, the state song, and a map of Oregon.

OREGON ALMANAC

Abbreviations, Oregon: OR (postal)

Airports: 97 public; 366 private

Altitudes
  Highest: Mt. Hood (11,239')
  Lowest: Pacific Ocean (sea level)

Animal, State

The American Beaver *(Castor canadensis)* was named Oregon state animal by the 1969 Legislature. Prized for its fur, the beaver was overtrapped by early settlers and eliminated from much of its original range. Through proper management and partial protection, the beaver has been reestablished in watercourses throughout the state and remains an important economic asset. The beaver has been referred to as "nature's engineer," and its dam-building activities are important to natural water flow and erosion control. Oregon is known as the "Beaver State" and Oregon State University's athletic teams are called the "Beavers."

Apportionment, US House of Representatives

1860-1880	1
1890-1900	2
1910-1930	3
1940-1970	4
1980-2004	5

Awards (Nobel, Pulitzer)

1934 - *Medford Mail Tribune* - Pulitzer, Journalism

1939 - Ronald Callvert, *The Oregonian* - Pulitzer, Editorial Writing

1954 - Linus Pauling - Nobel, Chemistry

1957 - Wallace Turner and William Lambert, *The Oregonian* - Pulitzer, Reporting (No Edition Time)

1962 - Linus Pauling - Nobel, Peace

1999 - Richard Read - *The Oregonian* - Pulitzer, Explanatory Writing

2001 - Carl Weiman - Nobel, Physics

2001 - *The Oregonian* - Pulitzer, Public Service

2001 - Tom Hallman Jr. - *The Oregonian* - Pulitzer, Feature Writing

Beverage, State

Milk was selected in 1997 as the state beverage. The legislature recognized that milk production and the manufacture of dairy products are major contributors to the economic well-being of Oregon agriculture.

Bird, State

The Western Meadowlark *(Sturnella neglecta)* was chosen state bird in 1927 by Oregon's school children in a poll sponsored by the Oregon Audubon Society. Native throughout western North America, the bird has brown plumage with buff and black markings. Its underside is bright yellow with a black crescent on the breast; its outer tail feathers are mainly white and are easily visible when it flies. The Western Meadowlark is known for its distinctive and beautiful song.

Births
  45,128 (2003)

Borders and Boundaries
  Washington on north
  California on south
  Idaho on east
  Pacific Ocean on west
  Nevada on southeast

Buildings, Tallest (Portland)
  Wells Fargo Tower, 546', 40 stories
  US Bancorp Tower, 536', 40 stories
  KOIN Tower, 509', 35 stories

Campsites (2004) overnight use:

Overnight campsites were used by Oregonians about 55 percent of the time, while non-residents made up the other 45 percent usage.

Cities, Total Incorporated: 241
  Largest Populations (July 2003)
  1. Portland (545,140)
  2. Eugene (143,910)
  3. Salem (142,940)
  4. Gresham (93,660)
  5. Hillsboro (79,340)
  6. Beaverton (79,010)

Counties, Total: 36
  Largest Area, Sq. Mi.
  1. Harney (10,228)
  2. Malheur (9,926)
  3. Lake (8,359)
  4. Klamath (6,135)
  5. Douglas (5,071)
  Smallest Area, Sq. Mi.
  1. Multnomah (465)
  2. Hood River (533)
  3. Benton (679)
  4. Columbia (687)
  5. Yamhill (718)
  Largest Population
  1. Multnomah (677,850)
  2. Washington (472,600)
  3. Clackamas (353,450)
  4. Lane (329,400)
  5. Marion (295,900)

Dance, State

In 1977 the legislature declared the Square Dance to be the official state dance. The dance is a combination of various steps and figures danced with four couples grouped in a square. The pioneer origins of the dance and the characteristic dress are deemed to reflect Oregon's heritage; the lively spirit of the dance exemplifies the friendly, free nature and enthusiasm that are a part of the Oregon Character.

Deaths
  28,339 (2003 preliminary)

Divorces

15,401 (2003 preliminary)

Electoral Votes for President: 7

Father of Oregon

The 1957 Legislature bestowed upon Dr. John McLoughlin the honorary title of "Father of Oregon" in recognition of his great contributions to the early development of the Oregon Country. Dr. McLoughlin originally came to the Northwest region in 1824 as a representative of the Hudson's Bay Company.

Fish, State

The Chinook Salmon *(Oncorhynchus tshawytscha)*, also known as spring, king and tyee salmon, is the largest of the Pacific salmons and the most highly prized for the fresh fish trade. Declared state fish by the 1961 Legislature, the Chinook Salmon is found from southern California to the Canadian Arctic. Record catches of 53 inches and 126 pounds have been reported.

Flag, State

The Oregon state flag, adopted in 1925, is navy blue with gold lettering and symbols. Blue and gold are the state colors. On the flag's face the legend "STATE OF OREGON" is written above a shield which is surrounded by 33 stars. Below the shield, which is part of the state seal, is written "1859" the year of Oregon's admission to the union as the 33rd state. The flag's reverse side depicts a beaver. Oregon has the distinction of being the only state in the union whose flag has a different pattern on the reverse side. The dress or parade flag has a gold fringe, and the utility flag has a plain border.

Flower, State

The legislature designated the Oregon Grape *(Mahonia aquifolium)* as the Oregon state flower by resolution in 1899. A low growing plant, the Oregon Grape is native to much of the Pacific Coast and is found sparsely east of the Cascades. Its year-round foliage of pinnated, waxy green leaves resembles holly. The plant bears dainty yellow flowers in early summer and a dark blue berry that ripens late in the fall. The fruit can be used in cooking.

Gemstone, State

The 1987 Legislature designated the Oregon sunstone as the official state gemstone. Uncommon in its composition, clarity, and colors, it is a large, brightly colored transparent gem in the feldspar family. The Oregon sunstone attracts collectors and miners and has been identified as a boon to tourism and economic development in southeastern Oregon counties.

Geographic Center

In Crook County, 25 miles south-southeast of Prineville.

Geysers

Old Perpetual, north edge of Lakeview - erupts up to 60' in the air every 90 seconds.

Crump Geyser, between Crump and Pelican Lakes in Lake County.

Gorge, Deepest

Hell's Canyon - Wallowa County. Up to 7,900' in depth, the deepest gorge in North America.

Historian Laureate

For his years as keeper of Oregon's memory and heritage, the 1989 Legislature named Thomas Vaughan historian laureate of Oregon. His dedicated leadership and distinguished record of professional study and publication have brought worldwide recognition to the Oregon Historical Society and contributed greatly to historical interest and knowledge.

Hot Springs

Alvord, Antelope, Bagby, Baker's Bar M Ranch (guests only), Belknap, Breitenbush, Cove, Crystal Crane, Hunter's, Jackson, Kah-Nee-Ta, Kitson (Boy Scouts only), Lehman, McCredie Springs, McKenzie River, Mitchell, Radium, Snively, Summer Lake, Terwilliger, Umpqua, Wall Creek, Whitehorse.

Hydropower Power Projects, Largest

Bonneville Dam - Columbia River - 1938
The Dalles Dam - Columbia River - 1957
John Day Dam - Columbia River - 1971
Other Major Dams in Oregon
Owyhee Dam - Owyhee River - 1932
McNary Dam - Columbia River - 1954

Insect, State

In 1979 the legislature designated the Oregon Swallowtail *(Papilio oregonius)* as Oregon's official insect. A true native of the Northwest, the Oregon Swallowtail is at home in the lower sagebrush canyons of the Columbia River and its tributaries, including the Snake River drainage. This strikingly beautiful butterfly, predominantly yellow, is a wary, strong flier not easily captured.

Jails/Correctional Institutions

106 County operated jails; temporary holds; lockups; local correctional and juvenile detention facilities

11 county work and restitution centers

12 state institutions (including release, work centers and camps)

1 federal penal institution

Judicial Districts: 27

Lake, Deepest

Crater Lake - 1,996' (deepest in U.S.)

Lakes, Total

Approximately 1,773

Legal Holidays and Days of Special Observance

New Year's Day
12/31/04; 1/2/06; 1/1/07
Martin Luther King Jr.'s Birthday
1/17/05; 1/16/06; 1/15/07

President's Day
2/21/05; 2/20/06; 2/19/07
Memorial Day
5/30/05; 5/29/06; 5/28/07
Independence Day
7/4/05; 7/4/06; 7/4/07
Labor Day
9/5/05; 9/4/06; 9/3/07
Veterans Day
11/11/05; 11/10/06; 11/12/07
Thanksgiving Day
11/24/05; 11/23/06; 11/22/07
Christmas Day
12/26/05; 12/25/06; 12/25/07

In addition to the standing holidays described above, other days may be legal holidays in Oregon. These are: every day appointed by the governor as a holiday; and every day appointed by the president of the United States as a day of mourning, rejoicing or other special observance when the governor also appoints that day as a holiday.

Whenever a holiday falls on a Sunday, the following Monday shall be observed as the holiday. Whenever a holiday falls on a Saturday, the preceding Friday shall be observed as the holiday.

At various intervals throughout the year, the governor may also proclaim days or weeks to give special recognition and attention to individuals or groups and to promote issues and causes.

Lighthouses

Cape Arago Lighthouse - Coos Bay
Cape Blanco Lighthouse - Port Orford
Cape Meares Lighthouse - Tillamook
Cleft of the Rock Lighthouse - Yachats (privately-owned, not open to the public)
Coquille River Lighthouse - Bandon
Heceta Head Lighthouse - Florence
Port of Brookings Lighthouse - Brookings (privately-owned, not open to the public)
Tillamook Rock Lighthouse - Cannon Beach
Umpqua River Lighthouse - Reedsport
Yaquina Bay Lighthouse - Newport
Yaquina Head Lighthouse - Newport

Marriages

25,580 (2003 preliminary)

Mileage Distances, Road (from Portland)

Albuquerque, NM	1363
Atlanta, GA	2583
Boise, ID	429
Chicago, IL	2085
Denver, CO	1248
Fargo, ND	1449
Houston, TX	2206
Los Angeles, CA	962
Miami, FL	3226
New York, NY	2875
Omaha, NE	1646
Phoenix, AZ	1237
St. Louis, MO	2018
Salt Lake City, UT	765

San Francisco, CA	633
Seattle, WA	173

Mother of Oregon

Honored by the 1987 Legislature as Mother of Oregon, Tabitha Moffatt Brown "represents the distinctive pioneer heritage and the charitable and compassionate nature of Oregon's people." At 66 years of age, she financed her own wagon for the trip from Missouri to Oregon. The boarding school for orphans that she established later became known as Tualatin Academy and eventually was chartered as Pacific University.

Motto, State

"She Flies With Her Own Wings" was adopted by the 1987 Legislature as the state motto. The phrase originated with Judge Jessie Quinn Thornton and was pictured on the territorial seal in Latin: *Alis Volat Propiis*. The new motto replaces "The Union", which was adopted in 1957.

Mountains, Major

Coast Range: Highest Elevations: (north of Coquille) - Mary's Peak, Benton County: 4,097'; (south of Coquille) - Mt. Bolivar, Coos and Curry Counties: 4,319'. The Coast Range runs the length of the state along the western Coastline, from the Columbia River in the north to the Rogue River in the south. These mountains contain dense softwood forests, which historically made lumbering an important economic activity. Their eastern slopes mark the western edge of the Willamette Valley.

Klamath Mountains: The Klamath Mountains in southwestern Oregon are sometimes included as part of the Coast Range. These mountains include numerous national forest and wildlife preserves, and contain scenic portions of the Klamath River. Mt. Ashland, Jackson County, is generally regarded as the highest peak of these mountains, at 7,532'.

Cascade Range: Highest Elevations: Mt. Hood, Clackamas and Hood River Counties: 11,239'; and Mt. Jefferson, Jefferson, Linn and Marion Counties: 10,495'. This lofty mountain range extends the entire north-south length of Oregon east of the Willamette Valley. It lies about 100 to 150 miles inland from the coastline. It forms an important climactic divide, with the western slopes receiving abundant precipitation, but the eastern slopes very little. The western slopes are thus heavily wooded, with the eastern section mainly covered by grass and scrub plants. Many lakes and several large rivers are in the mountains, the latter harnessed for hydroelectric power. It is used frequently for outdoor recreation, including camping, hiking and skiing.

Blue Mountains: This northeastern Oregon mountain chain is part of the Columbia Plateau which also extends into southeastern Washington. Lava flows cover much of the surface, and the upper, wooded slopes have been used for lumbering. Recreation and livestock grazing are the mountains principal economic uses. The highest elevation is

Rock Creek Butte (9,105'), located on the Elkhorn Ridge a few miles west of Baker City.

Steens Mountain: This is a massive, 30-mile-long mountain in the Alvord Valley featuring valleys and U-shaped gorges that were cut by glaciers one million years ago. It is located in Harney County in southeastern Oregon, and is 9,773' in elevation.

Name of Oregon

The first written record of the name "Oregon" comes to us from a 1765 proposal for a journey written by Major Robert Rogers, an English army officer. It reads, "The rout . . . is from the Great Lakes towards the Head of the Mississippi, and from thence to the River called by the Indians Ouragon. . . ." His proposal rejected, Rogers re-applied in 1772, using the spelling "Ourigan." The first printed use of the current spelling appeared in Captain Jonathan Carver's 1778 book, "Travels Through the Interior Parts of North America 1766, 1767 and 1768." He listed the four great rivers of the continent, including "the River Oregon, or the River of the West, that falls into the Pacific Ocean at the Straits of Annian."

National Cemeteries

Willamette - Portland
Eagle Point - Eagle Point
Roseburg - Roseburg

National Fish Hatcheries

Eagle Creek - Estacada
Warm Springs - Warm Springs

National Forests

Deschutes, Fremont, Klamath, Malheur, Mt. Hood, Ochoco, Rogue River, Siskiyou, Siuslaw, Umatilla, Umpqua, Wallowa-Whitman, Willamette, Winema

National Monuments

John Day Fossil Beds - near Kimberly.
Newberry National Volcanic Monument - near Bend.
Oregon Caves - near Cave Junction.

National Parks

Crater Lake
Lewis & Clark National Historical Park
Nez Perce National Historical Park (Oregon, Idaho, Montana, Washington)

National Recreation Areas

Hell's Canyon National Recreation Area (Oregon, Idaho)
Oregon Dunes National Recreation Area

National Scenic Area

Columbia River Gorge

National Trails

California National Historic Trail
Lewis and Clark National Historic Trail
Oregon National Historic Trail - Length: 2,170 miles, from Independence, Missouri to the Willamette Valley, Oregon. Passes through Missouri, Kansas, Nebraska, Wyoming, Idaho, Oregon.

National Wildlife Refuges

Ankeny - near Jefferson.
Bandon Marsh - near Bandon.
Baskett Slough - near Dallas.
Bear Valley - near Klamath Falls.
Cape Meares - near Tillamook.
Cold Springs - near Hermiston.
Hart Mountain National Antelope Refuge - northeast of Lakeview.
Klamath Marsh - near Chiloquin.
Lewis and Clark - islands in lower Columbia River.
Malheur - southeast of Burns.
McKay Creek - near Pendleton.
Mid-Columbia River complex.
Nestucca Bay - near Pacific City.
Oregon Islands - off central and south-central Oregon coast.
Siletz Bay - near Lincoln City.
Three Arch Rocks - off coast near Oceanside.
Tualatin - near Sherwood.
Umatilla - near Irrigon.
Upper Klamath - northwest of Klamath Falls.
Western Oregon complex.
William L. Finley - southwest of Corvallis.

Native Americans

10 federally-recognized tribes:
Burns Paiute Tribe
Confederated Tribes of Coos, Lower Umpqua and Siuslaw Indians
Confederated Tribes of Grand Ronde
Confederated Tribes of Siletz
Confederated Tribes of the Umatilla Indian Reservation
Confederated Tribes of Warm Springs Reservation
Coquille Indian Tribe
Cow Creek Band of Umpqua Indians
Fort McDermitt Shoshone-Paiute (Oregon, Idaho)
Klamath Tribe
5 reservations
48,341 individuals (2000 Census)

Nut, State

The hazelnut *(Corylus avellana)* was named state nut by the 1989 Legislature. Oregon grows 99 percent of the entire U.S. commercial crop. The Oregon hazelnut, unlike wild varieties, grows on single-trunked trees up to 30 or 40 feet tall. Adding a unique texture and flavor to recipes and products, hazelnuts are preferred by chefs, bakers, confectioners, food manufacturers and homemakers worldwide.

Park Areas, State

240 (2004)

Physical Dimensions

U.S. Rank in Area = 10
Land Area = 96,002 sq. mi.
Water Area = 1,129 sq. mi.
Coastline = 296 miles

Population

1850 = 12,093	1960 = 1,768,687
1860 = 52,465	1970 = 2,091,533
1870 = 90,923	1980 = 2,633,321
1880 = 174,768	1990 = 2,842,321
1890 = 317,704	1994 = 3,082,000
1900 = 413,536	1996 = 3,181,000
1910 = 672,765	1999 = 3,393,410
1920 = 783,389	2000 = 3,421,399
1930 = 953,786	2001 = 3,471,700
1940 = 1,089,684	2002 = 3,504,700
1950 = 1,521,341	2003 = 3,541,500

Precipitation, Record Maximum

(24 hours, through 1998)

Measured at Elk River Fish Hatchery near Port Orford: 11.65", 11/19/96.

Average yearly precipitation at Salem: 40.22"

Reservoir, Longest: Lake Owyhee - 52 miles

Rivers, Longest

Partially in the State of Oregon:

Columbia River - 1,243 miles

Snake River - 1,038 miles

Entirely in the State of Oregon:

Willamette River - approx. 300 miles

John Day River - 281 miles

Rock, State

The Thunder-egg (geode) was named state rock by the 1965 Legislature after rockhounds throughout Oregon voted it first choice. Thunder-eggs range in diameter from less than one inch to over four feet. Nondescript on the outside, they reveal exquisite designs in a wide range of colors when cut and polished. They are found chiefly in Crook, Jefferson, Malheur, Wasco and Wheeler counties.

Schools (2003)

Education Service Districts	20
School Districts	198
Student population, public schools	551,290

Seal, State

The state seal consists of an escutcheon, or shield, supported by 33 stars and divided by an ordinary, or ribbon, with the inscription "The Union". Above the ordinary are the mountains and forests of Oregon, an elk with branching antlers, a covered wagon and ox team, the Pacific Ocean with setting sun, a departing British man-of-war signifying the departure of British influence in the region and an arriving American merchant ship signifying the rise of American power. Below the ordinary is a quartering with a sheaf of wheat, plow and pickax, which represent Oregon's mining and agricultural resources. The crest is the American Eagle. Around the perimeter of the seal is the legend "State of Oregon 1859". A resolution adopted by the Constitutional Convention in session on September 17, 1857, authorized the president to appoint a committee of three—Benjamin F. Burch, L.F. Grover and James K. Kelly—to report on a proper device for the seal of the state of Oregon. Harvey Gordon created a draft, to which the committee recommended certain additions that are all incorporated in the state seal.

Seashell, State

In 1848, a conchologist (shell expert) named Redfield named the *Fusitriton oregonensis* after the Oregon Territory. Commonly called the Oregon hairy triton, the shell is one of the largest found in the state, reaching lengths up to five inches. The shells are found from Alaska to California and wash up on the Oregon coast at high tide. The legislature named the state shell in 1991.

Shoes, Oldest

9,000-year-old sandals made of sagebrush and bark found at Fort Rock Cave in central Oregon in 1938 by archaeologist Luther Cressman.

Skiing

Downhill

Anthony Lakes - near Union.

Ski Ashland - near Ashland.

Mt. Bachelor - near Bend.

Mt. Bailey snocat skiing - east of Roseburg.

Cooper Spur - Mt. Hood.

Ferguson Ridge - near Joseph.

Hoodoo - west of Sisters.

Mt. Hood Meadows - Mt. Hood.

SkiBowl - Mt. Hood.

Summit - Government Camp.

Timberline - Mt. Hood.

Warner Canyon - near Lakeview.

Willamette Pass - near Oakridge.

Cross Country

National Forests: Deschutes; Malheur; Mt. Hood; Ochoco; Rogue River; Umatilla; Umpqua; Wallowa-Whitman; Willamette; Winema. Also Crater Lake National Park and Hell's Canyon National Recreation Area.

Song, State

J.A. Buchanan of Astoria and Henry B. Murtagh of Portland wrote "Oregon, My Oregon," in 1920. With this song, Buchanan and Murtagh won a statewide competition sponsored by the Society of Oregon Composers, gaining statewide recognition. The song became the official state song in 1927.

Standard of Time

The officially adopted standard established by Congress in 1918;

Exception: Pacific Daylight Time begins every spring at 2:00 a.m. on the first Sunday in April:

4/3/05

4/2/06

4/1/07

Reverts back to Pacific Standard Time at 2:00 a.m. on the last Sunday in October:

10/30/05

10/29/06

10/28/07

Most of Malheur County along the Idaho border is in the Mountain Time Zone.

Temperatures, Record
Highest: 119°F on August 10, 1898 in Pendleton
Lowest: -54°F on February 10, 1933 in Seneca
Average Jan/July Temp.:

Burns........................... Jan 30.5°/July 73.1°
Grants Pass .... Jan 39.3°/July 69.2°
Newport .... Jan 45.0°/July 57.9°
Redmond..................... Jan 33.3°/July 66.7°
Salem .... Jan 40.3°/July 66.8°

Tree, State
The Douglas-fir *(Pseudotsuga menziesii)*, named for David Douglas, a 19th century Scottish botanist, was designated state tree in 1939. Great strength, stiffness and moderate weight make it an invaluable timber product said to be stronger than concrete. Averaging up to 200' in height and six feet in diameter, heights of 325' and diameters of 15' can also be found.

Trees, Giant (National Champions located in Oregon from the National Register of Big Trees)
Arroyo Willow: 3' 7" circumference, 27' tall, located near Sheep Creek, 8.226 USGC marker.

Baker Cypress: 10' 9" circumference, 129' tall, located in Rogue River National Forest.

Big Leaf Maple: 34' 11" circumference, 101' tall, located south of Jewell on Hwy. 103.

Big Sagebrush: 1' 8" circumference, 13' tall, located in Crooked River National Grassland.

Birchleaf Cercocarpus: 3' 8" circumference, 34' tall, located about 3 miles west of Central Point.

Black Cottonwood: 26' 8" circumference, 158' tall, located north of Salem in Willamette Mission State Park.

Black Walnut: 23' 2" circumference, 130' tall, located on Sauvies Island off NW Gillihan Rd.

Blackbead Elder: 3' 3" circumference, 42' tall, located on Hwy. 30 near Prescott.

Blueblossom (Blue-Myrtle): 2' 8" circumference, 41' tall, located on Rogue River near Agness.

Buckthorn Cascara: Co-champions - 8' 3" circumference, 37' tall, located in Clatsop County; 9' 1" circumference, 27' tall, located in Lane County.

California Black Oak: 28' 2" circumference, 124' tall, located 62 miles northwest of Grants Pass.

California Hazelnut: 5' 6" circumference, 50' tall, located at 567 N Bear Creek Rd. in Otis.

Chickasaw Plum: 10' 10" circumference, 86' tall, located in Clatsop State Forest.

Garden Plum: 10' 10" circumference, 47' tall, located at 434 NW 19th Ave. in Portland.

Hinds Willow: 4' 10" circumference, 50' tall, located on Parker Ranch in Jackson County.

Hooker Willow: 5' 5" circumference, 50' tall, located off Miami Forest Rd. north of Tillamook.

Klamath Plum: 3' 6" circumference, 28' tall, located at 1141 Lake Shore Dr. at south end of Klamath Lake.

Monterey Pine: 17' 4" circumference, 95' tall, located in Shore Acres State Park, Coos County.

Narrowleaf Cottonwood: 26' 2" circumference, 79' tall, located in Ironside, Malheur County.

Northwestern Paper Birch: 3' 10" circumference, 66' tall, located on state land near the Minam River.

Oregon Ash: 23' 8" circumference, 65' tall, located on Sauvies Island.

Oregon White Oak: 22' 8" circumference, 98' tall, located off Hwy. 42 in Douglas County.

Pacific Dogwood: 14' 1" circumference, 60' tall, located on Rutters Rd. near Old Quincy Grade School north of Clatskanie.

Pacific Red Elder: 4' 8" circumference, 27' tall, located along Hwy. 101 between Hemlock and Beaver.

Pacific Yew: 13' 4" circumference, 70' tall, located in Washington County.

Port Orford Cedar: 37' 7" circumference, 219' tall, located in Siskiyou National Forest about 10 miles southeast of Powers on the Elk Creek Rd.

Quaking Aspen: 10' circumference, 136' tall, located in Umatilla National Forest.

Red Alder: 20' 5" circumference, 104' tall, located about 15 miles southeast of Astoria off Hwy. 202 along the Klaskanine River.

Rocky Mountain Douglas-Fir: 26' 4" circumference, 139' tall, located in Deschutes National Forest near Jefferson Lake Trail.

Silver Buffaloberry: 6' 6" circumference, 22' tall, located near the Oregon/Nevada state line in Malheur County.

Sitka Mountain Ash: 1' 7" circumference, 50' tall, located one mile east of Coquille.

Sitka Spruce: 56' 1" circumference, 206' tall, located in Klootchy Creek Park, Clatsop County.

Tanoak: 22' 11" circumference, 144' tall, located near Ophir in Curry County.

Tracy Willow: 3' 0" circumference, 20' tall, located at 75 Dean Dr. in Central Point.

Vine Maple: 4' 8" circumference, 40' tall, located near Nehalem Fish Hatchery in Tillamook County.

Water Birch: 9' 5" circumference, 53' tall, located near Milepost 11 on Little Sheep Creek Hwy. between Joseph and Imnaha.

Wavyleaf Silktassel: 2' 4" circumference, 29' tall, located in Azalea Park at Brookings.

White Alder: 12' 5" circumference, 92' tall, located in West Salem near Eola.

Water, Largest Natural Bodies (surface acres)
Upper Klamath Lake - 58,922
Malheur Lake - 49,000
Note: Size varies depending on the season, so at times Malheur Lake may have a larger surface area than Upper Klamath Lake.

Waterfall, Highest
Multnomah Falls - 620'

Oregon Olympic Medalists
(1906–2004)

1906

Kerrigan, Bert H.W.	High Jump	Bronze

1908

Gilbert, Alfred C.	Pole Vault	Gold
Kelly, Dan	Long Jump	Silver
Smithson, Forrest	Hurdles	Gold

1912

Hawkins, Martin	Hurdles	Bronze

1920

Balbach, Louis J.	Diving	Bronze
Kuehn, Louis (Hap)	Diving	Gold
Ross, Norman	Swimming	Gold (3)
Samborn-Payne, Thelma	Diving	Bronze
Sears, Robert	Fencing	Bronze

1924

Newton, Chester	Wrestling	Silver
Reed, Robin	Wrestling	Gold

1928

Hamm, Edward B.	Broad Jump	Gold

1932

Graham, Norris	Rowing	Gold
Hill, Ralph	Track and Field	Silver
LaBorde, Henri J.	Discus	Silver

1936

Dunn, Gordon G.	Discus	Silver

1948

Beck, Lewis W. Jr.	Basketball	Gold
Brown, David P.	Rowing	Gold
Gordien, Fortune	Discus	Bronze
Helser (DeMorelos), Brenda	Swimming	Gold
Zimmerman-Edwards, Suzanne	Swimming	Silver

1952

Proctor, Hank	Rowing	Gold
Smith, William T.	Wrestling	Gold

1956

Fifer, James	Rowing	Gold
Gordien, Fortune	Discus	Silver
Tarala, Harold	Ice Hockey	Gold

1960

Dischinger, Terry G.	Basketball	Gold
Imhoff, Darrall	Basketball	Gold

1964

Carr, Ken	Basketball	Gold
Counts, Mel G.	Basketball	Gold
Dellinger, William S.	Track and Field	Bronze
Freeman, Kevin	Equestrian	Silver
Saubert, Jean M.	Skiing	Silver/Bronze
Schollander, Don	Swimming	Gold (4)

1968

Fosbury, Richard D.	High Jump	Gold

Freeman, Kevin	Equestrian	Silver
Garrigus, Thomas I.	Trapshooting	Silver
Sanders, Richard J.	Wrestling	Silver
Schollander, Don	Swimming	Gold/Bronze

1972

Freeman, Kevin	Equestrian	Silver
Peyton McDonald, Kim	Swimming	Gold
Sanders, Richard J.	Wrestling	Silver

1976

Peyton McDonald, Kim	Swimming	Gold
Wilkins, Mac M.	Discus	Gold

1984

Burke, Douglas L.	Water Polo	Silver
Herland, Douglas J.	Rowing	Bronze
Huntley (Ruete), Joni	High Jump	Bronze
Johnson, William D.	Skiing	Gold
King (Brown), Judith	Track and Field	Silver
Menken-Schaudt, Carol	Basketball	Gold
Schultz, Mark P.	Wrestling	Gold
Wilkins, Mac M.	Discus	Silver

1988

Brown, Cynthia L.	Basketball	Gold
Lang, Brent	Swimming	Gold

1992

Jorgenson, Dan	Swimming	Bronze

1994

Street, Picabo	Skiing	Silver

1996

Deal, Lance	Hammer	Silver
MacMillan, Shannon	Soccer	Gold
Milbrett, Tiffany	Soccer	Gold
Schneider, Marcus	Rowing	Bronze
Steding, Katy	Basketball	Gold

1998

Street, Picabo	Skiing	Gold

2000

French, Michelle	Soccer	Silver
Kinkade, Mike	Baseball	Gold
Lindland, Matt	Wrestling	Silver
MacMillan, Shannon	Soccer	Silver
Milbrett, Tiffany	Soccer	Silver
Thompson, Chris	Swimming	Bronze

2002

Steele, Dan	Bobsled	Bronze
Klug, Chris	Snow Board	Bronze

2004

Hansen, Joey	Rowing	Gold
Johnson, Kate	Rowing	Silver
Zagunis, Mariel	Fencing	Gold

Olympic medal information courtesy of Jack Elder, Olympian, Luge 1972.

State Song

Words
J.A. Buchanan

Music
Henry B. Murtagh

"Oregon, My Oregon"

Land of the
Land of the

Empire Builders, Land of the Gold-en   West;   Con-quered and held by free men,
rose and sunshine, Land of the sum-mer's breeze;   Lad - en with health and vig-or,

Fair - est   and the best.   On-ward and up-ward ev - er,   Forward and on, and
Fresh from the Western seas.   Blest by the blood of mar - tyrs,   Land of the set-ting

on;   Hail to thee, Land of He - roes, My O - re - gon.
sun;   Hail to thee, Land of Prom - ise, My O - re - gon.

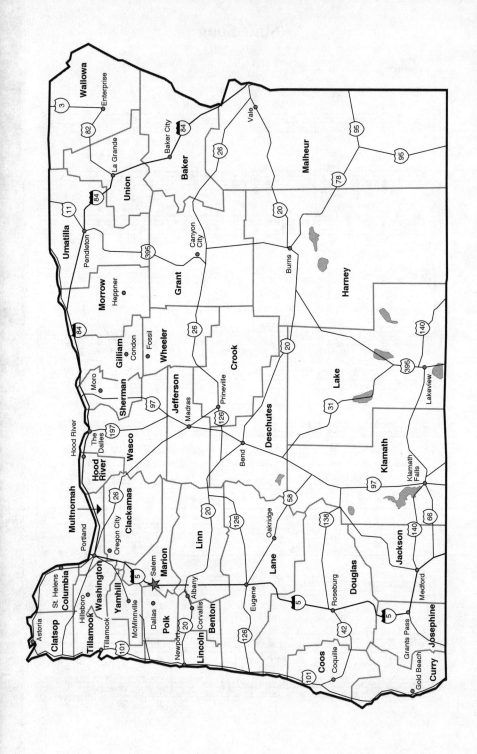

Tugboat pulls log raft on Umpqua River near Reedsport—Oregon State Archives Photograph, OHD-5322

Oregonians elect six statewide officials to manage the executive branch of government. These officials are the governor, secretary of state, treasurer, attorney general, commissioner of labor and industries, and superintendent of public instruction. This section describes the executive branch of government and introduces these six statewide officials.

THEODORE R. KULONGOSKI was born in rural Missouri on November 5, 1940. After graduating from high school, he enlisted in the U.S. Marine Corps. Kulongoski was honorably discharged and, on returning from overseas duty and with the help of the GI bill, he put himself through the University of Missouri, where he earned both his undergraduate and law degrees.

Kulongoski moved to Oregon in 1970 and began practicing law in Eugene. He was elected to the House of Representatives (1974) and to the State Senate (1978), representing parts of Lane and Douglas counties. In 1987, he was appointed Insurance Commissioner.

Kulongoski was elected Attorney General in 1992 and he was elected to the Oregon Supreme Court in 1996 where he served for 4 1/2 years. With the distinction of having served in all three branches of state government, Kulongoski brings legal, administrative and legislative knowledge and expertise to the office of governor.

In his 30 years of public service, Kulongoski has brought together the people of Oregon to solve some of our state's most difficult issues, from protecting older Oregonians from fraud and abuse, to improving minimum wage and worker safety laws, to ensuring that Oregon's children are well-educated, healthy and safe.

Kulongoski and his wife, Mary, have three grown children.

Governor Theodore R. Kulongoski

254 State Capitol, Salem 97310; 503-378-3111

Governor Theodore R. Kulongoski, Salem; Democrat; elected 2002; inaugurated January 13, 2003; term expires January 2007.

The governor is elected to a four-year term and is limited to two terms in office. The governor must be a U.S. citizen, at least 30 years old, and an Oregon resident for three years before taking office.

The governor provides leadership, planning and coordination for the executive branch of state government. He appoints many department and agency heads within the executive branch and appoints members to more than 200 policymaking, regulatory and advisory boards and commissions.

The governor proposes a two-year budget to the legislature, recommends a legislative program to each regular session and may also call special sessions. He reviews all bills passed by the legislature and may veto measures he believes are not in the public interest.

The governor chairs both the State Land Board, which manages state-owned lands, and the Progress Board, which sets strategic goals for Oregon. The governor directs state government's coordination with local and federal governments and is commander-in-chief of the state's military forces.

The governor appoints judges to fill vacancies in judicial office, has extradition authority and may grant reprieves, commutations and pardons of criminal sentences.

If the office of governor becomes vacant, the office passes, in order, to the secretary of state, state treasurer, president of the Senate and speaker of the House of Representatives. There is no lieutenant governor in Oregon.

For additional information, see page 18.

BILL BRADBURY *was born in Chicago, Illinois. He graduated from the University of Chicago Laboratory High School and attended Antioch College in Yellow Springs, Ohio.*

Before entering public life, Bradbury owned a restaurant in Bandon and worked as a television news reporter, director and producer in San Francisco, Bandon, Eugene, Coos Bay and Portland. He was elected to represent the south coast in the legislature, both as a State Representative and a State Senator. Bradbury served in the legislature from 1981 to 1995 and during his tenure he was Senate Majority Leader and Senate President.

Prior to becoming Secretary of State, Bradbury served as Executive Director of For the Sake of the Salmon—*a nonprofit organization dedicated to finding common ground for salmon restoration in Oregon, Washington and California.*

In November 1999, Governor Kitzhaber appointed him Secretary of State and in November 2000, Bradbury was elected to a four-year term. Secretary Bradbury's continued priorities include protecting the integrity of Oregon's election process and increasing voter participation, improving the performance of government through strategic auditing, facilitating business operations, protecting public access to government records and ensuring the responsible stewardship of state-owned lands. He also continues to emphasize making the information assets of the Secretary of State's office more readily available on the Internet.

Bill Bradbury is married to Katy Eymann of Mohawk Valley, Oregon. He has two grown daughters from a prior marriage, Abby and Zoe.

Secretary of State Bill Bradbury

136 State Capitol, Salem 97310-0722; 503-986-1523

Bill Bradbury, Bandon; Democrat; appointed 1999; elected 2000; reelected 2004; term expires January 2009. The secretary of state is the auditor of public accounts and chief elections officer, chair of the Oregon Sustainability Board, keeps records of official acts of the legislature and Executive Department, is custodian of the state seal, oversees the State Archives and the Corporation Division and serves on the State Land Board.

As auditor, the secretary examines and audits accounts of all publicly funded boards, commissions and agencies. As chief elections officer, he interprets and applies state election laws and supervises all elections, local and statewide. The secretary codifies, edits and publishes the administrative rules for state agencies, processes public documents, prepares notary applications and serves as filing officer for Uniform Commercial Code financial statements and security agreements.

The Archives Division, established in 1947, houses and provides access to the permanently valuable records of Oregon government. The oldest documents in the archives include records of the provisional and territorial governments and the original Oregon Constitution. The division provides records management advice and assistance to state agencies and political subdivisions and operates the State Records Center, which provides storage for inactive state agency records. The division also files, codifies and publishes state agency administrative rules and publishes the *Oregon Blue Book*.

The Corporation Division registers all domestic and foreign businesses, profit and nonprofit corporations, assumed business names and trade and service marks.

As a member of the State Land Board, the secretary shares responsibility with the governor and state treasurer in supervising management of state-owned lands, including offshore, grazing and timberlands; coastal estuarine tidelands and submerged and submersible lands along the state's navigable waterways.

For additional information, see page 19.

RANDALL EDWARDS was born in Eugene, Oregon on August 13, 1961 and raised in Walla Walla, Washington where he spent his summers working the wheat and pea harvests. Edwards earned a Bachelor's degree in economics from Colorado College in 1983 and a Masters of Business Administration from George Washington University in 1990.

Edwards was elected to the House of Representatives in 1996. In the legislature, he was a financial leader—improving school funding, saving taxpayers money through the creation of the Oregon School Bond Guaranty Act, and pushing into law an innovative financing plan to rebuild Oregon's State Parks. He also authored the Treasury's College Savings Plan, which allows Oregonians to save $2,000 a year tax free for college. From 1992–96, Edwards was a manager and senior advisor at the Oregon Treasury. Edwards was elected State Treasurer in 2000.

Edwards' professional experience also includes tenures as managing partner for EDJE Consulting and as an International Trade Analyst, U.S. Department of Commerce.

He and his wife, Julia Brim-Edwards, live in Portland with their three young children. Edwards is a school volunteer, and he serves on the Citizen Education Commission and the Trillium Family Services Board.

State Treasurer Randall Edwards

900 Court St. NE, Rm. 159, Salem 97301-4043; 503-378-4329

Randall Edwards, Portland; Democrat; elected 2000; reelected 2004; term expires January 2009. The state treasurer is a constitutional officer and a statewide elected official. The treasurer serves a four-year term and, if re-elected, can hold office for two terms.

The treasurer serves as the chief financial officer for the state and is responsible for the prudent financial management of billions of taxpayer dollars. The treasurer also serves as the state's chief investment officer, and has the duty of investing the moneys of the Public Employees Retirement Fund, the State Accident Insurance Fund, the Common School Fund and numerous smaller funds.

The treasurer serves on a variety of state financial boards and on the State Land Board which has a fiduciary duty to manage state trust lands for the benefit of the Common School Fund.

Over the years, the Treasury has evolved into a highly sophisticated organization with a wide range of financial responsibilities, including managing the investment of state funds, issuing state bonds, serving as the central bank for state agencies and administering the Oregon 529 College Savings Network.

The Treasury manages a portfolio of approximately $56 billion, with investments ranging from common stock, bonds, and real estate to alternative equity investments, foreign stocks, and U.S. Treasuries.

For additional information, see page 21.

HARDY MYERS was born in Electric Mills, Mississippi on October 25, 1939. He was educated in the public schools of Bend and Prineville before graduating from the University of Oregon in 1964 with an LL.B.

Myers served as law clerk to United States District Judge William East from 1964–65. He has been in private law practice with Stoel Rives and predecessor firms since 1965 specializing in labor and employment law and government affairs law. He is a member of the Oregon State Bar and Multnomah County Bar Association.

First elected to the House of Representatives in 1975, Myers served as a state representative for 10 years and as Speaker of the House from 1979–83. He also served as a Councilor for the Metropolitan Service District from 1985–86.

Other professional activities include serving as co-chair of the Governor's Task Force on State Employee Compensation (1995), chair of the Governor's Task Force on State Employee Benefits (1994), chair of the Oregon Criminal Justice Council (1987–91), chair of the Oregon Jail Project (1984–86) and chair of the Citizen's Task Force on Mass Transit Policy.

Married to Mary Ann Thalhofer of Prineville, the attorney general and his wife live in Portland and have three children.

Attorney General Hardy Myers

Justice Building, Salem 97310; 503-378-4400

Hardy Myers, Portland; Democrat; elected 1996; reelected 2000; reelected 2004; term expires January 2009. The attorney general is the chief legal officer of the state of Oregon and heads the Department of Justice and its six operating divisions.

The attorney general controls and supervises all court actions and legal proceedings in which the state of Oregon is a party or has an interest. The attorney general also has full charge and control of all legal business of all state departments, boards and commissions that require the services of legal counsel. He prepares ballot titles for measures to be voted upon by the people of Oregon and appoints the assistant attorneys general to act as counsel for the various state departments, boards and commissions.

The attorney general gives written opinions upon any question of law in which the state or any public subdivision may have an interest when requested by the governor, any state agency official or any member of the legislature. The attorney general and his assistants are prohibited by law from rendering opinions or giving legal advice to any other persons or agencies.

Services and responsibilities of the attorney general and the Department of Justice are: representation of the state's interests in all civil and criminal cases before the state and federal courts; consumer protection and information services; supervision of charitable trusts and solicitations; enforcement of state and federal antitrust laws in Oregon; assistance to the state's district attorneys; administration of the state crime victims' compensation program; investigations of organized crime and public corruption; and the establishment and enforcement of child support obligations for families who receive public assistance.

The term of office for attorney general is four years.

For additional information, see page 23.

DAN GARDNER was born in Peoria, Illinois on November 23, 1958.

Gardner was first elected to represent Oregon's 13th house district in 1996, where he served until 2002. He was unanimously chosen by his colleagues to serve as House Democratic Leader in 2000, and he served as Assistant Democratic Leader during the 1999 session.

Gardner is a third generation journeyman electrician. He has been a licensed electrician for 28 years, and served as vice-president of the International Brotherhood of Electrical Workers (IBEW) Local 48. He completed his National Joint Electrical Apprenticeship in 1985. He attended Illinois Central College, Portland Community and Mt. Hood Community Colleges.

Gardner lives in Milwaukie with his wife and children. He was elected Labor Commissioner May 21, 2002.

Commissioner of Labor and Industries Dan Gardner

800 NE Oregon St., #32, Portland 97232; 503-731-4070

The commissioner is chief executive of the Bureau of Labor and Industries. The commissioner also serves as chairperson of the State Apprenticeship and Training Council and executive secretary of the Wage and Hour Commission. The term of the commissioner is four years.

The commissioner enforces state laws prohibiting discrimination in employment, housing, public accommodation, and vocational, professional and trade schools, and has authority to initiate a "commissioner's complaint" on behalf of victims of discrimination.

Through the Wage and Hour Division, the commissioner administers state laws relating to wages, hours of employment, basic working conditions, child labor and prevailing wage rates; and licenses certain industries to ensure quality professional services. The division administers the Wage Security Fund that covers workers for unpaid wages in

certain business closure situations, and enforces group-health insurance termination-notification provisions.

The commissioner also oversees the state's registered apprenticeship-training system through giving workers the opportunity to learn a job skill while earning a living. The program benefits employers with a pool of skilled workers to meet business and industry demands.

Through administrative services, the commissioner provides public education programs to help employers comply with the law, and conducts administrative hearings. A hearings unit convenes administrative law proceedings in contested cases for wage and hour and civil rights determinations. Final orders in contested cases are issued by the commissioner.

For additional information, see page 25.

SUSAN CASTILLO was born in Los Angeles, California on August 14, 1951. She received a Bachelor of Arts in Communications from Oregon State University. Prior to entering public office, she enjoyed a long career as an award-winning television journalist.

The first Hispanic woman in the Oregon Legislative Assembly, Castillo served in the State Senate from 1997 to 2002. She was Vice-Chair of the Senate Education Committee and Assistant Democratic Leader for the 1999 and 2001 legislative sessions. She also served on the Health and Human Services Committee, Governor's Advisory Committee on DUII, Oregon Commission on Hispanic Affairs, Advisory Committee on Agricultural Labor, and the Transportation Committee.

During her legislative career, Castillo was recognized by the Oregon Library Association, the Oregon Nurses Association, the Oregon League of Conservation Voters, Centro LatinoAmericano, the Oregon Youth Authority, and Soroptomist International of the Americas.

Castillo is a member of the Lane Business Education Compact and the American Leadership Forum, and she has served as a board member for the Oregon State Commission on Hispanic Affairs. She is also a dedicated board member of Birth to Three, a nationally recognized nonprofit organization devoted to educating and supporting new parents.

Castillo and her husband, Paul Machu, live in Eugene.

Superintendent of Public Instruction Susan Castillo

255 Capitol St. NE, Salem 97310-0203; 503-378-3600

Susan Castillo, Eugene; Democrat; elected in 2002; term expires January 2007. The Oregon Constitution, Article VIII established the office of the State Superintendent of Public Instruction. The superintendent is elected by the people of Oregon and acts as administrative officer of the State Board of Education and executive head of the Department of Education. The term of office for superintendent is four years.

The superintendent is responsible for providing statewide leadership for some 551,290 elementary and secondary students in Oregon's 198 school districts. The responsibility also extends to public preschool programs, the state Schools for the Blind and the Deaf, regional programs for children with disabilities and education programs for young people in statewide juvenile corrections facilities. The superintendent recommends policy to the State Board of Education, which adopts rules affecting local schools. The department also coordinates with 20 education service districts that provide specialized resources and programs to school districts in their regions.

The Oregon Department of Education is responsible for providing leadership in statewide curriculum programs, school improvement efforts and statewide testing. In addition, the department acts as a liaison and monitors implementation for a variety of state and federal programs.

In conjunction with the legislature's actions, the superintendent and State Board of Education set priorities designed to lead the state's efforts in early childhood education; improve education, particularly in reading, for all students in Oregon's public elementary and secondary schools; close the achievement gap; and improving high school graduation rate and further reducing the drop-out rate.

For additional information, see page 27.

OFFICE OF THE GOVERNOR

Theodore R. Kulongoski, Governor
Address: State Capitol Bldg., 900 Court St. NE, Salem 97301-4047
Phone: 503-378-3111
Fax: 503-378-8970
Web: www.governor.oregon.gov
Duties and Responsibilities: The governor is the chief executive of Oregon. The Oregon Constitution charges the governor with faithfully executing the laws, making recommendations to the legislature and transacting all necessary business of government. The governor may veto bills of the legislature and shall fill vacancies by appointment.

Theresa McHugh is Governor Kulongoski's Chief of Staff. Peter Cogswell is the Deputy Chief of Staff. Stephen Schneider is Senior Advisor. The governor's policy advisors include: MardiLyn Saathoff, Legal Counsel; Erinn Kelley-Siel, Health and Human Services; Jim Brown, Natural Resources; Craig Campbell, Public Safety; Chris Warner, Legislative Liaison; Nancy Goss Duran, Executive Appointments; James Sager, Education and Workforce; Tom Chamberlain, Labor; and Ray Naff, Intergovernmental Affairs. Mary Ellen Glynn is Communications Director/Press Secretary, Teri Lemman is the governor's assistant and scheduler, and Leann Wilcox is the office administrator.

Advocate's Office for Minority, Women and Emerging Small Businesses

Address: 155 Cottage St. NE, Salem 97301
Phone: 503-378-3506
Contact: Lydia Muniz, Advocate
Duties and Responsibilities: The Advocate is appointed by the governor and serves as a policy advisor to the governor on issues related to minority, women and emerging small businesses, and creates access to contracting opportunities for certified firms.

Affirmative Action Office

Address: 155 Cottage St. NE, Salem 97301
Phone: 503-373-7444
Fax: 503-378-3139
Contact: Peggy C. Ross, Director
Duties and Responsibilities: The Affirmative Action Office directs and monitors affirmative action programs in all state agencies, a large portion of which is done on the basis of plans developed by state agencies. The director of affirmative action works closely with each state agency to assess its recruitment, placement, promotion and training practices with respect to achieving affirmative action goals. The director recommends and participates in affirmative action and equal opportunity training for state employees at all levels.

Arrest and Return (Extradition)

Address: 155 Cottage St. NE, U50, Salem 97301-3969
Phone: 503-378-3156, ext. 225
Fax: 503-378-3518
E-mail: frances.lushenko@state.or.us
Contact: Fran Lushenko, Extradition Officer
Duties and Responsibilities: Arrest and Return provides administrative services for Oregon's extradition program.

Citizens' Representative Office

Address: State Capitol Bldg., 900 Court St. NE, Salem 97301-4047
Phone: 503-378-4582
Fax: 503-378-4863
Contact: Liz Kiren, Citizens' Representative
Duties and Responsibilities: The Citizens' Representative Office provides access and help for citizens who have problems, questions, ideas or suggestions about state government. The office uses supervised student interns and volunteer help to work with the heavy volume of mail and telephone calls. The citizens' representative reports regularly to the governor, noting issues in state government that need attention. The Citizens' Representative Office aims to treat all inquiries fairly, to examine each situation objectively and to respond in a clear and helpful way.

Economic Revitalization Team

Address: Public Service Bldg., Rm. 126, 255 Capitol St. NE, Salem 97301
Phone: 503-986-6520
Fax: 503-378-3225
E-mail: maryanne.engle@state.or.us
Contact: Ray Naff, Intergovernmental Relations
Duties and Responsibilities: The Economic Revitalization Team provides coordinated state agency services to help local communities with their high-priority challenges, including a streamlined process to certify industrial lands and ready the state for a more aggressive and coordinated economic development plan.

Natural Resource Office

Address: State Capitol Building, 900 Court St. NE, Salem 97301-4047
Phone: 503-986-6525
Fax: 503-378-3225
Web: www.governor.oregon.gov
Contact: Mike Carrier, Governor's Natural Resource Policy Director
Statutory Authority: ORS 173.610
Duties and Responsibilities: The governor's Natural Resource Office develops and coordinates State of Oregon policies for federal forest and natural resource planning and endangered species issues.

Office of Education and Workforce Policy

Address: Public Service Bldg., Rm. 126, 255 Capitol St. NE, Salem 97301
Phone: 503-986-6545
Fax: 503-378-3225
E-mail: cheryl.yehling@state.or.us
Contact: James Sager, Education and Workforce Policy Advisor
Statutory Authority: Chapter 652, Oregon Laws 1997
Duties and Responsibilities: The Office of Education and Workforce Policy supports the governor's mission to be proactive in addressing important education and workforce issues.

Office of Rural Policy

Address: 900 Court St. NE, Salem 97301-4047
Phone: 503-986-6535
Fax: 503-378-3225
Contact: James F. Azumano, Director
Duties and Responsibilities: Created in 2004, the office will coordinate the formulation of rural policy for the state and will serve as a clearinghouse for the collection and dissemination of information about issues that are of special interest to rural Oregon. The office will also serve as a liason between elected officials in rural Oregon, the executive branch and the state legislature.

OFFICE OF THE SECRETARY OF STATE

Bill Bradbury, Secretary of State
Paddy McGuire, Deputy Secretary of State
Address: 136 State Capitol, Salem 97310-0722
Phone: 503-986-1500
Fax: 503-986-1616
E-mail: executive-office@sosinet.sos.state.or.us
Web: www.sos.state.or.us
Statutory Authority: Oregon Constitution Article VI section 2; ORS Chapters 177, 240
Duties and Responsibilities: The Office of Secretary of State is one of three constitutional offices established at statehood. The secretary of state is the custodian of the state seal and oversees the functions of seven divisions.

As auditor of public accounts, the secretary evaluates and reports on the financial condition and operations of state government and administers the Municipal Audit law.

The secretary of state is the chief elections officer. He is responsible for uniformly interpreting and applying state election laws. He also acts as the filing officer for state offices, initiative and referendum petitions, campaign finance reports and other election documents. In addition, the secretary publishes and distributes the Voters' Pamphlet and investigates and prosecutes election law violations.

The secretary is the public records administrator for Oregon, a role that includes preserving official acts of the Legislative Assembly and state agencies, supervising the state archivist, publishing the administrative rules for state agencies and producing the *Oregon Blue Book*.

The secretary of state registers domestic and foreign corporations assumed business names, and trade and service marks. The secretary prepares notarial applications and serves as filing officer for Uniform Commercial Code transactions.

The secretary of state serves with the governor and state treasurer on the State Land Board, managing state-owned lands for the benefit of the Common School Fund. He also serves as chair of the Oregon Sustainability Board.

Archives Division

Address: 800 Summer St. NE, Salem 97310
Phone: 503-373-0701
Fax: 503-373-0953
E-mail: archives.info@state.or.us
Web: http://arcweb.sos.state.or.us
Contact: Roy C. Turnbaugh, State Archivist
Statutory Authority: ORS 192.001, 357.815
Duties and Responsibilities: The Archives Division, established in 1947, houses and provides access to the permanently valuable records of Oregon government. Oldest documents at the archives include records of the provisional and territorial governments and the Oregon Constitution.

The division authorizes disposition of the public records of Oregon government, provides records management advice and assistance to state agencies and political subdivisions and operates the State Records Center which provides inexpensive storage for inactive state agency records. The division also files, codifies and publishes state agency administrative rules and publishes the *Oregon Blue Book*.

Historical Records Advisory Board

Address: 800 Summer St. NE, Salem 97310
Phone: 503-373-0701
Fax: 503-373-0953
Contact: Roy C. Turnbaugh, State Coordinator

Audits Division

Address: Public Service Bldg., 255 Capitol St. NE, Suite 500, Salem 97310
Phone: 503-986-2255; Hotline: 1-800-336-8218
Fax: 503-378-6767
E-mail: sos.audits@state.or.us
Web: www.sos.state.or.us/audits/audithp.htm
Contact: Cathy Pollino, State Auditor
Statutory Authority: ORS Chapter 297; 177.170–177.180, 692.285, 128.400–128.440, 97.810–97.920
Duties and Responsibilities: The Audits Division was created in 1929 to carry out the duties of the

secretary of state as the constitutional Auditor of Public Accounts. It is the only independent auditing organization in the state with authority to review programs of agencies in all three branches of government: executive, legislative and judicial. The division performs financial, performance, information technology, and other financial-related audits of state agencies and state-aided institutions in accordance with professional standards for government audits. The division administers the Municipal Audit law through administrative rules and review of municipal audits, and also conducts special investigations regarding potential misuse of state resources.

Business Services Division

Address: 255 Capitol St. NE, Suite 180, Salem 97310
Phone: 503-986-2204
Fax: 503-378-4991
Contact: Jeff Morgan, Director
Statutory Authority: ORS Chapter 177
Duties and Responsibilities: The Business Services Division provides centralized business and administrative support for the agency. The activities performed by the division include accounting, budgeting, cashiering, payroll, purchasing, contract administration, safety and risk management, fixed assets and inventory control, and mail service.

Corporation Division

Address: 255 Capitol St. NE, Salem 97310
Phone: 503-986-2200
Fax: 503-986-6355
Web: www.filinginoregon.com
Contact: Peter Threlkel, Director
Statutory Authority: ORS Chapters 56, 58, 60, 62, 63, 65, 67, 68, 79, 80, 87, 128, 194, 554, 647, 648
Duties and Responsibilities: The Corporation Division ensures the integrity of commercial transactions by facilitating business operations and reducing costs by enabling the creation of business identities, streamlining access to government services and regulatory requirements, preventing and deterring fraud through the commission of notaries public and the recording of secured debt. The division provides step-by-step information about how to start a business in Oregon.

Elections Division

Address: State Capitol Bldg., Suite 141, Salem 97310
Phone: 503-986-1518
Fax: 503-373-7414
E-mail: elections-division@sosinet.sos.state.or.us
Web: www.sos.state.or.us/elections/elechp.htm
Contact: John Lindback, Director
Statutory Authority: ORS Chapters 246–260

Duties and Responsibilities: The Elections Division assures the uniform interpretation and application of Oregon's election laws. The division provides the public, elected officials, candidates, the media and interested parties with advice and assistance in all matters related to elections.

The division receives candidate filings for state offices, initiative and referendum petitions, campaign contribution and expenditure reports, and other election documents. The division publishes and distributes the state Voters' Pamphlet for primary and general elections. Complaints of alleged election law violations are investigated and processed by the Elections Division.

Human Resources Division

Address: 255 Capitol St. NE, Suite 105, Salem 97310
Phone: 503-986-2173
Fax: 503-986-2175
Web: www.sos.state.or.us
Contact: Jen Coney, Director
Duties and Responsibilities: The Human Resources Division provides human resource services consisting of advice and assistance in the interpretation and application of state and federal laws and policies, and Secretary of State policies and procedures, maintaining a complete and confidential personnel record system, and monitoring human resource management activities in the agency. Additional division services include policy development, implementation, and compliance; recruitment and selection; employee discipline and grievance; dispute resolution; performance management; agency-wide training; compensation and classification; union relations; affirmative action planning and monitoring; employee orientation and benefits; employee records; and employee layoff and out-placement assistance.

Information Systems Division

Address: Public Service Bldg., Suite 103, 255 Capitol St. NE, Salem 97310
Phone: 503-986-0521
Fax: 503-986-2249
Contact: Jean Straight, Director
Statutory Authority: ORS 177.050, 177.120
Duties and Responsibilities: The Information Systems Division provides centralized technology services for the agency which include design, installation, configuration, maintenance and trouble-shooting services for hardware, software, telephony and networks; security administration; analysis for hardware and software purchases; production support; and, backup and recovery. The division also provides database administration, standards administration, data management, project and contractor management, Internet development, and application development and maintenance.

STATE TREASURY

Randall Edwards, State Treasurer
Linda Haglund, Deputy State Treasurer
Address: 350 Winter St. NE, Suite 100, Salem 97301-3896; (Office of the Treasurer: 900 Court St. NE, Rm. 159, Salem 97301-4043)
Phone: 503-378-4329
Fax: 503-373-7051
E-mail: oregon.treasury@state.or.us
Web: www.ost.state.or.us
Duties and Responsibilities: The State Treasurer is a constitutional officer and a statewide elected official. The treasurer serves as the chief financial officer for the State and is responsible for the prudent financial management of billions of taxpayer dollars. The treasurer serves a four-year term and may serve two terms only. Over the years, the Treasury has evolved into a highly sophisticated organization with a wide range of financial responsibilities, including managing the investment of state funds, issuing all state bonds, serving as the central bank for state agencies, and administering the Oregon 529 College Savings Network.

Debt Management Division

Address: 350 Winter St. NE, Suite 100, Salem 97301-3896
Phone: 503-378-4930
Fax: 503-378-2870
Contact: Laura Lockwood-McCall, Director
Duties and Responsibilities: The Debt Management Division provides central coordination and approval for the issuance of all state agency and authority bonds, which at year-end totaled $6 billion outstanding. This requires monitoring the local and national bond markets and the financing and economic trends that impact bond issuance structures and interest rates. The division staffs the Municipal Debt Advisory Commission, the Private Activity Bond Committee, and the State Debt Policy Advisory Commission. The division also provides information to private credit rating agencies.

Oregon Baccalaureate Bond Program

Address: 350 Winter St. NE, Suite 100, Salem 97301-3896
Phone: 503-378-4930
Fax: 503-378-2870
Contact: Laura Lockwood-McCall, Debt Management Division Director
Duties and Responsibilities: To assist anyone wishing to save for a child's future educational expenses, the State of Oregon periodically sells Oregon Baccalaureate Bonds. ORBAC bonds are issued as "deferred interest" bonds. Unlike most tax-exempt bonds, which pay interest every six months, ORBAC bonds pay interest only at matu-

rity. Interest on ORBAC bonds is compounded annually at a fixed rate until maturity. At maturity, an ORBAC bond is redeemed at face value.

Oregon Municipal Debt Advisory Commission

Address: 350 Winter St. NE, Suite 100, Salem 97301-3896
Phone: 503-378-4930
Fax: 503-378-2870
Contact: Laura Lockwood-McCall, Debt Management Division Director
Statutory Authority: ORS 287.030
Duties and Responsibilities: Assists local governments in the issuance of municipal debt and provides information on such debt. Promotes methods of reducing the cost of issuing municipal bonds.

Private Activity Bond Committee

Address: 350 Winter St. NE, Suite 100, Salem 97301-3896
Phone: 503-378-4930
Fax: 503-378-2870
Contact: Laura Lockwood-McCall, Debt Management Division Director
Duties and Responsibilities: The 1986 Tax Reform Act limited the number of bonds that each state may issue for "private activity" purposes. Consisting of a representative of the State Department of Administrative Services, the Oregon State Treasury, and a public member appointed by the governor, the three-member committee allocates to local governments a portion of the state private activity bond limit pursuant to ORS 286.625 and the 1986 Tax Reform Act.

State Debt Policy Advisory Commission

Address: 350 Winter St. NE, Suite 100, Salem 97301-3896
Phone: 503-378-4930
Fax: 503-378-2870
Contact: Laura Lockwood-McCall, Debt Management Division Director
Statutory Authority: ORS 286.550–286.555
Duties and Responsibilities: Advises the governor and the Legislative Assembly regarding policies and actions that enhance and preserve the State's credit rating and maintains the future availability of low-cost capital financing.

State Land Board

Address: Department of State Lands (DSL), 775 Summer St. NE, Suite 100, Salem 97301-1279
Phone: 503-378-3805
Fax: 503-378-4844
Contact: Ann Hanus, Director, Department of State Lands

Duties and Responsibilities: The State Land Board is comprised of the governor, treasurer, and secretary of state. The board has a fiduciary duty to manage state trust lands for the benefit of the Common School Fund, which provides funding to K-12 public schools in accordance with the distribution policy set by the board. The board's land base consists of nearly two million acres of land resource assets. The Department of State Lands serves as staff to the board.

Executive Division

Address: 900 Court St. NE, Rm. 159, Salem 97301-4043
Phone: 503-378-4329
Contact: Kate Cooper Richardson, Chief of Staff
Duties and Responsibilities: The Executive Division coordinates policy development, strategic planning, quality initiatives, legislative initiatives, media relations, internal auditing functions, human resource functions, and the publication of all Treasury financial reports. The State Treasurer, by constitutional authority, serves on the State Land Board and, by statute, on a number of public financial boards and councils. Executive Division staff consists of the State Treasurer, Deputy State Treasurer, Chief of Staff, Director of Legislative and Public Affairs, Communications Director, Director of Strategic Business Programs, Director of Executive Services, Internal Audit Manager/Information Security Officer, Senior Internal Auditor, Human Resource Manager, and support staff.

Finance Division

Address: 350 Winter St. NE, Suite 100, Salem 97301-3896
Phone: 503-378-4633
Fax: 503-373-1179
Contact: Darren Q. Bond, Director
Duties and Responsibilities: The Finance Division is the central bank for all state agencies. Virtually all money that flows to and from Oregon state government passes through this division. The Finance Division has a wide range of responsibilities, which include the processing of more than 9.8 million checks, 4.1 million electronic funds transfers, and more than 317,000 deposits made by state government annually. The division provides an automated banking system to state agencies to help manage these activities. The division also administers the $4 billion Local Government Investment Pool, which provides a short-term investment vehicle for local governments' idle cash. The Investment Accounting section, which reports on agency investments in 47 portfolios with a market value of $56 billion on December 31, 2003, is also part of the Finance Division. In addition, the division provides centralized support services that include payroll, safety, purchasing, facility and equipment maintenance, telecommunications, records retention and retrieval, administrative rules coordination, travel coordination, mail services, and recycling.

Oregon Short Term Fund Board

Address: 350 Winter St. NE, Suite 100, Salem 97301-3896
Phone: 503-378-4633
Fax: 503-373-1179
Contact: Darren Q. Bond, Finance Division Director
Statutory Authority: ORS 294.885
Duties and Responsibilities: In seeking to best serve local governments in Oregon, the Oregon Legislature established the Oregon Short Term Fund Board. The purpose of the board is to advise the Oregon Investment Council and the Oregon State Treasury in the management and investments of the Oregon Short Term Fund and the Local Government Investment Pool. The treasurer serves as an ex-officio member and appoints three members to the board. The governor appoints the remaining three members.

Information Services Division

Address: 350 Winter St. NE, Suite 100, Salem 97301-3896
Phone: 503-378-3436
Contact: Ron Pope, Director
Duties and Responsibilities: The Information Services Division is the information technology management center for the Treasury. The division designs, develops, and maintains the information technology infrastructure that supports Treasury's business operations. It provides the network, applications, telecommunications, and professional IT services to conduct business between Treasury, state agencies, local governments, banks, and other financial firms. Disaster recovery preparation is a key component of the division's efforts to ensure the provision of vital services to Treasury customers.

Investment Division

Address: 350 Winter St. NE, Suite 100, Salem 97301-3896
Phone: 503-378-4111
Contact: Ron Schmitz, Director
Duties and Responsibilities: The Investment Division manages the investment of the Oregon Public Employees Retirement Fund (OPERF), the State Accident Insurance Fund (SAIF), the Oregon Short Term Fund, and numerous smaller funds such as the Insurance Fund, the Common School Fund, and the Oregon Growth Account. OPERF is Treasury's largest fund under management, currently standing at approximately $44 billion. The total portfolio managed by Treasury has a market value of $56 billion and ranges in diversity from foreign

stocks to real estate. The Investment Division strives to save taxpayers money by earning the highest risk-adjusted return on its investments. The division also manages the investment program for the state's deferred compensation plan and is staff to the Oregon Investment Council and the Oregon Growth Account Board.

Oregon Growth Account Board

Address: 350 Winter St. NE, Suite 100, Salem 97301-3896
Phone: 503-378-4111
Contact: Michael Mueller, Assistant Director of Investments
Statutory Authority: ORS 348.702
Duties and Responsibilities: The Oregon Growth Account Board governs the investment of funds in the Oregon Growth Account, which earns returns for the Education Stability Fund by making investments in or to provide seed capital for emerging growth businesses in key industries in Oregon. Selects and oversees a management company to manage the funds. The Treasurer or a designee serves as the Chair of the Board, and the governor appoints the remaining six board members.

Oregon Investment Council

Address: 350 Winter St. NE, Suite 100, Salem 97301-3896
Phone: 503-378-4111
Contact: Ron Schmitz, Director of Investments
Statutory Authority: ORS 293.706
Duties and Responsibilities: The Oregon Investment Council is responsible for the investment of all state funds. The state treasurer serves as a member of the council. Monies are invested in accordance with the "Prudent Person Rule" to achieve the investment objectives of the various funds and to make the monies as productive as possible. The governor appoints council members to four-year terms, subject to Senate confirmation.

Oregon Facilities Authority

Address: 1700 Pacwest Center, 1211 SW 5th Ave., Portland 97204-3795
Phone: 503-228-6127
Contact: William E. Love, Executive Director
Statutory Authority: ORS 289.100
Duties and Responsibilities: OFA (formerly the Health, Housing, Educational and Cultural Facilities Authority) was created by the legislature in 1989. OFA is empowered to assist with the assembling and financing of lands for health, housing, educational and cultural uses, and for the construction and financing of facilities for such uses. All bonds issued by the State Treasurer upon recommendation of OFA are repaid solely from revenues generated by the projects or from other sources available to the applying institution. Interest on the bonds is tax-exempt from federal income taxes and is also exempt from personal income taxes imposed by the state. The State Treasurer appoints five members who serve a term of four years.

Oregon 529 College Savings Network

Address: 900 Court St. NE, Room 159, Salem 97301-4043
Phone: 503-373-1903
Contact: Michael Parker, Executive Director
Duties and Responsibilities: The Oregon 529 College Savings Network was created by the 1999 Oregon Legislature to help families save for higher education expenses. The plan is a unique investment vehicle that provides significant state and federal tax advantages and more flexibility than many other college savings tools. State law and section 529 of the Internal Revenue Code govern the plan. A five-member public board, chaired by the treasurer, administers the plan. The board sets investment policies for the plan and oversees the private-sector vendors that manage plan assets.

Oregon 529 College Savings Board

Address: 900 Court St. NE, Room 159, Salem 97301-4043
Phone: 503-373-1903
Contact: Michael Parker, Executive Director
Statutory Authority: ORS 348.849
Duties and Responsibilities: The Oregon 529 College Savings Board administers plans in the Oregon 529 College Savings Network.

OREGON DEPARTMENT OF JUSTICE

Hardy Myers, Attorney General
Address: 1162 Court St. NE, Salem 97301-4096
Phone: 503-378-4400; TTY: 503-378-5938
Fax: 503-378-4017
Web: www.doj.state.or.us
Statutory Authority: ORS Chapter 180
Duties and Responsibilities: The Department of Justice, established by statute in 1891, is Oregon state government's law firm. Administered by the attorney general, it represents and advises all state elected and appointed officials, agencies, boards and commissions. The attorney general, by statute, has control and supervision of all court actions in which the state is a party or has an interest.

In addition to legal services, the department has various program-service functions including child-support enforcement, technical and investigative assistance to district attorneys, organized crime investigation, consumer protection and service, charitable trust supervision, and crime-victim compensation. In all, the department and attorney general have responsibility and authority under more than 350 state statutes.

Appellate Division

Address: 1162 Court St. NE, Salem 97301-4096
Phone: 503-378-4402
Web: www.doj.state.or.us
Contact: Mary Williams, Solicitor General
Duties and Responsibilities: The Appellate Division generally is responsible for representing the state's interests in all civil, criminal and administrative cases before all state and federal appellate courts. Under supervision of the solicitor general, division attorneys articulate and defend the state's legal policies in written briefs and oral arguments before the Oregon Court of Appeals and Supreme Court; and the U.S. Court of Appeals and Supreme Court.

Child Support Division

Address: 1495 Edgewater St. NW, Suite 120, Salem 97304-4660
Phone: 503-373-7300
Web: www.dcs.state.or.us
Contact: Cynthia Chinnock, Administrator
Duties and Responsibilities: The Child Support Division establishes, modifies and enforces child-support obligations for families who receive public assistance. Since its inception in 1957 as the Welfare Recovery Division, the program has grown steadily in size, effectiveness and national stature. The division's activities are an integral part of Oregon's "Self-Sufficiency Strategy" for low-income families.

Civil Enforcement Division

Address: 1162 Court St. NE, Salem 97301-4096
Phone: 503-947-4400
Web: www.doj.state.or.us
Contact: Frederick M. Boss, Chief Counsel
Duties and Responsibilities: The Civil Enforcement Division handles civil law enforcement. Its purpose is to identify and eliminate violations of laws that regulate the commercial and labor markets. The Charitable Activities Section enforces laws regarding charitable trusts and solicitations. It also licenses and regulates bingo and raffle operations. The Civil Recovery Section is responsible for reducing to judgment and collecting debts owed to state agencies. It also protects the state's interests in bankruptcy proceedings. The Family Law Section provides legal services to the Child Support Division in establishing and enforcing child support and paternity orders in cases where children are receiving public assistance. It also operates a statewide program to assist the State Office for Services to Children and Families in its Permanent Planning Program. The Financial Fraud/Consumer Protection Section's responsibilities

include enforcement of Oregon's antitrust, securities, civil racketeering, unlawful trade practices and charitable solicitations laws. Its purpose is to protect Oregon consumers from predatory marketplace practices. The Medicaid Fraud Unit is part of a federally subsidized program created to deter and prosecute fraud committed by Medicaid healthcare service providers. It detects and prosecutes cases of criminal abuse or neglect of patients or residents of healthcare facilities who receive Medicaid funds.

Consumer Advisory Council

Address: 1162 Court St. NE, Salem 97301-4096
Phone: 503-378-4320 (Salem); 503-229-5576 (Portland); Toll-free 1-877-877-9392
Web: www.doj.state.or.us
Contact: Jan Margosian, Consumer Information Coordinator
Statutory Authority: ORS 180.520
Duties and Responsibilities: The Consumer Advisory Council was created in 1971 under the auspices of the Department of Commerce and transferred to the Department of Justice in 1981 when Consumer Services and Consumer Protection merged under ORS 180.520. Appointed by the attorney general, it consists of seven members—two representing business, two representing labor and three representing voluntary consumer agencies. Meetings are held quarterly and are open to the public. The council was created to assist the Financial Fraud/Consumer Protection Section of the Civil Enforcement Division. Functions include statewide promotion of Consumer Week; working with staff to coordinate state, local and federal agencies; conducting studies and research in consumer services; and advising Executive and Legislative branches in consumer matters.

Criminal Justice Division

Address: 1162 Court St. NE, Salem 97301-4096
Phone: 503-378-6347
Fax: 503-373-1936
Web: www.doj.state.or.us
Contact: Byron Chatfield, Chief Counsel
Duties and Responsibilities: The Criminal Justice Division serves as a statewide, multipurpose catalyst to the law-enforcement community. Among its many functions is serving as counsel to the Board on Public Safety Standards and Training and providing staff for the Oregon District Attorneys Association. Each of these functions is closely related and assists in creating a climate of quality law enforcement in Oregon. The division houses the Crime Victims' Compensation Program, established to provide certain benefits to innocent victims of violent crimes. The District Attorney Assistance Program provides to district attorneys and their deputies extensive statewide training in the techniques of criminal prosecution, uniform manuals,

forms, case digests, expert trial assistance and other coordinated services. The Organized Crime Section's primary purpose is to prevent infiltration of organized criminal enterprises into Oregon and to detect and combat existing organized criminal activities in the state. The unit also is charged with the specific responsibility of coordinating law-enforcement efforts in organized crime and has established a viable, cooperative network.

General Counsel Division

Address: 1162 Court St. NE, Salem 97301-4096
Phone: 503-947-4540
Web: www.doj.state.or.us
Contact: Donald C. Arnold, Chief Counsel
Duties and Responsibilities: The General Counsel Division provides a broad range of legal services to state agencies, boards and commissions, including day-to-day legal advice necessary for the state's operation. The division is composed of the following sections, headed by attorneys-in-charge. They are Business Activities; Business Transactions; Education; Government Services; Human Services; Labor and Employment; Natural Resources; Regulated Utility and Business; and Tax and Finance.

Trial Division

Address: 1162 Court St. NE, Salem 97301-4096
Phone: 503-378-6313
Web: www.doj.state.or.us
Contact: Timothy Wood, Chief Trial Counsel
Duties and Responsibilities: The Trial Division represents the state and all of its agencies, boards and commissions in state and federal trial courts in Oregon. It defends all state officers, officials, employees, agents and all elected officers, judges and legislators from tort claims filed against them for acts within the scope of their official duties. In addition, it defends the state against claims made by inmates challenging their underlying conviction and conditions of confinement.

BUREAU OF LABOR AND INDUSTRIES

Dan Gardner, Commissioner of Labor and Industries
Address: 800 NE Oregon St., #32, Portland 97232
Phone: 503-731-4200; TDD-Portland: 503-731-4106
Fax: 503-731-4103
Web: www.oregon.gov/BOLI/
Statutory Authority: ORS Chapter 651
Duties and Responsibilities: The Bureau of Labor and Industries was created by the legislature in 1903 and the first labor commissioner was elected in 1906. Historically the bureau was created to oversee the rapidly developing industrial workplace and to protect workers, especially minors. Its original responsibilities included inspecting mills, factories and schools as well as enforcing pay regulations and helping workers collect wages.

Today the bureau's mission is to promote the development of a highly skilled, competitive workforce in Oregon through partnerships with government, labor, business, and education; to protect the rights of workers and citizens to equal, nondiscriminatory treatment; to encourage and enforce compliance with state laws relating to wages, hours, terms and conditions of employment; and to advocate policies that balance the demands of the workplace and employers with the protections of workers and their families.

The bureau has regional offices in Bend, Eugene, Medford, Pendleton, Portland and Salem.

Commissioner's Office and Program Services Division

Address: 800 NE Oregon St., #32, Portland 97232
Phone: 503-731-4070
Fax: 503-731-4103
Web: www.oregon.gov/BOLI/
Contact: Annette Talbot, Deputy Labor Commissioner
Statutory Authority: ORS Chapter 651
Duties and Responsibilities: The Commissioner's Office and Program Services Division provides policy direction, resources and accountability to assist the operating units in encouraging compliance and in enforcing wage and hour and civil rights laws and apprenticeship standards. Administrative services include policy development, strategic planning, intergovernmental relations and public information. Business services include budget management, accounting, data processing and human resources. A Hearings Unit convenes administrative law proceedings in contested case hearings for wage and hour, and civil rights determinations. The Technical Assistance for Employers Program provides employers with a telephone information line; pamphlets, handbooks and printed materials; and public or company-based seminars and workshops to keep the business community informed about employment laws. Employers can call 503-731-4073 for immediate answers.

Apprenticeship and Training Division

Address: Portland (Main office): 800 NE Oregon, #32, Portland 97232
Phone: 503-731-4072; TDD-Portland: 503-731-4106
Fax: 503-731-4606
Web: www.oregon.gov/BOLI/
Contact: Stephen Simms

Statutory Authority: ORS Chapter 660; 334.745–334.750

Duties and Responsibilities: The Apprenticeship and Training Division promotes apprenticeship in a variety of occupations and trades and works with business, labor, government and education to increase training and employment opportunities in apprenticeable occupations. Apprenticeship is occupational training that combines on-the-job experience with classroom training. Industry and individual employers design and control the training programs, and pay apprentices' wages. The division registers occupational skill standards and agreements between apprentices and employers and works with local apprenticeship committees across the state to ensure that apprenticeship programs provide quality training and equal employment opportunities, particularly for women and minorities in technical and craft occupations.

Address: Central Oregon Intergovernmental Council, 2480 NE Twin Knolls Dr., Bend 97701
Phone: 541-322-2436
Fax: 541-389-8265

Address: Eugene: 1400 Executive Pkwy., Suite 200, Eugene 97401
Phone: 541-686-7623
Fax: 541-686-7980

Address: Medford: 191 N Oakdale Ave., Medford 97501-2629
Phone: 541-776-6270
Fax: 541-776-6284

State Apprenticeship and Training Council

Address: 800 NE Oregon St., #32, Portland 97232
Phone: 503-731-4072
Contact: Stephen Simms, Secretary; Dan Gardner, Chair
Statutory Authority: ORS 660.110
Duties and Responsibilities: The Oregon State Apprenticeship and Training Council (OSATC) is made up of ten members appointed by the governor and confirmed by the senate. The board sets policy for apprenticeship training and registers individual apprenticeship programs.

Four of the council members are from the service/industrial occupations, four from the construction occupations, and two from the public. The service/industrial and construction members are equally divided among employee representatives and management. The council has statutory authority to oversee apprenticeship committees, programs and policies and to approve apprenticeship committee members. The commissioner of the Bureau of Labor and Industries serves as the chairperson; the director of the bureau's Apprenticeship and Training Division serves as its secretary.

Civil Rights Division

Address: Portland (Main office): 800 NE Oregon, #32, Portland 97232
Phone: 503-731-4075; TDD-Portland: 503-731-4106
Fax: 503-731-4606
Web: www.oregon.gov/BOLI/
Contact: Amy Klare
Statutory Authority: ORS 654.062, Chapter 659A, 30.670, 30.685, 345.240
Duties and Responsibilities: The Civil Rights Division enforces laws granting individuals equal access jobs, career schools, promotions, and a work environment free from discrimination and harassment. These laws ensure that workers' jobs are protected when they report worksite safety violations, use family leave or the workers' compensation system. Civil rights laws also provide protection for those seeking housing or using public facilities such as retail establishments, or transportation.

Address: Eugene: 1400 Executive Pkwy., Suite 200, Eugene 97401
Phone: 541-686-7623
Fax: 541-686-7980

Address: Medford: 700 E Main, Suite 105, Medford 97504
Phone: 541-776-6270
Fax: 541-776-6284

Address: Pendleton: 1327 SE 3rd St., Rm. 110; PO Box 459, Pendleton 97801
Phone: 541-276-7884
Fax: 541-276-5767

Address: Salem: 3865 Wolverine St. NE, E-1, Salem 97305-1268
Phone: 503-378-3292
Fax: 503-373-7636

Oregon Council on Civil and Human Rights

Address: 800 NE Oregon St., #32, Portland 97232
Phone: 503-731-4075
Contact: Amy Klare
Statutory Authority: ORS 659A.815
Duties and Responsibilities: The mission of the Oregon Council on Civil and Human Rights is to provide leadership, advocacy, and education in coordinating statewide efforts to promote justice and equity for all people in Oregon. The council is an advisory group to the labor commissioner. It studies problems of discrimination, fosters goodwill, cooperation and conciliation among all groups and takes action to develop public policies and procedures and formal or informal educational programs that safeguard the civil and human rights of all Oregon residents. The labor commissioner appoints members who serve two-, three- or four-year terms.

Wage and Hour Division

Address: Portland (Main office): 800 NE Oregon, #32, Portland 97232
Phone: 503-731-4074; TDD-Portland: 503-731-4106
Fax: 503-731-4606
Web: www.oregon.gov/BOLI/
Contact: Christine Hammond, Administrator
Statutory Authority: ORS Chapters 279, 652, 653, 658; 654.251
Duties and Responsibilities: The Wage and Hour Division serves Oregon wage earners by enforcing laws covering state minimum wage and overtime requirements, wage collection, working conditions, child labor, farm and forest labor contracting, and private employment agencies. The division also regulates the employment of workers on public works projects.

Address: Eugene: 1400 Executive Pkwy., Suite 200, Eugene 97401
Phone: 541-686-7623
Fax: 541-686-7980

Address: Medford: 700 E Main, Suite 105, Medford 97504
Phone: 541-776-6270
Fax: 541-776-6284

Address: Salem: 3865 Wolverine St. NE, E-1, Salem 97305-1268
Phone: 503-378-3292
Fax: 503-373-7636

Prevailing Wage Advisory Committee

Address: 800 NE Oregon St., #32, Portland 97232
Phone: 503-731-4074
Contact: Christine Hammond; Norman Malbin, Chair
Statutory Authority: ORS 279.380
Duties and Responsibilities: The labor commissioner appoints a 12-member committee to assist in the administration of prevailing wage rate laws. This committee includes an equal number of management and labor members who are involved in the building and construction industry who work on public works contracts. The commissioner may also appoint other members from the public.

Wage and Hour Commission

Address: 800 NE Oregon St., #32, Portland 97232
Phone: 503-731-4074
Contact: Christine Hammond; Jeff Anderson, John Fyre and Kathy Nishimoto, Commission members
Statutory Authority: ORS 653.505
Duties and Responsibilities: The Wage and Hour Commission sets minimum standards for the working conditions of minors and may grant specific exceptions to child labor laws. The governor

appoints the three members of this commission to four-year terms. The commissioner of the Bureau of Labor and Industries acts as executive officer of the commission.

DEPARTMENT OF EDUCATION

Susan Castillo, Superintendent of Public Instruction; Vickie Fleming, Deputy Superintendent
Address: 255 Capitol St. NE, Salem 97310-0203
Phone: 503-378-3600; TDD: 503-378-2892
Fax: 503-378-5156
Web: www.ode.state.or.us
Statutory Authority: ORS 326.111
Duties and Responsibilities: The Department of Education is directed by the State Board of Education to implement state policies regarding public kindergarten through community colleges. The superintendent of public instruction is the executive head of the Department of Education, serving 198 elementary and secondary school districts and 20 education service districts, which in turn serve some 551,290 elementary and secondary school students. In addition, the department manages the Oregon School for the Blind, Oregon School for the Deaf, and education programs for adjudicated youth. The department carries out educational policies set by the legislature and State Board of Education and assists districts in complying with applicable statutes and rules.

State Board of Education

Address: 255 Capitol St. NE, Salem 97310-0203
Phone: 503-378-3600 ext. 2223; TDD: 503-378-2892
Fax: 503-378-5156
Contact: Randy Harnisch, Executive Director
Statutory Authority: ORS 326.011–326.075
Duties and Responsibilities: In 1951, the legislature created the State Board of Education, consisting of seven members appointed by the governor for up to two consecutive four-year terms. One member is selected from each of the five congressional districts and two members are selected from the state at large. Board members are unsalaried and cannot engage in teaching, school administration or operation while they serve on the board. The board sets educational policies and standards for 198 school districts, 17 community colleges and 20 education service districts.

The K–12 system serves some 551,290 students and the community college system served 330,595 students in 2003–04. School districts, community colleges and education services districts all have their own boards responsible for transacting business within their districts.

The mission of the board is to advance the education of every Oregon student. It does this by working in partnership with school districts, education service districts, community colleges, parents, teachers, administrators and other concerned citizens to provide educational opportunities for students that develop their skills and knowledge, motivation for lifelong learning, and their prospects for productive employment. The policies and decisions of the board are founded on the goals that it endorses for Oregon learners. These goals are crafted to assure that every student will have the opportunity to learn to function effectively in six life roles: individual, learner, producer, citizen, consumer, and family member.

The board is called upon by the legislature to implement the Oregon Educational Act for the 21st Century; implement state standards for public schools; adopt rules governing public elementary and secondary schools and community colleges; and distribute state education funds to school districts meeting all state requirements.

Fair Dismissal Appeals Board
Address: 255 Capitol St. NE, Salem 97310-0203
Phone: 503-378-3600, ext. 2350; TDD: 503-378-2892
Fax: 503-378-5156
Contact: Randy Harnisch, Executive Secretary
Statutory Authority: ORS 342.930
Duties and Responsibilities: The Fair Dismissal Law was enacted by the Legislative Assembly in 1971. It replaced the Teacher Tenure Law and established the Fair Dismissal Appeals Board (FDAB). A permanent teacher or administrator dismissed by a school board may appeal that decision to the FDAB, which holds a hearing on the dismissal. The 20-member board is appointed by the governor and is subject to confirmation by the senate.

OTHER STATE AGENCIES, BOARDS AND COMMISSIONS

This section of the *Oregon Blue Book* contains descriptions of duties and responsibilities of other state agencies, boards and commissions. Each description includes, when available: address, phone number, fax number, e-mail address, web address, director's name, and statutory authority. Listings are organized alphabetically by the substantive name of the organization. For example, the Department of Administrative Services appears as Administrative Services, Department of. Substantive parts of an organization are listed under that organization, so that Risk Management Division will appear under the Department of Administrative Services heading. The Index to the *Oregon Blue Book* may help find an agency.

ACCOUNTANCY, BOARD OF
Address: 3218 Pringle Rd. SE, Suite 110, Salem 97302-6307
Phone: 503-378-4181
Fax: 503-378-3575
Web: www.boa.state.or.us
Contact: Carol Rives, Administrator; Alan Steiger, CPA, Chair
Statutory Authority: ORS Chapter 673
Duties and Responsibilities: The Board of Accountancy assures that approximately 8,000 CPAs, PAs and municipal auditors registered to practice in Oregon demonstrate and maintain knowledge of professional standards and practices to serve the needs of their clients and other users of their services.

The board is authorized to establish and enforce standards and regulations, examine candidates and license qualified applicants in the field of public accounting. The Uniform CPA Examination is offered continuously at approved testing centers throughout each year as a computer based examination

ADMINISTRATIVE SERVICES, DEPARTMENT OF
Address: 155 Cottage St. NE, U20, Salem 97301-3966
Phone: 503-378-5967
Fax: 503-373-7643
E-mail: oregon.info@state.or.us
Web: www.oregon.gov/DAS/index.shtml
Contact: Laurie Warner, Acting Director
Statutory Authority: ORS 184.305
Duties and Responsibilities: The Department of Administrative Services administers the governor's programs and provides administrative and support services to state agencies and Oregonians. The department serves the governor, legislature, and state agencies, boards, commissions, employees, retirees of state government and the general public. Selective services may also be provided to the Legislative Assembly and the constitutional officers, at their option, as well as local governments and nonprofit organizations. Funded primarily by assessments or user fees paid by state agencies, the department has nine operating divisions that provide services to all state agencies. In addition, they have management oversight responsibility for Executive Branch agencies. There is one "policy office" within the department that provides policy development and guidance to the Governor's Office.

Director's Office
Address: 155 Cottage St. NE, U20, Salem 97301-3966
Phone: 503-378-3104

Fax: 503-373-7643
E-mail: oregon.info@state.or.us
Web: www.oregon.gov/DAS/index.shtml
Contact: Laurie Warner, Acting Director
Statutory Authority: ORS 184.315
Duties and Responsibilities: The Director's Office administers the governor's programs and provides administrative services to state agencies and the State of Oregon.

Budget and Management Division

Address: 155 Cottage St. NE, U10, Salem 97301-3965
Phone: 503-378-3106
Fax: 503-373-7643
E-mail: BAM.Info@das.state.or.us
Web: www.oregon.gov/DAS/BAM
Contact: Daron Hill, Administrator
Statutory Authority: ORS 184.335
Duties and Responsibilities: The Budget and Management Division is the primary central staff involved in preparing the Governor's Recommended Budget and in monitoring the development and execution of state agency budgets. The division provides management review services, issues Certificates of Participation, Tax Anticipation Notes and lottery bonds to finance capital and infrastructure projects, and maintains the central budget system.

Facilities Division

Address: 1225 Ferry St. SE, U100, Salem 97301-4281
Phone: 503-378-4138
Fax: 503-373-7210
E-mail: fac.info@state.or.us
Web: www.facilities.das.state.or.us
Contact: Bill Foster, Acting Administrator
Statutory Authority: ORS Chapter 276
Duties and Responsibilities: The Facilities Division acquires and maintains space for state agencies. It provides property management, real property transaction services (buy, sell and leasing), project management, space planning, lands management analysis and coordination, real property sales, building operations and maintenance, and landscape maintenance to state agencies. It manages parking and commuter programs for state employees in Salem and Portland. The statewide program provides assistance to all agencies in their efforts to achieve Oregon's facilities management and resource conservation goals.

Public Lands Advisory Committee

Address: 1225 Ferry St. SE, U100, Salem 97301-4281
Phone: 503-378-2865, ext. 251
Fax: 503-373-7210
E-mail: John.H.Wales@state.or.us
Contact: Scott Taylor, Chair
Statutory Authority: ORS 270.120, 270.100 (1)(d)
Duties and Responsibilities: The Public Lands Advisory Committee's primary role is to advise the Department of Administrative Services (DAS) on all real property acquisitions, exchanges or terminal dispositions valued at $100,000 or more for which the department must give its consent.

Human Resource Services Division

Address: 155 Cottage St. NE, U30, Salem 97301-3967
Phone: 503-378-8344
Fax: 503-378-7684
E-mail: hrsd.information@state.or.us
Web: www.hrdas.state.or.us
Contact: Susan Wilson, Administrator
Statutory Authority: ORS 240.055
Duties and Responsibilities: The Human Resource Services Division provides leadership, direction, and services to achieve an effective, efficient, and diversified workforce in Oregon state government. It manages employee compensation, recruitment, training programs, and personnel records. It represents state agencies in collective bargaining negotiations with representatives of organized labor.

Employee Suggestion Awards Commission

Address: 155 Cottage St. NE, U30, Salem 97301-3967
Phone: 503-378-4477
Fax: 503-373-7684
E-mail: Kathy.J.Shepherd@state.or.us
Web: www.das.state.or.us/das/hr/awards.shtml
Contact: Kathy Shepherd, Program Coordinator
Statutory Authority: ORS 182.320

Public Officials Compensation Commission

Address: 155 Cottage St. NE, U30, Salem 97301-3967
Phone: 503-378-2766
Fax: 503-373-7684
E-mail: Mia.M.Bullock@state.or.us
Contact: Mia Bullock
Statutory Authority: ORS 292.907

Information Resource Management Division

Address: 1225 Ferry St. SE, Salem 97301
Phone: 503-378-3795
Fax: 503-378-5200
E-mail: irmd.info@state.or.us
Web: irmd.das.state.or.us

Contact: Donald Fleming, Chief Information Officer
Statutory Authority: ORS 171.852, 171.855, 190.240, 190.250, 192.850
Duties and Responsibilities: The Information Resource Management Division operates the state's telecommunications, voice, video, and data networks and information technology. It also operates the state's General Government Data Center; plans, develops and manages large-scale databases and applications; conducts reviews of agency technology activities and plans; provides system development consulting and programming services to state agencies; develops and implements statewide information technology standards and protocols; and delivers technical training to state agencies and organizations.

Office for Oregon Health Policy and Research

Address: 255 Capitol St. NE, Fifth Flr., Salem 97310
Phone: 503-378-2422, ext. 407
Fax: 503-378-5511
E-mail: bruce.goldberg@state.or.us
Web: www.ohpr.state.or.us/
Contact: Bruce Goldberg, MD, Administrator
Statutory Authority: ORS 442.011
Duties and Responsibilities: The Office for Oregon Health Policy and Research advises the legislature and the governor on health policy issues. The office analyzes and recommends options for Oregon's health care reform efforts, as well as providing interagency coordination and oversight efforts.

Oregon Health Policy Commission

Address: 255 Capitol St. NE, Fifth Flr., Salem 97310
Phone: 503-378-2422, ext. 411
Fax: 503-378-5511
E-mail: Mike.Bonetto@state.or.us
Web: www.ohpr.state.or.us/ohpc/index.htm
Contact: Kerry Barnett, Chair; Jonathan Ater, Vice-Chair
Statutory Authority: ORS 442.035

Health Resources Commission

Address: 255 Capitol St. NE, Fifth Flr., Salem 97310
Phone: 503-378-2422, ext. 401
Fax: 503-378-5511
E-mail: Kathy.Weaver@state.or.us
Web: www.ohpr.state.or.us/ohrc/index.htm
Contact: Dr. Frank Baumeister, Chair; Diane Lovell, Vice-Chair
Statutory Authority: ORS 442.580

Health Services Commission

Address: 255 Capitol St. NE, Fifth Flr., Salem 97310
Phone: 503-378-2422, ext. 413
Fax: 503-378-5511
E-mail: Darren.D.Coffman@state.or.us
Web: www.ohpr.state.or.us/index~hsc.htm
Contact: Eric Walsh, MD, Chair
Statutory Authority: ORS 414.715

Office of Economic Analysis

Address: 155 Cottage St. NE, U20, Salem 97301-3966
Phone: 503-378-3405
Fax: 503-373-7643
E-mail: OEA.info@das.state.or.us
Web: www.oea.das.state.or.us
Contact: Thomas Potiowsky, State Economist
Duties and Responsibilities: The Office of Economic Analysis prepares state economic and revenue forecasts. It prepares the long-term population and employment forecast.

The office assesses long-term economic and demographic trends, evaluates their implications, and conducts special economic and demographic studies. The office prepares state criminal and juvenile population forecasting. It also manages the Highway Cost Allocation Study.

Governor's Council of Economic Advisors

Address: 155 Cottage St. NE, U20, Salem 97301-3966
Phone: 503-378-3405
Fax: 503-373-7643
Contact: Ralph Shaw, Chair

Operations Division

Address: 155 Cottage St. NE, U90, Salem 97301-3972
Phone: 503-378-2350, ext. 315
Fax: 503-373-1273
E-mail: William.T.Fink@state.or.us
Web: www.oregon.gov/DAS/OP
Contact: William T. Fink, Administrator
Duties and Responsibilities: The Operations Division provides administrative and operational support to the divisions of the Department of Administrative Services as well as the Office of the Governor and select commissions and agencies. There are five functional areas within the Operations Division: Accounting Services, Financial Services, Purchasing, Payroll, and Administration. These areas are responsible for administering the accounting, payroll, fiscal management, employee services, personnel, and safety and wellness programs.

Office of Information Technology

Address: 155 Cottage St. NE, U70, Salem 97301-3966
Phone: 503-378-3255
Fax: 503-378-5543
E-mail: steve.noel@state.or.us
Contact: Steve Noel, Manager
Duties and Responsibilities: The Office of Information Technology provides central technology services to all divisions of the department. The office supports more than 800 full-time equivalent positions engaged in diverse and geographically dispersed business activities.

Office of Personnel Services

Address: 155 Cottage St. NE, U130, Salem 97301-3974
Phone: 503-378-3622
Fax: 503-378-6879
E-mail: Jerry.F.Korson@state.or.us
Web: www.oregonjobs.org
Contact: Jerry Korson, Personnel Manager
Duties and Responsibilities: The Office of Personnel Services provides the full range of human resource management support for agency staff. The office also provides safety management and training programs.

Oregon Progress Board

Address: 155 Cottage St. NE, U20, Salem 97301-3966
Phone: 503-378-3201
Fax: 503-378-4048
E-mail: zoe.a.johnson@state.or.us
Web: www.oregon.gov/DAS/OPB
Contact: Jeffrey Tryens, Executive Director; Governor Theodore R. Kulongoski, Chair
Statutory Authority: ORS 285A.153
Duties and Responsibilities: The Oregon Progress Board is charged with developing and overseeing the implementation of a strategic vision for the state. The strategic vision, known as Oregon Shines, was developed in 1989 and updated in 1997. The board gauges Oregon's success achieving its goals by monitoring the Oregon Benchmarks, a set of outcome-based indicators of economic, social and environmental well-being. The board's mission is to make Oregon Shines a reality and the Benchmarks useful tools for Oregonians working to improve their communities. Helping state agencies, local governments and citizen groups achieve these goals is the core activity of the board. The board also supports efforts to develop outcome-based strategic plans at the city, county, regional and state agency level. The board is required by law to report on progress every two years and to update the strategic vision every eight years.

Public Employees' Benefit Board

Address: 775 Court St. NE, Salem 97301-3802
Phone: 503-373-1102; Toll-free: 1-800-788-0520
Fax: 503-373-1654
E-mail: inquiries.pebb@state.or.us
Web: http://pebb.das.state.or.us
Contact: Jean Thorne, Administrator
Statutory Authority: ORS 243.125
Duties and Responsibilities: The Public Employees' Benefit Board (PEBB) is responsible for the design, purchase and administration of benefit plans for approximately 44,550 state employees, 65,450 dependents, 600 COBRA-eligible former state employees, 3,000 pre-Medicare eligible retirees, and 27 semi-independent agencies. The benefit plans include contracts for medical, dental, life, accidental death, disability, long-term care and other insurance. PEBB is also responsible for providing education, training and ongoing communication to state employees, dependents and agencies regarding benefits, services offered and federal and state health benefit policy.

Risk Management Division

Address: 1225 Ferry St. SE, U150, Salem 97301-4287
Phone: 503-373-7475
Fax: 503-373-7337
E-mail: risk.management@state.or.us
Web: risk.das.state.or.us
Contact: David Hartwig, Administrator
Statutory Authority: ORS 278.405
Duties and Responsibilities: The Risk Management Division administers the state's Insurance Fund to minimize state risk and the cost of claims. It forecasts, allocates, and reduces costs that arise from accidental and malicious events, and from tort claims made against state government. State managers are provided with guidance to avoid needless and wasteful costs of loss.

State Controller's Division

Address: 155 Cottage St. NE, U50, Salem 97301-3969
Phone: 503-378-3156
Fax: 503-378-3518
E-mail: John.J.Radford@state.or.us
Web: www.scd.das.state.or.us/scd.htm
Contact: John Radford, Administrator
Statutory Authority: ORS 291.042
Duties and Responsibilities: The State Controller's Division manages the financial system infrastructure for state government which includes accounting, payroll, and financial reporting. The division develops policies, training and other fiscal services on behalf of state government. The division monitors compliance with federal regulations.

Executive

State Procurement Office

Address: 1225 Ferry St. SE, U140, Salem 97301-4285
Phone: 503-378-4642
Fax: 503-373-1626
E-mail: purchasing.info@state.or.us
Web: http://www.das.state.or.us/DAS/PFSS/ SPO /index.shtml
Contact: Dugan Petty, Administrator
Statutory Authority: ORS Chapter 279
Duties and Responsibilities: The State Procurement Office (SPO) combines state and local procurement power to ensure the cost-effective acquisition of commodities and services. SPO consults with and trains state and local governments, and vendors and contractors on procurement laws, rules, procedures and policies. SPO administers a training and certification program. The SPO audit and compliance program monitors (a) state agency compliance with procurement laws, rules and guidelines; (b) agency compliance with delegated procurement authority agreements; (c) procurement-related audit findings; and (d) the effectiveness and adequacy of the SPO training and certification program.

AGRICULTURE, DEPARTMENT OF

Address: 635 Capitol St. NE, Salem 97301-2532
Phone: 503-986-4550; TTY: 503-986-4762
Fax: 503-986-4747
E-mail: info@oda.state.or.us
Web: http://oregon.gov/ODA
Contact: Katy Coba, Director
Statutory Authority: ORS Chapter 576
Duties and Responsibilities: The Oregon Department of Agriculture was created in 1931 to provide leadership, service, and regulatory functions for food production and processing. Its mission has been expanded to provide food safety and consumer protection at all levels of production and marketing, to protect the agricultural natural resource base, and to promote economic development and develop markets for agriculture and food products. The director of the department is appointed by the governor. A ten-member State Board of Agriculture, also appointed by the governor, serves as advisory to the director. The department is divided into nine divisions that oversee 36 chapters of Oregon laws.

Agricultural Development and Marketing Division

Address: 1207 NW Naito Pkwy., Suite 104, Portland 97209-2832
Phone: 503-872-6600
Fax: 503-872-6601
E-mail: agmarket@oda.state.or.us
Web: www.oregon.gov/ODA/ADMD/
Contact: Dalton Hobbs, Administrator
Statutory Authority: ORS Chapter 576
Duties and Responsibilities: The Agricultural Development and Marketing Division promotes, develops and expands world markets for Oregon agricultural products. It conducts market research and promotional events and serves as a link between buyers and sellers of Oregon's agricultural products. The division provides legislative oversight of Oregon's Commodity Commissions, and monitors their activities, contractual obligations and budget development.

Animal Health and Identification Division

Address: 635 Capitol St. NE, Salem 97301-2532
Phone: Animal Health: 503-986-4680; Livestock Identification: 503-986-4681
Fax: 503-986-4734
E-mail: rhuffman@oda.state.or.us
Web: http://egov.oregon.gov/ODA/AHID/index. shtml
Contact: Rodger Huffman, Administrator
Statutory Authority: ORS Chapters 596, 599, 604, 607, 609, 633
Duties and Responsibilities: The Animal Health and Identification Division strives to prevent, control, and, if possible, eradicate livestock diseases harmful to humans and animals; to deter livestock theft by recording brands and inspecting cattle and horses for ownership; to educate ranchers, law enforcement officials, and livestock owners about livestock theft prevention; and to assure that all commercial livestock feeds meet label statements and are free from adulteration.

Commodity Inspection Division

Address: 635 Capitol St. NE, Salem 97301-2532
Phone: 503-986-4620
Fax: 503-986-4737
E-mail: jcramer@oda.state.or.us
Web: www.oregon.gov/ODA/CID/
Contact: James A. Cramer, Administrator
Statutory Authority: ORS Chapters 561, 570, 585, 586, 602, 632, 633
Duties and Responsibilities: The Commodity Inspection Division facilitates the movement of Oregon commodities in domestic and international markets through third party inspection and certification. The division provides a self-supporting system of grading agricultural commodities for quality and uniformity; ensures proper labeling of seed and produce; certifies grass seed and straw for export; and protects grain depositors in the event of failure of grain elevators.

Food Safety Division

Address: 635 Capitol St. NE, Salem 97301-2532
Phone: 503-986-4720
Fax: 503-986-4729
E-mail: rmckay@oda.state.or.us
Web: www.oregon.gov/ODA/FSD/
Contact: Ronald W. McKay, Administrator
Statutory Authority: ORS Chapters 603, 616, 619, 621, 622, 625, 628, 632, 635
Duties and Responsibilities: The Food Safety Division is responsible for assuring that Oregon consumers have a safe, wholesome and properly labeled food supply. It accomplishes this through inspection, sampling, education and consultation.

Laboratory Services

Address: 1207 NW Naito Pkwy., Suite 204, Portland 97209-2835
Phone: 503-872-6644 (Regulatory Lab)
Fax: 503-872-6615
E-mail: kwickman@oda.state.or.us
Web: www.oregon.gov/ODA/LAB/
Contact: Kathleen Wickman, Lab Manager
Duties and Responsibilities: Laboratory Services provides chemical, microbiological and pesticide residue analytical support to the agency and to other governmental entities. Samples include food, feed, fertilizer, water and environmental samples. Together with the Department of Environmental Quality and the Oregon Health Division, the laboratory certifies environmental testing labs under the EPA NELAP program. The laboratory also certifies dairy laboratories for FDA's Interstate Milk Shippers program. The laboratory participates in Food Innovation Center projects.

Export Service Center

Address: 1207 NW Naito Pkwy., Suite 224, Portland 97209-2835
Phone: 503-872-6630
Fax: 503-872-6615
E-mail: esc-food@oda.state.or.us
Web: www.oregon.gov/ODA/LAB/
Contact: Jeff Hyatt, Lab Manager
Duties and Responsibilities: The Export Service Center (ESC) is a one-of-a-kind analytical laboratory certified to test food products and determine compliance with foreign country regulations. The ESC certifies U.S. foods shipped to Japan, Korea and Taiwan. Seventeen other countries also accept ESC analytical results in lieu of port testing at the destination country. The ESC also provides analysis and consultation to export companies.

Measurement Standards Division

Address: 635 Capitol St. NE, Salem 97301-2532
Phone: 503-986-4670

Fax: 503-986-4784
E-mail: gshefche@oda.state.or.us
Web: www.oregon.gov/ODA/MSD/
Contact: George Shefcheck, Administrator
Statutory Authority: ORS 618.010–618.551, 646.905–646.925, 646.945–646.963
Duties and Responsibilities: The Measurement Standards Division seeks to prevent consumer fraud and ensure fair competition by assuring that goods such as groceries, fuels, and package products are accurately weighed and measured. The division also ensures that motor fuels meet the national standards for quality, and provides official calibration services to users of mass, volume and length standards to Oregon businesses.

Natural Resources Division

Address: 635 Capitol St. NE, Salem 97301-2532
Phone: 503-986-4700
Fax: 503-986-4730
E-mail: dgorham@oda.state.or.us
Web: www.oregon.gov/ODA/NRD/
Contact: Debbie Gorham, Administrator
Statutory Authority: ORS 468A.550–468A.620, 468B.200–468B.230, 561.175, 561.190–561.191, 561.400–561.407, 564.010–564.994, 568.210–568.890, 568.900–568.933, 622.010–622.992
Duties and Responsibilities: The Natural Resources Division provides guidance and technical assistance to 45 local soil and water conservation districts as they assist farmers with conservation plans and farming practices; permits confined animal feeding operations to assist them in meeting state and federal water quality laws; manages the state's threatened and endangered plant species program; manages a smoke management program to assist the grass seed industry with field burning; develops practical agricultural water quality management plans and rules for Oregon's priority watersheds; and leases submerged estuary land for commercial oyster cultivation.

Pesticides Division

Address: 635 Capitol St. NE, Salem 97301-2532
Phone: 503-986-4635
Fax: 503-986-4735
E-mail: pestx@oda.state.or.us
Web: www.oregon.gov/ODA/PEST/
Contact: Christopher K. Kirby, Administrator
Statutory Authority: ORS Chapters 633, 634
Duties and Responsibilities: The Pesticides Division registers pesticide and fertilizer products for distribution in Oregon; examines, licenses and recertifies individuals who use pesticides; licenses companies that apply pesticides; licenses outlets that sell pesticides; obtains and maintains records of pesticide use; and conducts investigations for compliance with federal and state pesticide laws.

Plant Division

Address: 635 Capitol St. NE, Salem 97301-2532
Phone: 503-986-4644
Fax: 503-986-4786
E-mail: dhilburn@oda.state.or.us
Web: www.oregon.gov/ODA/PLANT/
Contact: Daniel J. Hilburn, Administrator
Statutory Authority: ORS Chapters 561, 570, 571
Duties and Responsibilities: Plant Division programs include exclusion, detection and eradication of exotic weeds, plant pests and pathogens. Inspection and certification services are available for nursery stock, Christmas trees and seed crops. Sightings of potentially invasive species can be reported to the invasive species hotline: 1-866-INVADER.

Advisory Groups:

State Board of Agriculture

Address: 635 Capitol St. NE, Salem 97301-2532
Phone: 503-986-4619
Fax: 503-986-4750
Contact: Sherry Kudna, Assistant to the Board; Bernie Faber, Vice-Chair
Statutory Authority: ORS Chapter 561
Duties and Responsibilities: The State Board of Agriculture advises the director of the department and assists in determining policies. Ten members and two ex-officio members are appointed by the governor to four-year terms; not more than five members may be from one political party.

Ginseng Advisory Committee

Address: 635 Capitol St. NE, Salem 97301-2532
Phone: 503-986-4644
Contact: Daniel J. Hilburn
Statutory Authority: ORS 576.810
Duties and Responsibilities: The Ginseng Advisory Committee was created to provide assistance to the department in the administration of the ginseng management program. It consists of five members appointed by the director.

Minor Crops Advisory Committee

Address: 635 Capitol St. NE, Salem 97301-2532
Phone: 503-986-4635
Contact: Janet Fults
Statutory Authority: ORS 634.600

New Crops Development Board

Address: 635 Capitol St. NE, Salem 97301-2532
Phone: 503-986-4620
Contact: Jim Cramer
Statutory Authority: ORS Chapter 561
Duties and Responsibilities: The New Crops Development Board identifies, endorses and promotes worthy new and alternative crops for Oregon, and acts as a clearinghouse for new ideas and resources in the development of new crops. The board consists of seven members appointed by the director and one ex-officio member.

Nursery Research and Regulatory Committee

Address: 635 Capitol St. NE, Salem 97301-2532
Phone: 503-986-4644
Contact: Gary McAninch
Statutory Authority: ORS 571.025
Duties and Responsibilities: The Nursery Research and Regulatory Committee was created to provide close contact between the department and the nursery industry. The committee is composed of seven members appointed by the director.

Oregon Invasive Species Council

Address: 635 Capitol St. NE, Salem 97301-2532
Phone: 503-986-4644
Contact: Daniel J. Hilburn
Statutory Authority: ORS 561.685–561.695
Duties and Responsibilities: Oregon's Invasive Species Council provides educational material, encourages reporting of sightings, facilitates eradication programs, and promotes cooperation between state agencies and other parties concerned with harmful, non-indigenous species.

Pesticide Analytical and Response Center

Address: 800 NE Oregon St., Suite 772, Portland 97232-2162
Phone: 503-731-4025
Contact: Deborah Profant, Ph.D.
Statutory Authority: ORS 634.550
Duties and Responsibilities: The Pesticide Analytical and Response Center (PARC) was established in 1978 to coordinate state-agency investigations of health and environmental incidents involving pesticides. PARC serves as a clearinghouse of information and complaints; assesses pesticide incidents; conducts sample analyses; and publishes a yearly report of its findings. PARC analyzes the pesticide exposure data in order to identify patterns in the causes of exposures and to develop and implement population-based interventions. PARC is authorized by statute, and its board is composed of representatives from eight agencies and a citizen representative.

Soil and Water Conservation Commission

Address: 635 Capitol St. NE, Salem 97301-2532
Phone: 503-986-4705
Contact: Larry Ojua
Statutory Authority: ORS Chapter 568
Duties and Responsibilities: The primary function of the state Soil and Water Conservation Commission is to advise the Oregon Department of Agriculture (ODA) on policy and administration of the

state's conservation programs. The commission consists of seven soil and water conservation district directors appointed by the ODA Director. The commission provides assistance to and represents the interests of Oregon's 45 conservation districts, and coordinates its activities with the ODA Natural Resources Division. Each conservation district is governed by five or seven locally elected officials. Conservation districts develop and implement local conservation programs to address water quality and other identified natural resources issues utilizing local, state and federal resources. The commission also works closely with the Oregon Association of Conservation Districts, the U.S. Department of Agriculture, and state and federal agencies with responsibilities relating to natural resource management.

State Christmas Tree Advisory Committee

Address: 635 Capitol St. NE, Salem 97301-2532
Phone: 503-986-4644
Contact: Gary McAninch
Statutory Authority: ORS 571.515
Duties and Responsibilities: The State Christmas Tree Advisory Committee was created to provide close contact between the department and the Christmas tree industry. The committee is composed of six members appointed by the director.

State Weed Board

Address: 635 Capitol St. NE, Salem 97301-2532
Phone: 503-986-4621
Contact: Tim Butler
Statutory Authority: ORS 561.650–561.680
Duties and Responsibilities: The State Weed Board establishes a list of priority weeds for the state; awards grants for noxious weed control projects; assists the director in allocating money for weed control efforts; helps coordinate county, state and federal weed control programs; and advises the director on performing weed control duties assigned to the department. The board consists of seven members appointed by the director.

Agricultural Commodity Commissions

Most commodity commissions conduct promotional, educational, production and market research projects. The commissions are authorized by ORS chapters 576, 577 and 578. They are funded by assessments on the producers of the commodities. The director of the State Department of Agriculture appoints the members of all 28 commissions. Although the Wine Advisory Board is not a commodity commission, it is listed in this section.

Oregon Albacore Commission

Address: PO Box 1160, Coos Bay 97420-0301

Phone: 541-267-5810
Contact: Nick Furman, Administrator

Oregon Alfalfa Seed Commission

Address: PO Box 688, Ontario 97914-0688
Phone: 541-881-1335
Contact: Edith Kressley, Administrator

Oregon Bartlett Pear Commission

Address: 4382 SE International Way, Suite A, Milwaukie 97222-4635
Phone: 503-652-9720
Contact: Linda Bailey, Administrator

Oregon Beef Council

Address: 1200 NW Naito Parkway, Suite 290, Portland 97209
Phone: 503-274-2333
Contact: Nichole Bechtel, Executive Director

Oregon Blueberry Commission

Address: PO Box 3366, Salem 97302-0366
Phone: 503-364-2944
Contact: Bryan Ostlund, Administrator

Oregon Clover Seed Commission

Address: PO Box 2042, Salem 97308-2042
Phone: 503-370-7019
Contact: John McCulley, Administrator

Oregon Dairy Products Commission

Address: 10505 SW Barbur Blvd., Portland 97219-6853
Phone: 503-229-5033
Contact: Sheldon Pratt, Administrator

Oregon Dungeness Crab Commission

Address: PO Box 1160, Coos Bay 97420-0301
Phone: 541-267-5810
Contact: Nick Furman, Administrator

Oregon Fine Fescue Commission

Address: 1193 Royvonne Ave. SE, Suite 11, Salem 97302-1932
Phone: 503-585-1157
Contact: David S. Nelson, Administrator

Oregon Fryer Commission

Address: 11220 SE Stark, Suite 12, Portland 97216-3355
Phone: 503-256-1151
Contact: Julie Durand, Administrator

Oregon Grains Commission

Address: PO Box 1086, Pendleton 97801-1086
Phone: 541-276-4609
Contact: Tammy Dennee, Administrator

Oregon Hazelnut Commission

Address: 21595-A Dolores Way NE, Aurora 97002

Phone: 503-678-6823
Contact: Polly Owen, Administrator

Oregon Highland Bentgrass Commission

Address: PO Box 3366, Salem 97302-0366
Phone: 503-364-2944
Contact: Bryan Ostlund, Administrator

Oregon Hop Commission

Address: PO Box 198, Aurora 97002
Phone: 503-633-2922
Contact: Michelle Palacios, Administrator

Oregon Mint Commission

Address: PO Box 3366, Salem 97302-0366
Phone: 503-364-2944
Contact: Bryan Ostlund, Administrator

Oregon Orchardgrass Seed Producers Commission

Address: PO Box 2042, Salem 97308-2042
Phone: 503-370-7019
Contact: John McCulley, Administrator

Oregon Potato Commission

Address: 700 NE Multnomah, Suite 460, Portland 97232-4104
Phone: 503-731-3300
Contact: William Wise, Administrator

Oregon Processed Vegetable Commission

Address: PO Box 2042, Salem 97308-2042
Phone: 503-370-7019
Contact: John McCulley, Administrator

Oregon Raspberry and Blackberry Commission

Address: 4845 B SW Dresden, Corvallis 97333
Phone: 541-758-4043
Contact: Philip Gütt, Administrator

Oregon Ryegrass Growers Seed Commission

Address: PO Box 3366, Salem 97302-0366
Phone: 503-364-2944
Contact: Bryan Ostlund, Administrator

Oregon Salmon Commission

Address: PO Box 983, Lincoln City 97367-0983
Phone: 541-994-2647
Contact: Nancy Fitzpatrick, Administrator

Oregon Sheep Commission

Address: 1270 Chemeketa St. NE, Salem 97301
Phone: 503-364-5462
Contact: Richard Kosesan, Administrator

Oregon Strawberry Commission

Address: 4845 B SW Dresden, Corvallis 97333
Phone: 541-758-4043
Contact: Philip Gütt, Administrator

Oregon Sweet Cherry Commission

Address: 2527 Reed Rd., Hood River 97031
Phone: 541-386-5761
Contact: Dana Branson, Administrator

Oregon Tall Fescue Commission

Address: 1193 Royvonne Ave. SE, Suite 11, Salem 97302-1932
Phone: 503-585-1157
Contact: David S. Nelson, Administrator

Oregon Trawl Commission

Address: PO Box 569, Astoria 97103-0569
Phone: 503-325-3384
Contact: Brad Pettinger, Administrator

Oregon Wheat Commission

Address: 1200 NW Naito Parkway, Suite 520, Portland 97209-2800
Phone: 503-229-6665
Contact: Tana Simpson, Administrator

Western Oregon Onion Commission

Address: 3228 Journeay Court, West Linn 97068
Phone: 503-510-2632
Contact: Bruce Andrews, Administrator

Wine Advisory Board

Address: 1200 NW Naito Parkway, Suite 400, Portland 97209-2829
Phone: 503-228-8336
Fax: 503-228-8337
Contact: Ted Farthing, Executive Director

APPRAISER CERTIFICATION AND LICENSURE BOARD

Address: 1860 Hawthorne Ave. NE, Suite 200, Salem 97303
Phone: 503-485-2555
Fax: 503-485-2559
E-mail: bob@oregonaclb.org
Web: www.oregonaclb.org
Contact: Bob Keith, Administrator
Statutory Authority: ORS Chapter 674
Duties and Responsibilities: The Appraiser Certification and Licensure Board (ACLB) licenses and certifies real estate appraisers in Oregon and develops and establishes appraisal education and experience requirements in accordance with state and federal law, standards and guidelines.

The board was created in 1991 to implement Title XI of the Federal Financial Institutions Reform Recovery and Enforcement Act of 1989 (Public Law 101-73) in Oregon. The regulatory functions of the board are independent of other realty-related regulatory agencies. The ACLB consists of ten members, nine of whom are appointed by the governor. Five of these nine are appraisers, two are from the banking industry, and two are members of the public. The tenth member is the Department of Consumer and Business Services director or designee, who serves as a non-voting member.

ARCHITECT EXAMINERS, BOARD OF

Address: 205 Liberty St. NE, Suite A, Salem 97301
Phone: 503-763-0662
Fax: 503-364-0510
E-mail: architectboard@orbae.com
Web: www.orbae.com
Contact: Carol Halford, Administrator
Statutory Authority: ORS 671.010–671.220
Duties and Responsibilities: The Oregon Board of Architect Examiners (OBAE) was established in 1919 and consists of seven members—five members are resident architects and two members represent the general public. The board ensures that only competent persons and firms are permitted to practice architecture in Oregon and that all practicing architects follow prescribed professional standards of conduct. The board establishes qualifications and examines architects who want to practice in Oregon, registers architectural firms, investigates complaints and alleged violations of the Architectural Practice Act, and is authorized to deny, suspend, or revoke registrations and to assess civil penalties.

The OBAE is self-supporting and receives the majority of its revenue from application, registration and renewal fees.

AVIATION, OREGON DEPARTMENT OF

Address: 3040 25th St. SE, Salem 97302-1125
Phone: 503-378-4880
Fax: 503-373-1688
Web: www.aviation.state.or.us/
Contact: John Wilson
Statutory Authority: ORS 835.100
Duties and Responsibilities: The goals of the Oregon Department of Aviation include developing aviation as an integral part of Oregon's transportation network; creating and implementing strategies to protect and improve Oregon's aviation system; encouraging aviation related economic development; supporting aviation safety and education; and increasing commercial air service and general aviation in Oregon.

The department owns and operates 29 Oregon airports and annually licenses or registers more than 450 public or private airports, heliports, or landing areas. It also registers all pilots and non-military aircraft based in Oregon; oversees statewide aviation system planning and helps with community airport planning; administers a pavement maintenance program for airports around the state; administers a small community grant program; and conducts aviation safety and public education programs.

BLACK AFFAIRS, COMMISSION ON

Address: 800 NE Oregon St., Suite 930, Portland 97232-2162
Phone: 503-731-4002, ext. 312
Fax: 503-731-4078
E-mail: Everette.L.Rice@state.or.us
Web: www.ocba.state.or.us
Contact: Everette L. Rice, Commissioner, former Executive Director; Johnny Lake, Chair, Eugene
Statutory Authority: ORS 185.410
Duties and Responsibilities: Created by executive order in October 1980, the Oregon Commission on Black Affairs (OCBA) became a statutory commission in 1983. The commission works for the implementation and establishment of economic, social, legal and political equality for Oregon's African American and Black populations.

The commission monitors state and local programs and legislation; researches and identifies issues and concerns affecting the African American and Black communities, and recommends appropriate action, programs and legislation to the governor, Legislative Assembly, and state agencies. It maintains a liaison relationship between African American and Black communities, and Oregon government. It encourages, through outreach, education and presentation, African American and Black employment and representation on state boards, commissions, and government. It serves as an advocate, analyst, and advisor to the governor, Legislative Assembly, state agencies, officials, African Americans and Blacks throughout the state.

The commission is also authorized to produce or assist in the production of events that promote African American and Black heritage, cross-cultural and multicultural experiences such as Juneteenth Celebrations, Martin Luther King Jr. Holiday celebrations, Kwanzaa, Holocaust Remembrance celebrations, Cinco De Mayo celebrations, and development of an Oregon Black History Museum and business registry.

All funding for the Oregon Commission on Black Affairs was cut by the legislature on April 1, 2003. The commission and its commissioners have been operating as volunteers without funding.

BLIND, COMMISSION FOR THE

Address: 535 SE 12th, Portland 97214-2488
Phone: 503-731-3221, 888-202-5463; TTY: 503-731-3224
Fax: 503-731-3230
E-mail: ocbmail@state.or.us
Web: www.cfb.state.or.us
Contact: Linda R. Mock, Administrator
Statutory Authority: ORS 346.110–346.270
Duties and Responsibilities: Through a state-federal partnership under the Rehabilitation Act, the Commission for the Blind assists eligible blind Oregonians to achieve full inclusion in society. The commission provides a wide range of individualized services to legally blind Oregonians so that they may prepare for and secure employment, and trains eligible Oregonians, including older blind citizens, to maximize their ability to live independently in their homes and communities.

CHILDREN AND FAMILIES, OREGON COMMISSION ON

Address: 530 Center St. NE, Suite 405, Salem 97301
Phone: 503-373-1283
Fax: 503-378-8395
Web: www.ccf.state.or.us
Contact: Mickey Lansing
Statutory Authority: ORS 417.705–417.825, 417.900, 419.170
Duties and Responsibilities: The Oregon Commission on Children and Families (OCCF) is the largest umbrella advocacy group for children and families in Oregon. Created by legislation in 1993, and further defined by SB555 in 1999, OCCF promotes positive outcomes for children and families through a process driven by local decision-making. Commission members are appointed by the governor to four-year terms.

The commission provides no direct services, but is responsible for statewide planning, standards setting and policy development, and provides communities with research-based best practices on which to base local programs for children and families. All 36 Oregon counties have a local Commission on Children and Families, which is responsible for a local coordinated comprehensive plan; community mobilization; and coordination among community groups, government agencies, private providers and other parties, of programs and initiatives for children 0–18 years of age and their families.

Funds administered through the commission include: **Great Start,** designed to help ensure Oregon's youngest children, prenatal through eight years of age, reach the first grade with good physi-

cal, social, intellectual and emotional development; **Court Appointed Special Advocates (CASA),** a cadre of citizens appointed on a case-by-case basis to represent the best interests of children who are victims of abuse and neglect in Oregon's juvenile courts; **Children, Youth and Families,** supporting prevention initiatives for children prenatal to 18 and their families; **Youth Investment,** a federal grant focusing on non-delinquent youth, 11–18 years of age, who are acting out or who are victims of neglect. Equal consideration must be given to girls in the design of services; **Healthy Start Family Support Services,** which provides voluntary comprehensive risk assessment and support services, including community-based home visiting and referral to other community resources to all newly born children and their families; **Child Care and Development Fund,** a federal grant to benefit children and working parents by increasing the supply and enhancing the quality of child care services and supports in communities; **Safe and Stable Families,** a federal grant that promotes the expansion of family support and family preservation services; **Crisis/Relief Nurseries,** based on a model system of comprehensive family services, including parenting education, mental health services, substance abuse assessment and counseling, respite from parenting and therapeutic early childhood programs; **Family Resource Centers,** family friendly environments providing information, support activities and a single point of entry into the service delivery system; **Together for Children,** pilot parenting education programs in three counties.

CHILDREN'S TRUST FUND OF OREGON

Address: 1410 SW Morrison St., Suite 502, Portland 97205
Phone: 503-222-7102
Fax: 503-222-6975
E-mail: info@ctfo.org
Web: www.ctfo.org
Contact: Cynthia Thompson, Executive Director
Statutory Authority: ORS 418.187–418.199
Duties and Responsibilities: The Children's Trust Fund of Oregon (CTFO) was established in 1985 to eliminate child abuse and neglect in Oregon by awarding annual grants to effective, local primary prevention programs in communities throughout the state. The CTFO also provides public education and advocacy for the needs of families and children. In addition to the Trust Fund which comprises the annual funding available for grant awards, the organization acts as steward for the Children's Trust Endowment Fund, which is available for the long-term funding needs of primary prevention. The CTFO receives donations from the sale of heirloom birth certificates, employee fund drives,

private and corporate donations, and the income tax checkoff. The administrative expenses of the agency are funded through a fractional percentage of general funds, which also funds the Endowment Fund.

CHIROPRACTIC EXAMINERS, BOARD OF

Address: 3218 Pringle Rd. SE, Suite 150, Salem 97302-6311
Phone: 503-378-5816
Fax: 503-362-1260
E-mail: oregon.obce@state.or.us
Web: www.obce.state.or.us
Contact: Dave McTeague, Executive Director
Statutory Authority: ORS Chapter 684
Duties and Responsibilities: The Oregon Board of Chiropractic Examiners (OBCE) was created in 1915 and is responsible for administering the Chiropractic Practice Act and establishing the rules and regulations governing the practice of chiropractic in Oregon. The seven-member board is composed of five chiropractic physicians and two public members who are appointed by the governor to three-year terms.

The OBCE's mission is to protect and benefit the public health and safety, and promote quality in the chiropractic profession. The board currently licenses over 1,150 active and 325 inactive chiropractic physicians, and over 500 certified chiropractic assistants. The board's programs include application, examination, continuing education, public information, and investigation of complaints. If violations are found the board issues disciplinary actions and/or rehabilitation plans to meet competency standards. The OBCE also promotes diversity on the board and in the profession.

CLINICAL SOCIAL WORKERS, STATE BOARD OF

Address: 3218 Pringle Rd. SE, Suite 240, Salem 97302-6130
Phone: 503-378-5735
Fax: 503-373-1427
E-mail: oregon.bcsw@state.or.us
Web: www.bcsw.state.or.us
Contact: Jon F. Langenwalter, Administrator
Statutory Authority: ORS 675.510–675.600
Duties and Responsibilities: The State Board of Clinical Social Workers was created in 1979 and is composed of four Licensed Clinical Social Workers and three public members. The board regulates clinical social workers by certifying associates working toward licensure through two-year Plans of Supervision, and licenses clinical social workers by means of a national examination with a self-test on Oregon laws and rules. The board sets policy,

writes and adopts rules, renews licenses annually, and audits continuing education as a part of the renewal process. The board has the authority to discipline licensees, to deny, suspend, revoke, or refuse to renew a certificate or license. Monthly board meetings are held in Salem and are open to the public.

COLUMBIA RIVER GORGE COMMISSION

Address: PO Box 730, White Salmon, WA 98672
Phone: 509-493-3323
Fax: 509-493-2229
E-mail: crgc@gorge.net
Web: www.gorgecommission.org
Contact: Martha J. Bennett, Executive Director
Statutory Authority: ORS 196.150
Duties and Responsibilities: The Columbia River Gorge Commission was established by a bi-state compact between the states of Oregon and Washington in 1987. The commission was created in response to federal legislation that established the 300,000-acre Columbia River Gorge National Scenic Area in 1986. The purposes of the legislation are to protect and provide for the enhancement of the scenic, natural, cultural and recreational resources of the Columbia River Gorge, and to protect and support the area's economy by encouraging growth within existing areas and allowing future economic development elsewhere when consistent with the areas' important resources.

The commission works in partnership with the U.S. Forest Service, six counties and four tribes to implement a regional management plan.

CONSTRUCTION CONTRACTORS BOARD

Address: 700 Summer St. NE, Suite 300, PO Box 14140, Salem 97309-5052
Phone: 503-378-4621
Fax: 503-373-2007
E-mail: craig.p.smith@state.or.us
Web: www.ccb.state.or.us
Contact: Craig P. Smith, Administrator
Statutory Authority: ORS 701.205
Duties and Responsibilities: The Construction Contractors Board was created in 1971 as the Builders Board and is responsible for safeguarding the security and property of the citizens of Oregon by preventing and resolving construction contracting problems, and by ensuring contractors' compliance with the law. The board administers the Oregon Contractors Law that provides for licensing of all residential and commercial construction contractors and subcontractors, investigation and adjudication of complaints filed against licensees, and assessment of civil penalties against contractors

who are not licensed. The board tests applicants on a 16-hour course in construction laws and business practices. The board also tests and licenses home inspectors, engages in education activities aimed at preventing construction problems and publishes pamphlets that explain its role in helping citizens resolve problems.

CONSUMER AND BUSINESS SERVICES, DEPARTMENT OF

Address: 350 Winter St. NE, Salem 97301-3878; PO Box 14480, Salem 97309-0405
Phone: 503-378-4100; TTY: 503-378-4100
Fax: 503-378-6444
E-mail: dcbs.director@state.or.us
Web: www.oregon.gov/DCBS
Contact: Cory Streisinger, Director
Statutory Authority: ORS 705.010–705.350
Duties and Responsibilities: The Department of Consumer and Business Services (DCBS) fulfills wide-ranging regulatory and consumer-protection functions that significantly affect living and doing business in Oregon. The agency administers laws and rules governing workers' compensation (Workers' Compensation Division), occupational safety and health (OR-OSHA), building codes (Building Codes Division), the operation of insurance companies (Insurance Division), and financial institutions and securities offerings (Division of Finance and Corporate Securities).

The department has several programs and two ombudsmen to help consumers, injured workers, and businesses. The state-government-wide Office of Regulatory Streamlining is within the department. DCBS administers the Oregon Medical Insurance Pool and provides staff and support for the Workers' Compensation Management-Labor Advisory Committee. The Workers' Compensation Board, an independent adjudicatory body, shares fiscal and management services with the department. DCBS has three internal-support divisions: Business Administration, Information Management, and the Director's Office. DCBS has 1,088 staff positions and a biennial budget of about $560 million.

Building Codes Division

Address: 1535 Edgewater St. NW, PO Box 14470, Salem 97309-0404
Phone: 503-378-4133
Fax: 503-378-2322
E-mail: bcd.webmaster@state.or.us
Web: www.cbs.state.or.us/external/bcd/
Contact: Mark Long, Administrator
Statutory Authority: ORS Chapter 455
Duties and Responsibilities: The mission of the Building Codes Division is to work with Oregonians to ensure safe building construction while supporting a positive business climate. The division is charged with adopting and enforcing a uniform statewide building code relating to construction, reconstruction, alteration and repair of structures, and to the installation of mechanical, plumbing, and electrical devices and equipment. The director of the Department of Consumer and Business Services appoints the division administrator. The division adopts and administers seven specialty codes, provides technical assistance, enforcement, dispute resolution services, and oversight to ensure that local building department programs meet state standards. It examines, certifies, registers, and licenses 11 professions or trades, and issues operating permits for three industries. In addition to its West Salem headquarters, the division maintains full-service field offices in Coquille, Pendleton, and The Dalles, and a Tri-County Service Center in Portland.

The division works with, provides staff support to, and receives advice from the following seven boards.

Board of Boiler Rules

Address: PO Box 14470, Salem 97309-0404
Phone: 503-373-1216
Contact: Ray Andrus, Board Secretary
Statutory Authority: ORS 480.535
Duties and Responsibilities: The Board of Boiler Rules assists in adopting, amending and enforcing rules, certifications and minimum safety standards for boilers, pressure vessels and pressure piping; approves related division fees and training programs; hears code appeals; and makes scientific and technical findings related to code interpretations. The governor appoints the board's 11 members to four-year terms, subject to senate confirmation.

Building Codes Structures Board

Address: PO Box 14470, Salem 97309-0404
Phone: 503-378-4472
Contact: Richard Rogers, Board Secretary
Statutory Authority: ORS 455.132
Duties and Responsibilities: The Building Codes Structures Board assists the DCBS director in the administration of the commercial structural prefabricated structure and energy programs described in ORS chapter 455, as well as programs described in ORS 447.210–447.310 which promote accessibility for persons with physical disabilities. The board hears code appeals and makes scientific and technical findings related to code interpretations. The governor appoints the board's nine members to four-year terms, subject to senate confirmation.

Electrical and Elevator Board

Address: PO Box 14470, Salem 97309-0404
Phone: 503-373-7509
Contact: John Powell, Board Secretary

Statutory Authority: ORS 455.138

Duties and Responsibilities: The Electrical and Elevator Board assists in administering the state's electrical safety law and advises and approves electrical rules and codes, as well as revocations or suspensions of electrical licenses. The board advises on rules governing elevator safety and hears appeals. The board also approves related division fees and training programs, hears code appeals, and makes scientific and technical findings related to code interpretations. The governor appoints the board's 15 members, subject to senate confirmation.

Manufactured Structures and Parks Advisory Board

Address: PO Box 14470, Salem 97309-0404
Phone: 503-373-1326
Contact: Larry Iverson, Board Secretary
Statutory Authority: ORS 446.280
Duties and Responsibilities: The Manufactured Structures and Parks Advisory Board advises the DCBS director on adopting, administering and enforcing the standards for the national manufactured housing, manufactured dwelling park, recreational vehicle, recreation park, and organizational camp and picnic park programs. The board approves related division fees, licensing, and training programs, hears code appeals, and makes scientific and technical findings related to code interpretations. The DCBS director appoints the board's 12 members to four-year terms.

Mechanical Board

Address: PO Box 14470, Salem 97309-0404
Phone: 503-373-7529
Contact: Mike Ewert, Board Secretary
Statutory Authority: ORS 455.140
Duties and Responsibilities: The Mechanical Board assists in adopting and administering the state's mechanical code. The board advises on rules governing the mechanical code and approves related division fees and training programs, hears code appeals, and makes scientific and technical findings related to code interpretations. The governor appoints the board's nine members, subject to senate confirmation.

Plumbing Board

Address: PO Box 14470, Salem 97309-0404
Phone: 503-373-7488
Contact: Terry Swisher, Board Secretary
Statutory Authority: ORS 693.115
Duties and Responsibilities: The Plumbing Board advises on plumbing products, approves related division fees and training programs, hears code appeals, and makes scientific and technical findings related to code interpretations. The board also administers examinations to plumbers and issues

licenses. The governor appoints the board's seven members to four-year terms, subject to senate confirmation.

Residential Structures Board

Address: PO Box 14470, Salem 97309-0404
Phone: 503-373-1354
Contact: Ravi Majahan, Board Secretary
Statutory Authority: ORS 455.135
Duties and Responsibilities: The Residential Structures Board assists in adopting and administering the state's residential code. The board advises on rules governing the residential code and approves related division fees and training programs, hears code appeals, and makes scientific and technical findings related to code interpretations. The governor appoints the board's nine members, subject to senate confirmation.

Division of Finance and Corporate Securities

Address: 350 Winter St. NE, Salem 97301-3881; PO Box 14480, Salem 97309-0405
Phone: 503-378-4140; TTY: 503-378-7387
Fax: 503-947-7862
E-mail: dcbs.dfcsmail@state.or.us
Web: http://dfcs.oregon.gov
Contact: Floyd Lanter, Administrator
Statutory Authority: ORS Chapters 59, 97, 192, 646, 697, 705–717, 722, 723, 725, 726
Duties and Responsibilities: The Division of Finance and Corporate Securities regulates Oregon's state-chartered financial institutions, including banks, trust companies, savings and loan associations, credit unions, consumer finance companies, mortgage bankers and brokers, and credit service organizations. It regulates and registers public offerings of securities, and licenses securities broker-dealers, investment advisors, and salespersons. The division also regulates money transmitters, electronic signatures, sellers of travel, debt collection agencies, debt consolidating agencies, pawnbrokers, pre-need funeral trusts, and endowment care cemeteries. The division answers questions regarding laws, rules, and licensing requirements and provides consumers and businesses with public records about financial institutions, registered securities offerings, and the employment and discipline record of investment advisors and salespersons as well as securities dealers.

Insurance Division

Address: 350 Winter St. NE, Room 440, Salem 97301-3883; PO Box 14480, 97309-0405
Phone: 503-947-7980; Consumer Advocacy Unit: 503-947-7984; SHIBA: 1-800-722-4134
Fax: 503-378-4351
E-mail: dcbs.insmail@state.or.us
Web: http://insurance.oregon.gov

Contact: Joel Ario, Administrator
Statutory Authority: ORS 731.004–731.016
Duties and Responsibilities: The Insurance Division ensures the financial soundness of insurance companies, the availability and affordability of insurance, and the fair treatment of policyholders. The division disciplines violators of Oregon's insurance code, licenses insurance companies and agents doing business in Oregon, examines insurers for solvency and compliance with insurance law, and approves insurance products to be offered to the public. The division also reviews rates charged for insurance products, prepares publications and information to help consumers make informed decisions about insurance, and investigates consumer complaints against insurance companies and agents. The division also manages the Senior Health Insurance Benefits Assistance (SHIBA) program, which helps Medicare beneficiaries make informed health insurance decisions. SHIBA volunteers in many Oregon communities provide one-on-one assistance to help Medicare beneficiaries compare insurance policies, file claims and make appeals.

Office of Minority, Women and Emerging Small Business

Address: 350 Winter St. NE, Salem 97301-3878; PO Box 14480, Salem 97309-0405
Phone: 503-947-7922
Fax: 503-373-7041
E-mail: gabriel.m.silva@state.or.us
Web: http://oregon.gov/DCBS/OMWESB
Contact: Gabriel M. Silva, Administrator
Statutory Authority: ORS 200.055
Duties and Responsibilities: The Office of Minority, Women and Emerging Small Business (OMWESB) administers the state's certification programs for disadvantaged businesses, minority- and women-owned businesses and emerging small businesses. The programs help ensure that these businesses have access to contracting opportunities in the public and private sectors. OMWESB maintains online directories of certified firms for public jurisdictions, prime contractors, and private industries soliciting firms for projects with contracting goals.

Office of Regulatory Streamlining

Address: 350 Winter St. NE, Salem 97301-3878; PO Box 14480, 97309-0405
Phone: 503-947-7061
Fax: 503-378-6444
E-mail: patrick.allen@state.or.us
Web: http://streamline.oregon.gov
Statutory Authority: Executive Order 03-01

Duties and Responsibilities: The Office of Regulatory Streamlining was established in 2003 to facilitate state government's effort to simplify business regulations. The office provides ongoing research to identify streamlining opportunities and serves as a clearinghouse for agency streamlining practices, offering facilitation, process-improvement support, and resource referrals.

Oregon Medical Insurance Pool

Address: 250 Church St. SE, Suite 200, Salem 97301-3921
Phone: 503-373-1692; Toll-free: 1-800-542-3104
Fax: 503-378-8365
E-mail: omip.mail@state.or.us
Web: www.omip.state.or.us
Contact: Howard "Rocky" King, Administrator
Statutory Authority: ORS 735.600–735.650
Duties and Responsibilities: The Oregon Medical Insurance Pool (OMIP) was established in 1987 by the Oregon legislature to provide medical insurance coverage for all Oregonians unable to obtain medical insurance because of health conditions. OMIP also provides health benefit portability coverage to Oregonians who have exhausted Consolidated Omnibus Budget Reconciliation Act (COBRA) benefits and have no other portability options. OMIP offers enrollees four medical plans from which to choose. Since the first policy was issued, OMIP has insured more than 35,000 Oregonians who would have had no health benefit coverage. A citizen board of directors guides policy for OMIP, which is administered as part of Oregon's Department of Consumer and Business Services.

Oregon Occupational Safety and Health Division

Address: 350 Winter St. NE, Rm. 430, Salem 97301-3882; PO Box 14480, Salem 97309-0405
Phone: 503-378-3272 (Voice/TTY); Toll-free in Oregon only: 1-800-922-2689 (Voice/TTY)
Fax: 503-947-7461
E-mail: admin.web@state.or.us
Web: www.orosha.org
Contact: Peter De Luca, Administrator
Statutory Authority: ORS 654.001–654.295, 654.750–654.780, 654.991
Duties and Responsibilities: The Oregon Occupational Safety and Health Division (OR-OSHA) administers the Oregon Safe Employment Act and enforces the state's occupational safety and health rules, which establish minimum safety and health standards for Oregon employers. The division's enforcement staff inspects workplaces for occupational-safety-and-health hazards, investigates complaints about safety and health issues on the job, and investigates fatal accidents to determine if the

Oregon Safe Employment Act has been violated. The division has five major programs: Consultative Services, Public Education, Enforcement, Standards and Technical Resources, and Administration. These programs provide technical, educational and consultative services to help employers and their employees implement and improve injury-and-illness-prevention plans.

Workers' Compensation Board

Address: 2601 25th St. SE, Salem 97302-1282
Phone: 503-378-3308
Fax: 503-373-1684
E-mail: maureen.bock@state.or.us
Web: www.cbs.state.or.us/wcb
Contact: Maureen Bock, Chair
Statutory Authority: ORS Chapter 656
Duties and Responsibilities: The Workers' Compensation Board is an independent adjudicatory agency within DCBS. The board provides timely and impartial resolution of disputes arising under Oregon workers' compensation law and the Oregon Safe Employment Act. The five-member, full-time board consists of one public member, two members with backgrounds in business, and two members with backgrounds in labor. Members are appointed by the governor to four-year terms and confirmed by the senate. The board chair oversees the agency, including the work of the Hearings Division, whose administrative law judges conduct contested-case hearings and provide mediation on cases within the board's jurisdiction. The Board Review Division, which includes the board members, processes appeals of workers' compensation orders issued by the Hearings Division and approves alternative settlements such as claim disposition agreements, and hears appeals under the Oregon Crime Victims' Compensation Program.

Workers' Compensation Division

Address: 350 Winter St. NE, Salem 97301-3879; PO Box 14480, Salem 97309-0405
Phone: 503-947-7810
Fax: 503-947-7514
E-mail: dcbs.wcdmail@state.or.us
Web: http://oregonwcd.org
Contact: John L. Shilts, Administrator
Statutory Authority: ORS Chapter 656
Duties and Responsibilities: The Workers' Compensation Division administers and enforces Oregon's workers' compensation law to ensure that employers provide coverage for their workers, that workers with occupational injuries or diseases receive their entitled benefits, and that parties are provided with resources and procedures for fair resolution of disputes.

The division monitors, supervises, and regulates various service providers and the claims management of insurers and self-insured employers. This regulatory responsibility is balanced with fair and consistent policies that encourage a healthy business climate for companies regulated by the division. The division also administers the Worker Benefit Fund. One use of the fund provides incentives to employers in the form of reduced workers' compensation and operation costs for employing or re-employing injured workers.

Ombudsman for Injured Workers

Address: 350 Winter St. NE, Salem 97301-3878; PO Box 14480, Salem 97309-0405
Phone: 503-378-3351; Toll-free: 1-800-927-1271
Fax: 503-373-7639
E-mail: wallst@cbs.state.or.us
Web: http://oregon.gov/DCBS/OIW
Contact: S. Travis Wall, Ombudsman
Statutory Authority: ORS 656.709
Duties and Responsibilities: The office of the Ombudsman for Injured Workers (OIW) was established by the legislature in 1987. The ombudsman is appointed by the director of DCBS, with the concurrence of the governor, and serves as an independent advocate for injured workers. OIW investigates and attempts to resolve workers'-compensation-related complaints and problems through problem solving, informal mediation, negotiation, and other forms of administrative advocacy. In addition, OIW informs and educates workers and others about the rights and benefits to which injured workers are entitled under the state workers' compensation system.

Small Business Ombudsman for Workers' Compensation

Address: 350 Winter St. NE, Salem 97301-3878; PO Box 14480, Salem 97309-0405
Phone: 503-378-4209
Fax: 503-373-7639
Web: www.cbs.state.or.us/sbo
Statutory Authority: ORS 656.709
Duties and Responsibilities: The Small Business Ombudsman for Workers' Compensation, established by the legislature's special session in 1990, advises the DCBS director on all aspects of the workers' compensation system. The ombudsman is responsible for developing education programs and materials for small-business operators, identifying trends in consumer complaints, and proposing solutions. The ombudsman is the small-business advocate at workers' compensation ratemaking and rulemaking hearings.

Workers' Compensation Management-Labor Advisory Committee

Address: 350 Winter St. NE, Salem 97301-3878; PO Box 14480, Salem 97309-0405
Phone: 503-947-7867
Fax: 503-378-6444
E-mail: Louis.D.Savage@state.or.us
Web: www.cbs.state.or.us/mlac
Contact: Lou Savage, Administrator
Statutory Authority: ORS 656.790
Duties and Responsibilities: The Workers' Compensation Management-Labor Advisory Committee was created by Senate Bill 1197 during the legislature's 1990 special session. Members of the committee are appointed by the governor and subject to senate confirmation. The committee comprises five management and five labor representatives. The DCBS director serves as an ex officio member. The committee is charged with reviewing and making recommendations on workers' compensation issues to the governor, the director of DCBS, and the legislature.

CORRECTIONS, DEPARTMENT OF

Address: 2575 Center St. NE, Salem 97301-4667
Phone: 503-945-0920
Fax: 503-373-1173
E-mail: doc.info@doc.state.or.us
Web: www.oregon.gov/DOC
Contact: Max Williams, Director
Statutory Authority: ORS Chapter 423
Duties and Responsibilities: The Department of Corrections was created by the 64th Legislative Assembly in 1987. The department has custody of offenders sentenced to prison for more than 12 months. Oregon houses offenders in 12 state prisons; one new prison broke ground in 2002. The Department of Corrections is recognized nationally among correctional agencies for providing inmates with the cognitive, behavioral and job skills they need to become productive citizens. Oregon's recidivism rate is about 30 percent. It is inspired by the department's mission of public safety, offender accountability, and crime prevention.

Because of a rapidly growing inmate population, the state embarked on an ambitious prison construction and expansion program in 1995. As of mid-2004, the prison population numbers over 13,000; two new prisons have been opened since 2000 and major expansions of several others have been completed or are in process. New prison construction has begun in Lakeview.

The Department of Corrections provides administrative oversight and funding for the community corrections activities of Oregon's 36 counties. Oregon counties manage their own offenders who are subject to jail, parole, post-prison supervision and/or probation. The department provides interstate compact administration and jail inspections as well as central information and data services regarding felons statewide. It is also responsible for evaluating the performance of community corrections.

Budget Section

Address: 2575 Center St. NE, Salem 97301-4667
Phone: 503-945-9007
Fax: 503-373-1173
Web: http://oregon.gov/DOC/GENSVC/fiscal_services.shtml
Contact: Sue Acuff, Administrator
Duties and Responsibilities: The Budget Section is responsible for the planning, budget, fiscal services and facilities management activities of the agency. The section provides budget development and financial analysis.

General Services Division

Address: 2575 Center St. NE, Salem 97301-4667
Phone: 503-378-3798
Fax: 503-589-0427
Web: http://oregon.gov/DOC/GENSVC
Contact: John Koreski, Assistant Director
Duties and Responsibilities: The General Services Division supports the department's use of information technology. The division is composed of the Information Systems Unit, Facility Services, Central Distribution and Fiscal Services.

The Information Systems Unit (ISU) is responsible for computer center operations and the department's network, desktop technical support, and applications development and maintenance. Centrally, the unit manages data that is used for budget and planning purposes, policy development, prison population projections, and research and program evaluation. Other users of the department's automated systems include law enforcement agencies, county corrections agencies, the Board of Parole and Post-Prison Supervision, district attorneys and the courts.

Fiscal Services manages the accounting, central trust, purchasing and warehouse operations for the entire department. The Facilities Services Section oversees planning and implementation of new prison construction, as well as maintenance of current institutions.

Human Resources Division

Address: 2575 Center St. NE, Salem 97301-4667
Phone: 503-945-9006
Fax: 503-378-6427
Web: http://oregon.gov/DOC/HR
Contact: Shelli Honeywell, Assistant Director
Duties and Responsibilities: The Human Resources Division manages the personnel-related services of recruitment, affirmative action, employee development and training, employee safety and

risk management, and organization and leadership development for several thousand employees, volunteers, and contractors. It provides consultation and assistance in administering the department's classification, compensation, human resources' policies, and labor contracts.

Inspections Division

Address: 2575 Center St. NE, Salem 97301-4667
Phone: 503-945-0930
Fax: 503-373-7092
Web: http://oregon.gov/DOC/INSPEC
Contact: Rebecca Prinslow, Administrator
Duties and Responsibilities: The Inspections Division provides an oversight function on behalf of the director and deputy director of the department. The division is comprised of two units: Investigations and Rules/Compliance/Hearings.

The Investigations Unit is responsible for investigating allegations of inmate, employee, and visitor misconduct; collecting evidence of criminal behavior for referral to the State Police; investigating conspiracies to introduce contraband into the prisons; monitoring inmate communications; searching for fugitives; and performing other functions as requested by the director.

The Rules/Compliance/Hearings Unit prepares and distributes the agency rules and procedures. This unit is the department's liaison with the Department of Justice and performs official archival duties for the department. Hearings officers assigned to the unit adjudicate inmate misconduct.

Operations Division

Address: 2575 Center St. NE, Salem 97301-0470
Phone: 503-945-0950
Fax: 503-373-1173
Web: http://oregon.gov/DOC/OPS
Contact: Stan Czerniak, Assistant Director
Duties and Responsibilities: Oregon's adult prisons are centrally administered by the assistant director of Institutions. The Operations Division's responsibilities encompass prison management, inmate classification, transfers, inmate transportation, security threat group (gang) management, emergency preparedness, most inmate work crew activities, and inmate physical and mental health treatment.

Inmate Work Crews

Web: http://oregon.gov/DOC/WRKFRC
Duties and Responsibilities: Crews of supervised minimum-custody inmates perform work such as park maintenance, flood control and clean-up, upkeep of parkways, litter control of community roads, grounds-keeping, community beautification projects, seasonal gleaning of field crops for use in local food banks, fire fighting, forest lands restoration and hazardous fuels removal.

Emergency Preparedness

Duties and Responsibilities: Corrections Department's emergency preparedness efforts are designed to protect the lives and property of the public, staff, and inmates. Through a well-planned and coordinated system that includes department and community resources, the department considers emergency preparedness the responsibility of every staff member, contractor and volunteer.

Components of emergency preparedness include planning, prevention, prediction, preparation and practice. Department plans define the roles of central administration, prisons, and the community in emergencies. These plans identify emergency command structures, support functions and options to resolve emergencies. A strong emphasis on prevention of emergencies is achieved by involving employees, contractors, volunteers and citizens in the consistent enforcement of directives, effective communications, appropriate inmate programs and services, and maintaining good safety, security and sanitation standards. The department conducts emergency exercises and security audits to sharpen skills and ensure the evolution and effectiveness of the emergency preparedness system.

Oregon Corrections Enterprises

Address: 3691 State St., Salem 97301
Phone: 503-373-7604
Fax: 503-378-5592
Web: http://oregon.gov/DOC/WRKFRC
Contact: Rob Killgore, Administrator
Duties and Responsibilities: Oregon Corrections Enterprises (OCE) was created by the voters in 1999 to streamline the department's efforts to put all inmates to work as defined by 1994's Ballot Measure 17 and 1997's Ballot Measure 49. OCE is a semi-independent state agency. Its administrator reports to the director of the Oregon Department of Corrections.

Inmate work opportunities are divided into three categories: prison industries, private partnerships, and inmate work crews. OCE manages the first two. Inmate work crews are managed by the Operations Division (see Operations Division description). OCE also does business under the name, "Inside Oregon Enterprises."

In general, inmate work reduces inmate idleness and lowers the cost of operating government. Work is a major component of the Oregon Accountability Model, teaching inmates valuable skills while they are engaged in meaningful work. OCE focuses on providing work experience that translates into gainful employment upon release, potentially reducing repeat offenses and lowering recidivism rates.

Most DOC inmates are required to participate in work and training assignments 40 hours each week.

Inmates earn monetary credits for participating in work-skill development programs and for actual work performed.

OCE's ventures include:

Laundry. Commercial laundry operations at Oregon State Penitentiary in Salem, Eastern Oregon Correctional Institution in Pendleton, Snake River Correctional Institution in Ontario, and Two Rivers Correctional Institution in Umatilla provide sorting, cleaning, and packaging of linens (including pick-up and delivery) to public and private hospitals, institutions and businesses throughout the state.

Garment Factory. At Eastern Oregon Correctional Institution in Pendleton, inmates produce the Prison Blues™ line of denim jeans, jackets, t-shirts, sweatshirts, work shirts, and hats. All DOC inmates wear Prison Blues jeans stamped in orange with the word "INMATE."

Furniture Factory. Inmates at Oregon State Penitentiary in Salem manufacture stock and custom office furniture from oak and other woods in a variety of finishes. They also make bedroom and dormitory furniture, ergonomic office chairs, upholstered office furniture, modular panel systems, mattresses, and pillows.

Metal Shop. Metal items are fabricated at Oregon State Penitentiary and Mill Creek Correctional Facility. Products include gates, doors, tables, bed frames, lockers/secure storage, park products, boat docks, and custom work such as the decorative overpass fencing at the Chenowith interchange on I-84 near The Dalles.

Services. Inmates inside Oregon's prisons are interviewed, hired, and trained to provide public- and private-sector customers with professional services, including two printing operations, three telecommunication centers, computer-aided design and mapping (CAD/CAM), mailing, desktop publishing, Web page design, and general office services.

Private Partnerships. OCE can partner with private-sector businesses to use inmate labor both inside and outside of correctional facilities. OCE may provide industrial space and other related incentives to businesses to encourage successful partnerships.

Transitional Services Division

Address: 2575 Center St. NE, Salem 97301-4667
Phone: 503-945-9050
Fax: 503-373-7810
Web: http://oregon.gov/DOC/TRANS
Contact: Ginger Martin, Assistant Director
Duties and Responsibilities: Through intergovernmental agreements with the counties, the Transitional Services Division oversees, advocates for, and works in partnership with all the community corrections offices throughout the state. The local county community corrections offices provide supervision, services and sanctions to felony offenders in their communities. Parole/probations officers (PO's) monitor the behavior and compliance of more than 30,000 felony offenders living in Oregon's communities, enforcing conditions of supervision set by the court for those on probation and by the Board of Parole and Post-Prison Supervision for those who have been released from prison. State funding, administered through the DOC's Transitional Services Division, supports both the supervision of felony offenders and the development of community-based sanctions and correctional treatment programs.

The Transitional Services Division develops and delivers effective outcome-based interventions to inmates in Oregon's prisons. Using seven criminogenic risk factors, staff assess each inmate during the intake process at Coffee Creek Correctional Facility and create an individualized corrections plan. Correctional programs specified in an inmate's corrections plan may include work skills development, parenting, education, training, thinking changes, health care, mental health care, alcohol and drug treatment, work experience and re-entry services such as job placement, to support their transition back into the community. Additionally, all inmates are eligible to participate in religious services. Automated systems track inmates' progress in pursuing their plans as well as their behavior and conduct.

The Offender Information and Sentence Calculation Unit (OISC) calculates and updates the length of all prison terms, based on information provided by the courts. OISC also is the repository for all legal files pertaining to offenders who have been, or currently are, under the custody or supervision of the department. The unit is responsible for the maintenance of the department's official offender records.

The Classification Unit contributes to the safety of the general public and security of the prisons by supervising inmate classifications, prison transfers, earned time and security threat group (gang) issues. The unit assigns inmates to institutions based upon their level of risk. There are approximately 18,000 transfers each year. The unit separates inmates for safety reasons and balances the inmate population throughout Oregon's 12 prisons and in other states via Interstate Compact.

Corrections Education Advisory Board

Address: 1793 13th St. SE, Salem 97302-2595
Phone: 503-378-6482, ext. 7131
Fax: 503-378-5815
Contact: Nichole Brown, Workforce Development Education and Training Administrator

State Prisons

Coffee Creek Correctional Facility

Address: 24499 SW Grahams Ferry Rd., PO Box 9000, Wilsonville 97070-9000
Phone: 503-570-6400
Fax: 503-570-6417
Web: http://oregon.gov/DOC/OPS/PRISON/cccf. shtml
Contact: Bill Hoefel, Superintendent
Duties and Responsibilities: Coffee Creek Correctional Facility (CCCF) is a 1,360-bed dual-mission facility that comprises Oregon Corrections Intake Center for men and women as well as the state's only multi-custody full-service women's prison. Coffee Creek's minimum facility opened on October 15, 2001. The medium facility and intake center opened on April 18, 2002.

Virtually all inmates entering Oregon's prisons are initially housed at Coffee Creek. During a 22-day assessment period, individual plans are designed for each inmate.

Following the development of their corrections plans, inmates are assigned to a prison.

Women serving their sentences at CCCF have access to a full spectrum of programs to prepare them for their transition and re-entry to the community, including parenting programs and an on-site Early Head Start facility to help strengthen families and teach parental responsibility.

Columbia River Correctional Institution

Address: 9111 NE Sunderland Ave., Portland 97211-1799
Phone: 503-280-6646
Fax: 503-280-6012
Web: http://oregon.gov/DOC/OPS/PRISON/ crci. shtml
Contact: Mike Gower, Superintendent
Duties and Responsibilities: Columbia River Correctional Institution (CRCI) is a 540-bed minimum security prison located in Northeast Portland. The prison opened in September 1990, and houses 500 male inmates in dormitories.

Major program activities for most inmates include community service work projects, institution support and maintenance work, and educational and cognitive skills classes.

Fifty inmates are housed in a separate living area designed specifically for use as a residential alcohol and drug treatment center. Another 50 participate in the Bridgepoint Program, a residential alcohol, drug and mental health treatment program. Inmates participate in these therapeutic community programs designed to address serious addiction and substance abuse problems.

Eastern Oregon Correctional Institution

Address: 2500 Westgate, Pendleton 97801-9699
Phone: 541-276-0700
Fax: 541-276-1841
Web: http://oregon.gov/DOC/OPS/PRISON/eoci. shtml
Contact: Sharon Blacketter, Superintendent
Duties and Responsibilities: Eastern Oregon Correctional Institution (EOCI) was authorized in 1983 as the first medium-security adult male correctional facility established outside of Marion County. Until its conversion to a prison, EOCI had been a state mental hospital, with most of the buildings originally constructed in 1913. The 1,600-bed facility is Pendleton's second largest employer.

EOCI provides a variety of work opportunities to inmates. The internationally recognized "Prison Blues" line of blue denim clothing is manufactured in the Garment Factory. The commercial laundry meets the needs of the facility as well as several local public service agencies and large industries. EOCI's Physical Plant's mission is to teach marketable job skills to inmates in the fields of electricity, plumbing and carpentry. In 1999 the creative arts, wood working and metal shops were established to provide services to the community. The Physical Plant is also committed to environmental sustainability. With the permitted ecological auto shop, EOCI has minimized environmental impact while performing auto repairs; and, with the recent installation of solar panels, the facility has reduced emission of greenhouse gases by preheating water for boiler use.

Blue Mountain Community College provides GED and Adult Basic Education services for the inmates at the prison. In addition to these education classes, EOCI offers the STEPS to Freedom Program which is a 4–6 month pre-release alcohol and drug day treatment program serving 70 inmates. The COPE Program provides mental health day treatment services to inmates who experience moderate to severe mental health problems and have difficulty adjusting to prison life.

Mill Creek Correctional Facility

Address: 5465 Turner Rd. SE, Salem 97301-9400
Phone: 503-378-2600, ext. 221
Fax: 503-378-8235
Web: http://oregon.gov/DOC/OPS/PRISON/ mccf.shtml
Contact: Frank Thompson, Superintendent
Duties and Responsibilities: Mill Creek Correctional Facility (MCCF) is a minimum-security prison housing 310 inmates. The facility has been operated by the Department of Corrections since 1929. All inmates are within three years of release and most have successfully completed required correctional programs prior to being assigned to

MCCF. The facility prepares inmates for transition and release to the community by providing a variety of work programs and training opportunities.

Oregon State Correctional Institution

Address: 3405 Deer Park Dr. SE, Salem 97310-9385
Phone: 503-373-0100
Fax: 503-378-8919
Web: http://oregon.gov/DOC/OPS/PRISON/osci.shtml
Contact: Nancy Howton, Superintendent
Duties and Responsibilities: Oregon State Correctional Institution (OSCI), a men's medium-security transitional release facility located three miles east of Salem, was established by the 1955 Legislature and became fully operational on June 1, 1959.

The 880-bed facility confines males serving sentences for felony convictions from all counties of Oregon. OSCI focuses on providing transition programs and work skills to inmates who have less than three years to serve but are not suitable for housing in a minimum-security environment. Some of the work and skills training opportunities available to inmates at OSCI include Geographical Information Systems (GIS), Engineering Support Unit (ESU), printing, and telecommunication services for the Oregon Health Plan and the Oregon Secretary of State's Office.

Oregon State Penitentiary

Address: 2605 State St., Salem 97310-0505
Phone: 503-378-2445
Fax: 503-378-3897
Web: http://oregon.gov/DOC/OPS/PRISON/osp.shtml
Contact: Brian Belleque, Superintendent
Duties and Responsibilities: Oregon State Penitentiary (OSP), Oregon's first state prison, was originally located in Portland in 1851. In 1866 it was moved to a 26-acre site in Salem and enclosed by a 25 foot-tall reinforced concrete wall. OSP is the state's only maximum security prison.

The penitentiary accommodates up to 2,150 inmates. Housing for the general inmate population in the penitentiary is in large cell blocks with most people assigned to double cells. In addition to its general population housing, the penitentiary also has a disciplinary segregation unit, a special management unit, and an infirmary.

The penitentiary's 196-bed, self-contained Intensive Management Unit provides programs, housing and control for maximum-custody male inmates who are disruptive or pose a substantial threat to staff and other inmates, as well as those inmates with a sentence of death. Executions, using lethal injection, are conducted at the penitentiary.

Penitentiary inmates may work in Oregon Corrections Enterprises' shops including a furniture factory, metal shop, upholstery shop, or the state's third-largest commercial laundry. Several job skills training programs and comprehensive education programs are available.

The OSP Minimum Facility (OSPM) occupies the grounds formerly used by the Oregon Women's Correctional Center. It was recommissioned in April 2002 to accommodate 176 minimum-custody male inmates. This self-contained unit, managed by the Oregon State Penitentiary, provides support for other DOC facilities.

Powder River Correctional Facility

Address: 3600 13th St., Baker City 97814-1346
Phone: 541-523-6680
Fax: 541-523-6678
Web: http://oregon.gov/DOC/OPS/PRISON/prcf.shtml
Contact: Dan Johnson, Superintendent
Duties and Responsibilities: Powder River was opened in1989 and houses 286 adult male inmates. The facility operates a 178-bed alternative incarceration addictions treatment program. Inmates are assigned to institution and/or community-based work programs. Inmates assigned to the alternative incarceration addictions treatment program follow a strict regimen of work, education, treatment, physical exercise, service to the community and other program activities 16 hours daily. Inmates are assigned to perform institution-based and/or community based work projects for governmental, private sector, and non-profit organizations in Baker and surrounding counties. Inmates also serve on fire crews in support of the Oregon Department of Forestry. All inmates are expected to participate in and successfully complete transition programming designed to address their individual needs as part of their correctional plan.

Powder River serves as a transition/re-entry facility for selected minimum-security inmates preparing for transition from prison to community.

Santiam Correctional Institution

Address: 4005 Aumsville Hwy. SE, Salem 97301-9112
Phone: 503-378-5558, ext. 259
Fax: 503-378-8235
Web: http://oregon.gov/DOC/OPS/PRISON/sci.shtml
Contact: Frank Thompson, Superintendent
Duties and Responsibilities: Santiam Correctional Institution (SCI) is a minimum security prison located in southeast Salem that accommodates 390 male inmates in four dormitories. The department has operated the building as a correctional institution since 1977. SCI houses men who are within six months of release. The prison emphasizes programs

that enhance the inmates' chances of successful re-entry into their communities. In addition to transitional programs, the prison's work crews provide inmates with experience at state, county and city agencies and other department facilities.

Shutter Creek Correctional Institution

Address: 95200 Shutters Landing Ln., North Bend 97459-0303
Phone: 541-756-6666
Fax: 541-756-6888
Web: http://oregon.gov/DOC/OPS/PRISON/scci.shtml
Contact: Tim Causey, Superintendent
Duties and Responsibilities: Acquired from the Federal Government at no cost to Oregon taxpayers, this former Air National Guard radar station was converted into a 230-bed minimum security prison that opened in February 1990. Shutter Creek Correctional Institution (SCCI) consists of 56 acres and 20 buildings surrounded by forestland and is located approximately 15 miles north of North Bend on the Oregon coast. Inmate housing consists of four 50-bed dormitory units in two buildings and a small women's dorm. The Shutter Creek Work Center, located in North Bend, is managed by SCCI and provides housing for 50 additional inmates.

The facility accommodates 100 general population male inmates who work on-site in the physical plant, warehouse, laundry, and kitchen areas and provide off-site public service in forests, parks, highways, and beaches.

An additional 180 male and female inmates are participants in the Oregon SUMMIT Alternative Incarceration Program, which was implemented in March 1994. Offenders volunteer for the intensive cognitive-based program and, if successful, they can reduce their prison term by 30 months or less. Inmates are evaluated daily, and inmates who fail to maintain adequate standards of progress are removed from the program and returned to general population. The program and sentence reduction were authorized by the legislature in 1993.

Snake River Correctional Institution

Address: 777 Stanton Blvd., Ontario 97914-0595
Phone: 541-881-5000
Fax: 541-881-5460
Web: http://oregon.gov/DOC/OPS/PRISON/srci.shtml
Contact: Jean Hill, Superintendent
Duties and Responsibilities: Snake River Correctional Institution (SRCI) is a multi-security facility that opened in August 1991. Although sited for 3,000 beds, only 576 medium security and 72 minimum-security beds were constructed in Phase I. In 1995 the Oregon Legislative Assembly approved construction of the remaining 2,352 beds at a cost of $175 million, representing the largest state General Funded public works project in Oregon's history.

The largest prison in Oregon, Snake River has 105 acres inside the perimeter and 23.4 acres of buildings. SRCI has 2,336 medium-security beds, 154 minimum-security beds and 470 special-housing beds, (disciplinary segregation, intensive management, infirmary, administrative segregation and special management units). SRCI employs more than 900 corrections professionals.

SRCI has a construction trades technology program where inmates build modular buildings. Other work-related programs include a state-of-the-art call center, and training in various building maintenance trades and construction technology.

South Fork Forest Camp

Address: 48300 Wilson River Hwy., Tillamook 97141-9799
Phone: 503-842-2811
Fax: 503-842-6572
Web: http://oregon.gov/DOC/OPS/PRISON/sffc.shtml
Contact: Mike Gower, Superintendent
Duties and Responsibilities: South Fork Forest Camp (SFFC) stands alone in its unique mission and operation within the Department of Corrections. The camp was established in 1951 following the catastrophic Tillamook Burn and is operated in partnership with the State Forestry Department. Inmates housed at SFFC perform numerous reforestation projects in the Tillamook Burn area and are screened, selected, trained and deployed to fight wild fires throughout the state.

SFFC is located 28 miles east of Tillamook and two miles south of Highway 6. It houses 200 minimum-security inmates. SFFC also operates an on-site salmon/steelhead rearing pond in cooperation with the Department of Fish and Wildlife. The prison's boot shop saves taxpayers approximately $35,000 per year by repairing and recycling boots for the department.

Two Rivers Correctional Institution

Address: 82911 Beach Access Rd., Umatilla 97882
Phone: 541-922-2001
Fax: 541-922-2011
Web: http://oregon.gov/DOC/OPS/PRISON/trci.shtml
Contact: Guy Hall, Superintendent
Duties and Responsibilities: Two Rivers Correctional Institution's groundbreaking occurred on April 5, 1997. The institution was substantially complete on March 10, 2000. Operation of the housing units was phased in between December 1999 and September 2001 for an inmate capacity of 1,632. In 2004 the addition of 180 beds brought the population up to 1,812. These include 32 additional beds in Minimum Security, 30 single cells converted to

double cells to add 60 beds, and a dormitory unit created in Workforce adding 88 beds.

TRCI is designated as an education/work facility for long-term inmates. The focus of its programs is Adult Basic Education and GEDs.

COUNSELORS AND THERAPISTS, OREGON BOARD OF LICENSED PROFESSIONAL

Address: 3218 Pringle Rd. SE, Suite 250, Salem 97302-6312
Phone: 503-378-5499
E-mail: lpc.lmft@state.or.us
Web: www.oregon.gov/OBLPCT/
Contact: Julia M. Cooley, Administrator
Statutory Authority: ORS 675.775
Duties and Responsibilities: The Oregon Board of Licensed Professional Counselors and Therapists was created in 1989. The board determines professional qualifications and issues licenses to counselors and marriage and family therapists; sets standards for and regulates the practice of licensees and registered interns working toward licensure; sets and enforces continuing education requirements; publishes an annual directory; and investigates alleged violations and complaints against applicants and licensees. It consists of seven members appointed for three-year terms by the governor: three licensed professional counselors, two licensed marriage and family therapists, a faculty member, and a public representative.

CRIMINAL JUSTICE COMMISSION, OREGON

Address: 635 Capitol St. NE, Suite 350, Salem 97301-2524
Phone: 503-986-6494
Fax: 503-986-4574
E-mail: Phil.Lemman@state.or.us
Web: www.ocjc.state.or.us
Contact: Phillip Lemman, Executive Director
Statutory Authority: ORS 137.651–137.673
Duties and Responsibilities: The Criminal Justice Commission's purpose is to improve the efficiency and effectiveness of state and local criminal justice systems by providing a centralized and impartial forum for statewide policy development and planning. The commission is charged with developing a long-range public safety plan for Oregon, which includes making recommendations on the capacity and use of state prisons and local jails, implementation of community corrections programs and methods to reduce future criminal conduct. The commission also administers juvenile crime prevention grants, conducts research, develops impact estimates of crime-related legislation, acts as a statistical and data clearinghouse, administers Oregon's felony sentencing guidelines and provides staff to advisory committees regarding juvenile crime prevention, asset forfeiture, and racial profiling.

Commission members are appointed to four-year terms by the governor and confirmed by the senate.

DENTISTRY, OREGON BOARD OF

Address: 1600 SW 4th Ave., Suite 770, Portland 97201-5451
Phone: 503-229-5520
Fax: 503-229-6606
E-mail: information@oregondentistry.org
Web: www.oregon.gov/Dentistry/
Contact: Patrick Braatz, Executive Director
Statutory Authority: ORS Chapter 679; 680.010–680.205
Duties and Responsibilities: The Oregon Board of Dentistry was created in 1887 and administers the Dental Practice Act and rules of the board, establishes standards for licensure, and examines and licenses dentists and dental hygienists. The board regulates the use of anesthesia in the dental office and certifies dental assistants in radiologic proficiency and expanded functions. The board investigates alleged violations of the Dental Practice Act and may discipline licensees. Members of the Board of Dentistry are appointed by the governor and confirmed by the senate. There are nine board members: six dentists, one of whom must be a specialist, two dental hygienists and one public member. Members serve for four years.

The board is supported solely by revenues received from licensees, including application, license, permit and certification fees.

DIETITIANS, BOARD OF EXAMINERS OF LICENSED

Address: 800 NE Oregon St., #21, Suite 407, Portland 97232-2187
Phone: 503-731-4085
Fax: 503-731-4207
E-mail: doug.vanfleet@state.or.us
Web: www.bld.state.or.us
Contact: Douglas Van Fleet, Executive Officer
Statutory Authority: ORS 691.405
Duties and Responsibilities: The Board of Examiners of Licensed Dietitians oversees the practice of licensed dietitians by determining the qualifications of applicants for licensure, setting standards of practice, and investigating complaints of alleged violations of practice. The board also provides a consumer information brochure which is available to the public.

DISABILITIES COMMISSION, OREGON

Address: 1257 Ferry St. SE, Salem 97301-4279
Phone: 503-378-3142 (Voice/TTY); Toll-free Instate: 1-800-358-3117 (Voice/TTY)
Fax: 503-378-3599
Web: www.odc.state.or.us
Contact: Janine DeLaunay, Executive Director
Statutory Authority: ORS 185.120
Duties and Responsibilities: The Oregon Disabilities Commission identifies and publicizes the needs and rights of individuals with disabilities; advises the legislature, the governor, state agencies and other public and private agencies on disability issues; coordinates inter-agency efforts in the delivery of disability-related services, and promotes the rehabilitation and employment of the disabled. The commission conducts Oregon's Client Assistance Program, which helps clients in federally funded rehabilitation programs by explaining rules and procedures, client rights and responsibilities, and mediating conflicts. The Deaf and Hard of Hearing Access Program assists state agencies in ensuring that programs and services are accessible to deaf and hearing impaired persons.

The commission has been designated the coordinator for implementing the American with Disabilities Act in Oregon. The Oregon Disabilities Commission also administers Technology Access for Life Needs (TALN). TALN provides information and advocacy on assistive technology for people with disabilities. Commissioners are appointed by the governor and confirmed by the senate for not more than two consecutive three-year terms.

ECONOMIC AND COMMUNITY DEVELOPMENT DEPARTMENT, OREGON

Address: 755 Summer St. NE, Suite 200, Salem 97301-1280
Phone: 503-986-0123
Fax: 503-581-5115
E-mail: oedd.info@state.or.us
Web: www.econ.state.or.us
Contact: Marty Brantley, Director
Statutory Authority: ORS 285A.070
Duties and Responsibilities: The Oregon Economic and Community Development Department (OECDD) provides economic and community development and cultural enhancement throughout the state, and administers programs that assist businesses, communities and people. Oregon's economic development system is designed to meet the state's changing economy, provide flexibility in funding statewide and regional needs, and focus on funding economic and community development services for rural and distressed communities.

The five-member Oregon Economic and Community Development Commission, appointed by the governor, guides department policies and strategies to implement its mission: Assist Oregon businesses and governments to create economic opportunities and build quality communities throughout Oregon.

The department works cooperatively with state and federal agencies, non-profit community groups and organizations, businesses, industry, cities, counties, local economic development districts, ports and other organizations to help solve community and business problems. OECDD is also one of five state agencies that make up the governor's Economic Revitalization Team. The agencies, which include Transportation, Housing, Human Services and Environmental Quality, work together to more efficiently and effectively resolve community issues.

The department helps communities meet needs and standards for clean water and wastewater disposal and other public infrastructure and community facilities, develop telecommunications services and infrastructure, particularly in the areas of rural Oregon that lack adequate service, and support community-identified economic and community development programs.

Five regional teams work collaboratively with local partners to assist businesses, improve local business climate, build community infrastructure and provide training and technical assistance. There are also 12 regional development officers who live in communities throughout Oregon where they serve as key contacts with local and regional partners.

Regional office numbers are:
Baker/Morrow/Umatilla/Union/Wallowa—541-963-8676
Benton/Lane/Lincoln/Linn—541-242-2380
Clackamas/Hood River—503-353-4411
Clatsop/Columbia/Tillamook—503-388-4473
Coos/Curry/Douglas—541-267-4651
Crook/Deschutes/Jefferson—541-388-6266
Gilliam/Sherman/Wasco/Wheeler—541-298-4140
Grant/Harney/Malheur—541-575-1050
Jackson/Josephine—541-776-6234
Klamath/Lake—541-882-9600
Marion/Polk/Yamhill—503-485-9806
Multnomah/Washington—503-229-5115; 503-229-5113

The 2003–05 Legislatively Adopted Budget for the department's program services is $24.6 million ($15.2 million lottery funds, $7.9 million other funds, $1.5 million federal funds) and 107.38 FTE, not including affiliated boards and commissions.

The agency also provides administrative support to the Oregon Arts Commission and distributes funds to the semi-privatized Oregon Film and Video Office. The Oregon Progress Board was transferred from OECDD to the Department of Administrative Services in 2001. The Oregon Tourism Commission became a semi-independent agency in November 2003. The department disbursed the first year of operating funds to the Tourism Commission ($1.3 million of lottery funds).

Oregon Arts Commission

Address: 775 Summer St. NE, Suite 200, Salem 97301-1284
Phone: 503-986-0082
Fax: 503-986-0260
E-mail: oregon.artscomm@state.or.us
Web: www.oregonartscommission.org
Contact: Christine T. D'Arcy, Executive Director
Statutory Authority: ORS 359.020
Duties and Responsibilities: The Oregon Arts Commission works with a variety of customers to promote the arts in Oregon. From the individual artist to organizations and educational institutions, the commission acts as an advisor and catalyst. Commission staff help build local ability to improve community involvement in the arts and annually undertakes specific projects serving Oregon's cultural community. The commission provides grants to non-profit arts organizations and individual artists, information about arts resources in Oregon and support for lifelong arts education experiences. The commission works in partnership with 11 regional program providers.

Oregon Cultural Trust

Address: 775 Summer St. NE, Suite 200. Salem 97301
Phone: 503-986-0088
Fax: 503-986-0260
E-mail: cultural.trust@state.or.us
Web: www.culturaltrust.org
Contact: Christine T. D'Arcy, Executive Director
Statutory Authority: ORS 359.020
Duties and Responsibilities: The Oregon Cultural Trust is a statewide cultural plan to raise significant new funds to invest in Oregon's arts, humanities and heritage. The Trust provides resources needed to guarantee that every Oregonian benefits from our state's cultural assets. By 2011, Cultural Trust's goal is to build an endowment of over $200 million to provide long-term funding for Oregon's culture. Over the same ten years, the Trust plans to distribute $90 million in new funding for cultural initiatives.

Funds from the Trust are distributed to counties and tribes to support local cultural projects, granted to nonprofit cultural organizations for projects of regional and statewide significance, and appropriated to Oregon's existing cultural agencies to support ongoing programs. Funds for the Trust are raised through sales of a distinctive license plate, and surplus state-owned properties, and contributions from private citizens and businesses. Donations to the Trust qualify donors for a 100% credit on their Oregon taxes—up to $500 for individuals and $2500 for corporations—when a matching gift is also made to a qualified cultural nonprofit organization.

The Trust works in partnership with the Oregon Arts Commission, Oregon Council for the Humanities, Oregon Historical Society, State Historic Preservation Office and the Oregon Heritage Commission. It is governed by a nine member board of directors, comprised of citizens from around the state, all of whom are committed to the cultural development of Oregon. The seven citizens appointed by the governor serve as voting members of the board. The Speaker of the House of Representatives and the President of the Senate each appoint a member of the Legislative Assembly as non-voting advisory members. The Trust is administered by the Oregon Arts Commission, which reports to the citizen board of directors.

Oregon Film and Video Office

Address: One World Trade Center, 121 SW Salmon St., Suite 1205, Portland 97204
Phone: 503-229-5832
Fax: 503-229-6869
Web: www.oregonfilm.org
Contact: Veronica Rinard, Executive Director
Statutory Authority: ORS 284.305
Duties and Responsibilities: The Oregon Film and Video Office acts as a liaison between production companies and Oregon businesses, citizens and government. The office markets film locations and the film and television workforce within Oregon in addition to promoting Oregon companies and workers in the emerging areas of multimedia. The office also recruits film and video related businesses to relocate to Oregon on a permanent basis and serves as a resource for local communities interested in attracting film production.

Oregon Tourism Commission

Address: 775 Summer St. NE, Suite 200, Salem 97301-1282
Phone: 503-986-0000
Fax: 503-986-0001
E-mail: info.oregontourism@state.or.us
Web: www.traveloregon.com
Contact: Todd Davidson, Executive Director
Statutory Authority: ORS 285A.261
Duties and Responsibilities: The Oregon Tourism Commission, created in 1995, encourages economic growth through a strengthened economic

impact of tourism throughout the state. Staff work closely with Oregon communities, providing expertise and assistance in the development, marketing and evaluation of tourism products and resources. Governed by nine appointed commissioners, staff work to address environmental, developmental and long-range planning issues. The commission provides statewide leadership in addressing the needs of the tourism industry and plays an "umbrella" role in marketing the state through its publications, public relations, international marketing, research, tourism development, and the state's Welcome Centers.

EMPLOYMENT DEPARTMENT

Address: 875 Union St. NE, Salem 97311
Phone: 503-947-1470; Toll-free: 1-800-237-3710
Fax: 503-947-1472
E-mail: info@cmp.state.or.us
Web: www.oregon.gov/EMPLOY/
Contact: Deborah Lincoln, Director
Statutory Authority: ORS 657.601
Duties and Responsibilities: The Employment Department was created in 1993. The department is an active partner in the development of the state's workforce. The mission of the Employment Department is to promote employment of Oregonians through developing a diversified, multi-skilled workforce, promoting quality child care, and providing support during periods of unemployment. Through 48 offices across the state, the department serves business and promotes employment by: helping workers find suitable employment; providing qualified applicants for employers; supplying statewide and local labor market information; providing unemployment insurance benefits to workers temporarily unemployed through no fault of their own, and assuring safe and quality child care.

The department offers a number of services. It serves employers through timely recruitment of a qualified workforce, customizing state and local labor market information for use as a business planning tool, and by offering job-matching services based on the need of each employer. Labor market economists and research analysts identify major workforce policy areas that require additional research and present their findings and ideas for solutions to decision makers. Statewide, regional, and local economic information is prepared for use by employers, community leaders, and policy makers. The department helps job seekers find jobs that match their skills and employers' needs, provides them with up-to-date information about trends in occupations and skills needed for success in the job market, and works with other agencies to direct them to appropriate training programs and job experiences.

Employment Appeals Board

Address: 875 Union St. NE, Salem 97311
Phone: 503-947-1500
Fax: 503-947-1504
Contact: Mary Feldbruegge, Chair
Statutory Authority: ORS 657.685–657.690
Duties and Responsibilities: The three-member Employment Appeals Board (EAB) is appointed by the governor to review hearing decisions issued in contested unemployment insurance claims cases. The board performs new revisions of 2,500 to 3,000 cases per year, with authority to affirm, modify or reverse the decisions of Administrative Law Judges of the Employment Department, or to remand for additional evidence. Final written decisions of the EAB are subject to review by the Oregon Court of Appeals.

Employment Department Advisory Council

Address: 875 Union St. NE, Salem 97311
Phone: 503-947-1734
Contact: Tammy Adkins, Coordinator
Statutory Authority: ORS 657.695
Duties and Responsibilities: The Employment Department Advisory Council includes volunteer representatives of the public, management and labor. Council members are appointed by the governor. The council assists the director of the Employment Department in the effective development of policies and programs with respect to unemployment insurance, employment services, labor market information, and child care.

Oregon Employer Council

Address: 875 Union St. NE, Salem 97311
Phone: 503-947-1305
Contact: Marney Roddick, Coordinator
Duties and Responsibilities: The Oregon Employer Council is a partnership between Oregon employers and the Employment Department. The council brings together volunteer employer representatives who serve as advisors to the Employment Department to identify and address employment issues, primarily in the areas of employment services and other business needs. The council also provides educational seminars and job fairs for employers.

Child Care Division

Address: 875 Union St. NE, Salem 97311
Phone: 503-947-1407; 1-800-556-6616
Fax: 503-947-1428
E-mail: child_care@emp.state.or.us
Web: www.oregon.gov/EMPLOY/CCD/
Contact: Tom Olsen, Administrator
Statutory Authority: ORS 657A.010
Duties and Responsibilities: The Child Care Division is responsible for regulating child care

centers and family child care homes. The division also administers the federal Child Care and Development Fund (CCDF) which provides support and assistance to low-income working families, child care resource and referral agencies, community-based child care programs, and training and technical assistance to child care providers. The division also uses CCDF funds to support child care for high risk populations including migrant and seasonal workers, parents in substance abuse treatment, teen and post secondary student parents, and children with special needs.

Commission for Child Care

Address: 875 Union St. NE, Salem 97311
Phone: 503-947-1891
Web: www.findit.emp.state.or.us/occc/
Contact: Claudia Grimm, Executive Officer
Statutory Authority: ORS 657A.600–657A.640
Duties and Responsibilities: The Commission for Child Care was established in 1985, and moved to the Employment Department in 1993. The commission serves as an advisory board to the governor and the legislature on the issues, problems, and alternative solutions that are critical to the development of accessible, affordable, and quality child care services. The commission is comprised of 18 members. Three members represent the legislature, are appointed to two-year terms and are non-voting. The 15 voting members represent specific areas of expertise, and are appointed to three-year terms. The commission collaborates with public- and private-sector partners to advocate and provide information statewide for creative solutions to address Oregon's child care challenges.

Office of Administrative Hearings

Address: 605 Cottage St. NE, Salem 97301
Phone: 503-378-5432
Contact: Thomas E. Ewing, Chief Administrative Law Judge
Duties and Responsibilities: The Office of Administrative Hearings was created by the legislature in 1999, to provide an independent and impartial forum for citizens and businesses to dispute state agency action against them. Seventy professional administrative law judges hold over 37,000 hearings a year for approximately 70 state agencies. By statute, all administrative law judges are required to be "impartial in the performance of their duties, and to remain fair in all hearings." Oregon is the 22nd state in the nation with an independent central panel of administrative law judges.

EMPLOYMENT RELATIONS BOARD

Address: Old Garfield School Bldg., 528 Cottage St. NE, Suite 400, Salem 97301-3807
Phone: 503-378-3807
Fax: 503-373-0021
E-mail: emprel.board@state.or.us
Web: www.erb.state.or.us
Contact: Paul B. Gamson, Chair
Statutory Authority: ORS Chapter 240; 243.650–243.782, 662.405–662.445, 663.005–663.325
Duties and Responsibilities: The Employment Relations Board was established in 1977. The board determines appropriate bargaining units for state and local governments and private companies not involved in interstate commerce. The board also conducts elections to determine which labor organization, if any, the employees want to represent them in collective bargaining. It resolves unfair labor practice complaints and determines whether strikes are lawful. The board's Conciliation Service Division provides mediation services for resolving collective bargaining disputes in public and private employment and provides lists of fact-finders and arbitrators for the resolution of labor disputes. The board reviews personnel actions alleged to be arbitrary, contrary to law or rule, or taken for political reasons that affect unrepresented, classified state employees. The board consists of three members appointed by the governor for four-year terms.

ENERGY, DEPARTMENT OF

Address: 625 Marion St. NE, Salem 97301-3737
Phone: 503-378-4040; 1-800-221-8035 (Toll-free in Oregon)
Fax: 503-373-7806
E-mail: energy.in.internet@state.or.us
Web: www.energy.state.or.us
Contact: Michael Grainey, Director
Statutory Authority: ORS Chapters 469, 470
Duties and Responsibilities: The Department of Energy was created in 1975. The department ensures Oregon has an adequate supply of reliable and affordable energy and is safe from nuclear contamination, by helping Oregonians save energy, develop clean energy resources, promote renewable energy and clean up nuclear waste. To encourage investments in energy efficiency and conservation, the department offers loans, tax credits, information and technical expertise to households, businesses, schools and governments. The department works to ensure that Oregon's mix of energy resources minimizes harm to the environment and reliably meets the state's needs. To meet this commitment, the department formulates energy policies, advances the development of renewable energy resources, and evaluates whether proposed energy facilities are safe

and environmentally acceptable. The department also oversees the cleanup and safe transport of radioactive waste, and develops and implements emergency plans in the event of an accident involving radioactive materials. A major focus is the cleanup of radioactive waste at the Hanford nuclear site on the Columbia River in eastern Washington and the Trojan nuclear plant in Columbia County. The department staffs two energy policy and regulatory boards. The Energy Facility Siting Council is a board of citizens that determines whether energy facilities may be built in Oregon. The Hanford Cleanup Board represents Oregon's interests related to the Hanford site.

Energy Facility Siting Council
Address: 625 Marion St. NE, Salem 97301-3737
Phone: 503-378-4040; 1-800-221-8035 (Toll-free in Oregon)
Contact: Karen Green, Chair

Hanford Cleanup Board
Address: 625 Marion St. NE, Salem 97301-3737
Phone: 503-378-4040; 1-800-221-8035 (Toll-free in Oregon)
Contact: Barbara Jarvis, Chair

ENGINEERING AND LAND SURVEYING, STATE BOARD OF EXAMINERS FOR

Address: 728 Hawthorne Ave. NE, Salem 97301
Phone: 503-362-2666
Fax: 503-362-5454
E-mail: osbeels@osbeels.org
Web: www.osbeels.org
Contact: Mari Lopez, Executive Secretary
Statutory Authority: ORS 672.240
Duties and Responsibilities: The State Board of Examiners for Engineering and Land Surveying regulates the practices of engineering and land surveying in the state in order to safeguard the public's life, health and property. Activities are supported entirely by fees received from applicants and licensed professionals.

ENVIRONMENTAL QUALITY, DEPARTMENT OF

Address: 811 SW 6th Ave., Portland 97204-1390
Phone: 503-229-5696; TDD: 503-229-6993; Toll-free (Oregon only): 1-800-452-4011
Fax: 503-229-6124
Web: www.deq.state.or.us
Contact: Stephanie Hallock, Director
Statutory Authority: ORS Chapters 454, 459, 466, 467, 468
Duties and Responsibilities: The Department of Environmental Quality (DEQ) was created in 1969

when the State Sanitary Authority was dissolved. The Sanitary Authority was created in 1938 when outraged citizens overwhelmingly supported an initiative petition to clean up the Willamette River. Today, DEQ is responsible for protecting and enhancing Oregon's water and air quality and for managing the proper disposal of solid and hazardous wastes.

The DEQ consists of approximately 700 scientists, engineers, technicians, administrators, and environmental specialists. The agency's headquarters are in Portland with regional administrative offices in Bend, Eugene, and Portland; and field offices in Coos Bay, Grants Pass, Hermiston, Medford, Pendleton, Roseburg, Salem, and The Dalles. A modern pollution-control laboratory operates on the Portland State University campus. The agency completed a major reorganization during the 1995–97 budget period that transferred about 50 percent of the Portland headquarters staff to positions in the field.

The DEQ director has the authority to issue civil penalties (fines) for violation of pollution laws and standards. The DEQ relies on several advisory committees of citizens and government officials to help guide its decision-making.

Environmental Quality Commission
Address: 811 SW 6th Ave., Portland 97204
Phone: 503-229-5301
Fax: 503-229-6762
Contact: Mark Reeve, Chair
Duties and Responsibilities: The Environmental Quality Commission, DEQ's policy and rulemaking board, adopts administrative rules, issues orders and judges appeals of fines or other department actions, and hires the DEQ director. Commission members are appointed to four-year terms by the governor.

Air Quality Division
Address: 811 SW 6th Ave., Portland 97204-1380
Phone: 503-229-5397
Fax: 503-229-5675
Web: www.deq.state.or.us
Contact: Andy Ginsburg, Administrator
Duties and Responsibilities: The Air Quality Division's goal is to achieve clean and healthy air for all Oregonians. DEQ works to ensure that federal clean air standards are met, that the public is protected from toxic air pollutants and that our scenic vistas are visible. To meet these goals, DEQ develops and implements strategies to reduce emissions from industry, cars, burning and other sources of air pollution. Among other strategies, DEQ regulates some 1,200 sources of industrial air pollution through permits, operates a vehicle emission inspection program in the Portland area and in the Rogue Valley, and protects the public from asbestos in buildings that are being demolished or remodeled.

Land Quality Division

Address: 811 SW 6th Ave., Portland 97204-1380
Phone: 503-229-5332
Fax: 503-229-6977
Web: www.deq.state.or.us/wmc
Contact: Alan Kiphut, Administrator
Duties and Responsibilities: The Land Quality Division oversees agency programs in environmental cleanup and site assessment, hazardous and solid waste, spill response and underground storage tanks.

The division maintains an inventory of all sites in the state with a confirmed release of hazardous material into the environment. DEQ assesses these sites for potential threats to human health and the environment and, where appropriate, supervises development and implementation of cleanup strategies.

The emergency response program provides DEQ's all-hours, seven-days-a-week capability to deal with releases of hazardous materials and oil to both land and water. As the state's lead agency for cleanup of hazardous material and oil, the program provides on-scene incident commanders for major cleanups in coordination with the U.S. Environmental Protection Agency and the U.S. Coast Guard.

DEQ oversees Oregon's only hazardous waste landfill, located in Arlington, and regulates hazardous waste disposal from the point of origin until final disposal. The department emphasizes pollution prevention techniques and offers technical assistance to businesses to minimize the amount of hazardous waste generated. A special section regulates underground storage tanks which can pose a major threat to the environment because of the potential for tank contents to leak and pollute groundwater. Solid waste landfills are regulated by DEQ permits which set requirements for design, operation and monitoring. DEQ promotes solid waste reduction education and implements a statewide recycling law that requires cities to provide curbside recycling collection and reduce garbage volume going into landfills.

Water Quality Division

Address: 811 SW 6th Ave., Portland 97204-1380
Phone: 503-229-6785
Fax: 503-229-5408
Web: www.deq.state.or.us
Contact: Holly Schroeder, Administrator
Duties and Responsibilities: The Water Quality Division sets and enforces water quality standards and monitors 19 river basins for water quality. DEQ also monitors and assesses groundwater and implements strategies to protect this valuable resource. Oregon law prohibits discharging pollution into

Oregon water without a DEQ permit. DEQ regulates more than 3,800 waste discharges from city sewage treatment plants, industrial facilities and stormwater discharges. DEQ develops strategies to reduce pollution carried by runoff from urban areas, agriculture, forest practices, and construction. The program provides loans to local governments for sewage treatment systems and nonpoint control. DEQ also regulates the installation of onsite sewage disposal.

FISH AND WILDLIFE, OREGON DEPARTMENT OF

Address: 3406 Cherry Ave. NE, Salem 97303-4924
Phone: 503-947-6000; Toll-free: 1-800-720-6339 (ODFW); TDD (Hearing Impaired Access): 503-947-6339; Licensing: 503-947-6101; Controlled Hunts Hotline (Recorded): 503-947-6102
E-mail: Odfw.Info@state.or.us
Web: www.dfw.state.or.us

Director's Office

Address: 3406 Cherry Ave. NE, Salem 97303-4924
Phone: 503-947-6044
Fax: 503-947-6042
Contact: Lindsay A. Ball, Director; Roy Elicker, Deputy Director for Fish and Wildlife Programs; Kris Kautz, Deputy Director for Administration Programs
Statutory Authority: ORS 496.080–496.166
Duties and Responsibilities: The Oregon Department of Fish and Wildlife (ODFW) is responsible for all Oregon fish and wildlife resources and their habitats for use and enjoyment by present and future generations. The agency's responsibilities include operating hatcheries, selling hunting and angling licenses, advising on habitat protection for Oregon's diverse wildlife populations and educating the public on natural resource issues. ODFW works closely with other federal and state agencies, tribes, volunteers, property owners, hunters and anglers to balance protection of fish and wildlife with the economic, social and recreational needs of Oregonians.

Oregon Fish and Wildlife Commission

Address: 3406 Cherry Ave. NE, Salem 97303-4924
Phone: 503-947-6044
Contact: Marla Rae, Chair
Statutory Authority: ORS 496.090

Administrative Services Division

Address: 3406 Cherry Ave. NE, Salem 97303-4924

Phone: 503-947-6151

Fax: 503-947-6156

Contact: Deanne Depew, Administrator

Duties and Responsibilities: The Administrative Services Division oversees the department's fishing and hunting licensing responsibilities, fiscal management, budget and contracts management, and economic forecasting and monitoring for the agency.

Fish Division

Address: 3406 Cherry Ave. NE, Salem 97303-4924

Phone: 503-947-6201

Fax: 503-947-6202

Contact: Edward Bowles, Administrator

Duties and Responsibilities: The Fish Division manages fish populations by setting regulations for gamefish species, monitoring populations and operating 34 fish hatcheries which produce up to 80 percent of all salmon, trout and steelhead caught in Oregon each year. The division works cooperatively with other state and federal agencies and tribes on habitat and fishery management issues for inland and ocean waters, works with landowners to improve and protect habitat and coordinates law enforcement needs and activities with the Oregon State Police.

Restoration and Enhancement Board

Address: 3406 Cherry Ave. NE, Salem 97303-4924

Phone: 503-947-6232

Contact: Gary Galovich, Coordinator

Human Resources Division

Address: 3406 Cherry Ave. NE, Salem 97303-4924

Phone: 503-947-6051

Fax: 503-947-6050

Contact: Roxie Burns, Administrator

Duties and Responsibilities: The Human Resources Division serves 1,300 employees statewide. The division provides programs to recruit, maintain, train and reward an effective and diverse workforce in a safe environment.

Information and Education Division

Address: 3406 Cherry Ave. NE, Salem 97303-4924

Phone: 503-947-6000; Recorded Information: 503-947-6001

Fax: 503-947-6009

Contact: Ann Snyder, Administrator

Duties and Responsibilities: The Information and Education Division teaches individuals the skills needed to safely participate in aquatic, angling, hunting and other outdoor activities. The division also informs the public about recreational opportunities throughout the state, fishing and hunting regulations, wildlife viewing opportunities, habitat issues, and other issues related to the state's fish and wildlife resources.

Information Systems Division

Address: 3406 Cherry Ave. NE, Salem 97303-4924

Phone: 503-947-6271

Fax: 503-947-6265

Contact: Doug Juergensen, Administrator

Duties and Responsibilities: Information Systems Division is responsible for developing and supporting information processing systems services and training, coordinating development and use of information systems technology, and maintaining the Point-of-Sale computer system for license sales.

Wildlife Division

Address: 3406 Cherry Ave. NE, Salem 97303-4924

Phone: 503-947-6300

Fax: 503-947-6330

Contact: Ron Anglin, Administrator

Duties and Responsibilities: The Wildlife Division manages all game and non-game wildlife species in Oregon, manages game species by setting hunting and trapping regulations, and relocating wildlife or applying other management techniques. The division manages non-hunted species through the Wildlife Diversity Program, works cooperatively with other state and federal agencies and tribes on habitat and wildlife management issues, works with landowners to improve habitat or manage animal damage complaints, and coordinates law enforcement needs and activities with the Oregon State Police.

Access and Habitat Board

Address: 3406 Cherry Ave. NE, Salem 97303-4924

Phone: 503-947-6087

Contact: Nick Myatt, Coordinator

Statutory Authority: ORS 496.228

FORESTRY DEPARTMENT, STATE

Address: 2600 State St., Salem 97310

Phone: 503-945-7200; TTY: 1-800-437-4490

Fax: 503-945-7212

E-mail: info.odf@state.or.us

Web: www.odf.state.or.us
Contact: Marvin Brown, State Forester
Statutory Authority: ORS 526.008
Duties and Responsibilities: The State Forestry Department was established in 1911. It is under the direction of the state forester who is appointed by the State Board of Forestry. The statutes direct the state forester to act on all matters pertaining to forestry, including collecting and sharing information about the conditions of Oregon's forests, protecting forestlands and conserving forest resources. Specific activities include fire protection for 16 million acres of private, state and federal forests; regulation of forest practices (under the Oregon Forest Practices Act) and promotion of forest stewardship; implementation of the Oregon Plan for Salmon and Watersheds; detection and control of harmful forest insect pests and forest tree diseases on 12 million acres of state and private lands; management of 780,000 acres of state-owned forestlands; operation of a 15-million-tree forest nursery; forestry assistance to Oregon's 166,000 non-industrial private woodland owners; forest resource planning; and community and urban forestry assistance.

State Board of Forestry

Contact: Stephen Hobbs, Chair
Statutory Authority: ORS Chapter 526
Duties and Responsibilities: The Board of Forestry is a seven-member citizen board appointed by the governor and confirmed by the senate. It is charged by law to represent the public interest. No more than three members of the board may receive any significant portion of their income from the forest products industry. At least one member must reside in each of the three major forest regions of the state. The term of office is four years and no member of the board can serve more than two consecutive full terms.

The Board of Forestry is empowered by the Oregon Legislature to oversee all matters of forest policy within the jurisdiction of the state. Additionally, the board appoints the state forester, adopts rules regulating forest practices and other forestry programs, and provides general supervision of the state forester's duties in managing the Forestry Department. Therefore, the board supervises many actions: policymaking, public debate facilitation, environmental regulation, management of state-owned and private forestland, wildland firefighting, and most importantly, advocacy for the sustainable management of Oregon's forests. The board does not limit its scope to state or private forestlands. Its policies and leadership are designed to include federal lands and to have a positive influence over all of the state's 27.5 million acre forests.

The board periodically develops a strategic plan called the Forestry Program for Oregon (FPFO).

The FPFO describes the Board of Forestry's guidance to the state forester, legislature, governor and to the citizens on matters of forest policy the board considers important. It guides the actions of the board itself and the Forestry Department as they work with the public, the legislature, the forest landowner community, non-governmental organizations, and other agencies in implementing sound forest policy. With nearly 45 percent of Oregon's land base covered by forests, the successful implementation of this vision can profoundly affect the lives of all Oregonians.

County Forestland Classification Committees

Address: 2600 State St., Salem 97310
Phone: 503-945-7205
Contact: Charlie Stone, Assistant State Forester
Statutory Authority: ORS 526.305–526.350
Duties and Responsibilities: Each county may establish a County Forestland Classification Committee of five persons, one appointed by the state forester, one by the director of the Oregon State University Extension Service and three by the county governing body. At least one member must be an owner of forestland and at least one an owner of grazing land. These committees are charged with investigating forestlands to determine how the lands are to be classified. The classifications are used by the Board of Forestry and the state forester in administering all of Oregon's forest and fire laws, promoting the primary use for which that land is classified. Class 1 includes all forestland primarily suitable for timber production, Class 2 includes all forestland suitable for joint timber and livestock grazing, and Class 3 includes all forestland suitable primarily for grazing and other agricultural uses.

The committee must hold public hearings before final classifications and reclassification. Appeals by landowners may be taken to the circuit court. When no classification of forestland is made by a committee, the state forester may make this determination.

Emergency Fire Cost Committee

Address: 2600 State St., Salem 97310
Phone: 503-945-7449
Contact: Tom Lane, Fund Administrator
Statutory Authority: ORS 477.750
Duties and Responsibilities: The Emergency Fire Cost Committee supervises and controls the distribution of monies from the Oregon Forest Land Protection Fund which was established for emergency firefighting expenditures in controlling forest fires. Four members are appointed to the committee by the State Board of Forestry to serve four-year terms.

Forest Resource Trust
Advisory Committee

Address: 2600 State St., Salem 97310
Phone: 503-945-7493
Contact: Jim Cathcart
Statutory Authority: ORS 526.700
Duties and Responsibilities: The Forest Resource Trust Advisory Committee was established in 1993. The Forest Resource Trust provides funds for financial, technical and related assistance to private non-industrial forest landowners. This assistance is used for timber stand establishment and improved management of forestlands for timber production as well as for wildlife, water quality and other environmental purposes. The Board of Forestry has responsibility for managing the trust. The committee assists the board in setting policy for the best use and investment of funds available to the trust and otherwise assisting board members in carrying out trustee duties. The state forester is responsible for implementing board policies and trust programs.

Forest Trust Land
Advisory Committee

Address: 2600 State St., Salem 97310
Phone: 503-945-7204
Contact: Steve Thomas, Assistant State Forester
Statutory Authority: ORS 530.010–530.170
Duties and Responsibilities: The 1987 Legislature established the Forest Trust Land Advisory Committee to advise the State Board of Forestry and the state forester on the management of lands subject to the provisions of statutes, and on other matters in which the counties may have a responsibility pertaining to forestland. The 1997 Legislature amended the statutes pertaining to the composition of the committee; the committee is now composed of the Board of Directors of the Council of Forest Trust Land Counties. The council represents the 15 state/county forest trust land counties in policy matters related to the management of the forestlands and distribution of revenues produced from those lands.

Regional Forest Practice Committees

Address: 2600 State St., Salem 97310
Phone: 503-945-7482
Contact: Gregg Cline, Private and Community Forests Program Director
Statutory Authority: ORS 527.650
Duties and Responsibilities: The Northwest Oregon, Southwest Oregon and Eastern Oregon Regional Forest Practice Committees make recommendations to the Board of Forestry on forest practice rules appropriate to the forest conditions in their regions. The Board of Forestry appoints nine members to each committee, to serve three-year terms.

FOREST RESOURCES INSTITUTE, OREGON

Address: 317 SW 6th Ave., Suite 400, Portland 97204
Phone: 503-229-6718; 1-800-719-9195
Fax: 503-229-5823
E-mail: info@ofri.com
Web: www.oregonforests.org
Contact: Leslie Lehmann, Executive Director
Statutory Authority: ORS 526.600–526.685
Duties and Responsibilities: The Oregon Forest Resources Institute (OFRI) was created in 1991 by the legislature to improve public understanding of Oregon's forest resources—including how our forests can be managed to meet environmental, social and economic needs—and to provide landowner training in environmentally sound forest practices. OFRI is funded by a portion of the harvest tax on forest products producers and is under the direction of a Board of Directors representing small, medium and large forest products producers, small woodland owners and forestry employees. A public representative and the dean of the Oregon State University College of Forestry also serve on the board.

OFRI's programs include workshops and curriculum support programs for teachers, forest tours that provide opportunities to learn about modern forest practices, publications on a wide range of subjects, a web site, support for scientific research, conferences and workshops, displays and interpretive programs, and workplace forestry education for forestry employees and their families.

GEOLOGIST EXAMINERS, STATE BOARD OF

Address: 1193 Royvonne Ave. SE, #24, Salem 97302
Phone: 503-566-2837
Fax: 503-485-2947
E-mail: osbge@osbge.org
Web: www.osbge.org
Contact: Susanna Knight, Administrator
Statutory Authority: ORS 672.615
Duties and Responsibilities: The purpose of the State Board of Geologist Examiners, established in 1977, is to safeguard the health, welfare and property of Oregonians affected by the geologic fields of ground water, land-use planning, mineral exploration and development, geologic hazards and the further development of the science of geology through the regulation of professional practice.

The board evaluates qualifications, examines and registers geologists, certifies those with engineering specialty, and suspends, revokes or refuses to renew registration or certification, and assesses civil penalties when warranted. The board practices cooperative registration with other states that register geologists.

GEOLOGY AND MINERAL INDUSTRIES, OREGON DEPARTMENT OF

Address: 800 NE Oregon St., Suite 965, Portland 97232
Phone: 503-731-4100
Fax: 503-731-4066
Web: www.oregongeology.com
Contact: Vicki McConnell, State Geologist
Statutory Authority: ORS Chapters 516, 517, 520, 522
Duties and Responsibilities: The Oregon Department of Geology and Mineral Industries was created in 1937, and is Oregon's centralized source of geologic information. It produces maps and reports that can be used by the public and by government to reduce the loss of life and property due to geologic hazards and to manage geologic resources, including water. It helps Oregonians understand and prepare for earthquakes, tsunamis, coastal erosion, landslides, floods, and other geologic hazards. It is lead regulator for geologic resources (oil; gas; geothermal energy; metallic and industrial minerals; and sand, gravel, and crushed stone), with attention paid to environmental, reclamation, conservation, and related economic, engineering, and technical issues.

The department provides geologic data to assist in policy development through publications and release of electronic data, and through department participation in and coordination with state, federal, and local governmental natural resource agencies as well as with industry and other private sector groups. The department's library is a specialized central repository for both published and unpublished state geologic information.

The Mineral Land Regulation and Reclamation Program (which is located at 229 Broadalbin St. SE, Albany 97321, phone 541-967-2039, fax 541-523-5992), is the lead coordinating agency for state mining regulation, operating through an interagency team-permit process. In Oregon, exploration and operating permits and bonds are required to ensure reclamation of land disturbed by mining.

Field Offices:

Baker City
Address: 1510 Campbell St., Baker City 97814
Phone: 541-523-3133
Fax: 541-523-5992

Coastal Field Office
Address: 313 SW 2nd St., Suite D, Newport 97365

Phone: 541-574-6642
Fax: 541-265-5241

Grants Pass
Address: 5375 Monument Dr., Grants Pass 97526
Phone: 541-476-2496
Fax: 541-474-3158

Geology and Mineral Industries Governing Board

Contact: Vera Simonton, Chair
Duties and Responsibilities: The Geology and Mineral Industries Governing Board appoints the State Geologist and approves the agency budget. The governor appoints five members to four-year terms.

The Nature of the Northwest Information Center

Address: 800 NE Oregon St., Suite 177, Portland 97232
Phone: 503-872-2750; TDD: 503-872-2752
Fax: 503-731-4066
E-mail: info@naturenw.org
Web: www.naturenw.org
Contact: Don Haines, Center Administrator
Duties and Responsibilities: The Nature of the Northwest Information Center is operated by the Department of Geology and Mineral Industries in partnership with the USDA Forest Service on behalf of other state natural resource agencies. The center provides "one-stop shopping" for natural resource, natural science, and outdoor recreation maps, books, and brochures (some for sale, some free), which are primarily produced by state, federal, and local government natural resource agencies.

GOVERNMENT STANDARDS AND PRACTICES COMMISSION, OREGON

Address: 100 High St. SE, Suite 220, Salem 97301-3607
Phone: 503-378-5105
Fax: 503-373-1456
E-mail: gspc.mail@state.or.us
Contact: L. Patrick Hearn, Executive Director
Web: www.oregon.gov/GSPC/
Statutory Authority: ORS, 171.725–171.785, 192.660, 192.685, Chapter 244
Duties and Responsibilities: The Oregon Government Standards and Practices Commission (GSPC), established by vote of the people in 1974, is a seven-member citizen commission charged with enforcing government standards and practices (ethics) laws. Government standards and practices laws prohibit public officials from using office for financial gain, and require public disclosure of economic conflict

of interest. The GSPC also enforces state laws which require lobbyists and the entities they represent to register and periodically report their expenditures. The third area of GSPC jurisdiction is the executive session provisions of public meetings law. Before 1993, the agency was known as the Oregon Government Ethics Commission.

HEALTH LICENSING OFFICE

Address: 700 Summer St. NE, Suite 320, Salem 97301-1287
Phone: 503-378-8667; TTY: 503-373-2114
Fax: 503-585-9114
E-mail: hlo.info@state.or.us
Web: www.hlo.state.or.us
Contact: Susan K. Wilson, Director
Statutory Authority: ORS 676.600–676.992
Duties and Responsibilities: The Health Licensing Office (HLO) is an independent consumer protection agency providing centralized regulatory oversight for multiple citizens' boards, advisory councils and licensing programs of health and related professions. The agency's mission is to protect the health and safety of Oregon citizens by setting, communicating and enforcing uniform regulatory standards.

The agency works to actively promote consumer protection through education, enforcement and partnerships; to promote a positive business environment by reducing barriers to professional practice; and to provide excellent customer service to all agency clients and stakeholders.

The boards and councils under the agency's administration set educational and professional scope of practice requirements but are not responsible for central agency operations. The agency director assumes ultimate responsibility for the accountability of the agency, for achieving outcomes, complying with state law and ensuring stewardship of the funds entrusted for agency operations by the legislature. The director provides overall vision and leadership for the agency budget, legislative agenda and determination of policy formulation.

The agency proactively pursues regulatory streamlining initiatives in an effort to make regulations simpler and cheaper for both individuals and business owners. The agency's performance measures, which can be accessed online, provide a quick snapshot of how well it is achieving its mission and accomplishing its public service goals.

The following volunteer citizens' boards and councils—and one licensing program, body piercing, with no professional representation—are under the agency's administrative oversight. For more information on HLO-regulated professions, please visit the agency web site. For specific inquiries, please contact the Health Licensing Office.

Advisory Council for Electrologists, Permanent Color Technicians and Tattoo Artists

Statutory Authority: ORS 690.350–690.992
Duties and Responsibilities: This governor-appointed council consists of two practicing electrologists, one permanent color technician or tattoo artist with two years of experience, one licensed physician and one public member.

Electrologists, through a series of treatments, permanently remove hair from the skin by inserting a sterile needle-conductor into the hair follicle and directing electrical energy toward the hair cell. Electrologists work in beauty salons, in collaboration with dermatologists, and in private practice.

Tattoo artists and permanent color technicians mark or color the skin by inserting nontoxic dyes or pigments into or under the subcutaneous portion of the skin using single-use or sterile needles to form indelible marks for figurative, decorative, cosmetic or medical purposes.

Advisory Council on Hearing Aids

Statutory Authority: ORS 694.015–694.991
Duties and Responsibilities: This governor-appointed council consists of four hearing aid specialists, one licensed physician certified in otolaryngology (ear, nose, throat), one certified audiologist and one public member who is a consumer of hearing aids.

Anyone who sells, leases or rents hearing aids in conjunction with the evaluation or measurement of human hearing must be licensed as a hearing aid specialist. Hearing aid specialists recommend, select or adapt hearing aids and may alter, adjust or reconstruct hearing aids specifications for proper functionality, such as taking ear impressions for proper fit.

Board of Athletic Trainers

Statutory Authority: Oregon Laws 1999, 2003, Chapter 547
Duties and Responsibilities: This governor-appointed board consists of three practicing athletic trainers, one physician and one public member.

Athletic trainers prevent, recognize and evaluate athletic injuries and provide immediate care, rehabilitation and reconditioning services to athletes. Athletic trainers work in cooperation with physicians and other allied health personnel and function as an integral member of the athletic health care team at secondary schools, colleges and universities, sports medicine clinics, professional sports programs and other athletic health care settings.

Board of Cosmetology

Statutory Authority: ORS 690.005–690.992

Duties and Responsibilities: This governor-appointed board consists of six certified practitioners and one public member.

Cosmetologists earn certification in one or more of four separate fields of practice: barbering, hair design, facial technology and nail technology. As defined in state statute, "cosmetology" means the art or science of beautifying and improving the skin, nails and hair, and includes the study of cosmetics and their application.

Board of Denture Technology
Statutory Authority: ORS 680.500–680.990
Duties and Responsibilities: This governor-appointed board consists of four denturists, one dentist and two public members.

Denturists construct, repair, reline, reproduce, duplicate, supply, fit or alter removable prosthetic dental appliances—otherwise known as dentures. In the fitting process, denturists also take impressions, bite registrations, try-ins or insertions. Denturists provide full dentures to replace complete sets of original teeth that are missing in the upper, lower or both sections of the mouth, or partial dentures which fit sections of the mouth in which some of the original teeth remain.

Board of Direct Entry Midwifery
Statutory Authority: ORS 687.405–687.991
Duties and Responsibilities: This governor-appointed board consists of four licensed direct entry midwives, two certified nurse midwives and one licensed physician involved at the time of appointment in obstetrical care or education. All appointments are subject to confirmation by the senate.

A licensed direct entry midwife (LDM) supervises the conduct and labor of childbirth, advises the parent as to the progress of childbirth, and renders prenatal, intrapartum and postpartum care, usually in the home or at birthing centers or clinics. Licensure is voluntary, and unlicensed midwives may practice in Oregon. However, state statute allows for reimbursement under the Oregon Health Plan only if a licensed midwife provides birthing assistance. Only LDMs are legally authorized to administer legend drugs and devices.

Body Piercing Licensing Program
Statutory Authority: ORS 690.500–690.992
Duties and Responsibilities: No statutorily legislated representative body exists for this profession.

Body piercing technicians perform piercing services, including earlobe piercing, in licensed facilities. Body piercing technicians must be registered and adhere to stringent universal precautions for sterilization of needles and equipment, biohazard waste disposal and infection control practices formulated to state and national standards.

Environmental Health Registration Board
Statutory Authority: ORS 700.005–700.995
Duties and Responsibilities: This governor-appointed board consists of four registered environmental health specialists, one physician licensed in Oregon to practice medicine or surgery and certified by the American Board of Preventive Medicine and Public Health, one representative of the food or food/alcoholic beverage retail industry and one public member.

Environmental health specialists promote the control of infectious disease through environmental hygiene by enforcing health and safety standards relating to food, water and consumer products. Environmental health specialists collect, analyze, interpret and disseminate information about health events through public health "surveillance" to track and anticipate possible health problems, such as outbreaks of food-borne illness or disease.

Respiratory Therapists Licensing Board
Statutory Authority: ORS 688.800–688.995
Duties and Responsibilities: This governor-appointed board consists of five members who must be Oregon citizens who have engaged in the practice of respiratory care for a period of five or more years immediately preceding appointment to the board.

Respiratory care therapists provide services to patients with abnormalities associated with the cardiopulmonary system under the direction of a licensed physician and as part of a health care team. Respiratory care therapists administer therapeutic or diagnostic drugs to patients as part of a physician-prescribed treatment plan, implement a physician's orders for respiratory treatments, observe and monitor patient symptoms, and assist with administering medical gases.

HOUSING AND COMMUNITY SERVICES DEPARTMENT
Address: 725 Summer St. NE, Suite B, Salem 97301; Mail: PO Box 14508, Salem 97309-0409
Phone: 503-986-2000; TTY: 503-986-2100
Fax: 503-986-2020
E-mail: info@hcs.state.or.us
Web: www.oregon.gov/OHCS/
Contact: Bob Repine, Director
Statutory Authority: ORS 456.555
Duties and Responsibilities: The Housing and Community Services Department (OHCSD) is the state's housing financing agency, assisting in the financing of single family homes, the new construction or rehabilitation of multi-family affordable housing developments, and grants and tax

credits to promote affordable housing. The current agency was created in 1991, when the legislature merged the Oregon Housing Agency with State Community Services. The coordination between housing and services creates a continuum of programs that can assist and empower lower-income individuals and families in their efforts to become self-reliant.

Community Action Directors of Oregon (CADO)

Address: 12th St. Cutoff, Suite 110, Salem 97302
Phone: 503-316-3951
Contact: Mike Fieldman, President; Wendy Van Elverdinghe, Executive Director
Statutory Authority: ORS 458.505

Manufactured Dwelling Park Community Relations

Address: PO Box 14508, Salem 97309-0409
Phone: 503-986-2145; 1-800-453-5511
Web: www.hcs.state.or.us/mdpcr/
Contact: Eve Ford, Section Manager
Statutory Authority: ORS 446.453

State Housing Council

Address: PO Box 14508, Salem 97309-0409
Phone: 503-986-2005
Contact: Bob Repine, Director OHCS
Statutory Authority: ORS 456.567

Director's Office

Address: PO Box 14508, Salem 97309-0409
Phone: 503-986-2005
Fax: 503-986-2132
Web: www.ohcs.oregon.gov
Contact: Bob Repine, Director
Duties and Responsibilities: The Director's Office oversees the operations of the department with specific responsibility for three areas: the Governor's Economic Revitalization Team (GERT) Liaison, Human Resources Management, and the Regional Advisors to the Director (RADs).

The GERT Liaison represents the department and, along with the Director, participates in the Governor's Economic Revitalization Team. The department has worked with the GERT network to promote collaborative problem solving between state agencies and state and local partners to advance community and economic development goals, particularly the Governor's Industrial Lands Certification process.

The Human Resources Management Section is responsible for the implementation of a comprehensive human resources program.

The RADs provide overall technical assistance to financial institutions, not-for-profit and for-profit sponsors, community groups, local government and concerned individuals involved in developing "needs driven" affordable housing throughout the state. The RADs are the department's field representatives on the GERT, and provide links to other state agencies. The six RADs are located in the communities they serve (Ashland, Bend, Milton-Freewater, Portland (2) and Salem) and assist in the identification of program needs, development partners, financial resources, appropriate site placement, and preparation of funding applications.

Asset and Property Management Division

Address: PO Box 14508, Salem 97309-0409
Phone: 503-986-2000
Fax: 503-986-0959
Web: www.ohcs.oregon.gov
Contact: Marlys Laver, Administrator
Statutory Authority: ORS 317.097, 456.515–456.723, 458.305–458.310, 458.600–458.650
Duties and Responsibilities: The Asset and Property Management Division ensures that the department's financial security is maintained and the investment (the property) is maintained in a decent, safe and sanitary condition through scheduled financial reviews and inspections. The division includes two departmental sections: The Housing Programs Management Section, and the HUD Contract Administration Section.

The former monitors the loan, grant and low-income housing tax credit properties after the file is closed and the projects are in operation.

The latter monitors and completes inspections of Housing and Urban Development properties located within the state.

Community Resources Division

Address: PO Box 14508, Salem 97309-0409
Phone: 503-986-2000
Fax: 503-986-2020
Web: www.ohcs.oregon.gov
Contact: Jeanne Arana, Administrator
Statutory Authority: ORS 90.800–90.840, 446.525–446.543, 458.210–458.240, 458.350–458.365, 458.505–458.545, 458.600–458.650, 458.670–458.700
Duties and Responsibilities: The Community Resources Division oversees the community service programs of the department and includes two departmental sections: The Community Service Section and Services Outreach Section.

The former serves as the link between the federal government and local community action agencies (CAAs). The section supports community-based housing development and agency delivery of services to low-income individuals. This section is responsible for setting standards, compliance monitoring, performance evaluation, and providing training and technical assistance to each of its providers and vendors. The section provides such programs as homeless assistance, food programs and emergency housing.

The latter provides services including dispute resolution and mediation services to landlords and tenants of manufactured dwelling parks in the Manufactured Dwelling Park Community Relations Unit; and the Energy Unit works with Community Action Agencies and other community-based organizations to provide weatherization and energy assistance.

Financial Management Division

Address: PO Box 14508, Salem 97309-0409
Phone: 503-986-2000
Fax: 503-986-2020
Web: www.ohcs.oregon.gov
Contact: Rick Crager, Chief Financial Officer
Statutory Authority: ORS 456.515–456.578, 456.640–456.723
Duties and Responsibilities: The Financial Management Division oversees the financial viability of the department and includes four departmental sections: Business Services, Debt Management, Financial Operations, and Financial Services.

The Business Services Section provides guidance to the department on the administrative functions relating to facilities management, records and administrative rule development, internal communication and conference planning, mail service, and front-line customer service. The section also participates in the development of internal policies relating to activities specific to the agency.

The Debt Management Section directly supports the department's mission to create affordable housing through the issuance of bonded debt to acquire mortgage loans at below-market interest rates for Oregonians at or below median income.

The Financial Operations Section coordinates the department's financial activities related to budget preparation and tracking, disbursements, federal grant monitoring and reporting, and federal cash management and cost allocation. The section oversees the department's purchasing and contracting functions and also provides training and technical assistance to subgrantees and department staff.

The Financial Services Section maintains the department's accounting records and provides financial reporting both internally, for management purposes, and externally to bond trustees, the state, the federal government, and the financial community. The section manages the department's investment portfolio by analyzing, monitoring, reporting and controlling all activities related to making trades with various financial entities; provides sound financial analysis and establishes and maintains internal controls related to all fiduciary activities; receives and deposits all agency cash receipts; and handles the payroll and benefit functions for the department staff in accordance with federal and state rules and regulations.

Housing Division

Address: PO Box 14508, Salem 97309-0409
Phone: 503-986-2000
Fax: 503-986-2020
Contact: Bob Gillespie, Administrator
Statutory Authority: ORS 317.097, 456.515–456.723, 458.308–458.310, 458.600–458.650
Duties and Responsibilities: The Housing Division oversees the housing finance program operations of the department and includes three departmental sections: The Housing Finance Section, the Housing Resource Section and the Single Family Finance Section.

The Housing Finance Section provides permanent financing for new and/or rehabilitated affordable housing using multi-family tax-exempt or taxable bond proceeds and other financing program resources. The section is responsible for soliciting, reviewing, underwriting and closing loan, and loan guarantee applications for the financing of multi-family and elderly and disabled housing.

The Housing Resource Section administers multiple development programs that provide grants, loans and tax credits to address the locally defined housing need for low and very low-income residents. Approved developments provide lower rent housing opportunities for the general public, single parent households, farmworker populations, the elderly, as well as special needs populations. The section administers the Community Development Block Grant housing rehabilitation program that through our partners provide grants and loans for the rehabilitation of owner-occupied homes and for rental property owners with one or two units. The section develops the HUD required Consolidated Plan for Housing and Community Development which brings $26 million in community development resources to the state.

The Single Family Finance Section provides low- and moderate-income households access to below-market rate home loans, closing cost assistance and homebuyer training. Home loan funds are made available to the public through participating lenders and with the support of non-profit organizations. For more information about these services call 1-877-ST8-BOND or visit www.OregonBond.us

Information Services Division

Address: 725 Summer St. NE, Suite B, Salem 97301; Mail: PO Box 14508, Salem 97309-0409
Phone: 503-986-2128
Fax: 503-986-2020
Web: www.ohcs.oregon.gov
Contact: Bill Carpenter, Administrator

Duties and Responsibilities: The Information Services Division oversees the operations of the department's Information Systems (IS) Section, Communications Section, and the Planning, Policy and Research (PP&R) Section.

The IS Section is responsible for the department's applications, computers and networks and provides support and technical assistance to sub-grantee agencies with computer systems that interface with department programs.

The Communications Section implements the department's communication plan and policies, and works collaboratively with each division to develop specific documents and publications to inform and assist the public, our partners, legislators, and congressional representatives in their decision-making.

The PP&R Section advises and supports administration and partners through planning, policy development and by analyzing data and preparing research reports.

HUMAN SERVICES, DEPARTMENT OF

Address: 500 Summer St. NE, E-15, Salem 97301-1097
Phone: 503-945-5944; TTY: 503-947-5330
Fax: 503-378-2897
E-mail: dhs.info@state.or.us
Web: www.dhs.state.or.us
Contact: Gary Weeks, Director
Statutory Authority: ORS 409.010
Duties and Responsibilities: The Department of Human Services (DHS) is the state's health and human services agency. It is the largest department in state government, employing more than 9,000 people and operating with a budget of $9.2 billion during 2003–05. The agency served approximately 1 million people during 2002.

Working with local governments and other service providers, DHS strives to integrate programs and services, bringing a broader range of supports within easy reach of clients, many of whom have multiple needs. The DHS statewide integration strategy for human services is recognized nationally.

The department's mission is "helping people to become independent, healthy and safe." DHS strategies aimed at accomplishing these goals include:

- Helping low-income families achieve self-sufficiency, through services such as the JOBS employment and training program, Temporary Assistance for Needy Families (TANF) and food stamps.
- Protecting vulnerable Oregonians from abuse and neglect through child protective services, foster care and adoption programs, and

investigations into abuse of seniors and people with disabilities.
- Helping Oregonians obtain needed health care through the Oregon Health Plan, Medicaid, mental health and addiction treatment, and operation of mental health institutions.
- Helping seniors and people with disabilities live as independently as possible through in-home services, state-operated group homes, vocational rehabilitation services and senior employment programs.
- Protecting public health through such services as water-quality monitoring, restaurant inspections, monitoring and controlling communicable diseases, maintaining vital records and preparing for bioterrorism attack.

Phone numbers for many DHS services are listed in the "Government" pages of local phone directories under State of Oregon, Department of Human Services.

Director's Office

Address: 500 Summer St. NE, E-15, Salem 97301-1097
Phone: 503-945-5944; TTY: 503-947-5330
Fax: 503-378-2897
Contact: Gary Weeks, Director
Duties and Responsibilities: The Director's Office provides overall guidance and direction for DHS. The office also contains the Governor's Advocacy Office, which evaluates and resolves the public's issues and concerns about the department's programs and services.

Local Government Advisory Committee
Address: 500 Summer St. NE, E-25, Salem 97301
Phone: 503-947-5107; TTY: 503-947-5330
Contact: Office of Public Affairs

Administrative Services

Address: 500 Summer St. NE, E-94, Salem 97301-1098
Phone: 503-945-5733; TTY: 503-947-5330
Fax: 503-378-2897
Contact: Clyde Saiki, Administrative Officer
Duties and Responsibilities: This group provides department-wide support services in areas such as human resources, training, information technology, contracts, facilities management, financial services and forms and document management. The group also coordinates key agency-wide initiatives, including work to enhance security and privacy of information.

Children, Adults and Families

Address: 500 Summer St. NE, E-62, Salem 97301-1067
Phone: 503-945-5651; TTY: 503-945-5896
Fax: 503-527-6198

Contact: Ramona Foley, DHS Assistant Director for Children, Adults and Families
Duties and Responsibilities: This group oversees self-sufficiency and child protection programs. These include JOBS, Temporary Assistance for Needy Families, Employment-related Day Care, food stamps, child-abuse investigation and intervention, foster care and adoptions.

The group also administers vocational rehabilitation services which provide training and other supports that help people with disabilities become employed.

Child Welfare Advisory Committee
Address: 500 Summer St. NE, E-62, Salem 97301-1067
Phone: 503-945-5650; TTY: 503-945-5896
Fax: 503-581-6198
Contact: Marie Jacobsen
Statutory Authority: ORS 418.005

Family Services Review Commission
Address: 500 Summer St. NE, E-62, Salem 97301-1067
Phone: 503-945-5660; TTY: 503-945-5896
Fax: 503-581-6198
Contact: Dena Comer
Statutory Authority: ORS 411.125

Disability Services Advisory Council
Address: 500 Summer St. NE, E-02, Salem 97301
Phone: 503-945-6444; TTY: 1-800-282-8096
Fax: 503-373-7828
Contact: Jane-ellen Weidanz
Statutory Authority: ORS 410.210

State Rehabilitation Council
Address: 500 Summer St. NE, E-87, Salem 97301
Phone: 503-945-6256; TTY: 503-945-5896
Fax: 503-945-8991
Contact: Rhoda Hunter
Statutory Authority: ORS 344.735

Statewide Independent Living Council
Address: 500 Summer St. NE, E-87, Salem 97301
Phone: 503-945-6204; TTY: 503-945-6204
Fax: 503-945-8991
Contact: Shelly Emery
Statutory Authority: Exec. Order EO 94-12

Finance and Policy Analysis
Address: 500 Summer St. NE, E-23, Salem 97301-1098
Phone: 503-945-6933; TTY: 503-947-5330
Fax: 503-378-2897
Contact: Vic Todd, DHS Assistant Director for Finance and Policy Analysis

Duties and Responsibilities: This group provides budget and forecasting services, monitors federal and state policies for their impact on the department's budget, and develops the rates paid to providers in DHS programs.

Health Services
Address: 500 Summer St. NE, E-41, Salem 97301
Phone: 503-947-1175; TTY: 503-945-5895
Fax: 503-947-5104
Contact: Barry S. Kast, DHS Assistant Director for Health Services
Duties and Responsibilities: This group administers and develops policy for low-income medical programs, such as the Medicaid portion of the Oregon Health Plan, and for mental health and substance abuse services. It provides public health services such as monitoring drinking water quality, inspecting restaurants and promoting healthy behaviors. It also maintains the state's vital records, and operates Oregon State Hospital and the Eastern Oregon Psychiatric Center. Many of this group's services, such as immunizations, the Women Infants and Children nutrition program, and mental-health and substance-abuse treatment, are delivered through county health departments.

Conference of Local Health Officials
Address: 800 NE Oregon St., Suite 930, Portland 97232
Phone: 503-731-4017
Fax: 503-731-4078
Contact: Tom Engle
Statutory Authority: ORS 431.330–431.350

Governor's Council on Alcohol and Drug Abuse
Address: 500 Summer St. NE, E-86, Salem 97301
Phone: 503-945-5764
Fax: 503-378-8467
Contact: Karen Wheeler, Shauna McDaniel, staff
Statutory Authority: ORS 430.250–430.257

Medicaid Advisory Committee
Address: 500 Summer St. NE, E-49, Salem 97301-1079
Phone: 503-945-5769
Fax: 503-373-7689
Contact: Mary Reitan
Statutory Authority: ORS 414.211–414.225

Mental Health Planning and Management Advisory Council
Address: 500 Summer St. NE, E-86, Salem 97301
Phone: 503-945-5763; TTY: 503-945-9836
Fax: 503-378-8467
Contact: Office of Mental Health and Addiction Services
Statutory Authority: 42 USC 300x–3

Problem Gambling Services Advisory Committee
Address: 500 Summer St. NE, E-86, Salem 97301
Phone: 503-945-5763; **TTY:** 503-945-9836
Fax: 503-378-8467
Contact: Jeff Marotta
Statutory Authority: ORS 431.195

Public Health Advisory Committee
Address: 800 NE Oregon St., Suite 930, Portland 97232
Phone: 503-731-4017, ext. 877; **TTY:** 503-731-4031
Fax: 503-731-4078
Contact: Tom Engle
Statutory Authority: ORS 431.195

Radiation Advisory Board
Address: 800 NE Oregon St., Suite 260, Portland 97232
Phone: 503-731-4014
Fax: 503-731-4081
Contact: Terry Lindsey

Seniors and People with Disabilities
Address: 500 Summer St. NE, E-02, Salem 97301
Phone: 503-945-5811; **TTY:** 503-945-9782; **Toll-free:** 1-800-282-8096
Fax: 503-373-7823
Contact: James Toews, DHS Assistant Director for Seniors and People with Disabilities
Duties and Responsibilities: SPD is responsible for the administration of programs that increase the independence of, and help protect, seniors and people with disabilities. These include abuse investigation, licensing of long-term care facilities, help in arranging and paying for in-home services, Oregon Project Independence, and Lifespan Respite. Many of the services are provided to clients through local Area Agency on Aging (AAA) offices.

SPD also handles in-home, group-home and crisis services for people with developmental disabilities. Another SPD function is eligibility determination for federal Social Security disability benefits.

Continuing Care Retirement Community Advisory Council
Address: 500 Summer St. NE, E-13, Salem 97301
Phone: 503-945-6407; **TTY:** 503-945-9782; **Toll-free:** 1-800-232-3020
Fax: 503-378-8966
Contact: Seniors and People with Disabilities
Statutory Authority: ORS Chapter 101

Family Support Council
Address: 500 Summer St. NE, E-02, Salem 97301
Phone: 503-945-9787

Fax: 503-947-4245
Contact: Marylee Fay
Statutory Authority: ORS 417.346

Governor's Commission on Senior Services
Address: 500 Summer St. NE, E-02, Salem 97301
Phone: 503-945-6444; **TTY:** 1-800-282-8096
Fax: 503-373-7828
Contact: Jane-ellen Weidanz
Statutory Authority: ORS 410.320

Medicaid Long-Term Care Quality and Reimbursement Advisory Council
Address: 500 Summer St. NE, E-18, Salem 97301
Phone: 503-945-6465; **TTY:** 503-945-5896
Fax: 503-947-5043
Contact: Sarah Hansen
Statutory Authority: ORS 410.550

Oregon Council on Developmental Disabilities
Address: 540 24th Place NE, Salem 97310
Phone: 503-945-9941; **TTY:** 503-945-6790
Fax: 503-945-9947
Contact: Bill Lynch, Executive Director
Statutory Authority: 42 USC 6024

INSURANCE POOL GOVERNING BOARD
Address: 250 Church St. SE, Suite 200, Salem 97301-3921
Phone: 503-373-1692; **Toll-free (in Oregon):** 1-800-542-3104
Fax: 503-378-8365
E-mail: ipgb.mail@state.or.us
Web: www.ipgb.state.or.us
Contact: Howard "Rocky" King, Administrator
Statutory Authority: ORS 735.700
Duties and Responsibilities: The Insurance Pool Governing Board (IPGB) was established in 1987 to increase the number of employers who voluntarily provide health care coverage for employees and their dependents by certifying and marketing affordable health insurance plans. In 1999, the legislature removed the certified plan function of the IPGB, leaving the agency to concentrate its efforts in providing information and other resources to small businesses and the self-employed seeking health insurance coverage. The agency also administers the Family Health Insurance Assistance Program.

Family Health Insurance Assistance Program

Address: 250 Church St. SE, Suite 200, Salem 97301
Phone: 503-373-1692; Toll-free (in Oregon): 1-888-564-9669
Fax: 503-373-7704
E-mail: ipgb.mail@state.or.us
Web: www.ipgb.state.or.us
Contact: Craig C. Kuhn, Program Manager
Statutory Authority: ORS 735.720
Duties and Responsibilities: The Family Health Insurance Assistance Program (FHIAP) was created in 1997 to increase health care access to low-income, uninsured Oregonians through the private health insurance market. FHIAP offers subsidy assistance to qualified Oregon individuals and families to help pay the cost of health insurance premiums of plans purchased primarily through an employer or the individual market. Depending on the income and family size of the FHIAP member, 50 to 95 percent of the premium is paid for with the subsidy.

LAND CONSERVATION AND DEVELOPMENT, DEPARTMENT OF

Address: 635 Capitol St. NE, Suite 150, Salem 97301-2540
Phone: 503-373-0050, ext. 271
Fax: 503-378-5518
Web: www.lcd.state.or.us
Contact: Lane Shetterly, Director
Statutory Authority: ORS Chapters 92, 195, 196, 197, 215, 222, 227, 268, 308
Duties and Responsibilities: The Land Conservation and Development Commission (LCDC) has seven members who are appointed by the governor and confirmed by the senate. LCDC's administrative arm is the Department of Land Conservation and Development (DLCD). The department administers Oregon's statewide land-use planning program and Oregon's federally approved coastal-management program. The department's director is appointed by LCDC. Oregon's statewide planning program was created in 1973 when the legislature passed the Oregon Land Use Act (Senate Bill 100). Under that program all cities and counties have adopted comprehensive plans that meet mandatory state standards. The standards are 19 statewide planning goals that deal with land use, development, housing, transportation, and conservation of natural resources. Periodic review of plans and technical assistance in the form of grants to local jurisdictions are key elements of the program.

Citizen Involvement Advisory Committee

Address: 635 Capitol St. NE, Suite 150, Salem 97301-2540
Phone: 503-373-0050, ext. 268
Contact: Cliff Voliva

Local Officials Advisory Committee

Address: 635 Capitol St. NE, Suite 200, Salem 97301-2540
Phone: 503-373-0050, ext. 268
Statutory Authority: ORS 197.165

Community Services Division

Address: 635 Capitol St. NE, Suite 150, Salem 97301-2540; and Bend and Central Point Field Offices
Phone: 503-373-0050, ext. 239
Fax: 503-378-5518
Web: www.lcd.state.or.us
Contact: Rob Hallyburton, Manager
Duties and Responsibilities: The Community Services Division administers the Rural Community Program which includes efforts to conserve farmlands and forested areas, rural land use planning, elements of the Oregon Plan for Salmon and Watersheds, floodplain assessments and hazards management, and mineral and aggregate resource management.

Ocean/Coastal Division

Address: 635 Capitol St. NE, Suite 150, Salem 97301-2540
Phone: 503-373-0050, ext. 281
Fax: 503-378-6033
Web: www.lcd.state.or.us
Contact: Bob Bailey, Manager
Duties and Responsibilities: The Ocean/Coastal Division administers Oregon's Ocean Resources Management Program, co-sponsors the Pacific Northwest Coastal Ecosystem Regional Study, implements a coastal hazards assessment and management program, and manages the Coastal Dynamic Estuary Management Information System, the Coastal Public Access Inventory, the Coastal Nonpoint Pollution Control Program, the Coastal Management Program Information System, and the Coastal Visual Quality Project.

Planning Services Division

Address: 635 Capitol St. NE, Suite 150, Salem 97301-2540
Phone: 503-373-0050, ext. 255
Fax: 503-378-5518
Web: www.lcd.state.or.us
Contact: Ann Beier, Manager
Duties and Responsibilities: The Planning Services Division administers the Transportation Program and the Urban Growth Management

Program. Program emphases include transportation and growth management, urban livability, smart development, Main Street enhancement and enhanced public transportation options.

LAND USE BOARD OF APPEALS

Address: Public Utility Commission Bldg., 550 Capitol St. NE, Suite 235, Salem 97301-2552
Phone: 503-373-1265; TTY: 503-373-1265
Fax: 503-373-1580
Web: luba.state.or.us
Contact: Michael A. Holstun, Board Chair
Statutory Authority: ORS 197.810
Duties and Responsibilities: The Land Use Board of Appeals (LUBA) was created by legislation in 1979 and has exclusive jurisdiction to review all governmental land-use decisions, whether legislative or quasi-judicial in nature. LUBA was created to simplify the appeal process, speed resolution of land-use disputes and provide consistent interpretation of state and local land-use laws. The governor appoints the three-member board to serve four-year terms, subject to senate confirmation. The board members serving on LUBA must be members of the Oregon State Bar.

LANDSCAPE ARCHITECT BOARD, STATE

Address: 1193 Royvonne Ave. SE, #19, Salem 97302
Phone: 503-589-0093
Fax: 503-589-0545
E-mail: OSLAB@qwest.net
Contact: Leslie Clement, Administrator
Statutory Authority: ORS 671.459
Duties and Responsibilities: Since 1981 the State Landscape Architect Board has registered landscape architects either by examination or by reciprocity. The board consists of three registered landscape architects and two public members appointed by the governor, each serving a four-year term. More than 350 landscape architects are registered in Oregon.

LANDSCAPE CONTRACTORS BOARD, STATE

Address: 235 Union St. NE, Salem 97301
Phone: 503-986-6561
Fax: 503-986-6582
E-mail: LCB.info@state.or.us
Web: www.lcb.state.or.us
Contact: Michael A. Snyder, Administrator
Statutory Authority: ORS Chapter 671
Duties and Responsibilities: Created in 1972, the State Landscape Contractors Board licenses landscaping businesses and individual landscape

contractors. Individual landscape contractors must meet experience and/or educational requirements and pass a comprehensive competency exam. Landscaping businesses must post a security bond, submit evidence of liability insurance and workers' compensation if applicable and either employ an individual licensed landscape contractor or be owned by an individual licensed landscape contractor. The board receives and investigates consumer complaints, answers consumer and contractor questions and enforces compliance with the licensing law.

Approximately 1,400 individual landscape contractors and 1,100 landscaping businesses are licensed in Oregon. The governor appoints the seven-member board to serve three-year terms. Five members are from the landscape industry and two are public members.

LANE COUNTY LOCAL GOVERNMENT BOUNDARY COMMISSION

Address: 99 E Broadway, Suite 400, Eugene 97401-3111
Phone: 541-682-4425
Fax: 541-682-2635
E-mail: ptaylor@lane.cog.or.us
Web: www.lcog.org
Contact: Paula L. Taylor, Executive Officer
Statutory Authority: ORS Chapter 199
Duties and Responsibilities: Operating under ORS 199.410–199.540, the commission's purpose is to guide the creation and growth of cities, special service districts and privately owned community water and sewer systems.

LIBRARY, OREGON STATE

Address: 250 Winter St. NE, Salem 97301-3950
Phone: 503-378-4243
Fax: 503-585-8059
Web: www.osl.state.or.us/home
Contact: Jim Scheppke, State Librarian
Statutory Authority: ORS Chapter 357
Duties and Responsibilities: The State Library was established as the Oregon Library Commission in 1905 and today provides information services to approximately 27,000 state government employees. The State Library also circulates library materials in cassette and Braille format to approximately 7,000 print-disabled Oregonians and provides grants and assistance to help develop and improve local library services, and to foster greater cooperation among all of Oregon's libraries.

Since its founding, the State Library has been governed by an independent Board of Trustees. The present board consists of seven citizens from throughout the state who are appointed by the governor to serve four-year terms.

LIQUOR CONTROL COMMISSION, OREGON

Address: 9079 SE McLoughlin Blvd., Portland 97222-7355
Phone: 503-872-5000; Toll-free: 1-800-452-6522
Fax: 503-872-5266
E-mail: joli.whitney@state.or.us
Web: www.olcc.state.or.us
Contact: Teresa L. Kaiser, Executive Director
Statutory Authority: ORS Chpaters 471, 472, 473
Duties and Responsibilities: The five citizen commissioners are appointed by the governor to four-year terms, subject to senate confirmation. Commissioners provide policy direction for the Oregon Liquor Control Commission (OLCC). Each commissioner represents a state congressional district, and one is from the food and beverage industry. Together they appoint the OLCC Director who oversees the agency's 205 employees.

The Oregon Liquor Control Commission regulates the sale, distribution, and responsible use of alcoholic beverages in order to protect Oregon's public health, safety and community livability. The OLCC was created in 1933 by a special session of the legislature after national prohibition ended. Oregon chose a control-state system, giving the state the exclusive right to sell packaged distilled spirits, which are sold through 239 retail liquor stores operated by contracted agents.

The OLCC also licenses private businesses that sell beer and wine by the drink or by the package. The Liquor Control Act passed by the voters in 1953 permits the sale of distilled spirits by the drink in restaurants and private clubs. These Full On Premises Sales Licenses are issued by the OLCC. In addition, the OLCC administers the Alcohol Server Education Program which focuses on responsible alcohol service. All alcohol servers must complete the course every five years. The OLCC also enforces the Bottle Bill. Under this law, any malt or carbonated beverage sold in Oregon must have a refund value of not less than five cents.

Liquor store sales in fiscal year 2002–03 were $267.8 million. Another $16.5 million was collected in liquor license fees, privilege taxes on beer and wine, and in fines paid for liquor-law violations. Of the net revenue generated by the OLCC, 56 percent goes to the state's general fund; cities receive 20 percent, counties 10 percent, and the City Revenue Sharing gets 14 percent. Half of the privilege taxes collected go to the Mental Health Alcoholism and Drug Services account. The Wine Advisory Board receives a special two-cent tax on all wines to promote the development and marketing of Oregon wines. Allocations from liquor revenues for the 2002–03 fiscal year totaled $111.75 million.

The OLCC has headquarters in Portland and regional offices in Bend, Eugene, Medford and Salem.

LONG-TERM CARE OMBUDSMAN, OFFICE OF THE

Address: 3855 Wolverine St. NE, Suite 6, Salem 97305-1251
Phone: 503-378-6533; Toll-free: 1-800-522-2602; TTY: 503-378-5847
Fax: 503-373-0852
E-mail: LTCO.contact@state.or.us
Contact: Judith Roth, State Long-Term Care Ombudsman
Statutory Authority: ORS 441.100–441.153
Duties and Responsibilities: The Office of the Long-Term Care Ombudsman is an independent state agency with a resident-centered mission to enhance the quality of life, improve the level of care, protect the individual rights and promote the dignity of each Oregon citizen housed in a nursing facility, adult foster care home, residential care facility or assisted living facility. Specifically, the office is charged with investigating and resolving complaints made by or on behalf of long-term care facility residents. This objective is achieved by trained volunteers who are a routine presence in long-term care facilities throughout the state.

LOTTERY, OREGON STATE

Address: PO Box 12649, Salem 97309
Phone: 503-540-1000; TTY: 503-540-1068
Fax: 503-540-1009
E-mail: lottery.webcenter@state.or.us
Web: www.oregonlottery.org
Contact: Dale Penn, Director
Statutory Authority: ORS Chapter 461
Duties and Responsibilities: The Oregon State Lottery is operated under the direction of a five-member citizen commission. Commissioners are appointed by the governor and confirmed by the senate. By law, one commissioner must be a certified public accountant, and one must have at least five years experience in law enforcement.

The Oregon State Lottery was created through the initiative process in November 1984 when voters amended the Oregon Constitution to require the establishment and operation of a state lottery. Profits were to be used exclusively for economic development and job creation. In May 1995, voters enabled profits to be used to finance public education, and in November 1998, voters approved another initiative which directed 15 percent of Lottery net proceeds to go to parks and salmon restoration programs. The Oregon State Lottery's purpose is to provide additional revenue to those public purposes without the imposition of additional or increased taxes. The Oregon State Lottery is entirely self-financed through its sales, and does not receive any General Fund or other tax dollars.

The Lottery's duty is to develop, produce, and market its games; to pay its winners and operating expenses; and to turn the remaining net profits over to the state. The legislature is responsible for allocating Oregon State Lottery funds for economic development, public education and parks and salmon restoration programs. Since 1985 over $8.5 billion his been won in prizes, and over $3.4 billion in earnings has gone to public education and economic development programs. Another $2 billion has been paid to Oregon businesses and citizens for services and supplies needed to operate the Lottery.

MARINE BOARD, OREGON STATE

Address: PO Box 14145, Salem 97309-5065
Phone: 503-378-8587; TTY: 503-378-8587 (press space bar to begin)
Fax: 503-378-4597
E-mail: marine.board@state.or.us
Web: www.boatoregon.com
Contact: Paul Donheffner, Director; Wayne Shuyler, Policy and Planning Analyst
Statutory Authority: ORS 830.105
Duties and Responsibilities: The Oregon State Marine Board was established in 1959. The board is Oregon's recreational boating agency, dedicated to safety, education and access in an enhanced environment. The Marine Board returns user fees (marine fuel tax and title and registration fees) to boaters in the form of boating safety educational programs, marine law enforcement and improved boating facilities.

The board titles and registers recreational vessels, which currently number more than 195,000. The board also registers outfitters and guides and licenses ocean charterboats. The board establishes statewide boating regulations and contracts with county sheriffs and the Oregon State Police to enforce marine laws. The board provides technical training to marine patrol officers and supplies their equipment. The board also provides grants and engineering services to local governments (cities, counties, park districts, port districts) to develop and maintain accessible boating facilities and protect water quality.

The board actively promotes safe and sustainable boating through several programs. The Mandatory Boater Education program, when fully phased in, will require powerboat operators to complete a boating safety course. Sustainable boating campaigns encourage boaters to upgrade to clean-burning marine engines, adopt clean-boating practices and avoid spreading aquatic nuisance species. The

board also provides numerous safety publications and access information.

MASSAGE THERAPISTS, BOARD OF

Address: 748 Hawthorne Ave. NE, Salem 97301
Phone: 503-365-8657
Fax: 503-385-4465
E-mail: patty@oregonmassage.org
Web: www.oregonmassage.org
Contact: Patricia Glenn, Executive Director
Statutory Authority: ORS 687.011–687.991
Duties and Responsibilities: The Board of Massage Therapists regulates the practice of massage. This is accomplished by licensing, establishing continuing education requirements, promoting education, administering tests to establish minimum competency to practice, and enforcing professional behavior and standards.

MEDICAL EXAMINERS FOR THE STATE OF OREGON, BOARD OF

Address: 1500 SW 1st Ave., #620, Portland 97201-5826
Phone: 503-229-5770
Fax: 503-229-6543
E-mail: bme.info@state.or.us
Web: www.bme.state.or.us
Contact: Kathleen Haley, Executive Director
Statutory Authority: ORS Chapter 677
Duties and Responsibilities: The Board of Medical Examiners was created in 1889 and is responsible for administering the Medical Practice Act and establishing the rules and regulations pertaining to the practice of medicine in Oregon. The board determines requirements for Oregon licensure as a Medical Doctor (MD), Doctor of Osteopathy (DO), Doctor of Podiatric Medicine (DPM), Physician Assistant (PA), and Acupuncturist (LAc); ensures that all applicants granted licensure meet all Oregon requirements; investigates complaints against licensees and takes disciplinary action when a violation of the Medical Practice Act occurs; monitors licensees who have come under disciplinary action to ensure compliance with their terms of probation and ensure that it is safe for them to practice medicine; works to rehabilitate and educate "problem" licensees whenever appropriate; and takes an active stance in preventing practice problems which endanger patients, primarily through diversion programs for licensees with substance abuse disorders, by educational outreach, and by monitoring the prescribing practices of certain licensees.

MILITARY DEPARTMENT, OREGON

Address: 1776 Militia Way SE, Salem 97309
Phone: 503-584-3980
Fax: 503-584-3962
Web: www.or.ngb.army.mil
Contact: Brigadier General Raymond C. Byrne Jr., Acting Adjutant General; Brigadier General James E. Cunningham, Assistant Adjutant General (Air)
Statutory Authority: ORS 396.305
Duties and Responsibilities: The Oregon Military Department/National Guard serves the governor with its active command and administration vested in the Adjutant General. The Oregon Guard is available to the federal government upon receipt of order from the President in accordance with Section 102, Title 32 of the United States Code.

Military Council

Address: PO Box 14350, Salem 97309-5047
Phone: 503-945-3637
Contact: Major Alaine Encabo

Oregon Air National Guard

Starbase

Address: 6801 NE Cornfoot Rd., Portland 97218-2797
Phone: 503-945-3646
Contact: Brigadier General James E. Cunningham
Duties and Responsibilities: Starbase teaches math and science skills related to aviation to elementary school students in Portland and Klamath Falls in partnership with local school districts.

Oregon Army National Guard

Innovative Readiness Training Program (IRT)

Address: PO Box 14350, Salem 97309-5047
Phone: 503-945-3171
Contact: Daniel L. Brewer, MAJ
Duties and Responsibilities: The Innovative Readiness Training Program (IRT) provides engineer projects to help Oregon.

Counter Drug and Drug Demand Reduction Programs (CD) (DDR)

Address: 1921 Turner Rd. SE, Salem 97302-2099
Phone: 503-945-3865
Contact: Richard D. Williams, COL
Duties and Responsibilities: Counter Drug and Drug Demand Reduction Programs oversee counter drug assistance to agencies and local schools to teach students throughout Oregon that "Drug Abuse is Life Abuse." Programs also aid local law enforcement agencies in drug control and eradication efforts and provide local law enforcement

agencies, through the Oregon State Police as the lead agency, with military equipment and personnel support. The equipment includes helicopters, light armored vehicles, night vision equipment and transportation equipment.

Military Construction Program

Address: PO Box 14350, Salem 97309-5047
Phone: 503-945-3871
Contact: David Ferre, COL
Duties and Responsibilities: Military Construction Program projects include all armories for the Oregon National Guard including the Armed Forces Reserve Centers in Salem and Eugene.

Training Sites

Address: PO Box 14350, Salem 97309-5047
Phone: 503-945-3903
Contact: Donald Bond, COL
Duties and Responsibilities: Oregon National Guard training sites are located at Camp Rilea in Warrenton, the High Desert Training Center in Redmond, Umatilla Army Depot, Camp Withycombe in Clackamas, and Camp Adair in Corvallis.

Youth Challenge Program

Address: 23881 Dodds Rd., Bend 97850
Phone: 541-317-9623
Contact: Richard Demars
Duties and Responsibilities: The Youth Challenge Program provides a 22-week residential training camp for at-risk youth in Oregon.

MORTUARY AND CEMETERY BOARD, STATE

Address: State Office Bldg., Suite 430, 800 NE Oregon St., Box #19, Portland 97232-2195
Phone: 503-731-4040
Fax: 503-731-4494
E-mail: mortuary.board@state.or.us
Contact: David J. Koach, Executive Director
Statutory Authority: ORS 692.300, 97.931
Duties and Responsibilities: The Mortuary and Cemetery Board is composed of 11 members appointed by the governor: two funeral service practitioners, one embalmer, three cemetery representatives, one crematory representative and four public members.

It is the board's responsibility to regulate the practice of individuals and establishments engaged in the sale of funeral, cemetery, and crematory goods and services as well as the care, preparation, processing, transportation and final disposition of human remains. The board's licensees include funeral service practitioners, embalmers, apprentices, pre-need sales people, funeral establishments, immediate disposition companies, cemeteries and crematories.

The board's programs include background investigation, apprenticeship, practitioner examination, licensing, facility inspection, complaint investigation and education.

The board's financing is derived from licensing, examination and death registration fees.

NATUROPATHIC EXAMINERS, BOARD OF

Address: 800 NE Oregon St., Suite 407, Portland 97232
Phone: 503-731-4045
Fax: 503-731-4207
E-mail: obne.info@state.or.us
Web: www.obne.state.or.us
Contact: Anne Walsh, Executive Director
Statutory Authority: ORS Chapter 685
Duties and Responsibilities: The Board of Naturopathic Examiners, consisting of seven members, was established by the 1927 Legislature to protect the public by setting and enforcing standards in the practice of Naturopathic Medicine. It carries out the provision of its authority by examining, licensing, educating, promoting excellence in care, and investigating complaints and taking appropriate action when necessary.

NURSING, OREGON STATE BOARD OF

Address: 800 NE Oregon St., Suite 465, Portland 97232-2162
Phone: 503-731-4745
Fax: 503-731-4755
E-mail: oregon.bn.info@state.or.us
Web: www.oregon.gov/OSBN
Contact: Joan C. Bouchard, Executive Director
Statutory Authority: ORS 678.010–678.445
Duties and Responsibilities: The Oregon State Board of Nursing was established in 1911 to regulate nursing practice and education to protect the public's health, safety and well being. The board examines, licenses and renews licenses of qualified registered professional nurses and licensed practical nurses; certifies all nursing assistants and establishes standards for their training and certification; licenses nurse practitioners and grants prescriptive and dispensing authority to qualified nurse practitioners; licenses Certified Registered Nurse Anesthetists and Clinical Nurse Specialists; prescribes essential curricula and standards for nursing education programs; surveys and approves nursing education programs which meet board standards; and investigates complaints about nurses and nursing assistants to determine whether there have been violations of the law or administrative rules. Members are appointed by the governor to serve no more than two consecutive three-year terms.

License fees finance all board programs.

NURSING HOME ADMINISTRATORS, BOARD OF EXAMINERS OF

Address: 800 NE Oregon St., Suite 407, Portland 97232
Phone: 503-731-4046
Fax: 503-731-4207
E-mail: janet.bartel@state.or.us
Contact: Janet Bartel, Executive Officer
Statutory Authority: ORS 678.800
Duties and Responsibilities: The Board of Examiners of Nursing Home Administrators develops and enforces standards for nursing home administrators; formulates appropriate examinations; and issues, revokes and suspends licenses. The board investigates complaints; evaluates and approves continuing education courses to meet license renewal requirements; controls an ongoing trainee program for prospective nursing home administrators; and maintains a register of all licensed nursing home administrators and trainees.

OCCUPATIONAL THERAPY LICENSING BOARD

Address: 800 NE Oregon St., Suite 407, Portland 97232-2162
Phone: 503-731-4048
Fax: 503-731-4207
E-mail: felicia.m.holgate@state.or.us
Web: www.otlb.state.or.us
Contact: Felicia Holgate, Executive Director
Statutory Authority: ORS 675.210–675.340
Duties and Responsibilities: The Occupational Therapy Licensing Board, created in 1977, regulates occupational therapy practice to assure that only qualified persons provide occupational therapy services. The board sets the standards of practice and examines applicants for licensure, issues licenses to qualified applicants, investigates complaints and takes appropriate disciplinary action when violations are found to have occurred.

OPTOMETRY, OREGON BOARD OF

Address: 3218 Pringle Rd. SE, Suite 270, Salem 97302-6306
Phone: 503-373-7721
Fax: 503-378-3616
E-mail: board@oregonobo.org
Web: http://oregonobo.org
Contact: David W. Plunkett, Executive Director
Statutory Authority: ORS Chapter 683
Duties and Responsibilities: The Board of Optometry was created in 1905 and makes rules and enforces professional standards for the practice

of optometry in Oregon. The board examines applicants for licensure as optometrists; suspends, revokes or imposes probation on licensees; and limits the practice or imposes a civil penalty for violation of the statutes.

Activities are supported by fees assessed applicants and licensed optometrists.

PACIFIC NORTHWEST ELECTRIC POWER AND CONSERVATION PLANNING COUNCIL

Address: Oregon Office: 851 SW 6th Ave., Suite 1020, Portland 97204-1347
Phone: 503-229-5171
Fax: 503-229-5173
Web: www.nwcouncil.org
Contact: Joan M. Dukes, Oregon Council Member (Jan. 2008); Melinda S. Eden, Oregon Council Member (Jan. 2007)
Statutory Authority: ORS 469.805
Duties and Responsibilities: Through the Northwest Power Act of 1980 (PL 96-502), the U.S. Congress authorized Idaho, Montana, Washington and Oregon to create the Pacific Northwest Electric Power and Conservation Planning Council (commonly known as the Northwest Power and Conservation Council), a planning and policy-making body. The four state governors each appoint two members to the council. Council members serve three-year terms and can be reappointed.

Congress charged the council with developing a program to protect, mitigate and enhance fish and wildlife affected by the development, operation, and management of hydroelectric facilities in the Columbia River Basin while assuring the Pacific Northwest an adequate, efficient, economical, and reliable power supply; developing a power plan that included a 20-year demand forecast, an energy conservation program, and the fish and wildlife program; and involving the public extensively in the decision-making process.

PACIFIC STATES MARINE FISHERIES COMMISSION

Address: 205 SE Spokane St., Suite 100, Portland 97202
Phone: 503-595-3100
Fax: 503-595-3232
Web: www.psmfc.org
Contact: Randy Fisher, Executive Director
Statutory Authority: Compact entered into by the states with the consent of the United States Congress, July 1947. ORS 507.040
Duties and Responsibilities: The Pacific States Marine Fisheries Commission (PSMFC) is dedicated to resolving fishing issues and represents California, Oregon, Washington, Idaho and Alaska. PSMFC promotes and supports policies and actions directed at the conservation, development and management of fishery resources. PSMFC serves as a primary contractor on state and government funded grants and contracts. In addition, PSMFC collects data and maintains databases on salmon, steelhead and other marine fish for fishery managers and the fishing industry.

PARKS AND RECREATION DEPARTMENT, STATE

Address: 725 Summer St. NE, Suite C, Salem 97301
Phone: 503-986-0707; Campground Reservations: 1-800-452-5687; Parks Information: 1-800-551-6949
Fax: 503-986-0794
E-mail: tim.wood@state.or.us
Web: www.oregon.gov/OPRD
Contact: Tim Wood, Director
Statutory Authority: ORS Chapters 97, 358, 390
Duties and Responsibilities: The mission of the State Parks and Recreation Department is to "provide and protect outstanding, natural, scenic, cultural, historic and recreational sites for the enjoyment and education of present and future generations." The department operates Oregon's state parks through a headquarters staff in Salem and six administrative areas. The department was initially created as a branch of the Highway Department in 1921. The 1989 Legislature created a separate Parks and Recreation Department effective January 1, 1990.

Oregon's state parks are among the most popular in the U.S. Their combined day-use and camping attendance of 39.6 million visitors (2001) consistently ranks the system among the ten most visited in the nation.

Special programs also protect outstanding resources—the State Historic Preservation Office, Oregon Heritage Commission, Oregon Commission on Historic Cemeteries, Recreation Trails, the Ocean Shores Recreation Area, Scenic Waterways and the Willamette River Greenway. Department activities are funded primarily by Oregon Lottery dollars, state park user fees and recreation vehicle license fees.

State Parks and Recreation Commission

Contact: John Blackwell, Chair
Statutory Authority: ORS 390.114
Duties and Responsibilities: The State Parks and Recreation Commission sets policy for the department and has specific authority to purchase and sell property and set fees for use of parks facilities.

Members serve rotating four-year terms and are appointed by the governor, with senate confirmation. The seven-member commission represents citizens from each of Oregon's five congressional districts, as well as citizens on the east side of the Cascade Range and citizens west of the summit of the Coastal Range.

Oregon Heritage Commission

Address: 725 Summer St. NE, Suite C, Salem 97301-1271
Phone: 503-986-0673
Fax: 503-986-0794
E-mail: kyle.jansson@state.or.us
Contact: Kyle Jansson, Coordinator
Statutory Authority: ORS 358.570
Duties and Responsibilities: The mission of the Oregon Heritage Commission is to secure, sustain, enhance and promote Oregon's heritage. The commission serves as a connector and catalyst for the hundreds of organizations and thousands of Oregonians devoted to preserving and interpreting Oregon's heritage resources. OHC services for Oregon communities include heritage grants, museum grants, and the annual Heritage Conference.

The Oregon Heritage Commission is comprised of nine members of the public appointed by the governor and eight *ex-officio* members from state-level organizations with heritage interests. Commission members have varied heritage backgrounds and interests. *Ex-officio* members represent the Oregon Economic and Community Development Department, Oregon Education Department, Oregon Historical Society, Oregon Land Conservation and Development Department, Oregon State Archives, Oregon State Historic Preservation Office, Oregon State Library, and Oregon University System.

Oregon Historic Trails Advisory Council

Address: 725 Summer St. NE, Suite C, Salem 97301
Phone: 503-986-0669
Fax: 503-986-0796
Contact: James M. Hamrick Jr.

Oregon Recreation Trails Advisory Council

Address: 725 Summer St. NE, Suite C, Salem 97301
Phone: 503-986-0750
Fax: 503-986-0792
E-mail: sean.loughran@state.or.us
Contact: Ernie Drapela, Chair
Statutory Authority: ORS 390.950

State Advisory Committee on Historic Preservation

Address: 725 Summer St. NE, Suite C, Salem 97301
Phone: 503-986-0669
Fax: 503-986-0794
E-Mail: james.hamrick@state.or.us
Contact: James M. Hamrick Jr., Deputy State Historic Preservation Officer
Statutory Authority: ORS 358.622
Duties and Responsibilities: The State Advisory Committee on Historic Preservation is a nine-member committee appointed by the governor that reviews nominations to the National Register of Historic Places in Oregon and votes on their eligibility. When the committee determines that a nomination is eligible, it recommends that the State Historic Preservation Officer sign the nomination and forward it to the National Register office in Washington, D.C. for its review and listing. The committee meets three times a year to review nominations brought forward by the State Historic Preservation Office's National Register coordinator. The committee also advises SHPO on matters of program policy and budget.

State Historic Preservation Office

Address: 725 Summer St. NE, Suite C, Salem 97301
Phone: 503-986-0669
Fax: 503-986-0794
E-mail: james.hamrick@state.or.us
Contact: James M. Hamrick Jr., Deputy State Historic Preservation Officer
Duties and Responsibilities: The State Historic Preservation Office (SHPO) was established in 1967 under the terms of the National Historic Preservation Act of 1966. Under a mandate from the federal government as well as state administrative rules and laws, the office manages programs that allow Oregonians as individuals, organizations and local governments to become directly involved in the protection of significant historic and cultural resources. State and federal grants are available for the rehabilitation of historic properties as well as for other preservation related activities.

Programs of the SHPO include: National Register of Historic Places, Certified Local Governments, Historic/Prehistoric Survey and Inventory, Archaeological Permit Process, Historic Preservation Special Assessment for Historic Properties, Federal Historic Rehabilitation Tax Credit, Historic Preservation Comprehensive Planning, Section 106 Review and Compliance.

Executive

Parole and Post-Prison Supervision, State Board of

Address: 2575 Center St. NE, Salem 97310-0470
Phone: 503-945-0900
Fax: 503-373-7558
Web: www.oregon.gov/BOPPPS/
Contact: Aaron East, Executive Director
Statutory Authority: ORS Chapter 144
Duties and Responsibilities: The Board of Parole and Post-Prison Supervision works in partnership with the Department of Corrections and local supervisory authorities to protect the public and reduce the risk of repeat criminal behavior. The board imposes prison terms and makes release decisions only on offenders whose criminal conduct occurred prior to November 1, 1989. The board sets conditions of supervision for all offenders being released from prison; imposes sanctions for violations of supervision; and determines whether discharge from parole supervision is compatible with public safety. Discharge from supervision for offenders sentenced under sentencing guidelines occurs automatically upon expiration of the statutory period of post-prison supervision. The board's decisions are based on applicable laws, victims' interests, public safety and the recognized principles of offender behavioral change.

The governor appoints the members for four-year terms and also appoints the chair and vice-chair. The full-time board was authorized in 1969. In 1975, the board was enlarged to five members, with the stipulation that at least one member must be a woman. The membership was reduced to three in 1992.

Advisory Commission on Prison Terms and Parole Standards

Address: 2575 Center St. NE, Salem 97310
Phone: 503-945-0919
Fax: 503-373-7558
E-mail: aaron.w.east@doc.state.or.us
Contact: Aaron East, Executive Secretary
Statutory Authority: ORS 144.775

Pharmacy, State Board of

Address: Portland State Office Bldg., Suite 425, 800 NE Oregon St., Portland 97232-2162
Phone: 503-731-4032
Fax: 503-731-4067
E-mail: pharmacy.board@state.or.us
Web: www.oregon.gov/Pharmacy/
Contact: Gary Schnabel, Executive Director
Statutory Authority: ORS Chapters 475, 689

Duties and Responsibilities: The Board of Pharmacy was created in 1891 and it regulates pharmacy practice to assure that only qualified individuals practice pharmacy in Oregon. The board licenses pharmacists by examination or through reciprocity with other states, registers and inspects hospital and retail pharmacies, drug wholesalers and manufacturers, and over-the-counter drug outlets. It investigates drug diversion and violations of its rules, and regulates the quality and distribution of controlled substances, prescription and over-the-counter drugs within the state. The board enforces compliance by administrative procedures and by court action.

Board activities are financed by license fees.

Physical Therapist Licensing Board

Address: 800 NE Oregon St., Suite 407, Portland 97232-2162
Phone: 503-731-4047
Fax: 503-731-4207
Web: www.oregon.gov/PTBrd/
Contact: James Heider, Executive Director
Statutory Authority: ORS 688.160
Duties and Responsibilities: The Physical Therapist Licensing Board was created in 1971 to regulate the practice of physical therapy in Oregon. The board's purpose is public protection and to establish professional standards of practice which assure that physical therapists and physical therapist assistants are properly educated, hold valid/current licenses, practice within their scope of practice and continue to receive ongoing training throughout their careers. Physical therapy practice is governed by state statutes and rules, which define the scope of practice.

The board issues licenses, promulgates rules, monitors continuing education, investigates complaints, issues civil penalties for violations and may revoke, suspend or impose probation on a licensee or limit his/her practice.

The board is comprised of seven volunteer members: four physical therapists, one physical therapist assistant, one physician member and one public member. Each member is appointed by the governor and may serve a four-year term, with a maximum of two terms.

The board is self-supporting and activities are financed solely from licensure and related fees.

Police, Department of State

Address: 400 Public Service Bldg., Salem 97310
Phone: 503-378-3720
Fax: 503-378-8282
E-mail: asksupt@osp.state.or.us
Web: www.oregon.gov/OSP/

Contact: Ronald Ruecker, Superintendent; Gregory Willeford, Lieutenant Colonel; Timothy McLain, Lieutenant Colonel

Statutory Authority: ORS 181.020

Duties and Responsibilities: The Department of State Police was created in 1931 to serve as a rural patrol and to assist local city police and sheriffs' departments. The current mission of the department is to develop, promote and provide protection to the people, property and natural resources of the state, along with ensuring the state's safety and livability by serving, protecting and educating its citizens and visitors through leadership, action and coordination of Oregon's public safety resources.

The department is organized into three bureaus: Intergovernmental Services Bureau, Bureau of Investigations, and Central Operations Command. Some of the agency's specialized programs and services include: transportation safety; major crime investigations; forensic services including DNA identification, automated fingerprint identification, and computerized criminal history files; drug investigation; fish and wildlife enforcement; gambling enforcement and regulation; state emergency response coordination; state Fire Marshal Service and Conflagration Act coordination; statewide Law Enforcement Data System; coordination of federal grants for public safety issues; coordination of Criminal Justice Information Standards; medical examiner services; Special Weapons and Tactics (SWAT), and serves as the point of contact to the National Office of Homeland Security.

Criminal Investigation Services Division

Address: 400 Public Service Bldg., Salem 97310
Phone: 503-378-3720
Fax: 503-363-5475
E-mail: edward.mouery@state.or.us
Web: www.oregon.gov/OSP/
Contact: Ed Mouery, Captain
Statutory Authority: ORS 181.030

Duties and Responsibilities: The Criminal Investigation Services Division is committed to upholding public safety by providing leadership, investigative expertise, specialized services, statewide response, and assistance to the criminal justice system. The primary function of the division is the protection of the lives and property of the citizens of this state. Detectives are assigned throughout the state, and direct their efforts toward the violent and major offender participation in local major crime teams, multi-disciplinary teams, fire investigation teams, district attorney support programs, and interagency narcotic teams. Members of the field and local law enforcement agencies are supported by State Police specialized services in the areas of: Arson/Explosives, Drug

investigations, Missing Children Clearinghouse, Polygraph examinations, Sex Offender Registration, Sexually Exploited Children, Homicide Incident Tracking System (HITS), Computer crimes, and Tobacco Compliance.

Criminal Justice Services Division

Address: 400 Public Service Bldg., Salem 97310
Phone: 503-378-3720
Fax: 503-378-6993
E-mail: carmen.merlo@state.or.us
Web: www.oregon.gov/OSP/
Contact: Carmen Merlo
Statutory Authority: ORS 181.010–181.560

Duties and Responsibilities: The Criminal Justice Services Division was transferred from the Department of Administrative Services in 1995. The division is responsible for administering approximately $40 million in federal grants each biennium through numerous grant programs. The division funds programs under juvenile violence prevention, multijurisdictional narcotics task forces, domestic and family violence prevention, offender alcohol and drug treatment, and statewide criminal justice information systems. The division is also responsible for oversight of the Governor's Council on Domestic Violence.

Governor's Council on Domestic Violence

Address: 400 Public Service Bldg., Salem 97310
Phone: 503-378-3720
Contact: Linda Atkin

Governor's Drug and Violent Crime Advisory Board

Address: 400 Public Service Bldg., Salem 97310
Phone: 503-378-3720
Contact: Karen Green, Grants Manager

Fish and Wildlife Division

Address: 400 Public Service Bldg., Salem 97310
Phone: 503-378-3720, ext. 4300
Fax: 503-363-5475 or 503-378-8282
E-mail: cynthia.kok@state.or.us
Web: www.oregon.gov/OSP/
Contact: Cynthia Kok, Captain
Statutory Authority: ORS 181.020

Duties and Responsibilities: The Fish and Wildlife Division is charged with the detection and investigation of fish and wildlife, and commercial fish laws, rules, and regulations. The division is also charged with enforcement of boating, livestock, criminal and traffic laws and the protection of the state's natural resources.

Forensic Services Division

Address: 400 Public Service Bldg., Salem 97310
Phone: 503-378-3720
Fax: 503-363-5475
E-mail: dave.schmierbach@state.or.us
Web: www.oregon.gov/OSP/
Contact: Dave Schmierbach, Director
Statutory Authority: ORS 181.066–181.080
Duties and Responsibilities: The Crime Laboratory was created in 1939 as a support unit at the University of Oregon Medical School. Today, the Forensic Services Division consists of regional laboratories located in Bend, Central Point, Ontario, Pendleton, Portland, Salem and Springfield. The division utilizes information systems to solve crimes. These systems include Automated Fingerprint Identification System (AFIS), Computerized Criminal History files, National Combined Offender DNA Information System (CODIS) and the Integrated Ballistics Identification System. In 1997, the division successfully established the Forensic Academy to train law enforcement personnel in basic crime scene techniques. A liaison committee was established as a communication tool with the state's law enforcement associations. In 1998, a Laboratory Information Management System (LIMS) was installed to meet the increased demand of laboratory services.

Gaming Enforcement Division

Address: 400 Public Service Bldg., Salem 97310
Phone: 503-378-3720
Fax: 503-378-8282
E-mail: robert.sundstrom@state.or.us
Web: www.oregon.gov/OSP/
Contact: Robert Sundstrom, Captain
Statutory Authority: ORS 181.050, 461.130, Chapter 463
Duties and Responsibilities: The Gaming Enforcement Division was created to assure the fairness, honesty, integrity and security of the Oregon State Lottery and the Tribal Gaming Centers operating in Oregon. Security is the cornerstone of the Oregon State Lottery and the Tribal Gaming Centers.

The division consists of two gambling regulatory programs, the Lottery Security and Tribal Gaming sections. There is also a Boxing and Wrestling unit which was created to ensure the integrity and honesty of licensing of boxing and wrestling applicants and to ensure events are conducted in a manner that protects the public and participants. The division is directed and administered by a captain who also serves as a member of the Governor's Tribal Compact Negotiating Team.

Human Resource Services Division

Address: 400 Public Service Bldg., Salem 97310
Phone: 503-378-3720, ext. 4600
Fax: 503-378-2360
E-mail: roelin.smith@state.or.us
Web: www.oregon.gov/OSP/
Contact: Roelin Smith
Statutory Authority: ORS Chapter 181
Duties and Responsibilities: The Human Resource Services Division, consisting of five sections, provides administrative support to the department. Financial management services are provided by the Fiscal Services section which includes the payroll function. The Personnel section provides all the normal human resource services for the non-sworn employees and selected services for sworn employees. Fleet Management section purchases, prepares and maintains all law enforcement vehicles. The Purchasing/Stockroom section ensures adequate supplies and stocked items are on-hand to support operational needs, as well as mail distribution for the department. Additionally, this division provides business services to the department by managing facility leases, service contracts, personal service contracts and other agreements. The Training section recruits, selects and trains an effective sworn officer workforce.

Information Management Division

Address: 3225 State St., Salem 97301
Phone: 503-378-3055
Fax: 503-363-8249
E-mail: david.c.yandell@state.or.us
Web: www.oregon.gov/OSP/
Contact: David C. Yandell, Director
Statutory Authority: ORS 181.730
Duties and Responsibilities: The Information Management Division, including the Law Enforcement Data System (LEDS), is the focal point and "control agency" for access by law enforcement and criminal justice agencies in Oregon to the online information in the FBI's National Crime Information Center (NCIC), and to the interstate law enforcement message switching network, the National Law Enforcement Telecommunications System (NLETS), which is operated by a consortium of the states.

The central LEDS message switching computer system processes between 17 and 18 million messages per month, serving over 11,000 user devices in Oregon. The central LEDS online database contains a variety of information that is entered and accessed by criminal justice agencies throughout the state and in other states and Canada. This information includes arrest warrants, offenders on parole/probation, criminal histories, sex offender registrants, domestic restraining orders, concealed handgun licenses, and stolen vehicles and other property.

The division also operates the Oregon Uniform Crime Reporting Program (OUCR), which processes and distributes Oregon crime and arrest statistics and provides Oregon data to the FBI for the national crime statistics program. This information is published in a regular series of reports and is used by researchers and others in both the public and private communities.

LEDS Advisory Committee
Address: 400 Public Service Bldg., Salem 97310
Phone: 503-378-3054
Contact: David C. Yandell

Office of Emergency Management
Address: 3225 State St., Salem 97301; Mail: PO Box 14370, Salem 97309-5062
Phone: 503-378-2911; TTY: 503-373-7857
Fax: 503-588-1378
Web: www.oregon.gov/OSP/OEM/
Contact: Kenneth Murphy, Director
Statutory Authority: ORS Chapter 401
Duties and Responsibilities: The purpose of the Office of Emergency Management is to coordinate and maintain the governor's statewide emergency services system. This system is intended to facilitate, coordinate, organize, staff, and manage both pre-event and post-event activities that support the state's ability to prepare for, respond to, and recover from a disaster. This mandate requires that all state agencies having a responsibility to provide service during or following a disaster, do so in a planned, coordinated, and cooperative manner.

State Emergency Coordination Center
Address: 3225 State St., Salem 97301; Mail: PO Box 14370, Salem 97309-5062
Phone: 503-378-2911, ext. 225
Contact: Kenneth Murphy, Director
Statutory Authority: ORS 401.270(6)

9-1-1 Advisory Council
Address: 3225 State St., Salem 97301; Mail: PO Box 14370, Salem 97309-5062
Phone: 503-378-2911, ext. 242
Contact: Ken Keim, Technology and Response Section Director
Statutory Authority: ORS 401.635

Chemical Stockpile Emergency Program
Address: 125 SW 1st St., Pendleton 97801
Phone: 541-966-9640
Contact: Chris Brown, Program Manager

Domestic Preparedness and Citizen Corps Program
Address: 3225 State St., Salem 97301; Mail: PO Box 14370, Salem 97309-5062
Phone: 503-378-2911, ext. 226
Contact: Dave Cassel, Plans and Training Services Section Director

Financial and Recovery Services Section
Address: 3225 State St., Salem 97301; Mail: PO Box 14370, Salem 97309-5062
Phone: 503-378-2911, ext. 227
Contact: Abby Kershaw, Director

Oregon Emergency Response System (OERS)
Address: 3225 State St., Salem 97301; Mail: PO Box 14370, Salem 97309-5062
Phone: 503-378-2911, ext. 242
Contact: David Yandell, Information Management Division Director
Statutory Authority: ORS 401.275(1)–(5)

Oregon Emergency Response System Council
Address: 3225 State St., Salem 97301; Mail: PO Box 14370, Salem 97309-5062
Phone: 503-378-2911, ext. 226
Contact: Dave Cassel, Plans and Training Section Director

Oregon Seismic Safety Policy Advisory Committee
Address: 3225 State St., Salem 97301; Mail: PO Box 14370, Salem 97309-5062
Phone: 503-378-2911, ext. 237
Contact: Dave Cassel
Statutory Authority: ORS 401.337

Oregon Showcase State Initiative
Address: 3225 State St., Salem 97301; Mail: PO Box 14370, Salem 97309-5062
Phone: 503-378-2911, ext. 227
Contact: Abby Kershaw, Financial and Recovery Services Section Director

Plans and Training Services Section
Address: 3225 State St., Salem 97301; Mail: PO Box 14370, Salem 97309-5062
Phone: 503-378-2911, ext. 226
Contact: Dave Cassel, Director

Search and Rescue Program
Address: 3225 State St., Salem 97301; Mail: PO Box 14370, Salem 97309-5062
Phone: 503-378-2911, ext. 238
Contact: Georges Kleinbaum, SAR Coordinator
Statutory Authority: ORS 401.550–401.635

Patrol Services Division

Address: 400 Public Service Bldg., Salem 97310
Phone: 503-378-3720
Fax: 503-391-5910
E-mail: dan.durbin@state.or.us
Web: www.oregon.gov/OSP/
Contact: Dan Durbin, Captain
Statutory Authority: ORS 181.010–181.560
Duties and Responsibilities: The Patrol Services Division functions under the Operations Services Bureau for the purpose of providing a uniform police presence and law enforcement services throughout the state, with a primary responsibility for traffic safety and response to emergency calls-for-service on Oregon's 6,000 miles of state and federal highways. Some of the services provided include augmenting and supporting local enforcement and meeting the needs of the public for criminal investigation and transportation safety.

State Fire Marshal

Address: 4760 Portland Rd. NE, Salem 97305-1760
Phone: 503-378-3473; TTY: 503-390-4661
Fax: 503-373-1825
E-mail: oregon.sfm@state.or.us
Web: www.oregon.gov/OSP/SFM/
Contact: Nancy Orr, State Fire Marshal
Statutory Authority: ORS 476.020
Duties and Responsibilities: The Office of State Fire Marshal was created in 1917 and was consolidated in 1993 into the Department of State Police under the public safety umbrella. The office is charged with reducing the loss of life and property from fire, explosion and hazardous materials; and minimizing the fire and life-safety hazards of structures, equipment and materials exposed to fire risks. Program areas cover fire prevention and investigation; uniform fire and life safety code development, adoption and interpretation; Community Right to Know; public education and firesetter intervention; industry licensing and permits relating to liquefied petroleum gas, fireworks and explosives; licensing and surveying non-retail gasoline dispensing; Regional Hazardous Materials Emergency Response Team system; Fire Incident Reporting system; and the Oregon Home Fire Sprinkler Coalition.

State Medical Examiner

Address: 301 NE Knott St., Portland 97212-3092
Phone: 503-280-6061
Fax: 503-280-6041
E-mail: karen.gunson@state.or.us
Web: www.oregon.gov/OSP/
Contact: Karen Gunson, M.D.
Statutory Authority: ORS Chapter 146
Duties and Responsibilities: The State Medical Examiner's office is responsible for managing all aspects of the State Medical Examiner program. Staffed by four full-time forensic pathologists and three support staff, the office's duties include the certification of the cause and manner of a death requiring investigation. The office provides forensic medical support and general supervision to each county medical examiner office; files and maintains appropriate reports on all deaths requiring investigation; performs post-mortem examinations and alcohol and drug analyses of deceased persons; and provides lectures and training on legal medicine and death investigation to medical school physicians, law students, police officers, and emergency medical technicians. The State Medical Examiner appoints the county medical examiners with the approval of the Board of Commissioners.

State Medical Examiner
Advisory Board

Address: 301 NE Knott St., Portland 97212-3091
Phone: 503-280-6061
Contact: William Rogers, M.D., Chair
Statutory Authority: ORS 146.015

Training Section

Address: 4760 Portland Rd. NE, Salem 97305
Phone: 503-378-2626
Fax: 503-373-0700
E-mail: fred.douthit@state.or.us
Web: www.oregon.gov/OSP/
Contact: Fred Douthit, Lieutenant
Statutory Authority: ORS Chapter 181
Duties and Responsibilities: The purpose of the Training Section is to recruit, select, and retain an effective sworn workforce and to provide the highest quality training and education to all department employees through mandatory, essential, desirable, and discretionary workforce development skills programs.

The section is comprised of the Training Unit, and the Sworn Applicant Processing Unit. The Training Unit is responsible for identifying and providing training to all employees. The primary function is workforce development. Safety of the public, officer and employee safety, and high exposure to vicarious liability require extensive and high quality training for employees. Secondary responsibilities are to provide training and education to other law enforcement, public safety, and criminal justice agencies, and communities served.

PSYCHIATRIC SECURITY REVIEW BOARD

Address: 620 SW 5th Ave., Suite 907, Portland 97204
Phone: 503-229-5596
Fax: 503-229-5085
E-mail: psrb@oregonvos.net

Contact: Mary Claire Buckley, J.D., Executive Director
Statutory Authority: ORS 161.327
Duties and Responsibilities: The Psychiatric Security Review Board was created in 1978 to assume jurisdiction over persons in Oregon found to be "guilty except for insanity" of a crime. The board's jurisdiction is equal to the maximum sentence provided by statute for the crime for which the person was found "guilty except for insanity."

The board's primary purpose is to protect the public through the on-going review of the progress of those placed under its jurisdiction and a determination of their appropriate placement. The board has the authority to: commit a person to a state hospital designated by the Department of Human Services; conditionally release a person from a state hospital to a community-based program with close monitoring and supervision; discharge a person from its jurisdiction; and, when appropriate, revoke the conditional release of a person under its jurisdiction and order the person's return to a state hospital pending a full hearing before the board. The five board members are appointed by the governor for four-year terms.

PSYCHOLOGIST EXAMINERS, STATE BOARD OF

Address: 3218 Pringle Rd. SE, Suite 130, Salem 97302-6309
Phone: 503-378-4154
Fax: 503-378-3575
Web: www.obpe.state.or.us
Contact: Martin Pittioni, Executive Director
Statutory Authority: ORS 675.010–675.150
Duties and Responsibilities: The State Board of Psychologist Examiners was created in 1973 to determine qualifications, examine and license individuals to practice psychology in Oregon. The board may deny, suspend, revoke or restore licenses. It investigates alleged violations of the statutes and imposes appropriate sanctions, adopts a code of ethics, and enforces continuing education requirements.

PUBLIC EMPLOYEES RETIREMENT SYSTEM

Address: PERS, PO Box 23700, Tigard 97281-3700
Phone: 503-598-7377; Toll-free: 1-888-320-7377; TTY: 503-603-7766
Fax: 503-598-1218
Web: www.pers.state.or.us
Contact: Paul R. Cleary, Executive Director
Statutory Authority: ORS 237.350–237.980, 238.005–238.750, 243.401–243.507

Duties and Responsibilities: The Public Employees Retirement System (PERS) was established in 1946 to provide service and disability retirement income and death benefits to Oregon public employees. Membership includes employees of the state, school districts and local governments. On June 1, 2004, there were 209,954 PERS members and 101,000 retired members or beneficiaries. PERS is administered by a five-member Board of Trustees (three from the private sector and two from the public sector representing both employer and employee) that also administers the Oregon Savings Growth Plan, a deferred compensation program available to all Oregon public employees. The Public Employees Retirement Board members are appointed by the governor and confirmed by the senate. Terms are for three years. The PERS Fund is managed by the Oregon Investment Council under the oversight of the state treasurer.

Public Employees Retirement Board
Address: PERS, PO Box 23700, Tigard 97281-3700
Phone: 503-598-7377
Contact: Michael Pittman, Chair
Statutory Authority: ORS 238.630

Oregon Savings Growth Plan Advisory Committee
Address: 800 Summer St. NE, Suite 200, Salem 97310
Phone: 503-378-3730
Contact: Gerard Drummond, Chair

PUBLIC SAFETY STANDARDS AND TRAINING, DEPARTMENT OF

Address: 550 N Monmouth Ave., Monmouth 97361
Phone: 503-378-2100
Fax: 503-378-3306
Web: www.oregon.gov/DPSST
Contact: John Minnis, Director
Statutory Authority: ORS 181.610–181.991, 206.010–206.015, 243.950–243.974, 703.010–703.325
Duties and Responsibilities: The Department of Public Safety Standards and Training (DPSST) implements minimum standards established by the Board on Public Safety Standards and Training for recruitment and training of city, county and state police, corrections officers, parole and probation officers, fire service personnel, emergency telecommunicators and private security providers. DPSST conducts public safety training throughout Oregon and at the central academy in Monmouth; certifies qualified officers at various levels from basic through executive; certifies qualified instructors;

and inspects and accredits training programs throughout the state based on standards established by the Public Safety Standards and Training Board.

Board on Public Safety Standards and Training

Address: 550 N Monmouth Ave., Monmouth 97361
Phone: 503-378-2100
Web: www.oregon.gov/DPSST
Contact: Robert Tardiff, Chair; Bob Wolfe, Vice Chair
Duties and Responsibilities: The Board on Public Safety Standards and Training consists of 24 members representing city, county and state administrators, professionals representing each of the public safety disciplines and a private citizen appointed by the governor. The board establishes minimum standards for recruitment and training of city, county and state police, corrections officers, parole and probation officers, fire service personnel, emergency telecommunicators and private security providers, and makes determinations on waiver requests. The board operates in close partnership with the Department of Public Safety Standards and Training which implements the standards set by the board. The board is supported by six advisory and policy committees representing the public safety disciplines, which provide technical expertise and serve as vital links to local public safety organizations.

PUBLIC UTILITY COMMISSION

Address: 550 Capitol St. NE, Suite 215, Salem 97301-2551; Mail: PO Box 2148, Salem 97308
Phone: 503-378-6611
Fax: 503-378-5505
E-mail: puc.commission@state.or.us
Web: www.puc.state.or.us
Contact: Rick Willis, Executive Director; Lee Beyer, Chair
Statutory Authority: ORS Chapters 756, 757, 758, 759, 772
Duties and Responsibilities: The Public Utility Commission of Oregon (PUC) regulates customer rates and services of the state's investor-owned electric, natural gas and telephone utilities; and certain water companies. The commission does not regulate people's utility districts, cooperatives or municipally-owned utilities except in matters of safety. The PUC conducts its business in public meetings scheduled every two weeks at its headquarters in Salem, and it encourages public involvement in its decisions. The PUC also conducts public hearings on specific issues. The commission's regulatory responsibilities are carried out by a staff of 120 employees. Each year, the PUC

issues a variety of reports including statistical reports on utility companies.

RACING COMMISSION, OREGON

Address: 800 NE Oregon St., Suite 310, Portland 97232
Phone: 503-731-4052
Fax: 503-731-4053
E-mail: jodi.hanson@state.or.us
Web: http://racing.oregon.gov
Contact: Jodi Hanson, Executive Director
Statutory Authority: ORS 462.210
Duties and Responsibilities: The Oregon Racing Commission was established in 1933 as part of the Pari-Mutuel Wagering Act. The agency regulates all aspects of the pari-mutuel industry in Oregon. The commission currently regulates all horse and greyhound racing where pari-mutuel wagering is conducted. Regulation occurs both on track and at off-track wagering facilities and covers all aspects of the operation. In addition, the commission regulates multi-jurisdictional hubs (currently five) located in the state. Proceeds from pari-mutuel racing not used for the commission's operation are transferred to the state general fund. The executive director, supervisor of horse racing, supervisor of greyhound racing, supervisor of pari-mutuels, chief of investigations and other officials appointed by the commission currently administer seven horse and one greyhound pari-mutuel race meets which are conducted annually at various locations throughout the state. Members of the commission are appointed by the governor and confirmed by the senate.

RADIOLOGIC TECHNOLOGY, BOARD OF

Address: 800 NE Oregon St., Suite 407, Portland 97232
Phone: 503-731-4088
Fax: 503-872-6831
E-mail: Linda.Russell@state.or.us
Web: www.obrt.state.or.us/
Contact: Linda A. Russell, Executive Officer
Statutory Authority: ORS 688.405–688.605, 688.915
Duties and Responsibilities: The Board of Radiologic Technology was established in 1977 to ensure the quality of radiation therapy, fluoroscopy, CT scans, mammography, bone densitometry and other means of medical imaging by assuring the quality of radiologic technology operators. The board licenses diagnostic or therapeutic technologists and diagnostic technicians, administers Limited Permit Examinations to determine initial competence to practice for radiologic technicians, and approves

continuing education offerings to assure continuing competence for both technologists and technicians.

REAL ESTATE AGENCY

Address: 1177 Center St. NE, Salem 97301-2505
Phone: 503-378-4170
Fax: 503-378-2491
Web: www.rea.state.or.us
Contact: Scott W. Taylor, Commissioner
Statutory Authority: ORS 696.375
Duties and Responsibilities: The Real Estate Agency was established in 1919. The agency is administered by the Real Estate Commissioner who is appointed by the governor.

The agency is responsible for the licensing, education and enforcement of Oregon's real estate laws applicable to brokers, salespersons, property managers, real estate marketing organizations; licensing and regulation of escrow agents (ORS chapter 696); and subdivision (ORS chapter 92), condominium (ORS chapter 100), timeshare and campground (ORS chapter 94) registration/public report issuance.

Each year the agency processes and tests more than 2,500 license applicants and monitors regulated activities in over 4,400 escrow and real estate offices. Land developers with offerings to Oregon citizens have thousands of disclosure filings with the agency.

The agency provides educational material and seminars for real estate professionals. The agency also conducts investigations and hearings when complaints are filed against licensees, registrants and real property developers.

Real Estate Board

Address: 1177 Center St. NE, Salem 97301-2505
Phone: 503-378-4170
Contact: Marguerite Kenagy
Statutory Authority: ORS 696.405
Duties and Responsibilities: The Real Estate Board meets bi-monthly to review experience and education waivers of real estate licensing applicants. The governor appoints the nine-member advisory board, which consists of seven industry members and two public members. Board members serve four-year terms and through the chair advise the governor when appropriate.

REVENUE, DEPARTMENT OF

Address: 955 Center St. NE, Salem 97301-2555
Phone: 503-945-8214; TTY: 503-945-8617
Fax: 503-945-8738
Web: www.dor.state.or.us
Contact: Elizabeth S. Harchenko, Director
Statutory Authority: ORS 305.025
Duties and Responsibilities: The Department of Revenue administers more than 30 tax programs in addition to the personal income tax. These programs include corporation income and excise taxes; gift and inheritance taxes; and tobacco taxes. Additionally, the department collects and distributes revenues for TriMet and Lane transit districts.

In fiscal year 2002, $4.2 billion was raised through personal and corporation income tax. The department processes about 4.5 million documents a year, of which 1.6 million are income tax returns. In tax year 2003, the department received more than 535,000 electronic returns—a record number.

The department collects delinquent accounts for more than 275 state agencies, programs and boards, including the departments of Human Services, Justice, and Higher Education; community colleges; and state courts. Collections for these other agencies totaled more than $56.3 million for the 2001–03 biennium.

Though the department does not collect property taxes, it is responsible for seeing that property tax laws are applied fairly and equitably throughout the state. It also provides training and assistance for county assessors, tax collectors, treasurers and local government budget officials. The department appraises and establishes values for utility property, forestland and most large industrial property for county tax rolls. It collects taxes on harvested timber for distribution to schools, county taxing districts, and state programs related to timber.

SPEECH-LANGUAGE PATHOLOGY AND AUDIOLOGY, STATE BOARD OF EXAMINERS FOR

Address: 800 NE Oregon St., Suite 407, Portland 97232-2162
Phone: 503-731-4050; TDD: 503-731-4031
Fax: 503-731-4207
E-mail: speechaud.board@state.or.us
Web: bspa.state.or.us
Contact: Brenda Felber, Executive Officer
Statutory Authority: ORS 681.205–681.991
Duties and Responsibilities: The Board of Examiners for Speech-Language Pathology and Audiology was established in 1973 to license and regulate the performance of speech-language pathologists and audiologists for consumer protection.

STATE FAIR AND EXPOSITION CENTER, OREGON

Address: 2330 17th St. NE, Salem 97303-3201
Phone: 503-947-3247
Fax: 503-947-3206
E-mail: lin.wolfe@fair.state.or.us
Web: www.oregonstatefair.org

Contact: Katie Cannon, Director
Statutory Authority: ORS 565.040
Duties and Responsibilities: The Oregon State Fair disseminates knowledge about and encourages the growth and prosperity of all agricultural, stock raising, horticultural, mining, mechanical, artistic and industrial pursuits in this state, including animal racing. The director of the Oregon State Fair and Exposition Center operates the business and properties of the center as a year-round fair and exposition center.

STATE LANDS, DEPARTMENT OF

Address: 775 Summer St. NE, Salem 97301-1279
Phone: 503-378-3805
Fax: 503-378-4844
Web: www.oregonstatelands.us
Contact: Ann Hanus, Director
Statutory Authority: ORS Chapter 273
Duties and Responsibilities: The Department of State Lands, one of Oregon's oldest agencies, manages more than 630,000 acres of grazing and agricultural land; 133,000 acres of forest land, including the Elliott State Forest in Coos and Douglas counties; 800,000 acres of off-shore land, estuarine tidelands, and submerged and submersible lands of the state's extensive navigable waterway system. The department's director is appointed by the State Land Board. The department currently has 85 employees and a 2003–05 operating budget of $16 million. Proceeds from management of lands and waterways and other activities of the department and the Land Board become part of Common School Fund principal. The Fund's market value exceeded $702 million as of June 30, 2003. Earnings from fund investments is distributed semi-annually to school districts through county treasurers' offices. The funds are distributed based on the school-age population of each county. In the 2001–03 biennium $48 million in Common School Fund investment earnings were distributed.

In addition to its land and fiscal management functions, the department provides other public services. It is responsible for administering the state's removal-fill law, which protects Oregon's waterways and wetlands from uncontrolled alteration.

Under the Unclaimed Property Act, the department director also acts as trust agent for "abandoned funds" such as bank accounts and uncashed checks. Additionally, Oregon's probate law designates the director of the Department of State Lands as the personal representative in the probate of an estate of a deceased person who has left neither a will nor known heirs.

Other department responsibilities include: leasing state-owned mineral rights for exploration and production of oil, gas, hard minerals and geothermal energy; providing opportunities to lease or buy state land; maintenance of historical records related to early land transactions, including deeds, leases and plats; performance of administrative functions for the Natural Heritage Advisory Council; management oversight and performance of administrative services for the South Slough National Estuarine Research Reserve; lead state agency for the protection and maintenance of Oregon's unique wetlands resources; and management of coastal resources seaward of the mean high tide line.

State Land Board

Statutory Authority: ORS 273.031
Duties and Responsibilities: The State Land Board is composed of the governor, who serves as chair, the secretary of state and the state treasurer. Under constitutional and statutory guidelines, the board is responsible for managing the assets of the Common School Fund (land and money) as well as for additional functions assigned by the legislature.

The Common School Fund was established as a constitutional trust when Oregon was admitted to the union on February 14, 1859. At that time, the federal government granted to the state the 16th and 36th sections of every township, or other lands "in lieu" of these sections, to support the public schools.

Natural Heritage Advisory Council

Address: 1322 SE Morrison St., Portland 97214
Phone: 503-731-3070
Fax: 503-378-4844
Contact: Gary Fowles, Chair
Web: www.oregonstate.edu/ornhic
Statutory Authority: ORS 273.571

South Slough National Estuarine Research Reserve/South Slough National Estuarine Research Reserve Management Commission

Address: PO Box 5417, Charleston 97420
Phone: 541-888-5558
Fax: 541-888-5559
Web: www.southsloughestuary.com
Contact: Michael Graybill, Manager
Statutory Authority: ORS 273.554
Duties and Responsibilities: Under policy guidance from the State Land Board, the reserve is managed through a cooperative agreement between the state and federal governments. An eight-member South Slough National Estuarine Research Reserve Management Commission, appointed by the governor, provides management oversight. The director of the Department of State Lands chairs the commission.

Established in 1974, South Slough National Estuarine Research Reserve was the first reserve created under the 1972 federal Coastal Zone Management Act.

STUDENT ASSISTANCE COMMISSION, OREGON

Address: 1500 Valley River Dr., Suite 100, Eugene 97401
Phone: 541-687-7400; 1-800-452-8807
Fax: 541-687-7419
E-mail: public_information@mercury.osac.state.or.us
Web: www.osac.state.or.us
Contact: Margie Lowe, Executive Director
Statutory Authority: ORS Chapter 348
Duties and Responsibilities: The Oregon Student Assistance Commission (OSAC) was created by the Oregon Legislature in 1959 and administers a variety of state, federal, and privately funded student financial aid programs for the benefit of Oregonians attending institutions of postsecondary education. The mission of the commission is to assist Oregon students and their families in attaining a postsecondary education and to enhance the value, integrity, and diversity of Oregon's college programs.

The Oregon Student Assistance Commission:

- Guarantees student loans from private lenders
- Educates students to prevent loan defaults
- Develops and administers scholarships, and administers the state-funded need based grant program
- Manages the ASPIRE (Access to Student assistance Programs in Reach of Everyone) program: volunteers advising high school students on postsecondary education and financial aid options
- Provides computer-based information services
- Performs collection activities on student loans in default
- Provides authorization of postsecondary degree programs offered by out-of-state and unaccredited colleges

Over 220,000 students are enrolled in authorized degree programs in colleges and universities in Oregon, and every year more than 20,000 more students will begin postsecondary education. In the past year the commission helped over 50,000 Oregon students work toward their educational goals.

Administration Division

Address: 1500 Valley River Dr., Suite 100, Eugene 97401
Phone: 541-687-7400
Fax: 541-687-7419
Web: www.osac.state.or.us
Contact: Jeff Svejcar, Executive Director

Duties and Responsibilities: The Administration Division includes Outreach, Accounting, Human Resources, and Policy and Research, and is responsible for agency direction, new business development, personnel and research. Staff reviews and evaluates financial aid programs and makes recommendations to the governor and the Legislative Assembly. In addition, this division works with the public, the media, lenders and schools, and annually recognizes academically excellent high school seniors as Oregon Scholars.

Claims and Collections Division

Address: 1500 Valley River Dr., Suite 100, Eugene 97401
Phone: 541-687-7366
Fax: 541-687-7426
Web: www.osac.state.or.us
Contact: Robert Barley, Director

Duties and Responsibilities: The Claims and Collections Division reviews lender claims for reimbursement based upon borrower delinquency, death, disability, bankruptcy, or false certification. If the claim is approved, the lender is reimbursed for the outstanding borrower balance. The division then performs collection activities to recover the collectible defaulted student loans.

Grants and Scholarships Division

Address: 1500 Valley River Dr., Suite 100, Eugene 97401
Phone: 541-687-7395
Fax: 541-687-7426
Web: www.osac.state.or.us
Contact: Vicki Merkel, Director

Duties and Responsibilities: The Grants and Scholarships Division administers over 250 scholarships totaling more than $9 million for Oregon residents and several federal and state-funded grant and loan programs for specific populations. In addition, Grants and Scholarships staff delivers more than $20 million of state funds to needy students through the Oregon Opportunity Grant. The staff manages the ASPIRE program, now expanded to 39 Oregon high schools, the Rural Health and Nursing Services Programs, the Jobs Plus Individual Education Accounts for Oregon's "welfare-to-work" program, the Barber/Hairdresser Grant and the Deceased or Disabled Public Safety Officer Grant. Contact this division for assistance setting up a privately funded scholarship program.

Guarantee Services/ Default Prevention Divisions

Address: 1500 Valley River Dr., Suite 100, Eugene 97401

Phone: 541-687-7375
Fax: 541-687-7391
Web: www.osac.state.or.us
Contact: Kat Kordon, Operations Director
Duties and Responsibilities: The Guarantee Services Division provides training and assistance to schools and lenders. Since 1967, OSAC has guaranteed more than $1.8 billion in loans from private lenders, keeping low-cost loans available for Oregon students. The Default Prevention Division works with borrowers and lenders to resolve delinquencies and prevent student loans from defaulting.

Information Technology Division

Address: 1500 Valley River Dr., Suite 100, Eugene 97401
Phone: 541-687-7428
Fax: 541-687-7419
Web: www.osac.state.or.us
Contact: Pat Downey, Director
Duties and Responsibilities: The Information Technology Division (IT) staff manages the on-line system for the agency that administers loan, grants and scholarship programs, as well as the agency's web site. In addition, this division works with a variety of financial aid offices and organizations throughout the state to provide support of their computer systems, networks and websites.

Office of Degree Authorization

Address: 1500 Valley River Dr., Suite 100, Eugene 97401
Phone: 541-687-7452
Fax: 541-687-7419
Web: www.osac.state.or.us/oda/
Contact: Alan Contreras, Administrator
Duties and Responsibilities: The Office of Degree Authorization has four functions: to evaluate requests to start new colleges or degree programs within Oregon; to protect Oregonians from illegal diploma mills; to determine whether individuals in Oregon are using such fraudulent degrees; and to protect existing degree programs from adverse impacts associated with new publicly funded degree programs.

TAX PRACTITIONERS, BOARD OF

Address: 3218 Pringle Rd. SE, Suite 120, Salem 97302-6308
Phone: 503-378-4034
Fax: 503-378-3575
E-mail: tax.bd@state.or.us
Web: www.open.org/~ortaxbrd/

Contact: Ronald A. Bersin, Director; Donna Gilmour, Chair
Statutory Authority: ORS 673.605–673.740
Duties and Responsibilities: The Board of Tax Practitioners protects Oregon consumers by ensuring Oregon tax practitioners are competent and ethical in their professional activities. The board accomplishes its mission by issuing license credentials, conducting a program of examination and continuing education, and by consumer awareness and compliance enforcement activities. All persons who prepare, advise or assist in the preparation of personal income tax returns for a fee must be licensed. Licensed Tax Consultants have proven their competency through experience and examination to the extent they can be in their own office. Licensed Tax Preparers are apprentice-level practitioners who must work under supervision of Licensed Tax Consultants.

TAX SUPERVISING AND CONSERVATION COMMISSION

Address: PO Box 8428, Portland 97207
Phone: 503-988-3054
Fax: 503-988-3053
E-mail: tscc@co.multnomah.or.us
Web: www.co.multnomah.or.us/orgs/tscc
Contact: Tom Linhares, Director
Statutory Authority: ORS 294.605–294.705
Duties and Responsibilities: The Tax Supervising and Conservation Commission was established in 1919 and exercises jurisdiction over 36 municipal corporations that are subject to Local Budget Law. The commission certifies the legality of budgets and tax levies; conducts public hearings on budgets, tax levies and bonding proposals; provides advisory services; and collects and reports financial data from the local units.

Activities are funded by appropriations from the Multnomah County general fund.

TEACHER STANDARDS AND PRACTICES COMMISSION

Address: 465 Commercial St. NE, Salem 97301
Phone: 503-378-3586; TTY: 503-378-6961
Fax: 503-378-4448 or 503-378-3758
E-mail: contact.tspc@state.or.us
Web: www.tspc.state.or.us
Contact: Victoria Chamberlain, Executive Director
Statutory Authority: ORS 342.350
Duties and Responsibilities: The Teacher Standards and Practices Commission was established in 1965 to maintain and improve performance in the education profession by approving teacher

preparation programs offered by Oregon colleges and universities; by licensing teachers, administrators and other personnel employed in Oregon schools; and by taking disciplinary actions when educators commit crimes or violate Standards for Competent and Ethical Performance.

TRANSPORTATION, DEPARTMENT OF

Address: 355 Capitol St. NE, Rm. 135, Salem 97301-3871
Phone: 503-986-3289; 1-888-ASK-ODOT for questions, comments or concerns
Fax: 503-986-3432
Web: www.oregon.gov/ODOT/
Contact: Bruce Warner, Director
Statutory Authority: ORS 184.615
Duties and Responsibilities: The Department of Transportation's (ODOT) mission is to provide Oregonians with a safe, efficient transportation system that supports economic opportunity and livable communities. ODOT is actively involved in developing Oregon's system of highways and bridges, public transit services, rail passenger and freight systems, and bicycle and pedestrian paths. ODOT manages driver licensing and vehicle registration programs, motor carrier operations, and transportation safety programs.

Office of the Director

Address: 355 Capitol St. NE, Rm. 135, Salem 97301-3871
Phone: 503-986-3452
Fax: 503-986-3432
Contact: Lori Sundstrom, Chief of Staff
Duties and Responsibilities: The Office of the Director is composed of the ODOT Director, the Chief of Staff, Government Relations Section, and the Office of Employee Safety. The ODOT Director oversees the agency's biennial budget and manages Oregon's statewide transportation policy and development of surface transportation, driver and vehicle safety and licensing, and motor carrier programs. The Chief of Staff directs the activities of the ODOT Executive Team in setting overall policy and strategic direction. The Government Relations section analyzes local, state, and federal laws and rules that affect transportation. The Office of Employee Safety works to develop and implement employee safety and risk management programs.

Oregon Board of Maritime Pilots

Address: 800 NE Oregon St., #15, Portland 97232
Phone: 503-731-4044
Web: www.oregon.gov/ODOT/BMP/
Contact: Susan Johnson, Administrator
Duties and Responsibilities: Oregon has had a policy of licensing pilots to navigate ships on certain waters since 1846. The Board of Maritime

Pilots is an independent occupational licensing agency for pilots, and exists today as Oregon's oldest state agency. A pilot is a local navigational and ship-handling expert, engaging in a professional occupation that requires education and licensure. Pilots command salaries commensurate with other professionals, such as physicians and attorneys.

Oregon Transportation Commission

Address: 355 Capitol St. NE, Rm. 135, Salem 97301-3871
Phone: 503-986-3450
Contact: Stuart Foster, Chair
Statutory Authority: ORS 184.615–184.620
Duties and Responsibilities: The Oregon Transportation Commission is a five-member, volunteer citizens board. Its members are appointed by the governor, with the consent of the senate. Members serve a four-year term and may be re-appointed. When making appointments, the governor considers the geographic regions of the state and ensures that at least one member is a resident east of the Cascades. In addition, not more than three members may belong to any one political party.

Central Services Division

Address: 355 Capitol St. NE, Rm. 101, Salem 97301
Phone: 503-986-4060
Fax: 503-986-3291
Contact: Mike Marsh, Deputy Director
Statutory Authority: ORS 184.615
Duties and Responsibilities: The Central Services Division is comprised of six branches that provide core services to support all operations within ODOT. These branches include Financial Services, which provides stewardship of public funds and assures that resources are effectively and efficiently directed to the priority needs of ODOT; Human Resources, which provides staffing and development support; Civil Rights, which manages several related federal and state regulatory programs; Information Systems, which is responsible for technology solutions; Support Services, which oversees business services, facilities management, fleet management, and purchasing and contract management; and Internal Audit Services, performing audits to assure appropriate functioning.

Communications Division

Address: 355 Capitol St. NE, Rm. 135, Salem 97301-3871
Phone: 503-986-3455
Fax: 503-986-3432
Contact: Patrick J. Cooney, Administrator
Duties and Responsibilities: The Communications Division helps citizens understand transportation programs and issues through the department's overall outreach and information efforts, which include

community and government relations, public information, employee communications, and media relations. The division also provides support for the Office of the Director, the Oregon Transportation Commission, and numerous advisory committees.

Driver and Motor Vehicle Services

Address: 1905 Lana Ave. NE, Salem 97314-0100
Phone: Statewide: 503-945-5000; Toll-free (Portland): 503-299-9999
Fax: 503-945-5254
Web: www.oregon.gov/ODOT/DMV/
Contact: Lorna Youngs, Administrator
Statutory Authority: ORS 184.615(3)
Duties and Responsibilities: Driver and Motor Vehicle Services (DMV) contributes to public safety by licensing only qualified persons and vehicles to drive on streets and highways. DMV issues titles to protect the financial and ownership interests in vehicles. There are currently 2.9 million licensed drivers and 4.0 million registered vehicles in Oregon. The fees collected for licensing and registration are dedicated to the Oregon Highway Fund. Law enforcement uses DMV computer records thousands of times daily. DMV also licenses commercial driving schools and instructors, snowmobile dealers and instructors, and vehicle dealers and wreckers. Each day, more than 15,000 customers are served at DMV's 64 offices statewide, and more than 7,000 customers are served by telephone.

Highway Division

Address: 355 Capitol St. NE, Rm. 135, Salem 97301-3871
Phone: 503-986-3435
Fax: 503-986-3432
Web: www.oregon.gov/ODOT/
Contact: John Rosenberger, Deputy Director
Statutory Authority: ORS 184.615(3)
Duties and Responsibilities: The Highway Division is responsible for design, maintenance, operation and construction of about 7,500 miles of state highways. The division's activities include identifying highway needs; maintaining state highway routes; acquiring rights of way; designing highways, bridges and related structures; awarding highway construction and modernization contracts; supervising contractors; obtaining federal highway funds; helping counties and cities improve roads and streets; testing materials; evaluating environmental impacts of proposed projects; and conducting traffic studies and other research projects.

ODOT's five regional offices are responsible for transportation operations in their area. Each region has several district offices responsible for transportation system maintenance.

Region 1 (Portland Metropolitan Area)
Address: 123 NW Flanders, Portland 97209-4012
Phone: 503-731-8200
Fax: 503-731-8259

Region 2 (Willamette Valley, North and Central Coast, Western Cascades)
Address: 455 Airport Rd. SE, Bldg. B, Salem 97301-5395
Phone: 503-986-2600
Fax: 503-986-2630

Region 3 (Southwestern Oregon)
Address: 3500 NW Stewart Pkwy., Roseburg 97470-1687
Phone: 541-957-3500
Fax: 541-957-3547

Region 4 (Central Oregon)
Address: 63055 N Hwy. 97, Bend 97701-5765
Phone: 541-388-6180
Fax: 541-388-6231

Region 5 (Eastern Oregon)
Address: 3012 Island Ave., La Grande 97850-9497
Phone: 541-963-3177
Fax: 541-963-9079

Bicycle and Pedestrian Advisory Committee

Address: 355 Capitol St. NE, Fifth Floor, Salem 97301-3871
Phone: 503-986-3555
Contact: Michael Ronkin, Program Manager

Historic Columbia River Highway Advisory Committee

Address: 123 NW Flanders, Portland 97209-4037
Phone: 503-731-8234
Contact: Jeanette Kloos, Scenic Area Coordinator

Winter Recreation Advisory Committee

Address: 800 Airport Rd., Salem 97301-4798
Phone: 503-986-3006
Contact: Karen Morrison, Program Coordinator

Motor Carrier Transportation Division

Address: 550 Capitol St. NE, Salem 97301-2530
Phone: 503-378-5849
Fax: 503-373-1940
Web: www.oregon.gov/ODOT/
Contact: Gregg Dal Ponte, Administrator
Statutory Authority: ORS Chapters 803, 810, 818, 823, 825, 826

Duties and Responsibilities: The Motor Carrier Transportation Division is responsible for issuing operating authority to motor carriers, collecting highway use taxes, conducting motor carrier tax, IFTA (International Fuel Tax Agreements) and IRP (International Registration Plan) audits, registering heavy vehicles, enforcing motor carrier safety regulations to protect Oregon motorists, and enforcing truck size and weight laws to protect Oregon's highways, roads and bridges.

Public Transit Division

Address: 555 13th St. NE, Suite 3, Salem 97301-4179
Phone: 503-986-3300
Fax: 503-986-4189
Web: www.oregon.gov/ODOT/
Contact: Martin Loring, Administrator
Statutory Authority: ORS 184.615(3)
Duties and Responsibilities: The Public Transit Division develops and encourages the use of public transportation, ridesharing, telecommuting and other alternatives to driving alone. The division provides financial and technical help to small-city and rural transit service providers; to providers of transportation to elderly people and people with disabilities; and to inter-city passenger service providers. Planning staff support statewide and metropolitan transit planning.

The Rural Technical Assistance Program provides technical help and training resources. A nine-person committee oversees this program, identifying needs and recommending priorities.

Rail Division

Address: 555 13th St. NE, Suite 3, Salem 97301-4179
Phone: 503-986-4321
Fax: 503-986-3183
Web: www.oregon.gov/ODOT/
Contact: Kelly Taylor, Administrator
Statutory Authority: ORS 823.009, Chapter 824
Duties and Responsibilities: The Rail Division works for high-quality passenger and freight rail service. It regulates the industry for safety and service, and has jurisdiction over all public highway-rail grade crossings. The division also manages Oregon's inter-city passenger rail service and invests in railroad improvement projects.

Oregon Passenger Rail Advisory Council

Address: 555 13th St. NE, Salem 97310-1333
Phone: 503-986-4125
Contact: Ruth Bascom, Chair

Transportation Development Division

Address: 555 13th St. NE, Suite 2, Salem 97310-1333
Phone: 503-986-3421
Fax: 503-986-4173
Web: www.oregon.gov/ODOT/
Contact: Craig Greenleaf, Administrator
Statutory Authority: ORS 814.615
Duties and Responsibilities: The Transportation Development Division coordinates the future use of transportation resources among federal, state, regional and local agencies to design and operate an efficient transportation system.

Transportation Safety Division

Address: 235 Union St. NE, Salem 97310-1054
Phone: 503-986-4190 or 1-800-922-2022
Fax: 503-986-4341
Web: www.oregon.gov/ODOT/
Contact: Troy E. Costales, Administrator
Statutory Authority: ORS 184.615(3), 802.300
Duties and Responsibilities: The Transportation Safety Division organizes, plans and conducts a statewide transportation safety program that focuses on occupant protection, driving under the influence of intoxicants, speeding, youthful drivers, pedestrians, bicyclists, motorcyclists and driver education. The division operates these programs by annually awarding more than 500 grants and contracts to service providers.

Oregon Transportation Safety Committee (OTSC)

Address: 235 Union St. NE, Salem 97310-1054
Phone: 503-986-4188
Contact: Dr. John Tongue, Chair

Governor's Advisory Committee on DUII

Address: 235 Union St. NE, Salem 97310-1054
Phone: 503-986-4188
Contact: Jerome S. Cooper, Chair

Governor's Advisory Committee on Motorcycle Safety

Address: 235 Union St. NE, Salem 97310-1054
Phone: 503-986-4188
Contact: Guy "Mitch" Putman, Chair

TRAVEL INFORMATION COUNCIL

Address: 229 Madrona Ave. SE, Salem 97302-4609
Phone: 503-378-4508 or 1-800-574-9397
Fax: 503-378-6282
E-mail: angie@oregontic.com

Contact: Cheryl Gribskov, Executive Director
Statutory Authority: ORS 377.835
Duties and Responsibilities: The Travel Information Council administers the State Highway Logo Program; the Tourist Oriented Directional Program; Museum signs and General Service signs; the Historical Marker and Heritage Tree programs; and the Travel InfoCenters in 15 rest areas.

VETERANS' AFFAIRS, DEPARTMENT OF

Address: 700 Summer St. NE, Salem 97301-1285
Phone: 503-373-2000, 1-800-828-8801; TTY: 503-373-2217
Fax: 503-373-2362
Web: www.odva.state.or.us
Contact: Jim Willis, Director
Statutory Authority: ORS 406.020
Duties and Responsibilities: The Department of Veterans' Affairs has been serving Oregon's military veterans since 1945. The legislature created the department in answer to the citizens' mandate to provide veterans' benefits and services for Oregon soldiers, sailors and airmen returning from duty in World War II. Since then, benefits managed by the department have been extended to include veterans of later eras.

In addition to providing veterans' benefits counseling, claims preparation, and conservatorship services to veterans, their dependents and survivors, the department administers the Veterans' Home Loan and Oregon Educational Aid programs. The loan program was designed to answer a need for equity for returning war veterans. Oregon Senate Concurrent Resolution Number 2, passed in 1943, said, in part, ". . . it would not be fitting that those who remained at home should by reason thereof gain economic advantage over our patriotic defenders." The resolution continued, "Let it be in the declared policy of the State of Oregon to place our returning military and naval forces as nearly as possible on the same economic equality as those who remained at home."

That policy, resulting in the program to provide below-market home loans to qualified veterans, has not changed, although the program itself has been revised and expanded.

Advisory Committee to the Director of Veterans' Affairs

Address: 700 Summer St. NE, Salem 97301-1285
Phone: 503-373-2383
Contact: Evelyn F. Anderson, Chair
Statutory Authority: ORS 406.210

Oregon Veterans' Home

Address: 700 Veterans Dr., The Dalles 97058
Phone: 541-296-7190; Toll-free: 1-800-846-8460

Contact: John Hutchison, Executive Officer
Statutory Authority: ORS 408.360
Duties and Responsibilities: Opening its doors in 1997, the Oregon Veterans' Home is a state-of-the-art, 151-bed long-term health care facility that provides professional Alzheimer and other dementia, nursing, rehabilitative, recreational, social, and other support services for Oregon veterans. The Home is the first and only state-mandated nursing home to provide comprehensive nursing care specifically for Oregon's veterans. The Oregon Veterans' Home is a tax-exempt organization and accepts donations to help meet operating expenses.

Veterans' Services Division

Address: 700 Summer St. NE, Salem 97301-1289
Contact: Valerie Conley, Administrator
Duties and Responsibilities: The Veterans' Services Division provides a variety of services to Oregon's veterans, their dependents, and survivors through its Veterans' Benefits Counseling and Claims, Veterans' Home Loans, Conservatorship, and Oregon Educational Aid programs. Through the Counseling and Claims program, veterans' benefits consultants (VBC) provide assistance to veterans, their dependents, and survivors with obtaining federal, state and local veterans benefits. VBCs are located in Salem and Portland, and offer outreach to nursing homes, correctional facilities, other state institutions, and private residences. The Veterans' Loan program provides home acquisition and home improvement loans to veterans at favorable interest rates. Through the Conservatorship program, the Director provides Conservatorship service, including total estate management to certain veterans and their survivors who are legally determined to be "protected persons" by various Oregon probate courts. The Oregon Educational Aid program provides a financial benefit to help offset the educational expenses of honorably discharged Oregon veterans whose active military duty included service in a theatre of operations for which a campaign or expeditionary medal is authorized.

Benefits Counseling and Educational Aid Programs

Address: 700 Summer St. NE, Salem 97301-1289
Phone: 503-373-2085; Toll-free: 1-800-692-9666
Fax: 503-373-2392
Contact: Dianne Kangas

Claims Program

Address: 1220 SW 3rd Ave., Suite 1610, Portland 97204
Phone: 503-326-2611
Fax: 503-497-1053
Contact: Edward Van Dyke

Conservatorship Program

Address: 700 Summer St. NE, Salem 97301-1289
Phone: 503-373-2085; Toll-free: 1-800-692-9666
Fax: 503-373-2392
Contact: Kathy Andreas

Loan Program

Address: 700 Summer St. NE, Salem 97301-1285
Phone: 503-373-2373; Toll-free: 1-800-828-8801
Fax: 503-373-2088
Contact: Dona Lanterman

VETERINARY MEDICAL EXAMINING BOARD, OREGON STATE

Address: 800 NE Oregon St., Suite 407, Portland 97232
Phone: 503-731-4051
Fax: 503-731-4207
E-mail: ovmeb.info@state.or.us
Web: www.ovmed.state.or.us
Contact: Lori Makinen, Executive Director
Statutory Authority: ORS 686.210
Duties and Responsibilities: The Veterinary Medical Examining Board regulates the veterinary professions in Oregon through enforcement of the Veterinary Practice Act. The board establishes licensing requirements and monitors the professional conduct of veterinarians, veterinary technicians, euthanasia shelters and euthanasia technicians. The board investigates consumer complaints and takes appropriate remedial or disciplinary action. The board monitors consumer issues and advances in the profession, and identifies and establishes minimum practice standards to ensure that quality veterinary care is available to the public.

WATER RESOURCES DEPARTMENT

Address: 725 Summer St. NE, Suite A, Salem 97301-1271
Phone: 503-986-0900
Fax: 503-986-0903
E-mail: webmaster@wrd.state.or.us
Web: www.oregon.gov/OWRD/
Contact: Phillip C. Ward, Director
Statutory Authority: ORS 536.039
Duties and Responsibilities: The Water Resources Department (WRD) was established in 1909 and is authorized by the Water Rights Act. By law, all surface and ground water in Oregon belongs to the public. The department's mission is to serve the public by practicing and promoting wise long-term water management. The department strives to restore and protect streamflows in order to ensure the long-term sustainability of Oregon's ecosystems, economy, and quality of life, and to directly address Oregon's water supply needs. The department's core functions are to protect existing water rights, facilitate voluntary streamflow restoration, increase the understanding of the demands on the state's water resources, provide accurate and accessible water resource data, and facilitate water supply solutions.

As administrative chief of the WRD, the director is charged with carrying out the water management policies set by the Water Resources Commission and with overseeing the enforcement of Oregon's water laws. The director is appointed by the governor for a four-year term, subject to confirmation by the senate.

WRD employs a wide variety of experts, including hydrologists, engineers, geologists, technicians, and administrative specialists. Agency staff monitor streamflows at hundreds of gaging stations, map and study ground water aquifers and help design long-term water plans for Oregon's river basins. They supply local governments and citizen groups with information and technical assistance to make and carry out their own water programs.

The agency is organized into five divisions: Field Services, Technical Services, Water Rights and Adjudications, Director's Office, and Administrative Services. Agency headquarters and the Northwest Regional office are in Salem.

The department is represented throughout the state by a network of five regional and 15 field offices from which watermasters carry out their responsibilities. Among a variety of other duties, regional managers meet with user groups to explain current water law and how local practices fit in and develop working agreements with other agencies for data collection. Watermasters, under the direction of regional managers, enforce water laws and measure the waters of the state.

Water Resources Commission

Contact: Dan Thorndike, Chair
Statutory Authority: ORS 536.022
Duties and Responsibilities: This seven-member citizen board oversees the activities of the Water Resources Department. Consistent with state law, the commission sets water policy.

Through the department, the commission authorizes diversions and appropriations of surface and ground water; issues and records permits, licenses and certificates allowing use of water; establishes instream water rights; and determines critical ground water areas.

Commission members are appointed by the governor for four-year terms, subject to confirmation by the senate.

Ground Water Advisory Committee

Address: 725 Summer St. NE, Suite A, Salem 97301-1271
Phone: 503-986-0845
Contact: Donn Miller, Department Liaison; Malia Kupillas, Chair
Statutory Authority: ORS 536.090

Klamath River Basin Compact

Address: 280 Main St., Klamath Falls 97601
Phone: 541-882-4436
Web: www.water.ca.gov/nd/oregon/index.html
Contact: Richard Fairclo, Esq., Commission Counsel; Alice Kilham, Chair, Klamath Falls, appointed by President Clinton to represent the federal government; Phillip C. Ward, representative for Oregon; and Dwight Russell, representative for California.
Duties and Responsibilities: Members facilitate and promote intergovernmental cooperation to assist in the development and proper use of the water resources of the Klamath River Basin.

Water Development Loan Program

Address: 725 Summer St. NE, Suite A, Salem 97301-1271
Phone: 503-986-0920
Web: www.wrd.state.or.us
Contact: Michael Auman
Duties and Responsibilities: The Water Development Loan Program was enacted by the 1977 Legislature to finance low-interest loans for irrigation and drainage projects in Oregon. Since that time, the constitution has been amended to allow the funding of loans for community water-supply projects, fish protection and watershed enhancement. Since 1977, the loan program has issued $43,511,000 in bonds and funded 180 loans for various projects.

Western States Water Council

Address: Creekview Plaza, #A-201, 942 E, 7145 S, Midvale, UT 84047
Phone: 801-561-5300
Web: www.westgov.org/wswc
Contact: Craig Bell, Executive Director
Duties and Responsibilities: The WSWC was established by the Western Governors' Conference to foster cooperation among western states in the management of their water resources. Member states are Alaska, Arizona, California, Colorado, Idaho, Kansas, Montana, Nebraska, Nevada, New Mexico, North Dakota, Oklahoma, Oregon, South Dakota, Texas, Utah, Washington and Wyoming. Delegates to the council are appointed by and serve at the discretion of the governors. Oregon's delegate is Phillip C. Ward, Salem.

WATERSHED ENHANCEMENT BOARD, OREGON

Address: 775 Summer St. NE, Suite 360, Salem 97301-1290
Phone: 503-986-0178
Fax: 503-986-0199
E-mail: bonnie.ashford@state.or.us
Web: www.oweb.state.or.us
Contact: Tom Byler, Acting Director
Statutory Authority: ORS Chapter 541
Duties and Responsibilities: The Oregon Watershed Enhancement Board (OWEB) was created by the 1999 Legislature to promote the restoration and enhancement of Oregon's watersheds. OWEB evolved from the Governor's Watershed Enhancement Board (GWEB), created in 1987. OWEB provides watershed improvement grants, technical guidance, training and tools to groups working statewide to improve watershed health, and supports the voluntary restoration efforts of landowners and citizens. OWEB also partners with state and federal agencies, local governments, tribes, industries and others to increase support for watershed restoration.

In the 2003–05 biennium, OWEB expects to award over $33 million to landowners, watershed councils, soil and water conservation districts and others for watershed enhancement work. Ballot Measure 66, approved by Oregonians in November 1998, dedicated these funds to support salmon, watershed and habitat restoration. In addition, OWEB administers federal funds to support the Oregon Plan for Salmon and Watersheds, allocated to Oregon for the Pacific Coastal Salmon Recovery Program. OWEB grants fund watershed restoration projects, assessments, monitoring efforts, support for watershed councils, and education/outreach activities. OWEB maintains a Watershed Restoration Inventory of all funded projects to track local restoration efforts and report investment results. The 2001 Legislature added the responsibility to monitor watershed conditions and provide leadership for natural resource data management. The agency reports progress of the Oregon Plan for Salmon and Watersheds biennially to the governor and legislature.

OWEB is administered by an Executive Director and staff in Salem with five regional field offices.

Oregon Watershed Enhancement Board

Address: 775 Summer St. NE, Suite 360, Salem 97301-1290
Phone: 503-986-0178

Fax: 503-986-0199
Contact: Dan Heagerty, Jane O'Keeffe, Co-Chairs
Statutory Authority: ORS 541.360
Duties and Responsibilities: OWEB is guided by a 17-member board, made up of 11 voting members and six advisory members. Voting members represent five state natural resource agency boards and commissions: Board of Forestry, Board of Agriculture, Water Resources Commission, Environmental Quality Commission, and Fish and Wildlife Commission, and six public members representing all regions of the state. Nonvoting, advisory members represent federal natural resource agencies, including the U.S. Forest Service, Bureau of Land Management, Environmental Protection Agency, Natural Resources Conservation Service, NOAA Fisheries, and the Oregon State University Extension Service. This interagency/citizen group is unique in Oregon state government, and was created to foster intergovernmental collaboration. The board acts on applications for funds to accomplish watershed restoration activities, and is responsible for establishing Oregon's long-term strategy for achieving sustainable watershed health.

WOMEN, COMMISSION FOR

Address: PO Box 751-CW, Portland 97207
Phone: 503-725-5889
Fax: 503-725-8152
E-mail: ocfw@pdx.edu
Contact: Roslyn Farrington, Executive Director
Statutory Authority: ORS 185.510–185.570
Duties and Responsibilities: The Oregon Commission for Women was legislatively established in 1983 to work for women's equality. The commission does this by advocating for women in the community, providing information on women to the governor and state legislature, serving as a link for women to state agencies, and providing services to individual women in Oregon. The commission meets at various locations around the state to gather information about women. It also publishes a handbook called Oregon Women and the Law, as well as holding an annual fundraiser to honor Oregon's outstanding women. The commission's women's educational program provides seminars statewide on women's health, wellness and financial literacy. The commission produces a quarterly newsletter.

The commission also administers Communities in Partnership to Stop Violence Against Women and Children (CPSVAWC), an AmeriCorps program focusing on creating communities where violence against women and children is not tolerated or ignored. AmeriCorps members serve for one year.

YOUTH AUTHORITY, OREGON

Address: 530 Center St. NE, Suite 200, Salem 97301-3765
Phone: 503-373-7205
Fax: 503-373-7622
E-mail: oya.info@oya.state.or.us
Web: www.oya.state.or.us
Contact: Robert Jester, Director
Statutory Authority: ORS 419A, 419C, 420, 420A
Duties and Responsibilities: The Oregon Youth Authority (OYA) was created by the 68th Legislative Assembly in July, 1995 and established as an independent department of state government on January 1, 1996. The OYA is responsible for the supervision, management and administration of youth correction facilities, state parole and probation services, community out-of-home placements for youth offenders, and other functions related to state programs for youth corrections. The OYA exercises legal and physical custody over youth offenders between the ages of 12 and 18 who have been committed to the OYA by county juvenile courts. Juvenile court-committed youth offenders may remain in the OYA's legal and physical custody up to age 25. Juveniles, ages 15, 16 or 17, who commit crimes for which they have been waived to and convicted in adult court or for which the state's mandatory minimum sentences apply, are in the legal custody of the Oregon Department of Corrections (adult corrections), but can be placed in the physical custody of the OYA up to age 25.

The goal of the Oregon Youth Authority is to protect the public by holding youth offenders accountable and providing opportunities for youth to reform. This is accomplished through the provision of evidence-based rehabilitation and treatment programming in a multi-tiered system of secure facilities. The goal of facility-based treatment, education and vocational training is to provide youth offenders with needed daily-living skills to successfully transition back into their communities.

Complementing facility programs, OYA provides community-based parole and probation services to youth committed to the OYA for out-of-home placements. State parole and probation services are available in all 36 Oregon counties. In 2003, approximately 1,400 youth offenders were under state parole or probation supervision. Approximately 600 of these youth were placed in out-of-home care including foster care (the OYA is responsible for certifying youth offender foster homes), contracted provider homes, and residential treatment centers. Over 800 youth offenders were supervised on parole or probation while remaining at home.

The following facilities comprise OYA's tiered secure custody system:

Youth Correctional Facilities: MacLaren, Woodburn—345 beds; Hillcrest, Salem—180 beds; Eastern Oregon, Burns—25 state beds; North Coast, Warrenton—25 state beds; Rogue Valley, Grants Pass—100 beds; Tillamook Youth Correctional Facility, Tillamook—50 beds.

Transition Programs: Camp Florence, Florence—25 beds; Camp Tillamook, Tillamook—25 beds; Corvallis House Young Women's Transition Program, Corvallis—25 beds; River Bend, La Grande—50 beds.

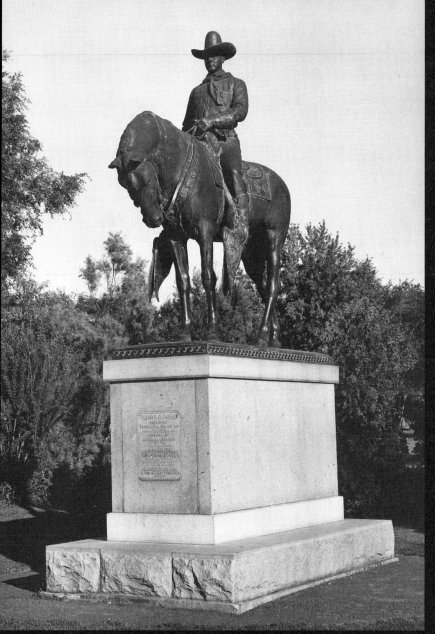

Statue in Pendleton of Umatilla County Sheriff, Til Taylor—Oregon State Archives Photograph, OHD-5294

Oregon's judicial branch of government helps people, business and government resolve disputes, protects their rights and enforces their legal duties as state and federal constitutions and laws require. Oregon judges review the actions of the executive and legislative branches of government for compliance with the Oregon Constitution. This section describes Oregon's judiciary and introduces its members.

OREGON SUPREME COURT

Address: Supreme Court Bldg., 1163 State St., Salem 97301-2563
Records and Case Information: 503-986-5555; TTY: 503-986-5561
Fax: 503-986-5560

The Supreme Court of Oregon has seven justices elected by nonpartisan statewide ballot to serve six-year terms. Justices elected to the Supreme Court must be United States citizens and members of the Oregon State Bar and must have resided in the state three years. The court has its offices and courtroom in the Supreme Court Building just east of the State Capitol in Salem. The members of the court elect one of their number to serve as chief justice for a six-year term.

Powers and Authority

The Supreme Court is created, and its role largely defined, by Amended Article VII of the Oregon Constitution. It is primarily a court of review; that is, it reviews the decisions of the Court of Appeals in selected cases. The Supreme Court decides which Court of Appeals cases to review, usually selecting those with significant legal issues calling for interpretation of laws or legal principles affecting many citizens and institutions of society. When the Supreme Court decides not to review a Court of Appeals case, the Court of Appeals' decision becomes final. In addition to its discretionary review function, the Supreme Court hears direct appeals in death penalty, lawyer and judicial discipline, and tax court cases. It may accept original jurisdiction in mandamus, quo warranto and habeas corpus proceedings. It also reviews ballot measure titles, prison siting disputes, reapportionment of legislative districts, and legal questions on Oregon law referred by federal courts.

Administrative Authority

The chief justice is the administrative head of the judicial department and, as such, exercises administrative authority over and supervises the appellate, circuit, and tax courts. The chief justice makes rules and issues orders to carry out necessary duties and requires appropriate reports from judges and other officers and employees of the courts. As head of the judicial department, the chief justice appoints the chief judge of the Court of Appeals and the presiding judges of all state trial courts from the judges elected to those courts. The chief justice adopts certain rules and regulations respecting procedures for state courts. The chief justice must also supervise a statewide plan for budgeting, accounting and fiscal management of the judicial department.

The chief justice and the Supreme Court have the authority to appoint lawyers, elected judges, and retired judges to serve in temporary judicial assignments.

Admission, Discipline of Lawyers and Judges

The Supreme Court has responsibility for admitting lawyers to practice law in Oregon and the power to reprimand, suspend, or disbar lawyers investigated and prosecuted by the Oregon State Bar. In admitting lawyers, the Supreme Court acts on the recommendation of the Board of Bar Examiners, which conducts examinations for lawyer applicants each February and July and screens applicants for character and fitness to practice law. The Supreme Court appoints at least 14 members to the Board of Bar Examiners. The board includes two "public" members who are not lawyers. The Supreme Court also has the power to censure, suspend, or remove judges after investigation and recommendation by the Commission on Judicial Fitness and Disability.

OREGON COURT OF APPEALS

Address: Supreme Court Bldg., 1163 State St., Salem 97301-2563
Records and Case Information: 503-986-5555; TTY: 503-986-5561
Fax: 503-986-5560

Created in 1969 as a five-judge court, the Court of Appeals was expanded to six judges in 1973 and to ten in 1977. Its judges, elected on a statewide, nonpartisan basis for six-year terms, must be United States citizens, members of the Oregon State Bar and qualified electors of their county of residence. The chief justice of the Supreme Court appoints a chief judge from among the judges of the Court of Appeals.

Court of Appeals judges have their offices in the Justice Building in Salem and usually hear cases in the courtroom of the Supreme Court Building. The court ordinarily sits in panels of three judges. The Supreme Court has authority to appoint a Supreme Court justice, a circuit court judge or a tax court judge to serve as a judge pro tempore of the Court of Appeals. The 1997 Legislature created an appellate mediation program; see ORS 2.560(3).

Jurisdiction

The Court of Appeals has jurisdiction of all civil and criminal appeals, except death-penalty cases and appeals from the Tax Court, and for review of most state administrative agency actions.

Reviews and Decisions

A party aggrieved by a decision of the Court of Appeals may petition the Supreme Court for review within 35 days after the Court of Appeals issues its decision. The Supreme Court determines whether to review the case. The Court allows a petition for

continued on page 98

Supreme Court

Carson, Wallace P. Jr.
Chief Justice
Position 6
Served since 1982
Term expires 1/2007

Balmer, Thomas A.
Associate Justice
Position 1
Served since 2001
Term expires 1/2009

De Muniz, Paul J.
Associate Justice
Position 2
Served Since 2001
Term expires 1/2007

Durham, Robert D.
Associate Justice
Position 3
Served since 1994
Term expires 1/2007

Gillette, W. Michael
Associate Justice
Position 5
Served since 1986
Term expires 1/2011

Kistler, Rives
Associate Justice
Position 4
Served since 2003
Term expires 1/2011

Riggs, R. William
Associate Justice
Position 7
Served since 1998
Term expires 1/2011

Judicial

continued from page 96

review whenever one less than a majority of the Supreme Court judges participating vote to allow it.

OREGON TAX COURT

Address: Robertson Bldg., 1241 State St., 4th Floor, Salem 97301-2563
Phone: 503-986-5645; TTY: 503-986-5651
Fax: 503-986-5507

The Oregon Tax Court has exclusive, statewide jurisdiction in all questions of law or fact arising under state tax laws, i.e., income taxes, corporate excise taxes, property taxes, timber taxes, cigarette taxes, local budget law, and property tax limitations.

Magistrate Division

Address: Robertson Bldg., 1241 State St., 3rd Floor, Salem 97301-2563
Phone: 503-986-5650

As of September 1, 1997, the Tax Court consists of two divisions: the Magistrate Division and the Regular Division (ORS chapter 650, Or Laws 1995). The judge of the Tax Court appoints one presiding magistrate and one or more individuals to sit as magistrates of the Magistrate Division.

Trials in the Magistrate Division are informal proceedings. Statutory rules of evidence do not apply, and the trials are not reported. The proceedings may be conducted by telephone or in person. A taxpayer may be represented by a lawyer, public accountant, real estate broker or appraiser.

The filing fee is $25 unless a taxpayer elects to file as a small claims procedure for $10. The decisions of magistrates in small claims procedures are final and may not be appealed. All other decisions of the magistrates may be appealed to the Regular Division of the Tax Court.

Regular Division

Appeals from the Magistrate Division are made directly to the Regular Division of the Tax Court. The judge of the Tax Court presides over trials in the Regular Division. The Regular Division is comparable to a circuit court and exercises equivalent powers. All trials are before the judge only (no jury) and are reported. The parties must either represent themselves or be represented by an attorney. Appeals from the judge's decision are made directly to the Oregon Supreme Court. The filing fee is $50.

The judge serves a six-year term and is elected on the statewide, nonpartisan judicial ballot.

CIRCUIT COURTS

Effective January 15, 1998, district court jurisdiction, authority, powers, functions, and duties were transferred to circuit court (ORS chapter 658, Or Laws 1995). The circuit courts are the state trial courts of general jurisdiction. The circuit courts have juvenile jurisdiction in all counties except Gilliam, Morrow, Sherman and Wheeler, where the county court exercises juvenile jurisdiction except for termination of parental rights proceedings, over which the circuit court has exclusive jurisdiction. The circuit courts also exercise jurisdiction in probate, adoptions, guardianship and conservatorship cases in all counties except Gilliam, Grant, Harney, Malheur, Sherman and Wheeler.

continued on page 100

Court of Appeals

Brewer, David
Chief Judge
Position 6
Served since 1999
Term expires 1/2007

Armstrong, Rex
Associate Judge
Position 10
Served since 1995
Term expires 1/2007

Edmonds, Walter I. Jr.
Associate Judge
Position 2
Served since 1989
Term expires 1/2009

Haselton, Rick T.
Associate Judge
Position 5
Served since 1994
Term expires 1/2007

Landau, Jack L.
Associate Judge
Position 8
Served since 1993
Term expires 1/2007

Linder, Virginia L.
Associate Judge
Position 4
Served since 1997
Term expires 1/2011

Ortega, Darleen
Associate Judge
Position 3
Served Since 2003
Term expires 1/2011

Schuman, David
Associate Judge
Position 1
Served since 2001
Term expires 1/2009

Wollheim, Robert D.
Associate Judge
Position 7
Served since 1998
Term expires 1/2011

Vacant
Associate Judge
Position 9

Tax Court

Breithaupt, Henry C.
Tax Judge
Served since 2001
Term expires 1/2009

Cases Filed in Oregon Courts 1998-2003

	1998	1999	2000	2001	2002	2003
Oregon Supreme Court	266	297	314	338	285	260
Oregon Court of Appeals	4,876	4,830	4,073	4,297	3,277	3,314
Tax Court—Regular Division	111	184	78	32	47	55
Tax Court—Magistrate Division	3,164	1,497	1,200	1,186	1,245	1,047
Circuit/District Courts	623,593	635,501	653,367	654,822	645,956	655,574

Notes:
1. Data on Supreme Court filings do not include petition for reviews or original jurisdiction petitions that the Supreme Court has denied.
3. Effective January 15, 1998, all district courts were abolished and the powers and functions and judges of the district courts were transferred to the circuit courts.
4. Data on filings do not include preindictment felony filings in district courts.

continued from page 98

Circuit court judges are elected on a nonpartisan ballot for a term of six years. They must be citizens of the United States, members of the Oregon State Bar, residents of Oregon at least three years and residents of their judicial district at least one year (except Multnomah County judges, who may reside within ten miles of the county). As of January 1, 2005, there are 169 circuit judges serving the 36 Oregon counties. The circuit judges are grouped in 27 geographical areas called judicial districts. Multnomah County district has 38 circuit judges; Lane, 15; Marion, 14; Washington, 14; Clackamas, 10. One district has eight judges, one district has seven judges, one district has six judges, three districts have five judges, four districts have four judges, five districts have three judges, four districts have two judges and three districts have one judge.

To expedite judicial business, the chief justice of the Supreme Court may assign any circuit judge to sit in any judicial district in the state.

Senior Judges

Under Oregon law, a judge who retires from the circuit court, Oregon Tax Court, Court of Appeals or Supreme Court, except a judge retired under the provisions of ORS 1.310, may be designated a senior judge of the state by the Supreme Court, eligible for temporary assignment by the Supreme Court to any state court at or below the level in which he or she last served as a full-time judge. The current roster of senior judges follows:

From Supreme Court—Ralph M. Holman, Berkeley Lent, Hans Linde, Edwin Peterson, Betty Roberts, Gordon W. Sloan, Richard L. Unis, George Van Hoomissen.

From Court of Appeals—Edward Branchfield, John H. Buttler, George M. Joseph, William L. Richardson, Kurt C. Rossman, Herbert M. Schwab,

Robert Y. Thornton, John Warden, Edward H. Warren.

From Circuit Court—Philip T. Abraham, Ted Abram, Raymond Bagley, Richard D. Barber, John C. Beatty, William A. Beckett, Richard C. Beesley, Alan C. Bonebrake, Winston L. Bradshaw, Sid Brockley, Clarke C. Brown, Carl N. Byers, Joseph F. Ceniceros, John M. Copenhaver, Charles Crookham, L.A. Cushing, Ross G. Davis, Mercedes F. Deiz, Henry R. Dickinson Jr., Jim Donnell, Jeff Dorroh, James R. Ellis, Duane R. Ertsgaard, Charles H. Foster, Karl W. Freerksen Jr., Jackson L. Frost, Robert S. Gardner, James C. Goode, Charles B. Guinasso, James Hargreaves, Wayne R. Harris, Stephen B. Herrell, Alan R. Jack, Dale Jacobs, Lee Johnson, Donald Kalberer, Mitchell A. Karaman, Frank D. Knight, Harlow F. Lenon, William O. Lewis, Jon B. Lund, William S. Mackay, James A. Mason, Robert B. McConville, William McLennan, L.A. Merryman, Rodney W. Miller, Gregory E. Milnes, Robert J. Morgan, Thomas M. Mosgrove, Thomas L. Moultrie, Albert R. Musick, Kathleen B. Nachtigal, J. Loyd O'Neal, Clifford Olsen, Jack F. Olsen, Hollie M. Pihl, Milo Pope, Robert Redding, Charles A. Sams, Don H. Sanders, Loren L. Sawyer, William C. Snouffer, Douglas R. Spencer, Wendell H. Tompkins, Eric Valentine, Pierre L. Van Rysselberghe, Robert F. Walberg, Stephen S. Walker, C. Gregory West, Darrell J. Williams, Lyle R. Wolff, George J. Woodrich, Frank J. Yraguen.

From District Court—Frank R. Alderson, Robert H. Anderson, H. William Barlow, Wayne H. Blair, Aaron Brown Jr., Anthony L. Casciato, George F. Cole, Richard J. Courson, Walter W. Foster, Robert L. Gilliland, Robert E. Jones, Winfrid K. Liepe, Charles H. Reeves, Joseph J. Thalhofer.

continued on page 123

Circuit Court

Abernethy, Pamela L.
Marion
Dist. 3—Pos. 5

Adkisson, Marci W.
Klamath
Dist. 13—Pos. 3

Adler, A. Michael
Deschutes
Dist. 11—Pos. 4

Ahern, Daniel J.
Crook, Jefferson
Dist. 22—Pos. 2

Alexander, Timothy P.
Washington
Dist. 20—Pos. 7

Amiton, Marshall L.
Multnomah
Dist. 4—Pos. 22

Judicial

Arnold, G. Philip
Jackson
Dist. 1—Pos. 3

Avera, Fred
Polk
Dist. 12—Pos. 3

Baisinger, Glen D.
Linn
Dist. 23—Pos. 5

Baker, Lindi L.
Josephine (P)
Dist. 14—Pos. 4

Baldwin, Richard C.
Multnomah
Dist. 4—Pos. 14

Barron, Richard L.
Coos, Curry (P)
Dist. 15—Pos. 2

Baxter, Greg
Baker (P)
Dist. 8—Pos. 1

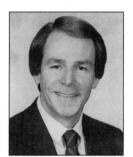

Bearden, Frank L.
Multnomah
Dist. 4—Pos. 9

Bearden, Mary Ann
Lane (P)
Dist. 2—Pos. 7

Bechtold, Paula M.
Coos, Curry
Dist. 15—Pos. 5

Beckman, Douglas G.
Multnomah
Dist. 4—Pos. 27

Bergman, Linda L.
Multnomah
Dist. 4—Pos. 11

Billings, Jack
Lane
Dist. 2—Pos. 8

Bispham, Carol R.
Linn
Dist. 23—Pos. 1

Bloch, Eric J.
Multnomah
Dist. 4—Pos. 20

Brady, Alta J.
Deschutes
Dist. 11—Pos. 1

Branford, Thomas O.
Lincoln
Dist. 17—Pos. 3

Brownhill, Paula J.
Clatsop (P)
Dist. 18—Pos. 1

Burton, Claudia M.
Marion
Dist. 3—Pos. 4

Campbell, Nancy W.
Washington
Dist. 20—Pos. 12

Carlson, Charles D.
Lane
Dist. 2—Pos. 2

Carlson, Cynthia D.
Lane
Dist. 2—Pos. 13

Carp, Ted
Lane
Dist. 2—Pos. 12

Cinniger, Ronald E.
Multnomah
Dist. 4—Pos. 21

Collins, John L.
Yamhill (P)
Dist. 25—Pos. 1

Connell, David B.
Benton
Dist. 21—Pos. 3

Coon, Allan H.
Josephine
Dist. 14—Pos. 2

Crain, Patricia
Jackson
Dist. 1—Pos. 4

Cramer, William D. Jr.
Grant, Harney (P)
Dist. 24—Pos. 1

Crowley, Paul G.
Gilliam, Hood River,
Sherman, Wasco, Wheeler
Dist. 7—Pos. 3

Dailey, Kathleen M.
Multnomah
Dist. 4—Pos. 25

Darling, Deanne L.
Clackamas
Dist. 5—Pos. 9

Dickey, Don A.
Marion
Dist. 3—Pos. 12

Downer, Hugh C. Jr.
Coos, Curry
Dist. 15—Pos. 3

Foote, Gregory G.
Lane
Dist. 2—Pos. 9

Forte, Stephen P.
Deschutes
Dist. 11—Pos. 7

Judicial

Frantz, Julie
Multnomah
Dist. 4—Pos. 10

Freeman, Clifford
Multnomah
Dist. 4—Pos. 28

Fuchs, Alicia A.
Multnomah
Dist. 4—Pos. 15

Galton, Sid
Multnomah
Dist. 4—Pos. 4

Gardner, Mark
Washington
Dist. 20—Pos. 4

Garrison, Randolph Lee
Douglas
Dist. 16—Pos. 3

Gernant, David
Multnomah
Dist. 4—Pos. 31

Gillespie, Michael J.
Coos, Curry
Dist. 15—Pos. 4

Gilroy, Patrick D.
Clackamas
Dist. 5—Pos. 1

Graves, Dennis J.
Marion
Dist. 3—Pos. 7

Photo
Not
Submitted

Grove, Ted
Columbia
Dist. 19—Pos. 2

Photo
Not
Submitted

Guimond, Joseph C.
Marion
Dist. 3—Pos. 8

Hantke, David W.
Tillamook (P)
Dist. 27—Pos. 2

Harris, Daniel L.
Jackson
Dist. 1—Pos. 2

Hart, Thomas M.
Marion
Dist. 3—Pos. 13

Haslinger, Barbara A.
Deschutes
Dist. 11—Pos. 5

Henry, Eveleen
Lane
Dist. 2—Pos. 15

Hernandez, Marco A.
Washington (P)
Dist. 20—Pos. 11

Photo
Not
Submitted

Herndon, Robert D.
Clackamas
Dist. 5—Pos. 7

Hill, Daniel J.
Morrow, Umatilla
Dist. 6—Pos. 3

Hodges, Bryan T.
Lane
Dist. 2—Pos. 14

Holcomb, Janet S.
Benton (P)
Dist. 21—Pos. 2

Holland, Lauren S.
Lane
Dist. 2—Pos. 11

Horner, William
Polk
Dist. 12—Pos. 1

Huckleberry, Robert J.
Lincoln (P)
Dist. 17—Pos. 1

Hull, Donald W.
Gilliam, Hood River,
Sherman, Wasco, Wheeler
(P)
Dist. 7—Pos. 1

Isaacson, Rodger J.
Klamath
Dist. 13—Pos. 1

James, Mary
Marion
Dist. 3—Pos. 6

Johnson, Nely L.
Multnomah
Dist. 4—Pos. 6

Jones, Carol E.
Yamhill
Dist. 25—Pos. 3

Jones, Edward J.
Multnomah
Dist. 4—Pos. 23

Kantor, Henry
Multnomah
Dist. 4—Pos. 30

Kelly, John V.
Gilliam, Hood River,
Sherman, Wasco, Wheeler
Dist. 7—Pos. 2

Knapp, Rick
Washington
Dist. 20—Pos. 14

Koch, Dale R.
Multnomah (P)
Dist. 4—Pos. 26

Kohl, Thomas W.
Washington
Dist. 20—Pos. 1

Kurshner, Paula J.
Multnomah
Dist. 4—Pos. 35

LaBarre, Jerome
Multnomah
Dist. 4—Pos. 7

LaMar, Kristena A.
Multnomah
Dist. 4—Pos. 17

Larson, Darryl
Lane
Dist. 2—Pos. 4

Photo
Not
Submitted

Lasswell, William L.
Douglas
Dist. 16—Pos. 4

Leggert, Terry A.
Marion
Dist. 3—Pos. 9

Leonard, Kip W.
Lane
Dist. 2—Pos. 5

Letourneau, Donald R.
Washington
Dist. 20—Pos. 3

Lewis, John B.
Washington
Dist. 20—Pos. 13

Lipscomb, Paul J.
Marion (P)
Dist. 3—Pos. 2

Littlehales, Charles
Lincoln
Dist. 17—Pos. 2

Litzenberger, Marilyn
Multnomah
Dist. 4—Pos. 38

Lowe, John K.
Clackamas
Dist. 5—Pos. 6

Loy, Michael S.
Multnomah
Dist. 4—Pos. 33

Luukinen, Charles
Polk (P)
Dist. 12—Pos. 2

Marcus, Michael H.
Multnomah
Dist. 4—Pos. 34

Marshall, Christopher J.
Multnomah
Dist. 4—Pos. 5

Maurer, Jean Kerr
Multnomah
Dist. 4—Pos. 24

Maurer, Steven L.
Clackamas
Dist. 5—Pos. 8

McCormick, John A.
Linn
Dist. 23—Pos. 4

McCormick, Rick J.
Linn (P)
Dist. 23—Pos. 2

Judicial

McElligott, Michael J.
Washington
Dist. 20—Pos. 6

McKnight, Maureen H.
Multnomah
Dist. 4—Pos. 13

McShane, Michael J.
Multnomah
Dist. 4—Pos. 19

Meisenheimer, Keith E.
Multnomah
Dist. 4—Pos. 29

Mejia, Lorenzo A.
Jackson
Dist. 1—Pos. 1

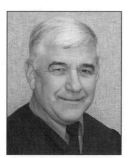

Mendiguren, Phillip A.
Union, Wallowa (P)
Dist. 10—Pos.1

Photo
Not
Submitted

Merten, Maurice K.
Lane
Dist. 2—Pos. 6

Mickelson, Richard K.
Coos, Curry
Dist. 15—Pos. 6

Miller, Eve L.
Clackamas
Dist. 5—Pos. 2

Millikan, Robert C.
Douglas (P)
Dist. 16—Pos. 5

Mitchell, Douglas S.
Lane
Dist. 2—Pos. 10

Murphy, Daniel R.
Linn
Dist. 23—Pos. 3

Nachtigal, Gayle A.
Washington
Dist. 20—Pos. 8

Neilson, George W.
Crook, Jefferson (P)
Dist. 22—Pos. 1

Nelson, Philip L.
Clatsop
Dist. 18—Pos. 2

Neufeld, Gerald C.
Josephine
Dist. 14—Pos. 1

Newman, Michael
Josephine
Dist. 14—Pos. 3

Norblad, Albin W.
Marion
Dist. 3—Pos. 3

Ochoa, Joseph V.
Marion
Dist. 3—Pos. 11

Orf, Rebecca G.
Jackson
Dist. 1—Pos. 6

Osborne, Roxanne Burgett
Klamath
Dist. 13—Pos. 2

Pahl, Ronald J.
Morrow, Umatilla
Dist. 6—Pos. 2

Perkins, Edward L.
Deschutes
Dist. 11—Pos. 6

Poole, Ronald
Douglas
Dist. 16—Pos. 1

Pratt, J. Burdette
Malheur (P)
Dist. 9—Pos. 2

Price, Steven L.
Washington
Dist. 20—Pos. 9

Purdy, William G
Jackson
Dist. 1—Pos. 8

Raines, Keith R.
Washington
Dist. 20—Pos. 5

Rambo, Richard B.
Klamath
Dist. 13—Pos. 5

Rasmussen, Karsten H.
Lane
Dist. 2—Pos. 1

Rastetter, Thomas
Clackamas
Dist. 5—Pos. 10

Reed, Steven B.
Columbia (P)
Dist. 19—Pos. 1

Reynolds, Garry L.
Morrow, Umatilla
Dist. 6—Pos. 1

Judicial

Rhoades, Jamese L.
Marion
Dist. 3—Pos. 1

Photo
Not
Submitted

Roll, Rick W.
Tillamook
Dist. 27—Pos. 1

Rosenblum, Ellen F.
Multnomah
Dist. 4—Pos. 8

Schiveley, Mark
Jackson (P)
Dist. 1—Pos. 7

Seitz, Joan G.
Douglas
Dist. 16—Pos. 2

Selander, Robert
Clackamas (P)
Dist. 5—Pos. 5

Simpson, Lane W.
Lake (P)
Dist. 26—Pos. 1

Smith, Berkeley A.
Columbia
Dist. 19—Pos. 3

Smith, Bernard L.
Gilliam, Hood River,
Sherman, Wasco, Wheeler
Dist. 7—Pos. 4

Stone, Martin E.
Coos, Curry
Dist. 15—Pos. 1

Stone, Ronald W.
Yamhill
Dist. 25—Pos. 2

Sullivan, Michael C.
Deschutes (P)
Dist. 11—Pos. 2

Sullivan, Patricia
Malheur
Dist. 9—Pos. 1

Svetkey, Susan M.
Multnomah
Dist. 4—Pos. 16

Tennyson, Katherine
Multnomah
Dist. 4—Pos. 1

Thom, Ronald D.
Clackamas
Dist. 5—Pos. 3

Thompson, Gary S.
Crook, Jefferson
Dist. 22—Pos. 3

Thompson, Kirsten E.
Washington
Dist. 20—Pos. 2

Tichenor, Carroll J.
Yamhill
Dist. 25—Pos. 4

Tiktin, Stephen N.
Deschutes
Dist. 11—Pos. 3

Tripp, Susan
Marion
Dist. 3—Pos. 14

Judicial

Upton, Suzanne
Washington
Dist. 20—Pos. 10

Van Dyk, Douglas V.
Clackamas
Dist. 5—Pos. 4

Velure, Lyle C.
Lane
Dist. 2—Pos. 3

Wallace, Jeffrey M.
Morrow, Umatilla (P)
Dist. 6—Pos. 4

Waller, Nan G.
Multnomah
Dist. 4—Pos. 2

Welch, Elizabeth
Multnomah
Dist. 4—Pos. 18

West, Russell B.
Union, Wallowa
Dist. 10—Pos. 2

White, Raymond B.
Jackson
Dist. 1—Pos. 5

Williams, Locke A.
Benton
Dist. 21—Pos. 1

Wilson, Janice R.
Multnomah
Dist. 4—Pos. 12

Wilson, John B.
Marion
Dist. 3—Pos. 10

Wittmayer, John
Multnomah
Dist. 4—Pos. 36

Wogan, Cameron F.
Klamath (P)
Dist. 13—Pos. 4

Wyatt, Merri Souther
Multnomah
Dist. 4—Pos. 32

Wyers, Jan
Multnomah
Dist. 4—Pos. 37

CIRCUIT COURT JUDGES BY DISTRICT

Dist. 1—Jackson
Justice Bldg., 100 S Oakdale, Medford 97501

Arnold, G. Philip
Pos. 3, Exp. 1-3-11, 541-776-7171 (173)

Crain, Patricia
Pos. 4, Exp. 1-3-11, 541-776-7171 (164)

Harris, Daniel L.
Pos. 2, Exp. 1-3-11, 541-776-7171 (168)

Mejia, Lorenzo A.
Pos. 1, Exp. 1-3-11, 541-776-7171 (169)

Orf, Rebecca G.
Pos. 6, Exp. 1-5-09, 541-776-7171 (172)

Purdy, William G.
Pos. 8, Exp. 1-5-09, 541-770-5466

Schiveley, Mark (P)
Pos. 7, Exp. 1-5-09, 541-776-7171 (108)

White, Raymond B.
Pos. 5, Exp. 1-1-07, 541-776-7171 (163)

Dist. 2—Lane
Lane County Courthouse, Eugene 97401

Bearden, Mary Ann (P)
Pos. 7, Exp. 1-3-11, 541-682-4240

Billings, Jack
Pos. 8, Exp. 1-5-09, 541-682-4250

Carlson, Charles D.
Pos. 2, Exp. 1-5-09, 541-682-4257

Carlson, Cynthia D.
Pos. 13, Exp. 1-1-07, 541-682-4218

Carp, Ted
Pos. 12, Exp. 1-5-09, 541-682-4497

Foote, Gregory G.
Pos. 9, Exp. 1-1-07, 541-682-4427

Henry, Eveleen
Pos. 15, Exp. 1-5-09, 541-682-4300

Hodges, Bryan T.
Pos. 14, Exp. 1-1-07, 541-682-4027

Holland, Lauren S.
Pos. 11, Exp. 1-3-11, 541-682-4415

Larson, Darryl
Pos. 4, Exp. 1-5-09, 541-682-4259

Leonard, Kip W.
Pos. 5, Exp. 1-5-09, 541-682-4254

Merten, Maurice K.
Pos. 6, Exp. 1-3-11, 541-682-4258

Mitchell, Douglas S.
Pos. 10, Exp. 1-1-07, 541-682-4753

Rasmussen, Karsten H.
Pos. 1, Exp. 1-1-07, 541-682-4253

Velure, Lyle C.
Pos. 3, Exp. 1-1-07, 541-682-4256

Dist. 3—Marion
PO Box 12869, Salem 97309-0869

Abernethy, Pamela L.
Pos. 5, Exp.1-5-09, 503-566-2974

Burton, Claudia M.
Pos. 4, Exp. 1-3-11, 503-588-5033

Dickey, Don A.
Pos. 12, Exp. 1-5-09, 503-373-4445

Graves, Dennis J.
Pos. 7, Exp. 1-1-07, 503-588-5497

Guimond, Joseph C.
Pos. 8, Exp. 1-5-09, 503-588-5160

Hart, Thomas M.
Pos. 13, Exp. 1-3-11, 503-584-7749

James, Mary
Pos. 6, Exp. 1-3-11, 503-588-5135

Leggert, Terry A.
Pos. 9, Exp. 1-1-07, 503-588-5492

Lipscomb, Paul J. (P)
Pos. 2, Exp. 1-1-07, 503-588-5024

Norblad, Albin W.
Pos. 3, Exp. 1-1-07, 503-588-5028

Ochoa, Joseph V.
Pos. 11, Exp. 1-1-07, 503-373-4361

Rhoades, Jamese L.
Pos. 1, Exp. 1-1-07, 503-588-7950

Tripp, Susan
Pos. 14, Exp. 1-5-09, 503-588-8484

Wilson, John B.
Pos. 10, Exp. 1-3-11, 503-588-5030

Dist. 4—Multnomah
Multnomah County Courthouse, Portland 97204

Amiton, Marshall L.
Pos. 22, Exp. 1-1-07, 503-988-3068

Baldwin, Richard C.
Pos. 14, Exp. 1-5-09, 503-988-3052

Bearden, Frank L.
Pos. 9, Exp. 1-1-07, 503-988-3803

Beckman, Douglas G.
Pos. 27, Exp. 1-1-07, 503-988-3201

Bergman, Linda L.
Pos. 11, Exp. 1-5-09, 503-988-3041

Bloch, Eric J.
Pos. 20, Exp. 1-3-11, 503-988-3954

Cinniger, Ronald E.
Pos. 21, Exp. 1-1-07, 503-988-3546

Dailey, Kathleen M.
Pos. 25, Exp. 1-3-11, 503-988-3062

Frantz, Julie
Pos. 10, Exp. 1-5-09, 503-988-3045

Freeman, Clifford
Pos. 28, Exp. 1-5-09, 503-988-3227

Fuchs, Alicia A.
Pos. 15, Exp. 1-3-11, 503-988-3731

Galton, Sid
Pos. 4, Exp. 1-3-11, 503-988-5047

Gernant, David
Pos. 31, Exp. 1-1-07, 503-988-3835

Johnson, Nely L.
Pos. 6, Exp. 1-5-09, 503-988-3404

Jones, Edward J.
Pos. 23, Exp. 1-1-07, 503-988-3540

Kantor, Henry
Pos. 30, Exp. 1-5-09, 503-988-3972

Koch, Dale R. (P)
Pos. 26, Exp. 1-1-07, 503-988-5008

Kurshner, Paula J.
Pos. 35, Exp. 1-1-07, 503-988-5010

LaBarre, Jerome
Pos. 7, Exp. 1-1-07, 503-988-3348

LaMar, Kristena A.
Pos. 17, Exp. 1-5-09, 503-988-3204

Litzenberger, Marilyn
Pos. 38, Exp. 6-30-09, 503-988-3957

Loy, Michael S.
Pos. 33, Exp. 1-5-09, 503-988-3813

Marcus, Michael H.
Pos. 34, Exp. 1-5-09, 503-988-3250

Marshall, Christopher J.
Pos. 5, Exp. 1-5-09, 503-988-3274

Maurer, Jean Kerr
Pos. 24, Exp. 1-5-09, 503-988-3804

McKnight, Maureen H.
Pos. 13, Exp. 1-5-09 503-988-3986

McShane, Michael J.
Pos. 19, Exp. 1-5-09 503-988-3214

Meisenheimer, Keith E.
Pos. 29, Exp. 1-1-07, 503-988-3985

Rosenblum, Ellen F.
Pos. 8, Exp. 1-1-07, 503-988-5029

Svetkey, Susan M.
Pos. 16, Exp. 1-1-07, 503-988-3060

Tennyson, Katherine
Pos. 1, Exp. 1-5-09, 503-988-3078

Waller, Nan G.
Pos. 2, Exp. 1-3-11, 503-988-3038

Welch, Elizabeth
Pos. 18, Exp. 1-1-07, 503-988-3008

Wilson, Janice R.
Pos. 12, Exp. 1-1-07, 503-988-3069

Wittmayer, John
Pos. 36, Exp. 1-5-09, 503-988-3165

Wyatt, Merri Souther
Pos. 32, Exp. 1-1-07, 503-988-3029

Wyers, Jan
Pos. 37, Exp. 1-3-11, 503-988-6760

Vacant
Pos. 3, 503-988-5101

Dist. 5—Clackamas

Clackamas County Courthouse, Oregon City 97045

Darling, Deanne L.
Pos. 9, Exp. 1-5-09, 503-655-8643

Gilroy, Patrick D.
Pos. 1, Exp. 1-1-07, 503-655-8687

Herndon, Robert D.
Pos. 7, Exp. 1-3-11, 503-655-8643

Lowe, John K.
Pos. 6, Exp. 1-1-07, 503-655-8678

Maurer, Steven L.
Pos. 8, Exp. 1-1-07, 503-655-8643

Miller, Eve L.
Pos. 2, Exp. 1-3-11, 503-655-8686

Rastetter, Thomas
Pos. 10, Exp. 1-3-11, 503-655-8643

Selander, Robert (P)
Pos. 5, Exp. 1-5-09, 503-655-8623

Thom, Ronald D.
Pos. 3, Exp. 1-1-07, 503-655-8685

Van Dyk, Douglas V.
Pos. 4, Exp. 1-3-11, 503-655-8688

Dist. 6—Morrow, Umatilla

Hill, Daniel J.
Pos. 3, Exp. 1-3-11, 541-278-0341 (232); PO
PO Box 1307, Pendleton 97801

Pahl, Ronald J.
Pos. 2, Exp. 1-3-11, 541-278-0341 (225);
PO Box 1307, Pendleton 97801

Reynolds, Garry L.
Pos. 1, Exp. 1-5-09, 541-278-0341 (222);
PO Box 1307, Pendleton 97801

Wallace, Jeffrey M. (P)
Pos. 4, Exp. 1-3-11, 541-567-5225 (225);
243-B E Main St., Hermiston 97838

Dist. 7—Gilliam, Hood River, Sherman, Wasco, Wheeler

Crowley, Paul G.
Pos. 3, Exp. 1-3-11, 541-386-1862; Hood
River County Courthouse, Hood River 97031

Hull, Donald W. (P)
Pos. 1, Exp. 1-3-11, 541-386-2676; Hood
River County Courthouse, Hood River 97031
Moro 97039, 541-565-3650

Kelly, John V.
Pos. 2, Exp. 1-3-11, 541-296-3196 (21);
Wasco County Courthouse, The Dalles 97058

Smith, Bernard L.
Pos. 4, Exp. 1-3-11, 541-296-2209 (14);
Wasco County Courthouse, The Dalles 97058

Dist. 8—Baker

Baxter, Greg (P)
Pos. 1, Exp. 1-1-07, 541-523-6303; Baker
County Courthouse, Baker City 97814

Dist. 9—Malheur

251 B St. W, Box 3, Vale 97918

Pratt, J. Burdette (P)
Pos. 2, Exp. 1-5-09, 541-473-5194

Sullivan, Patricia
Pos. 1, Exp. 1-1-07, 541-473-5178

Dist. 10—Union, Wallowa

Mendiguren, Phillip A. (P)
Pos. 1, Exp. 1-5-09, 541-962-9500 (231);
Joseph Bldg., 1108 K Ave., La Grande 97850
Enterprise 97828, 541-426-4991

West, Russell B.
Pos. 2, Exp. 1-5-09, 541-962-9500 (232);
Joseph Bldg., 1108 K Ave., La Grande 97850;
541-426-4991; Wallowa County Courthouse,
Enterprise 97828

Dist. 11—Deschutes

Deschutes County Courthouse, Bend 97701

Adler, A. Michael
Pos. 4, Exp. 1-3-11, 541-388-5300 (249)

Brady, Alta J.
Pos. 1, Exp. 1-1-07, 541-388-5300 (245)

Forte, Stephen P.
Pos. 7, Exp. 6-30-09, 541-388-5300

Haslinger, Barbara A.
Pos. 5, Exp. 1-5-09, 541-388-5300 (255)

Perkins, Edward L.
Pos. 6, Exp. 1-3-11, 541-388-5300 (252)

Sullivan, Michael C. (P)
Pos. 2, Exp. 1-1-07, 541-388-5300 (241)

Tiktin, Stephen N.
Pos. 3, Exp. 1-5-09, 541-388-5300 (237)

Judicial

Dist. 12—Polk

Polk County Courthouse, Dallas 97338

Avera, Fred
Pos. 3, Exp. 1-3-11, 503-623-5235

Horner, William
Pos. 1, Exp. 1-1-07, 503-623-9266

Luukinen, Charles (P)
Pos. 2, Exp. 1-1-07, 503-623-9245

Dist. 13—Klamath

Klamath County Courthouse, Klamath Falls 97601

Adkisson, Marci Warner
Pos. 3, Exp. 1-3-11, 541-883-5503 (251)

Isaacson, Rodger J.
Pos. 1, Exp. 1-5-09, 541-883-5503 (247)

Osborne, Roxanne Burgett
Pos. 2, Exp. 1-3-11, 541-883-5503 (257)

Rambo, Richard B.
Pos. 5, Exp. 1-1-07, 541-883-5503 (255)

Wogan, Cameron F. (P)
Pos. 4, Exp. 1-3-11, 541-883-5503 (244)

Dist. 14—Josephine

Josephine County Courthouse, Grants Pass 97526

Baker, Lindi L. (P)
Pos. 4, exp. 1-3-11, 541-475-2309

Coon, Allan H.
Pos. 2, Exp. 1-5-09, 541-476-2309

Neufeld, Gerald C.
Pos. 1, Exp. 1-1-07, 541-476-2309

Newman, Michael
Pos. 3, Exp. 1-3-11, 541-476-2309

Dist. 15—Coos, Curry

Coos County Courthouse, Coquille 97423

Barron, Richard L. (P)
Pos. 2, Exp. 1-3-11, 541-396-3121 (244)

Bechtold, Paula M.
Pos. 5, Exp. 1-1-07, PO Box 324, North Bend 97459, 541-756-2020

Downer, Hugh C. Jr.
Pos. 3, Exp. 1-3-11, 541-247-2742;
Curry County Courthouse, PO Box H, Gold Beach 97444

Gillespie, Michael J.
Pos. 4, Exp. 1-3-11, 541-396-3121 (261)

Mickelson, Richard K.
Pos. 6, Exp. 1-3-11, 541-247-2812;
Curry County Courthouse, PO Box H, Gold Beach 97444

Stone, Martin E.
Pos. 1, Exp. 1-3-11, 541-396-3121 (238)

Dist. 16—Douglas

Justice Bldg., Rm. 201, Roseburg 97470

Garrison, Randolph Lee
Pos. 3, Exp. 1-3-11, 541-957-2433

Lasswell, William L.
Pos. 4, Exp. 1-1-07, 541-957-2420

Millikan, Robert C. (P)
Pos. 5, Exp. 1-5-09, 541-957-2422

Poole, Ronald
Pos. 1, Exp. 1-5-09, 541-957-2430

Seitz, Joan G.
Pos. 2, Exp. 1-5-09, 541-957-2436

Dist. 17—Lincoln

PO Box 100, Newport 97365

Branford, Thomas O.
Pos. 3, Exp. 1-1-07, 541-265-4236 (223)

Huckleberry, Robert J. (P)
Pos. 1, Exp. 1-1-07, 541-265-4236 (252)

Littlehales, Charles
Pos. 2, Exp. 1-1-07, 541-265-4236 (224)

Dist. 18—Clatsop

Clatsop County Courthouse, Astoria 97103

Brownhill, Paula J. (P)
Pos. 1, Exp. 1-5-09, 503-325-8555 (304);

Nelson, Philip L.
Pos. 2, Exp. 1-3-11, 503-325-8536 (318);

Dist. 19—Columbia

Columbia County Courthouse, St. Helens 97051

Grove, Ted
Pos. 2, Exp. 1-5-09, 503-397-2327 (314)

Reed, Steven B. (P)
Pos. 1, Exp. 1-5-09; 503-397-2327 (313)

Smith, Berkeley A.
Pos. 3, Exp. 1-3-11, 503-397-1660 (317)

Dist. 20—Washington

Washington County Courthouse, Hillsboro 97124

Alexander, Timothy P.
Pos. 7, Exp. 1-5-09, 503-846-8772

Campbell, Nancy W.
Pos. 12, Exp. 1-1-07, 503-846-3443

Gardner, Mark
Pos. 4, Exp. 1-1-07, 503-846-3503

Hernandez, Marco A. (P)
Pos. 11, Exp. 1-5-09, 503-846-3851

Knapp, Rick
Pos. 14, Exp. 6-30-09, 503-846-8787

Kohl, Thomas W.
Pos. 1, Exp. 1-3-11, 503-846-3589

Letourneau, Donald R.
Pos. 3, Exp. 1-1-07, 503-846-3418

Lewis, John B.
Pos. 13, Exp. 1-1-07, 503-846-4403

McElligott, Michael J.
Pos. 6, Exp. 1-1-07, 503-846-8675

Nachtigal, Gayle A.
Pos. 8, Exp. 1-3-11, 503-846-4562

Price, Steven L.
Pos. 9, Exp. 1-5-09, 503-846-4999

Raines, Keith R.
Pos. 5, Exp. 1-5-09, 503-846-3457

Thompson, Kirsten E.
Pos. 2, Exp. 1-5-09, 503-846-8872

Upton, Suzanne
Pos. 10, Exp. 1-3-11, 503-846-3590

Dist. 21—Benton
Benton County Courthouse, Corvallis 97330

Connell, David B.
Pos. 3, Exp. 1-3-11, 541-766-6830

Holcomb, Janet S. (P)
Pos. 2, Exp. 1-3-11, 541-766-6843

Williams, Locke A.
Pos. 1, Exp. 1-5-09, 541-766-6827

Dist. 22—Crook, Jefferson
County Courthouse, 75 SE "C" St., Madras 97741-1794

Ahern, Daniel J.
Pos. 2, Exp. 1-5-09, 541-475-3317; 541-447-6541

Neilson, George W. (P)
Pos. 1, Exp. 1-5-09, 541-475-3317; 541-447-6541

Thompson, Gary S.
Pos. 3, Exp. 1-5-09, 541-475-3317; 541-447-6541

Dist. 23—Linn
PO Box 1749, Albany 97321

Baisinger, Glen D.
Pos. 5, Exp. 1-1-07, 541-967-3844

Bispham, Carol R.
Pos. 1, Exp. 1-3-11, 541-967-3848

McCormick, John A.
Pos. 4, Exp. 1-1-07, 541-967-3844

McCormick, Rick J. (P)
Pos. 2, Exp. 1-1-07, 541-967-3848

Murphy, Daniel R.
Pos. 3, Exp. 1-1-07, 541-967-3848

Dist. 24—Grant, Harney
Grant County Courthouse, Canyon City 97820
Harney County Courthouse, Burns 97720

Cramer, William D. Jr. (P)
Pos. 1, Exp. 1-5-09, 541-573-5207

Dist. 25—Yamhill
Yamhill County Courthouse, McMinnville 97128

Collins, John L. (P)
Pos. 1, Exp. 1-3-11, 503-434-7530 (4272)

Jones, Carol E.
Pos. 3, Exp. 1-3-11, 503-434-7530 (4286)

Stone, Ronald W
Pos. 2, Exp. 1-1-07, 503-434-7530 (4251)

Tichenor, Carroll J.
Pos. 4, Exp. 1-5-09, 503-434-7530

Dist. 26—Lake
Lake County Courthouse, Lakeview 97630

Simpson, Lane W. (P)
Pos. 1, Exp. 1-5-09, 541-947-6051

Dist. 27—Tillamook
Tillamook County Courthouse, Tillamook 97141

Hantke, David W. (P)
Pos. 2, Exp. 1-3-11, 503-842-7914 (114)

Roll, Rick W.
Pos. 1, Exp. 1-3-11, 503-842-2598 (112)

(P) = Presiding Judge

Circuit Judges Association:
President—Hon. Karsten H. Rasmussen
Vice President—Hon. Mark Gardner
Secretary—Hon. Daniel L. Harris
Treasurer—Hon. William D. Cramer Jr.
Immediate Past President—Jean Kerr Maurer

continued from page 100

JUDICIAL CONFERENCE

The Judicial Conference, created under ORS 1.810, is composed of all judges of the Supreme Court, Court of Appeals, Tax Court, circuit courts and all senior judges certified under ORS 1.300. The chief justice of the Supreme Court is chair of the conference, and the state court administrator acts as executive secretary. The conference is directed to make a continuous survey and study of the organization, jurisdiction, procedure, practice and methods of administration and operation of the various courts within the state.

Under the direction of an executive committee, the conference usually works under a committee structure in such subject areas as judicial administration, judicial education, judicial conduct and special courts.

The Judicial Conference meets yearly to conduct their annual business meeting, educational seminars, issue committee reports and adopt recommendations.

STATE COURT ADMINISTRATOR

Source: Kingsley W. Click, State Court Admin.
Address: 510 Justice Bldg. (mail: Supreme Court Bldg., 1163 State St., Salem 97301-2563)
Phone: 503-986-5500; TTY: 503-986-5504
Fax: 503-986-5503

The state court administrator, a statutory position created by the 1971 Legislature, assists the chief justice in exercising administrative authority and supervision over the courts of the state. Among the specific duties are: supervision of the personnel plan for nonjudge staff of the state courts; supervision of the accounting system for the state courts; preparation of the consolidated budget for the state courts and management of that budget; management of the legislative program for the judicial department; maintenance of the inventory of state property in the control of the courts; collection and compilation of statistics relating to the courts in Oregon; establishment and supervision of a statewide automated information system; establishment and supervision of education programs for judges and nonjudge staff; continuing evaluation of the administrative methods and activities, records, business and facilities of the courts; development of statewide administrative, personnel, fiscal and records policies and procedures concerning the courts; and preparing and maintaining a continuing long-range plan for the future needs of the courts.

In addition, the state court administrator supervises staff responsible for daily management of the records of all cases on appeal to the Court of Appeals and Supreme Court, publication of the Oregon Reports, Oregon Reports Court of Appeals and the Tax Court opinions, as well as advance sheets for the opinions of all three courts. The administrator also has responsibility for administrative management of the Supreme Court, Court of Appeals, Tax Court, Office of the State Court Administrator and the State Citizen Review Board program.

The state court administrator is secretary to the Oregon Judicial Conference and is responsible for maintaining the roster of lawyers authorized to practice law in Oregon and for coordinating with the Oregon State Bar for admission of new lawyers.

STATE OF OREGON LAW LIBRARY

Source: Joe K. Stephens, Law Librarian
Address: Supreme Court Bldg., Salem 97301-2563
Phone: 503-986-5640; TTY: 503-986-5561
Fax: 503-986-5623

The State of Oregon Law Library traces its origins to the organization of the territorial government of Oregon. The Territorial Act of 1848 provided for the establishment of a library "to be kept at the seat of government." An 1851 act provided for the appointment of a librarian, and defined the librarian's duties. The library served a broad constituency from its beginnings: "Members of the Legislature, and its clerks and officers; Judges of the Supreme and District Courts, and their clerks; Attorney-general and Marshall of the Territory; attorneys-at-law, secretary of the Territory; and all other persons, shall have access to the library, and the privileges allowed by law." This inclusive policy was continued with statehood in 1859, and after charge and control of the library was transferred to the Supreme Court in 1905.

Today, the mission of the library is to provide the comprehensive legal resources that the executive, legislative, and judicial branches of state government require to serve the public effectively, and to afford all Oregonians access to legal information.

The library provides the largest collection of legal information resources in state government. The collection includes the primary law of all U.S. jurisdictions, historical and current; secondary material in virtually all areas of law, and many legal periodicals.

The library operates under the administrative authority of the State Court Administrator.

Related Organizations

BOARD OF BAR EXAMINERS

Source: Marlyce A. Gholston, Executive Director
Address: PO Box 1689, Lake Oswego 97035-0889
Phone: 503-620-0222
Fax: 503-598-6990

Jeanne Loftis, chair, Portland, 2005, Brian Talcott, vice chair, Portland, 2005, Michelle Holman Kerin, Portland, 2007, Darren Lee, Eugene, 2005, William H. Martin, Eugene, 2005, Steven L. McIntire, Eugene, 2007, Erin K. Olson, Portland, 2006, Simeon D. Rapoport, Portland, 2006, Tara J. Schleicher, Portland, 2006, Elizabeth Schwartz, Portland, 2007, Paul Stoltzfus, Salem, 2005, Theresa M. Wade, Salem, 2007, Eleanor Wallace, Salem, 2006.

The Board of Bar Examiners, established in 1913, acts for the Supreme Court in evaluating an applicant's qualifications to practice law in Oregon. Board activities in determining an applicant's qualifications for admission to the Bar include preparation, grading and evaluation of a bar examination; and investigation and evaluation of the character and fitness of each applicant.

OREGON STATE BAR

Source: Karen L. Garst, Executive Director
Address: 5200 SW Meadows Rd., PO Box 1689, Lake Oswego 97035

Phone: 503-620-0222; Toll-free: 1-800-452-8260
Fax: 503-624-8326
E-mail: kgarst@osbar.org
Web: www.osbar.org

Nena Cook, president, Portland, 2005; Mark B. Comstock, Salem, 2006; Phyllis Edmundson, public member, Portland, 2007; Dr. John Enbom, public member, Corvallis, 2006; Linda K. Eyerman, Portland, 2007; Marva Fabien, Salem, 2007; Gerry Gaydos, Eugene, 2005; Timothy C. Gerking, Medford, 2008; Jonathan Hill, public member, Roseburg, 2005; Frank H. Hilton, Portland, 2005; Albert Manashe, Portland, 2007; Lauren J. Paulson, Aloha, 2006; Dennis P. Rawlinson, Portland, 2006; Carol DeHaven Skerjanec, Vale, 2008; Richard S. Yugler, Portland, 2008.

The Oregon State Bar was established in 1935 to license and discipline lawyers. The bar organization is a large public corporation with diverse program responsibilities for the benefit of the public, lawyers, government and the courts. The state bar plays a key role in the admission and discipline of lawyers in Oregon. It also operates a lawyer referral service and Tel-law program; conducts continuing legal education programs; publishes a wide variety of legal and public service material; sponsors a legislative program to improve the laws and judicial system of Oregon; provides malpractice coverage for lawyers in private practice; and funds and supports numerous law-related and public service programs through Oregon Law Foundation.

The Oregon State Bar is a full-service professional organization having not only regulatory, but significant public service and law improvement responsibilities.

COUNCIL ON COURT PROCEDURES

Source: Maurice Holland, Executive Director
Address: University of Oregon School of Law, Eugene 97403-1221
Phone: 541-346-3990
Fax: 541-346-1564

The council, established in 1977 by ORS 1.725–1.750, promulgates rules governing pleading, practice and procedure in all civil proceedings in all courts of the state. The rules are submitted to the legislature and go into effect on January 1 of the following year unless amended, repealed or supplemented by the legislature. The following is a list of members, term-expiration dates and the statutory appointing authority:

Kathryn H. Clarke, chair, Portland, 2007 (practitioner member appointed by the Board of Governors of the Oregon State Bar); Connie Elkins McKelvey, vice-chair, Portland, 2005 (practitioner member appointed by the Board of Governors of the Oregon State Bar); Nicolette D. Johnston,

treasurer, Portland, 2005 (public member appointed by the Oregon Supreme Court); Justice Robert D. Durham, Salem, 2005 (judicial member appointed by the Oregon Supreme Court); Judge David Schuman, Eugene, 2007 (judicial member appointed by the Oregon Court of Appeals); Judge Richard L. Barron, Coquille, 2007; Judge Eric J. Bloch, Portland, 2007; Judge Ted Carp, Eugene, 2005; Judge Allan H. Coon, Grants Pass, 2005; Judge Daniel L. Harris, Medford, 2005; Judge Nely L. Johnson, Portland, 2005; Judge Ronald D. Thom, Oregon City, 2007; Judge Russell B. West, La Grande, 2007 (judicial members appointed by the Executive Committee of the Circuit Judges Association); Lisa A. Amato, Portland, 2005; Benjamin M. Bloom, Medford, 2007; Bruce J. Brothers, Bend, 2005; Eugene H. Buckle, Portland, 2005; Don Corson, Eugene, 2007; Martin E. Hansen, Bend, 2007; Alexander D. Libmann, Lake Oswego, 2005; Shelley D. Russell, Portland, 2005; David F. Sugerman, Portland, 2007; John Svoboda, Eugene, 2005 (practitioner members appointed by the Board of Governors of the Oregon State Bar).

COMMISSION ON JUDICIAL FITNESS AND DISABILITY

Source: Susan D. Isaacs, Executive Director
Address: P.O. Box 1130, Beaverton 97075-1130
Phone: 503-626-6776
Fax: 503-626-6787
Web: www.ojd.state.or.us/aboutus/cjfd/

Mariann Hyland, chair, Portland, 2008; Lois Barry, La Grande, 2005; William Barton, Newport, 2006; Hon. David Brewer, Salem, 2006; Tom Christ, Portland, 2007; Richard Feeney, Portland, 2006; Hon. Henry Kantor, Portland, 2005; Hon. Roxanne Osborne, Klamath Falls, 2005; Caroline Wilkins, Corvallis, 2008.

Commission members, serving four-year terms, are three judges appointed by the Supreme Court, three lawyers appointed by the Oregon State Bar and three citizens appointed by the governor subject to Senate confirmation.

The purpose of the commission, operating under ORS 1.410–1.480, is to investigate complaints of misconduct, as defined in the Oregon Constitution and the Rules of Judicial Conduct, by Oregon judges. If the commission believes there is substantial evidence of misconduct, a public hearing is held. At the conclusion of the hearing the commission recommends to the Supreme Court whether disciplinary action is warranted. A judge may be censured, suspended or removed from office by the Supreme Court. The commission cannot change the decision of a judge, and does not have jurisdiction over arbitrators, mediators, or municipal court judges.

COUNTY COURTS

At one time, county courts existed in all 36 Oregon counties. The title "county judge" is retained in some counties as the title of the chair of the board of county commissioners. There is no requirement that county judges be members of the bar.

Where a county judge's judicial function still exists, it is limited to juvenile and probate matters and occupies only a portion of the judge's time, which is primarily devoted to nonjudicial administrative responsibilities as a member of the county board.

Only seven counties, all east of the Cascades, now have county judges who retain any judicial authority: Gilliam, Sherman and Wheeler (both juvenile and probate jurisdiction); Grant, Harney, and Malheur (probate only); and Morrow (juvenile only).

JUSTICE COURT

Justice court is held by a justice of the peace within the district for which he or she is elected. The county commissioners have power to establish justice court district boundaries. The justice of the peace is a remnant of territorial days when each precinct of the state was entitled to a justice court. Thirty justice courts currently administer justice in 19 counties.

Justice courts have jurisdiction within their county concurrent with the circuit court in all criminal prosecutions except felony trials. Actions at law in justice courts are conducted using the mode of proceeding and rules of evidence similar to those used in the circuit courts, except where otherwise specifically provided.

Justice courts have jurisdiction over traffic, boating, wildlife, and other violations occurring in their county. Justices of the peace also perform weddings at no charge if performed at their offices during regular business hours.

The justice court has small claims/civil jurisdiction nonexclusive where the money or damages claimed does not exceed $2,500, except in actions involving title to real property, false imprisonment, libel, slander or malicious prosecution.

A justice of the peace must be a citizen of the United States, a resident of Oregon three years, and a resident of the justice court district one year prior to becoming a nonpartisan candidate for election to that office. The names of the Oregon justices of the peace can be found in the Local Government chapter in the section titled "County Government."

MUNICIPAL COURT

Most incorporated cities in Oregon have a municipal court, as authorized by state law.

Municipal courts have jurisdiction over violations of the city's municipal ordinances and over criminal cases occurring within the city limits or on city-owned or controlled property. The usual types of cases adjudicated by municipal courts are criminal misdemeanors, including misdemeanor traffic crimes where the maximum penalty does not exceed a $2,500 fine or one year in jail, or both; other minor traffic infractions; certain minor liquor and drug violations; parking violations; and municipal code violations such as animal and fire violations. Municipal judges can perform weddings within their jurisdiction. Although municipal courts are not courts of record, the procedures in such courts are controlled to a large extent by state statute.

Municipal judges are appointed by the city council in most instances except for a few judges who are elected by the city's voters. The qualifications of a municipal judge are determined by the city council or the city charter. A municipal judge need not be an attorney.

OFFICE OF PUBLIC DEFENSE SERVICES

Source: Peter Ozanne, Executive Director
Address: 1320 Capitol St. NE, Suite 200, Salem 97303
Phone: 503-378-3349
Fax: 503-375-9701

The Office of Public Defense Services is governed by the Public Defense Services Commission, which in turn is appointed by the Chief Justice. The office is managed by the Executive Director whose duties under ORS 151.219 include representation of indigent persons in the Court of Appeals and the Supreme Court, on felony, misdemeanor and parole appeals, and the negotiation and administration of contracts for public defense services across the state on criminal, juvenile, civil and post conviction relief cases.

The PDSC consists of seven members appointed to four-year terms. The current Chair is Barnes Ellis, Portland. The merger of all indigent defense services under the PDSC occurred in July, 2003 with the statutory transfer of the State Indigent Defense Program from the Office of the State Court Administrator. The commission was created in 2001 and is authorized by ORS 151.211–151.225.

Oregon Caves—Oregon State Archives Photograph, OHD-G297

Oregon's Legislative Assembly first met in 1860 for 40 days. Since 1860, legislative sessions have grown longer and legislative business has become more complex, but the tradition of citizen involvement has remained constant. This section describes Oregon's Legislative Assembly and introduces its members.

Oregon's Legislative Assembly

Source: Legislative Administration
Address: 900 Court St. NE, Rm. 140-A, Salem 97301
Phone: 503-986-1848
Web: www.leg.state.or.us

Senate President

Peter Courtney, Senate President
Address: 900 Court St. NE, Rm. S-203, Salem 97301
Phone: 503-986-1600

The Senate President is elected by members of the Senate to select committee chairs and membership, preside over its daily sessions, and coordinate its administrative operations. Subject to the rules of the Senate, the President refers measures to committees, directs Senate personnel, and mediates questions on internal operations.

The Senate President's staff assists in carrying out responsibilities of the office. The office helps coordinate Senate operations and provides a variety of public information services. In cooperation with the Speaker of the House, the President coordinates and supervises the work product of the legislative branch of Oregon state government and represents that branch in contacts with the executive branch. The President's office works closely with both parties to ensure session goals are met.

Senator Peter Courtney is currently serving as Senate President, by election of the members.

Secretary of the Senate

Judy Hall, Secretary of the Senate
Address: 900 Court St. NE, Rm. 233, Salem 97301
Phone: 503-986-1851

The Secretary of the Senate is an elected officer of the State Senate. The Secretary is responsible for and supervises Senate employees engaged in keeping measures, papers, and records of proceedings and actions of the Senate; supervises preparation of the daily agenda, all measures, histories, journals, and related publications; and is in charge of publication of documents related to the Senate. In addition, the Secretary has custody of all measures, official papers, and records of the Senate except when released to authorized persons by signed receipt. The Secretary also serves as parliamentary consultant to the Senate, advises officers of the Senate on parliamentary procedure, and manages the Honorary Page program.

During the interim, the Secretary receives messages from the governor announcing executive appointments requiring Senate confirmation, prepares the agenda for the convening of the Senate, and supervises publication of the official record of proceedings.

Speaker of the House of Representatives

Karen Minnis, Speaker of the House
Address: 900 Court St. NE, Rm. 269, Salem 97301
Phone: 503-986-1200

The Speaker of the House is elected by House members to preside over the deliberations of the House, preserve order and decorum, and decide questions of order. The Speaker appoints chairs and members to each committee and refers measures to appropriate committees in accordance with provisions of the Rules of the House. In the additional capacity as an elected state representative, the Speaker responds to the needs and requests of their House District constituents.

The House Speaker's staff assists in conducting duties of the office. The staff helps coordinate operations of the Speaker's Office, assists the presiding officer in performing official duties, provides research and policy support in issue areas, provides information to the news media, assists legislators in solving constituent problems, and performs other duties. In conjunction with the Senate President's office, the Speaker's office coordinates and supervises operations of the legislative branch of government, joint statutory committees, and joint interim committees and task forces.

Representative Karen Minnis of Wood Village is currently serving as House Speaker, by election of the members.

Chief Clerk of the House of Representatives

Ramona Kenady, Chief Clerk
Address: 900 Court St. NE, Rm. H-271, Salem 97301
Phone: 503-986-1870

The Chief Clerk, elected by members of the House of Representatives, is responsible to supervise the keeping of a correct journal and is the official custodian of all other records of House proceedings. The Chief Clerk notifies the Senate of all acts of the House; certifies and transmits all bills, resolutions, and papers requiring Senate concurrence immediately upon their passage or adoption; and secures proper authentication of bills that have passed both houses and transmits them to the governor.

Under the Oregon system, the Chief Clerk also prepares the agenda and coordinates details for the opening organization of the House, and acts as parliamentarian as directed by House Rules. In addition, the Chief Clerk supervises and authenticates the revision and printing of the House Journal at the end of the legislative session, and prepares all legislative records that are to be permanently filed with the state archivist.

Caucus Offices

Kate Brown, Senate Majority Leader
Address: 900 Court St. NE, Rm. S-223 Salem 97301
Phone: 503-986-1950

Ted Ferrioli, Senate Republican Leader
Address: 900 Court St. NE, Rm. S-323, Salem 97301
Phone: 503-986-1700

Wayne Scott, House Majority Leader
Address: 900 Court St. NE, Rm. H-295, Salem 97301
Phone: 503-986-1400

Jeff Merkley, House Democratic Leader
Address: 900 Court St. NE, Rm. H-395, Salem 97301
Phone: 503-986-1900

Caucus offices provide many services to their members during both session and interim periods. Each office is directed by a leader chosen by the respective political party. The operations of the four offices are not identical, but typical services include conducting research; writing speeches and press releases, and providing other public information services; serving as liaison to state and federal agencies to help solve constituent problems; organizing caucus activities; and circulating information about legislative business among caucus members during both session and interim periods.

Organization

Oregon's Legislative Assembly is composed of two houses—the Senate and House of Representatives. The Senate consists of 30 members elected to four-year terms. Half of the Senate seats are filled every two years. The House consists of 60 representatives elected to two-year terms. Except in cases of persons selected to fill vacancies, legislators are elected in even-numbered years from single-member districts. Election by single-member district means that each Oregonian is represented by one senator and one representative. To qualify for a seat in the Legislature, one must be 21 years of age, a U.S. citizen, and reside in the legislative district for at least one year prior to election. Each house elects a presiding officer to preside over daily sessions; oversee operations; and perform other duties set by rule, custom, and law. These officers are known as President of the Senate and Speaker of the House.

Functions

The primary functions of the Legislature are to enact new laws and revise existing ones, make decisions that keep the state in good economic and environmental condition, and provide a forum for discussion of public issues. The latter function frequently occurs without enactment of any new laws.

The Legislature reviews and revises the governor's proposed budget and passes tax laws to provide needed revenue. The Oregon Constitution provides that the state must not spend money in excess of revenue.

The Legislature also influences executive branch decisions. Laws enacted by the Legislature, along with adoption of the budget, establish state policy that directs all state agency activity. The Senate confirms gubernatorial appointments to certain offices. To ensure that legislative intent is followed, the Legislative Counsel Committee reviews administrative rules of state agencies.

Legislative Process

During a regular session, some 3,000 measures are introduced in the Legislature. Nearly one-third of these become law. Most of the discussion and revision of bills and other measures is done in committees. The process begins when a measure is introduced and referred to a committee. The committee may hear testimony on the measure, frequently from members of the public, and may amend the measure and send it to the floor of its house for debate. The committee can also table the measure and end its consideration. Unlike many state legislatures, Oregon does not amend measures during floor debate.

After a measure has been considered by a committee and passed by the house in which it was introduced, it is sent to the other house where a similar procedure is followed.

If both houses pass a bill in identical form, including any amendments approved by the other house, it is enrolled (printed in final form) for the signatures of the presiding officers and governor. The governor may sign the bill, veto it or let it become law without signature. The governor may also veto line items of appropriation bills but may not veto an act referred for a vote of the people or an act initiated by the people.

The Oregon Constitution and state law require that deliberations of the Legislative Assembly and its committees be open to the public. The law also requires public notice of meetings and maintenance of public meeting records. These practices ensure that the legislative process is open to public scrutiny.

Effective Date of Laws

The regular effective date of a measure is January 1 of the year following passage of the measure. Some measures may contain a provision, such as an emergency clause, that specifies an earlier effective date. The Oregon Constitution prohibits tax measures from having an emergency clause. This means that the people have the right to refer a tax measure by petition before it goes into effect.

Session Schedule

The Legislature convenes in the State Capitol at Salem on the second Monday of each odd-numbered year (January 10, 2005). The constitution does not limit the length of sessions, but recent sessions have lasted approximately six months.

Chronology of Legislative Sessions in Oregon

Ses.	Year	Date	Length in Days	Ses.	Year	Date	Length in Days
1	1860	Sept. 10–Oct. 19	40	40	1939	Jan. 9–Mar. 15	66
2	1862	Sept. 8–Oct. 17	40	41	1941	Jan. 13–Mar. 15	62
3	1864	Sept. 12–Oct. 22	41	42	1943	Jan. 11–Mar. 10	59
4	1866	Sept. 10–Oct. 20	41	43	1945	Jan. 8–Mar. 17	69
5	1868	Sept. 14–Oct. 28	44	44	1947	Jan. 13–Apr. 5	83
6	1870	Sept. 12–Oct. 20	39	45	1949	Jan. 10–Apr. 16	100
7	1872	Sept. 9–Oct. 23	45	46	1951	Jan. 8–May 3	116
8	1874	Sept. 14–Oct. 21	38	47	1953	Jan. 12–Apr. 21	100
9	1876	Sept. 11–Oct. 20	40	48	1955	Jan. 10–May 4	115
10	1878	Sept. 9–Oct. 18	40	49	1957	Jan. 14–May 21	128
11	1880	Sept. 13–Oct. 23	41	50	1959	Jan. 12–May 6	115
12	1882	Sept. 11–Oct. 19	39	51	1961	Jan. 9–May 10	124
13	1885	Jan. 12–Feb. 21	40	52	1963	Jan. 14–June 3	143
14	1887	Jan. 10–Feb. 18	39	53	1965	Jan. 11–May 14	127
15	1889	Jan. 14–Feb. 22	39	54	1967	Jan. 11–June 14	157
16	1891	Jan. 12–Feb. 20	39	55	1969	Jan. 13–May 23	131
17	1893	Jan. 9–Feb. 17	39	56	1971	Jan. 11–June 10	151
18	1895	Jan. 14–Feb. 23	40	57	1973	Jan. 8–July 6	180
19	1897	Jan. 11–Mar. 2	*	58	1975	Jan. 13–June 14	153
20	1899	Jan. 9–Feb. 18	40	59	1977	Jan. 10–July 5	177
21	1901	Jan. 14–Mar. 4	50	60	1979	Jan. 8–July 4	178
22	1903	Jan. 12–Feb. 20	39	61	1981	Jan. 13–Aug. 1	202
23	1905	Jan. 9–Feb. 17	40	62	1983	Jan. 10–July 15	187
24	1907	Jan. 14–Feb. 23	41	63	1985	Jan. 14–June 21	159
25	1909	Jan. 11–Feb. 20	41	64	1987	Jan. 12–June 28	168
26	1911	Jan. 9–Feb. 18	41	65	1989	Jan. 9–July 4	177
27	1913	Jan. 13–Mar. 5	51	66	1991	Jan. 14–June 30	168
28	1915	Jan. 11–Feb. 20	41	67	1993	Jan. 11–August 5	207
29	1917	Jan. 8–Feb. 19	43	68	1995	Jan. 9–June 10	153
30	1919	Jan. 13–Feb. 27	46	69	1997	Jan. 13–July 5	174
31	1921	Jan. 10–Feb. 23	45	70	1999	Jan. 11–July 24	195
32	1923	Jan. 8–Feb. 22	46	71	2001	Jan. 8–July 7	181
33	1925	Jan. 12–Feb. 26	46	72	2003	Jan. 13–August 27	227
34	1927	Jan. 10–Feb. 25	47	73	2005	Jan. 10–	
35	1929	Jan. 14–Mar. 5	50				
36	1931	Jan. 12–Mar. 6	54				
37	1933	Jan. 9–Mar. 9	60				
38	1935	Jan. 14–Mar. 13	59				
39	1937	Jan. 11–Mar. 8	57				

The House of Representatives never formally convened as its members failed to reach agreement on organization.

Special sessions to deal with emergencies may be called by the governor or by a majority of each house. Oregon governors can convene special sessions. For example, Gov. John Kitzhaber called one special session in 1995, one in 1996, and five in 2002. The Legislative Assembly called itself into special session once in 2002.

Contacting a Legislator and Obtaining Legislative Information

During session, the following numbers are available to reach your legislator or for legislative information:

• Outside Salem: 1-800-332-2313
• Within Salem: 503-986-1187

During the interim, individual legislators may be reached by calling the telephone numbers listed on pages 137–139 and 145–149. Legislative information may be obtained by calling the Legislative Liaison at 503-986-1000.

Interim between Sessions

After adjournment of regular sessions, the work of the Legislature continues. Legislators study issues likely to be important during future sessions, become acquainted with new issues, prepare drafts of legislation, and exercise legislative oversight.

Convening of the Senate to Act on Executive Appointments

The Senate convenes at the call of the President to act on executive appointments made during legislative interim periods. This procedure was adopted to assist compliance with Article III, Section 4, of the Oregon Constitution. A gubernatorial appointment must be confirmed before the appointee can take office. A statutory committee on executive appointments was created by the Legislature in 1929 to act on gubernatorial appointments to the Board of Higher Education. Subsequent Legislatures added to the governor's authority to appoint, but retained the Senate's authority to confirm or deny approval on most appointments. Gubernatorial appointments made during a regular session of the Legislature or at a special session are acted on by the Senate prior to adjourning *sine die*.

History

The present legislative system began when Oregon's Provisional Legislature met formally for the first time in Oregon City, December 2–19, 1845. However, an earlier pre-provisional committee met in August of the same year after the formal ratification of Oregon's Organic Articles and Laws of 1843 and the inauguration of George Abernethy as governor. The first Provisional Legislature, a unicameral body with autonomous powers, conducted its sessions in a rather casual manner and frequently suspended its rules to take care of unexpected situations. It met annually or more frequently until February 1849, five months before the first Territorial Legislature met July 16–24, 1849, also in Oregon City.

The Territorial Legislature was bicameral. It had both an upper "council" of nine members and a lower house of 18 members elected from the eight existing county divisions that had regular annual meetings. Unlike the Provisional Legislature, its actions were subject to review in Washington, D.C. At the time of statehood and adoption of the constitution in 1859, the present bicameral system was adopted. The Legislature then met in the fall of even-numbered years until 1885, when the sessions were moved to the early winter months of odd-numbered years to accommodate members who farmed.

Statistical Summary
Seventy-Second Legislative Assembly

Source of Information: Legislative Counsel

Regular Session

Session Length	227 Calendar Days
Convened	Jan. 13, 2003
Adjourned	August 27, 2003
Bills Introduced	2,769
Other Measures	153
Total	2,922

Senate Total Membership	30
Democrats	15
Republicans	15
President: Peter Courtney (D), Salem	

House Total Membership	60
Democrats	25
Republicans	35
Speaker: Karen Minnis (R), Wood Village	

Bills	House	Senate	Total
Introduced	1,756	1,013	2,769
Passed Both Houses	477	347	824
Vetoed	5	2	7
Became Law	472	345	817
Unsigned by Governor	5	2	7

Resolutions and Memorials			
Introduced	96	57	153
Adopted	26	19	45

Senate-Representative District Numbers

Sen.	Rep. Dist.	Sen.	Rep. Dist.	Sen.	Rep. Dist.	Sen.	Rep. Dist.
1	1 and 2	9	17 and 18	17	33 and 34	25	49 and 50
2	3 and 4	10	19 and 20	18	35 and 36	26	51 and 52
3	5 and 6	11	21 and 22	19	37 and 38	27	53 and 54
4	7 and 8	12	23 and 24	20	39 and 40	28	55 and 56
5	9 and 10	13	25 and 26	21	41 and 42	29	57 and 58
6	11 and 12	14	27 and 28	22	43 and 44	30	59 and 60
7	13 and 14	15	29 and 30	23	45 and 46		
8	15 and 16	16	31 and 32	24	47 and 48		

Legislative

Senate Districts

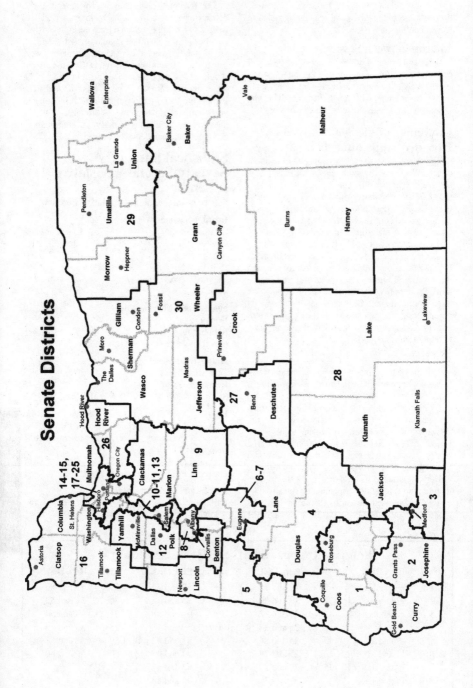

Representative Districts

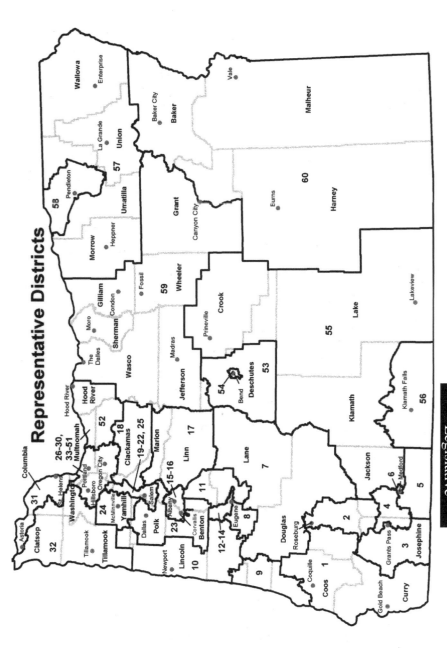

President of the Senate

Peter Courtney (D, District 11) was born in Philadelphia, Pennsylvania on June 18, 1943. He graduated with Bachelor and Master degrees from the University of Rhode Island and received a law degree from Boston University. Courtney was first elected to the Salem City Council in 1974, where he served until 1981. He began serving in the House of Representatives in 1981 and was first elected to the Senate in 1998. Courtney has worked at Western Oregon University since 1985. He currently is employed as a professor. He has served on the Salem Mass Transit Board and the United Way Board, coached for the Boys and Girls club, and currently sits on the Board of Directors for the YMCA.

Courtney has worked as a political commentator for the 10 o'clock news at KPTV, Channel 12, Portland and KSLM Radio, Salem. He married his wife, Margie, in 1976. They have three sons, Peter, Sean and Adam.

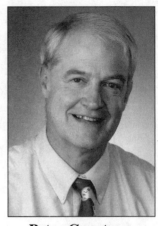

Peter Courtney

Atkinson, Jason
R—Dist. 2

Bates, Alan
D—Dist. 3

Beyer, Roger
R—Dist. 9

Brown, Kate
D—Dist. 21

Burdick, Ginny
D—Dist. 18

Carter, Margaret
D—Dist. 22

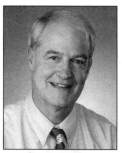

Courtney, Peter
D—Dist. 11

Deckert, Ryan
D—Dist. 14

Devlin, Richard
D—Dist. 19

Dukes, Joan, D—Dist. 16
Replaced by Betsy Johnson 1/05

Ferrioli, Ted
R—Dist. 30

George, Gary
R—Dist. 12

Gordly, Avel
D—Dist. 23

Kruse, Jeff
R—Dist. 1

Metsger, Rick
D—Dist. 26

Monnes Anderson, Laurie
D—Dist. 25

Morrisette, Bill
D—Dist. 6

Morse, Frank
R—Dist. 8

Legislative

Nelson, David
R—Dist. 29

Prozanski, Floyd
D—Dist. 4

Ringo, Charlie
D—Dist. 17

Schrader, Kurt
D—Dist. 20

Shields, Frank
D—Dist. 24

Starr, Bruce
R—Dist. 15

Starr, Charles
R—Dist. 13

Verger, Joanne
D—Dist. 5

Walker, Vicki
D—Dist. 7

Westlund, Ben
R—Dist. 27

Whitsett, Doug
R—Dist. 28

Winters, Jackie
R—Dist. 10

State Senators by District

District/Counties	Name/Address/Phone	Occupation/Terms*	Birthplace/Date
1. Curry and portions of Douglas, Jackson and Josephine	Jeff Kruse (R) 174 Burkhart Rapids Lane Roseburg 97470 541-673-7201	Co-owner Kruse Farms 2005 (1997-2004)	Roseburg, OR 9/1951
2. Portions of Jackson and Josephine	Jason Atkinson (R) PO Box 1704 Ashland 97528 541-955-0911	Business Consultant 2001/2005 (1997/1999)	Sacramento, CA 11/1970
3. Portion of Jackson	Alan Bates (D) 886 Oak Street Ashland 97520 541-482-1427	Family Physician 2005 (2001/2003)	Seattle, WA 3/1945
4. Portions of Douglas and Lane	Floyd Prozanski (D) PO Box 11511 Eugene 97440 541-342-2447	Attorney 2005 (1995-2003)	Lubbock, TX 10/1954
5. Lincoln and portions of Coos, Douglas, Lane, Polk, Tillamook and Yamhill	Joanne Verger (D) 2285 N 13th Ct. Coos Bay 97420 541-267-7611	Business Owner 2005 (2001/2003)	Amite, LA 7/1930
6. Portion of Lane and Linn	Bill Morrisette (D) 348 'G' Street Springfield 97477 541-746-1378	Legislator; Retired High School Teacher 2003 (1999/2001)	Anaconda, MT 10/1931
7. Portion of Lane	Vicki Walker (D) PO Box 10314 Eugene 97440 541-302-9533	Court Reporter/Small Business Owner 2003 (1999/2001)	Monroe, WA 5/1956
8. Portions of Benton and Linn	Frank Morse (R) 221 NW 2nd Street Corvallis 97330 541-738-8763	Business Owner 2003	Lebanon, OR 9/1943
9. Portions of Clackamas, Linn and Marion	Roger Beyer (R) 39486 S Cooper Rd. Molalla 97038 503-829-6910	Managing Partner of Beyer Tree Farm 2001/2005 (1997/1999)	Oregon City, OR 9/1960
10. Portions of Marion and Polk	Jackie Winters (R) PO Box 126 Salem 97308 503-986-1710	Restaurant Owner 2003 (1999/2001)	Topeka, KS 4/1937
11. Portion of Marion	Peter Courtney (D) 900 Court St NE, S-203 Salem 97301 503-986-1600	Asst. to Pres., Western Oregon University 1999/2003(1981/1983/1989/1991/1993/1995/1997)	Philadelphia, PA 6/1943
12. Portions of Benton, Linn, Marion, Polk, and Yamhill	Gary George (R) 15195 NE Ribbon Ridge Rd. Newberg 97132 503-538-4122	Farmer/Small Business Owner 1997/2001/2005	Dos Palos, CA 10/1943

Senate terms are four years unless appointed; (representative terms are two years).

Legislative

District/Counties	Name/Address/Phone	Occupation/Terms*	Birthplace/Date
13. Portions of Clackamas, Marion, Washington and Yamhill	Charles Starr (R) 8330 SW River Rd. Hillsboro 97123 503-642-2024	General Contractor 1999/2003 (1993/1995/ 1997)	Eastland, TX 10/1932
14. Portions of Multnomah and Washington	Ryan Deckert (D) PO Box 2247 Beaverton 97075 503-977-1609	Development Director 2001/2003/2005 (1997/1999)	Corpus Christi, TX 3/1971
15. Portion of Washington	Bruce Starr (R) 22115 NW Imbrie Dr. #290 Hillsboro 97124 503-640-3780	Small Business Owner 2003 (1999/2001)	Portland, OR 1/1969
16. Clatsop, Columbia and portions of Multnomah, Tillamook and Washington	Joan Dukes (D) S-318 State Capitol Salem 97301 503-986-1716	Legislator 1987/1991/1995/1999/ 2003; Replaced by Betsy Johnson 1-20-05	Tacoma, WA 10/1947
17. Portions of Multnomah and Washington	Charlie Ringo (D) 4085 SW 109th Ave. Beaverton 97005 503-643-7500	Attorney 2003 (2001)	Corvallis, OR 6/1958
18. Portions of Multnomah and Washington	Ginny Burdick (D) 4641 SW Dosch Rd. Portland 97239 503-244-1444	Policy and Communica- tion Adviser/Legislator 1997/2001/2003/2005	Portland, OR 12/1947
19. Portions of Clackamas, Multnomah and Washington	Richard Devlin (D) 10290 SW Anderson Ct. Tualatin 97062 503-691-2026	Legal Investigator/ Legislator 2003 (1997/1999/2001)	Eugene, OR 9/1952
20. Portion of Clackamas	Kurt Schrader (D) 2525 N Baker Dr. Canby 97013 503-263-2585	Veterinarian/Farmer/ Businessman 2003 (1997/1999/2001)	Bridgeport, CT 10/1951
21. Portions of Clackamas and Multnomah	Kate Brown (D) 900 Court St NE, S-323 Salem 97301 503-986-1700	State Senator/Attorney 1997/2001/2003/2005 (Appt.1991/1993/1995)	Spain 6/1960
22. Portion of Multnomah	Margaret Carter (D) PO Box 3277 Portland 97208 503-282-6846	Counselor 2001/2003/2005 (1985/1987/1989/1991/ 1993/1995/1997)	Shreveport, LA 12/1935
23. Portion of Multnomah	Avel Gordly (D) 10809 NE Fremont Portland 97220 503-288-0837	Legislator 1997/2001/2005 (Appt. 1991/ 1993/1995)	Portland, OR 2/1947
24. Portions of Clackamas and Multnomah	Frank Shields (D) 7802 SE 111th Ave. Portland 97266 503-762-4008	Legislator 1999/2003 (1993/ 1995/1997)	New Castle, PA 3/1945
25. Portion of Multnomah	Laurie Monnes Anderson (D) PO Box 1531 Gresham 97030 503-618-3071	Nurse 2005 (2001/2003)	San Diego, CA 12/1945

District/Counties	Name/Address/Phone	Occupation/Terms*	Birthplace/Date
26. Hood River and portions of Clackamas and Multnomah	Rick Metsger (D) PO Box 287 Welches 97067 503-668-4378	Journalist/Educator 1999/2003	Sandy, OR 8/1951
27. Portion of Deschutes	Ben Westlund (R) 20590 Arrowhead Dr. Bend 97701 503-986-1727	Small Businessman 2005 (1997/1999/2001/ 2003)	Long Beach, CA 9/1949
28. Crook, Klamath, Lake and portions of Deschutes and Jackson	Doug Whitsett (R) 23131 North Poe Valley Rd. Klamath Falls 97603 541-882-1315	Retired Veterinarian 2005	Carmel, CA 3/1943
29. Morrow, Umatilla, Union, and Wallowa	David Nelson (R) 1407 NW Horn Ave. Pendleton 97801 541-278-2332	Farmer 1997/2001/2005	Pendleton, OR 8/1941
30. Baker, Gilliam, Grant, Harney, Jefferson, Malheur, Sherman, Wasco, Wheeler, and portions of Clackamas, Deschutes and Marion	Ted Ferrioli (R) 750 W Main John Day 97845 541-575-2321	Natural Resource Association Director 1997/2001/2005	Spokane, WA 2/1951

MEMBERS OF THE OREGON HOUSE OF REPRESENTATIVES

Speaker of the House

Born and raised in Portland, Representative Karen Minnis is serving her third term in the Oregon House representing the cities of Fairview, Gresham, Troutdale and Wood Village in East Multnomah County. Representative Minnis has extensive legislative experience. Before being elected to her first term in 1998, she served for six terms as Legislative Assistant to State Representative John Minnis, her husband.

Representative Minnis has previously served as House Majority Leader and Chair of the Ways and Means subcommittee on Education. She has also served on the Emergency Board in both the 1999–2000 and 2001–02 interims, the Ways and Means subcommittee on Public Safety, the Commission on Black Affairs and the Spinal Cord Research Board.

Karen is a graduate of James Monroe High School, and has attended Clark Community College. Married since 1972, Representative Minnis and her husband have two sons and a daughter.

Karen Minnis

Legislative

Ackerman, Robert
D—Dist. 13

Anderson, Gordon
R—Dist. 3

Avakian, Brad
D—Dist. 34

Barker, Jeff
D—Dist. 28

Barnhart, Phil
D—Dist. 11

Berger, Vicki
R—Dist. 20

Beyer, Elizabeth Terry
D—Dist. 12

Boone, Deborah
D—Dist. 32

Boquist, Brian
R—Dist. 23

Brown, Alan
R—Dist. 10

Bruun, Scott
R—Dist. 37

Buckley, Peter
D—Dist. 5

2005–2006 Oregon Blue Book

Burley, Chuck
R—Dist. 54

Butler, R. Tom
R—Dist. 60

Dallum, John
R—Dist. 59

Dalto, Billy
R—Dist. 21

Dingfelder, Jackie
D—Dist. 45

Doyle, Dan, R—Dist. 19
Resigned 1/31/05

Esquivel, Sal
R—Dist. 6

Farr, Debi
R—Dist. 14

Flores, Linda
R—Dist. 51

Galizio, Larry
D—Dist. 35

Garrard, Bill
R—Dist. 56

Gilman, George
R—Dist. 55

Legislative

Greenlick, Mitch
D—Dist. 33

Hanna, Bruce
R—Dist. 7

Hansen, Gary D.
D—Dist. 44

Hass, Mark
D—Dist. 27

Holvey, Paul
D—Dist. 8

Hunt, Dave
D—Dist. 40

Jenson, Bob
R—Dist. 58

Johnson, Betsy, D—Dist. 31
Replaced by Brad Witt 1/05

Kitts, Derrick
R—Dist. 30

Komp, Betty
D—Dist. 22

Krieger, Wayne
R—Dist. 1

Kropf, Jeff
R—Dist. 17

Krummel, Jerry
R—Dist. 26

Lim, John
R—Dist. 50

Macpherson, Greg
D—Dist. 38

March, Steve
D—Dist. 46

Merkley, Jeff
D—Dist. 47

Minnis, Karen
R—Dist. 49

Morgan, Susan
R—Dist. 2

Nelson, Donna
R—Dist. 24

Nolan, Mary
D—Dist. 36

Olson, Andy
R—Dist. 15

Richardson, Dennis
R—Dist. 4

Riley, Chuck
D—Dist. 29

Roblan, Arnie
D—Dist. 9

Rosenbaum, Diane
D—Dist. 42

Schaufler, Mike
D—Dist. 48

Scott, Wayne
R—Dist. 39

Shields, Chip
D—Dist. 43

Smith, Greg
R—Dist. 57

Smith, Patti
R—Dist. 52

Sumner, Mac
R—Dist. 18

Thatcher, Kim
R—Dist. 25

Tomei, Carolyn
D—Dist. 41

Whisnant, Gene
R—Dist. 53

Wirth, Kelley
D—Dist. 16

State Representatives by District

District/Counties	Name/Address/Phone	Occupation/Terms*	Birthplace/Date
1. Curry and portions of Coos and Douglas	Wayne Krieger (R) 95702 Skyview Ranch Rd. Gold Beach 97444 541-247-7990	Legislator 2001/2003/2005	Portland, OR 9/1940
2. Portions of Douglas, Jackson and Josephine	Susan Morgan (R) PO Box 2223 Myrtle Creek 97457 541-784-3503	Small Business Owner 1999/2001/2003/2005	Nanaimo, B.C. Canada 9/1949
3. Portion of Josephine	Gordon Anderson (R) PO Box 1389 Grants Pass 97526 541-476-3059	Small Business Owner 2003/2005	Chicago, IL 12/1934
4. Portions of Jackson and Josephine	Dennis Richardson (R) 55 S 5th St. Central Point 97502 541-665-9203	Business Man/Attorney 2003/2005	Los Angeles, CA 7/1949
5. Portion of Jackson	Peter Buckley (D) 840 Roca St. Ashland 97520 541-621-7195	Manager of Non-profit 2005	San Francisco, CA 5/1957
6. Portion of Jackson	Sal Esquivel (R) 711 Medford Center #178 Medford 97504 541-734-4369	Real Estate Broker 2005	Pittsburg, CA 5/1948
7. Portion of Douglas and Lane	Bruce Hanna (R) 612 NW Cecil Ave. Roseburg 97470 541-440-9004	Business Owner 2005	Roseburg, OR 4/1960
8. Portion of Lane	Paul Holvey (D) PO Box 51048 Eugene 97405 541-344-5636	Carpenters' Union Rep. 2005	Eugene, OR 1/1954
9. Portions of Coos, Douglas and Lane	Arnie Roblan (D) PO Box 1410 Coos Bay 97420 541-267-6609	Teacher 2005	Port Angeles, WA 4/1948
10. Lincoln and portions of Lane, Polk, Tillamook and Yamhill	Alan Brown (R) 1155 SW Coast Hwy. Newport 97365 541-265-8060	Small Business Owner 2001/2003/2005	Medford, OR 11/1936
11. Portions of Lane and Linn	Phil Barnhart (D) PO Box 71188 Eugene 97401 541-484-5119	State Representative 2001/2003/2005	New Rochelle, NY 8/1946
12. Portion of Lane	Terry Beyer (D) PO Box 131 Springfield 97477 541-726-2533	Legislator 2003/2005	Eugene, OR 1/1951

Representative terms are two years unless appointed.

District/Counties	Name/Address/Phone	Occupation/Terms*	Birthplace/Date
13. Portion of Lane	Robert Ackerman (D) PO Box 41749 Eugene 97404 541-242-6486	Attorney/Legislator 2001/2003/2005	San Francisco, CA 3/1937
14. Portion of Lane	Debi Farr (R) 4257 Barger Dr. #272 Eugene 97402 541-461-4091	Educational Assistant 2005	Portland, OR 3/1955
15. Portions of Benton and Linn	Andy Olson (R) 34499 Mountain View Pl. NE Albany 97321 541-967-0393	Law Enforcement 2005	Norfolk, NE 11/1952
16. Portion of Benton	Kelley Wirth (D) PO Box 607 Corvallis 97333 541-738-8707	Systems Analyst/ Legislator 2001/2003/2005	Panorama City, CA 8/1965
17. Portions of Linn and Marion	Jeff Kropf (R) 900 Court St. NE, H-386 Salem 97301 503-767-8910	Grass Seed Farmer/ Small Business Owner 1999/2001/2003/2005	Albany, OR 2/1959
18. Portions of Clackamas and Marion	Mac Sumner (R) 1442 Meadowlawn Pl. Molalla 97038 503-829-8861	Warehouseman/ Real Estate 2005	Sedalia, MO 3/1940
19. Portion of Marion	Dan Doyle (R) 3995 Hagers Grove Rd. SE. Salem 97302 503-391-1231	Attorney/Legislator 2001/2003/2005 Resigned 1-31-05	Fullerton, CA 9/1957
20. Portion of Marion and Polk	Vicki Berger (R) 900 Court St. NE, H-488 Salem 97301 503-581-9969	Retired Business Owner 2003/2005	Salem, OR 3/1949
21. Portion of Marion	Billy Dalto (R) PO Box 943 Salem 97308 503-540-7405	Small Business Owner 2003/2005	New York City, NY 10/1976
22. Portion of Marion	Betty Komp (D) 885 Garfield St. Woodburn 97071 503-981-6160	Teacher/Principal 2005	Silverton, OR 6/1949
23. Portions of Benton, Linn, Marion, Polk and Yamhill	Brian Boquist (R) 17080 Butler Hill Rd. Dallas 97338 503-623-4426	Businessman/Rancher 2005	Tillamook, OR 10/1958
24. Portions of Polk and Yamhill	Donna G. Nelson (R) 2150 St. Andrews Dr. NW McMinnville 97128 503-474-7446	Small Business Owner/ Legislator 2001/2003/2005	Paducha, TX 6/1943
25. Portion of Marion and Yamhill	Kim Thatcher (R) PO Box 9111 Salem 97303 503-932-2330	Small Business Owner 2005	Pocatello, ID 10/1964

District/Counties	Name/Address/Phone	Occupation/Terms*	Birthplace/Date
26. Portions of Clackamas and Washington	Jerry Krummel (R) 7544 SW Roanoke Dr. Wilsonville 97070 503-682-7872	Senior Account Executive 1999/2001/2003/2005	Walla Walla, WA 1/1953
27. Portions of Multnomah and Washington	Mark Hass (D) 6505 SW 90th Ave. Portland 97223 503-986-1427	Journalist/Legislator 2001/2003/2005	Newport, RI 12/1956
28. Portion of Washington	Jeff Barker (D) PO Box 6751 Aloha 97007 503-986-1428	Retired Police Lieutenant 2003/2005	Portland, OR 4/1943
29. Portion of Washington	Chuck Riley (R) 250 NE Hillwood Dr. Hillsboro 97124 503-640-8689	Retired Computer Consultant 2005	Jefferson County, IL 5/1939
30. Portion of Washington	Derrick Kitts (R) PO Box 1946 Hillsboro 97123 503-312-8146	Small Business Owner 2003/2005	Tacoma, WA 7/1973
31. Portions of Clatsop, Columbia and Mult-nomah	Elizabeth (Betsy) Johnson (D) PO Box R Scappoose 97056 503-543-4046	Aviation Executive/ Legislator 2001/2003/ 2005; Replaced by Brad Witt 1-27-05	Bend, OR 1/1951
32. Portions of Clatsop, Columbia, Tillamook and Washington	Deborah Boone (D) PO Box 637 Cannon Beach 97110 503-717-4655	Business Owner 2005	Portland, OR 6/1951
33. Portions of Multnomah and Washington	Mitch Greenlick (D) 712 NW Spring Ave. Portland 97229 503-297-2416	Professor Emeritus, OHSU 2003/2005	Detroit, MI 3/1935
34. Portion of Washington	Brad Avakian (D) 17915 NW Lonerock Dr. Portland 97229 503-645-9830	Attorney/Small Business Owner 2003/2005	Fresno, CA 2/1961
35. Portions of Multnomah and Washington	Larry Galizio (D) PO Box 231161 Tigard 97281 503-516-1101	Teacher 2005	Los Angeles, CA 1/1964
36. Portion of Multnomah	Mary Nolan (D) PO Box 1686 Portland 97207 503-221-4999	Business Owner 2001/2003/2005	Chicago, IL 11/1954
37. Portions of Clackamas and Washington	Scott Bruun (R) 2020 8th Ave., PMB 160 West Linn 97068 503-697-3525	Banker 2005	Portland, OR 5/1966
38. Portions of Clackamas, Multnomah and Wash-ington	Greg Macpherson (D) 322 Second St. Lake Oswego 97034 503-635-2648	Attorney 2003/2005	Corvallis, OR 5/1950

District/Counties	Name/Address/Phone	Occupation/Terms*	Birthplace/Date
39. Portion of Clackamas	Wayne Scott (R) PO Box 664 Canby 97013 503-266-3837	Business Owner 2003/2005	Wallis, ID 1/1947
40. Portion of Clackamas	Dave Hunt (D) PO Box 67190 Oak Grove 97268 503-650-5900	Executive Director 2003/2005	Port Angeles, WA 11/1967
41. Portions of Clackamas and Multnomah	Carolyn Tomei (D) 11907 SE 19th Ave. Milwaukie 97222 503-653-5180	Legislator; Psychiatric Social Worker 2001/2003/2005	Charleston, WV 1/1936
42. Portion of Multnomah	Diane Rosenbaum (D) 1125 SE Madison St. #100B Portland 97214 503-231-9970	Legislator 1999/2001/2003/2005	Berkeley, CA 11/1949
43. Portion of Multnomah	Chip Shields (D) 6606 NE Mallory Ave. Portland 97211 503-281-3378	Consultant 2005	St. Louis, MO 9/1967
44. Portion of Multnomah	Gary Hansen (D) 628 N Tomahawk Isl. Dr. Portland 97217 503-289-3995	Business Owner/ Legislator 1999/2001/2003/2005	Portland, OR 4/1944
45 Portion of Multnomah	Jackie Dingfelder (D) 2104 NE 45th Ave. Portland 97213 503-493-2804	Environmental Consultant/Legislator 2001/2003/2005	New York City, NY 12/1960
46. Portion of Multnomah	Steve March (D) 842 NE 44th Ave. Portland 97213 503-233-4157	Legislator 2001/2003/2005	Woodland, CA 9/1946
47. Portion of Multnomah	Jeff Merkley (D) PO Box 33167 Portland 97292 503-261-7826	Executive Director World Affairs Council of Oregon/Legislator 1999/2001/2003/2005	Eugene, OR 10/1956
48. Portions of Clackamas and Multnomah	Mike Schaufler (D) 12910 SE Ridgecrest Rd. Happy Valley 97236 503-760-4446	Contractor 2003/2005	Buffalo, MN 11/1959
49. Portion of Multnomah	Karen Minnis (R) 900 Court St. NE, Rm. 269 Salem 97301 503-666-7186	Legislator 1999/2001/2003/2005	Portland, OR 7/1954
50. Portion of Multnomah	John Lim (R) PO Box 1616 Gresham 97030 503-667-3647	Businessman 2005(1993/1995/1997/ 1999)	YeoJu, S. Korea 12/1935
51. Portions of Clackamas and Multnomah	Linda Flores (R) PO Box 55 Clackamas 97015 503-658-6735	Small Business Owner 2003/2005	Portland, OR 8/1947

District/Counties	Name/Address/Phone	Occupation/Terms*	Birthplace/Date
52. Hood River and portions of Clackamas and Multnomah	Patti Smith (R) PO Box 209 Corbett 97019 503-695-6385	Farmer/Small Business Owner 2005	Portland, OR 10/1946
53. Portion of Deschutes	Gene Whisnant (R) PO Box 3565 Sunriver 97707 541-593-7437	USAF Colonel, retired 2005	Caroleen, NC 12/1943
54. Portion of Deschutes	Chuck Burley (R) PO Box 9424 Bend 97701 541-383-8598	Forester/Small Business Owner 2005	Cleveland, OH 1/1956
55. Crook, Lake and portions of Deschutes, Jackson, and Klamath	George Gilman (R) 3695 Dodson Dr. Medford 97504 541-858-1726	Foster Grandparent/ Program Director 2003/2005	Portland, OR 5/1939
56. Portion of Klamath	Bill Garrard (R) 906 N 8th St. Klamath Falls 97601 541-882-0490	Legislator 2001/2003/2005	Rochester, NY 5/1940
57. Morrow, Wallowa and portions of Umatilla and Union	Greg Smith (R) PO Box 219 Heppner 97836 541-676-8719	Small Business Owner/ Legislator 2001/2003/2005	Portland, OR 11/1968
58. Portions of Umatilla and Union	Bob Jenson (R) 2126 NW Despain Ave. Pendleton 97801 541-276-2707	Legislator 1997/1999/2001/2003/ 2005	Omaha, NE 5/1931
59. Gilliam, Jefferson, Sherman, Wasco, Wheeler and portions of Clackamas, Deschutes, Grant and Marion	John Dallum (R) 1900 W 13th St. The Dalles 97058 541-506-9284	Retired School Superintendent 2005	Aberdeen, SD 3/1944
60. Baker, Harney, Malheur and portion of Grant	R. Tom Butler (R) PO Box "E" Ontario 97914-0106 541-889-3014	Certified Public Accountant 1999/2001/2003/2005	Ontario, OR 4/1946

STATUTORY COMMITTEES AND INTERIM OFFICES

Source: Legislative Administration
Address: 900 Court St. NE, Rm. 140-A, Salem 97301
Phone: 503-986-1848
Web: www.leg.state.or.us/comm/

Legislative Administration Committee

Dave Henderson, Legislative Administrator

The Legislative Administration Committee (LAC) provides services to the Legislative Assembly, its support staff, and the public. The committee, authorized by ORS 173.710, is composed of the President of the Senate, the Speaker of the House, three senators appointed by the President, and four representatives appointed by the Speaker. The committee appoints an administrator to serve as its executive officer. The administrator's office coordinates and oversees the operation of the following administrative units:

Committee Services

Address: 900 Court St. NE, Rm. 453, Salem 97301
Phone: 503-986-1813
Web: www.leg.state.or.us/comm/

Special Legislative Sessions in Oregon[1]

Year	Date	Length in Days
1860	Oct. 1–Oct. 2	2
1865	Dec. 5–Dec. 18	14
1885	Nov. 11–Nov. 24	14
1898	Sept. 28–Oct. 15	20
1903	Dec. 21–Dec. 23	3
1909	Mar. 15–Mar. 16	2
1920	Jan. 12–Jan. 17	6
1921	Dec. 19–Dec. 24	6
1933	Jan. 3–Jan. 7	5
1933	Nov. 20–Dec. 9	20
1935	Oct. 21–Nov. 9	20
1957	Oct. 28–Nov. 15	19
1963	Nov. 11–Dec. 2	13[2]
1965	May 21–May 25	5
1967	Oct. 30–Nov. 21	23
1971	Nov. 16–Nov. 22	7
1974	Jan. 24–Feb. 24	14[3]
1975	Sept. 16–Sept. 16	1
1978	Sept. 5–Sept. 9	5
1980	Aug. 4–Aug. 8	5
1981	Oct. 24–Oct. 24	1
1982	Jan. 18–Mar. 1	37
1982	June 14–June 14	1
1982	Sept. 3–Sept. 3	1
1983	Sept. 14–Oct. 4	21
1984	July 30–July 30	1
1990	May 7–May 7	1
1992	July 1–July 3	3
1995	July 28–Aug. 4	8
1996	Feb. 1–Feb. 1	1
2002	Feb. 8–Feb. 11	4
2002	Feb. 25–Mar. 2	6
2002	June 12–June 30	19
2002	Aug. 16–Aug. 20	5
2002	Sept. 1–Sept. 18	18

[1]Historical records are not consistent on actual dates.
[2]Nine-day recess, Nov. 22 to Dec. 2, due to death of President Kennedy.
[3]Does not include recess from Jan. 24 to Feb. 11.

Committee Services supports the Legislative Assembly by providing professional services to legislative committees, legislators, legislative offices and staff, government agencies, and the public. Staff responsibilities include administration of standing, session, and interim committees; research projects; public notification; measure analyses; and session staff coordination and training. Committee Services also includes Committee Records and the Legislative Library.

Committee Records
Address: 900 Court St. NE, Rm. 453, Salem 97301
Phone: 503-986-1182
Committee Records maintains minutes, exhibits, and audio tapes of all legislative committee proceedings from the current session or interim.

Legislative Library
Address: 900 Court St. NE, Rm. 347, Salem 97301
Phone: 503-986-1668
The Legislative Library provides information services to members, staff, government agencies, other legislatures, and to the public. The library contains more than 4,000 catalogued documents on legislative issues; 50 periodicals and newspaper subscriptions; measure analyses from recent sessions and interims, as well as legislative calendars, journals, and laws from past sessions. These items are available primarily for use by legislators and legislative staff.

Employee Services
Address: 900 Court St. NE, Rm. 140-B, Salem 97301
Phone: 503-986-1373
Web: www.leg.state.or.us/jobs
Employee Services provides human resource administration to all legislative employees and legislative job seekers.

Facility Services
Address: 900 Court St. NE, Rm. 60-H, Salem 97301
Phone: 503-986-1360
Facility Services is responsible for operational support within the State Capitol, oversight of security and food service, Capitol room reservations, risk management, and historic preservation. Services are provided through two sections: Legislative Publications and Distribution Services, and Operations and Maintenance.

Legislative Publications
Address: 900 Court St. NE, Rm. 49, Salem 97301
Phone: 503-986-1180
In addition to serving as the Legislature's central mail and publication distribution office, Legislative Publications is the site at which the public may receive copies of legislative measures and publications. This unit also issues office supplies to legislative staff.

Operations and Maintenance

Address: 900 Court St. NE, Rm. 60H, Salem 97301

Phone: 503-986-1360

The Operations and Maintenance unit of Facility Services provides custodial and recycling services, building maintenance, heating/cooling plant operations, office furniture, and equipment.

Financial Services

Address: 900 Court St. NE, Rm. 140-C, Salem 97301

Phone: 503-986-1695

Financial Services provides budgeting, accounting, and financial reporting services for the Legislative Assembly, Legislative Administration, and the Legislative Commission on Indian Services. Accounting services are provided for the Legislative Fiscal and Revenue offices.

Information Systems/Computer and Legislative Media

Address: 900 Court St. NE, Rm. S-424, Salem 97301

Phone: 503-986-1914

Information Systems/Computer and Legislative Media supports the Legislative Assembly by collecting, processing, and distributing information. This unit improves internal and external communications and enhances the decision-making process by promoting awareness of what, how, when, and where information is available; simplifying access to all legislative information; providing audio, video, internet, computer, and print technologies to the legislative community; and providing job-related training.

Visitor Services

Address: 900 Court St. NE, Rotunda Area, Salem 97301

Phone: 503-986-1388

Web: www.leg.state.or.us/capinfo

Visitor Services provides guided tours and video presentations on the legislative process and Capitol history. The unit also schedules and coordinates various Capitol special events and disseminates a wide range of information to legislators, staff, and the public. It operates the Capitol Gift Shop, which markets Oregon products, crafts, and art.

Committee on Executive Appointments

Address: c/o Secretary of the Senate; 900 Court St. NE, Rm. 233, Salem 97301

Phone: 503-986-1851

Article III, Section 4, of the Oregon Constitution provides that the Legislative Assembly, in the manner provided by law, may require that all appointments and reappointments to state public office made by the governor shall be subject to confirmation by the Senate.

During the legislative session, the Senate President refers executive appointments to an appropriate standing or special committee. The committee has the duty and responsibility of reviewing the background and qualifications of appointees to ensure statutory requirements are met. Each appointee appears before the committee for a personal interview unless such appearance is waived in accordance with Senate Rules. The committee submits its specific recommendations to the full Senate for its vote on confirmation.

During the interim period between legislative sessions, pursuant to ORS 171.565, the Senate reviews the governor's appointments and reappointments. An interim standing committee is appointed by the Senate President, in accordance with Senate Rules, and has at least five, but no more than 11 members. The committee generally meets the day prior to convening of the Senate to consider the governor's appointments and then submits its recommendations to the full Senate for a vote. The Senate convenes seven or eight times during an interim period for the purpose of considering the governor's appointments.

Emergency Board

Ken Rocco, Legislative Fiscal Officer

Address: 900 Court St. NE, Rm. H-178, Salem 97301

Phone: 503-986-1828

The Emergency Board, created under ORS 291.324, has 19 members consisting of the President of the Senate, the Speaker of the House of Representatives, the co-chairs of the Joint Committee on Ways and Means, seven other Senate members, and eight other House members. Between sessions, the Emergency Board may allocate to any state agency, out of emergency funds appropriated to the board, additional monies to carry on an activity required by law for which an appropriation was not made. The board may authorize an agency to expend from funds dedicated or continuously appropriated for the purpose of the agency sums in excess of the amount budgeted for the agency; may approve a budget for a new activity coming into existence at a time that would preclude submission of a budget to the Legislature; and may revise the budgets of state agencies to the extent of authorizing transfers between expenditure classifications within an agency.

Joint Committee on Ways and Means

Ken Rocco, Legislative Fiscal Officer

Address: 900 Court St. NE, Rm. H-178, Salem 97301

Phone: 503-986-1828

The Joint Committee on Ways and Means, created under ORS 171.555, is the legislative entity charged with the responsibility of making recommendations to the Legislative Assembly with regard to its constitutional requirement to adopt a balanced budget. The joint committee is made up of members appointed by the President of the Senate and the Speaker of the House. This appropriation process structure, employed in Oregon and several other states, is especially effective in resolving budgetary differences. The Legislative Fiscal Office provides staff assistance to the committee.

Joint Legislative Audit Committee

Dallas Weyand, Committee Administrator
Address: 900 Court St. NE, Rm. H-178, Salem 97301
Phone: 503-986-1828

The Joint Legislative Audit Committee was created in 1989 pursuant to ORS 171.580 to 171.590. The committee consists of ten members: the cochairs of the Joint Committee on Ways and Means and four other members each from the House and from the Senate. The committee reviews financial and compliance audits for the purpose of recommending changes in the agency operations or state financial and other systems. The committee also sets priorities for program evaluations and performance audits and determines the type of audit, evaluation, or review to be performed. The Legislative Fiscal Office provides staff assistance to the committee.

Joint Legislative Committee on Information Management and Technology

Dallas Weyand, Committee Administrator
Address: 900 Court St. NE, Rm. H-178, Salem 97301
Phone: 503-986-1828

The Joint Legislative Committee on Information Management and Technology was created to establish statewide information systems goals and policies; to make recommendations regarding established and proposed information resource management programs and information technology acquisitions; and to conduct studies of data processing efficiency and security. The committee consists of seven members: four appointed by the Speaker of the House of Representatives and three appointed by the President of the Senate. The committee operates pursuant to ORS 171.852 to 171.855, and is staffed by the Legislative Fiscal Office.

Legislative Commission on Indian Services

Karen Quigley, Executive Officer
Address: 900 Court St. NE, Rm. 167, Salem 97301

Phone: 503-986-1067
E-mail: karen.m.quigley@state.or.us

The Commission on Indian Services was created in 1975 under ORS 172.100 et seq. and operates as a small agency within the legislative branch of state government. Because of all the sovereigns represented, the Commission is an advisory, not an advocacy body.

The commission's specific statutory responsibilities include: compiling information about services for Indians; developing programs that inform Indians about available services, and that make Indian needs and concerns known to public and private agencies whose activities affect Indians; encouraging and supporting agencies to expand and improve services for Indians; and evaluating state services to Indians, reporting biennially to the governor and the Legislature on matters concerning Indians in Oregon.

Since the commission was created, it has assumed responsibility for coordinating issues of cultural resources protection. It is also the main agency to monitor and facilitate state/tribal relations.

The commission normally consists of 13 members appointed by the legislative leadership to two-year terms of office. Each of Oregon's nine federally-recognized Indian tribal groups is entitled to one member each. There is also a member from the Portland-area Indian community and one from the Willamette Valley. One state senator and one state representative are also seated on the commission.

Legislative Counsel Committee

David Heynderickx, Acting Legislative Counsel
Address: 900 Court St. NE, Rm. S-101, Salem 97301
Phone: 503-986-1243

The Legislative Counsel Committee is a joint legislative committee established under ORS 173.111. The committee consists of the President of the Senate, four senators appointed by the President, the Speaker of the House of Representatives, and five representatives appointed by the Speaker. The Legislative Counsel, who is selected by the committee, serves as executive officer to the committee. The Legislative Counsel manages the Office of the Legislative Counsel and employs a legal and professional staff.

One of the principal duties of the Office of the Legislative Counsel is the drafting of measures for legislators, legislative committees, and state agencies. The office also provides research services and legal advice to legislators and legislative committees. During legislative sessions, the office prepares amendments to the measures being considered by the Legislative Assembly.

The Office of the Legislative Counsel prepares indexes and tables for all measures introduced during a legislative session. At the end of each regular session, the office publishes the official compilation of that session's laws, *Oregon Laws*. The office also prepares and publishes every two years the official codification of Oregon's statute laws, *Oregon Revised Statutes* (ORS). Each edition of ORS incorporates the new statutory provisions and amendments to statutory provisions passed by the Legislative Assembly in the preceding regular session.

Pursuant to ORS 183.710 to 183.725, the Office of Legislative Counsel conducts a review of all new administrative rules adopted by state agencies. This review allows the Legislative Assembly to monitor whether an agency's rules are consistent with the agency's statutory authority.

Legislative Fiscal Office

Ken Rocco, Legislative Fiscal Officer
Address: 900 Court St. NE, Rm. H-178, Salem 97301
Phone: 503-986-1828

The Legislative Fiscal Office is a permanent, nonpartisan legislative agency created in 1959 pursuant to ORS 173.410 to 173.450 to serve legislators and legislative committees on matters related to the state's fiscal affairs. The office provides research, analysis, evaluation, and recommendations concerning state expenditures, budget issues, agency organization, and program administration. The Legislative Fiscal Office also provides fiscal impact assessment of proposed legislation, and staff assistance to the Joint Legislative Committee on Information Management and Technology and the Joint Legislative Audit Committee. The Legislative Fiscal Office staffs the Joint Committee on Ways and Means during the session and to the Emergency Board during the interim.

Legislative Revenue Office

Paul Warner, Legislative Revenue Officer
Address: 900 Court St. NE, Rm. H-197, Salem 97301
Phone: 503-986-1266

The Legislative Revenue Office was established by the 1975 Oregon Legislature to provide nonpartisan analysis of tax and school-finance issues pursuant to ORS 173.810 to 173.850.

The Legislative Revenue Officer is appointed by and responsible to the House and Senate committees that deal with revenue and school finance.

The Office staffs the House and Senate Revenue committees, writes revenue impact statements for proposed legislation and researches tax and school finance issues.

Oregon Law Commission

Lane P. Shetterly, Chair
David R. Kenagy, Executive Director
Address: Willamette University College of Law, 245 Winter St. SE, Salem 97301
Phone: 503-370-6973
Web: www.willamette.edu/wucl/oregonlawcommission

The Oregon Law Commission was formally established in 1997 to conduct an ongoing, substantive law revision program. The Commission replaced the Law Improvement Committee.

The Oregon Law Commission consists of 13 Commissioners: two persons appointed by the President of the Senate (one of whom must be a Senator), two persons appointed by the Speaker of the House of Representatives (one of whom must be a Representative), the deans, or an appointee from each of Oregon's three law schools, three persons appointed by the Oregon State Bar, the Attorney General, the Chief Justice of the Supreme Court, and one person appointed by the Governor.

The principal function of the Commission is to study Oregon law and to recommend law reform needed to correct defects and anachronisms in the law. The Commission reviews current judicial decisions to identify problems in the law, and considers reform proposals from judges, public officials, lawyers, and members of the public. The commission is also directed to study the repeal of statutes held unconstitutional by the courts.

The Commission recommends legislation as needed to implement its reform proposals and submits a biennial report to the Legislative Assembly. *[Pursuant to ORS 173.335, the Office of Legislative Counsel assists the Commission in carrying out its duties.]*

Legislative

Fishing on Umpqua River—Oregon State Archives Photograph, OHD-G435

Government finance—where government gets its money and how it spends it—affects all Oregonians. The connections between state and local government revenues and state and local government services are important. This section describes revenue sources and distribution.

STATE AND LOCAL GOVERNMENT FINANCE

State Government

Oregon has a two-year, or biennial budget. Each budget begins July 1 of odd-numbered years and lasts for two years. Oregon law requires all governments—state and local—to balance their budgets. How does state government's budget work? The state receives money from a variety of sources, which are grouped into 'funds.' These funds are known as the General Fund, Lottery Fund, Federal Funds, and Other Funds.

The total Legislatively Adopted Budget for the 2003–05 biennium was $37.290 billion. This is essentially even with 2001–03 total estimated expenditures of $37.251 billion. The General and Lottery Fund part of the budget amounted to $11.496 billion. Voter rejection of the temporary income tax surcharge (Ballot Measure 30) reduced this funding to $10.966 billion.

General Fund

The 2003–05 Legislatively Adopted Budget included $10.7 billion in General Fund, for a 28.8 percent share of the total budget. The General Fund is largely made up of personal and corporate income tax, collected by the Oregon Department of Revenue. General Fund appropriations provide funding to agencies that do not generate revenues, receive federal funds, or generate sufficient funds to meet their approved programs. Agencies do not actually receive money from the General Fund.

Corporate income taxes are eight percent of the total revenue amount. Other sources make up the remainder. The largest of these are the cigarette tax and the liquor apportionment transfer. Because General Fund monies can be used for any public purpose and the amount of General Fund is limited, competition for these monies is keen.

In 1990, voters approved Ballot Measure 5. This reduced property tax rates, especially for schools, and shifted much of the responsibility for funding public schools to the state's General Fund. The 2003–05 Legislatively Adopted Budget had $6.7 billion, or 58.4 percent of the General and Lottery Funds being spent on education.

As of the Close of Session 2003, projected General Fund revenues for the 2003–05 biennium totaled $10.7 billion and the balance carried over from the prior biennium was $57.1 million. At an expected $9.4 billion, personal income tax accounted for 87.5 percent of total revenues. Anticipated corporate income tax of $539.7 million was an additional 5.0 percent. The revenue forecast included $780 million derived from increases in personal income tax rates, changes to the corporate income tax, and transfers from county property tax collections, passed collectively by the 2003 Legislature as House Bill 2152. In February 2004, Oregon voters repealed HB 2152. For the September 2004 forecast, the revenue forecast equaled $10.2 billion, $527.0 million below the Close of Session forecast. The beginning balance was revised up to $129.9 million, bringing total resources to $10.3 billion. The projected ending balance for 2003–05 equaled $137.3 million.

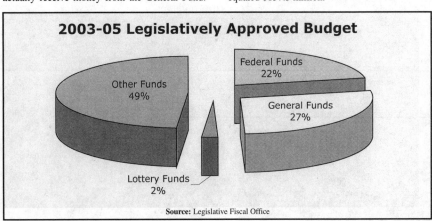

2003-05 Legislatively Approved Budget

Other Funds 49%

Federal Funds 22%

General Funds 27%

Lottery Funds 2%

Source: Legislative Fiscal Office

Instead, they expend against an appropriation from the General Fund that is established for general government purposes, up to the amount approved in their budget bill. The personal income tax makes up the largest share of General Fund revenue. It accounts for 85 percent of projected revenue.

Lottery Fund

The 2003–05 Legislatively Adopted Budget included $756.9 million in Lottery Fund, for a 2.0 percent share of the total budget. The Lottery Fund receives its money from the games run by the Oregon State Lottery. State law requires the Lottery to

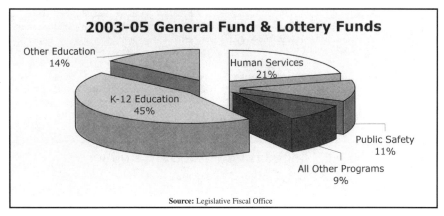

2003-05 General Fund & Lottery Funds

Other Education 14%

Human Services 21%

K-12 Education 45%

Public Safety 11%

All Other Programs 9%

Source: Legislative Fiscal Office

award at least 50 percent of the money it receives as prizes. The remainder goes into the Lottery Fund.

Other Funds

The 2003–05 Legislatively Adopted Budget included $17.7 billion in Other Funds, for a 47.6 percent share of the total budget. Other Fund revenue generally refers to money collected by agencies in return for services. Legislative actions may allow an agency to levy taxes, provide services for a fee, license individuals, or otherwise earn revenues to pay for programs. These other funds are often separate and distinct from monies collected

from one major program to another. Consequently, competition for these monies is limited.

Federal Funds

The 2003–05 Legislatively Adopted Budget included $8.1 billion in Federal Funds, for a 21.6 percent share of the total budget. Federal Funds are monies received from the federal government. The Legislative Assembly may authorize receipt of federal funds for specific purposes. Federal funds may be used to match General Fund dollars, used for specific programs, or passed through to local governments.

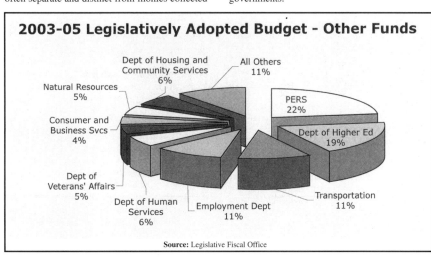

2003-05 Legislatively Adopted Budget - Other Funds

Dept of Housing and Community Services 6%

All Others 11%

Natural Resources 5%

PERS 22%

Consumer and Business Svcs 4%

Dept of Higher Ed 19%

Dept of Veterans' Affairs 5%

Dept of Human Services 6%

Employment Dept 11%

Transportation 11%

Source: Legislative Fiscal Office

for general government purposes (general funds), and they may be based on statutory language, federal mandate, and legal requirements or for specific business reasons. Some funds are "dedicated" in that the income and disbursements are limited by the state's constitution or by law (for example, the Highway Fund). Other Funds may not be moved

State Budget Process

In Oregon state government, agencies develop biennial budgets according to instructions provided by the Department of Administrative Services, Budget and Management Division. This budget development process occurs in even-numbered years, well before the Legislative Assembly convenes in January of the odd-numbered years. Agencies are required to prepare and submit their budget requests for review by the Budget and Management Division by September 1. These budget requests consist of narrative descriptions of agency programs, completed forms, and reports from the state's Automated Budget Information System (ABIS).

An agency begins with a base budget, which is the amount of money it will need in the new

When the Legislative Assembly is in session, a subcommittee of the Joint Ways and Means Committee hears each agency's budget. At the budget hearings, an agency presents its budget request and answers questions asked by members of the committee. Staff members from the Legislative Fiscal Office and the Budget and Management Division are also present at the budget hearings. Members of the public may attend the hearings and request an opportunity to testify. At the end of an agency's

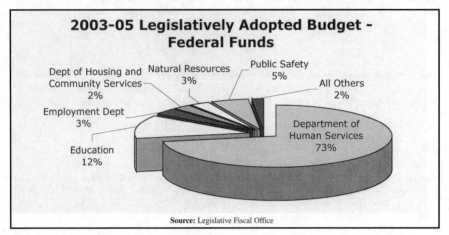

2003-05 Legislatively Adopted Budget - Federal Funds

Dept of Housing and Community Services 2%

Natural Resources 3%

Public Safety 5%

All Others 2%

Employment Dept 3%

Education 12%

Department of Human Services 73%

Source: Legislative Fiscal Office

biennium to continue its operations at the current service level. An agency may request increases to this base budget in the form of Program Option Packages, which are separate pieces of the budget, with the purpose and the amount needed specified. Agencies work with staff from the Department of Administrative Services, Budget and Management Division, as they develop their budgets. Agency budget requests follow a format established by the Budget and Management Division. This standard format, from agency to agency, is intended to facilitate understanding and review. For their 2005–07 budget requests, agencies began in March 2004 and submitted their completed requests no later than the beginning of September 2004. An agency's budget provides an outline of what an agency does, what it costs, and how many people are involved.

After they pass a review by the Governor's Office and the Budget and Management Division, the budget requests become part of the Governor's Recommended Budget. The Governor's Recommended Budget includes the proposed budgets for the Legislative Assembly, the Judicial Department, and the Secretary of State, although they are not subject to the governor's budget authority. This is because the governor has a legal obligation to submit a balanced budget for the state. The governor presents the Recommended Budget to the Legislative Assembly when it convenes in January of odd-numbered years.

budget hearings, the agency's budget goes to the full Ways and Means Committee for a vote and then on to the full House and Senate for a vote. The agency's budget may be amended at any point in this process, although typically changes occur during the subcommittee hearings. When both houses pass an agency's budget bill, it becomes the agency's Legislatively Adopted Budget for the biennium, and it goes into effect July 1 of odd-numbered years.

Kicker

The two percent surplus kicker was enacted by the 1979 Legislative Assembly. It gives taxpayers an income tax refund or credit if actual revenues are more than two percent higher than forecast at the time the state budget was adopted. The law divides General Fund money into two pots: 1) corporate taxes and 2) all other revenues. At the end of each biennium, if the actual collections in either of these pots is more than two percent higher than was forecast at the close of the regular legislative session, then a refund or credit must be paid. When triggered, all of the money in the pot greater than the forecast must be returned to taxpayers. Surpluses in the corporate pot result in a corporate tax credit. Surpluses in all the other revenues pot result in a personal income tax refund. Taxpayers receive a check by December 1 of the year the biennium ends (odd-numbered years). The refund is an identical proportion of each taxpayer's personal income tax liability for the prior year. During 2003–05, no personal or corporate kicker refunds were issued. As of the September 2004 forecast, a $68.1 million corporate kicker rebate was projected for tax year 2005.

State Spending Limit

The state spending limit was first enacted by the 1979 Legislative Assembly. It limited the growth of General Fund appropriations to the growth of personal income in Oregon. The 2001 Legislative Assembly replaced this spending limit with one tying appropriations for a biennium to personal income for that biennium. The appropriations subject to this limit may not exceed eight percent of projected personal income for the same biennium. The 2003–05 Legislatively Adopted Budget authorized an expenditure limit of 7.6 percent of projected personal income for the biennium, based on the May 2003 revenue forecast. The limit may be exceeded if the governor declares an emergency and three-fifths of the members of both houses vote to exceed it.

Local Government

Local government in Oregon is predominantly financed by the property tax, although there are other local taxes, such as hotel-motel taxes, transit taxes and, in Multnomah County, a business income tax.

Most local governments must prepare and adopt an annual budget. This includes schools, counties, cities, ports, rural fire protection districts, water districts, urban renewal agencies and special districts. Oregon's Local Budget Law establishes standard budget procedures and requires citizen participation in budget preparation and public disclosure of the budget before it is formally adopted. A budget officer must be appointed and a budget committee formed. The budget officer prepares a draft budget and the budget committee reviews and revises it before it is approved. Notices are then published, copies of the budget are made available for public review, and at least two opportunities for public comment are provided.

Local government budgets are usually for a fiscal year, beginning July 1 and ending June 30. However, local governments do have the option of doing a two-year biennial budget, like the state. The governing body must enact a resolution or an ordinance to formally adopt the budget, make appropriations, and levy and categorize any tax. This must be done no later than June 30. Budget revenues are divided into ensuing year property tax and non-property tax revenues.

The Oregon Constitution allows a local government to levy annually the amount that would be raised by its permanent rate limit without further authorization from the voters. When a local government has to increase the permanent rate limit or when the rate limit does not provide enough revenue to meet estimated expenditures, the government may request a local option levy from the voters. Approval requires a 'double majority.' This means that at least 50 percent of the registered voters must vote and a majority of those who vote must approve the levy. Since 1991, the Constitution has limited the maximum amount of taxes to support the public schools to $5 per $1,000 of real market value. The maximum amount to support other government operations is $10 per $1,000 of real market value.

Taxes

Personal Income Tax

Oregon residents and nonresidents who earn income in Oregon pay personal income tax. Oregon taxable income is the same as federal taxable income, with some adjustments. Tax rates range from 5 percent to 9 percent of taxable income. Taxable income is total income less exclusions and either the standard or itemized deductions. After deductions and credits, the average effective tax rate is about 5.6 percent of adjusted gross income. Since 1993, the income tax brackets have been indexed to changes in the U.S. Consumer Price Index. The standard deduction is $3,280 on a joint return, $1,640 on single and married filing separate returns, and $2,640 for a head of household return.

The personal income tax is the largest source of state tax revenue.

Business Taxes

Corporations that do or are authorized to do business in Oregon pay excise tax. Corporations not doing or authorized to do business in Oregon but having income from an Oregon source pay income tax. The tax rate is 6.6 percent of Oregon net income. There is a minimum excise tax of $10. The corporate excise and income tax is the second largest source of state tax revenue.

Property Tax

Property tax rates differ across Oregon. The rate depends on the tax rate approved by local voters and the limits established by the Oregon Constitution. Most properties are taxed by a number of districts, such as a city, county, school district, community college, fire district, and port. The total tax rate on any particular property is calculated by adding all the local taxing district rates in the area. The total tax rate is then multiplied by the assessed value of the property. The county assessor annually verifies the tax rates and levies submitted by each local taxing

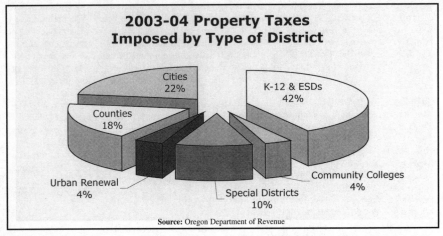

2003-04 Property Taxes Imposed by Type of District

Cities 22%

K-12 & ESDs 42%

Counties 18%

Urban Renewal 4%

Community Colleges 4%

Special Districts 10%

Source: Oregon Department of Revenue

district. The county tax collector collects the taxes and distributes the funds to the local districts.

Taxable property includes real property, mobile homes, and some tangible personal property used by business. The county assessor determines the value of property in each county. Measure 5 was passed by the voters in November 1990. Measure 5 restricted non-school taxes on any property to $10 per $1,000 of real market value. It restricted school taxes on any property to $5 per $1,000 of real market value.

Measure 50 was passed by the voters in May 1997. Measure 50 added another limit to the Measure 5 limits. Now each property has a real market value and an assessed value. Each taxing district has a fixed, permanent tax rate for operations. Districts may not increase this rate. Voters can approve local option levies for up to five years for operations and up to 10 years or the useful life of capital projects, whichever is less. Local option levies require a 'double majority' for approval. Measure 50 established the 1997–98 maximum assessed value as 90 percent of a property's 1995–96 real market value. In subsequent tax years, the assessed value is limited to three percent annual growth until it reaches real market value. The assessed value can never exceed real market value. New property is assessed at the average county ratio of assessed to real market value of existing property of the same class. For 2003–04, for all classes of property statewide, total assessed value was about 75 percent of real market value.

Resources

Oregon State Legislature (www.leg.state.or.us)

Legislative Fiscal Office (www.leg.state.or.us/comm/lfo)

The Legislative Fiscal Office publishes highlights and detailed analyses of the *Legislatively Adopted Budget,* as well as detailed analyses of the *Legislatively Adopted Budget* and the *Governor's Recommended Budget.*

Legislative Revenue Office
(www.leg.state.or.us/comm/lro)

The Legislative Revenue Office publishes a wide variety of reports on revenue-related issues. It publishes *Oregon Public Finance: Basic Facts,* which serves as an introduction to how Oregon government is financed.

Department of Administrative Services, Budget and Management Division
(www.oregon.gov/DAS/BAM/index.shtml)

The Budget and Management Division publishes a *Budget Process Overview,* as well as the *Governor's Recommended Budget.*

Department of Administrative Services, Office of Economic Analysis
(www.oregon.gov/DAS/OEA/index.shtml)

The Office of Economic Analysis publishes periodic *Economic and Revenue Forecasts,* as well as much related demographic data.

Department of Revenue,
(www.oregon.gov/DOR/index.shtml)

The Department of Revenue publishes a great deal of information about taxes in Oregon.

Neptune State Park—Oregon State Archives Photograph, OHD-5118

Education continues to be a central concern for Oregonians. As the state's population grows and its economy evolves, the future of educational institutions at all levels has been a significant public policy issue. This section describes public education in Oregon and also provides an overview of private colleges.

ELEMENTARY AND SECONDARY EDUCATION IN OREGON

Source: Department of Education
Address: 255 Capitol St. NE, Salem 97310-0203
Phone: 503-378-3569; TDD: 503-378-2892
Fax: 503-378-5156
Web: www.ode.state.or.us

Oregon's public school system was created by the Territorial Legislature in 1849. The Oregon Constitution assigns the legislature primary responsibility for establishing a public school system and provides for an elected state superintendent of public instruction. In 1951, the legislature established the State Board of Education, which is responsible for setting policy for administering and operating public elementary and secondary schools and community colleges.

The Department of Education serves 198 school districts, which educate 551,290 elementary and secondary students, and 20 education service districts, which offer expertise and specialized resources to school districts. In addition, the department manages the Oregon School for the Blind, the Oregon School for the Deaf and education programs for students in correctional facilities.

Oregon Educational Act for the 21st Century

Economically and socially, Oregon is becoming more dynamic and complex every day. As students graduate from high school, they enter an increasingly demanding world. Oregon schools are raising their academic standards to help students meet the challenges they will face after high school. Students in the Class of 2001 were the first group eligible to receive a Certificate of Initial Mastery for meeting the new high standards.

Traditional basics—reading, writing and arithmetic—are at the heart of Oregon's education plan, along with new basics—advanced mathematics, science and technology—necessary for college and work in the 21st Century.

The Oregon Educational Act for the 21st Century, passed by an overwhelming majority of the legislature in 1991 and clarified and strengthened by amendments in 1995, signals a concerted effort to improve the performance and accountability of Oregon schools. The law calls for:

• Rigorous academic standards;
• Classroom assignments and tests to measure student progress toward the standards;
• Annual public reports on student achievement of the standards;
• Increased parental involvement in schools;
• Less state regulation so teachers can help students achieve the standards without government interference.

Thousands of parents and teachers from across Oregon helped draft academic content standards specifying what students should know and be able to do in seven areas: English, mathematics, science, the social sciences (history, civics, geography and economics), the arts, a second language, and physical education. The standards, adopted by the State Board of Education in September 1996, contain requirements such as use correct spelling, grammar, punctuation, capitalization and paragraphing by the end of the fifth grade, perform numeric and algebraic calculations using paper and pencil, calculators and computer programs by the end of the tenth grade, and demonstrate other learning. Student progress toward the standards will be evaluated at grades 3–8, and in high school beginning at grade 10. Students who achieve high school standards will receive a Certificate of Initial Mastery. Students who achieve additional career-related learning standards and complete a focused area of study toward their future goals will receive a Certificate of Advanced Mastery.

Average Oregon SAT Results Compared Nationally

Verbal

	Oregon	National
2004	527	508
2003	526	507
2002	524	504
2001	526	506
2000	527	505
1999	523	505
1998	528	505
1997	525	505
1996	523	505
1995	525	504

Mathematics

	Oregon	National
2004	528	518
2003	527	519
2002	528	516
2001	526	514
2000	527	514
1999	525	511
1998	528	512
1997	524	511
1996	521	508
1995	522	506

Oregon students scored second in the nation on the SAT among the 23 states that had at least 50 percent of their high school graduates tested.

Early Childhood Education

Early childhood education is the foundation of school improvement. If children receive the support they need as they begin school, they will be better able to achieve high academic standards as they continue their education. The Oregon Educational Act for the 21st Century recommends that schools develop kindergarten through grade three programs that:

- Encourage parent participation;
- Apply successful teaching practices and sound educational research;
- Acknowledge children's individual differences such as learning styles and cultural backgrounds;
- Plan children's transitions from pre-kindergarten through grade three;
- Assist families who request such assistance with obtaining health care and other social services.

The Oregon Head Start Pre-kindergarten program, modeled after the federal Head Start program, fosters the healthy development of low-income three- and four-year-olds to enhance their chances for success in school. The greatest challenge for pre-kindergarten is meeting the growing need.

In 2003–04, the Oregon and federal Head Start programs together served 59 percent of Oregon's eligible children. The population of three- and four-year-old children has increased and the federal poverty rate for children under six has changed to 17.4 percent. Oregon's Head Start Pre-kindergarten Program and the federal Head Start Program serve Oregon's poorest children.

Professional Technical Education

Professional technical education (PTE) provides high school and community college students with opportunities to achieve high academic and technical skills standards as they prepare for productive, rewarding careers and lives. Professional Technical Education works closely with education sectors and workforce partners to connect K-12 education, postsecondary education and career opportunities. The Office of Professional Technical Education is responsible for PTE in Oregon and provides support to public schools and community colleges to:

- Connect rigorous academic content and career-related learning to real life applications;
- Equip students with the knowledge and skills they need to move successfully to post-secondary education and/or careers;
- Create smooth transitions for students between education levels and between education and careers; and
- Build partnerships among schools, communities, businesses and state and local governments that assist students to meet standards leading to success.

The office is responsible for the administration of the federal Carl D. Perkins Vocational and Technical Education Act (professional technical education) and Learn & Serve America (service learning) funds for Oregon.

Special Education

In 2003–04, 77,922 Oregon children and youth (birth–21) with disabilities received special education or other services. Of the 70,825 who were school-aged (5–21), 96 percent attended a regular public school where they participated in the general curriculum and received specially designed instruction and related services. Other students with disabilities received their education and special education services in a state-operated or state-supported program. The goal for these students is similar to that for all students: to receive an education that prepares them for living and working in an integrated community setting of their choice.

Oregon School for the Deaf
Jane Mulholland, Director
Address: 999 Locust St. NE, Salem 97303-5254
Phone: 503-378-3825 (Voice/TDD)
Fax: 503-373-7879

Established in 1870, the Oregon School for the Deaf (OSD) enrolls students who, because of hearing impairment, need a more comprehensive level of service and/or a more communication-rich environment than can be provided through their regular public school. OSD is funded by legislative appropriation and is operated by the Oregon Department of Education. In 2004–05, between 125–135 students were enrolled at the school, at no cost to their families.

Teachers certified to teach the deaf use American Sign Language or Total Communication in all instructional settings. Total Communication uses a variety of modes depending on individual student needs. Modes may include: American Sign Language, English-like signing, spoken English or print. The academic curriculum is enhanced by classes in speech, computer literacy, driver education, art and drama. OSD's high school is Oregon's only residential comprehensive secondary program designed exclusively for deaf students.

The school offers an equal opportunity for students to participate and excel. Daily socialization with deaf peers builds confidence. Student government and community activities develop leadership skills. Casco League football, basketball, track, golf and volleyball teams anchor a strong sports program and provide opportunities for interaction with hearing peers.

Students who cannot attend OSD as day students are eligible for residential services. Specially trained counselors give 24-hour guidance, teaching independent living, self-help, social and leisure-time skills. Older students have the opportunity to live in apartments within the residence halls, assuming all household tasks and learning skills required for successful transition to adulthood.

A center of deaf culture for more than 130 years, OSD features successful deaf adult role models on staff and deaf studies coursework.

Oregon School for the Blind
Donald A. Ouimet, Director
Address: 700 Church St. SE, Salem 97301-3795
Phone: 503-378-3820
Fax: 503-373-7537

The Oregon School for the Blind (OSB) provides intensive educational services for students who are visually impaired. OSB's mission includes a continuum of support to district and regional vision programs and to children and their parents.

Established in 1873, the school is operated by the Oregon Department of Education and funded by legislative appropriations. Students ages five through 21 who need a more intensive level of individualized special education than can be provided locally are served by OSB at no cost to their families. OSB's average annual enrollment in the school year program is 50 students. Through all program areas, approximately 400 visually impaired children in Oregon are served each year.

Compensatory academic, career education, independent living, and recreation/leisure skills are essential programming components for all OSB students. Students have opportunities to develop travel, social and technology skills. Students with low vision can receive programming to enable them to maximize visual efficiency.

OSB's services are provided by staff who have specialized skills in working with children who are visually impaired. Teachers (including adapted physical education, technology, orientation and mobility, and vocational), related service staff (including occupational and physical therapy, speech, autism, counseling, and nursing services), and residential service staff provide a 24-hour program that includes time in the community and inclusion with non-disabled peers.

As a statewide resource, the school shares materials and provides consultation and assessment services. The school coordinates the Lions Statewide Vision Clinic and administers the Elks preschool program, which serves visually impaired preschoolers throughout Oregon. Summer programming is available to visually impaired students who attend their local school during the regular school year. These thematic programs include Braille, technology, outdoor learning, creative enrichment, and work experience.

Juvenile Corrections Education Programs
Jay Gense, Director, Low Incidence Programs
Address: Office of Student Learning and Partnerships, Oregon Department of Education, 255 Capitol St. NE, Salem 97310-0203
Phone: 503-378-3600, ext. 2325
Fax: 503-378-5156

The Office of Special Education is responsible for educating youth housed in Oregon Youth Authority correctional facilities. More than 900 students, ages 12 to 25, are served at 10 youth correctional facilities across the state. Education services in all facilities are operated by local education agencies under contracts with the department.

The education program operates 220 days per year, emphasizing general education and professional/technical education. Eligible students receive special education services. In addition, art, second language, parenthood education, alcohol and drug education, health education, career development and other subjects help students prepare for a successful transition back into Oregon communities.

The Oregon Youth Authority is responsible for security, treatment, recreation, medical, residential and transition services supporting a safe, secure environment and providing opportunity for rehabilitation of youth offenders.

The Office of Student Learning and Partnerships is also charged with providing the education programs to 15 county juvenile detention programs, and contracts with local education agencies to provide education services.

Statewide Interagency Coordinating Council for Early Intervention Services
Diana Allen, Director
Address: Early Childhood Programs, Office of Student Learning and Partnerships, Oregon Department of Education, 255 Capitol St. NE, Salem 97310-0203
Phone: 503-378-3600, ext 2338
Fax: 503-378-5156

The State Interagency Coordinating Council for Early Intervention/Early Childhood Special Education was established in 1988. The council now advises the State Superintendent of Public Instruction and the State Board of Education on the needs of preschool children with disabilities, reviews any related administrative rules proposed by the State Board, comments on the distribution of funds for early intervention and early childhood special education, and helps develop and report data and evaluations of these programs.

Oregon began implementing a state-operated program for infants and preschoolers with disabilities in 1992. Early childhood special education services are available to eligible children following all the federal special education regulations. Early intervention services are provided with federal and state funds.

Education Service Districts

Senate Bill 26, 1993 placed all of Oregon's school districts in education service districts (ESD). ESDs provide school districts with expertise and specialized resources that few could provide on their own (ORS 334.005). In recent years, the legislature reduced education service districts from 29 to 20. The ESDs provide important links between the Department of Education, local districts and other governmental entities.

Local districts participate in deciding what services ESDs will offer, ensuring that the services reflect local needs. Support for special education, instruction, technology, instructional media, juvenile corrections, cooperative purchasing, graphic arts, printing, data processing and professional/technical services are typical needs ESDs provide.

Through their strong relationship with the Department of Education, ESDs coordinate and deliver department information and materials regarding curriculum, assessment, school improvement teams, child-find, data collection and other issues. ESDs coordinate nearly $300 million annually in local, state and federal resources to provide important equal educational opportunities to the children of Oregon.

The 2001 Legislative Assembly reviewed the recommendations of the ESD Task Force and enacted Senate Bills 259 and 260. This legislation clarified the role that ESDs play in Oregon education and created a more equitable funding mechanism.

COMMUNITY COLLEGES

Source: Cam Preus-Braly, Commissioner
Address: Department of Community Colleges and Workforce Development, 255 Capitol St. NE, Salem 97310
Phone: 503-378-8648, ext. 357
Fax: 503-378-8434
Web: www.odccwd.state.or.us

For the past half century, Oregon's community colleges have met a major share of the state's adult education needs. Today, Oregon's 17 community colleges serve more than 377,000 students a year and are an integral part of the postsecondary education system.

The community college student is generally older than the typical four-year college student, with an average age of 36 years. Many of these older students are returning to college to upgrade their job skills, with the goal of keeping current in their chosen field. Many returning students hold bachelor's or master's degrees.

The legislature has charged community colleges with three responsibilities:

Transfer education. Thousands of students each year take advantage of the two-year college transfer program that gives them the opportunity to stay home for the first two years of a four-year college education.

Professional technical education and training. Community colleges are responsible for providing technical job-related training to a large portion of Oregon's labor force. Developed in cooperation with local employers, community college programs are state-of-the-art. Students enrolled in a professional technical education program can work toward a one-year certificate or a two-year degree.

Developmental education. Community colleges also provide developmental education programs to help adult learners complete their high school education. Often, after earning a GED certificate or Adult High School Diploma, adults choose to continue their education in vocational or two-year transfer classes to upgrade job skills.

Every community college offers workshops, seminars and classes geared to the nontraditional student. These courses range from personal interest classes to on-site industry training.

The community college network is a primary delivery system for education programs that are essential to Oregon's economic health. Community colleges serve as the home for most Small Business Development Centers (SBDCs), which are linked as a statewide network created in 1983 by the legislature in cooperation with the U.S. Small Business Administration. SBDCs work with local businesses to foster entrepreneurship, good management skills, economic development, joint venture capital and creation of locally-based jobs.

Community colleges respond regularly to requests from business and industry for specialized training. The college contracts directly with firms, and the training programs take place either on campus or at the business site.

Using community college training programs, companies can save a considerable amount of start-up time by providing training for workers before the business is ready to go into production.

Community colleges work with the State Board of Education, under the leadership of the Commissioner for the Department of Community Colleges and Workforce Development. They are not a part of the Oregon University System.

When the legislature created community colleges in Oregon, it did not establish a series of institutions. Rather, it created a mechanism for residents of a community to form their own colleges through the initiative process.

The legislature consistently has supported the principle that community colleges should be controlled locally through locally-elected boards. These boards are required by statute to keep in touch with the needs of the people they serve and to assure development of programs to meet those needs.

Blue Mountain Community College
John Turner, Interim President
Address: PO Box 100, Pendleton 97801-1000
Phone: 541-276-1260
Web: www.bluecc.edu
2002–03 FTE enrollment: 2,983

Central Oregon Community College
Dr. James Middleton, President
Address: 2600 NW College Way, Bend 97701-5998
Phone: 541-383-7700
Web: www.cocc.edu
2002–03 FTE enrollment: 4,073

Chemeketa Community College
Dr. Gretchen Schuette, President
Address: PO Box 14007, Salem 97309-7070
Phone: 503-399-5000
Web: www.chemeketa.edu
2002–03 FTE enrollment: 11,712

Clackamas Community College
Dr. Joe Johnson, President
Address: 19600 S Molalla Ave., Oregon City 97045-7998
Phone: 503-657-6958 ext. 2401
Web: www.clackamas.edu
2002–03 FTE enrollment: 7,959

Clatsop Community College
Dr. Greg Hamann, President
Address: 1653 Jerome Ave., Astoria 97103-3698
Phone: 503-325-0910
Web: www.clatsopcc.edu
2002–03 FTE enrollment: 1,542

Columbia Gorge Community College
Dr. Frank Toda, President
Address: 400 E Scenic Dr., The Dalles 97058-3434
Phone: 541-296-6182
Web: www.cgcc.cc.or.us
2002–03 FTE enrollment: 1,055

Klamath Community College
Dr. Fred Smith, President
Address: 7390 S 6th St., Klamath Falls 97603-7121
Phone: 541-882-3521
Web: www.kcc.cc.or.us
2002–03 FTE enrollment: 1,285

Lane Community College
Dr. Mary Spilde, President
Address: 4000 E 30th Ave., Eugene 97405-0640
Phone: 541-463-3000
Web: www.lanecc.edu
2002–03 FTE enrollment: 12,364

Linn-Benton Community College
Dr. Rita Cavin, President
Address: 6500 Pacific Blvd. SW, Albany 97321-3779
Phone: 541-917-4999
Web: www.linnbenton.edu
2002–03 FTE enrollment: 6,866

Mt. Hood Community College
Dr. Robert Silverman, President
Address: 26000 SE Stark St., Gresham 97030-3300
Phone: 503-491-6422
Web: www.mhcc.edu
2002–03 FTE enrollment: 9,755

Oregon Coast Community College
Dr. Patrick O'Connor, President
Address: 332 SW Coast Hwy., Newport 97365-4928
Phone: 541-265-2283
Web: www.occc.cc.or.us
2002–03 FTE enrollment: 420

Portland Community College
Dr. Preston Pulliams, President
Address: PO Box 19000, Portland 97280-0990
Phone: 503-244-6111
Web: www.pcc.edu
2002–03 FTE enrollment: 26,244

Rogue Community College
Dr. Peter Angstadt, President
Address: 3345 Redwood Hwy., Grants Pass 97527-9298
Phone: 541-956-7500
Web: www.roguecc.edu
2002–03 FTE enrollment: 4,513

Southwestern Oregon Community College
Dr. Stephen J. Kridelbaugh, President
Address: 1988 Newmark, Coos Bay 97420-2971
Phone: 541-888-2525
Web: www.socc.edu
2002–3 FTE enrollment: 2,966

Tillamook Bay Community College
Ralph Orr, President
Address: 2510 First St., Tillamook 97141-2599
Phone: 503-842-8222
Web: www.tbcc.cc.or.us
2002–03 FTE enrollment: 350

Treasure Valley Community College
Dr. James Sorensen, President
Address: 650 College Blvd., Ontario 97914-3498
Phone: 541-881-8822
Web: www.tvcc.cc.or.us
2002–03 FTE enrollment: 2,384

Umpqua Community College
Dr. David Beyer, President
Address: PO Box 967, Roseburg 97470
Phone: 541-440-4600
Web: www.umpqua.edu
2002–03 FTE enrollment: 3,552

Total 2002–03 enrollment in Oregon community nity colleges was 100,023.

HIGHER EDUCATION IN OREGON

Source: Department of Higher Education
Address: PO Box 3175, Eugene 97403-0175
Phone: 541-346-5700
Fax: 541-346-5764
Web: www.ous.edu

The Oregon University System (OUS) is comprised of seven universities under the control of the governor-appointed State Board of Higher Education. The chancellor is the system's chief executive officer, with vice chancellors and deputies having responsibilities for Strategic Programs and Planning; Graduate and Research Policy; Enrollment Policy and Community Colleges Liaison; K–12 and Teacher Programs; and Finance and Administration. The three statewide universities, four regional universities, and one satellite campus within OUS include Eastern Oregon University (La Grande), Oregon Institute of Technology (Klamath Falls), Oregon State University (Corvallis and Bend), Portland State University (Portland), Southern Oregon University (Ashland), University of Oregon (Eugene), and Western Oregon University (Monmouth). Oregon Health and Science University (Portland) is an affiliated institution. In instruction, research and service, public higher education plays a key role in furthering Oregon's economic, intellectual, and cultural growth and diversity. In addition to the institutions' principal mission—instruction—they also perform important agricultural, high technology, research and other public services.

Each Oregon county has access to public higher education services offered by OUS institutions and their affiliated education centers. Total unduplicated headcount for the 2003–04 academic year was 108,972, which includes regular classes and continuing education courses.

OUS manages the wise investment of state dollars through consolidation of services, sharing of resources, and innovative uses of technology. The State Board of Higher Education and staff actively seek the advice and support of business, industry, government, K–12, and community college leaders in finding ways to provide cost-effective delivery of services that meet the changing needs of Oregonians.

The 2003–04 budget for the OUS institutions came from the following sources: General Fund, 17%; tuition and fees, 22%; sales and service fees, 18%; contracts, donations and grants, 16%; student loan funds, 13%; capital funds, 10%; and other, 4%.

State Board of Higher Education
George P. Pernsteiner, Acting Chancellor
Address: PO Box 3175, Eugene 97403-0175
Phone: 541-346-5795
Fax: 541-346-5764
Web: www.ous.edu

Henry Lorenzen, President, Pendleton, 2007; Kirby Dyess, Vice President, Eugene, 2008; Dr. Geri Richmond, Eugene (*Ex Officio*); Donald W. Blair, Beaverton, 2008; Bridget Burns, Eugene, 2005; Adriana Mendoza, La Grande, 2005; Tim Nesbitt, Salem, 2008; Dr. Gretchen S. Schuette,

---

Enrollment at Oregon University System Institutions

Academic year 2003–04 unduplicated headcount enrollment
(includes all students enrolling throughout school year)

Eastern Oregon University	5,114
Oregon Institute of Technology	4,217
Oregon State University (includes Cascades Campus)	23,087
Portland State University	37.854
Southern Oregon University	7,895
University of Oregon	24,091
Western Oregon University	6,714
Total Oregon University System enrollment for the year 2003–04	**108,972**

Salem, 2008; Howard F. Sohn, Roseburg, 2005; Tony Van Vliet, Corvallis, 2005; John E. von Schlegell, Portland, 2005. The governor appoints the 11 board members, subject to senate confirmation. Nine members are appointed for four-year terms, and two OUS students are appointed for two-year terms. The State Board of Higher Education, operating under ORS Chapter 351, appoints a chancellor as chief executive officer; establishes systemwide policy; sets institutional guidelines; approves curricular programs; reviews and approves budgets; and manages property and investments.

Western Interstate Commission for Higher Education

Address: PO Box 3175, Eugene 97403
Phone: 541-346-5729

The Western Interstate Commission for Higher Education (WICHE) is a public interstate agency created in 1953 by governors and legislators of the 15 western states. It was formed to help provide high-quality, cost-effective postsecondary education programs through cooperation and collaboration among the western states and their institutions of higher education.

WICHE has three student exchange programs: The Professional Student Exchange Program (PSEP), the Western Regional Graduate Program (WRGP), and the Western Undergraduate Exchange (WUE). PSEP provides preference in admission and financial assistance to a limited number of students who wish to enroll in selected professional programs not available in the student's home state. WRGP provides students in participating states access to selected master's and doctoral programs at resident tuition rates. WUE enables undergraduates to enroll in designated institutions and programs in other participating states on a space-available basis at 150 percent of resident tuition. WICHE also provides research and information services concerning higher education.

WICHE is funded by state dues, supplemented by grants and contracts, and governed by 45 commissioners: three appointed by the governor of each state.

Oregon's WICHE membership is authorized by ORS 351.770, and its commissioners are Ryan Deckert, Portland; Camille Preus-Braly, Salem; and Diane Vines, Portland.

Eastern Oregon University

Dr. Khosrow Fatemi, President
Address: One University Blvd., La Grande 97850
Phone: 541-962-3512; Toll-free: 1-800-452-8639
Fax: 541-962-3493
Web: www.eou.edu

Eastern Oregon University (EOU), was recently ranked number two in the nation as a "Best Value for Public Colleges and Universities" by *Consumers Digest* magazine. The university offers 26 bachelor's degree programs and has partnerships with Oregon Health and Science University, Portland State University, Oregon State University, and the Oregon Institute of Technology. With a national reputation and innovative new courses and program offerings both on campus and online, EOU strives for excellence in education.

Already well known as a student-centered university, EOU places the interests of all its students at the forefront of its academics, student services, and extracurricular activities. Under the leadership of President Khosrow Fatemi, EOU is strengthening its commitment to preparing students for today's global marketplace by providing opportunities for internships, international experiences, undergraduate research, and community involvement. As a nationally recognized leader in distance learning, EOU provides educational services from 16 statewide distance learning centers to students throughout Oregon and across the country.

Visitors to the region are impressed with the area's rugged scenic beauty, as were the pioneers who traveled west on the Oregon Trail, which passes along the southern edge of the campus. Located 260 miles east of Portland and 174 miles northwest of Boise, Idaho, EOU is the only four-year university in eastern Oregon, serving an area roughly the size of Pennsylvania. As a result, EOU plays a vital role in the social, economic, and cultural life of the region.

Oregon Health and Science University

Dr. Peter Kohler, President
Address: 3181 SW Sam Jackson Park Rd., Portland 97239-3098
Phone: 503-494-8311
Fax: 503-494-8935
Web: www.ohsu.edu

Oregon Health and Science University (OHSU) is a health and research university dedicated to the well-being of people in Oregon and beyond. As part of its multifaceted public mission, OHSU strives for excellence in education, research, clinical practice and community service.

OHSU includes the state's only academic health center. Through its schools of medicine, dentistry, nursing, and science and engineering, OHSU educates more than 2,600 health and high-technology professionals, scientists, environmental engineers and managers.

In addition to its four schools, Oregon Health and Science University includes OHSU Hospital and Doernbecher Children's Hospital, numerous primary care and speciality clinics, multiple research institutes and interdisciplinary centers, and several outreach and community service units. OHSU hospitals and clinics care for about 170,000 patients annually. More than 1,500 scientists conduct basic and applied research at OHSU in informational, environmental and biomedical sciences. OHSU improves access to care, education and information with hundreds of targeted community service programs.

In total, OHSU occupies more than five million square feet of space throughout Oregon, and will be adding close to 1 million more during the next two-and-a-half years, both at the main campus and in Portland's South Waterfront District.

With more than 11,300 employees, OHSU is Portland's largest corporate employer and the state's fourth largest. The majority of its billion-dollar budget is earned from clinical activities, grants, contracts and gifts. Less than four percent of the university's budget comes from state support. OHSU generates more than 41,000 jobs and fuels more than $2.7 billion in regional economic activity annually.

The university's research program is a major catalyst for Oregon's biotechnology industry. Competitive funding awards have nearly quadrupled during the last decade—from $65 million in 1993 to nearly $256 million in 2003. More than 96 percent of those dollars come from out-of-state sources. The National Institutes of Health ranks OHSU 31st among the 534 domestic higher education institutions competing for research dollars, or 14th among all public higher education institutions. OHSU receives more NIH funding than all other recipients in Oregon.

In 1995 OHSU transformed from a state agency to a public corporation with a governor-appointed board of directors. OHSU continues to coordinate educational activities within the state system of higher education, but is no longer governed by the State Board of Higher Education.

All of OHSU's schools, hospitals and clinics have received the highest accreditation granted nationally. OHSU Hospital has received the National Research Corporation's Consumer Choice Award for the fifth year in a row.

Oregon Institute of Technology
Dr. Martha Anne Dow, President
Address: 3201 Campus Dr., Klamath Falls 97601-8801
Phone: 541-885-1000
Fax: 541-885-1101
E-mail: oit@oit.edu
Web: www.oit.edu

Oregon Institute of Technology (OIT) provides computer-intensive, industry-responsive curricula, and is the only accredited public institute of technology in the Pacific Northwest. The institute offers bachelor's degree programs in engineering, engineering and health technologies, information technology, management, communications and applied sciences. A Master's program in Manufacturing

Engineering Technology will be offered beginning fall 2005. In conjunction with the Oregon Health and Science University, OIT hosts a program in nursing, and offers joint degrees with OHSU in clinical lab science and paramedic education.

The Center for Health Professions is expanding to meet the healthcare industry workforce needs in Oregon. A dental hygiene degree is offered in La Grande in a partnership with Oregon Dental Service and Eastern Oregon University. OIT also offers a Respiratory Care program at Rogue Community College.

OIT interacts regularly with the industries and businesses that employ its graduates. The placement rate for employment or graduate school continues to run above 95 percent, and the average starting salary of the Class of 2002 graduates was $45,000. The college's successful placement rate is based on the uncommon aspects of the university's program offerings and curricula, including extensive lab instructions, clinical and cooperative education experiences and senior projects.

The 2001 Legislature designated OIT as the home of the new Oregon Renewable Energy Center (OREC). OREC offers renewable energy systems applied research with emphasis in photovoltaic power, fuel cell technology, ground source heat exchange, and wind power generation. A bachelor of science degree in Renewable Energy Systems will be offered in Portland in 2005.

Startup funding for OREC came from PacifiCorp, JELD-WEN, Inc. and the U.S. Congress. In addition, OIT has been home to the internationally-known Geo-Heat Center for more than 25 years.

OIT also serves the Portland area with locations in Clackamas County and Washington County. At the Portland area locations, OIT offers bachelor's degree completion programs in electronics, software, manufacturing engineering technology, mechanical engineering technology, management information systems, information technology, and operations management.

Oregon State University
Edward J. Ray, President
Address: Corvallis 97331
Phone: 541-737-0123
Fax: 541-737-2400
Web: http://oregonstate.edu

Oregon State University (OSU) prepares students to excel as working professionals and world citizens by providing a unique blend of academic programs, exemplary scholarly research and an exceptional learning environment within the secure setting of one of the most beautiful campuses in the United States.

As Oregon's oldest state-assisted institution of higher education, founded in 1858 and chartered by the state of Oregon in 1868, OSU is a Carnegie Doctoral/Research-Extensive university. Respected for its teaching, research, and public service, OSU is the only land-, sea-, and space-grant university in the Pacific Northwest.

Undergraduate and graduate degrees can be earned in more than 220 distinct academic programs. With an enrollment of more than 19,000, OSU prepares students to achieve success in agricultural sciences, business, education, engineering, forestry, health and human sciences, liberal arts, oceanography and atmospheric sciences, pharmacy, science, and veterinary medicine. OSU's Honors College and International Studies degree program are available for students who seek additional challenges and opportunities.

A distinguished faculty of 3,200 scholars (including full-time and part-time faculty) attracts more than $175 million each year in external research grants and contracts. OSU faculty are at the forefront of developments in electronic communications, biotechnology, engineering and computer science, gene research, family studies, human and environmental health, forest research, marine science, applied agriculture, and nanotechnology.

OSU's Agricultural Experiment Station and Forest Research Laboratory conduct research and demonstrations in the areas of agriculture and forestry. OSU's Extension Service provides education and information based on timely research to help Oregonians solve problems and develop skills related to agriculture, energy, forestry, family and community development, marine resources, and 4-H youth development. The OSU Food Innovation Center in Portland, the OSU Mark O. Hatfield Marine Sciences Center in Newport and Seafood Laboratory in Astoria symbolize the University's programs in marine-related research, education, and extension activities.

Through the Extended Campus, OSU is making education more accessible. One can complete or start a degree program, retool job skills for professional development, increase employability, and satisfy intellectual curiosity. Most classes are offered through distance technology and are available to students throughout the state, the nation and the world.

Beginning Fall 2001, OSU was given responsibility for administering Oregon's first branch campus. The OSU Cascades Campus in Bend is a unique partnership between OSU, the Central Oregon Community College, the central Oregon community and three partner universities.

OSU energetically serves the people of Oregon, the nation, and the world with a commitment to provide excellent academic programs, educational experiences, and opportunities for creative scholarship.

Portland State University
Daniel O. Bernstine, President
Address: PO Box 751, Portland 97207-0751
Phone: 503-725-3000; Toll-free: 1-800-547-8887
Fax: 503-725-4882

Web: www.pdx.edu

Portland State University, Oregon's only urban university, is the largest and most diverse in the state system. The University's position in Oregon's economic and cultural center allows for deep community engagement and the creation of partnerships with hundreds of organizations throughout the region—partnerships that give PSU students valuable learning opportunities as they solve real-world problems of business and community. Portland State offers more than 100 undergraduate, master's, and doctoral degrees, as well as graduate certificates and continuing education programs. PSU serves more students and confers more master's degrees annually than any other Oregon university. Programs are offered through the College of Liberal Arts and Sciences, College of Urban and Public Affairs, Graduate School of Education, Graduate School of Social Work, Maseeh College of Engineering and Computer Science, School of Business Administration, School of Fine and Performing Arts, and through Extended Studies and Continuing Education programs.

Southern Oregon University
Elisabeth Zinser, President
Address: 1250 Siskiyou Blvd., Ashland 97520
Phone: 541-552-7672
Fax: 541-552-6337
E-mail: admissions@sou.edu
Web: www.sou.edu

Southern Oregon University is a contemporary public liberal arts and sciences university that is regionally responsive, nationally recognized and internationally engaged. It strives to make its top quality education accessible and affordable for students. SOU's rising national reputation is based on its faculty's notable research and creative talents, as well as its practical liberal learning. Its purpose is to provide intellectual and personal growth through quality education. Southern emphasizes critical thinking, career preparation, and capacity to live and lead in a multicultural, global society. SOU is proud of its emerging strengths in scientific fields, its tradition of preparing outstanding teachers and business leaders, and its designation as Oregon's Center of Excellence in the Fine and Performing Arts. It was recently selected to be one of only 21 member institutions in the national Council of Public Liberal Arts Colleges (COPLAC).

SOU offers 100 areas of study including 35 majors in the schools of arts and letters, sciences, social sciences, education, and business at the bachelor's level and 12 graduate programs including management, applied psychology, and several areas of study in education. An Accelerated Baccalaureate Degree Program, select certificates, and other special opportunities are also available. Students may take pre-professional programs for entry into medicine, dentistry, pharmacy, law, theology and other fields. SOU baccalaureate graduates are well-prepared for graduate and professional schools. The University offers nursing through its association with Oregon Health and Science University.

Students get valuable hands-on experiences in research and community projects, internships, and fieldwork that complement their classroom, laboratory, and studio learning. Multicultural opportunities exist with the International Student Exchange and study-abroad programs spanning over 20 countries. One-hundred-fifty international students from 30 countries enrolled for fall term 2003.

The combination of quality academics and a pleasing environment attracts nearly 5,500 students. SOU provides many advantages for students: small class sizes; a student/faculty ratio of 19:1; and classes taught by faculty who have their PhD or the highest degree in their fields (93%), including some who earn grants from the National Endowment for the Humanities and the National Science Foundation and Fullbright Fellowships.

Recent developments at SOU include a new Honors Program, the Center for Visual Arts, a 66,000 square foot complex for art exhibition and education, a newly acquired biotechnology center boasting state-of-the-art molecular biology instrumentation, and the Institute for Environmental Studies. Additionally, the University is nearing completion of a major renovation and expansion of the Hannon Library, slated for grand opening in May 2005. The project will nearly double the size of the library and yield a new learning center with contemporary services and technologies, ample study spaces, seminar rooms, reading areas with fireplaces, and a coffee shop.

The university's beautiful 175 acre campus is located in the community of Ashland, touted in popular guidebooks such as The 100 Best Small Arts Towns in America and Great Towns of America. The University itself was ranked 20th in the nation by Outside magazine (2003) as an ideal place to study, live and work.

University of Oregon
Dave Frohnmayer, President
Address: Eugene 97403
Phone: 541-346-3036
Fax: 541-346-3017
E-mail: pres@oregon.uoregon.edu
Web: www.uoregon.edu

The University of Oregon is a comprehensive teaching and research university that provides students a top-quality education in the liberal arts, sciences, social sciences and professions. As Oregon's flagship public university, it boasts the state's most comprehensive library, highest enrollment, and largest endowment. Recently named a "rising star" among public universities, the UO offers exceptional technological support for students and professors. It was also rated the nation's "Most

Wired" public university and has been judged a "Best Buy" in higher education for the past six years.

The UO's academic reputation is highlighted by its stature as Oregon's only member of the prestigious Association of American Universities, one of just 34 public universities in the United States so honored. Membership in this select group signifies preeminence in graduate and professional education and basic research. The quality of its faculty has been ranked 15th nationally among all U.S. public universities, and the UO's emphasis on top-quality teaching is highlighted by innovative new programs, such as the Oregon Model of small-class undergraduate education.

Located in the southern Willamette Valley city of Eugene, close to beaches, mountains, lakes and forests, the 280-acre main UO campus consists of 84 major buildings surrounded by an arboretum of more than 3,000 specimens of trees. Sunset magazine ranked Eugene one of the West's five best college towns

The combination of strong academic programs, beautiful setting and moderate size draws an annual enrollment of about 20,000, including international students from more than 80 countries.

In addition to a comprehensive College of Arts and Sciences, which includes the Clark Honors College, the university is composed of a graduate school and six professional schools: architecture and allied arts, business, education, journalism and communication, law and music. Degrees and certificates are offered in more than 110 academic majors and minors. The university is the only institution in the state offering doctoral degrees in the arts and humanities and the social sciences, and it places a strong emphasis on research programs in the most advanced areas of basic science. Internationally recognized institutes in molecular biology, neuroscience, materials science, and chemical physics foster interdisciplinary research at the vanguard of science.

Also included among the UO's institutes and research centers are the Oregon Humanities Center, the Institute on Violence and Destructive Behavior, the Center on Human Development, the Oregon Institute of Marine Biology at Charleston on the southern Oregon coast, and the Center for Asian and Pacific Studies.

Western Oregon University
Dr. Philip W. Conn, President
Address: 345 N Monmouth Ave., Monmouth 97361
Phone: 503-838-8000
Fax: 503-838-8474
Web: www.wou.edu

Western Oregon University (WOU) has a tradition of educational excellence dating back to 1856 when it was founded by pioneers who crossed the Oregon Trail. Today, it continues that tradition as a comprehensive liberal arts university. WOU is responding to the educational needs of Oregonians with a broad complement of degree programs, expanded service to the north Oregon coast, and extended distance learning offerings throughout the state.

The university offers more than 40 bachelor's and master's degree programs through its College of Liberal Arts and Sciences and College of Education. In addition to its two academic divisions, WOU's campus is home to the Division of Teaching Research and a Public Service Park. Teaching Research, which is funded annually by more than $6 million in grants, is nationally recognized for its research leading to innovative new methods in teaching and learning. The campus-based Oregon Military Academy and Oregon Public Service Academy make up the Public Service Park and are models for the mutually beneficial sharing of facilities and support services.

WOU athletics continues its competition in the NCAA Division II, after moving the Wolves up from NAIA membership to a higher level of competition.

As a cultural resource, WOU draws audiences from throughout Western Oregon for lectures, visual arts exhibitions, and performing arts programs.

INDEPENDENT COLLEGES AND UNIVERSITIES

Source: Dr. Gary Andeen, Executive Director
Address: Oregon Independent Colleges Association, 7150 SW Hampton St., #101, Portland 97223
Phone: 503-639-4541
Fax: 503-639-4851
E-mail: andeen@oicanet.org

Oregon's private colleges and universities fulfill an important public purpose by providing higher education to 30 percent of the state's four-year college students.

Early pioneers to the Oregon Territory established Willamette University as the first institution of higher learning west of St. Louis in 1842. Ever since, visionary Oregonians have been creating and nurturing high-quality independent colleges and universities supported by students, families, donors and community initiative rather than by taxes or government funding.

The diversity of Oregon's people is reflected in the diversity of these institutions, providing undergraduate liberal arts and sciences curricula, specialized two- and four-year professional and technical training, and a wide range of graduate studies.

Enrolling more than 30,000 students and employing some 5,500 tax-paying Oregonians, these institutions add a combined annual budget of more than $500 million to the state's economy. They keep thousands of Oregonians from leaving the state for specialized college experiences elsewhere, and also attract an additional 12,000 out-of-state students, making Oregon a net importer of high-quality college students.

Educating this number of additional students at our public colleges and universities would require at least $300 million more in state tax dollars per biennium. State taxpayers invest over 30 times more funds per year on an average public college student (in tuition subsidies) than they do on an average independent college student (in state student aid).

The Dividends of Independent Higher Education

Oregon's independent higher education institutions produced 7,698 graduates in the 2001–02 school year. This represented 29 percent of all bachelor's degrees awarded in the state, 35 percent of all master's degrees, and 64 percent of all first professional degrees.

Oregon's independent institutions:

- Convert annually $80 million of gifts from private capital to the public purpose of educating students.
- Attract more than $20 million per year from government contracts for research.
- Teach most classes with experienced professors, not graduate students.
- Sustain a four-year graduation rate more than twice that of public four-year institutions, saving families money in tuition and fees and giving students a head start on a career.
- Offer talented volunteer faculty and students to enrich our communities in government, schools, businesses, social services, religion, and the arts.

Affording a Private College

Independent colleges and universities generally believe the primary responsibility for funding one's higher education belongs to the student and his or her family, assisted as necessary with outside support from public and private aid.

Tuition, however, never covers all the costs of educating a student. Other support includes equipment and facilities donated by others over many years, as well as teachers supported by endowments, and field experiences donated by businesses, schools, and by health, social service and government agencies.

Most students at independent colleges depend on a wide array of direct financial assistance to meet their tuition and other costs. Among the sources of this aid are the colleges themselves, private donors, community scholarship funds, churches, foundations, corporations, and state and federal financial aid programs.

Eighty-five percent of all students at Oregon's independent colleges and universities receive financial assistance totaling more than $350 million per year. All students who desire the distinctive opportunities provided at an independent college or university are encouraged to apply to the colleges of their choice and to request financial aid at the same time. Many students accepted by a private college are surprised to find that the direct cost to them and their families is about the same or even less than that expected at a government-owned institution.

A general Web site for accessing specific information about each of these institutions is: www.ous.edu/one/4yrinsti.htm

The Art Institute of Portland*
Steven Goldman, President
Address: 2000 SW 5th Ave., Portland 97205
Phone: 503-228-6528
Fall 2003 enrollment: 1,326

Cascade College
Dennis Lynn, President
Address: 9101 E Burnside St., Portland 97216
Phone: 503-255-7060
Fall 2003 enrollment: 275

Concordia University*
Charles Schlimpert, President
Address: 2811 NE Holman, Portland 97211
Phone: 503-288-9371
Fall 2003 enrollment: 1,186

Eugene Bible College
David Cole, President
Address: 2155 Bailey Hill Rd., Eugene 97405
Phone: 541-485-1780
Fall 2003 enrollment: 160

George Fox University*
David Brandt, President
Address: 414 N Meridian, Newberg 97132
Phone: 503-538-8383
Fall 2003 enrollment: 2,968

Heald College
Stephen Prisay, Director
Address: 625 SW Broadway, 2nd Flr., Portland 97205
Phone: 503-229-0492
Fall 2003 enrollment: 298

ITT Technical Institute
Wayne Matulich, Director
Address: 6035 NE 78th Ct., Portland 97218
Phone: 503-255-6500
Fall 2003 enrollment: 562

Lewis and Clark College*
Paul Bragdon, President
Address: 0615 SW Palatine Hill Rd., Portland 97219
Phone: 503-768-7000
Fall 2003 enrollment: 3,032

Linfield College*
Vivian Bull, President
Address: 900 SE Baker St., McMinnville 97128
Phone: 503-434-2200
Fall 2003 enrollment: 2,549

Marylhurst University*
Nancy Wilgenbusch, President
Address: PO Box 261, Marylhurst 97036
Phone: 503-636-8141
Fall 2003 enrollment: 1,123

Mount Angel Seminary*
Very Rev. Richard Paperini, President, Rector
Address: St. Benedict 97373
Phone: 503-845-3951
Fall 2003 enrollment: 162

Multnomah Bible College*
Daniel Lockwood, President
Address: 8435 NE Glisan St., Portland 97220
Phone: 503-255-0332
Fall 2003 enrollment: 785

National College of Naturopathic Medicine*
Dr. William Keppler, President
Address: 049 SW Porter St., Portland 97201
Phone: 503-499-4343
Fall 2003 enrollment: 574

Northwest Christian College*
David Wilson, President
Address: 828 11th Ave. E, Eugene 97401
Phone: 541-343-1641
Fall 2003 enrollment: 476

Northwest Film Center
Ellen Thomas, President
Address: 1219 SW Park Ave., Portland 97205
Phone: 541-221-1156
Fall 2003 enrollment: 352

Oregon College of Art and Craft
Bonnie Laing-Malcomsen, President
Address: 8245 SW Barnes Rd., Portland 97225
Phone: 503-297-5544
Fall 2003 enrollment: 129

Oregon College of Oriental Medicine
Elizabeth Goldblatt, President

Address: 10525 SE Cherry Blossom Dr., Portland 97216
Phone: 503-253-3443
Fall 2003 enrollment: 249

Pacific Bible College
Rick Booye, President
Address: 670 Superior Ct., Suite 202, Medford 97504
Phone: 541-776-9942
Fall 2003 enrollment: 64

Pacific Northwest College of Art*
Sally Lawrence, President
Address: 1241 NW Johnson St., Portland 97209
Phone: 503-226-4391
Fall 2003 enrollment: 302

Pacific University*
Phil Creighton, President
Address: 2043 College Way, Forest Grove 97116
Phone: 503-357-6151
Fall 2003 enrollment: 2,376

Pioneer Pacific College
Raymond Gauthier, President
Address: 27501 SW Parkway Ave., Wilsonville 97070
Phone: 503-682-3903
Fall 2003 enrollment: 761

Process Work Center of Portland
Kara Wilde, Director
Address: 2049 NW Hoyt St., Portland 97209
Phone: 503-223-8188
Fall 2003 enrollment: 55

Reed College*
Colin Diver, President
Address: 3203 SE Woodstock Blvd., Portland 97202
Phone: 503-771-1112
Fall 2003 enrollment: 1,312

Salem Bible College
Carly Kendrick, President
Address: 4500 Lancaster Dr. NE, Salem 97305
Phone: 503-304-0092
Fall 2003 enrollment: 38

University of Phoenix
Pat Hardie, Administrator, Oregon Campus
Address: 13221 SW 68th Parkway #500, Tigard 97223
Phone: 503-670-0590
Fall 2003 enrollment: 1,544

University of Portland*
David Tyson, President
Address: 5000 N Willamette Blvd., Portland 97203
Phone: 503-283-7911
Fall 2003 enrollment: 3,195

Walla Walla College School of Nursing
Lucy Krull, Dean
Address: 10345 SE Market, Portland 97216
Phone: 503-251-6115
Fall 2003 enrollment: 93

Warner Pacific College*
Jay Barber Jr., President
Address: 2219 SE 68th Ave., Portland 97215
Phone: 503-517-1000
Fall 2003 enrollment: 510

Western Baptist College* ("Corban College" after May 2005)
Reno Hoff, President
Address: 5000 Deer Park Dr. SE, Salem 97301
Phone: 503-581-8600
Fall 2003 enrollment: 711

Western Business College
Mardell Lanfranco, Executive Director
Address: 425 SW Washington, Portland 97204
Phone: 503-222-3225
Fall 2003 enrollment: 761

Western Seminary*
Bert Downs, President
Address: 5511 SE Hawthorne Blvd., Portland 97215
Phone: 503-233-8561
Fall 2003 enrollment: 626

Western States Chiropractic College*
Joseph Brimhall, President
Address: 2900 NE 132nd Ave., Portland 97230
Phone: 503-256-3180
Fall 2003 enrollment: 372

Willamette University*
Lee Pelton, President
Address: 900 State St., Salem 97301
Phone: 503-370-6300
Fall 2003 enrollment: 2,603

Total Fall 2003 enrollment: 31,529

*Independent institutions accredited by Northwest Commission on Colleges and Universities.

Deer waits for handout—Oregon State Archives Photograph, OHD-G296

Oregon has a large number of organizations that promote greater understanding and appreciation of the arts, history, culture and the physical universe. These resources range greatly in size and location. This section describes some of the opportunities available to Oregonians with an interest in these areas.

CULTURE AND THE ARTS

Source: Christine D'Arcy, Executive Director
Address: Oregon Arts Commission, 775 Summer
St. NE, Suite 200, Salem 97301-1284
Phone: 503-986-0082; TDD: 1-800-735-2900
E-mail: oregon.artscomm@state.or.us
Web: www.oregonartscommission.org

Oregon's tremendous natural beauty is balanced by its citizens' participation in the arts and the value they place on arts, culture and education. Throughout the state, individuals, organizations and local communities collaborate to promote cultural activities for residents and visitors.

From Ashland to Astoria, from the Wallowa Valley Arts Council to the Port Orford Arts Council, Oregonians have ensured that the arts receive attention in their communities. Oregon's annual Governor's Arts Awards recognize the special contributions to the arts made by individuals and others each year.

The Oregon Arts Commission oversees a network of regional and local arts councils, non-profit arts groups as well as arts education programs and services. Providing grant support, technical assistance and information, the commission works to see that access to the arts exists across Oregon. Through regional partnerships it provides local arts programs and services. The commission's Arts Education program links Oregon youth to the arts through residencies with professional artists and training for teachers. The Arts Builds Communities initiative supports community cultural collaborations with funding and resource team training. Oregon's growing population of individual artists, writers and performers are assisted through its Fellowship program.

Oregonians recognize that maintaining their quality of life goes beyond protection of the natural environment. The legislature passed one of the first laws providing that one percent of funding for all new and remodeled state buildings be used to purchase or commission works of art. Communities in Multnomah and Lane Counties have also established art in public places programs, resulting in the integration of artwork in the designs for light rail, airports, streets and other public spaces.

Oregon's arts and cultural industry has economic value. The non-profit industry alone employs more than 28,000 people and generates $64 million annually. With indirect spending included, the arts contribute more than $250 million to the state's economy, and play an even more significant role in regional economic development areas such as tourism, graphic and product design, and other creative fields.

Oregon's Largest Arts Organizations

Oregon Shakespeare Festival

Libby Appel, Artistic Director
Paul Nicholson, Executive Director
Address: PO Box 158, Ashland 97520
Phone: 541-482-2111
Fax: 541-482-0446
Web: www.osfashland.org

The Oregon Shakespeare Festival is one of the largest non-profit theaters in the U.S. Established in 1935, it has an annual attendance of more than 340,000. It presents eleven plays in repertory from mid-February through October on its three stages. The festival also offers backstage tours, classes, lectures, concerts, and play readings.

Oregon Symphony Association

William Ryberg, President
Address: 921 SW Washington St., Suite 200, Portland 97205
Phone: 503-416-6339
Web: www.orsymphony.com

With Carlos Kalmar, music director, the association is a major professional orchestra performing an extensive and varied menu of musical services to an equally varied audience. Performances include the classical concert series, pops concerts, youth and educational concerts, family concerts and special performances, as well as touring concerts throughout the state.

Portland Art Museum

John E. Buchanan Jr., Executive Director
Address: 1219 SW Park Ave., Portland 97205
Phone: 503-226-2811
Web: www.portlandartmuseum.org

The Portland Art Museum, founded in 1892, is the region's oldest and largest visual and media arts center, and one of the state's greatest cultural assets. The museum's treasures span 35 centuries of international art.

The museum's strengths include: the renowned Rasmussen Collection of Northwest Coast Native American art; Chinese tomb figures and archaic bronzes; Japanese ukiyo-e prints and paintings; 22,000 prints, photographs and drawings housed in the Gilkey Center for Graphic Arts; European and American paintings and sculpture; and regional contemporary art.

The museum's Northwest Film Center is widely acclaimed for its school of film, statewide artist-in-schools programs and year-round exhibition program highlighted by the annual Portland International Film Festival held each February. The museum's Eye on Art school tours for children bring more than 30,000 students to the museum annually.

Portland Opera
Christopher Mattaliano, General Director
Address: 211 SE Caruthers St., Portland 97214
Phone: 503-241-1407
Fax: 503-241-4212
Web: www.portlandopera.org

Internationally renowned singers perform with the Portland Opera Orchestra and Chorus in a four-production season of opera. Although sung in their original languages, the operas are easily understandable to all patrons, thanks to the Opera's projected English translations. The Opera's efforts are not limited to the Keller Auditorium stage or the opera season. The company's Education and Outreach programs continue year-round, including fully staged traveling opera productions that tour the state, in-school programs, student dress rehearsals, pre- and post-performance lectures, and costume shop and backstage tours.

In addition to its Opera productions, the company also presents "Fred Meyer Broadway in Portland" which delights regional audiences with ten weeks of nationally touring Broadway productions each year.

Regional Arts Councils

Arts Central
Cate O'Hagan, Executive Director
Address: 875 NW Brooks St., Bend 97701
Phone: 541-317-9324
Fax: 541-317-5653
E-mail: info@artscentraloregon.org
Web: www.artscentraloregon.org

Serving Crook, Deschutes and Jefferson Counties.

Arts Council of Southern Oregon
Lyn Godsey, Executive Director
Address: 33 N Central, Suite 300, Medford 97501
Phone: 541-779-2820
Fax: 541-772-4945
E-mail: office@artscouncilso.org
Web: www.artscouncilso.org

Serving Josephine and Jackson Counties.

Columbia Gorge
Columbia Center for the Arts
Judie Hanel, Executive Director
Address: PO Box 1543, Hood River 97031
Phone: 541-387-8877
Fax: 541-386-6547
Web: www.artsinthegorge.org

Serving the Columbia River Gorge.

Columbia Gorge Arts in Education
Leith Gains, Executive Director
Address: PO Box 920, Hood River 97031

Phone: 541-387-5031
Fax: 541-386-7198
E-mail: lgains@hoodriver.k12.or.us

Eastern Oregon Regional Arts Council
Jane Howell, Executive Director
Address: EOU/131 Zabel Hall, La Grande 97850
Phone: 541-962-3624
Fax: 541-962-3596
E-mail: eorac@eou.edu
Web: www3.eou.edu/eorac

Serving Baker, Gilliam, Grant, Harney, Malheur, Morrow, Umatilla, Union, Wallowa and Wheeler Counties.

Lane Arts Council
Andrew Toney, Executive Director
Address: 99 W 10th Ave., Suite 100, Eugene 97401
Phone: 541-485-2278
Fax: 541-485-2478
E-mail: lanearts@lanearts.org
Web: www.lanearts.org

Serving Lane County.

Linn-Benton Arts Council
Victoria Fridley, Executive Director
Address: Corvallis Arts Center, 700 SW Madison Ave., Corvallis 97333
Phone: 541-754-1551
Fax: 541-754-1552
E-mail: victoria@artcentric.org
Web: html://artcentric.org

Serving Linn and Benton Counties.

Oregon Coast Council for the Arts
Frank Geltner, Executive Director
Address: PO Box 1315, Newport 97365
Phone: 541-265-9231; Toll-free: 1-888-701-7123
Fax: 541-265-9464
E-mail: occa@coastarts.org
Web: www.coastarts.org

Serving Clatsop, Coos, Curry, Lincoln and Tillamook Counties, and coastal parts of Lane and Douglas Counties.

Regional Arts and Culture Council
Eloise Damrosch, Executive Director
Address: 108 NW 9th Ave., Suite 300, Portland 97209
Phone: 503-823-5111
Fax: 503-823-5432
E-mail: info@racc.org
Web: www.racc.org

Serving Clackamas, Multnomah and Washington Counties.

Umpqua Valley Arts Association
Shawn Ramsey, Executive Director
Address: PO Box 1105, Roseburg 97470
Phone: 541-672-2532
Fax: 541-672-7696
E-mail: shawn@uvarts.com
Web: www.uvarts.com
Serving Douglas County.

Local and Regional Arts Agencies in Oregon

Astoria
Astor Street Opry Company
Address: 279 W Marine Dr., PO Box 743, Astoria 97103
Phone: 503-325-6104
Web: www.shanghaiedinastoria.com

Baker City
Crossroads Center for the Creative and Performing Arts
Address: 1901 Main St., Baker City 97814
Phone: 541-523-5369
E-mail: crossroads@webcom.com
Web: www.crossroads-arts.org

Beaverton
Beaverton Arts Commission
Address: PO Box 4755, Beaverton 97076
Phone: 503-526-2288
Fax: 503-526-2479
E-mail: jscott@ci.beaverton.or.us
Web: www.ci.beaverton.or.us/departments/arts

Brookings
Brookings Area Council for the Arts
Address: PO Box 1737, Brookings 97415
Phone: 541-469-3181
Fax: 541-469-4094
E-mail: chamber@brookingsor.com

Burns
Harney County Arts & Crafts
Address: 7555 Imperial, Burns 97720
Phone: 541-573-2610

Cannon Beach
Cannon Beach Arts Association
Address: 1064 S Hemlock, PO Box 684, Cannon Beach 97110
Phone: 503-436-0744
E-mail: info@cannonbeacharts.org

Condon
Greater Condon Arts Association
Address: PO Box 165, Condon 97823
Phone: 541-384-5114
Fax: 541-384-5114
E-mail: boydharris@jncable.com

Coquille
Coquille Valley Art Association
Address: 10144 Hwy. 42, Coquille 97423
Phone: 541-396-3294

Elgin
Elgin Opera House Theatre
Address: PO Box 894, Elgin 97827
Phone: 541-437-3456
Fax: 541-437-3456
E-mail: operahsetheatre@eoni.com

Enterprise
Wallowa Valley Arts Council
Address: PO Box 526, Joseph 97846
Phone: 541-432-7535
Fax: 541-432-7535
E-mail: gilbertc@starband.net

Florence
Florence Arts & Crafts Association
Address: PO Box 305, Florence 97439
Phone: 541-997-5034

Florence Performing Arts Association
Address: 715 Quince St., Florence 97439
Phone: 541-997-1994

Forest Grove
Valley Art Association
Address: 2022 Main St., PO Box 333, Forest Grove 97116
Phone: 503-357-3703

Gladstone
Clackamas County Arts Council
Address: 1777 SE Kirkwood Rd., Gladstone 97027
Phone: 503-656-9543

Grants Pass
Grants Pass Museum of Art
Address: PO Box 966, Grants Pass 97528
Phone: 541-479-3290
E-mail: museum@gpmuseum.com
Web: www.gpmuseum.com

Gresham
Gresham Art Advisory Committee
Address: 1333 NW Eastman Pkwy., Gresham 97030
Phone: 503-618-2360
Fax: 503-665-7692
E-mail: Connie.Otto@ci.gresham.or.us
Web: www.ci.gresham.or.us/departments/ocm/cacs/

Halfway
Cornucopia Arts Council
Address: PO Box 353, Halfway 97834
Phone: 541-742-6315

Harbor
Pelican Bay Arts Association
Address: PO Box 2568, Harbor 97415
Phone: 541-469-1807
E-mail: waterfrontart@aol.com

Hillsboro
Hillsboro Community Arts
Address: PO Box 3303, Hillsboro 97123
Phone: 503-648-3979
Fax: 503-648-5598
E-mail: info@HCAonline.org
Web: www.hcaonline.org

Hood River
Columbia Gorge Regional Arts Association
Address: 101 Fourth St., PO Box 516, Hood River 97031
Phone: 541-386-4512
E-mail: columbiaartgallery@gorge.net
Web: www.columbiaartgallery.org

Irrigon
Morrow County Arts Council
Address: PO Box 343, Irrigon 97844
Phone: 541-932-4799
Web: www3.eou.edu/eorac/organizations/morrow.html

John Day
Juniper Arts Council
Address: PO Box 101, John Day 97845
Phone: 541-575-2492

Joseph
Wallowa Valley Arts Council
Address: PO Box 526, Joseph 97846
Phone: 541-432-7535
Fax: 541-432-7535
E-mail: gilbertc@starband.net

Keizer
Keizer Art Association
Address: 980 Chemawa Rd. NE, Keizer 97307
Phone: 503-390-3010

Klamath Falls
Klamath Art Association
Address: 120 Riverside Dr., Klamath Falls 97601
Phone: 541-883-1833
E-mail: KlamathArtAssoc@aol.com
Web: http://hometown.aol.com/klamathartassoc/myhomepage/artgallery.html

Klamath Arts Council
Address: PO Box 1706, Klamath Falls 97601
Phone: 541-883-2009
E-mail: patzberg@jeffnet.org

Ross Ragland Theater
Address: 218 N 7th St., Klamath Falls 97601
Phone: 541-884-0651

Fax: 541-884-8574
E-mail: rrt@rrtheater.org
Web: www.rrtheater.org

Lake Oswego
Lake Oswego Arts Commission
Address: 1099 Cherry Circle, Lake Oswego 97034
Phone: 503-636-4189

Lake Oswego Crafts & Art League
Address: PO Box 1854, Lake Oswego 97035
Phone: 503-241-8939

Lincoln City
Coastal Communities Cultural Center (4 Cs)
Address: PO Box 752, Lincoln City 97367
Gallery: 801 SW Hyw 101
Phone: 541-994-9994

Madras
Jefferson County Arts Association
Address: PO Box 376, Madras 97741
Phone: 541-475-7701
E-mail: coraleepopp@yahoo.com

McMinnville
Arts Alliance of Yamhill County
Address: PO Box 898, McMinnville 97128
Phone: 503-472-3784
Fax: 503-472-2496
E-mail: marlenab@comcast.net
Web: www.artharveststudiotour.org

Medford
Medford Parks and Recreation Department
Address: 411 W 8th, Rm. 225, Medford 97501
Phone: 541-774-2400
Fax: 541-774-2560
Web: www.ci.medford.or.us

Rogue Gallery & Arts Center
Address: 40 S Bartlett, Medford 97501
Phone: 541-772-8118
Web: www.roguegallery.org

Milwaukie
North Clackamas Art Guild
Address: PO Box 22676, Milwaukie 97269
Phone: 503-654-1398

Monmouth
Monmouth/Independence Community Arts Association
Address: PO Box 114, Monmouth 97361
Phone: 503-838-5182

Nehalem
The Art Ranch
Address: 39450 Northfork Rd., Nehalem 97131
Phone: 503-368-7160
Fax: 503-368-7656
E-mail: lortiz@nehalemtel.net

Ontario

Four Rivers Cultural Center
Address: 676 SW 5th Ave., Ontario 97914
Phone: 541-889-8191
Fax: 541-889-7628
E-mail: sbriggs@fmtc.com
Web: www.4rcc.com

Oregon City

Arts Action Alliance of Clackamas County
Address: PO Box 2181, Oregon City 97045
Phone: 503-655-0525
E-mail: artsaction@hevanet.com
Web: www.co.clackamas.or.us/artsaction

Pendleton

Arts Council of Pendleton
Address: 214 N Main St., Pendleton 97801
Phone: 541-278-9201
Fax: 541-278-9202
E-mail: artscntr@uci.net
Web: www.pendletonarts.org

Port Orford

Port Orford Arts Council
Address: 736 Oregon St. (Hwy. 101), PO Box
771, Port Orford 97465
Phone: 541-332-1140
Fax: 541-332-8508
E-mail: info@portorfordart.com
Web: www.portorfordart.org

Salem

Arts In Oregon Council (AOC)
Address: 3445 Dogwood Dr. S, Salem 97302
Phone: 503-399-1194
E-mail: lee.andy@comcast.com

Salem Art Association
Address: 600 Mission St. SE, Salem 97302
Phone: 503-581-2228
Fax: 503-371-3342
E-mail: info@salemart.org
Web: www.salemart.org

Scappoose

Columbia Arts Guild
Address: PO Box 105, Scappoose 97056
Phone: 503-397-9174
Web: www.columbia-center.org/home/webs/art

Silverton

Silverton Arts Association
Address: 303 Coolidge St., Silverton 97381
Phone: 503-873-2480
E-mail: silverton.artist@verizon.net
Web: www.silvertonarts.org

Springfield

Emerald Empire Art Association
Address: 500 Main St., Springfield 97477
Phone: 541-726-8595

Fax: 541-726-2954
E-mail: emerald@eped.net
Web: www.emeraldartcenter.org

Springfield Arts Commission
Address: 225 Fifth St., Springfield 97477
Phone: 541-726-2287
Fax: 541-726-3747

Tillamook

Five River Gallery
Address: PO Box 634, Tillamook 97141
Phone: 503-842-1244

Tualatin

Tualatin Arts Advisory Committee
Address: 18880 SW Martinazzi Ave., Tualatin
97062
Phone: 503-691-3060
Fax: 503-691-9786
Web: www.ci.tualatin.or.us/living/arts/arts_index.htm

Welches

Wy'east Artisans Guild
Address: PO Box 272, Welches 97067
Phone: 503-622-3607

West Linn

West Linn Arts Commission
Address: 3910 Mapleton Dr., West Linn 97068
Phone: 503-675-9522
Web: westlinnartscommission.org

Wilsonville

Wilsonville Arts and Cultural Council
Address: PO Box 861, Wilsonville 97070
Phone: 503-638-6933
E-mail: c-music@pcez.com

Woodburn

Woodburn Art Center
Address: 2551 N Boones Ferry Rd., Woodburn
97071
Phone: 503-982-6450
E-mail: wbartctr@open.org
Web: www.open.org/~wbartctr

OREGON HISTORY ORGANIZATIONS

Oregonians are proud of their state's history.
Many organizations are dedicated to various
aspects of Oregon history. Some of these are listed
below.

Oregon's Major Heritage and History Organizations

Oregon State Archives
Roy Turnbaugh, State Archivist
Address: 800 Summer St. NE, Salem 97310

Phone: 503-373-0701
Fax: 503-373-0953
E-mail: archives.info@state.or.us
Web: arcweb.sos.state.or.us

The Archives Division, established in 1947, houses and provides access to the permanently valuable records of Oregon government. Oldest documents at the archives include records of the provisional and territorial governments and the Oregon Constitution.

The division authorizes disposition of the public records of Oregon government, provides records management advice and assistance to state agencies and political subdivisions and operates the State Records Center which provides inexpensive storage for inactive state agency records. The division also files, codifies and publishes state agency administrative rules and publishes the *Oregon Blue Book*.

End of the Oregon Trail Interpretive Center
David M. Porter, Executive Director
Address: 1726 Washington St., Oregon City 97045
Phone: For hours and admission: 503-657-9336
Fax: 503-557-8590
E-mail: trlboss@att.net
Web: www.endoftheoregontrail.org

At the End of the Oregon Trail Interpretive Center, visitors step back in time 160 years to those days when "Oregon Fever" swept the country like wildfire. Hundreds of thousands of people crossed this land on the Oregon Trail in search of a dream, in search of a new life, in search of the "land at Eden's Gate."

Visitors first enter the Missouri Provisioners Depot. Interpreters dressed in period clothing present the story about the struggles of the times and how pioneers were lured by tales of the bountiful Oregon Territory. Supplies and provisions were carefully selected for the long arduous journey.

The westward trip is recreated in the Cascade Theater. *Bound for Oregon*, a compelling digital experience, traces the journey of four real pioneers in their own words. Native voices and the narration of Dr. John McLoughlin complete the story. Daily life along the trail comes alive as fictitious characters recount the adventures, emotions and stories of their own journeys.

Arrival in Oregon City is the final stop. The Oregon City Gallery features a fine collection of artifacts such as a Barlow Road toll book, clothing, tools and household items. The George Abernethy Store offers a variety of Oregon products and heritage items. Living history interpreters engage visitors in "hands on" demonstrations and exhibits of daily life in pioneer times.

The Center site offers seasonal historic displays. In the gardens are two historic markers acknowledging the End of the Oregon Trail. The Willamette Chapter of the Daughters of the American Revolution erected a marker in 1917. The U.S. Congress recognized the western terminus of the trail in 1976.

The End of the Oregon Trail Interpretive Center, also the site of the I-205 State Welcome Center, is open daily, except Thanksgiving, Christmas and New Year's Day.

The Museum at Warm Springs
Carol Leone, Executive Director
Address: PO Box 909, Warm Springs 97761
Phone: 541-553-3331
Fax: 541-553-3338
Web: www.warmsprings.biz/museum/

Completed in early 1993, The Museum at Warm Springs was created by the Confederated Tribes of the Warm Springs Reservation of Oregon to preserve the traditions of the Warm Springs, Wasco and Paiute tribes and to keep alive their legacy. The museum's celebrated permanent collection includes treasured artifacts, historic photographs, narratives, graphics, murals and rare documents.

Traditional dwellings, a tule mat lodge, wickiup and plankhouse have been meticulously constructed to show life as it was long ago.

The changing exhibit gallery explores all dimensions of the Native American experience, past and present: exhibitions, programs and lectures by prominent Native American scholars, artists and poets are perfectly framed. The summer months feature live demonstrations of drumming, dancing, storytelling, bead-working and hide-tanning. A gift shop offers an impressive array of books and tapes on Native American cultures as well as traditional beadwork, silver jewelry, baskets and other Native American crafts.

Museum hours are 9 a.m. to 5 p.m. From March to November, the museum is open every day. During the winter, the museum is closed Mondays and Tuesdays, as well as Thanksgiving, Christmas and New Year's Day.

National Historic Oregon Trail Interpretive Center
Sarah LeCompte, Center Director
Address: PO Box 987, Baker City 97814
Phone: 541-523-1843
Fax: 541-523-1834
Web: http://oregontrail.blm.gov

Operated by the U.S. Department of Interior's Bureau of Land Management, the National Historic Oregon Trail Interpretive Center is located at Flagstaff Hill on Highway 86, five miles east of Baker City. The 509-acre site features a 23,000 square-foot facility with permanent exhibits offering audio, video, dioramas and artifacts to recreate the experiences of Oregon Trail emigrants. The Interpretive Center also includes exhibits on

Arts, History and Sciences

Native American culture, mining and history of the BLM. A 150-seat theater hosts an active schedule of lectures and performances.

From atop Flagstaff Hill, visitors see more than 13 miles of the Oregon Trail route. Visitors may also view close-up trail ruts at the base of Flagstaff Hill. During the summer, living history characters interpret pioneer life at a wagon encampment.

The center is open daily from 9 a.m. to 6 p.m., April 1 to October 31 and 9 a.m. to 4 p.m., November 1 to March 31. It is closed Thanksgiving, Christmas and New Year's Day. Please call for admission prices.

Oregon Commission on Historic Cemeteries
Mirra Meyer, Coordinator
Address: 725 Summer St. NE, Salem 97301
Phone: 503-986-0685
Fax: 503-986-0794
E-mail: Mirra.Meyer@state.or.us

The Oregon Commission on Historic Cemeteries (OCHC) consists of seven citizens who have broad knowledge of the issues relating to preservation, restoration and upkeep of historic burial sites, and to the importance of historic and pioneer era burial grounds in Oregon history. Old cemeteries are a visible record of community history, and frequently serve as outdoor museums that preserve the architecture, sculptural forms, traditional landscaping, and literary styles of the past.

In 1999 the Oregon Legislature established a statewide commission (ORS 97.772–97.784) to assist in the coordination of restoration, renovation and maintenance of historic cemeteries statewide. Originally named the Oregon Pioneer Cemetery Commission, in 2003 the board was re-titled Oregon Commission on Historic Cemeteries in recognition of the need for protection of all historic cemeteries.

The OCHC was empowered by the legislature to develop and maintain a listing of all pioneer and historic cemeteries and gravesites in Oregon; to make recommendations for funding, obtain grants funding, and seek legislative appropriations for historic cemeteries; and to assist in obtaining technical assistance on the care of artifacts such as grave markers, structures, railings and curbs, ironwork, fencing, and plantings. Landmark legislation was recently passed that provides stricter laws protecting historic cemeteries against vandalism.

Oregon Council for the Humanities
Christopher Zinn, Ph.D., Executive Director
Address: 812 SW Washington, Suite 225, Portland 97205
Phone: 503-241-0543; Toll-free: 1-800-735-0543
Fax: 503-241-0024
E-mail: och@oregonhum.org
Web: www.oregonhum.org

The Oregon Council for the Humanities (OCH) seeks to improve the quality of life for Oregonians by providing programs that enrich minds and broaden perspectives, foster positive human relationships, encourage civility and good citizenship, and bring together the diverse peoples who make up our statewide culture.

In carrying out its mission, the Council works to:
- Promote an understanding of the humanities, and the role of thoughts and ideas in our lives.
- Support scholarship and discussion that address social, cultural, and public issues.
- Build community and connectedness among Oregonians.
- Reach Oregonians of all ages, cultures, and backgrounds in all areas of the state.
- Encourage productive interaction between humanities scholars and the public.
- Advocate a widening role for the humanities in public and private life.

Council programs include Oregon Chautauqua, Humanity in Perspective, Young Scholars, *Oregon Humanities* magazine, Teacher Institutes, Public Program Grants, Research Grants, *Verso,* and *On Principle.*

OCH was established in 1971, and is an independent affiliate of the National Endowment for the Humanities. The NEH provides the organization's principal funding, with additional support from foundations, corporations and individuals throughout Oregon.

Oregon Geographic Names Board
Champ C. Vaughan, President; Sharon Nesbit, Vice-President; Dr. John C. Pierce, Secretary
Address: 1200 SW Park Ave., Portland 97205
Phone: 503-222-1741
Fax: 503-221-2035
E-mail: orhist@ohs.org

Founded in 1908, the board is an advisor to the United States Board on Geographic Names, and is associated with the Oregon Historical Society which maintains the board's correspondence and records. It is comprised of 25 appointed board members representing all geographic areas of the state and is served by advisors from government agencies and the private sector.

The board supervises the naming of all geographic features within the state to standardize geographic nomenclature, prevent confusion and duplication in naming geographic features, and correct previous naming errors. The board's recommendations are submitted to the U.S. Board in Washington, D.C. for final action.

Oregon Historical Society
Dr. John C. Pierce, Executive Director; Robert Gregg, President
Address: 1200 SW Park Ave., Portland 97205
Phone: 503-222-1741; TDD: 503-306-5194

Fax: 503-221-2035
E-mail: orhist@ohs.org
Web: www.ohs.org

For more than 100 years, the Oregon Historical Society (OHS) has provided a place for history—a home for Oregon heritage, culture, beginnings and future. The Society has expanded far beyond its original mission of collecting, preserving, publishing and sharing Oregon's rich history. Today, OHS offers a broad array of educational, interpretive, technical assistance and field services programs. Attractions include exhibits covering a wide range of historical topics; lectures and special events; a museum store; and the research library with its wealth of books, maps, documents, oral histories, photographs and film footage. OHS also publishes books about the history of Oregon and the Pacific Northwest, operates educational programs for children and adults, and provides outreach services to other historical societies. The Oregon Historical Society Museum is open Tuesday through Saturday from 10 a.m. to 5 p.m. and on Sunday from noon to 5 p.m. Museum Store is open Monday through Saturday, 10 a.m. to 5 p.m., and on Sunday from noon to 5 p.m. Admission is charged for the museum (OHS members free). The Research Library is open Wednesday 1–5 p.m. (OHS members only) and Thursday through Saturday from 1 to 5 p.m. Admission pays for access to both Museum and Research Library.

Oregon Historic Trails Advisory Council

James M. Hamrick, Deputy State Historic Preservation Officer
Address: 725 Summer St. NE, Suite C, Salem 97301
Phone: 503-986-0669
Fax: 503-986-0796
Web: http://egov.oregon.gov./OPRD/HCD/ohtac.shtml

The Oregon Historic Trails Advisory Council (OHTAC) was established by Executive Order 98–16 to recognize all Oregon historic trails as outlined in ORS 358.057. The council is a nine-member committee appointed by the governor and formed to promote public awareness of the significance of Oregon's historic trails as well as to advise a variety of public and private agencies and organizations on policy matters. The council is Oregon's official liaison to other states, associations and federal agencies in acquiring national as well as state recognition of Oregon's historic trails.

The OHTAC represents three National Historic Trails in Oregon—the Lewis and Clark Trail, the Applegate Trail and Nez Perce Trail—as well as five alternative routes to the Oregon Trail, and seven other major Oregon historic trails.

With the 1998 Oregon Historic Trails Report as a work program, the council also encourages the development, protection and interpretation of historical sites and outdoor recreation resources along their routes.

NATURAL SCIENCES AND TECHNOLOGY

Oregon has a varied set of facilities designed to help children and adults learn about a changing world. Along with the many visitors centers available in state and national parks and forest areas, other independent centers teach visitors about the natural world and encourage them to speculate about those things yet to be learned.

Oregon's Major Industry, Science and Technology Organizations

The High Desert Museum

Forrest B. Rodgers, President
Address: 59800 S Hwy. 97, Bend 97702-7963
Phone: 541-382-4754
Fax: 541-382-5256
Web: www.highdesertmuseum.org

The High Desert Museum, located just 3.5 miles south of Bend, is nationally acclaimed for its indoor and outdoor exhibits and naturalistic animal habitats—and for making the High Desert come alive through presentations on the region's people, cultures, science, art, and history.

The private, non-profit museum contributes to the Northwest's educational and cultural vitality through its permanent and changing exhibits, education programs for students in grades K–12, public education programs, and excursions to historically, culturally, and geologically significant locations throughout the High Desert region.

Major permanent exhibits include the Earle A. Chiles Center on the Spirit of the West, the Henry J. Casey Hall of Plateau Indians, and the Donald M. Kerr Birds of Prey Center featuring naturalistic habitats for its "Raptors of the Desert Sky" exhibit. Outdoors, the museum offers extensive natural trails and wildlife viewing areas, including the "Wind, Earth, and Fire" interpretive fire trail. North American river otters can be found frolicking in the stream at the naturalistic Autzen Otter Exhibit, and porcupines also make their daily appearance. The museum's 100-year-old working saw mill and pioneer homestead round out its outdoor highlights.

Truly a museum for the adventurous at heart, The High Desert Museum is open every day except Thanksgiving, Christmas, and New Year's Day. The museum is funded solely by visitors, members, and donors.

Malheur Field Station

Duncan Evered and Lyla Messick, Directors
Address: 34848 Sodhouse Ln., Princeton 97721
Phone: 541-493-2629
Fax: 541-493-2629

E-mail: mfs@oregontrail.net
Web: www.malheurfieldstation.org

Malheur Field Station is an environmental education and research center located in the northern Great Basin region in southeastern Oregon. It is operated by the Great Basin Society, a non-profit organization founded in 1985. Its mission is dedicated to the concept that learning is a lifelong process. This philosophy is achieved by providing public lectures, accredited and non-accredited courses, professional development workshops, Elderhostel programs, in-service teacher education, and scout projects. It also serves as host to individuals, families, birding groups, K-12 school groups, and other organizations and agencies. A member-based consortium of 19 northwest universities, colleges, and education organizations guides the academic programs. Individual and Family Membership (Friends of Malheur) benefits include newsletters, bookstore and lodging discounts.

Located on Malheur National Wildlife Refuge, 32 miles south of Burns the field station is surrounded by a unique and diverse setting of extensive marshland, desert basins, alkali playas, upland desert scrub steppe, volcanic and glacial landforms, and fault block mountains. As such, the Malheur Field Station provides a rich outdoor classroom for the biologist, geologist, archaeologist, artist, astronomer, environmental science student or visitor interested in the cultural or natural history of the region.

Lodging and food services are available to the public from April through September, with the option of limited lodging available during the winter season. Accommodations are basic but clean, ranging from dormitories and kitchenettes to trailers and RV hook-ups. Guests provide their own sleeping bag or linens, pillow and towel. The dining hall serves cafeteria-style, healthy breakfasts and dinners, and offers sack lunches for field trips.

Other facilities for group use include conference rooms, classrooms, darkrooms, audio visual room and equipment, a natural science library, and recreational buildings. The field station's Natural History Museum exhibits and bookstore are open to the public. The station also houses a significant collection of regional desert and mountain flora and fauna specimens used by researchers.

Oregon Coast Aquarium, Inc.

Patrick Helbling, Acting President; Cindy McEntee, Board Chair
Address: 2820 SE Ferry Slip Rd., Newport 97365
Phone: 541-867-3474
Fax: 541-867-6846
E-mail: info@aquarium.org
Web: www.aquarium.org

The Oregon Coast Aquarium, located in Newport, is a non-profit institution occupying a 32-acre site on Yaquina Bay, adjacent to the Oregon State University Mark O. Hatfield Marine Science Center. Aquarium exhibits are housed in an 80,000 square-foot building and on six acres of elaborately rocked pools, caves, cliffs and bluffs.

Indoor exhibits include four galleries replicating habitats found in coastal wetlands, sandy and rocky shores, and off Oregon's coast in deeper waters. Also indoors are a demonstration lab, US WEST Whale Theater, changing exhibit area, full-service cafe and gift shop. Outdoor exhibits include sea otters; harbor seals and sea lions; wave-pummeled tide pools; a coastal cave featuring a giant Pacific octopus; the largest walk-through seabird aviary in North America; a nature trail and a children's play area. The aquarium is open every day except Christmas and is handicap accessible.

Oregon Museum of Science and Industry (OMSI)

Nancy Stueber, President; Dave Vernier, Board Chair
Address: 1945 SE Water Ave., Portland 97214-3354
Phone: 503-797-4000
Fax: 503-797-4566
Web: www.omsi.edu

Established in 1944, the Oregon Museum of Science and Industry (OMSI) is an independent, non-tax-based educational and cultural resource center with an international reputation for excellence in science exhibitry and informal science education. OMSI is dedicated to improving the public's understanding of science and technology through a wide variety of innovative science programming. Approximately 870,000 people visit the museum and participate in OMSI's programs every year.

In 1992 OMSI moved to a beautiful, 18.5-acre riverside campus on the east bank of the Willamette River in downtown Portland. The complex includes five exhibit halls, seven interactive science labs, a state-of-the-art planetarium, a 300-seat, five-story, domed OMNIMAX Theater, and the 219-foot *USS Blueback* submarine moored just outside the building in the river. The museum also has a river view café, a science store stocked with hundreds of educational fun toys and an extensive bookstore.

In addition to the exhibits on permanent display, OMSI designs and builds science exhibits for travel to other science centers nationwide. Currently, OMSI has more than 25 exhibits in circulation — more than any other science museum in the country.

OMSI also boasts one of the most extensive science education programs in the world and serves 180,000 annually. OMSI Outreach brings a unique brand of traveling science education to more than 156,000 students in seven western states. OMSI Teacher Education programs provide programming to more than 1,300 teachers each year, and OMSI camps serve close to 10,200 children and provide approximately 328,000 hours of science instruction annually. OMSI's education programs also include classes, after-school science classes and camp-ins.

OMSI is open Tuesday through Sunday from 9:30 a.m. to 5:30 p.m. from Labor Day through mid-June and is open daily from 9:30 a.m. to 7:00 p.m. from mid-June through Labor Day. Open all holidays except Thanksgiving and Christmas. Museum admission is $8.50 for adults and $6.50 for youth (3–13) and seniors (63+). Group rates are available, and OMSI offers two-for-one discounts on Thursdays after 2:00 p.m. For theater schedules and general information visit our web site.

Oregon State University Hatfield Marine Science Center

Dr. George W. Boehlert, Director
Address: 2030 S Marine Science Dr., Newport 97365
Phone: 541-867-0212
Fax: 541-867-0138
E-mail: monita.cheever@oregonstate.edu
Web: http://hmsc.oregonstate.edu

The Hatfield Marine Science Center (HMSC) is a research center of Oregon State University (OSU) located on the south side of the Yaquina Bay estuary, adjacent to the Oregon Coast Aquarium. The public wing with its beloved touch pool and octopus tank was completely remodeled and redesigned in 1996 with the theme "Searching for Patterns in a Complex World." Frequently changing interactive exhibits and computer simulations enable visitors to play the role of scientific explorers using some of the current research underway at the center. Core exhibits highlight how people discover patterns at the global, bird's eye, human, and microscopic scale. Admission is free (though donations are encouraged).

The bookstore is stocked with marine, nearshore and estuarine books, posters, science kits and tools for all ages. Informal education programs are offered in the auditorium, along the estuary nature trail, beside the docks and in workshops. Hands-on laboratories are available for school and organized groups with prior reservations, and a dedicated corps of volunteers assists visitors with their individual explorations. The public wing accommodates those with special needs.

Behind the scenes, undergraduate and graduate courses are offered and the center serves as a coastal research park for scientists with OSU as well as with the Environmental Protection Agency, National Marine Fisheries Service, U.S. Fish and Wildlife Service, Oregon Department of Fish and Wildlife, the USDA's Agricultural Research Service, and the National Oceanic and Atmospheric Administration's Pacific Marine Environmental Laboratory. It is served by the Guin Library, the branch of the OSU Library that specializes in marine resource materials. The Coastal Oregon Marine Experiment Station and the Cooperative Institute for Marine Resources Studies are also located at the center. The general research theme involves understanding, conservation, and sustainable use of our coastal and ocean ecosystems.

Oregon Zoo

Tony Vecchio, Director
Address: 4001 SW Canyon Rd., Portland 97221
Phone: 503-226-1561
Fax: 503-226-6836
Web: www.oregonzoo.org

Nestled on 64 acres in the forested hills of Washington Park, the Oregon Zoo is just five minutes from downtown Portland, easily accessible by MAX light rail, TriMet bus #63 or by auto on Highway 26 West, the Sunset Highway. Parking costs $1.00.

The Oregon Zoo is home to more than 2,000 animals from around the world. The Great Northwest exhibit welcomes visitors to the zoo. The mountain village atmosphere of the entry plaza is complete with visitor amenities including the Cascade Grill and the Cascade Outfitters Gift Shop. The Cascade Crest exhibit is home to shaggy mountain goats living among a jumble of boulders, green grass and a crystal clear pond.

Farther down the trail visitors come to Steller Cove, which opened in 2000, home to sea lions, sea otters and an elephant seal. Visitors can get an underwater view of these graceful animals and explore the diversity of a kelp forest and tide pool.

The latest additions to the Great Northwest include two new exhibits opened in 2004. The Eagle Canyon exhibit surrounds visitors with the splendors of a natural watershed. Visitors have a fish-eye view of salmon, sturgeon and other native fish. Farther up the trail, magnificent bald eagles appear. Visitors discover the importance of rivers and streams and the interconnectedness of animals and the ecosystem.

Also new in 2004 is the Trillium Creek Family Farm, a recreation of an Oregon Century Farm, complete with farmhouse and barn. This interactive hands-on exhibit allows visitors of all ages a chance to see sheep, goats, chickens, and other farm animals.

The zoo is a perfect place to explore more exotic habitats. The Africa Savanna is home to rhinos, hippos, zebras, giraffes, and more. The Africa Rain Forest features fruit bats, monkeys, crocodiles, and many bright and colorful birds. The Amazon Flooded Forest gives visitors a peek at some of the many animals living in the most diverse ecosystem in the world. Other zoo residents include wolves, musk ox, polar bears, penguins, lorikeets, Amur tigers, and leopards all living in lush exhibits recreating their natural habitats.

In addition to exploring exhibits, visitors can hop aboard the Washington Park and Zoo Railway for a ride through the lush forest hillsides surrounding the zoo. During the summer, visitors may enjoy the four-mile loop or get off at the Rose Garden and take a stroll, enjoying a view of the city, and catch a later train back to the zoo. The zoo is Oregon's most popular paid attraction.

The Oregon Zoo is committed to conservation, research and education, home to more than 20 endangered and 50 threatened species. The zoo participates in more than 40 conservation breeding programs sponsored by the American Zoo and Aquarium Association. The zoo is internationally recognized for its successful Asian elephant breeding program with 27 elephant births to date and is a leader in animal environmental enrichment.

In recent years, the zoo has partnered with other conservation organizations to help with the preservation of Pacific Northwest species. The zoo is taking an active role in rearing Oregon silverspot butterflies, Columbia basin pygmy rabbits, and western pond turtles. In 2001, the Oregon Zoo joined the California Condor recovery program. In 2004 the first (and second) condor egg was laid in Oregon in more than 100 years!

Education programs involve participants from three years to senior citizens. A–Z Preschool classes, Zoomobile outreach, Discover Birds shows, Conservation Lecture Series, Zoo Animal Presenters, Urban Nature Overnights, ZooCamp, and many others reach over 150,000 people each year.

University of Oregon Museum of Natural History
C. Melvin Aikens, Director
Address: 1680 E 15th Ave., Eugene 97403-1224
Phone: 541-346-3024
Fax: 541-346-5334
E-mail: mnh@uoregon.edu
Web: http://natural-history.uoregon.edu

Founded by renowned University of Oregon archaeologist Luther Cressman in 1936, the Museum of Natural History links public programs and exhibits with strong archaeological and ethnographic collections and extensive research on the archaeology of Oregon.

The museum is the repository for all anthropological artifacts and specimens found on Oregon state lands, including the 10,000-year-old sagebrush sandals popularized as "Oregon's oldest running shoes." These collections are available for research, teaching, and loan to public museums. Under contract to public agencies, museum archaeologists conduct research at many threatened ancient sites to rescue and preserve as much as possible of Oregon's deep human past. The museum also holds the original paleontological collection of Thomas Condon, Oregon's first geologist and one of the University of Oregon's first faculty members.

The museum is reopening in February 2005 after a complete renovation and updating of its exhibit hall. The new displays will present 15,000 years of Native American cultural history, an account of the geological creation of Oregon, and a changing exhibit gallery to showcase the museum's extensive collection of traditional artifacts from the Northwest and around the world.

Exhibits and museum store are open on Tuesday– Sunday, 11 a.m. to 5 p.m.

World Forestry Center
Gary Hartshorn, President and CEO
Address: 4033 SW Canyon Rd., Portland 97221
Phone: 503-228-1367
Fax: 503-228-4608
E-mail: mail@worldforestry.org
Web: www.worldforestry.org

The World Forestry Center, located in Portland's Washington Park, is a private, non-profit forestry education organization. Through classes, tours, exhibits and demonstrations, it illustrates and interprets benefits of the forest environment and promotes appreciation and understanding of forests and forest resources worldwide.

Merlo Hall, added to the center's campus in 1989, houses the World Forest Institute. This facility was designed as an international forest information clearinghouse.

The center also operates the Magness Tree Farm, an 80-acre demonstration forest near Wilsonville, with a visitors' center and log bunkhouse used for summer camps. The area is also a wildlife sanctuary. Individuals and groups of all ages are welcome to visit and take advantage of the farm's varied educational activities, many of which are free of charge.

Cape Blanco Lighthouse—Oregon State Archives Photograph, OHD-5136

Economy

Oregon's rich natural resources fueled the state's economy for a long time. In recent years, high technology has assumed the role previously played by forest products, but forests, farms and ranches, retail trade, and tourism are significant elements of the state's economic profile. This section describes the Oregon economy.

OREGON'S ECONOMY

Oregon's economy has not yet recovered from the recession of 2001. Unemployment in Oregon grew from 4.3 percent in November 2000 to an average of 8.2 percent in 2003, but by November 2004, Oregon's seasonally adjusted unemployment rate had declined to 7.1 percent (124,791 unemployed Oregonians). The national unemployment rate in November 2004 was 5.4 percent. Competition for jobs was intensified by the state's continued population growth. From November 2000 to August 2004, Oregon's working age population grew 5.8 percent.

During the past two decades, Oregon has attempted to make the transition from a resource-based economy to a more mixed manufacturing and marketing economy, with an emphasis on high technology. Oregon's hard times of the early 1980s signaled basic changes had occurred in traditional resource sectors — timber, fishing, agriculture — and the state worked to develop new economic sectors to replace older ones. Most important, perhaps, at least in terms of perception, was the state's growing high-tech sector, centered in the three counties around Portland. However, rural Oregon counties were generally left out of any shift to a new economy. When the boom of the 1990s collapsed, Oregon was again confronted with high unemployment, widespread hunger, and a diminishing safety net of social services.

Despite the growth of the 1990s, however, Oregon's wages have continued to lag behind the rest of the United States. Oregon employment was impacted by a loss of exports to Asia, in part by the North American Free Trade Agreement (NAFTA). By 2000, work at 57 Oregon plants or portions of plants had been shifted to Mexico or Canada. Between 1999 and the middle of 2004, the U.S. government issued 168 Trade Adjustment Assistance certifications relating to Oregon layoffs. These certifications qualify laid-off workers for special help finding work. The Trade Act programs, Trade Adjustment Assistance (TAA), and Alternative Trade Adjustment Assistance (ATAA), help individuals who have become unemployed as a result of increased imports from, or shifts in production to, foreign countries.

In addition to TAA, the U.S. government operated another program called NAFTA-TAA to help workers regain employment after the loss of a job related to NAFTA. NAFTA decreased trade barriers between Canada, the United States, and Mexico, so layoffs covered by this program were limited to those related to trade with and production shifts to Canada and Mexico. Between 1997 and 2002, the U.S. government certified 112 of Oregon's NAFTA-TAA petitions, Of the 112 certifications, 84 attributed the layoff to imports from Canada or Mexico and 28 found the layoff to be due to a shift in production to Canada or Mexico. Of the 84 certified layoffs related to imports, 43 were due to imports from Canada, 26 were due to imports from Mexico, and 15 did not identify the country. Of the 28 certifications related to a shift in production, 12 said the shift was to Canada and 16 said the shift was to Mexico.

Employment

Professional and business services accounts for more than one in ten jobs in Oregon, and contains the fastest growing "subsector" in the state: business support services (up 14.8%; 1,900 jobs). The reason behind this sector's growth can be summed up in two words: call centers. Retail trade has added jobs over the past year, growing by a little less than two percent. Employment services (employment placement agencies, temp help firms, and employee leasing services) is another sector within professional and business services that has contributed to Oregon's job growth: 4,000 jobs since the end of the recession. Although seasonal and volatile, this sector has consistently posted gains since late 2003. As of September 2004, Oregon had the second fastest-growing manufacturing sector in the nation. Over the past year, it has added 4,600 jobs for a growth rate of 2.3 percent. Transportation equipment manufacturing has come back during the past year, regaining 1,800 of the 3,000-plus jobs lost during the recession. Primary metals manufacturing has recorded the second fastest growth rate of all the manufacturing industries that are tracked, growing by 8.4 percent or 700 jobs over the past year. This sector lost about 2,000 jobs between 2000 and 2003. High-tech manufacturing is growing, adding 1,600 jobs (up 4.0%) over the past year. Oregon's construction industry declined by almost ten percent or 8,000 jobs during the recession. In the past year, this sector has regained 2,900 jobs.

The top ten private sector employers in Oregon as of April, 2002 are:

1. Fred Meyer, Inc.
2. Providence Health System
3. Intel Corporation
4. Safeway Stores, Inc.
5. Oregon Health Sciences University
6. (tie) Legacy Emanuel Hospital & Health; Wal Mart Stores, Inc.
8. Kaiser Permanente
9. Hewlett-Packard Co.
10. Roseburg Forest Products Co.

Oregon has the fourth-highest statewide minimum wage rate in the nation. In 2004, its minimum wage was $7.05 per hour, only slightly lower than Washington's rate of $7.16, Alaska's $7.15, and Connecticut's $7.10. In January 2005, Oregon's rate rose to $7.25 and Washington's to $7.35 per hour. Oregon's average wage in 2002 (the most recent year data is available) was $33,684. Oregon ranked 22 in average wages (1 is high).

Data compiled by the Oregon Employment Department's research section suggests average wages vary widely by industry. The average annual wage in the leisure and hospitality sector was less than $14,000 in 2001, while the average annual wage in the information sector was nearly $50,000. Of course, the average wage for an industry does not reveal how many low- or high-wage jobs are in an industry. Of the 1.4 million wage records reported by Oregon's private employers during the first quarter of 2003, nearly one-third had an average wage of less than $10 per hour, while 13 percent had an average wage of $30 per hour or more. This suggests that more than half of all jobs paid between $10 and $30 per hour (with one-quarter paying $10 to $14.99 per hour).

Oregon's Economic and Community Development Department points out that Oregon has some of the most competitive labor costs in the western United States. Using data from 1999, the Department was able to show that average annual covered payroll per worker for Oregon was significantly lower than national average. When only rural counties were looked at, this number became even lower per worker.

Income
In the 2000 Census, Oregon ranked 27th in terms of the percentage of its population in poverty (1 was best). This represented an improvement since the 1990 Census. In 1990, 12.4 percent of Oregonians were in the poverty classification; by 2000 this had dwindled to 11.6 percent. The percentage of children under 18 in poverty decreased also, from 15.8 percent in 1990 to 14.7 percent in 2000. The prosperity of the 1990s had thus measurably affected the poor in Oregon. Unfortunately, this progress was reversed by the 2001 economic downturn. Even though per capita income in Oregon grew through the decade of the 1990s, it remained below the national average. When the recession hit, per capita income growth slowed and the gains of the 1990s were lost. In 2003, Oregon had a per capita personal income of $28,806. The per capita personal income for the United States was $31,459 and for the Far West region it was $32,894.

Until 2004, Oregon had the unenviable distinction of leading all other states in percentage of hungry citizens, despite its reputation for production of food. Housing prices increased 57.7 percent during the 1990s, and home ownership also increased, from 63.1 percent to 64.3 percent. However, the number of affordable housing units decreased. As the recession became felt, the number of Oregonians without health insurance grew to 15.9 percent in 2002. In 2003, Oregon's Department of Human Services estimated that 5.9 percent of the state's population has a serious mental health disorder. An earlier estimate, done in 1999 by the Department of Human Services, projected that 15.2 percent of the population abused or was dependent on illicit drugs or alcohol.

Revenue and Taxes
Oregon collects personal income taxes, corporate income taxes, property taxes and gasoline taxes. It does not have a state sales tax. The personal income tax rate ranges from 5 percent to 9 percent of taxable income. However, almost 70 percent of taxpayers fall into the top tax bracket. Individuals with incomes of $2,600 are at the bottom end of the personal income tax range. The corporate income tax is set at 6.6 percent of taxable business income. The minimum corporate tax is ten dollars. Fully 65 percent of Oregon corporations that pay state and federal income taxes paid the ten dollar minimum tax.

Property tax rates vary from community to community. Voters passed tax initiatives limiting the growth of property tax values to 3 percent a year. In addition, voters shifted responsibility for public schools from property taxes to the state's General Fund. This has depleted resources for other programs that are also dependent on the General Fund. When the 2001 recession struck, public education and human services were hit particularly hard. A significant part of the reason for the intensity of the downturn, at least as experienced by those who lost employment, was the restructuring of Oregon's tax system in the early 1990s. The demands on the state's general fund, when faced with a decline in revenues, meant pervasive truncation of government services. Perhaps the most conspicuous victim was public education. School districts throughout Oregon were faced with shorter school years, larger class sizes, and elimination of programs.

In 2004, voters passed Measure 37. This specified that the owner of private real property is entitled to receive just compensation when a land use regulation is enacted after the owner or a family member became the owner if the regulation restricts the use of the property and reduces its fair market value. The government responsible for the regulation may choose to pay the owner an amount equal to the reduction in value or modify, change or not apply the regulation to the owner's property.

Sources

Department of Consumer and Business Services
www.oregon.gov/DCBS/index.shtml

Economic and Community Development
  Department
www.oregon.gov/ECDD/index.shtml

Employment Department
www.oregon.gov/EMPLOY/index.shtml

Housing and Community Services Department
www.oregon.gov/OHCS/index.shtml

Department of Education
www.ode.state.or.us/

Department of Human Services
www.oregon.gov/DHS/index.shtml

Department of Agriculture
www.oregon.gov/ODA/index.shtml

Department of Energy
www.oregon.gov/ENERGY/index.shtml

Department of Environmental Quality
www.oregon.gov/DEQ/index.shtml

Forestry Department
www.oregon.gov/ODF/index.shtml

Land Conservation and Development Department
www.oregon.gov/LCD/index.shtml

River and swinging bridge—Oregon State Archives Photograph, OHD-G275

Oregon's long tradition of open government and citizen involvement depends in part on its citizens receiving accurate and timely information. The media play an important role in transmitting this information to Oregonians. This section lists Oregon's media resources.

Newspapers Published in Oregon

Source: Oregon Newspaper Publishers Association
Executive Director: J. LeRoy Yorgason
Address: 7150 SW Hampton St., Suite 111, Portland 97223
Phone: 503-624-6397
Fax: 503-639-9009
E-mail: onpa@orenews.com

Albany

Albany Democrat-Herald
PO Box 130, Albany 97321; 541-926-2211; Fax: 541-926-7209; Mon.–Sat. p.m., Sun. a.m.; Martha Wells (P); Hasso Hering (E); Circ.: 17,450 (M–Sat.) 18,025 (Sun); Estab.: 1865
E-mail: news@dhonline.com
Web: www.democratherald.com

Ashland

Ashland Daily Tidings
PO Box 7, Ashland 97520; 541-482-3456; Fax: 541-482-3688; Mon.–Sat. p.m.; J. Grady Singletary (P); Andrew Scot Bolsinger (E); Circ.: 5,106; Estab.: 1876
E-mail: tidings@mind.net
Web: www.dailytidings.com

Astoria

The Daily Astorian
PO Box 210, Astoria 97103; 503-325-3211; Fax: 503-325-6573; Mon.–Fri. p.m.; Steve Forrester (P&E); Circ.: 8,383; Estab.: 1873
E-mail: astorian@dailyastorian.com
Web: www.dailyastorian.info

Baker City

Baker City Herald
PO Box 805, Baker City 97814; 541-523-3673; Fax: 541-523-6426; Mon.–Fri. p.m.; Kari Borgen (P); Mark Furman (E); Circ.: 3,177 (M–Th), 3,426 (F); Estab.: 1870
E-mail: news@bakercityherald.com
Web: www.bakercityherald.com

The Record-Courier
PO Box 70, Baker City 97814; Phone/Fax: 541-523-5353; Thurs.; Byron C. Brinton (P); Byron D. Brinton (E); Circ.: 3,000; Estab.: 1901

Bandon

Western World
PO Box 248, Bandon 97411-0248; 541-347-2423; Fax: 541-347-2424; Wed.; Gregory L. Stevens (P); Jan Lee (E); Circ.: 2,278; Estab.: 1912
E-mail: westernworldnews@pulitzer.net
Web: www.bandonwesternworld.com

Beaverton

Beaverton Valley Times
PO Box 370, Beaverton 97075; 503-684-0360; Fax: 503-620-3433; Thurs.; Steven J. Clark (P); Mikel J. Kelly (E); Circ.: 7,011; Estab.: 1921
E-mail: email@commnewspapers.com
Web: www.beavertonvalleytimes.com

Bend

The Bulletin
PO Box 6020, Bend 97708; 541-382-1811; Fax: 541-385-5802; Mon.–Sun. a.m.; Gordon Black (P); John Costa (E); Circ.: 26,961 (M–Sat.), 28,348 (Sun.); Estab.: 1903
E-mail: bulletin@bendbulletin.com
Web: www.bendbulletin.com

Brookings

Curry Coastal Pilot
PO Box 700, Brookings 97415; 541-469-3123; Fax: 541-469-4679; Wed. and Sat.; Charles R. Kocher (P); Scott Graves (E); Circ.: 6,738; Estab.: 1946
E-mail: mail@currypilot.com
Web: www.currypilot.com

Brownsville

The Times
PO Box 278, Brownsville 97327; 541-466-5311; Fax: 541-466-5312; Wed.; Don and Wannell Ware (P); Don Ware (E); Circ.: 902; Estab.: 1888
E-mail: thetimes@peak.com

Burns

Burns Times-Herald
355 N Broadway, Burns 97720; 541-573-2022; Fax: 541-573-3915; Wed.; Scott Olson (P&E); Circ.: 2,873; Estab.: 1887
E-mail: btherald@burnstimes.com
Web: www.burnstimesherald.com

Canby

Canby Herald
PO Box 1108, Canby 97013; 503-266-6831; Fax: 503-266-6836; Wed. and Sat.; William D. Cassel (P); David Howell (E); Circ.: 4,674; Estab.: 1906
E-mail: cherald@eaglenewspapers.com
Web: www.canbyherald.com

Cave Junction

Illinois Valley News
PO Box 1370, Cave Junction 97523; 541-592-2541; Fax: 541-592-4330; Wed.; Robert R. and Jan Rodriguez (P&E); Circ.: 3,590; Estab.: 1937
E-mail: newsroom1@frontiernet.net

Clatskanie

The Clatskanie Chief
PO Box 8, Clatskanie 97016; 503-728-3350/1-800-340-3350; Fax: 503-728-3350; Thurs.; Deborah Steele Hazen (P&E); Circ.: 2,431; Estab.: 1891
E-mail: chief@clatskanie.com
Web: www.clatskanie.com/chiefonline

Condon

The Times-Journal
PO Box 746, Condon 97823; 541-384-2421; Fax: 541-384-2411; Thurs.; McLaren and Janet Stinchfield (P); McLaren Stinchfield (E); Circ.: 1,494; Estab.: 1886
E-mail: times-journal@jncable.com

Coos Bay

The World
PO Box 1840, Coos Bay 97420; 541-269-1222; Fax: 541-267-0294; Mon.–Fri. p.m., Sat. a.m.; Gregory L. Stevens (P); Kathy Erickson (E); Circ.: 13,080 (M–F), 15,060 (Sat.); Estab.: 1878
E-mail: theworldnews@pulitzer.net
Web: www.theworldlink.com

Coquille

The Coquille Valley Sentinel
PO Box 400, Coquille 97423; 541-396-3191; Fax: 541-396-3624; Wed.; Mikel Chavez (P); Anna Chavez (E); Circ.: 2,013; Estab.: 1882
E-mail: mikelchavez@webenet.net
Web: www.coquillevalleysentinel.com

Corvallis

Corvallis Gazette-Times
PO Box 368, Corvallis 97339; 541-753-2641; Fax: 541-758-9505; Mon.–Sun. a.m.; Brenda Speth (P); Rob Priewe (E); Circ.: 11,706 (M–Sat.), 12,509 (Sun.); Estab.: 1862
E-mail: news@gtconnect.com
Web: www.gazettetimes.com

Cottage Grove

Cottage Grove Sentinel
PO Box 35, Cottage Grove 97424; 541-942-3325; Fax: 541-942-3328; Wed.; Linda Powell (P); Jonni Gratton (E); Circ.: 3,834; Estab.: 1889
E-mail: news@cgsentinel.com
Web: www.cgsentinel.com

Creswell

Creswell Chronicle
PO Box 428, Creswell 97426; 541-895-2197; Fax: 541-895-2361; Wed.; Helen Hollyer (P); Circ.: 1,001; Estab.: 1965
E-mail: thechronicle@earthlink.net

Dallas

The Polk County Itemizer Observer
PO Box 108, Dallas 97338; 503-623-2373; Fax: 503-623-2395; Wed.; David W. Weston (P); Tom Henderson (E); Circ.: 5,615; Estab.: 1875
E-mail: dweston@eaglenewspapers.com
Web: www.itemizerobserver.com

Dayton

Dayton Tribune
PO Box 69, Dayton 97114; Phone/Fax: 503-864-2310; Thurs.; George and Edwina Meitzen (P&E); Circ.: 404; Estab.: 1912
E-mail: tribune@onlinemac.com

Drain

The Drain Enterprise
PO Box 26, Drain 97435; 541-836-2241; Fax: 541-836-2243; Thurs.; Betty Anderson (P); Sue Anderson (E); Circ.: 1,208; Estab.: 1951
E-mail: drainenterprise@earthlink.net

Enterprise

Wallowa County Chieftain
PO Box 338, Enterprise 97828; 541-426-4567; Fax: 541-426-3921; Thurs.; Dave Hassler (E); Circ.: 3,266; Estab.: 1884
E-mail: editor@wallowa.com
Web: www.wallowacountychieftain.info

Estacada

Clackamas County News
PO Box 549, Estacada 97023; 503-630-3241; Fax: 503-630-5840; Clinton Vining (E); Circ.: 1,970; Estab.: 1904
E-mail: email@clackamascountynews.com
Web: www.clackamascountynews.com

Eugene

The Register-Guard
PO Box 10188, Eugene 97440-2188; 541-485-1234; Fax: 541-984-4699; Mon.–Sun. a.m.; Alton F. Baker III (P&E); Circ.: 71,581 (M–F), 80,148 (Sat.), 76,308 (Sun.); Estab.: 1862
E-mail: tbaker@guardnet.com
Web: www.registerguard.com

Florence

Siuslaw News
PO Box 10, Florence 97439; 541-997-3441; Fax: 541-997-7979; Wed., Sat.; John Bartlett (P); Robert Serra (E); Circ.: 4,683; Estab.: 1890
E-mail: paperads@oregonfast.net

Forest Grove

News-Times
PO Box 408, Forest Grove 97116; 503-357-3181; Fax: 503-359-8456; Wed.; Linda D. Saari (P&E); Circ.: 4,435; Estab.: 1886

Media Directories

E-mail: news@forestgrovenewstimes.com
Web: www.forestgrovenewstimes.com

Gold Beach
Curry County Reporter
PO Box 766, Gold Beach 97444; 541-247-6643; Fax: 541-247-6644; Wed.; Jim and Molly Walker (P); Jim Walker (E); Circ.: 2,786; Estab.: 1914
E-mail: molly@currycountyreporter.com
Web: www.currycountyreporter.com

Grants Pass
Grants Pass Daily Courier
PO Box 1468, Grants Pass 97528-0330; 541-474-3700/1-800-228-0457; Fax: 541-474-3814; Mon.–Sat. p.m.; Dennis Mack (P); Dennis Roler (E); Circ.: 16,440; Estab.: 1885
E-mail: courier@thedailycourier.com
Web: www.thedailycourier.com

Gresham
The Outlook
PO Box 747, Gresham 97030; 503-665-2181; Fax: 503-669-2760; Wed. and Sat.; J. Mark Garber (P); Tiffany O'Dell (E); Circ.: 8,808; Estab.: 1911
E-mail: news@theoutlookonline.com
Web: www.theoutlookonline.com

Halfway
Hells Canyon Journal
PO Box 646, Halfway 97834; 541-742-7900; Fax: 541-742-7933; Wed.; Steve Backstrom (P&E); Circ.: 1,285; Estab.: 1984
E-mail: hcj@pinetel.com
Web: www.halfwayor.com/hcj

Heppner
Heppner Gazette-Times
PO Box 337, Heppner 97836; 541-676-9228; Wed.; David Sykes and April Hilton-Sykes (P); April Hilton-Sykes (E); Circ.: 1,489; Estab.: 1883
E-mail: gazette@heppner.net
Web: www.heppner.net

Hermiston
The Hermiston Herald
PO Box 46, Hermiston 97838; 541-567-6457; Fax: 541-567-4125; Tues. and Fri..; Rick Kennedy (P); Michael Kane (E); Circ.: 3,850; Estab.: 1906
E-mail: publisher@hermistonherald.com
Web: www.hermistonherald.com

Hillsboro
Hillsboro Argus
PO Box 588, Hillsboro 97123; 503-648-1131; Fax: 503-648-9191; Tues. and Thurs.; W. Clark Gallagher (P); Gary Stutzman (E); Circ.: 10,590; Estab.: 1873

E-mail: stutzman@hillsboroargus.com
Web: www.hillsboroargus.com/hillsboroargus

Hood River
Hood River News
PO Box 390, Hood River 97031; 541-386-1234; Fax: 541-386-6796; Wed. and Sat.; Tom Lanctot (P); Kirby Neumann-Rea (E); Circ.: 5,112; Estab.: 1905
E-mail: hrnews@eaglenewspapers.com
Web: www.hoodrivernews.com

Jefferson
Jefferson Review
PO Box 330, Jefferson 97352-0330; 541-327-1776; Fax: 541-327-2241; Thurs.; Glen Albrethsen (P); Marta Neilson (E); Circ.: 646; Estab.: 1890
E-mail: news@jeffersonreview.net

John Day
Blue Mountain Eagle
195 N Canyon Blvd., John Day 97845; 541-575-0710; Fax: 541-575-1244; Wed.; Diane Oster-Courtney (Gen. Mgr.); Hilary Miller (E); Circ.: 3,615; Estab.: 1898
E-mail: editor@bluemountaineagle.com
Web: www.bluemountaineagle.info

Junction City
Tri-County News
PO Box 340, Junction City 97448; 541-998-3877; Fax: 541-998-3878; Thurs.; Mike and Sandy Thoele (P); LaRae Ash (E); Circ.: 2,495; Estab.: 1977
E-mail: tceditor@triwestnews.com

Keizer
Keizertimes
PO Box 20025, Keizer 97307; 503-390-1051; Fax: 503-390-8023; Fri.; Scotta Callister (P&E); Circ.: 3,100; Estab.: 1979
E-mail: kt@keizertimes.com
Web: www.keizertimes.com

Klamath Falls
Herald and News
PO Box 788, Klamath Falls 97601; 541-885-4410; Fax: 541-885-4456; Mon.–Fri. p.m.; Sun. a.m.; Heidi Wright (P); Tim Fought (E); Circ.: 17,047 (M–F), 17,717 (Sun.); Estab.: 1906
E-mail: handnews@cdsnet.net
Web: www.heraldandnews.com

La Grande
The Observer
1406 Fifth St., La Grande 97850; 541-963-3161; Fax: 541-963-7804; Mon.–Sat. p.m.; Ron Horton (P); Ted Kramer (E); Circ.: 6,087; Estab.: 1896
E-mail: publisher@lagrandeobserver.com
Web: www.lagrandeobserver.com

Lake Oswego

Lake Oswego Review
PO Box 548, Lake Oswego 97034; 503-635-8811; Fax: 503-635-8817; Thurs.; J. Brian Monihan (P); Martin Forbes (E); Circ.: 7,247; Estab.: 1920
E-mail: email@lakeoswegoreview.com
Web: www.lakeoswegoreview.com

Lakeview

Lake County Examiner
PO Box 271, Lakeview 97630; 541-947-3378; Fax: 541-947-4359; Thurs.; Tillie Flynn (Gen. Mgr.); Vicki Reynolds (E); Circ.: 2,521; Estab.: 1880
E-mail: news@lakecountyexam.com
Web: www.lakecountyexam.com

Lebanon

Lebanon Express
PO Box 459, Lebanon 97355; 541-258-3151; Fax: 541 259 3569; Wed.; Martha Wells (P); A.K. Dugan (E); Circ.: 2,920; Estab.: 1887
E-mail: lebanon.express@lee.net
Web: www.lebanon-express.com

Lincoln City

The News Guard
PO Box 848, Lincoln City 97367; 541-994-2178; Fax: 541-994-7613; Wed.; Kathleen Newton (P); Laura Hardman Stanfill (E); Circ.: 4,484; Estab.: 1927
E-mail: news@thenewsguard.com
Web: www.thenewsguard.com

Madras

The Madras Pioneer
241 SE Sixth St., Madras 97741; 541-475-2275; Fax: 541-475-3710; Wed.; Tony Ahern (P); Susan Matheny (E); Circ.: 3,935; Estab.: 1904
E-mail: tahern@eaglenewspapers.com
Web: www.madraspioneer.com

McKenzie Bridge

McKenzie River Reflections
59059 Old McKenzie Hwy., McKenzie Bridge 97413; Phone/Fax: 541-822-3358; Wed.; Ken Engelman (P); Louise Engelman (E); Circ.: 960; Estab.: 1978
E-mail: rivref@aol.com
Web: mckenzie.orenews.com

McMinnville

News-Register
PO Box 727, McMinnville 97128; 503-472-5114; Fax: 503-472-9151; Tues., Thurs. and Sat.; Jeb Bladine (P); Steve Bagwell (E); Circ.: 8,946; Estab.: 1866
E-mail: news@newsregister.com
Web: www.newsregister.com

Medford

Mail Tribune
PO Box 1108, Medford 97501; 541-776-4411; Fax: 541-776-4415; Mon.–Sun. a.m.; J. Grady Singletary (P); Robert L. Hunter (E); Circ.: 30,674 (M–Th, Sat.), 38,868 (Fri.), 33,303 (Sun.); Estab.: 1906
E-mail: letters@mailtribune.com
Web: www.mailtribune.com

Mill City

Mill City Independent Press
PO Box 43, Mill City 97360; 503-897-4216; Fax: 503-897-2013; Wed.; Tree Fredrickson (P&E); Circ.: 1,248; Estab.: 1998
E-mail: mcipnews@wvi.com

Milton-Freewater

Valley Herald
112 NE 5th Ave., Milton-Freewater 97862; 541-938-6688; Fax: 541-938-6689; Fri.; Melanie Hall (P); Circ.: 713; Estab.: 2001
E-mail: valleyherald@qwest.net

Molalla

Molalla Pioneer
PO Box 168, Molalla 97038; 503-829-2301; Fax: 503-829-2317; Wed. and Sat.; William D. Cassel (P); Steve St. Amand (E); Circ.: 3,049; Estab.: 1911
E-mail: pioneer@eaglenewspapers.com
Web: www.molallapioneer.com

Myrtle Creek

The Douglas County Mail
PO Box 729, Myrtle Creek 97470; 541-863-5233; Fax: 541-863-5234; Thurs.; Robert L. Chaney Sr. (P); Steve Wicker (E); Circ.: 2,325; Estab.: 1902
E-mail: dcmail@pioneer-net.com

Myrtle Point

Myrtle Point Herald
PO Box 606, Myrtle Point 97458; 541-572-2717; Fax: 541-572-2828; Thurs.; Sherry Anderson (P); Mary Schamehorn (E); Circ.: 1,775; Estab.: 1889
E-mail: mpherald@harborside.com

Newberg

The Newberg Graphic
PO Box 700, Newberg 97132; 503-538-2181; Fax: 503-538-1632; Wed. and Sat.; Joe Petshow (P&E); Circ.: 2,850; Estab.: 1888
E-mail: thegraphic@eaglenewspapers.com
Web: www.newberggraphic.com

Newport

News-Times
PO Box 965, Newport 97365; 541-265-8571; Fax: 541-265-3103; Wed. and Fri.; Mark Bryan (P); Gail Kimberling (E); Circ.: 7,975; Estab.: 1882
Web: www.newportnewstimes.com

Oakridge

Dead Mountain Echo
PO Box 900, Oakridge 97463; 541-782-4241;
Fax: 541-782-3323; Thurs.; Larry and
Debra Roberts (P); Larry Roberts (E);
Circ.: 434; Estab.: 1973
E-mail: lroberts@efn.org

Ontario

Argus Observer
PO Box 130, Ontario 97914; 541-889-5387;
Fax: 541-889-3347; Mon.–Fri. p.m., Sun.
a.m.; Steve Krehl (P); Pat Caldwell (E);
Circ.: 6,912 (M–F), 7,803 (Sun.); Estab.:
1896
E-mail: stevek@argusobserver.com
Web: www.argusobserver.com

Pendleton

East Oregonian
PO Box 1089, Pendleton 97801; 541-276-
2211/1-800-522-0255; Fax: 541-276-8314;
Mon.–Sat. p.m., Sun. a.m.; David Balcom
(P); Rebecca Chambers (E); Circ.: 10,430
(M–Sat.), 10,761 (Sun.); Estab.: 1875
E-mail: eonews@eastoregonian.com
Web: www.eastoregonian.info

The Pendleton Record
PO Box 69, Pendleton 97801; 541-276-2853;
Fax: 541-278-2916; Thurs.; Marguerite M.
Maznaritz (P&E); Circ.: 856; Estab.: 1911
E-mail: penrecor@ucinet.com

Port Orford

Port Orford News
PO Box 5, Port Orford 97465; 541-332-2361;
Fax: 541-332-8101; Wed.; Matt and
Willowsong Hall (P); Circ.: 849; Estab.:
1958
E-mail: portorfordnews@earthlink.net
Web: www.portorfordnews.com

Portland

Daily Journal of Commerce
PO Box 10127, Portland 97296; 503-226-
1311; Fax: 503-226-2216; Mon.–Fri. a.m.;
Joan Ray (P); Joe Wilson (E); Circ.: 3,176;
Estab.: 1872
E-mail: newsroom@djc-or.com
Web: www.djc-or.com

The Oregonian
1320 SW Broadway, Portland 97201; 503-
221-8327; Fax: 503-227-5306; Mon.–Sun.
a.m.; Fred A. Stickel (P); Sandra Mims
Rowe (E); Circ.: 334,783 (M–F), 321,728
(Sat.), 409,554 (Sun.); Estab.: 1850
E-mail: publiceditor@news.oregonian.com
Web: www.oregonian.com

The Skanner
415 N. Killingsworth, Portland 97217; 503-
285-5555; Fax: 503-285-2900; Wed.;

Bernie Foster (P); Circ.: 20,000; Estab.:
1975
Web: www.theskanner.com

Prineville

Central Oregonian
558 N Main St., Prineville 97754; 541-447-
6205; Fax: 541-447-1754; Tues. and Fri.;
Bill Schaffer (P); Vance Tong (E); Circ.:
3,977; Estab.: 1881
E-mail: co@eaglenewspapers.com
Web: www.centraloregonian.com

Redmond

The Redmond Spokesman
PO Box 788, Redmond 97756; 541-548-
2184; Fax: 541-548-3203; Wed.; Gary
Husman (P); Eric Henry (E); Circ.: 3,889;
Estab.: 1910
Web: www.redmondspokesman.com

Reedsport

The Umpqua Post
PO Box 145, Reedsport 97467; 541-271-
7474; Fax: 541-271-6855; Wed.; Gregory
L. Stevens (P); Erik Hillstrom (E); Circ.:
1,802; Estab.: 1996
E-mail: umpquapost@harborside.com

Rogue River

Rogue River Press
PO Box 1485, Rogue River 97537; 541-582-
1707; Fax: 541-582-0201; Wed.; Dave and
Heidi Ehrhardt (P); Dave Ehrhardt (E);
Circ.: 1,923; Estab.: 1962
Web: www.rogueriverpress.com

Roseburg

The News-Review
PO Box 1248, Roseburg 97470; 541-672-
3321; Fax: 541-957-4265; Mon.–Fri. p.m.,
Sun. a.m.; Mark Raymond (P); Bart Smith
(E); Circ.: 19,331 (M–F), 20,123 (Sun.);
Estab.: 1867
E-mail: mraymond@newsreview.info
Web: www.newsreview.info

Salem

Statesman Journal
PO Box 13009, Salem 97309; 503-399-
6611/1-800-556-3975; Fax: 503-399-6706;
Mon.–Sun. a.m.; Sonja Sorensen Craig (P);
David Risser (E); Circ.: 55,986 (M–Sat.);
62,706 (Sun.); Estab.: 1851
Web: www.statesmanjournal.com

Sandy

The Sandy Post
PO Box 68, Sandy 97055; 503-668-5548;
Fax: 503-668-0748; Wed.; J. Mark Garber
(P); Lloyd Woods (E); Circ.: 2,548; Estab.:
1937
Web: www.sandypost.com

Scappoose

The South County Spotlight
PO Box C, Scappoose 97056; 503-543-6387;
Fax: 503-543-6380; Wed.; Art and Sally
Heerwagen (P); Art Heerwagen (E); Circ.:
3,637; Estab.: 1961
E-mail: newsspot@colcenter.org
Web: www.spotlightnews.net

Seaside

Seaside Signal
PO Box 848, Seaside 97138; 503-738-5561;
Fax: 503-738-5672; Thurs.; Kyle Larson
(P&E); Circ.: 2,536; Estab.: 1905
E-mail: signaleditor@orcoastnews.com
Web: www.seasidesignal.com

Sheridan

The Sun
PO Box 68, Sheridan 97378; 503-843-2312;
Fax: 503-843-3830; Wed.; George
Robertson (P&E); Circ.: 2,036; Estab.:
1890
E-mail: news@sheridansun.com
Web: www.sheridansun.com

Silverton

Silverton Appeal Tribune
PO Box 35, Silverton 97381; 503-873-8385;
Fax: 503-873-8064; Wed.; Brenna
Wiegand (Asst. E); Circ.: 3,702; Estab.:
1880
E-mail: sanews@salem.gannett.com
Web: www.eastvalleynews.com/appeal

Springfield

The Springfield News
PO Box 139, Springfield 97477; 541-746-
1671; Fax: 541-746-0633; Wed. and Fri.;
Harold Orsborn (P); Larry Berteau (E);
Circ.: 4,391; Estab.: 1903
E-mail: news@springfieldnews.com
Web: www.springfieldnews.com

St. Helens

The Chronicle
PO Box 1153, St. Helens 97051; 503-397-
0116; Fax: 503-397-4093; Wed. and Sat.;
Pamela A. Petersen (P); Circ.: 5,137;
Estab.: 1881
E-mail: news@thechronicleonline.com
Web: www.thechronicleonline.com

Stayton

The Stayton Mail
PO Box 400, Stayton 97383; 503-769-6338;
Fax: 503-769-6207; Wed.; Mary Owen (E);
Circ.: 3,478; Estab.: 1894
E-mail: smnews@salem.gannett.com
Web: www.eastvalleynews.com

Sutherlin

North County News
115 W Central, Sutherlin 97479; 541-459-
0716; Fax: 541-459-0283; Wed.; Jean Ivey
(P&E); Circ.: 1,000; Estab.: 2002
E-mail: ivey@internetcds.com

Sweet Home

The New Era
PO Box 39, Sweet Home 97386; 541-367-
2135; Fax: 541-367-2137; Wed.; Alex Paul
(P&E); Circ.: 2,175; Estab.: 1929
E-mail: newera@centurytel.net
Web: www.sweethomenews.com

The Dalles

The Dalles Chronicle
PO Box 1910, The Dalles 97058; 541-296-
2141; Fax: 541-298-1365; Mon.–Fri. p.m.,
Sun. a.m., Marilyn Roth (P); Dan Spatz
(E); Circ.: 4,635; Estab.: 1890
E-mail: tdchron@eaglenewspapers.com
Web: www.thedalleschronicle.com

Tigard

The Tigard Times and *Tualatin Times*
PO Box 370, Beaverton 97075; 503-684-
0360; Fax: 503-620-3433; Thurs.; Steven J.
Clark (P); Mikel J. Kelly (E); Circ.: 7,118;
Estab.: 1956
E-mail: email@commnewspapers.com
Web: www.tigardtimes.com; www.tualatin
times.com

Tillamook

Headlight-Herald
PO Box 444, Tillamook 97141; 503-842-
7535; Fax: 503-842-8842; Wed.; Kathleen
Newton (P); Joe Happ (E); Circ.: 7,126;
Estab.: 1888
E-mail: headlight@orcoastnews.com
Web: www.tillamookheadlightherald.com

Vale

Malheur Enterprise
PO Box 310, Vale 97918; 541-473-3377; Fax:
541-473-3268; Wed.; Julie Schaffeld (P);
Circ.: 1,410; Estab.: 1909
E-mail: malent@fmtc.com

Veneta

West Lane News
PO Box 188, Veneta 97487; 541-935-1882;
Fax: 541-935-4082; Thurs.; Mike and
Sandy Thoele (P); Jeneca Jones (E); Circ.:
1,876; Estab.: 1961
E-mail: westlanenews@aol.com

Warrenton

The Columbia Press
PO Box 130, Warrenton 97146; Phone/Fax: 503-861-3331; Fri.; Gary Nevan (P&E); Circ.: 960; Estab.: 1922
E-mail: columbiapress@seasurf.net

West Linn

West Linn Tidings
PO Box 548, Lake Oswego 97034; 503-635-8811; Fax: 503-635-8817; Thurs.; J. Brian Monihan (P); Ray Pitz (E); Circ.: 3,545; Estab.: 1981
Web: www.westlinntidings.com

Wilsonville

Wilsonville Spokesman
30250 SW Parkway Ave. #10, Wilsonville 97070; 503-682-3935; Fax: 503-682-6265; Wed.; William D. Cassel (P); Curt Kipp (E); Circ.: 3,100; Estab.: 1985
E-mail: wilsonvillespokesman@eaglenews papers.com
Web: www.wilsonvillenews.com

Woodburn

Woodburn Independent
PO Box 96, Woodburn 97071; 503-981-3441; Fax: 503-981-1253; Wed. and Sat.; Les Reitan (P); John Baker (E); Circ.: 4,003; Estab.: 1888
E-mail: woodburnindependent@eaglenews papers.com
Web: www.woodburnindependent.com

SELECTED PERIODICALS PUBLISHED IN OREGON

A representative sample of the many periodicals published in Oregon, compiled by the Oregon State Library.

Key: A—Annual; BM—Bi-monthly; BW—Bi-weekly; Irreg—Irregular publication schedule; M—Monthly; Q—Quarterly; SA—Semi-annual; SM—Semi-monthly; W—Weekly

Agri-Times Northwest (SM) 1984: Sterling Ag, LLC, PO Box 1626, Pendleton 97801-0189; 541-276-6202; Web: www.agritimes.com

Animal Law Review (A) 1995: Northwestern School of Law, 10015 SW Terwilliger Blvd., Portland 97219; 503-768-6798; Fax: 503-768-6671; Web: www.lclark.edu/org/animalaw

Automotive News of the Pacific Northwest (BM) 1919: 14789 SE 82nd Dr., Clackamas 97015; 503-656-1456; Fax: 503-656-1547; Web: www.anpw.com

Backwoods Home Magazine (BM) 1989: PO Box 712, Gold Beach 97444; 541-247-8900; Fax: 541-247-8600; Web: www.backwoodshome.com

Birth to Three Parenting Magazine (BM) 1978: 86 Centennial Loop, Eugene 97401-7909; 541-484-5316; Fax: 541-484-1449; Web: www.birthto3.org

Black Sheep Newsletter (Q) 1974: Black Sheep Press, 25455 NW Dixie Mountain Rd., Scappoose 97056; 503-621-3063; Fax: 503-621-3063; http://members.aol.com/jkbsnweb

Book Dealers World (Q) 1980: North American Exchange, PO Box 606, Cottage Grove 97424; 541-942-7455; Fax: 541-258-2625

Brainstorm NW (M) 1997: 393 N State St., Lake Oswego 97034; 503-675-7366; Fax: 503-675-7368; Web: www.brainstormnw.com

Calyx (SA) 1976: PO Box B, Corvallis 97339; 541-753-9384/1-888-336-2665; Fax: 541-753-0515; Web: www.proaxis.com/~calyx

Cascade Horseman (M) 1975: Klamath Publishing, PO Box 788, Klamath Falls 97601-1390; 541-883-4000/1-800-275-0788; Fax: 541-885-4447; Web: www.cascadehorseman.com

Cascades East (Q) 1976: Sun Publishing Co., PO Box 5784, Bend 97708; 541-382-0127; Web: www.sun-pub.com

Commercial Review (W) 1890: 2380 NW Roosevelt, Portland 97210-2323; 503-226-2758; Fax: 503-224-0947

Computer Bits (M) 1991: PO Box 329, Forest Grove 97116-0329; 503-359-9107/1-800-898-8886; Web: www.computerbits.com

Crow's Weekly Market Report (W) 1921: C.C. Crow Publications, Inc., PO Box 25749, Portland 97298-0749; 503-646-8075/1-800-800-9510; Fax: 503-646-9971; Web: www.crows.com

Dialogue (Q) 1961: Blindskills, Inc., PO Box 5181, Salem 97304-0181; 503-581-4224/1-800-860-4224; Fax: 503-581-0178; Web: www.blindskills.com

Digger (M) 1988: Oregon Nursery Association, 2780 SE Harrison, Suite 102, Milwaukie 97222; 503-653-8733/1-800-342-6401; Fax: 503-653-1528; Web: www.oan.org/publications/digger.html

El Hispanic (W) 1981: PO Box 306, Portland 97207-0306; 503-228-3139; Fax: 503-228-3384; Web: www.hispnews.com

El Latino de Hoy: Semanario Latinoamericano de Oregon (W) 1991: 7112 NE Sandy Blvd., Portland 97213; 503-493-1106; 503-493-1126; Fax: 503-493-1107; Web: www.ellatinodehoy.com

Environmental Law (Q) 1970: Northwestern School of Law, Lewis and Clark College, 10015 SW Terwilliger Blvd., Portland 97219; 503-768-6700; Fax: 503-768-6671; Web: www.lclark.edu/org/envtl

Eugene Weekly (W) 1993: 1251 Lincoln, Eugene 97401; 541-484-0519; Web: www.eugeneweekly.com

Fireweed: Poetry of Western Oregon (Q) 1990: 2917 NE 13th Ave., Portland 97212-3253; 503-284-0294

Flyfishing and Tying Journal (Q) 1978: Frank Amato Publications, PO Box 82112, Portland 97282; 503-653-8108/1-800-541-9498; Fax: 503-653-2766; Web: www.amatobooks.com

Heritage Newsletter (M) 1987: Linn County Genealogical Society, PO Box 1222, Albany 97321-0537; 541-928-2487

Home Power (BM) 1987: Home Power, PO Box 520, Ashland 97520-0520; 541-512-0220/1-800-707-6585; Fax: 541-512-0343; Web: www.home power.com

Journal of Pesticide Reform (Q) 1985: PO Box 1393, Eugene 97440; 541-344-5044; Fax: 541-344-6923; Web: www.pesticide.org/JPR.html

La Posta (BM) 1969: Posta Publications, 33470 Chinook Plaza, Suite 216, Scappoose 97056; 503-657-5685; Web: www.la-posta.com/journal.htm

Lane Electric Ruralite (M) 1953: Ruralite Services, Inc., PO Box 558, Forest Grove 97116-2333; 503-357-2105; Web: www.ruralite.org

Learning and Leading With Technology (M) 1995: International Society for Technology in Education, 1787 Agate St., Eugene 97403-1923; 541-346-4414/1-800-336-5191; Fax: 541-346-5890; Web: www.iste.org/LL/31/8/index.cfm

Lower Columbia Business (M) 1989: Walker & Company Marketing Communication, PO Box 1088, Seaside 97138-1088; 503-738-3398; Fax: 503-738-0172

Midwifery Today (Q) 1987: PO Box 2672, Eugene 97402; 541-344-7438/1-800-743-0974; Fax: 541-344-1422; Web: www.midwiferytoday.com

Northwest Labor Press (SM) 1987: PO Box 13150, Portland 97213; 503-288-3311; Fax: 503-288-3320; Web: http://nwlaborpress.org

Northwest Palate (BM) 1987: PO Box 10860, Portland 97296-0860; 503-224-6039/1-800-398-7842; Fax: 503-222-5312; Web: www.nwpalate. com

Northwest Travel (BM) 1991: Northwest Regional Magazines, 4969 Hwy. 101, # 2, Florence 97439-8896; 541-997-8401/1-800-348-8401; Fax: 541-902-0400; Web: www.northwestmagazines.com

Noticias Latinas! Latin News (BM) 1995: 524 SE 14th Ave., Portland 97214; Phone/Fax: 503-227-7780; Web: www.coho.net/~notilati

OLA Quarterly (Q) 1995: Oregon Library Association, PO Box 2042, Salem 97308; Web: http://olaweb.org/quarterly/index.shtml

Open Spaces: Views From the Northwest (Q) 1998: Open Spaces Publishing, 6327 SW Capitol Hwy., Suite 134, Portland 97239-1937; 503-227-3401; Fax: 503-227-5764; Web: www.open-spaces. com/index.php

Oregon Business Magazine (M) 1981: MIF Publications, Inc., 610 SW Broadway, Suite 200, Portland 97205-3431; 503-223-0304; Fax: 503-221-6544; Web:www.mediamerica.net/oregon_business_magazine.php

Oregon Coast (BM) 1982: Northwest Regional Magazines, 4969 Hwy. 101, #2, Florence 97439-0130; 541-997-8401/1-800-348-8401; Fax: 541-902-0400; Web: www.northwestmagazines.com

Oregon Grange Bulletin (M) 1990: Oregon State Grange, 643 Union St. NE, Salem 97301; 503-316-0106; Fax: 503-316-0109; Web: www.grange.org/Oregon/

Oregon Historical Quarterly (Q) 1900: Oregon Historical Society, 1200 SW Park Ave., Portland 97205; 503-222-1741; Fax: 503-221-2035; Web: www.ohs.org/publications/about_ohq.cfm

Oregon Home (BM) 1997: MediAmerica, 610 SW Broadway, Suite 200, Portland 97205; 503-223-0304; Fax: 503-221-6544; Web:www.medi america.net/oregon_home_magazine.php

Oregon Wheat (7/yr) 1962: Oregon Wheat Growers League, 115 SE 8th St., Pendleton 97801-2319; 541-276-7330; Fax: 541-276-1723; Web: www.owgl.org/index.cfm?show=10&mid=32

Oregon's Agricultural Progress (Q) 1953: OSU, Agricultural Experiment Station, 422 Kerr Administration Bldg., Corvallis 97331-2119; Web: http://extension.oregonstate.edu/oap

Oregon's Future (Q) 1996: Oregon's Future Magazine, 3129 SE Franklin, Portland 97202-1927; 503-234-6782; Web: www.willamette.edu/public policy/OregonsFuture

Over the Rainbow (Q) 1982: Mobility International USA, P.O. Box 10767, Eugene 97440-2767; 541-343-1284; Fax 541-343-6812

Random Lengths (W) 1944: PO Box 867, Eugene 97440; 541-686-9925; Fax: 800-874-7979; Web: www.randomlengths.com

Resource Recycling (M) 1982: Resource Recycling, PO Box 42270, Portland 97242-0270; 503-233-1305; Fax: 503-233-1356; Web: www.resource -recycling.com

Rubberstampmadness (BM) 1980: RSM Enterprises, Inc., PO Box 610, Corvallis 97339-0610; 541-752-0075/1-877-782-6762; Web: www.rsmad ness.com

Skipping Stones: A Multi-Cultural Children's Quarterly (Q) 1988: PO Box 3939, Eugene 97403-0939; 541-342-4956; Web: www.skippingstones.org

Small Farmers Journal (Q) 1976: PO Box 1627, Sisters 97759-1627; 541-549-2064/1-800-876-2893; Fax: 541-549-4403; Web: www.smallfarm ersjournal.com

Southern Oregon Heritage Today (M) 1995: Southern Oregon Historical Society, 106 N Central Ave., Medford 97501-5926; 541-773-6536; Fax: 541-773-7994

Tinnitus Today (Q) 1975: American Tinnitus Association, PO Box 5, Portland 97207; 503-248-9985/1-800-634-8978; Fax: 503-248-0024; Web: www.ata.org

Western Places (SA) 1992: PO Box 2093, Lake Grove 97035; 503-635-1379; Web: www.western places.net

Willamette Journal of International Law and Dispute Resolution (A) 1997: Willamette University College of Law, 245 Winter St. SE, Rm. 226, Salem 97301-3916; 503-370-6632; Fax: 503-370-6375; Web: http://willamette.edu/wucl/wjildr/

Willamette Law Review (Q) 1978: Willamette University College of Law, 245 Winter St. SE, Salem 97301; 503-375-5435; Fax: 503-375-5463; Web: www.willamette.edu/wucl/lawreview/

Willamette Week (W) 1974: 822 SW 10th, Portland 97205; 503-243-2122; Fax: 503-243-1115; Web: www.wweek.com

Willamette Writer (M) 1965: 9045 SW Barbur Blvd., Suite 5A, Portland 97219-4027; 503-452-1592; Web: www.willamettewriters.com

Writer's NW (Q) 1985: Media Weavers, Inc., PO Box 86190, Portland 97286-0190; 503-771-0428; Fax: 503-771-5186

OREGON RADIO STATIONS

Source: Oregon Association of Broadcasters
President/CEO: Bill Johnstone
Address: 7150 SW Hampton St., Suite 240, Portland 97223
Phone: 503-443-2299
Fax: 503-443-2488
Web: www.theoab.org

Albany
KHPE-FM (107.9), Contemporary Christian;
KWIL-AM (790), Christian Bible Teaching
   PO Box 278, Albany 97321; 541-926-2233; Fax: 541-926-3925; Bill Zipp

KRKT-FM (99.9), Country;
KTHH-AM (990), Classic Country
   2840 Marion St. SE, Albany 97321; 541-926-8628; Fax: 541-928-1261; Robert Dove

Astoria
KAQX-FM (94.3), Today's Hit Music;
KAST-AM (1370), News/Talk;
KAST-FM (92.9), Soft Rock;
KKEE-AM (1230), Oldies;
KVAS-FM (103.9), Country
   1006 West Marine Dr., Astoria 97103; 503-325-2911; Fax: 503-325-5570; Paul Mitchell

Baker City
KBKR-AM (1490)

KCMB-FM (104.7), Country
   2950 Church, Baker City 97814; 541-523-3400; Fax: 541-523-5481; Randy McKone

KKBC-FM (95.3)

Bandon
KBDN-FM (96.5), Classic Rock n' Roll
   PO Box 180, Coos Bay 97420; 541-267-2121; Fax: 541-267-5229; John Pundt

Banks (see Portland)

Bend
KBND-AM (1110), News/Talk;
KLRR-FM (101.7), Adult Contemporary/AAA;
KMTK-FM (99.7), Country;
KTWS-FM (98.3), Classic Rock
   PO Box 5037, Bend 97708; 541-382-5263; Fax: 541-388-0456; Mike Cheney

KICE-AM (940), Sports/Talk;
KMGX-FM (100.7), Adult Contemporary;
KSJJ-FM (102.9), Country;
KXIX-FM (94.1), CHR
   969 SW Colorado Ave., Bend 97702; 541-388-3300; Fax: 541-388-3303; Dana Horner

KNLR-FM (97.5), Contemporary Christian
   PO Box 7408, Bend 97708; 541-389-8873; Fax: 541-389-5291; Terry Cowan

KQAK-FM (105.7), Rock n' Roll Oldies;
KWPK-FM (104.1), Hot Adult Contemporary
   854 NE 4th, Bend 97701; 541-383-3825; Fax: 541-383-3403; Keith Shipman

Brookings
KURY-AM (910), Classic Country;
KURY-FM (95.3), Variety
   PO Box 1029, Brookings 97415; 541-469-2111; Fax: 541-469-6397; Vern Garvin

Burns
KQHC-FM (92.7), Classic Hits;
KZZR-AM (1230), Country/News-Information
   PO Box 877, Burns 97720; 541-573-2055; Fax: 541-573-5223; Stan Swol

Cannon Beach
KCBZ-FM (96.5) Adult Contemporary
   120 N Roosevelt, Seaside 97138; 503-738-8668; Fax: 503-738-8778; John Chapman

Cave Junction
KCNA-FM (102.7)

Coos Bay/North Bend
KACW-FM (107.3 & 107.7), Hot AC;
KBBR-AM (1340), News/Talk;
KOOS-FM (94.9), Country
   PO Box 180, Coos Bay 97420; 541-267-2121; Fax: 541-267-5229; John Pundt

KDCQ-FM (93.5), Oldies
   PO Box 478, Coos Bay 97420; 541-269-0935; Fax: 541-269-9376; Stephanie Kilmer

KHSN-AM (1230), ESPN-24 Hour Sports
PO Box 180, Coos Bay 97420; 541-267-2121; Fax: 541-267-5229; Laura Peck

KYSJ-FM (105.9), Smooth Jazz;

KYTT-FM (98.7), Contemporary Christian
580 Kingwood, Coos Bay 97420; 541-269-2022; Fax: 541-267-0114; Rick Stevens

Coquille

KSHR-FM (97.3), Hot New Country;

KWRO-AM (630), News/Talk
PO Box 180, Coos Bay 97420;. 541-267-2121; Fax: 541-267-5229; John Pundt

Corvallis

KEJO-AM (1240), Sports Talk;

KLOO-AM (1340), News/Talk;

KLOO-FM (106.3), Classic Rock
2840 Marion St. SE, Albany 97322; 541-926-8628; Fax: 541-928-1261; Robert Dove

Cottage Grove

KCGR-FM (100.5), Star Station/Mexicana Musicale;

KNND-AM (1400), Country Coast to Coast
321 Main St., Cottage Grove 97424; 541-942-2468; Fax: 541-942-5797; Diane O'Renick

Dallas

KWIP-AM (880), Regional Mexican Music
PO Box 469, Dallas 97338; 503-623-0245; Fax: 503-623-6733; Diane Burns

Eagle Point (see Medford)

Enterprise

KWVR-AM (1340), News/Talk/Sports;

KWVR-FM (92.1), Country
220 W Main St., Enterprise 97828; 541-426-4577; Fax: 541-426-4578; David Nelson

Eugene/Springfield

KDUK-FM (104.7), Top 40 Hits;

KFLY-FM (101.5), Album-oriented Rock;

KOOL-FM (99.1), Oldies;

KPNW-AM (1120), News/Talk/Sports
PO Box 1120, Eugene 97440; 541-485-1120; Fax: 541-484-5769; Robert Dove

KEED-AM (1600), News/Talk/Family
PO Box 278, Albany 97321; 541-683-1600; Fax: 541-607-8544; Bill Zipp

KEHK-FM (Star 102.3), Contemporary Rock;

KNRQ-FM (97.9), Alternative Rock;

KSCR-AM (1320), ESPN Sports;

KUGN-AM (590), News/Talk;

KUJZ-FM (95.3), Country;

KZEL-FM (96.1), Classic Rock
1200 Executive Pkwy, Suite 440, Eugene 97401; 541-284-8500; Fax: 541-485-4070; Steve Ries

KEUG-FM (105.5), 80's Oldies
925 Country Club Rd., Suite 200, Eugene 97401; 541-349-1055; Fax: 541-344-9424; John Tilson

KKNU-FM (93.1), New Country;

KKXO-AM (1450), Adult Standard;

KMGE-FM (94.5), Adult Contemporary
925 Country Club Rd., Suite 200, Eugene 97401; 541-484-9400; Fax: 541-344-9424; John Tilson

KKNX-AM (840), Oldies
945 Garfield St., Eugene 97402; 541-342-1012; Fax: 541-342-6201; John S. Mielke

KORE-AM (1050), Christian Programs/Talk
2080 Laura St., Springfield 97477-2197; 541-747-5673; Larry Knight

KQFE-FM (88.9)

Florence

KCST-AM (1250), Adult Standards/Net: Music of Your Life;

KCST-FM (106.9), Adult Contemporary/Country
PO Box 20000, Florence 97439; 541-997-9136; Fax: 541-997-9165; Jon Thompson

Gleneden Beach (see Newport)

Gold Beach

KGBR-FM (92.7), Adult Contemporary/Country
PO Box 787, Gold Beach 97444-0787; 541-247-7211; Fax: 541-247-4155; Dale St. Marie

Gold Hill

KRWQ-FM (100.3), Country .
3624 Avion Dr., Medford 97504; 541-772-4170; Fax: 541-857-0326; Bill Nielsen

Grants Pass

KAJO-AM (1270), Adult Standards/Talk
888 Rogue River Hwy., Grants Pass 97527; 541-476-6608; Fax: 541-476-4018; Carl Wilson

KLDR-FM (98.3), Adult CHR
888 Rogue River Hwy., Grants Pass 97527; 541-474-7292; Fax: 541-474-7300; Carl Wilson

KRRM-FM (94.7), Classic Country/Bluegrass/ Cowboy Music and Poetry
225 Rogue River Hwy., Grants Pass 97527; 541-479-6497; Fax: 541-479-5726; Herb Bell

201

Gresham (see Portland)

Hermiston
KOHU-AM (1360), Country;
KQFM-FM (100.5), Adult Contemporary
PO Box 145, Hermiston 97838-0145; 541-567-6500; Fax: 541-567-6068; Angela Pursel

Hillsboro (see Portland)

Hood River
KCGB-FM (105.5), Adult Contemporary;
KIHR-AM (1340), Country
PO Box 360, Hood River 97031; 541-386-1511; Fax: 541-386-7155; Gary Grossman

Jacksonville
KAPL-AM (1300)

John Day
KJDY-AM (1400), Country;
KJDY-FM (94.5), Country
PO Box 399, John Day 97845; 541-575-1400; Fax: 541-575-2313; Phil Gray

Junction City
KZTU-AM (660), News/Talk
283 Greenwood St., Junction City 97448; 541-995-9660; Fax: 541-995-8633; Mark Ail

Klamath Falls
KAGO-AM (1150), News/Talk;
KAGO-FM (99.5), Rock;
KKJX-AM (960) Hispanic (Regional);
KLAD-FM (92.5), Country;
KYSF-FM (102.9), Top 40
PO Box 339, Klamath Falls 97601; 541-882-8833; Fax: 541-882-8836; Greg Dourian

KFEG-FM (104.7) Classic Rock & Roll
PO Box 938, Klamath Falls 97601; 541-850-5242; 541-884-2845; Bill Ifft

KFLS-AM (1450), News/Sports;
KFLS-FM (96.5), Country;
KKRB-FM (106.9), Adult Contemporary
PO Box 1450, Klamath Falls 97601; 541-882-4656; Fax: 541-884-2845; Robert Wynne

KRAM-AM (1070)

KRAT-FM (97.7)

La Grande
KCMB-FM (104.7), Country;
KWRL-FM (99.9), Adult Contemporary
1009-C Adams Ave., La Grande 97850; 541-963-3405; Fax: 541-963-5090; Randy McKone

KLBM-AM (1450)
KUBQ-FM (98.7)

Lakeview
KQIK-AM (1230), Classic Hit Country;
KQIK-FM (93.5), Lite Rock
17968 Hwy. 395, Lakeview 97630; 541-947-3351; Fax: 541-947-3375; Tommie S. Dodd

Lake Oswego (see Portland)

Lebanon
KGAL-AM (1580), News/Talk/Sports
PO Box 749, Albany 97321; 541-926-5425; Fax: 541-451-5429; Charlie Eads

KSHO-AM (920), Adult Standards
PO Box 749, Albany 97321; 541-926-8683; Fax: 541-451-5429; Charlie Eads

KXPC-FM (103.7), Country
1207 9th Ave. SE, Albany 97322; 541-928-1926; Fax: 541-791-1054; Rich Coleman

Lincoln City
KBCH-AM (1400), Adult Standards/Talk/Sports;
KCRF-FM (96.7), Classic Rock
PO Box 1430, Newport 97365; 541-265-2266; Fax: 541-265-6397; Dave Miller

McMinnville
KLYC-AM (1260), Oldies
PO Box 1099, McMinnville 97128; 503-472-1260; Fax: 503-472-3243; Larry Bohnsack

Medford/Ashland/Phoenix
KAKT-FM (105.1), Country;
KBOY-FM (95.7), Classic Rock;
KCMX-AM (880), News/Talk;
KCMX-FM (101.9), Adult Contemporary;
KTMT-AM (580), Sports;
KTMT-FM (93.7), Contemporary Hits
1438 Rossanley Dr., Medford 97501; 541-779-1550; Fax: 541-776-2360; Ron Hren

KCNA-FM (102.7), Oldies;
KROG-FM (97.1), Adult Alternative;
KEZX-AM (730), Easy Listening;
KRTA-AM (610), Hispanic
511 Rossanley, Medford 97501; 541-772-0322; Fax: 541-772-4233; Brian Fraser

KDOV-FM (91.7), News/Talk - Christian
1236 Disk Dr., Suite E, Medford 97501; 541-776-5368; Fax: 541-776-0618; Perry Atkinson

KIFS-FM (107.5), Current Hit Radio
KLDZ-FM (103.5), 60's & 70's Superhits
3624 Avion Dr., Medford 97504; 541-774-1324; Fax: 541-857-0326; Bill Nielsen

KMED-AM (1440), News/Talk
3624 Avion Dr., Medford 97504; 541-773-1440; Fax: 541-857-0326; Bill Nielsen

KZZE-FM (106.3), Rock
3624 Avion Dr., Medford 97504; 541-857-0340; 541-857-0326; Bill Nielsen

Milton-Freewater
KTHK-FM (97.9)

Monmouth
KSND-FM (95.1), Adult Contemporary
285 Liberty St. NE, #340, Salem 97301; 503-763-9951; Fax: 503-763-2676; Ernie Hopseker

Myrtle Point
KOOZ-FM (94.1)

Newport
KNCU FM (92.7), Country;
KNPT-AM (1310), News/Talk/Sports;
KYTE-FM (102.7), Hot Adult Contemporary
PO Box 1430, Newport 97365; 541-265-2266; Fax: 541-265-6397; Dave Miller

KPPT-AM (1230), Nostalgia;
KPPT-FM (100.7), Classic Hits
PO Box 456, Newport 97365; 541-265-5000; Fax: 541-265-9576; Cheryl Harle

KSHL-FM (97.5), Country
PO Box 1180, Newport 97365; 541-265-6477; Fax: 541-265-6478; Dick Linn

Ontario
KSRV-AM (1380), Music;
KSRV-FM (96.1), Continuous Country Favorites
1725 N Oregon, Ontario 97914; 541-889-8651; Fax: 541-889-8733; Carrie Cornils

Pendleton
KTIX-AM (1240), Sports;
KUMA-AM (1290), News/Talk;
KUMA-FM (107.7), Adult Contemporary
2003 NW 56th Dr., Pendleton 97801; 541-276-1511; Fax: 541-276-1480; Randy McKone

KWHT-FM (103.5), Country
2003 NW 56th Dr., Pendleton 97801; 541-278-2500; Fax: 541-276-1480; Randy McKone

Portland
KBMS-AM (1480)

KBNP-AM (1410), All Business/Financial News
278 SW Arthur St., Portland 97201; 503-223-6769; Fax: 503-223-4305; Keith Lyons

KEX-AM (1190), News/Talk;
KPOJ-AM (620), Golden Oldies
4949 SW Macadam Ave., Portland 97201; 503-323-6400; Fax: 503-227-5873; Mary Lou Gunn

KFXX-AM (1080), Sports Talk;
KGON-FM (92.3), Classic Rock;
KNRK-FM (94.7), Alternative Rock;
KWJJ-FM (99.5), Country
0700 SW Bancroft St., Portland 97239; 503-223-1441; Fax: 503-223-6909; Jack Hutchison

KGDD-AM (1520), Spanish Regional;
KMUZ-AM (1230), Spanish Oldies;
KRMZ-AM (1150), Spanish Contemporary;
KZNY-AM (1010), English Oldies
5110 SE Stark, Portland 97215; 503-234-5550; Fax: 503-234-5583; Spencer French

KINK-FM (101.9), AAA
1501 SW Jefferson, Portland 97201; 503-517-6000; Fax: 503-517-6130; Stan Mak

KKCW-FM (103.3), Adult Contemporary
4949 SW Macadam Ave., Portland 97201; 503-323-6400; Fax: 503-222-0030; Mary Lou Gunn

KKPZ-AM (1330)

KKRZ-FM (100.3), Top 40;
KRVO-FM (105.9), Classic Rock
4949 SW Macadam Ave., Portland 97201; 503-323-6400; Fax: 503-323-6660; Mary Lou Gunn

KKSL-AM (1290)

KKSN-FM (97.1), Oldies;
KOTK-AM (910), Talk;
KRSK-FM (105.1), Adult Contemporary
0700 SW Bancroft St., Portland 97239; 503-223-1441; Fax: 503-223-6909; Erin Hubert

KLTH-FM (106.7), Light Rock
1501 SW Jefferson, Portland 97201; 503-223-0300; Fax: 503-223-6795; Stan Mak

KLVP-AM (1040);
KLVP-FM (88.7)

KPAM-AM (860), News/Talk
888 SW 5th Ave., Suite 790, Portland 97204; 503-223-4321; Fax: 503-294-0074; Kevin Young

KPDQ-AM (800)
KPDQ-FM (93.7)

KUFO-FM (101.1), Album Rock;
KVMX-FM (107.5), 80's
2040 SW First Ave., Portland 97201; 503-222-1011; Fax: 503-222-2047; Mark Walen

Media Directories

KUIK-AM (1360), News/Talk/Sports
PO Box 566, Hillsboro 97123; 503-640-1360;
Fax: 503-640-6108; Don McCoun

KUPL-AM (970), Country;
KUPL-FM (98.7), Country
222 SW Columbia, Suite 350, Portland
97201; 503-223-0300; Fax: 503-223-6795;
Mark Walen

KXJM-FM (95.5), Rhythmic Top 40;
KXL-AM (750), News/Talk/Sports
0234 SW Bancroft St., Portland 97239; 503-
243-7595; Fax: 503-417-7661; Tim
McNamara

Prineville
KLTW-FM (95.1), Soft Adult Contemporary;
KWLZ-FM (96.5), Active Rock
854 NE 4th, Bend 97701; 541-383-3825; Fax:
541-383-3403; Keith Shipman

KRCO-AM (690), Classic Country
854 NE 4th, Bend 97701; 541-447-6770; Fax:
541-383-3403; Keith Shipman

Redmond
KRDM-AM (1240), News/Talk
PO Box 1309, Redmond, 97756; 541-548-
7621; Fax: 541-504-8145; Bud Hutchinson

Reedsport
KDUN-AM (1030), Real Country
PO Box 168, Reedsport 97467; 541-271-
5558; Fax: 541-271-2598; Mark L. Ail

KJMX-FM (99.5), Adult Contemporary
PO Box 180, Coos Bay 97420; 541-267-
2121; Fax: 541-267-5229; John Pundt

Rogue River (see Grants Pass)

Roseburg
KAVJ-FM (101.1), Oldies;
KKMX-FM (104.5), Adult Contemporary;
KQEN-AM (1240), News/Talk/Sports;
KRSB-FM (103.1), Contemporary Country
1445 W Harvard, Roseburg 97470; 541-672-
6641; Fax: 541-673-7598; Pat Markham

KRNR-AM (1490), Country
PO Box 910, Roseburg 97470; 541-673-5553;
Fax: 541-673-3483; Faye Johnson

KTBR-AM (950)

St. Helens
KOHI-AM (1600), News/Talk/Country Rock
36200 N Columbia River Hwy., Suite E, St.
Helens 97051; 503-397-1600; Fax: 503-
397-1601; Marty Rowe

Salem
KBZY-AM (1490), Local Service/Adult
Contemporary

4340 Commercial St. SE, Salem 97302; 503-
362-1490; Fax: 503-362-6545; Roy
Dittman

KCCS-AM (1220), Christian Talk Radio
1850 45th Ave. NE, Salem 97305; 503-364-
1000; Fax: 503-364-1022; Don Wyant Jr.

KSLM-AM (1390), All Sports
0700 SW Bancroft St., Portland 97201; 503-
223-1441; Fax: 503-223-6909; Jack
Hutchison

KYKN-AM (1430), News/Talk
PO Box 1430, Salem 97308; 503-390-3014;
Fax: 503-390-3728; Mike Frith

Scappoose
KFIS-FM (104.1)

Seaside
KCRX-FM (102.3), Classic Rock
1006 West Marine Dr., Astoria 97103; 503-
325-2911; Fax: 503-325-5570; Paul
Mitchell

KCYS-FM (98.1), Hot Country
PO Box 1258, Astoria 97103; 503-717-9643;
Fax: 503-717-9578; Dave Heick

KSWB-AM (840), Adult Standards
1006 West Marine Dr., Astoria 97103; 503-
325-2911; Fax: 503-325-5570; Buz Kelly

Stayton
KCKX-AM (1460), Classic Country Western
PO Box 158, Woodburn 97071; 503-981-
9400; Fax: 503-981-3561; Don Coss

Sweet Home
KFIR-AM (720), Modern/Classic Country
PO Box 720, Sweet Home 97386; 541-367-
5115; Fax: 541-367-5233; Bob Ratter

KLVU-FM (107.1)

The Dalles
KACI-AM (1300), News/Talk;
KACI-FM (97.7), Oldies;
KMSW-FM (92.7), Rock Classics
PO Box 1517, The Dalles 97058; 541-296-
2211; Fax: 541-296-2213; Gary Grossman

KLCK-AM (1400), Oldies;
KYYT-FM (102.3), Country
PO Box 1023, The Dalles 97058; 541-296-
9102; Fax: 541-298-7775; Dan Manciu

KMCQ-FM (104.5), Adult Contemporary/
Contemporary Hits
PO Box 104, The Dalles 97058; 541-298-
5116; Fax: 541-298-5119; John Huffman

KODL-AM (1440), Adult Standards
PO Box 1488, The Dalles 97058; 541-296-
2101; Fax: 541-296-3766; Al Wynn

Tillamook

KDEP-FM (105.5), Light Rock
PO Box 669, Tillamook 97141; 503-842-3888; Fax: 541-842-5640; Chris Gilbreth

KMBD-AM (1590), News/Talk;
KTIL-FM (94.1), Adult Contemporary
PO Box 40, Tillamook 97141; 503-842-4422; Fax: 503-842-2755; Van Moe

Umatilla

KLWJ-AM (1090)

Waldport

KORC-AM (820), Adult Standards/Nostalgia
PO Box 495, Waldport 97394; 541-563-5100; Fax: 541-563-5116; Larry Profitt

Winston

KGRV-AM (700)

Woodburn

KWBY-AM (940), Mexican Regional
PO Box 158, Woodburn 97071; 503-981-9400; Fax: 503-981-3561; Dorecia Luse

OREGON COMMERCIAL TELEVISION STATIONS

Source: Oregon Association of Broadcasters
President/CEO: Bill Johnstone
Address: 7150 SW Hampton St., Suite 240, Portland 97223
Phone: 503-443-2299
Fax: 503-443-2488
Web: www.theoab.org

Bend

KFXO-TV (39); Fox
63140 Britta St., Suite D-101, Bend 97701; 541-382-7220; Fax: 541-382-5922; Teresa Burgess
Web: www.kfxo.com

KTVZ-TV (21); NBC
PO Box 6038, Bend 97708; 541-383-2121; Fax: 541-382-1616; Jim DeChant
Web: www.ktvz.com

Brookings

KBSC-TV (49); Independent
PO Box 1802, Brookings 97415; 541-469-4999; Fax: 541-469-0801; Michael McKenzie-Bahr

Coos Bay

KCBY-TV (11); CBS
PO Box 1156, Coos Bay 97420; 541-269-1111; Fax: 541-269-7464; Dave Weinkauf
Web: www.kcby.com

KMTZ-TV (23); NBC
Note: See KMTR-TV - Eugene

Eugene

KEVU-TV (25); Independent
2940 Chad Dr., Eugene 97408; 541-683-2525; Fax: 541-683-8016; Mark Metzger
Web: www.klsrtvfox.com

KEZI-TV (9); ABC
PO Box 7009, Eugene 97401; 541-485-5611; Fax: 541-342-1568; Scott Chambers
Web: www.kezi.com

KLSR-TV (34); Fox
2940 Chad Dr., Eugene 97408; 541-683-3434; Fax: 541-683-8016; Mark Metzger
Web: www.klsrtvfox.com

KMTR-TV (16); NBC
3825 International Court, Springfield 97477; 541-746-1600; Fax: 541-747-0866; Cambra Ward
Web: www.kmtr.com

KVAL-TV (13); CBS
PO Box 1313, Eugene 97440; 541-342-4961; Fax: 541-342-2635; Dave Weinkauf
Web: www.kval.com

Klamath Falls

KDKF-TV (31); ABC
231 E Main St., Klamath Falls 97601; 541-883-3131; Fax: 541-883-8931; Renard Maiuri

KOTI-TV (2); NBC
PO Box 2K, Klamath Falls 97601; 541-882-2222; Fax: 541-883-7664; Bob Wise
Web: www.localnewscomesfirst.com

Medford

KDRV-TV (12); ABC
PO Box 4220, Medford 97501; 541-773-1212; Fax: 541-779-9261; Renard Maiuri
Web: www.kdrv.com

KMVU-TV (26); Fox
820 Crater Lake Ave., #105, Medford 97504; 541-772-2600; Fax: 541-772-7364; Cary Jones

KOBI-TV (5); NBC
PO Box 1489, Medford 97501; 541-779-5555; Fax: 541-779-8888; Bob Wise
Web: www.kobi5.com

KTVL-TV (10); CBS
PO Box 10, Medford 97501-0202; 541-773-7373; Fax: 541-779-0451; Kingsley Kelley
Web: www.ktvl.com

Pendleton

KFFX-TV (11)

Portland

KATU-TV (2); ABC
PO Box 2, Portland 97207; 503-231-4222; Fax: 503-231-4233; Dave Olmsted
Web: www.katu.com

Media Directories

KGW-TV (8); NBC
  1501 SW Jefferson St., Portland 97201; 503-
  226-5000; Fax: 503-226-5059; Paul Fry
  Web: www.kgw.com

KMST-TV (4)

KNMT-TV (24); Independent
  432 NE 74th Ave., Portland 97213; 503-252-
  0792; Fax: 503-256-4205; Jane Duff

KOIN-TV (6); CBS
  222 SW Columbia, Portland 97201; 503-464-
  0600; Fax: 503-464-0717; David B.
  Lippoff
  Web: www.koin.com

KPDX-TV (49); UPN
  14975 NW Greenbrier Pkwy., Beaverton
  97006-5731; 503-906-1249; Fax: 503-548-
  6915; Teresa Burgess
  Web: www.kpdx.com

KPTV-TV (12); Fox
  14975 NW Greenbrier Pkwy., Beaverton
  97006-5731; 503-906-1249; Fax: 503-548-
  6915; Teresa Burgess
  Web: www.kptv.com

KWBP-TV (32); Warner Bros.
  10255 SW Arctic Dr., Beaverton 97005; 503-
  644-3232; Fax: 503-626-3576; Kieran
  Clarke
  Web: www.portlandswb.com

Roseburg

KMTX-TV (46); NBC
  Note: See KMTR-TV - Eugene

KPIC-TV (4); CBS
  PO Box 1345, Roseburg 97470; 541-672-4481;
  Fax: 541-672-4482; Connie Williamson
  Web: www.kpic.com

KTNU-TV (36)

Salem

KPXG-TV (22); Pax-Net
  1501 SW Jefferson, Portland 97201; 503-222-
  2221; Fax: 503-222-3732; Lee Warpack

The Dalles

KRHP-TV (14); Family Network, Worship
  3350 Columbia View Dr., The Dalles 97058;
  541-296-2711; Fax: 541-296-6158; Bob
  Pettitt

OREGON PUBLIC/EDUCATIONAL RADIO AND TELEVISION STATIONS

Source: Oregon Association of Broadcasters
President/CEO: Bill Johnstone
Address: 7150 SW Hampton St., Suite 240,
  Portland 97223

Phone: 503-443-2299
Fax: 503-443-2488
Web: www.theoab.org

Ashland

KSOR-FM (90.1);
KSMF-FM (89.1);
KSRG-FM (88.3)
  Southern Oregon University, 1250 Siskiyou
  Blvd., Ashland 97520; 541-552-6301; Fax:
  541-552-8565; Ron Kramer
  Web: www.jeffnet.org

Astoria

KMUN-FM (91.9)
  PO Box 269, Astoria 97103; 503-325-0010;
  Fax: 503-325-3956; Lisa Smith
  Web: www.kmun.org

Bend

KOAB-FM (91.3);
KOAB-TV (3)
  PO Box 509, Bend 97709; 541-382-1571;
  Max Culbertson

Burney/Redding, CA

KNCA-FM (89.7)
  Southern Oregon University, 1250 Siskiyou
  Blvd., Ashland 97520; 541-552-6301; Ron
  Kramer

Central Point

KCHC-FM (91.7)
  School District #6, Medford; 541-664-1241

Coos Bay

KSBA-FM (88.5)
  Southern Oregon University, 1250 Siskiyou
  Blvd., Ashland 97520; 541-552-6301; Ron
  Kramer

Corvallis

KBVR-FM (88.7);
KBVR-TV (99) (cable)
  Memorial Union East, Rm. 210, Oregon State
  University, Corvallis 97331; 541-737-
  4604; Fax: 541-737-4545; Ann Robinson

KOAC-AM (550);
KOAC-TV (7)
  239 Covell Hall, Oregon State University,
  Corvallis 97331; 541-737-4311; Fax: 541-
  737-4314; Lynne Clendenin
  Web: www.opb.org

Eagle Point

KEPO-FM (92.9)
  School District #9, PO Box 198, Eagle Point
  97524; 541-830-1345

Eugene

KLCC-FM (89.7)
Lane Community College, 4000 E 30th Ave., Eugene 97405; 541-463-6000; Fax: 541-463-6046; Steve Barton
Web: www.klcc.org

KRVM-FM (91.9);
KRVM-AM (1280)
Eugene Public School District 4J, 1574 Coburg Rd., PMB 237, Eugene 97401; 541-687-3370; Fax: 541-687-3573; Carl Sundberg

KWAX-FM (91.1)
University of Oregon, 75 Centennial Loop, Eugene 97401; 541-345-0800 or 800-422-4301; Paul Bjornstad
Web: www.kwax.com

Florence

K211BP (90.5)
Eugene Public School District 4J, 1574 Coburg Rd., PMB 237, Eugene 97401; 541-687-3370; Fax: 541-687-3573; Carl Sundberg

KLFO-FM (88.1)
Lane Community College, 4000 E 30th Ave., Eugene 97405; 541-463-6000; Fax: 541-463-6046; Steve Barton
www.klcc.org

Forest Grove

KPUR-FM (94.5)
Pacific University, 2043 College Way, Forest Grove 97116; 503-359-2255; Mike Geraci

Grants Pass

KAGI-AM (930)
Southern Oregon University, 1250 Siskiyou Blvd., Ashland 97520; 541-552-6301; Ron Kramer

Gresham

KMHD-FM (89.1)
Mt. Hood Community College, 26000 SE Stark St., Gresham 97030; 503-661-8900; Doug Sweet

Klamath Falls

KLMF-FM (88.5);
KSKF-FM (90.9)
Southern Oregon University, 1250 Siskiyou Blvd., Ashland 97520; 541-552-6301; Ronald Kramer

KTEC-FM (89.5)
Oregon Institute of Technology, PO Box 2009, Klamath Falls 97601; 541-885-1840; Fax: 541-885-1857; Jason Stec
www.oit.edu/~ktec/

La Grande

KEOL-FM (91.7)
Eastern Oregon University, La Grande 97850; 541-962-3698; Aaron Scott
Web: www.eou.edu/keol

KTVR-TV (13)
PO Box R, La Grande 97850; 541-963-3900; Fax: 541-963-7742; Maynard Orme

McMinnville

KSLC-FM (90.3)
Linfield College, #DD 900 S Baker, McMinnville 97128; 503-434-2550; Fax: 503-434-2666; Micah Shelton

Medford

KSYS-TV (8)
34 S Fir St., Medford 97501; 541-779-0808; Fax: 541-779-2178; Mark Stanislawski

Mendocino, CA

KPMO-AM (1300)
Southern Oregon University, 1250 Siskiyou Blvd., Ashland 97520; 541-552-6301; Ron Kramer

Mt. Shasta, CA

KMJC-AM (620)
KNSQ-FM (88.1)
Southern Oregon University, 1250 Siskiyou Blvd., Ashland 97520; 541-552-6301; Ron Kramer

Myrtle Point

KOOZ-FM (94.1)
Southern Oregon University, 1250 Siskiyou Blvd., Ashland 97520; 541-552-6301; Ron Kramer

Newberg

KFOX-AM (530)
George Fox College, Sub Box F, Newberg 97132; 503-554-3012; Brad Lau

Newport

KLCO-FM (90.5)
Lane Community College, 4000 E 30th Ave., Eugene 97405; 541-463-6000; Fax: 541-463-6046; Steve Barton
Web: www.klcc.org

Oakridge

KAVE-FM (92.1)
Eugene Public School District 4J, 1574 Coburg Rd., PMB 237, Eugene 97401; 541-687-3370; Fax: 541-687-3573; Debbie Gillespie

Ontario

KMBA-TV (19)
Treasure Valley Community College, Weese Bldg., 650 College Blvd., Ontario 97914; 541-889-6493, ext. 343; Fax: 541-881-2717; Russell Strawn

Media Directories

Pendleton

KRBM-FM (90.9)
Blue Mountain Community College, PO Box 100, Pendleton 97801; 541-276-1260; Fax: 541-276-6119; Maynard Orme

Portland

KBOO-FM (90.7)
20 SE 8th Ave., Portland 97214; 503-231-8032; Fax: 503-231-7145; Denise Kowalczyk
Web: www.kboo.fm

KBPS-AM (1450);
KBPS-FM (89.9)
School District #1, 515 NE 15th Ave., Portland 97232; 503-916-5828; Fax: 503-916-2642; Suzanne White
Web: www.allclassical.org

KBVM-FM (88.3)
PO Box 5888, Portland 97228; 503-285-5200; Fax: 503-285-3322; Steven Moffitt

KDUP-AM (860)
University of Portland Communications Dept., 5000 N Willamette Blvd., Portland 97203; 503-943-7121; Sally Click

KLC-FM (104.1)
Lewis and Clark College, PO Box 122, Portland 97219; 503-768-7132; Fax: 503-768-7130; Zac Tasjiau

KOPB-FM (91.5);
KOPB-TV (10)
Oregon Public Broadcasting, 7140 SW Macadam Ave., Portland 97219; 503-244-9900; Fax: 503-293-4165; Maynard Orme
Web: www.opb.org

KRRC-FM (97.9)
Reed College, Portland 97202; 503-517-7383; Ana Brown

Reedsport

KSYD-FM (92.1)
Eugene Public School District 4J, 1574 Coburg Rd., PMB 237, Eugene 97401; 541-687-3370; Fax: 541-687-3573; Carl Sundberg

Rio Dell/Eureka, CA

KNHT-FM (107.3)
Southern Oregon University, 1250 Siskiyou Blvd., Ashland 97520; 541-552-6301; Ron Kramer

Roseburg

KSRS-FM (91.5);
KTBR-AM (950)
Southern Oregon University, 1250 Siskiyou Blvd., Ashland 97520; 541-552-6301; Ron Kramer

Talent

KSJK-AM (1230)
Southern Oregon University, 1250 Siskiyou Blvd., Ashland 97520; 541-552-6301; Ron Kramer

Warm Springs

KWSO-FM (91.9)
PO Box 489, Warm Springs 97761; 541-553-1968; Fax: 541-553-3348; Mary Sando-Emhoolah

Yreka, CA

KNYR-FM (91.3);
KSYC-AM (1490)
Southern Oregon University, 1250 Siskiyou Blvd., Ashland 97520; 541-552-6301; Ron Kramer

CABLE TELEVISION

Source: Oregon Cable Telecommunications Association
Executive Director: Michael Dewey
Address: 1249 Commercial St. SE, Salem 97302
Phone: 503-362-8838
Fax: 503-399-1029
Web: www.oregoncable.com

Cable television was developed in the late 1940s in communities unable to receive broadcast TV signals because of terrain or distance from broadcast stations. In fact, Astoria is believed to be the site of the first cable TV system. Cable provides broadcast signals, satellite signals and public and leased access services to its subscribers.

Many Oregon cable companies have or are making significant technological changes to their infrastructure. Besides providing an array of television programming services on their analog or digital services, many cable companies are now providing high-speed data services to the Internet. And in some cases, especially in larger markets, local telephone service is delivered through the local cable company.

The Oregon Cable Telecommunications Association (OCTA) represents its Oregon members who are cable companies. It does not regulate cable TV or cable companies.

Fisherman with 40 pound Chinook salmon at Celilo—Oregon State Archives Photograph, OHDG208

The federal government owns more than half the land in Oregon. Oregon's position on the Pacific Rim has resulted in strong ties between Oregon and other nations. Oregon has nine federally recognized tribes of Native Americans, which have a distinct relationship with state government. This section contains information about the federal government, tribes, and representatives of other nations in Oregon.

Gordon H. Smith

Republican. Born in Pendleton, May 25, 1952. Brigham Young University, B.A., 1976; Southwestern University, law degree, 1979. Purchased Smith Frozen Foods in 1980, now one of the largest private label packers of frozen vegetables in the U.S. He and his wife, Sharon, have three children.

Elected to the Oregon Senate, 1992; became Senate President in 1994. Elected to the U.S. Senate, 1996; reelected 2002. Member, Finance; Energy and Natural Resources; Commerce, Science, and Transportation; Rules and Administration; and Indian Affairs Committees. Also serves on Special Committee on Aging. Term expires: 2009.

Washington, D.C. Office: 404 Russell, Senate Office Bldg., Washington, D.C. 20510; 202-224-3753; Fax: 202-228-3997; Web and E-mail: http://gsmith.senate.gov

District Offices: Portland: One World Trade Center, 121 SW Salmon St., Suite 1250, Portland 97204; 503-326-3386. **Eastern Oregon:** Jager Bldg., 116 S Main St., Suite 3, Pendleton 97801; 541-278-1129. **Western Oregon:** Federal Bldg., 211 E 7th Ave., Suite 202, Eugene 97401; 541-465-6750. **Southern Oregon:** Security Plaza, 1175 E Main, Suite 2D, Medford 97504; 541-608-9102. **Central Oregon:** Jamison Bldg., 131 NW Hawthorne Ave., Suite 208, Bend 97701; 541-318-1298.

Ron Wyden

Democrat. Born in Wichita, Kansas, May 3, 1949. Stanford University, A.B. in Political Science, 1971; University of Oregon School of Law, J.D., 1974. He has two children. Co-director, Oregon Gray Panthers, 1974–80; director, Oregon Legal Services for the Elderly, 1977–79; public member, Oregon Board of Examiners of Nursing Home Administrators, 1978–79.

Elected to Congress, 1980; reelected 1982, 1984, 1986, 1988, 1990, 1992, 1994. Elected to the U.S. Senate, 1996; reelected 1998 and 2004. Member, Finance; Commerce, Science and Transportation; Energy and Natural Resources; Environment and Public Works; Budget; Intelligence; and Aging Committees. Term expires 2011.

Washington, D.C. Office: 516 Hart, Senate Office Bldg., Washington, D.C. 20510; 202-224-5244; Fax: 202-228-2717; Web and E-mail: http://wyden.senate.gov

District Offices: Bend—The Jamison Bldg., 131 NW Hawthorne Ave., Suite 107, Bend 97701; 541-330-9142; Fax: 541-330-6266. **Eugene**—The Center Court Bldg., 151 W 7th Ave., Suite 435, Eugene 97401; 541-431-0229; Fax: 541-431-0610. **La Grande**—Sac Annex Bldg., 105 Fir. St., Suite 201, La Grande 97850; 541-962-7691; Fax: 541-963-0885. **Medford**—The Federal Courthouse, 310 W 6th St., Rm. 118, Medford 97501; 541-858-5122; Fax: 541-858-5126. **Portland**—700 NE Multnomah St., Suite 450, Portland 97232; 503-326-7525; Fax: 503-326-7528. **Salem**—777 13th St. SE, Suite 110, Salem 97301; 503-589-4555; Fax: 503-589-4749.

David Wu—First District

Counties: Clatsop, Columbia, Washington, Yamhill and part of Multnomah.

Democrat. Born in Taiwan, April 8, 1955. Stanford University, B.S., 1977; Yale Law School, J.D., 1982. Attorney, Cohen and Wu. He and his wife, Michelle, have two children, Matthew and Sarah. Commissioner, Portland Planning Commission; Judicial Clerk to Judge Alfred T. Goodwin; Staff to Deputy Assistant Secretary for Health, Education and Welfare; Executive Office of the President.

Elected to Congress, 1998; reelected 2000, 2002 and 2004; Member, House Education and Workforce Committee, Science Committee. Term expires 2006.

Washington, D.C. Office: 1023 Longworth Bldg., Washington, D.C. 20515; 202-225-0855; Fax: 202-225-9497; Web: www.house.gov/wu.

District Office: 620 SW Main St., Suite 606, Portland 97205; 503-326-2901; Toll-free: 1-800-422-4003; Fax: 503-326-5066

Greg Walden—Second District

Counties: All counties east of the Cascades, all of Jackson and the Grants Pass area of Josephine.

Republican. Born January 10, 1957. University of Oregon, B.S. Small Business owner, Columbia Gorge Broadcasters. He and his wife, Mylene, have one child. Press Secretary and Chief of Staff, Congressman Denny Smith, 1981–1987; Board of Directors, Oregon Health Sciences Foundation; Director, Columbia River Bancorp.

Elected to Oregon House of Representatives, 1988; served as House Majority Leader, 1991–93; appointed to Oregon Senate, 1995; served as Assistant Majority Leader.

Elected to Congress, 1998; reelected 2000, 2002 and 2004; Member, House Energy and Commerce Committee, and Resources Committee. Term expires 2006.

Washington, D.C. Office: 1210 Longworth Bldg., Washington, D.C. 20515; 202-225-6730; Fax: 202-225-5774; E-mail: greg.walden@mail.house.gov; Web: www.walden.house.gov

District Offices: Medford—843 E Main St., Suite 400, Medford 97504; 541-776-4646; Fax: 541-779-0204. **Bend**—Jamison Bldg., 131 NW Hawthorne Ave., Suite 201, Bend 97701; 541-389-4408; Fax: 541-389-4452.

Earl Blumenauer—Third District

Counties: Most of Multnomah and northern part of Clacka-mas.

Democrat. Born in Portland, August 16, 1948. Attended Lewis and Clark College, Portland State University, University of Colorado at Denver and Kennedy School of Government at Harvard. Received B.A., political science, 1970; law degree, 1976.

Elected to Oregon House of Representatives, 1972; reelected 1974 and 1976. Elected to Multnomah County Board of Commissioners, 1978; reelected 1982. Elected to Portland City Council, 1986; reelected 1990, 1994.

Elected to Congress, 1996; reelected 1998, 2000, 2002 and 2004; Member, Transportation and Infrastructure Committee, Ground and Water Subcommittees. Term expires 2006.

Washington, D.C. Office: 2446 Rayburn House Bldg., Washington, D.C. 20515; 202-225-4811; E-mail: write.earl@ mail.house.gov; Web: http://blumenauer.house.gov

District Office: 729 NE Oregon, Suite 115, Portland 97232; 503-231-2300; Fax: 503-230-5413.

Peter DeFazio—Fourth District

Counties: Coos, Curry, Douglas, Lane, Linn, northern part of Josephine and most of Benton.

Democrat. Born in Needham, Massachusetts, May 27, 1947. Tufts University, B.A., 1969; University of Oregon, M.A., 1977. Honorable discharge U.S. Air Force Reserve, 1971. He and his wife, Myrnie L. Daut, own a home and live in Springfield. Aide to Congressman Jim Weaver, 1977–82; elected to Lane County Board of Commissioners, 1982.

Elected to Congress, 1986; reelected 1988, 1990, 1992, 1994, 1996, 1998, 2000, 2002 and 2004; Member, House Transportation and Infrastructure Committees, Resources Committee; Aviation and Surface Transportation Subcommittees; ranking Democrat on Water and Power Subcommittee. Term expires 2006.

Washington, D.C. Office: 2134 Rayburn House Office Bldg., Washington, D.C. 20515; 202-225-6416; Fax: 202-225-0032; Web: www.house.gov/defazio/

District Offices: Coos Bay—125 Central, Rm. 350, Coos Bay 97420; 541-269-2609. **Eugene**—151 W 7th Ave., Suite 400, Eugene 97401; 541-465-6732; Toll-free: 1-800-944-9603. **Roseburg**—612 SE Jackson, Rm. #9, Roseburg 97470; 541-440-3523.

Darlene Hooley—Fifth District

Counties: Lincoln, Marion, Polk, Tillamook, northern Benton, most of Clackamas.

Democrat. Born in Williston, North Dakota, April 4, 1939. Oregon State University, B.S., 1961. Health and PE teacher at Woodburn and Gervais schools, 1962–65; Portland Public Schools, 1965–67; St. Mary's Academy, 1967–69. Served on West Linn City Council, 1977–80; Oregon House of Representatives, 1981–87; Clackamas County Board of Commissioners, 1987–96. Member of the Oregon Trail Foundation Board. Former member of Oregon Progress Board and Area Agencies on Aging, and former co-chair of Commission on Children and Families. Two adult children.

Elected to Congress,1996; reelected 1998, 2000, 2002 and 2004; Member of House Budget and Banking Committee. Financial Service, Capital Market, Insurance and Government Sponsored Enterprises; Financial Institutions and Consumer Credit; Domestic Policy, Technology and Economic Growth Subcommittees. Term expires 2006.

Washington, D.C. Office: 2430 Rayburn House Bldg., Washington, D.C. 20515; 202-225-5711; Fax: 202-225-5699; E-mail: darlene@mail.house.gov; Web: www.house.gov/hooley/

District Offices: 315 Mission St. SE, Suite 101, Salem 97302; 503-588-9100; Fax: 503-588-5517. **Portland**—21570 Willamette Dr., West Linn 97068.

Congressional Districts

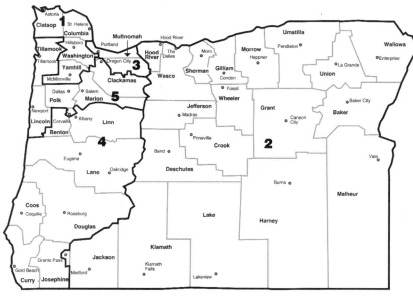

National/International/Tribal

U.S. GOVERNMENT OFFICIALS

President of the United States
George W. Bush
Address: The White House, 1600 Pennsylvania Ave., Washington, D.C. 20500
Phone: 202-456-1414
Fax: 202-456-2461
Web: www.whitehouse.gov

Occupational Background: Oil and gas exploration; major league baseball management. **Educational Background:** Yale University, Bachelor's degree, 1968; Harvard Business School, Master of Business Administration, 1975. **Governmental Experience:** Governor of Texas, 1995–2000. Elected President, 2000; reelected 2004.

Vice-President of the United States
Dick Cheney
Address: The White House, 1600 Pennsylvania Ave., Washington, D.C. 20500
Phone: 202-456-1414
Fax: 202-456-2461
Web: www.whitehouse.gov

Occupational Background: Business Executive. **Educational Background:** University of Wyoming, Bachelor of Arts, 1965; Master of Arts, 1966. **Governmental Experience:** Nixon and Ford administration positions from 1969–1977 including White House Chief of Staff from 1975–1977; U.S. House of Representatives, 1979–89; U.S. Secretary of Defense, 1989–93; Elected Vice-President, 2000; reelected 2004.

The Cabinet:

Chief of Staff
Andrew Card
Address: The White House, 1600 Pennsylvania Ave., Washington, D.C. 20500
Phone: 202-456-1414
Web: www.whitehouse.gov

Department of Agriculture
Mike Johanns, Secretary
Address: 810 Verm
Address: 1400 Independence Ave. SW, Washington, D.C. 20250
Phone: 202-720-2791
Web: www.usda.gov

Department of Commerce
Carlos Guttierrez, Secretary
Address: 14th and Constitution Ave. NW, Washington, D.C. 20230
Phone: 202-482-2112

Fax: 202-482-2741
Web: www.commerce.gov

Department of Defense
Donald Rumsfeld, Secretary
Address: 1000 Defense Pentagon, Washington, D.C. 20301-1000
Phone: 703-428-0711
Web: www.defenselink.mil

Department of Education
Margaret Spellings, Secretary
Address: 810 Verm
Address: 400 Maryland Ave. SW, Washington, D.C. 20202
Phone: 202-401-3000
Fax: 202-401-0596
Web: www.ed.gov

Department of Energy
Samuel Bodman, Secretary - subject to Senate confirmation
Address: 1000 Independence Ave. SW, Washington, D.C. 20585
Phone: 800-DIAL-DOE
Fax: 202-586-4403
Web: www.energy.gov

Department of Health and Human Services
Michael O. Leavitt, Secretary
Address: 200 Independence Ave. SW, Washington, D.C. 20201
Phone: 877-696-6775
Fax: 202-690-7203
Web: www.hhs.gov

Department of Homeland Security
Michael Chertoff, Secretary - subject to Senate confirmation
Address: Washington, D.C. 20410
Phone: 202-282-8000
Web: www.dhs.gov

Department of Housing and Urban Development
Alphonzo Jackson, Secretary
Address: 451 7th St. SW, Washington, D.C. 20410
Phone: 202-708-1112
Web: www.hud.gov

Department of Interior
Gale Norton, Secretary
Address: 1849 C St. NW, Washington, D.C. 20240
Phone: 202-208-1923
Fax: 202-208-1821
Web: www.doi.gov

Department of Justice
Alberto Gonzales, Attorney General - subject to Senate confirmation

Address: 950 Pennsylvania Ave. NW, Washington, D.C. 20530
Phone: 202-514-2000
Fax: 202-307-6777
Web: www.usdoj.gov

Department of Labor
Elaine L. Chao, Secretary
Address: 200 Constitution Ave. NW, Washington, D.C. 20210
Phone: 202-693-6000
Fax: 202-693-6111
Web: www.dol.gov

Department of State
Condoleezza Rice, Secretary
Address: 2201 C St. NW, Washington, D.C. 20520
Phone: 202-647-4000
Web: www.state.gov

Department of Transportation
Norman Mineta, Secretary
Address: 400 7th St. SW, Washington, D.C. 20590
Phone: 202-366-4000
Web: www.dot.gov

Department of the Treasury
John W. Snow, Secretary
Address: 1500 Pennsylvania Ave. NW, Washington, D.C. 20220
Phone: 202-622-2000
Fax: 202-622-6415
Web: www.treasury.gov

Department of Veterans Affairs
Jim Nicholson, Secretary
Address: 810 Vermont Ave. NW, Washington, D.C. 20420
Phone: 800-827-1000
Web: www.va.gov

Environmental Protection Agency
Vacant, Administrator
Address: 1200 Pennsylvania Ave. NW, Washington, D.C. 20460
Phone: 202-564-4700
Fax: 202-501-1450
Web: www.epa.gov

Office of Management and Budget
Joshua Bolten, Director
Address: 725 17th St. NW, Washington, D.C. 20503
Phone: 202-395-7254
Fax: 202-395-7298
Web: www.whitehouse.gov/omb

United Nations Ambassador
Vacant, Ambassador
Address: 140 E 45th St., New York, NY 10017

Phone: 212-415-4000
Fax: 212-415-4443
Web: www.un.int/usa/

United States Trade Representative
Vacant
Address: 600 17th St. NW, Washington, D.C. 20508
Phone: 1-888-473-8787
Web: www.ustr.gov

National Drug Control Policy
John P. Walters, Director
Address: Office of National Drug Control Policy, PO Box 6000, Rockville, MD 20849-6000
Phone: 1-800-666-3332
Fax: 301-519-5212
Web: www.whitehousedrugpolicy.gov

U.S. GOVERNMENT IN OREGON

For information about U.S. Government in Oregon, contact the Federal Information Center at 1-800-688-9889 (TTY 1-800-326-2996) or visit them on the internet at http://fic.info.gov/

MAJOR POLITICAL PARTIES IN OREGON

Democratic National Committee
Address: 430 S Capitol St. SE, Washington, D.C. 20003
Phone: 202-863-8000
E-mail: dnc@democrats.org
Web: www.democrats.org

Democratic State Central Committee of Oregon
Address: 232 NE 9th Ave., Portland 97232
Phone: 503-224-8200
Fax: 503-224-5335
E-mail: info@dpo.org
Web: www.dpo.org

Republican National Committee
Address: 310 1st St. SE, Washington, D.C. 20003
Phone: 202-863-8500
Fax: 202-863-8820
E-mail: info@gop.com
Web: www.rnc.org

Republican State Central Committee of Oregon
Address: Oregon Republican Party, PO Box 789, Salem 97308-0789
Phone: 503-587-9233
Fax: 503-587-9244
E-mail: info@orgop.org
Web: www.orgop.org

INDIAN TRIBES IN OREGON

Source: Legislative Commission on Indian Services

Address: 900 Court St. NE, Rm. 167, Salem 97301

Phone: 503-986-1067

Fax: 503-986-1071

Web: www.leg.state.or.us/cis

Indian tribes represent unique legal entities in the United States and are distinct political communities with extensive powers of self-government. Tribal sovereignty predates the U.S. government. Treaties, federal statutes and executive agreements over the past 200 years have established a special trust relationship between tribes and the federal government. The federal Bureau of Indian Affairs has been designated by the Secretary of the Interior as the primary agency to protect tribal interests and administer trust responsibilities.

During the 1950s, in a move to assimilate Native Americans into mainstream America, the U.S. government ended federal trusteeship of roughly three percent of the country's Native American population through a process called termination. Of the 109 tribes and bands terminated, 62 were native to Oregon. Even though the tone of the termination legislation was emancipation, the net effect of the policy on terminated tribes was cultural, political and economic devastation.

In recent years, however, vigorous efforts have been mounted by terminated tribes to reestablish or restore the trust relationship. In 1977, the Confederated Tribes of Siletz won restoration; followed by the Cow Creek Band of Umpqua Indians in 1982; the Confederated Tribes of Grand Ronde in 1983; the Confederated Tribes of Coos, Lower Umpqua and Siuslaw Indians in 1984; the Klamath Tribes in 1986 and the Coquille Tribe in 1989.

Oregon now has nine federally recognized tribes: the Burns Paiute Tribe; the Confederated Tribes of Coos, Lower Umpqua and Siuslaw Indians; the Confederated Tribes of Grand Ronde; the Confederated Tribes of Siletz; the Confederated Tribes of Warm Springs; the Confederated Tribes of Umatilla Indian Reservation; the Cow Creek Band of Umpqua Indians; the Klamath Tribes and the Coquille Tribe. On May 22, 1996 Governor John A. Kitzhaber signed Executive Order No. EO-96-30 which officially recognized state/tribal government-to-government relations. The 2001 session of the Oregon Legislature passed SB 770 which codified Executive Order 96-30. Oregon law also requires state agencies to develop and implement policies to include tribes when state agency policies and programs affect tribal interests. Oregon law requires state agencies to have a key contact for state/tribal relations, to promote communication with tribes and to promote positive government-to-government relations. The law requires certain training, an Annual Summit and an Annual Report to the Governor and the Legislative Commission on Indian

Services on state agency interactions with the tribes. Oregon's state/tribal government-to-government law can be found at ORS 182.162–182.168.

Oregon's Native American population is estimated at 45,211 according to the 2000 census. Many Native Americans in Oregon are not members of Oregon Tribes, but may be enrolled members of tribes located in other states. All Native Americans who reside in Oregon, regardless of tribal enrollment, are also Oregon citizens. Enrolled membership in Oregon Tribes totals 22,441 as of July 2004. Each tribe and organization has its own particular history, value system, government, language and ties. Many historically rural and reservation Indians have moved to urban centers, and this transition has resulted in continually evolving values and needs. Oregon Indians can be divided into two distinct groups:

Reservation/Nonreservation: Reservation Indians live on or near Oregon's Indian reservations. A reservation community includes enrolled members of the tribe or tribes for whom the reservation was established, as well as Indians from other tribes living on the reservation. The reservations are strikingly different in many aspects. Size is one example. Siletz is situated on 4,204 acres; Burns Paiute on 13,738 acres; Umatilla on 172,882 acres; Grand Ronde on 11,040 acres; and Warm Springs on more than 644,000 acres. By an Act of Congress in 1996, the Coquille Tribe now has reservation acreage totalling 6,512 acres.

Enrollment figures also vary widely. Burns Paiute has the smallest enrollment with 341; Warm Springs has 3,980; Siletz, 4,094; Umatilla, 2,447; Coquille, 819 and Grand Ronde is the largest with 4,926 members. Reservations differ markedly in other ways as well, including governing structure, resource base, range of available services and treaty provisions.

Nonreservation Indians are either from nonrecognized tribes, are members of recognized tribes not having a land base, or are members of Oregon Tribes living off-reservation. Reservations are in various stages of planning for the Klamath Tribes, Cow Creek Band of Umpqua Indians and the Confederated Tribes of Coos, Lower Umpqua and Siuslaw. The Klamath Tribe has 3,466 enrolled members; the Cow Creek has 1,289; and Coos, Lower Umpqua and Siuslaw has 754 members.

Recognized/Unrecognized: Recognized Indians are those who are enrolled members of tribes from whom the federal government has acknowledged treaty or statutory obligations. Recognized Indians include urban/rural or reservation/nonreservation Indians.

Unrecognized Indians include those from tribes with whom federal relations have been severed by congressional action (termination) and those whose tribe has never been recognized by the federal government. Tribal diversity notwithstanding, all Indians share common concerns. On the regional level, for example, the Columbia River Intertribal Fish

Commission (CRITFC) represents tribes in Washington, Oregon and Idaho on matters concerning fisheries management. On the statewide level, many intertribal organizations have been formed to deal with specific issues such as education, health, legal matters, aging, alcoholism and adoption.

One economic development tool available to tribes since passage of a 1988 federal law (The National Indian Gaming Regulatory Act (NIGRA)) is operation of gaming centers on trust land. All nine tribes in Oregon currently have gaming facilities. The gaming centers operate in accordance with the NIGRA and negotiated state compacts. Besides providing employment opportunities for tribal members and citizens of surrounding Oregon communities, revenues from this tribal enterprise go towards health clinics, education scholarships, housing and other services.

The Legislative Commission on Indian Services has developed the Oregon Directory of American Indian Resources, a resource guide for Indians to provide information about and for Oregon's Indian population. Copies of this directory are available on the Internet at: www.leg.state.or.us/cis/ along with other information about Oregon's state/tribal relations and Oregon Tribes, including links to tribal websites.

OREGON CONSULAR CORPS

A number of foreign nations maintain consulates in Oregon. A consul is an official appointed by a government to live in a foreign city to look after the business and other interests of the home country and to assist and protect its nationals within the consular territory.

A consular representative: promotes a country's trade within the assigned area; assists and protects a country's shipping interests, legalizes ships' papers, assists native seamen in distress and adjudicates on some shipping matters; administers oaths, legalizes foreign documents as required by a country's laws; issues passports and visas; and explains a country's policies, cultural achievements and its attractions for tourism.

Austria
Christopher R. Hermann, Honorary Consul
Address: 900 SW 5th Ave., Suite 2600, Portland 97204
Phone: 503-552-9733
Fax: 503-220-2480
E-mail: crhermann@stoel.com

Barbados
H. Desmond Johnson, Honorary Consul
Address: 10202 SE 32nd Ave., Suite 601, Milwaukie 97222
Phone: 503-659-0283
Fax: 503-653-4959
E-mail: bajandoc@hotmail.com

Belgium
John H. Herman, Honorary Consul
Address: 2121 NW Front Ave., 2nd Floor, Portland 97209
Phone: 503-226-2121
Fax: 971-544-0305
E-mail: jacherman@aol.com

Canada
Jim Baumgartner, Honorary Consul
Address: 805 SW Broadway, Suite 1900 Fox Tower, Portland 97205
Phone: 503-224-5560
Fax: 503-224-6148
E-mail: jmb@bhlaw.com

Cyprus
Alex Christy, Honorary Consul
Address: 1130 SW Morrison, Suite 510, Portland 97205
Phone: 503-227-1411
Fax: 503-227-2086
E-mail: alexchristy@qwest.net

Czech Republic
Marie Amicci, Honorary Consul
Address: PO Box 2851, Wilsonville 97070
Phone: 503-293-9545
Fax: 503-293-9546

Denmark
Ingolf Noto, Honorary Consul
Address: 1600 Pioneer Tower, 888 SW 5th Ave., Portland 97204
Phone: 503-802-2131
Fax: 503-972-3813
E-mail: ingolf@tonkon.com

Fiji
James W. Bosley, Honorary Consul
Address: 4129 Glacier Lily St., Lake Oswego 97035
Phone: 503-635-9430
E-mail: bozxcel@comcast.com

Finland
Paul M. Niskanen, Honorary Consul
Address: 2660 SW Cedar Hills Blvd., Beaverton 97005
Phone: 503-526-0391
Fax: 503-526-0902
E-mail: finnconsul@finevoyages.com

France
Claudine Fisher, Honorary Consul
Address: Neuberger Hall 479, Portland State University, PO Box 751, Portland 97207
Phone: 503-725-5298
Fax: 503-725-5276
E-mail: fisherc@pdx.edu

Germany
Guenther H. Hoffmann, Honorary Consul

Address: 200 SW Market St., Suite 1695, Portland 97201
Phone: 503-222-0490
Fax: 503-248-0138
E-mail: ghoffman1@aol.com

Guatemala
Serge D'Rovencourt, Honorary Consul
Address: 821 NW 11th Ave. #323, Portland 97209
Phone: 503-224-4193
Fax: 503-224-4886
E-mail: sergedr@earthlink.net

Iceland
Les Swanson, Honorary Consul
Address: Neuberger Hall 233, Portland State University, PO Box 751, Portland 97207-0751
Phone: 503-725-9705
Fax: 503-725-9174
E-mail: lswanson@pdx.edu

Italy
Andrea Bartoloni, Honorary Vice Consul
Address: One World Trade Center, 121 SW Salmon St., Suite 1030, Portland 97204
Phone: 503-225-0702
Fax: 503-227-0739
E-mail: ab@bartoloni.com

Ivory Coast
Elizabeth Hamilton-McFadden, Honorary Consul
Address: 4875 SW 78th Ave., Suite 350, Portland 97225
Phone: 503-224-2293

Japan
Tadashi Nagai, Consul General
Address: 1300 SW 5th Ave., Suite 2700, Portland 97201
Phone: 503-221-1811
Fax: 503-224-8936
E-mail: tadnagai@cgjpdx.org

Korea
Robert Donaldson, Honorary Consul General
Address: 805 SW Broadway, Suite 1900 Fox Tower, Portland 97205
Phone: 503-224-5560
Fax: 503-224-6148
E-mail: rwd@bhlaw.com

Lithuania
Randolph L. Miller, Honorary Consul
Address: 333 SE 2nd Ave., Portland 97214
Phone: 503-234-5600
Fax: 503-232-7447
E-mail: randy@mooreco.com

Luxembourg
Bill Failing, Honorary Consul
Address: 1708 SW Hawthorne Terrace, Portland 97201
Phone: 503-224-5268

Fax: 503-478-9848
E-mail: bfailing@europa.com

Malaysia
Jay A. Killeen, Honorary Consul General
Address: 18697 SE Semple Rd., Clackamas, 97015
Phone: 503-658-3633
Fax: 503-658-2210
E-mail: Forte@pcez.com

Mexico
Martin Alcala, Deputy Consul
Address: 1234 SW Morrison St., Portland 97205
Phone: 503-274-1442
Fax: 503-274-1540
E-mail: portland@sre.gob.mx

The Netherlands
Ted E. Runstein, Honorary Consul
Address: 520 SW Yamhill St., Suite 600, Portland 97204
Phone: 503-222-7957
Fax: 503-227-2980
E-mail: trunstein@kelrun.com

Norway
Larry K. Bruun, Honorary Consul
Address: 4380 SW Macadam, Suite 120, River Forum 1, Portland 97239
Phone: 503-221-0870
Fax: 503-221-0515
E-mail: lbruun@wbcatty.com

Poland
Ted Winnowski, Honorary Consul
Address: 11333 SW Northgate Ave., Portland 97219
Phone: 503-819-8198
Fax: 503-635-8615

Sweden
Mark O. Johnson, Honorary Consul
Address: 111 SW 5th Ave., Suite 3700, Portland 97204
Phone: 503-227-0634
Fax: 503-227-7956
E-mail: mark.johnson@milliman.com

Thailand
Nicholas J. Stanley, Honorary Consul
Address: 121 SW Salmon St., Suite 1430, Portland 97204
Phone: 503-221-0090
Fax: 503-221-0550
E-mail: nicks@siaminc.com

United Kingdom
Andrew MacRitchie, Honorary Consul
Address: 825 NE Multnomah, 20th Floor, Portland 97232
Phone: 503-227-5669
Fax: 503-813-5378
E-mail: andy.macritchie@pacificorp.com

Oregon State Symbols

State Flag: front *(Oregon State Archives)*

State Flag: reverse

State Seal

State Animal: American Beaver *(Castor canadensis)*
(Oregon Department of Fish and Wildlife)

State Gemstone: Oregon Sunstone
(Oregon Department of Geology and Mineral Industries)

State Insect: Oregon Swallowtail *(Papilio oregonius)*
(Oregon Capitol, Legislative Administration)

State Mushroom: *Cantharellus formosus*
(Richard F. Bishop)

State Nut: Hazelnut *(Corylus avellana)*
(Oregon State Archives)

State Shell: Hairy Triton *(Fusitriton oregonesis)*
(Bill Hanshumaker, Hatfield Marine Science Center)

State Bird: Western Meadowlark *(Sturnella neglecta)*
(Noah Strycker)

State Flower: Oregon Grape *(Mahonia Aquifolium)*
(Oregon State Archives)

State Rock: Thunderegg (geode)
(Oregon Department of Geology and Mineral Industries)

State Fish: Chinook Salmon *(Oncorhynchus tshawytscha)*
(Oregon Department of Fish and Wildlife)

State Tree: Douglas-fir *(Pseudotsuga menziesii)*
(World Forestry Center)

Dr. John McLoughlin,
Father of Oregon

Tabitha Moffatt Brown,
Mother of Oregon
(Oregon Tourism Commission)

Thomas Vaughan,
Historian Laureate

Oregon's Capitol

Oregon's present Capitol has its origins in two fires. On Dec. 30, 1855, fire swept through a newly occupied Statehouse, completely destroying the structure. The Holman Building, in the business section of Salem, served as a temporary Capitol from 1859 until another one was completed in 1876. On April 25, 1935, fire again destroyed the elegant Statehouse patterned after the U.S. Capitol.

(LA)

(LA)

(LA)

Francis Keally with the New York firm of Trowbridge & Livingston designed the current building, which was dedicated October 1, 1938. A four-story structure of Modern Greek architecture, it was completed at a cost of $2.5 million and is the fourth newest Capitol in the United States. The exterior is faced with white Danby Vermont marble. The rotunda, the halls, and all of the lobby areas are lined with a warm, delicately polished Rose Travertine from Montana. The floor and staircases of the rotunda utilize large squares of Phoenix Napoleon grey marble from Missouri with borders of Radio Black marble from Vermont.

(LA)

Capitol Entrances

A Capitol "Wings" project, completed in 1977 at a cost of $12.5 million, added further space for legislative offices, hearing rooms, support services, a first floor galleria, and underground parking.

The beauty of the entire Capitol plan is enhanced by its utility. The building houses several elected state officials—the Governor, the Secretary of State, and the State Treasurer—in addition to the entire Legislative Branch of state government. Spacious hearing rooms provide Oregonians an opportunity to participate in legislative decision making and to view state government at work.

(OSA)

(LA)

(OSA)

(LA)

The massive Vermont marble sculptures flanking the main entrance, by Leo Friedlander, depict The Covered Wagon (west) and Lewis and Clark led by Sacajawea (east). Intaglio maps outlining the Old Oregon Trail and the routes of Lewis and Clark appear on the backsides of these sculptures. Ulric Ellerhusen sculpted five relief marble works for the exterior of the building. Above the south entrance is a work by Oregon sculptor Tom Morandi. A wheelchair ramp is outside the east entrance. A Liberty Bell replica distinguishes the west entrance.

(OSA)

Capitol Rotunda (first floor)

In the center of the rotunda, embedded in the floor, is a large bronze replica of the *(LA)* Oregon State Seal sculpted by Ulric Ellerhusen, who also created the six cast bronze sculptures over the main entrance doors—three outside and three inside. Eight medallions painted near the top of the walls of the rotunda represent the eight objects in the state seal.

The Capitol dome rises 106 feet above the state seal in the floor of the spacious rotunda. The ceiling, painted by Frank H. Schwarz, features a design of 33 stars symbolizing Oregon as the 33rd state in the union.

(LA)

Capitol Rotunda Murals

Surrounding the rotunda are four large, colorful murals illustrating events in Oregon history: Captain Robert Gray at the mouth of the Columbia River in 1792; Lewis and Clark on their way to the Pacific in 1805; the first women to cross the continent by covered wagon, welcomed by Dr. John McLoughlin in 1836; and the first wagon train migration in 1843. Outstanding examples of Depression period art, the murals were painted by Barry Faulkner and Frank H. Schwarz.

Wagon Train Migration   *(LA)*

Dr. John McLoughlin   *(LA)*

Captain Robert Gray at the mouth of the Columbia River

Lewis and Clark (far right) at Celilo Falls

(OSA)

Four smaller murals alongside the stairways, including this one representing dairying and ranching, are symbolic of Oregon industries. The seal of the provisional government (1843–1848) is above the grand staircase leading to the Senate Chamber. The territorial seal (1848–1859) is above the opposite staircase leading to the House of Representatives.

(OSA)

Display cases containing exhibits relating to Oregon history, hearing rooms, traveling art exhibits and the visitors' information center highlight the galleria. The visitors' information center provides information about the Capitol, the Legislative Assembly and Oregon to the public. Historical building tours and videos are available. The Tower is open for tours seasonally.

House and Senate Chambers

The paneling and furniture in Oregon's 60-member House of Representatives is *(LA)* fashioned entirely of golden oak. Symbolic of Oregon's important wood products industry is the specially designed carpet featuring the Douglas-fir, Oregon's state tree. Behind the desk of the Speaker of the House, is a Barry Faulkner mural showing the historic meeting of Oregon pioneers at Champoeg in 1843, when the provisional government was established.

Oregon's 30 state Senators use the Senate Chamber that features paneling and fur- *(LA)* niture of matched black walnut. Alternating designs of wheat and salmon, symbolizing Oregon's agricultural and fishing industries are woven into the carpeting. The mural behind the Senate President's desk is by Frank H. Schwarz and shows a street scene in Salem when news of Oregon's admission to the Union was received in 1859.

Above the galleries in both the House and Senate Chambers are friezes inscribed with the names of 158 people prominent in the history and development of Oregon.

Governor's Suite

Between the two legislative chambers on the second floor is the Governor's Suite   *(LA)*
with a reception room, a public ceremonial office, and private staff offices. The paneling is
matched black walnut. The map of Oregon's geography above the fireplace in the ceremonial office is a work of Barry Faulkner. The ornate table in the reception area is made of
40 different types of wood and depicts the previous Capitol. It was created and given to the
citizens of Oregon by the architectural firm employing Francis Keally. The reception area
and ceremonial office are used frequently for art exhibits.

(OSA)

Tower and
Oregon Pioneer

The Oregon Pioneer statue that tops the
building is another work by Ulric Ellerhusen. This heroic figure represents the
spirit of Oregon's early settlers. Cast in
bronze and finished in gold leaf, it weighs
8.5 tons and is hollow inside. The base of
the 23-foot high statue is 140 feet above the
ground. The statue is reached by 121 steps
spiraling up into the tower from the fourth
floor of the building out onto a deck
providing a spectacular view of Salem.

Capitol Grounds

(OSA)   *(OSA)*

Ornamental and native trees and shrubs are featured in the landscaped areas surrounding the Capitol. To the east, Capitol Park is also the setting of three statues representing major forces in Oregon history: The Circuit Rider (above, right) by A. Phimister Proctor is symbolic of the many missionaries who came to Oregon; Gifford Proctor sculpted both Reverend Jason Lee (above, left), and Dr. John McLoughlin. Lee, a minister, played a major role in the American colonization of Oregon. He was also the founder of Oregon's oldest university, Willamette University, located south of the Capitol. McLoughlin was the chief factor of the Hudson's Bay Company and was the first man to govern the Oregon territory, although he held no official title. Recent additions to the Capitol Park are fragments of Corinthian columns salvaged from the Capitol destroyed by fire in 1935.

Willson Park, to the west, was a city park from 1853 until 1965 when it officially became part of the Capitol grounds. It is the setting for the Waite Fountain, Parade of Animals sculpture, a Liberty Bell replica, and a gazebo constructed in 1982.

(OSA)

These cast bronze sculptures by Ulric Ellerhusen greet visitors at the outside of the north entry.

These reliefs by Ulric Ellerhusen, representing historical land transportation modes, grace the inside of the north entry.

Capitol Rotunda Engraving

"In the souls of its citizens will be found the likeness of the state which if they be unjust and tyrannical than will it reflect their vices but if they be lovers of righteousness confident in their liberties so will it be clean in justice bold in freedom."

Portraits of former Oregon governors, such as this one of Governor Tom McCall, hang in the Capitol.

Capitol tour credits:
Text: Oregon State Capitol, Legislative Administration; Additional text: Oregon State Archives
Photographs: LA = Oregon State Capitol, Legislative Administration; OSA = Oregon State Archives

Lewis and Clark Exposition

A Centennial Exhibit of the 1905 Fair

Official Catalogue to the Lewis and Clark Exposition. *(Courtesy Oregon State Library)*

About the Exposition: Portland hosted the Lewis and Clark Exposition in the summer of 1905. Commemorating the Centennial of the "Corps of Discovery" it was the first exposition held in the western United States. It proved to be a successful undertaking and promoted Portland and the Pacific Northwest to a worldwide audience.

View of the Agricultural Palace. *(Courtesy Al Staehli)*

View of the Grand Stairway and lakefront looking across the lake to the U.S. Government Building. *(Courtesy Al Staehli)*

View from the entrance through the Sunken Gardens with monumental sculpture by Fredric Remington in the foreground. *(Courtesy Al Staehli)*

China plate depicting: Lewis, Clark, President Jefferson, the current President Theodore Roosevelt, the emblems for Oregon, Washington, Idaho, and Montana, and a view of Portland surrounding the center image of the fair emblem. *(Courtesy Gov. Victor Atiyeh)*

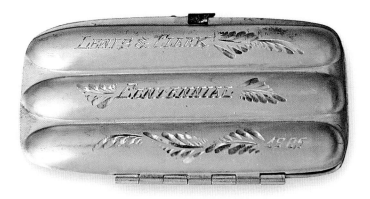

Souvenir cigar holder engraved with Lewis and Clark Exposition.
(Courtesy Gov. Victor Atiyeh)

Decorative ribbon with medallion celebrating July 29th as Scandinavian Day at the fair. *(Courtesy Gov. Victor Atiyeh)*

Brass letter opener embellished with the fair seal entitled "Into the Setting Sun." *(Courtesy Gov. Victor Atiyeh)*

Officers and operations directors of the Lewis and Clark Exposition Corporation, which oversaw the development and operation of the fair. A state commission worked in conjunction with the corporation to assure legislative support and accountability.
(Courtesy Oregon State Library)

Metal match safe embossed with an image of the fair's Forestry Building.
(Courtesy Gov. Victor Atiyeh)

Souvenir metal tray depicts major attractions from the fair, including the U.S. Government Building, Sunken Gardens, Forestry Building, Foreign Exhibit Building, Industrial and Liberal Arts Building, Agricultural Palace, and the Bridge of All Nations.
(Courtesy Gov. Victor Atiyeh)

Award banner presented to Oregon Agricultural College for a "collection of birds" exhibited at the fair. *(Courtesy Benton County Historical Museum)*

Commemorative stein with pewter lid and thumb rests. The stein incorporates several images, including Meriwether Lewis and the "Into the Setting Sun" seal.
(Courtesy Southern Oregon Historical Society)

Souvenir mother of pearl purse, imprinted with the fair name, location, and date. *(Courtesy Gov. Victor Atiyeh)*

Souvenir leather purse depicting the Art Palace at the fair. *(Courtesy Gov. Victor Atiyeh)*

WESTERN WORLD'S FAIR

OFFICIAL
DAILY
PROGRAM
LEWIS AND CLARK
CENTENNIAL
EXPOSITION

PORTLAND
OREGON~

SOUVENIR

THURSDAY 1905

Official Daily Program of the fair. The program included a map, schedule of events,
advertisements, and other promotional information on the fair and its host city.
(Courtesy Oregon State Library)

Participants ribbon for 33rd annual reunion of the Pioneer Association. Gilt braid adorns the bottom edge and an applied medallion depicts Lewis, Clark, and President Jefferson.
(Courtesy Gov. Victor Atiyeh)

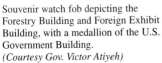

Souvenir watch fob depicting the Forestry Building and Foreign Exhibit Building, with a medallion of the U.S. Government Building.
(Courtesy Gov. Victor Atiyeh)

Paper lithographed fan. The fan features the seal used by the fair, depicting Lewis and Clark escorted by Lady Liberty, walking "into the setting sun."
(Courtesy Columbia Gorge Discovery Center)

Porcelain plate with gilt decoration and transfer image of Festival Hall.
(Courtesy Gov. Victor Atiyeh)

Pocket watch with an image of the fair seal "into the setting sun."
(Courtesy Gov. Victor Atiyeh)

Oversized diploma awarded by the State of Oregon to exhibitors at the fair. The image at the bottom represents a bird's-eye view of the fairgrounds.
(Courtesy Oregon State Archives)

Souvenir heart shaped pin embossed with a relief of the Forestry Building. *(Courtesy Gov. Victor Atiyeh)*

Bronze medal depicting the fair seal, Lewis and Clark being escorted "into the setting sun" by Lady Liberty. *(Courtesy Benton County Historical Museum)*

Souvenir pin back button commemorating Oakland and Alameda County Day at the fair. *(Courtesy Gov. Victor Atiyeh)*

Souvenir coin portraying Lewis and Clark in profile wearing expedition apparel. *(Courtesy Columbia Gorge Discovery Center)*

Wooden shingle plaque depicting the fair's Forestry Building, the "world's largest log cabin." *(Courtesy Southern Oregon Historical Society)*

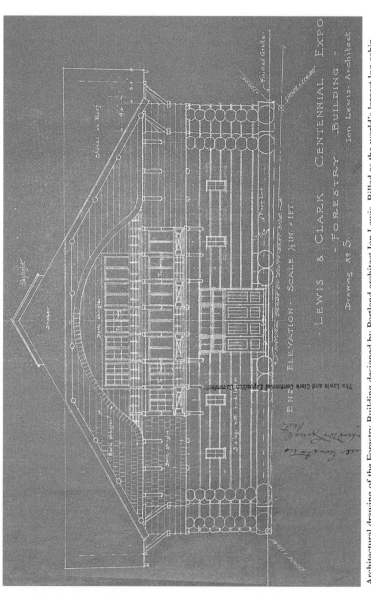

Architectural drawing of the Forestry Building designed by Portland architect Ion Lewis. Billed as the world's largest log cabin, the structure measured 105 feet by 209 feet and was constructed completely of unhewn logs. The largest foundation logs weighed 32 tons and measured 54 feet in length by 5 feet across. Fire destroyed the building in 1962. (*Courtesy Oregon State Archives*)

Panoramic view of the fairgrounds. The Forestry Building depicted in the middle stands out because of its brown color. The U.S. Government Building is shown to the left across the lake. The sprawling fair covered 400 acres of what is now an industrial area in Northwest Portland. (*Courtesy Al Staehli*)

Cover image from the "Lewis and Clark Centennial Exposition Illustrated" showing a view of the fairgrounds looking back from the Lake View Terrace. The bandstand, depicted in the lower left, is now located on the grounds of the Deepwood Estate in Salem. (*Courtesy Al Staehli*)

Physical Feature Names

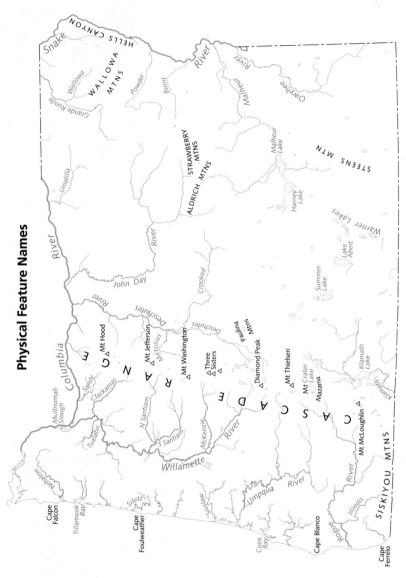

Image reproduced from the *Atlas of Oregon, Second Edition* courtesy of the University of Oregon Press.
© 2001 University of Oregon Press.

Fossil rocks showing shells—Oregon State Archives Photograph, OHD-G492

Oregon's towns, cities and counties contain the qualities that make Oregon a unique place. From the Pacific coast to the Willamette Valley and on to the mountain ranges and high desert, Oregon's rich geographic diversity is echoed by the places where people have chosen to live. This section, with information about Oregon cities and counties, local and regional governments, hints at this variety.

SALEM— OREGON'S CAPITAL

Salem, the state capital, is Oregon's third largest city with a population of 142,940. Salem is also the county seat of Marion County, but a small portion contained within its corporate limits of 44 square miles lies across the Willamette River in Polk County. Salem is situated on the 45th parallel in the center of the Willamette Valley—one of the most fertile and agriculturally productive regions in the world—47 miles south of Portland and 64 miles north of Eugene.

Salem serves as the hub of both state government and the surrounding farming communities. State government is the largest employer, with approximately 14,470 full-time employees and offices for 70 state agencies located in the immediate area. Salem is also one of the largest food-processing centers in the United States.

In addition, Salem is one of Oregon's oldest cities. The Indian name for the locality was Chemeketa, said to mean "meeting or resting place." It may also have been the name of one of the bands of Calapooya Indians. In 1840–41, the Jason Lee Mission was moved from the Willamette River upstream to a site on Mill Creek. In 1842, the missionaries established the Oregon Institute. When the mission was dissolved in 1844, it was decided to lay out a townsite on the Institute lands. Either David Leslie, one of the trustees who came to Oregon from Salem, Mass., or W.H. Willson, who filed plats in 1850–51 for what is now the main part of the city, selected the name "Salem." Salem is the anglicized form of the hebrew word Shalom, meaning peace.*

The location of the Oregon capital caused a spirited contest that lasted nearly 15 years. By an act of 1851, the territorial government moved the capital to Salem from Oregon City; in 1855 it was moved to Corvallis, only to move back to Salem the same year. Destruction of the Capitol at Salem on December 31, 1855, was considered an incendiary part of this controversy.

The close proximity of government provides Salem citizens with a distinct opportunity to be involved in the decision-making processes of the state. The citizens of Salem also have a long history of commitment to community improvement—a commitment recognized nationally through presentation of two All-America City Awards, one for 1960–61 and more recently for 1982–83.

*Early Salem history from **Oregon Geographic Names,** by Lewis A. McArthur.

State Buildings

Agriculture Building (1966)*
635 Capitol St. NE, Salem 97301

Capitol Mall Parking Structure (1991)
900 Chemeketa St. NE, Salem 97301

Cecil Edwards Archives Building (1991)
800 Summer St. NE, Salem 97310

Commerce Building (1931)
158 12th St. NE, Salem 97301

Commission for the Blind (1977)
535 SE 12th Ave., Portland 97204

Employment Building (1974)
875 Union St. NE, Salem 97311

Executive Building (1979)
155 Cottage St. NE, Salem 97301

Fish and Wildlife Building (2003)
3406 Cherry Ave. NE, Salem 97303

Forestry Buildings (1938)
2600 State St., Salem 97310

General Services Building (1954)
1225 Ferry St. SE, Salem 97301

General Services Building Annex (1967)
1257 Ferry St. SE, Salem 97301

Human Resources Building (1992)
550 Summer St. NE, Salem 97301

Justice Building (1930)
1162 Court St. NE, Salem 97301

Labor and Industries Building (1961)
350 Winter St. NE, Salem 97301

Liquor Control Commission Building (1955)
9201 SE McLoughlin Blvd., Milwaukie 97222

North Capitol Mall Office Building (2003)
725 Summer St. NE, Salem 97301

Public Employees' Retirement System Building (1998)
11410 SW 68th Parkway, Tigard 97281

Public Service Building (1949)
255 Capitol St. NE, Salem 97310

Public Utility Commission Building (1992)
550 Capitol St. NE, Salem 97301

Real Estate Building (1990)
1177 Center St. NE, Salem 97301

Revenue Building (1981)
955 Center St. NE, Salem 97301

State Fair Buildings, State Fairgrounds
2330 17th St. NE, Salem 97303

State Hospital Building (1883)
2600 Center St. NE, Salem 97301

State Lands Building (1990)
775 Summer St. NE, Salem 97301

State Library (1939)
250 Winter St. NE, Salem 97301

State Lottery Building (1996)
500 Airport Rd. SE, Salem 97301

State Office Building, Eugene (1961)
165 7th St. E, Eugene 97401

State Office Building, Pendleton (1963)
700 SE Emigrant St., Pendleton 97801

State Office Building, Portland (1992)
800 NE Oregon, Portland 97232

State Printing Plant (1980)
550 Airport Rd. SE, Salem 97301

Supreme Court Building (1914)
1163 State St., Salem 97301

Transportation Building (1951)
355 Capitol St. NE, Salem 97301

Veterans' Building (1984)
700 Summer St. NE, Salem 97301

*Year is date building was constructed, purchased or occupied by the state.

INCORPORATED CITIES AND TOWNS

Source: Ken Strobeck, Exec. Dir., League of Oregon Cities
Address: 1201 Court St. NE, Suite 200, Salem 97301; PO Box 928, Salem 97308
Phone: 503-588-6550
Fax: 503-399-4863
E-mail: loc@orcities.org
Web: www.orcities.org

In the 241 incorporated cities throughout Oregon, the city councils serve as the highest authority within city governments in deciding issues of public policy. In open public forums, city councils pass laws (ordinances), adopt resolutions and generally conduct discussions involving the governance of their communities and the welfare of their citizens.

Oregon cities have councils of fewer than ten members serving either four-year terms or, in a few cities, two-year terms. Councilors are elected to the council by district, ward or at-large.

Four forms of city government determine the administrative role of any city council. Most Oregon cities over 2,500 have the council/manager or council/administrator form, in which the council hires a chief executive officer to be responsible for the daily supervision of city affairs. Portland is the only city in the state with the commission form of government, where the elected commissioners function collectively as the city council and serve as administrators of city departments. Smaller Oregon cities typically have the mayor/council form, in which the legislative and policy-making body is a popularly elected council. Currently, Beaverton is the only city with the strong mayor form, in which the mayor, serving as the chief executive officer, has the authority to appoint administrative personnel, is responsible for city administration, and serves as the presiding officer at council meetings.

City administrators and other city employees often participate in the policy development process but are primarily responsible for effective delivery of municipal services and programs. Many local government activities and programs are directly related to federal or state mandates.

City governments typically provide such services as fire and police protection, streets and street maintenance, sewer and water treatment and collection systems, building permit activities, libraries, parks and recreation activities, and other numerous social service responsibilities determined locally. Cities also have considerable responsibilities for land-use planning within their city limits and urban growth boundaries.

Regardless of the type of government, cities find their strength in a cooperative relationship between the citizens, city officials, the private sector and other government entities. Cities recognize the positive impact of working together, both regionally and on a statewide basis, to enhance community livability.

City name origins are available from *Oregon Geographic Names,* by Lewis A. McArthur.

*County seat

Adair Village
County: Benton
Address: 6030 NE Wm. R. Carr Ave., 97330
Phone: 541-745-5507
Fax: 541-745-5508
E-mail: adairvillage@hotmail.com
Elevation: 328'
Incorporated: 1976
Mayor: Faye Abraham

Adams
County: Umatilla
Address: PO Box 20, 97810
Phone: 541-566-9380
Fax: 541-566-2077
E-mail: cityofadams@uci.net
Elevation: 1,526'
Incorporated: 1893
Mayor: Patrick Bryson

Adrian
County: Malheur
Address: PO Box 226, 97901
Phone: 541-372-2179
Elevation: 2,225'
Incorporated: 1972
Mayor: Jim Greene

*Albany
County: Benton/Linn
Address: PO Box 490, 97321
Phone: 541-917-7500
Fax: 541-917-7511
E-mail: info@cityofalbany.net
Web: www.cityofalbany.net
Elevation: 210'
Incorporated: 1864
Mayor: Chuck McLaran

Amity
County: Yamhill
Address: PO Box 159, 97101
Phone: 503-835-3711
Fax: 503-835-3780
E-mail: amity@viclink.com
Elevation: 162'
Incorporated: 1880
Mayor: Bob Wiro

Antelope
County: Wasco
Address: PO Box 105, 97001
Phone: 541-489-3201
E-mail: bbeas10010@aol.com
Elevation: 2,685'
Incorporated: 1901
Mayor: Brian Sheer

Arlington
County: Gilliam
Address: PO Box 68, 97812
Phone: 541-454-2743
Fax: 541-454-2753
E-mail: cityofa@oregontrail.net
Elevation: 285'
Incorporated: 1885
Mayor: Carmen Kontur-Gronquist

Ashland
County: Jackson
Address: 20 E Main St., 97520-1849
Phone: 541-488-6002
Fax: 541-488-5311
E-mail: berteauf@ashland.or.us
Web: www.ashland.or.us
Elevation: 1,895'
Incorporated: 1874
Mayor: John Morrison

*Astoria
County: Clatsop
Address: 1095 Duane St., 97103
Phone: 503-325-5821
Fax: 503-325-2997
E-mail: dbartlett@astoria.or.us
Web: www.astoria.or.us
Elevation: 23'
Incorporated: 1856
Mayor: Willis L. Van Dusen

Athena
County: Umatilla
Address: PO Box 686, 97813-0686
Phone: 541-566-3862
Fax: 541-566-2781
E-mail: athenacityhall@eoni.com
Web: www.jhmand.com/athena
Elevation: 296'
Incorporated: 1904
Mayor: Mark Seltmann

Aumsville
County: Marion
Address: 595 Main St., 97325
Phone: 503-749-2030
Fax: 503-749-1852
E-mail: mgatti@aumsville.us
Web: www.aumsville.us
Elevation: 366'
Incorporated: 1911
Mayor: Harold L. White

Aurora
County: Marion
Address: 21420 Main St. NE, 97002
Phone: 503-678-1283, ext. 2
Fax: 503-678-2758
E-mail: aurorarecorder@centurytel.net
Elevation: 136'
Incorporated: 1893
Mayor: Bill Carr

*Baker City
County: Baker
Address: PO Box 650, 97814
Phone: 541-523-6541
Fax: 541-524-2049
E-mail: sbogart@bakercity.com
Web: www.bakercity.com
Elevation: 3,451'
Incorporated: 1874
Mayor: Peter Ellingson

Bandon
County: Coos
Address: PO Box 67, 97411
Phone: 541-347-2437
Fax: 541-347-1415
E-mail: citymanager@ci.bandon.or.us
Web: www.ci.bandon.or.us
Elevation: 20'
Incorporated: 1891
Mayor: Mary Schamehorn

Banks
County: Washington
Address: 100 S Main St., 97106
Phone: 503-324-5112
Fax: 503-324-6674
E-mail: recorder@cityofbanks.org
Web: www.cityofbanks.org
Elevation: 250'
Incorporated: 1921
Mayor: Mike Lyda

Barlow
County: Clackamas
Address: 103 N Main St., 97013-9191
Phone: 503-266-1330
Fax: 503-266-1574
Elevation: 101'
Incorporated: 1903
Mayor: David Stegmeir

Bay City
County: Tillamook
Address: PO Box 3309, 97107
Phone: 503-377-2288
Fax: 503-377-4044
E-mail: baycity@oregoncoast.com
Web: www.ci.bay-city.or.us
Elevation: 17'
Incorporated: 1910
Mayor: Shaena Peterson

Beaverton
County: Washington
Address: PO Box 4755, 97076
Phone: 503-526-2222
Fax: 503-526-2479
E-mail: citymail@ci.beaverton.or.us
Web: www.ci.beaverton.or.us
Elevation: 189'
Incorporated: 1893
Mayor: Rob Drake

*Bend
County: Deschutes
Address: PO Box 431, 97709
Phone: 541-388-5505
Fax: 541-385-6676
E-mail: pstell@ci.bend.or.us
Web: www.ci.bend.or.us
Elevation: 3,628'
Incorporated: 1905
Mayor: Bill Friedman

Boardman
County: Morrow
Address: PO Box 229, 97818
Phone: 541-481-9252
Fax: 541-481-3244
E-mail: citymanager@cityofboardman.com
Web: www.cityofboardman.com
Elevation: 298'
Incorporated: 1927
Mayor: F.E. Glenn

Bonanza
County: Klamath
Address: PO Box 297, 97623
Phone: 541-545-6566
Fax: 541-545-1027
E-mail: bonanza@fireserve.net
Elevation: 4,120'
Incorporated: 1901
Mayor: Betty Tyree

Brookings
County: Curry
Address: 898 Elk Dr., 97415
Phone: 541-469-2163
Fax: 541-469-3650
E-mail: city@brookings.or.us
Web: www.brookings.or.us
Elevation: 129'

Incorporated: 1951
Mayor: Pat Sherman

Brownsville
County: Linn
Address: PO Box 188, 97327
Phone: 541-466-5666
Fax: 541-466-5118
E-mail: admin@ci.brownsville.or.us
Web: www.ci.brownsville.or.us
Elevation: 265'
Incorporated: 1876
Mayor: Rob Wingren

*Burns
County: Harney
Address: 242 S Broadway, 97720
Phone: 541-573-5255
Fax: 541-573-5622
E-mail: cen63649@centurytel.net
Elevation: 4,148'
Incorporated: 1891
Mayor: Laura Van Cleave

Butte Falls
County: Jackson
Address: PO Box 268, 97522
Phone: 541-865-3262
Fax: 541-865-3777
E-mail: bfcityhall@hotmail.com
Elevation: 2,536'
Incorporated: 1911
Mayor: Ron Ormond

Canby
County: Clackamas
Address: PO Box 930, 97013
Phone: 503-266-4021
Fax: 503-266-7961
E-mail: scheaferk@ci.canby.or.us
Web: www.ci.canby.or.us
Elevation: 153'
Incorporated: 1893
Mayor: Melody Thompson

Cannon Beach
County: Clatsop
Address: PO Box 368, 97110
Phone: 503-436-1581
Fax: 503-436-2050
E-mail: cityhall@ci.cannon-beach.or.us
Web: www.ci.cannon-beach.or.us
Elevation: 30'
Incorporated: 1956
Mayor: Dave Rouse

*Canyon City
County: Grant
Address: PO Box 276, 97820
Phone: 541-575-0509
Fax: 541-575-0515
E-mail: canyon.orgtelco.net
Web: http://grantcounty.cc/communities/canyonc/

Elevation: 3,194'
Incorporated: 1864
Mayor: Don Mooney

Canyonville
County: Douglas
Address: PO Box 765, 97417
Phone: 541-839-4258
Fax: 541-839-4680
E-mail: city@cityofcanyonville.com
Elevation: 750'
Incorporated: 1901
Mayor: Chuck Spindel

Carlton
County: Yamhill
Address: PO Box 458, 97111
Phone: 503-852-7575
Fax: 503-852-7761
E-mail: sweaver@carltonor.org
Web: www.carltonor.org
Elevation: 198'
Incorporated: 1899
Mayor: Kathie Oriet

Cascade Locks
County: Hood River
Address: PO Box 308, 97014
Phone: 541-374-8484
Fax: 541-374-8752
E-mail: kwoosie@cascade-locks.or.us
Web: www.clbb.net
Elevation: 170'
Incorporated: 1935
Mayor: Ralph Hesgard

Cave Junction
County: Josephine
Address: PO Box 1396, 97523
Phone: 541-592-2156
Fax: 541-592-6694
E-mail: cityofcj@cavenet.com
Elevation: 1,350'
Incorporated: 1948
Mayor: Tony Paulson

Central Point
County: Jackson
Address: 155 S 2nd St., 97502
Phone: 541-664-3321
Fax: 541-664-6384
E-mail: deannag@ci.central-point.or.us
Web: www.ci.central-point.or.us
Elevation: 1,272'
Incorporated: 1889
Mayor: Henry Williams

Chiloquin
County: Klamath
Address: PO Box 196, 97624
Phone: 541-783-2717
Fax: 541-783-2035
Elevation: 4,200'

Incorporated: 1926
Mayor: Mark Cobb

Clatskanie
County: Columbia
Address: PO Box 9, 97016
Phone: 503-728-2622
Fax: 503-728-3297
E-mail: clatscty@clatskanie.com
Web: www.clatskanie.com
Elevation: 59'
Incorporated: 1891
Mayor: Diane Pohl

Coburg
County: Lane
Address: PO Box 8316, 97408
Phone: 541-682-7851
Fax: 541-485-0655
E-mail: sammy.egbert@ci.coburg.or.us
Elevation: 398'
Incorporated: 1893
Mayor: Judy Volta

Columbia City
County: Columbia
Address: PO Box 189, 97018
Phone: 503-397-4010
Fax: 503-366-2870
E-mail: columbiacity@columbia-center.org
Web: www.columbia-center.org/colcity
Elevation: 71'
Incorporated: 1926
Mayor: Cheryl Young

*Condon
County: Gilliam
Address: PO Box 445, 97823
Phone: 541-384-2711
Fax: 541-384-2700
E-mail: cityofcondon@tds.net
Elevation: 2,900'
Incorporated: 1893
Mayor: N. Dale Thompson

Coos Bay
County: Coos
Address: 500 Central Ave., 97420
Phone: 541-269-1181
Fax: 541-267-5912
E-mail: smcclure@coosbay.org
Web: www.coosbay.org
Elevation: 10'
Incorporated: 1874
Mayor: Joe Benetti

*Coquille
County: Coos
Address: 99 E 2nd St., 97423
Phone: 541-396-2115
Fax: 541-396-5125
E-mail: cdufner@cityofcoquille.org
Web: www.cityofcoquille.org

Elevation: 40'
Incorporated: 1885
Mayor: Steve Britton

Cornelius
County: Washington
Address: 1355 N Barlow St., 97113
Phone: 503-357-9112
Fax: 503-357-7775
E-mail: info@ci.cornelius.or.us
Web: www.ci.cornelius.or.us
Elevation: 596'
Incorporated: 1893
Mayor: Terry Rilling

*Corvallis
County: Benton
Address: PO Box 1083, 97339-1083
Phone: 541-757-6900
Fax: 541-766-6780
E-mail: kathy.louie@ci.corvallis.or.us
Web: www.ci.corvallis.or.us
Elevation: 224'
Incorporated: 1857
Mayor: Helen Berg

Cottage Grove
County: Lane
Address: 400 E Main St., 97424
Phone: 541-942-5501
Fax: 541-942-1267
E-mail: cityrecorder@cottagegrove.org
Web: www.cottagegrove.org
Elevation: 640'
Incorporated: 1887
Mayor: Gary Williams

Cove
County: Union
Address: PO Box 8, 97824
Phone: 541-568-4566
Fax: 541-568-7747
E-mail: citycove@eoni.com
Elevation: 2,870'
Incorporated: 1904
Mayor: Richard H. Thew

Creswell
County: Lane
Address: PO Box 276, 97426
Phone: 541-895-2531
Fax: 541-895-3647
E-mail: layli.nichols@centurytel.net
Web: www.ci.creswell.or.us
Elevation: 542'
Incorporated: 1909
Mayor: Ron Petitti

Culver
County: Jefferson
Address: PO Box 256, 97734
Phone: 541-546-6494
Fax: 541-546-3624

E-mail: jjones701@aol.com
Elevation: 2,640'
Incorporated: 1946
Mayor: Daniel Harnden

*Dallas
County: Polk
Address: 187 SE Court St., 97338
Phone: 503-623-2338
Fax: 503-623-2339
E-mail: city.mgr@ci.dallas.or.us
Web: www.ci.dallas.or.us
Elevation: 312'
Incorporated: 1874
Mayor: Jim Fairchild

Damascus
County: Clackamas
Address: 19750 Damascus Lane, Boring 97009
Phone: 503-658-8545
Fax: 503-658-3395
Web: www.damascusstudy.org
Elevation: 530'
Incorporated: 2004
Mayor: Dee Wescott

Dayton
County: Yamhill
Address: PO Box 339, 97114-0339
Phone: 503-864-2221
Fax: 503-864-2956
E-mail: suehollis@ci.dayton.or.us
Elevation: 280'
Incorporated: 1880
Mayor: Jackie Brons

Dayville
County: Grant
Address: PO Box 321, 97825
Phone: 541-987-2188
Fax: 541-987-2187
E-mail: dbille@ortelco.net
Elevation: 2,348'
Incorporated: 1914
Mayor: Robert Waltenburg

Depoe Bay
County: Lincoln
Address: PO Box 8, 97341
Phone: 541-765-2361
Fax: 541-765-2129
E-mail: info@ci.depoe-bay.or.us
Web: www.ci.depoe-bay.or.us
Elevation: Sea level
Incorporated: 1973
Mayor: Jim White

Detroit
County: Marion
Address: PO Box 589, 97342
Phone: 503-854-3496
Fax: 503-854-3232
E-mail: detroit@open.org

Web: www.detroitlakeoregon.org
Elevation: 1,595'
Incorporated: 1952
Mayor: Connie LaMont

Donald
County: Marion
Address: PO Box 388, 97020
Phone: 503-678-5543
Fax: 503-678-2750
E-mail: donaldcity@cablerocket.com
Elevation: 198'
Incorporated: 1912
Mayor: Marci Spotanski

Drain
County: Douglas
Address: PO Box 158, 97435
Phone: 541-836-2417
Fax: 541-836-7330
E-mail: cityofdrain@centurytel.net
Web: www.354.com/drain
Elevation: 290'
Incorporated: 1887
Mayor: Sue Anderson

Dufur
County: Wasco
Address: PO Box 145, 97021
Phone: 541-467-2349
Fax: 541-467-2353
E-mail: dufurcity@ortelco.net
Elevation: 1,345'
Incorporated: 1893
Mayor: Darrel Wolff

Dundee
County: Yamhill
Address: PO Box 220, 97115-0220
Phone: 503-538-3922
Fax: 503-538-1958
E-mail: dundeecity3@comcast.net
Web: www.dundee-or.com
Elevation: 189'
Incorporated: 1895
Mayor: C. Diane Ragsdale

Dunes City
County: Lane
Address: PO Box 97, Westlake 97493
Phone: 541-997-3338
Fax: 541-997-5751
E-mail: joannedunescity@charterinternet.com
Web: www.dunescity.com
Elevation: 39'
Incorporated: 1963
Mayor: Robert B. Ward Jr.

Durham
County: Washington
Address: PO Box 23483, 97281-3483
Phone: 503-639-6851
Fax: 503-598-8595

E-mail: cityofdurham@comcast.net
Elevation: 197'
Incorporated: 1966
Mayor: Gary Schirado

Eagle Point
County: Jackson
Address: PO Box 779, 97524
Phone: 541-826-4212
Fax: 541-826-6155
E-mail: carolblackwell@cityofeaglepoint.org
Elevation: 1,310'
Incorporated: 1911
Mayor: Leon Sherman

Echo
County: Umatilla
Address: PO Box 9, 97826
Phone: 541-376-8411
Fax: 541-376-8218
E-mail: ecpl@centurytel.net
Web: www.echo-oregon.com
Elevation: 635'
Incorporated: 1904
Mayor: Richard Winter

Elgin
County: Union
Address: PO Box 128, 97827
Phone: 541-437-2253
Fax: 541-437-2253
E-mail: elgin1@eoni.com
Web: www.eoni.com/~elgin1
Elevation: 2,670'
Incorporated: 1891
Mayor: Carmen Gentry

Elkton
County: Douglas
Address: PO Box 508, 97436
Phone: 541-584-2547
Fax: 541-584-2547
E-mail: cityofelkton@cascadeaccess.com
Elevation: 130'
Incorporated: 1948
Mayor: Alfred S. Tyson

*Enterprise
County: Wallowa
Address: 108 NE 1st, 97828
Phone: 541-426-4196
Fax: 541-426-3395
E-mail: cityent@eoni.com
Elevation: 3,757'
Incorporated: 1889
Mayor: Irving Nuss Jr.

Estacada
County: Clackamas
Address: PO Box 958, 97023-0958
Phone: 503-630-8270
Fax: 503-630-8280
E-mail: carey@cityofestacada.org

Web: www.cityofestacada.org
Elevation: 426'
Incorporated: 1905
Mayor: Robert Austin

*Eugene
County: Lane
Address: 777 Pearl St., Rm. 105, 97401
Phone: 541-682-5010
Fax: 541-682-5414
E-mail: PSO@ci.eugene.or.us
Web: www.ci.eugene.or.us
Elevation: 426'
Incorporated: 1862
Mayor: Kitty Piercy

Fairview
County: Multnomah
Address: PO Box 337, 97024
Phone: 503-665-7929, ext. 224
Fax: 503-666-0888
E-mail: husonc@ci.fairview.or.us
Web: www.ci.fairview.or.us
Elevation: 114'
Incorporated: 1908
Mayor: Mike Weatherby

Falls City
County: Polk
Address: 299 Mill St., 97344
Phone: 503-787-3631
Fax: 503-787-3023
E-mail: fcutility@aol.com
Web: www.fallscity.org
Elevation: 370'
Incorporated: 1893
Mayor: Darren Fleener

Florence
County: Lane
Address: 250 Hwy. 101, 97439
Phone: 541-997-3436
Fax: 541-997-6814
E-mail: rodger.bennett@ci.florence.or.us
Web: www.ci.florence.or.us
Elevation: 14'
Incorporated: 1893
Mayor: Phil Brubaker

Forest Grove
County: Washington
Address: PO Box 326, 97116
Phone: 503-359-3200
Fax: 503-992-3207
E-mail: msykes@ci.forest-grove.or.us
Web: www.ci.forest-grove.or.us
Elevation: 210'
Incorporated: 1872
Mayor: Richard G. Kidd

*Fossil
County: Wheeler
Address: PO Box 467, 97830

Phone: 541-763-2698
Fax: 541-763-2124
E-mail: fossilcity@centurytel.net
Elevation: 2,654'
Incorporated: 1891
Mayor: Don Shipley

Garibaldi
County: Tillamook
Address: PO Box 708, 97118
Phone: 503-322-3327
Fax: 503-322-3737
E-mail: garibaldi.city@tillanet.com
Elevation: 22'
Incorporated: 1946
Mayor: Everett Brown

Gaston
County: Washington
Address: PO Box 129, 97119
Phone: 503-985-3340
Fax: 503-985-1014
E-mail: gaston.city@comcast.net
Elevation: 300'
Incorporated: 1911
Mayor: Rick Lorenz

Gates
County: Marion
Address: PO Box 577, 97346
Phone: 503-897-2669
Fax: 503-897-5046
E-mail: ctygtes@open.org
Elevation: 945'
Incorporated: 1950
Mayor: Kathy Sherman

Gearhart
County: Clatsop
Address: PO Box 2510, 97138
Phone: 503-738-5501
Fax: 503-738-9385
E-mail: cityadmin@freedomnw.com
Elevation: 16'
Incorporated: 1918
Mayor: Kent Smith

Gervais
County: Marion
Address: PO Box 329, 97026
Phone: 503-792-4222
Fax: 503-792-3791
E-mail: gervaiscityof@yahoo.com
Elevation: 187'
Incorporated: 1874
Mayor: Joe Simmons

Gladstone
County: Clackamas
Address: 525 Portland Ave., 97027
Phone: 503-656-5225
Fax: 503-650-8938
E-mail: block@ci.gladstone.or.us

Web: www.ci.gladstone.or.us
Elevation: 57'
Incorporated: 1911
Mayor: Wade Byers

Glendale
County: Douglas
Address: PO Box 361, 97442
Phone: 541-832-2106
Fax: 541-832-3221
E-mail: glendale@tymewyse.com
Web: www.cityofglendaleor.com
Elevation: 1,410'
Incorporated: 1901
Mayor: John Poore Sr.

*Gold Beach
County: Curry
Address: 29592 Ellensburg Ave., 97444
Phone: 541-247-7029
Fax: 541-247-2212
E-mail: cityadmin@harborside.com
Web: www.goldbeach.net
Elevation: 50'
Incorporated: 1945
Mayor: Karl Popoff

Gold Hill
County: Jackson
Address: PO Box 308, 97525
Phone: 541-855-1525
Fax: 541-855-4501
E-mail: recorder@ci.goldhill.or.us
Web: www.ci.goldhill.or.us
Elevation: 1,085'
Incorporated: 1895
Mayor: Sherry Young

Granite
County: Grant
Address: 1378 Main St., 97877
Phone: 541-755-5100
Fax: 541-755-5100
Elevation: 4,660'
Incorporated: 1901
Mayor: Patricia Fielding

*Grants Pass
County: Josephine
Address: 101 NW "A" St., 97526
Phone: 541-474-6360
Fax: 541-479-0812
E-mail: bpeterson@ci.grants-pass.or.us
Web: www.ci.grants-pass.or.us
Elevation: 960'
Incorporated: 1887
Mayor: Len Holzinger

Grass Valley
County: Sherman
Address: PO Box 191, 97029
Phone: 541-333-2434
Fax: 541-333-2776

E-mail: tfritts@oregontrail.net
Elevation: 2,257'
Incorporated: 1901
Mayor: Neil Pattee

Greenhorn
County: Baker
Address: 13605 Duane St., Oregon City 97045
Phone: 503-656-7945
Fax: 503-657-9399
E-mail: ocpoyser@hotmail.com
Elevation: 6,300'
Incorporated: 1903
Mayor: Lauren Hartman, Interim

Gresham
County: Multnomah
Address: 1333 NW Eastman Pkwy., 97030
Phone: 503-661-3000
Fax: 503-665-7692
E-mail: debbi.jermann@ci.gresham.or.us
Web: www.ci.gresham.or.us
Elevation: 301'
Incorporated: 1904
Mayor: Charles Becker

Haines
County: Baker
Address: PO Box 208, 97833
Phone: 541-856-3366
Fax: 541-856-3812
E-mail: haines@cascadeaccess.com
Web: www.hainesoregon.com
Elevation: 3,341'
Incorporated: 1909
Mayor: Tom Isaacson

Halfway
County: Baker
Address: PO Box 738, 97834-0738
Phone: 541-742-4741
Fax: 541-742-4742
E-mail: mayor@pinetel.com
Elevation: 2,651'
Incorporated: 1909
Mayor: Gordon Kaesemeyer

Halsey
County: Linn
Address: PO Box 10, 97348
Phone: 541-369-2522
Fax: 541-369-2521
E-mail: recorder@cityofhalsey.com
Web: www.cityofhalsey.com
Elevation: 280'
Incorporated: 1876
Mayor: Larry Nelsen

Happy Valley
County: Clackamas
Address: 12915 SE King Rd., Portland 97236
Phone: 503-760-3325
Fax: 503-760-9397

E-mail: wandak@ci.happy-valley.or.us
Web: www.happy-valley.org
Elevation: 497'
Incorporated: 1965
Mayor: Eugene Grant

Harrisburg
County: Linn
Address: PO Box 378, 97446
Phone: 541-995-6655
Fax: 541-995-9244
E-mail: cityhall@harrisburg.or.us
Web: www.ci.harrisburg.or.us
Elevation: 309'
Incorporated: 1866
Mayor: Robert Duncan

Helix
County: Umatilla
Address: PO Box 323, 97835
Phone: 541-457-2521
E-mail: cityofhelix@helixtel.com
Elevation: 1,754'
Incorporated: 1903
Mayor: Harry Schuening

*Heppner
County: Morrow
Address: PO Box 756, 97836
Phone: 541-676-9618
Fax: 541-676-9650
E-mail: heppner@centurytel.net
Web: www.heppner.net
Elevation: 1,955'
Incorporated: 1887
Mayor: Tim VanCleave

Hermiston
County: Umatilla
Address: 180 NE 2nd St., 97838
Phone: 541-567-5521
Fax: 541-567-5530
E-mail: city@hermiston.or.us
Web: www.hermiston.or.us
Elevation: 450'
Incorporated: 1907
Mayor: Robert Severson

*Hillsboro
County: Washington
Address: 123 W Main St., 97123
Phone: 503-681-6100
Fax: 503-681-6232
E-mail: gailw@ci.hillsboro.or.us
Web: www.ci.hillsboro.or.us
Elevation: 196'
Incorporated: 1876
Mayor: Tom Hughes

Hines
County: Harney
Address: PO Box 336, 97738
Phone: 541-573-2251

Fax: 541-573-5827
E-mail: cen73385@centurytel.net
Elevation: 4,155'
Incorporated: 1930
Mayor: Ruth Schultz

*Hood River
County: Hood River
Address: PO Box 27, 97031
Phone: 541-386-1488
Fax: 541-387-5289
Web: www.ci.Hood-River.or.us
Elevation: 160'
Incorporated: 1901
Mayor: Linda Rouches

Hubbard
County: Marion
Address: PO Box 380, 97032
Phone: 503-981-9633
Fax: 503-981-8743
E-mail: vlnogle@cityofhubbard.org
Web: www.open.org/~hubbard/
Elevation: 181'
Incorporated: 1891
Mayor: Tom McCain

Huntington
County: Baker
Address: PO Box 369, 97907
Phone: 541-869-2202
Fax: 541-869-2550
E-mail: hun101@oregontrail.net
Elevation: 2,110'
Incorporated: 1891
Mayor: Donna Rush

Idanha
County: Linn/Marion
Address: PO Box 430, 97350
Phone: 503-854-3313
Fax: 503-854-3114
E-mail: cityofid@open.org
Elevation: 1,718'
Incorporated: 1949
Mayor: Jeff Skeeters

Imbler
County: Union
Address: PO Box 40, 97841-0040
Phone: 541-534-6095
Fax: 541-534-2343
E-mail: imblerfd@uwtc.net
Elevation: 2,725'
Incorporated: 1922
Mayor: Joe Combe

Independence
County: Polk
Address: PO Box 7, 97351
Phone: 503-838-1212
Fax: 503-606-3282
E-mail: independ@open.org

Web: www.open.org/independ
Elevation: 168'
Incorporated: 1874
Mayor: John McArdle

Ione
County: Morrow
Address: PO Box 361, 97843
Phone: 541-422-7414
Fax: 541-422-7179
E-mail: cityofione@centurytel.net
Elevation: 1,080'
Incorporated: 1903
Mayor: Mark Bruno

Irrigon
County: Morrow
Address: PO Box 428, 97844
Phone: 541-922-3047
Fax: 541-922-9322
E-mail: irrigon@oregontrail.net
Elevation: 297'
Incorporated: 1957
Mayor: Don Baxter

Island City
County: Union
Address: 10605 Island Ave., 97851
Phone: 541-963-5017
Fax: 541-963-3482
E-mail: icity@uwtc.net
Elevation: 2,743'
Incorporated: 1904
Mayor: Dale DeLong

Jacksonville
County: Jackson
Address: PO Box 7, 97530
Phone: 541-899-1231
Fax: 541-899-7882
E-mail: jvillerecorder@charterinternet.com
Web: www.jacksonvilleoregon.org
Elevation: 1,569'
Incorporated: 1860
Mayor: James W. Lewis

Jefferson
County: Marion
Address: PO Box 83, 97352-0083
Phone: 541-327-2768
Fax: 541-327-3120
E-mail: jefferson@open.org
Web: www.ci.jefferson.or.us
Elevation: 240'
Incorporated: 1870
Mayor: Michael Myers

John Day
County: Grant
Address: 450 E Main, 97845
Phone: 541-575-0028
Fax: 541-575-3668
E-mail: cityjd@centurytel.net

Elevation: 3,120'
Incorporated: 1901
Mayor: Roger Simonsen

Johnson City
County: Clackamas
Address: 16121 SE 81st Ave., 97267
Phone: 503-655-9710
Fax: 503-723-0317
Elevation: 60'
Incorporated: 1970
Mayor: Kay Mordock

Jordan Valley
County: Malheur
Address: PO Box 187, 97910
Phone: 541-586-2460
Fax: 541-586-2460
E-mail: cityofjv@juno.com
Elevation: 4,385'
Incorporated: 1911
Mayor: Jake Roe

Joseph
County: Wallowa
Address: PO Box 15, 97846
Phone: 541-432-3832
Fax: 541-432-3832
E-mail: cityofjoseph@eoni.com
Web: www.josephoregon.com
Elevation: 4,200'
Incorporated: 1887
Mayor: Peggy Kite-Martin

Junction City
County: Lane
Address: PO Box 250, 97448-0250
Phone: 541-998-2153
Fax: 541-998-3140
E-mail: jmoore@ci.junction-city.or.us
Web: www.ci.junction-city.or.us
Elevation: 325'
Incorporated: 1872
Mayor: Larry Crowley

Keizer
County: Marion
Address: PO Box 21000, 97307-1000
Phone: 503-390-3700
Fax: 503-393-9437
E-mail: citycouncil@keizer.org
Web: www.keizer.org
Elevation: 132'
Incorporated: 1982
Mayor: Lore Christopher

King City
County: Washington
Address: 15300 SW 116th Ave., 97224
Phone: 503-639-4082
Fax: 503-639-3771
E-mail: jturner@ci.king-city.or.us
Elevation: 213'

Incorporated: 1966
Mayor: Chuck Faes

*Klamath Falls
County: Klamath
Address: PO Box 237, 97601
Phone: 541-883-5316
Fax: 541-883-5399
E-mail: lisa@ci.klamath-falls.or.us
Web: www.ci.klamath-falls.or.us
Elevation: 4,099'
Incorporated: 1893
Mayor: Todd Kellstrom

*La Grande
County: Union
Address: PO Box 670, 97850
Phone: 541-962-1302
Fax: 541-963-3333
E-mail: kshaw@uwtc.net
Web: www.ci.la-grande.or.us
Elevation: 2,785'
Incorporated: 1865
Mayor: Colleen F. Johnson

Lafayette
County: Yamhill
Address: PO Box 55, 97127
Phone: 503-864-2451
Fax: 503-864-4501
E-mail: trenam@ci.lafayette.or.us
Web: www.ci.lafayette.or.us
Elevation: 160'
Incorporated: 1878
Mayor: Don Leard

Lake Oswego
County: Clackamas
Address: PO Box 369, 97034
Phone: 503-635-0215
Fax: 503-697-6594
E-mail: rchristie@ci.oswego.or.us
Web: www.ci.oswego.or.us
Elevation: 100'
Incorporated: 1910
Mayor: Judie Hammerstad

Lakeside
County: Coos
Address: PO Box L, 97449
Phone: 541-759-3011
Fax: 541-759-3711
E-mail: lakeside@harborside.com
Web: http://tlbp.presys.com
Elevation: 28'
Incorporated: 1974
Mayor: Ed Gowan

*Lakeview
County: Lake
Address: 525 N 1st St., 97630
Phone: 541-947-2029
Fax: 541-947-2952

E-mail: townoflakeview@gooselake.com
Elevation: 4,802'
Incorporated: 1889
Mayor: Rick Watson

Lebanon
County: Linn
Address: 925 Main St., 97355
Phone: 541-258-4900
Fax: 541-258-4950
E-mail: jhitt@ci.lebanon.or.us
Web: www.ci.lebanon.or.us
Elevation: 347'
Incorporated: 1878
Mayor: Ken Toombs

Lexington
County: Morrow
Address: PO Box 416, 97839
Phone: 541-989-8515
Fax: 541-989-8515
E-mail: townlex@oregontrail.net
Elevation: 1,454'
Incorporated: 1903
Mayor: John Edwards

Lincoln City
County: Lincoln
Address: PO Box 50, 97367
Phone: 541-996-2152
Fax: 541-994-7232
E-mail: davidh@lincolncity.org
Web: www.lincolncity.org
Elevation: 11'
Incorporated: 1965
Mayor: Lori Hollingsworth

Lonerock
County: Gilliam
Address: Lonerock Rte., Condon 97823
Elevation: 2,800'
Incorporated: 1901
Mayor: Floyd Parrott

Long Creek
County: Grant
Address: PO Box 489, 97856
Phone: 541-421-3601
Fax: 541-421-3075
E-mail: citylc@ortelco.net
Elevation: 3,754'
Incorporated: 1891
Mayor: Clifford Smith

Lostine
County: Wallowa
Address: PO Box 181, 97857
Phone: 541-569-2415
Fax: 541-569-5116
E-mail: cityoflostine@eoni.com
Elevation: 3,200'
Incorporated: 1903
Mayor: Krag Norton

Lowell

County: Lane
Address: PO Box 490, 97452
Phone: 541-937-2157
Fax: 541-937-2936
E-mail: cityoflowell@lowell-or.gov
Elevation: 742'
Incorporated: 1954
Mayor: Warren Weathers

Lyons

County: Linn
Address: PO Box 10, 97358
Phone: 503-859-2167
Fax: 503-859-5167
E-mail: marym@wvi.com
Web: www.wvi.com/~marym/
Elevation: 660'
Incorporated: 1958
Mayor: William M. Hatt

*Madras

County: Jefferson
Address: 71 SE "D" St., 97741-1605
Phone: 541-475-2344
Fax: 541-475-7061
E-mail: Kcoleman@cci.madras.or.us
Web: www.ci.madras.or.us
Elevation: 2,242'
Incorporated: 1910
Mayor: Rick Allen

Malin

County: Klamath
Address: PO Box 61, 97632
Phone: 541-723-2021
Fax: 541-723-2011
E-mail: kayneumeyer@centurytel.net
Elevation: 4,058'
Incorporated: 1922
Mayor: Gary Zeig

Manzanita

County: Tillamook
Address: PO Box 129, 97130-0129
Phone: 503-368-5343
Fax: 503-368-4145
E-mail: manzbch@nehalemtel.net
Elevation: 78'
Incorporated: 1946
Mayor: Hugh McIsaac

Maupin

County: Wasco
Address: PO Box 308, 97037
Phone: 541-395-2698
Fax: 541-395-2499
E-mail: maupincity@centurytel.net
Elevation: 1,047'
Incorporated: 1922
Mayor: Dennis Ross

Maywood Park

County: Multnomah
Address: 10100 NE Prescott St., Suite 147, Portland, 97220
Phone: 503-255-9805
Fax: 503-667-6403
E-mail: julierisley@integraonline.com
Elevation: 77'
Incorporated: 1967
Mayor: Mark Hardie

*McMinnville

County: Yamhill
Address: 230 NE 2nd St., 97128
Phone: 503-434-7301
Fax: 503-472-4104
E-mail: benedictc@ci.mcminnville.or.us
Web: www.ci.mcminnville.or.us
Elevation: 157'
Incorporated: 1876
Mayor: Edward J. Gormley

*Medford

County: Jackson
Address: 411 W 8th St., 97501
Phone: 541-774-2000
Fax: 541-618-1700
E-mail: council@ci.medford.or.us
Web: www.ci.medford.or.us
Elevation: 1,382'
Incorporated: 1885
Mayor: Gary Wheeler

Merrill

County: Klamath
Address: PO Box 487, 97633
Phone: 541-798-5808
Fax: 541-798-0145
E-mail: cityofmerrill@centurytel.net
Elevation: 4,067'
Incorporated: 1903
Mayor: Ronda Lyon

Metolius

County: Jefferson
Address: 636 Jefferson Ave., 97741
Phone: 541-546-5533
Fax: 541-546-8809
E-mail: comet@bendnet.com
Web: www.cityofmetolius.com
Elevation: 2,530'
Incorporated: 1913
Mayor: Sandy Toms

Mill City

County: Linn/Marion
Address: PO Box 256, 97360
Phone: 503-897-2302
Fax: 503-897-3499
E-mail: millcity@wvi.com
Elevation: 832'
Incorporated: 1947
Mayor: Tim Kirsch

Millersburg
County: Linn
Address: 4222 NE Old Salem Rd., Albany 97321
Phone: 541-928-4523
Fax: 541-928-8945
E-mail: bcmburg@callatg.com
Elevation: 235'
Incorporated: 1974
Mayor: Clayton Wood

Milton-Freewater
County: Umatilla
Address: PO Box 6, 97862
Phone: 541-938-5531
Fax: 541-938-8224
E-mail: linda.hall@milton-freewater-or.gov
Web: www.mfcity.com
Elevation: 1,071'
Incorporated: 1950
Mayor: Lewis Key

Milwaukie
County: Clackamas
Address: 10722 SE Main St., 97222
Phone: 503-786-7502
Fax: 503-653-2444
E-mail: duvalp@ci.milwaukie.or.us
Web: www.cityofmilwaukie.org
Elevation: 39'
Incorporated: 1903
Mayor: James Bernard

Mitchell
County: Wheeler
Address: PO Box 97, 97750
Phone: 541-462-3045
Fax: 541-462-3045
E-mail: cityofmitchell@bendnet.com
Elevation: 2,777'
Incorporated: 1891
Mayor: Keifer Davis

Molalla
County: Clackamas
Address: PO Box 248, 97038
Phone: 503-829-6855
Fax: 503-829-3676
E-mail: city@molalla.net
Web: www.molalla.net/~city
Elevation: 371'
Incorporated: 1913
Mayor: Mike Clarke

Monmouth
County: Polk
Address: 151 W Main St., 97361
Phone: 503-838-0722
Fax: 503-838-0725
E-mail: ssalisbury@ci.monmouth.or.us
Elevation: 214'
Incorporated: 1859
Mayor: Larry Dalton

Monroe
County: Benton
Address: PO Box 486, 97456
Phone: 541-847-5175
Fax: 541-847-5177
E-mail: barbjd@99webstreet.com
Elevation: 288'
Incorporated: 1914
Mayor: Frank Thayer

Monument
County: Grant
Address: PO Box 426, 97864
Phone: 541-934-2025
Fax: 541-934-2025
E-mail: monument@oregontrail.net
Elevation: 2,000'
Incorporated: 1905
Mayor: Joe Duncan

*Moro
County: Sherman
Address: PO Box 231, 97039
Phone: 541-565-3535
Fax: 541-565-3535
E-mail: moro@netcnct.net
Elevation: 1,799'
Incorporated: 1899
Mayor: John Waldron

Mosier
County: Wasco
Address: PO Box 456, 97040
Phone: 541-478-3505
Fax: 541-478-3810
E-mail: mosiercityhall@gorge.net
Web: http://community.gorge.net/mosier
Elevation: 164'
Incorporated: 1914
Mayor: Marc Berry

Mt. Angel
County: Marion
Address: PO Box 960, 97362
Phone: 503-845-9291
Fax: 503-845-6261
E-mail: gmiles@ci.mt-angel.or.us
Web: www.ci.mt-angel.or.us
Elevation: 168'
Incorporated: 1893
Mayor: Thomas Bauman

Mt. Vernon
County: Grant
Address: PO Box 647, 97865
Phone: 541-932-4688
Fax: 541-932-4222
E-mail: cmtv@ortelco.net
Elevation: 2,865'
Incorporated: 1948
Mayor: Dennis Bradley

Myrtle Creek
County: Douglas
Address: PO Box 940, 97457
Phone: 541-863-3171
Fax: 541-863-7155
E-mail: mc.city@pioneer-net.com
Web: www.myrtlecreek-oregon.org
Elevation: 660'
Incorporated: 1893
Mayor: Jerry Pothier

Myrtle Point
County: Coos
Address: 424 5th St., 97458
Phone: 541-572-2626
Fax: 541-572-3838
E-mail: cityofmyrtlepoint@yahoo.com
Elevation: 90'
Incorporated: 1887
Mayor: Edward Cook

Nehalem
County: Tillamook
Address: PO Box 143, 97131
Phone: 503-368-5627
Fax: 503-368-4175
E-mail: nehalemch@nehalemtel.net
Elevation: 11'
Incorporated: 1899
Mayor: Shirley Kalkhoven

Newberg
County: Yamhill
Address: PO Box 970, 97132
Phone: 503-538-9421
Fax: 503-537-5393
E-mail: nctymgr@ci.newberg.or.us
Web: www.ci.newberg.or.us
Elevation: 175'
Incorporated: 1889
Mayor: Robert Stewart

*Newport
County: Lincoln
Address: 169 SW Coast Highway, 97365
Phone: 541-574-0603
Fax: 541-574-0609
E-mail: p.hawker@thecityofnewport.net
Web: www.thecityofnewport.net
Elevation: 134'
Incorporated: 1882
Mayor: Mark D. Jones

North Bend
County: Coos
Address: PO Box B, 97459
Phone: 541-756-8500
Fax: 541-756-8527
E-mail: janw@uci.net
Web: www.cityofnorthbend.org
Elevation: 41'
Incorporated: 1903
Mayor: Rick Wetherell

North Plains
County: Washington
Address: 31360 NW Commercial St., 97133
Phone: 503-647-5555
Fax: 503-647-2031
E-mail: debbie@northplains.org
Web: www.northplains.org
Elevation: 176'
Incorporated: 1963
Mayor: Cheryl Olson

North Powder
County: Union
Address: PO Box 309, 97867
Phone: 541-898-2185
Fax: 541-898-2647
E-mail: cityofnp@oregontrail.net
Elevation: 3,256'
Incorporated: 1903
Mayor: Carrie Crook

Nyssa
County: Malheur
Address: 14 S 3rd St., 97913
Phone: 541-372-2264
Fax: 541-372-2377
E-mail: cnyssa@cubewireless.com
Web: www.nyssacity.org
Elevation: 2,175'
Incorporated: 1903
Mayor: Diego Castellanoz

Oakland
County: Douglas
Address: PO Box 117, 97462
Phone: 541-459-4531
Fax: 541-459-4472
E-mail: oakland@tsioregon.net
Web: www.makewebs.com/oakland
Elevation: 430'
Incorporated: 1878
Mayor: James C. Baird

Oakridge
County: Lane
Address: PO Box 1410, 97463
Phone: 541-782-2258
Fax: 541-782-1081
E-mail: chantellhayson@ci.oakridge.or.us
Web: ci.oakridge.or.us
Elevation: 1,240'
Incorporated: 1935
Mayor: Sue Bond

Ontario
County: Malheur
Address: 444 SW 4th St., 97914
Phone: 541-889-7684
Fax: 541-889-7121
E-mail: tori.ankrum@ontariooregon.org
Web: www.ontariooregon.org
Elevation: 2,150'

Incorporated: 1899
Mayor: Leroy Cammack

*Oregon City
County: Clackamas
Address: PO Box 3040, 97045-0021
Phone: 503-657-0891
Fax: 503-657-7026
E-mail: recorder@ci.oregon-city.or.us
Web: www.orcity.org
Elevation: 55'
Incorporated: 1844
Mayor: Alice Norris

Paisley
County: Lake
Address: PO Box 100, 97636
Phone: 541-943-3173
Fax: 541-943-3982
Web: www.cityofpaisley@geocities.com
Elevation: 4,369'
Incorporated: 1911
Mayor: Dennis O'Leary

*Pendleton
County: Umatilla
Address: 500 SW Dorion Ave., 97801
Phone: 541-966-0200
Fax: 541-966-0231
E-mail: judi@ci.pendleton.or.us
Web: www.pendleton.or.us
Elevation: 1,200'
Incorporated: 1880
Mayor: Phillip Houk

Philomath
County: Benton
Address: PO Box 400, 97370
Phone: 541-929-6148
Fax: 541-929-3044
E-mail: philomath.admin@ci.philomath.or.us
Web: www.ci.philomath.or.us
Elevation: 279'
Incorporated: 1882
Mayor: Chris Nusbaum

Phoenix
County: Jackson
Address: 510 West 1st St., 97535
Phone: 541-535-1955
Fax: 541-535-5769
E-mail: phoenixadmbetty@charter.com
Web: www.phoenixoregon.net
Elevation: 1,543'
Incorporated: 1910
Mayor: Vicki Bear

Pilot Rock
County: Umatilla
Address: PO Box 130, 97868
Phone: 541-443-2811
Fax: 541-443-2253
E-mail: cityofpr@centurytel.net

Web: www.cityofpilotrock.org
Elevation: 1,637'
Incorporated: 1911
Mayor: Virginia Karnes

Port Orford
County: Curry
Address: PO Box 310, 97465
Phone: 541-332-3681
Fax: 541-332-3830
E-mail: portorfordcityh@harborside.com
Web: www.portorford.org
Elevation: 59'
Incorporated: 1935
Mayor: James Auborn

*Portland
County: Clackamas/Multnomah/Washington
Address: 1221 SW 4th Ave., Rm. 140, 97204
Phone: 503-823-4087
Fax: 503-823-4571
E-mail: gblackmer@ci.portland.or.us
Web: www.portlandonline.com
Elevation: 77'
Incorporated: 1851
Mayor: Tom Potter

Powers
County: Coos
Address: PO Box 250, 97466
Phone: 541-439-3331
Fax: 541-439-5555
E-mail: powersch@ucinet.com
Elevation: 286'
Incorporated: 1945
Mayor: Noble Adamek

Prairie City
County: Grant
Address: PO Box 370, 97869
Phone: 541-820-3605
Fax: 541-820-3566
E-mail: pchall@ortelco.net
Web: www.prairiecityoregon.com
Elevation: 3,535'
Incorporated: 1891
Mayor: Jim Hamsher

Prescott
County: Columbia
Address: 72742 Blakely St., Rainier 97048
E-mail: ckmiller@crpud.net
Elevation: 17'
Incorporated: 1947
Mayor: Kevin Miller

*Prineville
County: Crook
Address: 400 NE 3rd St., 97754
Phone: 541-447-5627
Fax: 541-447-5628
E-mail: cityhall@cityofprineville.com
Web: www.cityofprineville.or.gov

Elevation: 2,868'
Incorporated: 1880
Mayor: Mike Wendel

Rainier
County: Columbia
Address: PO Box 100, 97048-0100
Phone: 503-556-7301
Fax: 503-556-3200
E-mail: marchibald@cityofrainier.com
Web: http://www.7technw.com/rainier
Elevation: 51'
Incorporated: 1885
Mayor: Jerry Cole

Redmond
County: Deschutes
Address: PO Box 726, 97756
Phone: 541-923-7710
Fax: 541-548-0706
E-mail: info@ci.redmond.or.us
Web: www.ci.redmond.or.us
Elevation: 3,077'
Incorporated: 1910
Mayor: Alan Unger

Reedsport
County: Douglas
Address: 451 Winchester Ave., 97467
Phone: 541-271-3603
Fax: 541-271-2809
E-mail: citymanager@reedsport.or.us
Elevation: 10'
Incorporated: 1919
Mayor: Jim Hanson

Richland
County: Baker
Address: PO Box 266, 97870
Phone: 541-893-6141
Fax: 541-893-6267
E-mail: richcity@pinetel.com
Elevation: 2,231'
Incorporated: 1917
Mayor: Nancy Gover

Riddle
County: Douglas
Address: PO Box 143, 97469
Phone: 541-874-2571
Fax: 541-874-2625
E-mail: coriddle@pioneer-net.com
Elevation: 700'
Incorporated: 1893
Mayor: William G. Duckett

Rivergrove
County: Clackamas/Washington
Address: PO Box 1104, Lake Oswego 97035
Phone: 503-639-6919
Fax: 503-639-0899
Elevation: 132'
Incorporated: 1971
Mayor: Larry Barrett

Rockaway Beach
County: Tillamook
Address: PO Box 5, 97136
Phone: 503-355-2291
Fax: 503-355-8221
E-mail: rbeach@pacifier.com
Web: www.cityofrockawaybeach.com
Elevation: 17'
Incorporated: 1942
Mayor: Lisa Phipps

Rogue River
County: Jackson
Address: PO Box 1137, 97537
Phone: 541-582-4401
Fax: 541-582-0937
E-mail: mreagles@ci.rogue-river.or.us
Elevation: 1,000'
Incorporated: 1912
Mayor: Dick Skevington

*Roseburg
County: Douglas
Address: 900 SE Douglas Ave., 97470-3397
Phone: 541-672-7701
Fax: 541-673-2856
E-mail: scox@ci.roseburg.or.us
Web: www.ci.roseburg.or.us
Elevation: 480'
Incorporated: 1868
Mayor: Larry Rich

Rufus
County: Sherman
Address: PO Box 27, 97050
Phone: 541-739-2321
Fax: 541-739-2460
E-mail: rufuscity@faw.net
Elevation: 235'
Incorporated: 1965
Mayor: Clifford Jett

*Salem
County: Marion
Address: 555 Liberty St. SE, Suite 205, 97301
Phone: 503-588-6091
Fax: 503-361-2202
E-mail: manager@cityofsalem.net
Web: www.cityofsalem.net
Elevation: 154'
Incorporated: 1857
Mayor: Janet Taylor

Sandy
County: Clackamas
Address: 39250 Pioneer Blvd., 97055
Phone: 503-668-5533
Fax: 503-668-8714
E-mail: slazenby@ci.sandy.or.us
Web: www.ci.sandy.or.us
Elevation: 1,000'
Incorporated: 1911
Mayor: Linda Malone

Scappoose

County: Columbia
Address: PO Box P, 97056
Phone: 503-543-7146
Fax: 503-543-7182
E-mail: susanpentecost@ci.scappoose.or.us
Web: www.ci.scappoose.or.us
Elevation: 62'
Incorporated: 1921
Mayor: Glenn E. Dorschler

Scio

County: Linn
Address: PO Box 37, 97374-0037
Phone: 503-394-3342
Fax: 503-394-2340
E-mail: scio@smt-net.com
Elevation: 317'
Incorporated: 1866
Mayor: Dean Ferguson

Scotts Mills

County: Marion
Address: PO Box 220, 97375-0220
Phone: 503-873-5435
E-mail: smcity@open.org
Web: www.open.org/~smcity/
Elevation: 426'
Incorporated: 1916
Mayor: Larry Martin

Seaside

County: Clatsop
Address: 989 Broadway, 97138
Phone: 503-738-5511
Fax: 503-738-5514
E-mail: mwinstanley@cityofseaside.us
Web: www.cityofseaside.us
Elevation: 17'
Incorporated: 1899
Mayor: Don Larson

Seneca

County: Grant
Address: PO Box 208, 97873
Phone: 541-542-2161
Fax: 541-542-2161
E-mail: cseneca@ortelco.net
Elevation: 4,690'
Incorporated: 1970
Mayor: Linda Starbuck

Shady Cove

County: Jackson
Address: PO Box 1210, 97539
Phone: 541-878-2225
Fax: 541-878-2226
E-mail: shadycovecityhall@grrtech.com
Web: www.shadycove.net
Elevation: 1,406'
Incorporated: 1972
Mayor: Dick Bailey

Shaniko

County: Wasco
Address: PO Box 17, 97057
Phone: 541-489-3226
Fax: 541-489-3255
E-mail: jhogan@madras.net
Web: www.shaniko.com
Elevation: 3,344'
Incorporated: 1901
Mayor: Booker T. Pannell

Sheridan

County: Yamhill
Address: 120 SW Mill St., 97378
Phone: 503-843-2347
Fax: 503-843-3661
E-mail: tihenderson@cablerocket.com
Elevation: 189'
Incorporated: 1880
Mayor: Joe Fabiano

Sherwood

County: Washington
Address: 20 NW Washington St., 97140
Phone: 503-625-5522
Fax: 503-625-5524
E-mail: wileyc@ci.sherwood.or.us
Web: www.ci.sherwood.or.us
Elevation: 193'
Incorporated: 1893
Mayor: Keith Mays

Siletz

County: Lincoln
Address: PO Box 318, 97380
Phone: 541-444-2521
Fax: 541-444-7371
E-mail: chsiletz@qwest.net
Elevation: 130'
Incorporated: 1946
Mayor: Daniel A. Smith

Silverton

County: Marion
Address: 306 S Water St., 97381
Phone: 503-873-5321
Fax: 503-873-3210
E-mail: bcosgrove@silverton.or.us
Web: www.silverton.or.us
Elevation: 252'
Incorporated: 1885
Mayor: Kenneth J. Hector

Sisters

County: Deschutes
Address: PO Box 39, 97759
Phone: 541-549-6022
Fax: 541-549-0561
E-mail: enstein@ci.sisters.or.us
Web: www.ci.sisters.or.us
Elevation: 3,182'

Incorporated: 1946
Mayor: M. David Elliott

Sodaville
County: Linn
Address: 30723 Sodaville Rd., Sodaville 97355
Phone: 541-258-8882
Fax: 541-258-8882
E-mail: sodaville@centurytel.net
Elevation: 492'
Incorporated: 1880
Mayor: Karen Corrington

Spray
County: Wheeler
Address: PO Box 83, 97874
Phone: 541-468-2069
Fax: 541-468-2044
E-mail: cityofspray@centurytel.net
Elevation: 1,795'
Incorporated: 1958
Mayor: Terry Ingalls

Springfield
County: Lane
Address: 225 5th St., 97477
Phone: 541-726-3700
Fax: 541-726-2363
E-mail: asowa@ci.springfield.or.us
Web: www.ci.springfield.or.us
Elevation: 454'
Incorporated: 1885
Mayor: Sidney Leiken

*St. Helens
County: Columbia
Address: PO Box 278, 97051
Phone: 503-397-6272
Fax: 503-397-4016
E-mail: brianl@ci.st-helens.or.us
Web: www.ci.st-helens.or.us
Elevation: 39'
Incorporated: 1889
Mayor: Randy Peterson

St. Paul
County: Marion
Address: PO Box 7, 97137
Phone: 503-633-4971
Fax: 503-633-4972
E-mail: stpaulcity@stpaultel.com
Elevation: 169'
Incorporated: 1901
Mayor: Kathy Connor

Stanfield
County: Umatilla
Address: PO Box 369, 97875
Phone: 541-449-3831
Fax: 541-449-1828
E-mail: costnfld@uci.net
Elevation: 592'
Incorporated: 1910
Mayor: Thomas J. McCann

Stayton
County: Marion
Address: 362 N 3rd Ave., 97383
Phone: 503-769-3425
Fax: 503-769-1456
E-mail: cchilds@stayton.org
Web: www.open.org/~stayton
Elevation: 452'
Incorporated: 1901
Mayor: Gerry Aboud

Sublimity
County: Marion
Address: PO Box 146, 97385
Phone: 503-769-5475
Fax: 503-769-2206
E-mail: sublime@open.org
Web: www.open.org/~sublime
Elevation: 551'
Incorporated: 1903
Mayor: Raymond Heuberger

Summerville
County: Union
Address: PO Box 92, 97876
Phone: 541-534-6873
E-mail: summerville@eoni.com
Elevation: 2,705'
Incorporated: 1885
Mayor: Sheri Rogers

Sumpter
County: Baker
Address: PO Box 68, 97877
Phone: 541-894-2314
Fax: 541-894-2314
E-mail: sumpter@eoni.com
Web: www.historicsumpter.com
Elevation: 4,437'
Incorporated: 1901
Mayor: Jack Colton

Sutherlin
County: Douglas
Address: 126 E Central Ave., 97479
Phone: 541-459-2856
Fax: 541-459-9363
E-mail: vluther@ci.sutherlin.or.us
Elevation: 520'
Incorporated: 1911
Mayor: Joe Mongiovi

Sweet Home
County: Linn
Address: 1140 12th Ave., 97386
Phone: 541-367-5128
Fax: 541-367-5113
E-mail: shmanage@dnc.net
Web: www.ci.sweet-home.or.us
Elevation: 537'
Incorporated: 1893
Mayor: Tim McQueary

Talent
County: Jackson
Address: PO Box 445, 97540-0445
Phone: 541-535-1566
Fax: 541-535-7423
E-mail: betty@cityoftalent.org
Web: www.cityoftalent.org
Elevation: 1,635'
Incorporated: 1910
Mayor: Marian Telerski

Tangent
County: Linn
Address: PO Box 251, 97389
Phone: 541-928-1020
Fax: 541-928-4920
E-mail: tangent@quik.com
Elevation: 245'
Incorporated: 1893
Mayor: Chris Schaffner

*The Dalles
County: Wasco
Address: 313 Court St., 97058
Phone: 541-296-5481
Fax: 541-296-6906
E-mail: julie_krueger@ci.the-dalles.or.us
Web: www.ci.the-dalles.or.us
Elevation: 109'
Incorporated: 1857
Mayor: Rob Van Cleave

Tigard
County: Washington
Address: 13125 SW Hall Blvd., 97223
Phone: 503-639-4171
Fax: 503-684-7297
E-mail: cathy@ci.tigard.or.us
Web: www.ci.tigard.or.us
Elevation: 169'
Incorporated: 1961
Mayor: Craig Dirksen

*Tillamook
County: Tillamook
Address: 210 Laurel Ave., 97141
Phone: 503-842-2472
Fax: 503-842-3445
E-mail: mgervasi@tillamookor.gov
Web: www.tillamookor.gov
Elevation: 24'
Incorporated: 1891
Mayor: J. Robert McPheeters

Toledo
County: Lincoln
Address: PO Box 220, 97391
Phone: 541-336-2247
Fax: 541-336-3512
E-mail: manager@cityoftoledo.org
Web: www.cityoftoledo.org
Elevation: 59'

Incorporated: 1905
Mayor: Sharon R. Branstiter

Troutdale
County: Multnomah
Address: 104 SE Kibling Ave., 97060
Phone: 503-665-5175
Fax: 503-667-6403
E-mail: feedback@ci.troutdale.or.us
Web: www.troutdale.info
Elevation: 30'-200'
Incorporated: 1907
Mayor: Paul Thalhofer

Tualatin
County: Clackamas/Washington
Address: 18880 SW Martinazzi Ave., 97062
Phone: 503-692-2000
Fax: 503-692-5421
E-mail: swheeler@ci.tualatin.or.us
Web: www.ci.tualatin.or.us
Elevation: 123'
Incorporated: 1913
Mayor: Lou Ogden

Turner
County: Marion
Address: PO Box 456, 97392
Phone: 503-743-2155
Fax: 503-743-2140
E-mail: turner@open.org
Web: www.open.org/~turner
Elevation: 287'
Incorporated: 1905
Mayor: James Thompson

Ukiah
County: Umatilla
Address: PO Box 265, 97880
Phone: 541-427-3271
Fax: 541-427-3271
Elevation: 3,400'
Incorporated: 1969
Mayor: Clint Barber

Umatilla
County: Umatilla
Address: PO Box 130, 97882
Phone: 541-922-3226
Fax: 541-922-5758
E-mail: larry@umatilla–city.org
Elevation: 296'
Incorporated: 1864
Mayor: David Trott

Union
County: Union
Address: PO Box 529, 97883
Phone: 541-562-5197
Fax: 541-562-5196
E-mail: cityhall@cityofunion.com
Web: www.cityofunion.com
Elevation: 2,791'

Incorporated: 1878
Mayor: Deborah Clark

Unity
County: Baker
Address: PO Box 7, 97884
Phone: 541-446-3544
Fax: 541-446-3544
E-mail: cityofunity@ortelco.net
Elevation: 4,040'
Incorporated: 1972
Mayor: Tina Kandle

*Vale
County: Malheur
Address: 252 B St. W, 97918
Phone: 541-473-3133
Fax: 541-473-3895
E-mail: ddemayo@fmtc.com
Web: www.ci.vale.or.us
Elevation: 2,243'
Incorporated: 1889
Mayor: Jim Silence

Veneta
County: Lane
Address: PO Box 458, 97487
Phone: 541-935-2191
Fax: 541-935-1838
E-mail: ringham@ci.veneta.or.us
Web: www.ci.veneta.or.us
Elevation: 418'
Incorporated: 1962
Mayor: T.J. Brooker

Vernonia
County: Columbia
Address: 1001 Bridge St., 97064
Phone: 503-429-5291
Fax: 503-429-4232
E-mail: cityhall@vernonia-or.gov
Web: www.vernonia-or.gov
Elevation: 630'
Incorporated: 1891
Mayor: Sally Harrison

Waldport
County: Lincoln
Address: PO Box 1120, 97394
Phone: 541-563-3561
Fax: 541-563-5810
E-mail: reda.quinlan@waldport.org
Web: www.waldport.org
Elevation: 12'
Incorporated: 1911
Mayor: Scott Beckstead

Wallowa
County: Wallowa
Address: PO Box 487, 97885
Phone: 541-886-2422
Fax: 541-886-4215
E-mail: wallowam@oregontrail.net

Web: www.cityofwallowa.com
Elevation: 2,950'
Incorporated: 1899
Mayor: Ron Philbrook

Warrenton
County: Clatsop
Address: PO Box 250, 97146
Phone: 503-861-2233
Fax: 503-861-2351
E-mail: cityofwarrenton@ci.warrenton.or.us
Elevation: 8'
Incorporated: 1899
Mayor: Gilbert Gramson

Wasco
County: Sherman
Address: PO Box 26, 97065
Phone: 541-442-5515
Fax: 541-442-5001
E-mail: wascocty@pacifier.com
Elevation: 1,281'
Incorporated: 1901
Mayor: Karen Kellogg

Waterloo
County: Linn
Address: PO Box 1066, Lebanon 97355
Phone: 541-451-2245
Fax: 541-451-3133
E-mail: cityofwaterloo@centurytel.net
Elevation: 402'
Incorporated: 1893
Mayor: Jed Little

West Linn
County: Clackamas
Address: 22500 Salamo Rd. #100, 97068
Phone: 503-657-0331
Fax: 503-650-9041
E-mail: sfarley@ci.west-linn.or.us
Web: www.ci.west-linn.or.us
Elevation: 105'
Incorporated: 1913
Mayor: Norm King

Westfir
County: Lane
Address: PO Box 296, 97492
Phone: 541-782-3733
Fax: 541-782-3983
E-mail: westfircity@trip.net
Elevation: 1,075'
Incorporated: 1979
Mayor: Diana Tonkin

Weston
County: Umatilla
Address: PO Box 579, 97886
Phone: 541-566-3313
Fax: 541-566-2792
E-mail: weston2@bmi.net
Web: www.cityofweston.org

Elevation: 1,796'
Incorporated: 1878
Mayor: Barbara Byerley

Wheeler

County: Tillamook
Address: PO Box 177, 97147
Phone: 503-368-5767
Fax: 503-368-4273
E-mail: cityofwheeler@nehalemtel.net
Elevation: 37'
Incorporated: 1914
Mayor: Richard Hendricks

Willamina

County: Polk/Yamhill
Address: PO Box 629, 97396
Phone: 503-876-2242
Fax: 503-876-1121
E-mail: recorder@onlinemac.com
Elevation: 225'
Incorporated: 1903
Mayor: Rita Baller

Wilsonville

County: Clackamas
Address: 30000 SW Town Center Loop E, 97070
Phone: 503-682-1011
Fax: 503-682-1015
E-mail: king@ci.wilsonville.or.us
Web: www.ci.wilsonville.or.us
Elevation: 175'
Incorporated: 1969
Mayor: Charlotte Lehan

Winston

County: Douglas
Address: 201 NW Douglas Blvd., 97496
Phone: 541-679-6739
Fax: 541-679-0794
E-mail: winston@rosenet.net
Web: www.sova.org/cities/winston.htm
Elevation: 545'
Incorporated: 1953
Mayor: Rex Stevens

Wood Village

County: Multnomah
Address: 2055 NE 238th Dr., 97060
Phone: 503-667-6211

Fax: 503-669-8723
E-mail: city@ci.wood-village.or.us
Web: www.ci.wood-village.or.us
Elevation: 90'–330'
Incorporated: 1951
Mayor: David Fuller

Woodburn

County: Marion
Address: 270 Montgomery St., 97071
Phone: 503-982-5222
Fax: 503-980-2482
E-mail: mary.tennant@ci.woodburn.or..us
Web: www.ci.woodburn.or.us
Elevation: 186'
Incorporated: 1889
Mayor: Kathy Figley

Yachats

County: Lincoln
Address: PO Box 345, 97498
Phone: 541-547-3565
Fax: 541-547-3063
E-mail: cityhall@ci.yachats.or.us
Web: www.ci.yachats.or.us
Elevation: 45'
Incorporated: 1967
Mayor: Suzanne Smith

Yamhill

County: Yamhill
Address: PO Box 9, 97148
Phone: 503-662-3511
Fax: 503-662-4589
E-mail: recorder@cityofyamhill.com
Web: www.cityofyamhill.com
Elevation: 182'
Incorporated: 1891
Mayor: Randy Murphy

Yoncalla

County: Douglas
Address: PO Box 508, 97499
Phone: 541-849-2152
Fax: 541-849-2552
E-mail: yoncalla@rosenet.net
Elevation: 360'
Incorporated: 1901
Mayor: Stella Myers

CITY POPULATIONS: 1970–2003

Source: Population Research Center, Portland State University
Phone: 503-725-3922

Rank	City	% Change*	2003	2000	1990	1980	1970
147	Adair Village	56.7	840	536	554	589	0
178	Adams	11.1	330	297	223	240	219
192	Adrian	2.0	150	147	131	162	0
12	Albany	6.7	43,600	40,852	29,540	26,511	18,181
119	Amity	0.1	1,480	1,478	1,175	1,092	708
196	Antelope	1.7	60	59	34	39	51
165	Arlington	8.8	570	524	425	521	375
23	Ashland	4.7	20,430	19,522	16,252	14,943	12,342
44	Astoria	0.8	9,890	9,813	10,069	9,996	10,244
126	Athena	4.0	1,270	1,221	997	965	872
86	Aumsville	1.6	3,050	3,003	1,650	1,432	590
159	Aurora	0.8	660	655	567	523	306
45	Baker City	-0.2	9,840	9,860	9,140	9,471	9,354
88	Bandon	4.5	2,960	2,833	2,215	2,311	1,832
120	Banks	11.2	1,430	1,286	563	489	430
193	Barlow	0.00	140	140	118	105	105
129	Bay City	0.1	1,150	1,149	1,027	986	898
6	Beaverton	3.8	79,010	76,129	53,307	31,962	18,577
8	Bend	20.9	62,900	52,029	20,447	17,260	13,710
85	Boardman	7.9	3,080	2,855	1,387	1,261	192
172	Bonanza	1.2	420	415	323	270	230
65	Brookings	9.2	5,950	5,447	4,400	3,384	2,720
118	Brownsville	3.5	1,500	1,449	1,281	1,261	1,034
86	Burns	-0.5	3,050	3,064	2,913	3,579	3,293
170	Butte Falls	0.2	440	439	252	428	358
35	Canby	8.8	13,910	12,790	8,990	7,659	3,813
114	Cannon Beach	3.3	1,640	1,588	1,221	1,187	779
158	Canyon City	0.1	670	669	648	639	600
122	Canyonville	9.0	1,410	1,293	1,219	1,288	940
115	Carlton	2.4	1,550	1,514	1,289	1,302	1,126
130	Cascade Locks	2.2	1,140	1,115	930	838	574
121	Cave Junction	4.2	1,420	1,363	1,126	1,023	415
31	Central Point	18.1	14,750	12,493	7,512	6,357	4,004
155	Chiloquin	0.6	720	716	673	778	826
113	Clatskanie	8.0	1,650	1,528	1,629	1,648	1,286
136	Coburg	8.4	1.050	969	763	699	734
112	Columbia City	9.5	1,720	1,571	1,003	678	537
151	Condon	1.4	770	759	635	783	973
30	Coos Bay	1.8	15,650	15,374	15,076	14,424	13,466
78	Coquille	-0.1	4,180	4,184	4,121	4,481	4,437
43	Cornelius	5.2	10,150	9,652	6,148	4,402	1,903
10	Corvallis	7.4	52,950	49,322	44,757	40,960	35,056
48	Cottage Grove	5.5	8,910	8,445	7,403	7,148	6,004
160	Cove	7.7	640	594	507	451	363

Rank	City	% Change*	2003	2000	1990	1980	1970
79	Creswell	11.5	3,990	3,579	2,431	1,770	1,199
147	Culver	4.7	840	802	570	514	407
36	Dallas	6.5	13,270	12,459	9,422	8,530	6,361
98	Dayton	5.2	2,230	2,119	1,526	1,409	949
191	Dayville	15.9	160	138	144	199	197
127	Depoe Bay	4.8	1,230	1,174	870	723	0
184	Detroit	-4.6	250	262	331	367	328
160	Donald	2.4	640	608	316	267	231
135	Drain	3.8	1,060	1,021	1,086	1,148	1,204
164	Dufur	2.0	600	588	527	560	493
91	Dundee	10.1	2,860	2,598	1,663	1,223	588
124	Dunes City	5.6	1,310	1,241	1,081	1,124	976
123	Durham	1.3	1,400	1,382	748	707	410
58	Eagle Point	38.2	6,630	4,797	3,008	2,764	1,241
157	Echo	6.2	690	650	500	624	479
113	Elgin	-0.2	1,650	1,654	1,586	1,701	1,375
192	Elkton	2.0	150	147	172	155	176
106	Enterprise	1.3	1,920	1,895	1,905	2,003	1,680
95	Estacada	2.9	2,440	2,371	2,016	1,419	1,164
2	Eugene	4.4	143,910	137,893	112,733	105,664	79,028
49	Fairview	13.6	8,590	7,561	2,391	1,749	1,045
139	Falls City	-0.6	960	966	818	804	745
54	Florence	7.1	7,780	7,263	5,171	4,411	2,246
26	Forest Grove	8.0	19,130	17,708	13,559	11,499	8,175
168	Fossil	-1.9	460	469	399	535	511
143	Garibaldi	0.1	900	899	886	999	1,083
162	Gaston	3.3	620	600	563	471	429
167	Gates	4.0	490	471	499	455	250
137	Gearhart	4.5	1,040	995	1,027	967	829
100	Gervais	5.0	2,110	2,009	992	799	746
40	Gladstone	3.1	11,790	11,438	10,152	9,500	6,254
146	Glendale	0.6	860	855	707	712	709
105	Gold Beach	1.7	1,930	1,897	1,546	1,515	1,554
134	Gold Hill	-0.3	1,070	1,073	964	904	603
198	Granite	-16.7	20	24	8	17	4
18	Grants Pass	6.4	24,470	23,003	17,503	15,032	12,455
190	Grass Valley	-0.6	170	171	160	164	153
199	Greenhorn	0.0	0	0	0	0	0
4	Gresham	3.8	93,660	90,205	68,249	33,005	10,030
170	Haines	3.3	440	426	405	341	212
176	Halfway	3.9	350	337	311	380	317
153	Halsey	2.2	740	724	667	693	467
60	Happy Valley	41.0	6,370	4,519	1,519	1,499	1,392
89	Harrisburg	4.8	2,930	2,795	1,939	1,881	1,311
189	Helix	-1.6	180	183	150	155	152
122	Heppner	1.1	1,410	1,395	1,412	1,498	1,429
32	Hermiston	10.5	14,540	13,154	10,047	8,408	4,893
5	Hillsboro	13.0	79,340	70,186	37,598	27,664	14,675

Rank	City	% Change*	2003	2000	1990	1980	1970
111	Hines	7.2	1,740	1,623	1,452	1,632	1,407
61	Hood River	6.8	6,230	5,831	4,632	4,329	3,991
92	Hubbard	8.7	2,700	2,483	1,881	1,640	975
166	Huntington	1.0	520	515	522	539	507
186	Idanha	-0.9	230	232	289	319	382
181	Imbler	2.1	290	284	299	292	139
57	Independence	13.5	6,850	6,035	4,425	4,024	2,594
177	Ione	5.9	340	321	255	345	355
109	Irrigon	4.6	1,780	1,702	737	700	261
141	Island City	0.4	920	916	696	477	202
96	Jacksonville	6.0	2,370	2,235	1,896	2,030	1,611
94	Jefferson	-0.3	2,480	2,487	1,805	1,702	936
108	John Day	1.0	1,840	1,821	1,836	2,012	1,566
161	Johnson City	-0.6	630	634	586	378	0
185	Jordan Valley	0.4	240	239	364	473	196
133	Joseph	2.5	1,080	1,054	1,073	999	839
72	Junction City	3.2	4,870	4,721	3,670	3,320	2,373
14	Keizer	5.6	34,010	32,203	21,884	0	0
101	King City	7.7	2,100	1,949	2,060	1,853	1,427
24	Klamath Falls	3.8	20,190	19,460	17,737	16,661	15,775
38	La Grande	1.4	12,500	12,327	11,766	11,354	9,645
87	Lafayette	16.4	3,010	2,586	1,292	1,215	786
13	Lake Oswego	1.6	35,860	35,278	30,576	22,527	14,615
121	Lakeside	-0.1	1,420	1,421	1,437	1,453	0
94	Lakeview	0.2	2,480	2,474	2,526	2,770	2,705
37	Lebanon	1.5	13,140	12,950	10,950	10,413	7,277
183	Lexington	-1.1	260	263	286	307	230
55	Lincoln City	-0.2	7,420	7,437	5,908	5,469	4,196
198	Lonerock	-16.7	20	24	11	26	12
187	Long Creek	-3.5	220	228	249	252	196
184	Lostine	-4.9	250	263	231	250	196
144	Lowell	1.1	890	880	785	661	567
135	Lyons	5.2	1,060	1,008	938	877	645
70	Madras	5.8	5,370	5,078	3,443	2,235	1,689
149	Malin	25.0	800	640	725	539	486
163	Manzanita	8.2	610	564	513	443	261
169	Maupin	9.5	450	411	456	495	428
152	Maywood Park	-3.5	750	777	781	845	1,230
15	McMinnville	9.0	28,890	26,499	17,894	14,080	10,125
7	Medford	6.9	68,080	63,687	47,021	39,746	28,454
142	Merrill	1.4	910	897	837	822	722
150	Metolius	7.0	780	729	450	451	27
117	Mill City	-0.5	1,530	1,537	1,555	1,565	1,451
155	Millersburg	10.6	720	651	715	562	0
59	Milton-Freewater	0.5	6,500	6,470	5,533	5,086	4,105
21	Milwaukie	0.4	20,580	20,490	18,670	17,931	16,444
190	Mitchell	0.0	170	170	163	183	196
66	Molalla	2.7	5,800	5,647	3,651	2,992	2,005

Rank	City	% Change*	2003	2000	1990	1980	1970
52	Monmouth	4.4	8,080	7,741	6,288	5,594	5,237
163	Monroe	0.5	610	607	448	412	443
192	Monument	-0.7	150	151	162	192	161
177	Moro	0.9	340	337	292	336	290
171	Mosier	4.9	430	410	244	340	217
80	Mt. Angel	18.6	3,700	3,121	2,778	2,876	1,973
164	Mt. Vernon	0.8	600	595	549	569	423
83	Myrtle Creek	1.8	3,480	3,419	3,063	3,365	2,733
94	Myrtle Point	1.2	2,480	2,451	2,712	2,859	2,511
188	Nehalem	3.4	210	203	232	258	241
25	Newberg	8.1	19,530	18,064	13,086	10,394	6,507
46	Newport	2.2	9,740	9,532	8,437	7,519	5,188
47	North Bend	0.8	9,620	9,544	9,614	9,779	8,553
114	North Plains	2.2	1,640	1,605	997	715	690
167	North Powder	0.2	490	489	448	430	304
84	Nyssa	0.2	3,170	3,163	2,629	2,862	2,620
140	Oakland	-1.5	940	954	844	886	1,010
81	Oakridge	16.0	3,680	3,172	3,063	3,680	3,422
42	Ontario	1.7	11,170	10,985	9,394	8,814	6,523
16	Oregon City	9.1	28,100	25,754	14,698	14,673	9,176
184	Paisley	1.2	250	247	350	343	260
28	Pendleton	2.9	16,830	16,354	15,142	14,521	13,197
75	Philomath	12.3	4,310	3,838	2,983	2,673	1,688
73	Phoenix	11.1	4,510	4,060	3,239	2,309	1,287
116	Pilot Rock	0.5	1,540	1,532	1,478	1,630	1,612
128	Port Orford	3.2	1,190	1,153	1,025	1,061	1,037
1	Portland	3.0	545,140	529,121	438,802	366,383	379,967
154	Powers	-0.5	730	734	682	819	842
132	Prairie City	1.9	1,100	1,080	1,117	1,106	867
196	Prescott	-16.7	60	72	63	73	105
50	Prineville	15.5	8,500	7,358	5,355	5,276	4,101
110	Rainier	3.7	1,750	1,687	1,674	1,655	1,731
27	Redmond	29.4	17,450	13,481	7,165	6,452	3,721
77	Reedsport	-3.4	4,230	4,378	4,796	4,984	4,039
191	Richland	8.8	160	147	161	181	133
138	Riddle	0.6	1,020	1,014	1,143	1,265	1,042
179	Rivergrove	-1.2	320	324	294	314	0
125	Rockaway Beach	2.6	1,300	1,267	970	906	665
107	Rogue River	2.6	1,900	1,851	1,759	1,308	841
22	Roseburg	2.3	20,480	20,017	17,069	16,644	14,461
182	Rufus	0.7	270	268	295	352	317
3	Salem	4.4	142,940	136,924	107,793	89,091	68,725
62	Sandy	15.1	6,200	5,385	4,152	2,905	1,544
69	Scappoose	10.1	5,480	4,976	3,529	3,213	1,859
156	Scio	2.2	710	695	623	579	447
180	Scotts Mills	-3.8	300	312	283	249	208
64	Seaside	2.4	6,040	5,900	5,359	5,193	4,402
187	Seneca	-1.3	220	223	191	285	0

Rank	City	% Change*	2003	2000	1990	1980	1970
93	Shady Cove	10.1	2,540	2,307	1,351	1,097	0
197	Shaniko	15.4	30	26	26	30	58
68	Sheridan	1.1	5,620	5,561	3,979	2,249	1,881
34	Sherwood	19.2	14,050	11,791	3,093	2,386	1,396
131	Siletz	-0.3	1,130	1,133	992	1,001	596
53	Silverton	7.6	7,980	7,414	5,635	5,168	4,301
120	Sisters	49.1	1,430	959	708	696	516
181	Sodaville	0.0	290	290	192	171	125
193	Spray	0.0	140	140	149	155	161
9	Springfield	3.5	54,720	52,864	44,664	41,621	26,874
41	St. Helens	12.3	11,250	10,019	7,535	7,064	6,212
174	St. Paul	10.2	390	354	322	312	346
103	Stanfield	0.1	1,980	1,979	1,568	1,568	891
56	Stayton	7.1	7,300	6,816	5,011	4,396	3,170
99	Sublimity	0.6	2,160	2,148	1,491	1,077	634
195	Summerville	2.6	120	117	142	143	76
190	Sumpter	-0.6	170	171	119	133	120
56	Sutherlin	9.5	7,300	6,669	5,020	4,560	3,070
51	Sweet Home	3.9	8,330	8,016	6,850	6,921	3,799
67	Talent	2.0	5,700	5,589	3,274	2,577	1,389
141	Tangent	-1.4	920	933	556	478	0
39	The Dalles	1.6	12,350	12,156	11,021	10,820	10,423
11	Tigard	9.5	45,130	41,223	29,435	14,799	6,499
74	Tillamook	0.0	4,350	4,352	4,001	3,991	3,968
82	Toledo	3.1	3,580	3,472	3,174	3,151	2,818
33	Troutdale	3.8	14,300	13,777	7,852	5,908	1,661
17	Tualatin	8.8	24,790	22,791	14,664	7,483	750
119	Turner	23.4	1,480	1,199	1,281	1,116	846
183	Ukiah	2.0	260	255	250	249	0
63	Umatilla	21.9	6,070	4,978	3,046	3,199	679
104	Union	1.2	1,950	1,926	1,847	2,062	1,531
194	Unity	-0.8	130	131	87	115	0
103	Vale	0.2	1,980	1,976	1,491	1,558	1,448
83	Veneta	26.0	3,480	2,762	2,519	2,449	1,377
97	Vernonia	1.4	2,260	2,228	1,808	1,785	1,643
102	Waldport	0.5	2,060	2,050	1,595	1,274	700
145	Wallowa	0.1	870	869	748	847	811
76	Warrenton	5.0	4,300	4,096	2,681	2,493	1,825
175	Wasco	-0.3	380	381	374	415	412
185	Waterloo	0.4	240	239	191	211	186
19	West Linn	7.0	23,820	22,261	16,389	11,358	7,091
178	Westfir	17.9	330	280	278	312	0
155	Weston	0.4	720	717	606	719	660
173	Wheeler	4.9	410	391	335	319	262
108	Willamina	-0.2	1,840	1,844	1,748	1,749	1,193
29	Wilsonville	13.5	15,880	13,991	7,106	2,920	1,001
71	Winston	7.1	4,940	4,613	3,773	3,359	2,468
90	Wood Village	0.3	2,870	2,860	2,814	2,253	1,533

Rank	City	% Change*	2003	2000	1990	1980	1970
20	Woodburn	7.3	21,560	20,100	13,404	11,196	7,495
158	Yachats	8.6	670	617	533	482	441
148	Yamhill	3.3	820	794	867	690	516
133	Yoncalla	2.7	1,080	1,052	919	805	675

*Change in population between 2000 and 2003.

COUNTY POPULATIONS: 1970–2003

Rank	County	% Change*	2003	2000	1990	1980	1970
28	Baker	-1.4	16,500	16,741	15,317	16,134	14,919
11	Benton	3.0	80,500	78,153	70,811	68,211	53,776
3	Clackamas	4.5	353,450	338,391	278,850	241,911	166,088
19	Clatsop	1.9	36,300	35,630	33,301	32,489	28,473
18	Columbia	3.3	45,000	43,560	37,557	35,646	28,790
16	Coos	0.4	63,000	62,779	60,273	64,047	56,515
26	Crook	5.8	20,300	19,182	14,111	13,091	9,985
24	Curry	-0.2	21,100	21,137	19,327	16,992	13,006
7	Deschutes	13.1	130,500	115,367	74,958	62,142	30,442
9	Douglas	1.4	101,800	100,399	94,649	93,748	71,743
34	Gilliam	-0.8	1,900	1,915	1,717	2,057	2,342
30	Grant	-3.6	7,650	7,935	7,853	8,210	6,996
31	Harney	-4.1	7,300	7,609	7,060	8,314	7,215
25	Hood River	0.4	20,500	20,411	16,903	15,835	13,187
6	Jackson	4.3	189,100	181,269	146,389	132,456	94,533
27	Jefferson	4.7	19,900	19,009	13,676	11,599	8,548
12	Josephine	3.5	78,350	75,726	62,649	58,855	35,746
14	Klamath	1.3	64,600	63,775	57,702	59,117	50,021
32	Lake	-0.3	7,400	7,422	7,186	7,532	6,343
4	Lane	2.0	329,400	322,959	282,912	275,226	215,401
17	Lincoln	1.2	45,000	44,479	38,889	35,264	25,755
8	Linn	1.8	104,900	103,069	91,227	89,495	71,914
20	Malheur	1.2	32,000	31,615	26,038	26,896	23,169
5	Marion	3.9	295,900	284,834	228,483	204,692	151,309
29	Morrow	6.9	11,750	10,995	7,625	7,519	4,465
1	Multnomah	2.6	677,850	660,486	583,887	562,647	554,668
15	Polk	2.6	64,000	62,380	49,541	45,203	35,349
35	Sherman	-1.8	1,900	1,934	1,918	2,172	2,139
21	Tillamook	2.6	24,900	24,262	21,570	21,164	18,034
13	Umatilla	0.8	71,100	70,548	59,249	58,861	44,923
22	Union	0.5	24,650	24,530	23,598	23,921	19,377
33	Wallowa	-1.1	7,150	7,226	6,911	7,273	6,247
23	Wasco	-1.0	23,550	23,791	21,683	21,732	20,133
2	Washington	6.1	472,600	445,342	311,554	245,860	157,920
36	Wheeler	0.2	1,550	1,547	1,396	1,513	1,849
10	Yamhill	3.7	88,150	84,992	65,551	55,332	40,213
	Oregon	**3.5**	**3,541,500**	**3,421,399**	**2,842,321**	**2,633,156**	**2,091,533**

*Change in population between 2000 and 2003.

COUNTY GOVERNMENT

For more information contact individual counties.

The word county is from the French word "conte," meaning the domain of a count. However, the American county, defined by Webster as "the largest territorial division for local government within a state ...," is based on the Anglo-Saxon shire, which corresponds to the modern county. Counties were brought to America by the English colonists and were established in the central and western parts of the United States by the pioneers as they moved westward.

Early county governments in Oregon were very limited in the services they provided. Their primary responsibilities were forest and farm-to-market roads, law enforcement, courts, care for the needy and tax collections. In response to demands of a growing population and a more complex society, today's counties provide a wide range of important public services including: public health, mental health, community corrections, juvenile services, criminal prosecution, hospitals, nursing homes, airports, parks, libraries, land-use planning, building regulations, refuse disposal, elections, air-pollution control, veterans services, economic development, urban renewal, public housing, vector control, county fairs, museums, dog control, civil defense and senior services.

Until recently, counties functioned almost exclusively as agents of the state government. Their every activity had to be either authorized or mandated by state law. However, a 1958 constitutional amendment authorized counties to adopt "home rule" charters, and a 1973 state law granted all counties power to exercise broad "home rule" authority. As a result, the national Advisory Commission on Intergovernmental Relations has identified county government in Oregon as having the highest degree of local discretionary authority of any state in the nation.

Nine counties have adopted "home rule" charters, wherein voters have the power to adopt and amend their own county government organization. Lane and Washington were the first to adopt "home rule" in 1962, followed by Hood River (1964), Multnomah (1967), Benton (1972), Jackson (1978), Josephine (1980), Clatsop (1988) and Umatilla (1993).

Twenty-four of Oregon's 36 counties, including the nine with charters, operate under a "board of commissioners" with from three to five elected members. The remaining 12 less populated counties are governed by a "county court" consisting of a county judge and two commissioners.

Baker County

County Seat: 1995 3rd St., Baker City 97814
Phone: 541-523-8200 (General); 541-523-8207 (County Clerk)
Fax: 541-523-8240
E-mail: tgreen@bakercounty.org
Web: www.bakercounty.org
Established:
Sep. 22, 1862
Elev. at Baker City: 3,471'
Area: 3,089 sq. mi.
Average Temp.:
January 25.2°,
July 66.6°

Assessed Value: $946,658,071
Real Market Value: $1,112,740,350
Annual Precipitation: 10.63"
Economy: Agriculture, forest products, manufacturing and recreation.
Points of Interest: The Oregon Trail Interpretive Center and Old Oregon Trail, Sumpter Gold Dredge Park and ghost towns, Sumpter Valley Railroad, Baker City Restored Historic District (including Geiser Grand Hotel), Anthony Lakes Ski Resort and summer picnic areas, camping and hiking trails, Eagle Cap Wilderness area, Brownlee, Oxbow and Hells Canyon Reservoirs and Hells Canyon.

Baker County was established from part of Wasco County and named after Col. Edward D. Baker, a U.S. Senator from Oregon. A Union officer and close friend of President Lincoln, Colonel Baker was the only member of Congress to die in the Civil War. He was killed at Balls Bluff. Auburn, which no longer exists, was the first county seat. Baker City, which was incorporated in 1874 and which is the 17th oldest city in Oregon, became county seat in 1868.

Before 1861, the majority of immigrants only paused in Baker County on their way west, unaware of its vast agricultural and mineral resources. Then the great gold rush began and Baker County became one of the Northwest's largest gold producers. Farming, ranching, logging, and recreation have become the chief economic bases for an area that displays spectacular scenery, including the world's deepest gorge—Hells Canyon; an outstanding museum with the famous Cavin-Walfel rock collection; and numerous historic buildings with interesting architectural features.

County Officials: Commissioners—Tim L. Kerns (R) 2008; Carl E. Stiff (R) 2007; Fred Warner Jr. (D) 2007; Dist. Atty. Matthew Shirtcliff (NP) 2005; Assess. Harry Alan Phillips (NP) 2008; Clerk Tami Green (NP) 2006; Justices of the Peace Larry Cole (NP) 2007, Yvonne Riggs (NP) 2007, Beverly Robertson (NP) 2008; Sheriff Mitch Southwick (NP) 2008; Surv. Tom Hanley; Treas. Alice Durflinger (NP) 2006.

❖ ❖ ❖

Benton County

County Seat: 120 NW 4th St., Corvallis 97330
Phone: 541-766-6832 (General); 541-766-6859 (Court Administrator)
Fax: 541-766-6675
E-mail: bcrec@co.benton.or.us
Web: www.co.benton.or.us
Established:
  Dec. 23, 1847
Elev. at
  Corvallis: 224'
Area: 679 sq. mi.
Average Temp.:
  January 39.3°,
  July 65.6°

Assessed Value: $5,261,637,645
Real Market Value: $6,806,727,474
Annual Precipitation: 42.71"
Economy: Agriculture, forest products, research and development, electronics and wineries.
Points of Interest: Benton County Courthouse, Oregon State University Campus, Benton County Museum (Philomath), Alsea Falls, Mary's Peak, William L. Finley National Wildlife Refuge, Peavy Arboretum, McDonald Forest, Jackson Frazier Wetland.

Benton County was created from Polk County by an act of the Provisional Government of Oregon in 1847. It is one of seven counties in the United States to be named after Senator Thomas Hart Benton of Missouri, a longtime advocate of the development of the Oregon Territory. The county was created out of an area originally inhabited by the Klickitat Indians, who rented it from the Calapooia Indians for use as hunting grounds. At that time, the boundaries began at the intersection of Polk County and the Willamette River, ran as far south as the California border and as far west as the Pacific Ocean. Later, portions of Benton County were taken to form Coos, Curry, Douglas, Jackson, Josephine, Lane and Lincoln Counties, leaving it in its present form with 679 square miles of land area.

Oregon State University, agriculture, and lumber and wood products manufacturing form the basis of Benton County's economy. A substantial portion of the nation's research in forestry, agriculture, engineering, education and the sciences takes place at OSU.

County Officials: Commissioners—Jay Dixon (D) 2008, Annabelle Jaramillo (D) 2008, Linda Modrell (D) 2006; Dist. Atty. Scott Heiser (NP) 2007; Assess. Doug Hillpot; Clerk James Morales (NP); Sheriff Jim Swinyard (NP) 2007; Surv. Ray Wilson; Treas. Mary Otley; Admin. Services Director Ramona Rodamaker.

Clackamas County

County Seat: Board of Commissioners' Office, 2051 Kaen Rd., Oregon City 97045
Phone: 503-655-8656 (General); 503-655-8670 (Court Administrator)
Fax: 503-742-5919
E-mail: sherryh@co.clackamas.or.us
Web: www.co.clackamas.or.us
Established:
  July 5, 1843
Elev. at Oregon
  City: 55'
Area: 1,879 sq. mi.
Average Temp.:
  January 40.2°,
  July 68.4°
Assessed Value: $25,153,450,492
Real Market Value: $36,857,601,161
Annual Precipitation: 48.40"
Economy: Agriculture, metals manufacturing, trucking and warehousing, nursery stock, retail services, wholesale trade and construction.
Points of Interest: Mt. Hood and Timberline Lodge, End of the Oregon Trail Interpretive Center, Willamette Falls and locks, McLoughlin House, Canby Ferry, Molalla Buckaroo, driving tour of Old Barlow Road, Clackamas Town Center, Museum of the Oregon Territory, North Clackamas Aquatic Park.

Clackamas County was named for the resident Clackamas Indians and was one of the four original Oregon counties created in 1843. Oregon City, the county seat, was the first incorporated city west of the Rockies, the first capital of Oregon Territory, and the site of the first legislative session.

Oregon City was also the site of the only federal court west of the Rockies in 1849, when the city of San Francisco was platted. The plat was filed in 1850 in the first plat book of the first office of records in the West Coast and is still in Oregon City. The area's early history is featured at the End of the Oregon Trail Interpretive Center, a living history museum on an 8.5 acre site with three 50-foot high covered wagon-shaped buildings, an outdoor amphitheater and heritage garden.

From its 55-foot elevation at Oregon City, the county rises to 11,235 feet at the peak of Mt. Hood, the only year-round ski resort in the United States and the site of Timberline Lodge National Historical Landmark. The mountain, rivers and forests offer excellent outdoor recreation activities, from skiing and rafting to fishing and camping. The Clackamas Town Center, one of the largest shopping malls in Oregon, is the hub of eastside business.

County Officials: Commissioners—Bill Kennemer (R) 2008, Martha Schrader (D) 2008, Larry Sowa (D) 2006; Dist. Atty. John Foote (NP) 2008; Assess. Ray Erland (NP) 2008; Clerk Sherry Hall (NP) 2006; Sheriff Craig Roberts (NP) 2006; Surv. R. Charles Pearson; Treas. Shari Anderson (NP) 2006; Co. Admin. Jonathan Mantay.

Clatsop County

County Seat: 800 Exchange St., Astoria 97103
Phone: 503-325-8511 (General); 503-325-8536 (Court Administrator)
Fax: 503-325-9307
E-mail: nwwilliams@co.or.us
Web: www.co.clatsop.or.us
Established:
June 22, 1844
Elev. at Astoria:
19'
Area: 843 sq. mi.
Average Temp.:
January 41.9°,
July 60.1°

Assessed Value: $3,711,395,660
Real Market Value: $5,174,717,996
Annual Precipitation: 66.40"
Economy: Fishing, tourism and forest products.
Points of Interest: Astoria Column, Port of Astoria, Flavel Mansion Museum, Lewis and Clark Expedition Salt Cairn, Fort Clatsop, Fort Stevens, Columbia River Maritime Museum.

Clatsop County was created from the original Tuality District in 1844 and named for the Clatsop Indians, one of the many Chinook tribes living in Oregon. The Journals of Lewis and Clark mention the tribe. Fort Clatsop, Lewis and Clark's winter headquarters in 1805 and now a national memorial near the mouth of the Columbia River, also took the tribe's name.

Astoria, Oregon's oldest city, was established as a fur trading post in 1811 and named after John Jacob Astor. The first U.S. Post Office west of the Rocky Mountains was also established in Astoria in 1847. The first county courthouse was completed in 1855; the present courthouse was erected in 1904. Records show that the summer resort of Seaside was founded by Ben Holladay, pioneer Oregon railroad builder, in the early 1870s when he constructed the Seaside House, a famous luxury hotel for which the city was finally named. The Lewis and Clark Expedition reached the Pacific Ocean at this spot.

County Officials: Commissioners—Lylla Gaebel (NP) 2006, Richard Lee (NP) 2006, Sam Patrick (NP) 2008, Patricia Roberts (NP) 2008, Helen Westbrook (NP) 2006; Dist. Atty. Joshua Marquis (NP) 2006; Assess. Betsy Moes (NP); Clerk Nicole Williams (NP); Sheriff Thomas J. Bergin (NP) 2008; Surv. Steven Thornton (NP); Treas. Michael L. Robison (NP); Co. Admin. Scott Derickson (NP).

Columbia County

County Seat: Courthouse, 230 Strand St., St. Helens 97051-0010
Phone: 503-397-3796 (General); 503-397-2327 (Court Administrator)
Fax: 503-397-7266
E-mail: huserb@co.columbia.or.us
Web: www.co.columbia.or.us
Established:
Jan. 16, 1854
Elev. at St.
Helens: 42'
Area: 687 sq. mi.
Average Temp.:
January 39.0°,
July 68.4°

Assessed Value: $3,108,731,330
Real Market Value: $3,813,802,745
Annual Precipitation: 44.60"
Economy: Agriculture, forest products, manufacturing, surface mining and tourism.
Points of Interest: Lewis and Clark Heritage Canoe Trail, Vernonia/Banks Linear State Park, Jewell Elk Refuge, Sauvie Island Wildlife Area, Sand Island Park, Jones Beach near Clatskanie, Prescott Beach Park, St. Helens Golf Course, Vernonia Golf Course, Lewis and Clark Bridge at Rainier, Columbia County Fairgrounds, Trojan Nuclear Plant (operations ceased 1993).

Chinook and Clatskanie Indians inhabited this bountiful region centuries before Captain Robert Gray, commanding the *Columbia Rediviva,* landed on Columbia County's timbered shoreline in 1792. The Corps of Discovery expedition, led by Lewis and Clark, traveled and camped along the Columbia River shore in the area later known as Columbia County in late 1805 and early 1806.

The county has 62 miles of Columbia riverfront and contains deep water ports and some of the finest industrial property in the Pacific Northwest. The Columbia River is a major route for ocean-going vessels and is a popular playground for fishing, boating, camping and windsurfing. The county has two marine parks, Sand Island and J.J. Collins Memorial Marine Park. Columbia County has a strong economic and cultural heritage centered around industries such as forest products, shipbuilding, mining and agriculture. The rural lifestyle and scenic beauty of Columbia County, coupled with its proximity to Portland, have drawn many new residents to the area.

County Officials: Commissioners—Rita Bernhard (D) 2007, Joe Corsiglia (D) 2007, Anthony Hyde (R) 2007; Dist. Atty. Steve Atchison (NP) 2007; Assess. Sue Poling (D) 2007; Clerk Elizabeth Huser (NP) 2007; Justice of the Peace Rod McLean (NP) 2007; Sheriff Phil Derby (NP) 2007; Surv. Philip Dewey (D) 2007; Treas. Ruth Baker.

❖ ❖ ❖

Coos County

County Seat: Courthouse, 250 N Baxter, Coquille 97423
Phone: 541-396-3121 (General); 541-396-3121, ext. 344 or 343 (Court Administrator)
Fax: 541-396-6551
Web: www.co.coos.or.us
Established:
Dec. 22, 1853
Elev. at Coquille:
40'
Area: 1,629 sq. mi.
Average Temp.:
January 44.2°,
July 60.9°

Assessed Value: $3,299,830,560
Real Market Value: $4,392,674,448
Annual Precipitation: 56.8"
Economy: Forest products, fishing, agriculture, shipping, recreation and tourism.
Points of Interest: Lumber port, myrtlewood groves, Shore Acres State Park and Botanical Gardens, beaches, Oregon Dunes National Recreation Area, museums, fishing fleets, boat basins, scenic golf courses.

Coos County was created by the Territorial Legislature from parts of Umpqua and Jackson Counties in 1853 and included Curry County until 1855. The county seat was Empire City until 1896, when it was moved to Coquille. Although trappers had been in the area a quarter-century earlier, the first permanent settlement in present Coos County was at Empire City, now part of Coos Bay, by members of the Coos Bay Company in 1853. The name "Coos" derives from a native Coos Bay Indian tribe and translates to "lake" or "place of pines."

Forest products, tourism, fishing and agriculture dominate the Coos County economy. Boating, dairy farming, myrtlewood manufacturing, shipbuilding and repair, and agriculture specialty products including cranberries, also play an important role. The International Port of Coos Bay, considered the best natural harbor between Puget Sound and San Francisco, is the world's largest forest products shipping port.

County Officials: Commissioners—John Griffith (R) 2009, Gordon Ross (I) 2007, Nikki Whitty (D) 2007; Dist. Atty. Paul R. Burgett (NP) 2009; Assess. Robert Main (D) 2009; Clerk Terri Turi (NP) 2007; Sheriff Andy Jackson (NP) 2007; Surv. Karlas Seidel (D) 2009; Treas. Mary Barton (D) 2007.

Crook County

County Seat: Courthouse, 300 NE 3rd, Rm. 23, Prineville 97754
Phone: 541-447-6553 (General); 541-447-6555 (Court Administrator)
Fax: 541-416-2145
E-mail: dee.berman@co.crook.or.us
Web: www.co.crook.or.us
Established:
Oct. 24, 1882
Elev. at Prineville:
2,868'
Area: 2,991 sq. mi.
Average Temp.:
January 31.8°,
July 64.5°

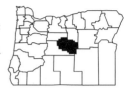

Assessed Value: $1,123,687,464
Real Market Value: $1,459,141,304
Annual Precipitation: 10.50"
Economy: Livestock, forest products, recreation, agriculture, manufacturing and wholesale trade.
Points of Interest: Pine Mills, Crooked River Canyon, Ochoco Mountains, Prineville and Ochoco Reservoirs, rockhound areas, county courthouse, Steins Pillar, Wildland Fire Fighter's Monument and geological formations.

Crook County was formed from Wasco County in 1882, and named for Maj. Gen. George Crook, U.S. Army. Geographically, the county is in the center of Oregon. It is unique in that it has only one incorporated population center, the city of Prineville, founded in 1868. Prineville's colorful past was the scene of Indian raids, range wars between sheepmen and cattlemen and vigilante justice. Other communities in this sparsely settled region are Powell Butte, Post and Paulina.

Forest products, agriculture, livestock raising and recreation/tourism services constitute most of Crook County's economy. Thousands of hunters, fishers, boaters, sightseers and rockhounds are annual visitors to its streams, reservoirs and the Ochoco Mountains. Rockhounds can dig for free agates, limb casts, jasper and thundereggs on more than 1,000 acres of mining claims provided by the Prineville Chamber of Commerce. Major annual events include the Prineville Rockhound Pow Wow, Crooked River Roundup, Crook County Fair, Old Fashioned Fourth of July Celebration, High Desert Celtic Festival and the Lord's Acre Sale.

County Officials: Commissioners—Judge Scott Cooper, chair (R) 2009, Mike McCabe (R) 2009, Mike Mohan (D) 2007; Dist. Atty. Gary Williams (NP) 2009; Assess. Tom Green (R) 2007; Clerk Deanna "Dee" Berman (NP) 2007; Sheriff Rodd Clark (NP) 2007; Surv. David Armstrong (D) 2009; Treas. Kathy Gray (NP) 2009.

❖❖❖   ❖❖❖

Curry County

County Seat: P.O. Box 746, Gold Beach 97444
Phone: 541-247-3295 (General); 541-396-3121, ext. 345 (Court Administrator)
Fax: 541-247-6440
E-mail: kolenr@co.curry.or.us
Web: www.co.curry.or.us
Established:
  Dec. 18, 1855
Elev. at Gold Beach: 60'
Area: 1,648 sq. mi.
Average Temp.:
  January 45.0°,
  July 65.0°
Assessed Value: $1,917,303,029
Real Market Value: $2,593,152,790
Annual Precipitation: 82.67"
Economy: Forest products, agriculture, commercial and sport fishing, recreation and tourism.
Points of Interest: Cape Blanco Lighthouse, Cape Sebastian and Samuel H. Boardman State Parks, Rogue River Japanese Bomb Site and coastal ports.

Named after Territorial Governor George L. Curry, the county was a part of "Coose" [sic] County until it was created in 1855. Port Orford was the county seat until 1859 when it was replaced by Ellensburg (later renamed Gold Beach).

Curry County contains valuable standing timber and also offers spectacular coastal scenery, clamming and crabbing, excellent fishing (freshwater and saltwater), upriver scenic boat trips, hiking trails, and gold for the fun of panning. The Port of Brookings is considered one of the safest harbors on the coast.

Agricultural products include sheep and cattle, cranberries, blueberries, Easter lilies and horticultural nursery stock. Curry County is also a prolific producer of myrtlewood.

County Officials: Commissioners—Ralph Brown (R) 2007, Lucie La Bonté (D) 2009, Marlyn A. Schafer (R) 2009; Dist. Atty. Alexandria Streich; Assess. James V. Kolen (NP) 2007; Clerk Renee Kolen (NP) 2009; Sheriff Mark Metcalf; Surv. Jerry Floyd (NP) 2007; Treas. Isabella Brock (NP) 2007.

Deschutes County

County Seat: 1300 NW Wall St., Suite 200, Bend 97701-1947
Phone: 541-388-6549 (General); 541-388-5300 (Court Administrator)
Fax: 541-389-6830
Web: www.deschutes.org
Established:
  Dec. 13, 1916
Elev. at Bend: 3,628'
Area: 3,055 sq. mi.
Average Temp.:
  January 30.5°,
  July 65.5°
Assessed Value: $12,212,561,314
Real Market Value: $17,617,229,049
Annual Precipitation: 12"
Economy: Tourism, retail trade, forest products, recreational equipment, aviation, software and high technology.
Points of Interest: Smith Rock State Park, Mt. Bachelor ski area, High Desert Museum, Lava Lands, Cascade Lakes Highway, Lava River Caves State Park, Lava Cast Forests, Newberry Crater, Pilot Butte, Three Sisters Wilderness, Central Oregon Community College, Deschutes County Fairgrounds, Redmond Airport, Pine Mountain Observatory.

French-Canadian fur trappers of the Hudson's Bay Company gave the name Riviere des Chutes (River of the Falls) to the Deschutes River, from which Deschutes County took its name. In 1916 Deschutes County was created from a part of Crook County.

Deschutes County is the outdoor recreation capital of Oregon. With noble, snow-capped peaks dominating the skyline to the west and the wide-open high desert extending to the east, the beauty and uniqueness of Deschutes County captures the awe of locals and visitors alike. Deschutes County has grown into a bustling, exciting place where progress and growth are hallmarks.

During the past ten years, Deschutes County has experienced the most rapid growth of any county in the state largely due to its invigorating climate and year-round recreation activities. Central Oregon offers downhill and cross-country skiing, snowboarding, fishing, hunting, hiking, rockclimbing, whitewater rafting, and golfing. Deschutes County is the host of diverse annual events including the Cascade Festival of Music, the Art Hop, Cascade Children's Festival, Pole Pedal Paddle, Sisters Rodeo, Sunriver Sunfest, and the Cascade Cycling Classic.

County Officials: Commissioners—Mike Daly (R) 2009, Tom DeWolf (R) 2007, Dennis R. Luke (R) 2007; Dist. Atty. Mike Dugan (NP) 2007; Assess. Scott Langton (NP) 2007; Clerk Nancy Blankenship (NP) 2007; Sheriff Les Stiles (NP) 2007; Surv. Jeff Kern; Treas. Marty Wynne (D) 2007.

Douglas County

County Seat: Courthouse, 1036 SE Douglas, Rm. 217, Roseburg 97470
Phone: 541-440-4323 (General); 541-957-2409 (Court Administrator)
Fax: 541-440-4408
E-mail: benielse@co.douglas.or.us
Web: www.co.douglas.or.us
Established: Jan. 7, 1852
Elev. at Roseburg: 479'
Area: 5,071 sq. mi.
Average Temp.: January 41.2°, July 68.4°

Assessed Value: $5,764,637,627
Real Market Value: $10,007,803,131
Annual Precipitation: 33.35"
Economy: Forest products, mining, agriculture, fishing and recreation
Points of Interest: Winchester Bay and Salmon Harbor, Oregon Dunes National Recreation Area, North Umpqua River, Diamond Lake, historic Oakland, Wildlife Safari, Douglas County Museum, wineries.

Douglas County was named for U.S. Senator Stephen A. Douglas, Abraham Lincoln's opponent in the presidential election of 1860 and an ardent congressional advocate for Oregon. Douglas County was created in 1852 from the portion of Umpqua County which lay east of the Coast Range summit. In 1862, Douglas County absorbed what remained of Umpqua County.

Douglas County extends from sea level at the Pacific Ocean to 9,182-foot Mt. Thielsen in the Cascade Range. The Umpqua River marks the dividing line between northern and southern Oregon, and its entire watershed lies within the county's boundaries. The county contains nearly 2.8 million acres of commercial forest lands and the largest stand of old growth timber in the world, which still provides the region's main livelihood. Approximately 25 percent of the labor force is employed in the forest products industry. Agriculture includes field crops, orchards and livestock. Over 50 percent of the land area of the county is owned by the federal government.

County Officials: Commissioners—Marilyn Kittelman (R) 2009, Doug Robertson (R) 2009, Dan Van Slyke (R) 2007; Dist. Atty. Jack Banta (NP) 2006; Assess. Ron Northcraft (NP) 2007; Clerk Barbara Nielsen; Justices of the Peace Candi Hissong (NP) 2008, Stephen H. Miller (NP) 2008, Carol Roberts (NP) 2008, Russell Trump (NP) 2008; Sheriff Chris Brown (NP) 2009; Surv. Romey Ware (NP) 2009; Treas. Sam Huff (NP) 2009.

Gilliam County

County Seat: Courthouse, 221 S Oregon St., Condon 97823-0427
Phone: 541-384-2311 (General); 541-384-3572 (Court Administrator)
Fax: 541-384-2166
Established: Feb. 25, 1885
Elev. at Condon: 2,844'
Area: 1,223 sq. mi.
Average Temp.: January 31.9°, July 71.3°
Assessed Value: $230,373,337
Real Market Value: $375,376,543
Annual Precipitation: 11.39"
Economy: Agriculture, recreation and environmental services.
Points of Interest: Old Oregon Trail, Arlington Bay and Marina, Lonerock area, Condon historic district, Indian pictographs.

Gilliam County was established in 1885 from a portion of Wasco County and was named after Col. Cornelius Gilliam, a veteran of the Cayuse Indian War. The first county seat was at Alkali, now Arlington. At the general election of 1890, voters chose to move the county seat to Condon, known to early settlers as "Summit Springs." A brick courthouse was built in Condon in 1903 but was destroyed by fire in 1954. The present courthouse, built on the same site, was constructed in 1955.

Gilliam County is in the heart of the Columbia Plateau wheat area. The economy is based mainly on agriculture, with an average farm size of about 4,200 acres. Wheat, barley and beef cattle are the principal crops. The largest individual employers in the county are two subsidiaries of Waste Management Inc., Chemical Waste Management of the Northwest and Oregon Waste Systems, Inc., two regional state-of-the-art waste disposal landfills.

With elevations of over 3,000 feet near Condon in the south of the county and 285 feet at Arlington, 38 miles north, the county offers a variety of climates and atmosphere. Hunting, fishing and tourism are secondary industries. Two major rivers, the John Day and Columbia, traverse the area east-to-west, as well as Interstate 84. Highway 19 connects the county's major cities north-to-south and serves as gateway to the John Day Valley.
County Officials: Commissioners—Frank Bettencourt (R) 2009, Dennis Gronquist (D) 2007, Judge Laura M. Pryor, chair (D) 2007; Dist. Atty. Marion Weatherford (NP) 2007; Assess. Patricia Shaw (NP) 2009; Clerk Rena Kennedy (NP) 2007; Justice of the Peace Cris Patnode (NP) 2009; Sheriff Mike Parker (NP) 2007; Surv. Robert Bagett (NP) 2007; Treas. Alcenia Byrd (NP) 2007.

Grant County

County Seat: Courthouse, 201 S Humbolt, Canyon City 97820
Phone: 541-575-1675 (General); 541-575-1438 (Court Administrator)
Fax: 541-575-2248
E-mail: grantco.@oregontrail.net
Web: www.grantcounty.cc
Established:
Oct. 14, 1864

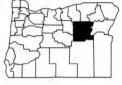

Elev. at Canyon
City: 3,194'
Area: 4,528 sq. mi.
Average Temp.:
January 30.7°,
July 68.4°
Assessed Value: $353,513,120
Real Market Value: $720,423,920
Annual Precipitation: 14.28"
Economy: Forest products, agriculture, hunting, livestock and recreation.
Points of Interest: John Day Fossil Beds National Monument, Veteran's Memorial, Kam Wah Chung Museum, Joaquin Miller Cabin, Grant County Historical Museum, Sacred Totem Pole, Grant County Historical Mural, Dewitt Museum, Depot Park, Sumpter Valley Railroad, Strawberry Mountain Wilderness and North Fork John Day River Wilderness.

Grant County was created in 1864 from Wasco and Umatilla Counties and was named for Gen. Ulysses S. Grant. It shares boundaries with more counties (eight) than any other county in Oregon.

Grant County contains the headwaters of the John Day River, which has more miles of Wild and Scenic designation than any other river in the United States. More than 60 percent of the land in the county is in public ownership.

County Officials: Commissioners—Boyd Briton (R) 2007, Scott Myers (R) 2009, Judge Dennis Reynolds, chair (R) 2006; Dist. Atty. Lee Carter (NP) 2007; Assess. Lane Burton (D) 2009; Clerk Kathy McKinnon (R) 2009; Justice of the Peace Terrance Ferrell (NP) 2006; Sheriff Glenn Palmer (NP) 2009; Surv. Robert Bagett (D) 2009; Treas. Kathy Smith (R) 2009.

Harney County

County Seat: Courthouse, 450 N Buena Vista, Burns 97720
Phone: 541-573-6641 (General); 541-573-5207 (Court Administrator)
Fax: 541-573-8370
E-mail: clerk@co.harney.or.us
Web: www.co.harney.or.us
Established:
Feb. 25, 1889

Elev. at Burns:
4,148'
Area: 10,228 sq. mi.
Average Temp.:
January 27.5°,
July 69.4°
Assessed Value: $340,709,269
Real Market Value: $708,907,244
Annual Precipitation: 10.13"
Economy: Forest products, manufacturing, livestock and agriculture.
Points of Interest: Steens Mountain, Malheur Cave, Malheur Wildlife Refuge, Alvord Desert and Lake, Squaw Butte Experimental Station, "P" Ranch Round Barn, Frenchglen.

In 1826, Peter Skene Ogden became the first white man to explore this area when he led a fur brigade for the Hudson's Bay Company. In 1889, Harney, the largest county in Oregon, was carved out of Grant County and named for Harney Lake. The lake, in turn, was named for Maj. Gen. William S. Harney, commander of the Department of Oregon, U.S. Army, from 1858–59. Harney was instrumental in opening areas of eastern Oregon for settlement.

A fierce political battle, with armed night riders who spirited county records from Harney to Burns, ended with Burns as the county seat in 1890. The courthouse was constructed five years later. Burns' first newspaper was established in 1884 and its first church in 1887.

Harney County shares the largest Ponderosa pine forest in the nation with Grant County and has more than 100,000 head of beef cattle on its vast ranges. Its abundance of game, numerous campsites and excellent fishing have stimulated fast-growing recreational activities.

County Officials: Commissioners—Jack Drinkwater (R) 2007, Judge Steven E. Grasty (NP) 2011, Dan Nichols (R) 2009; Dist. Atty. Timothy Colahan (NP) 2009; Assess. Ted Tiller (NP) 2007; Clerk Maria Iturriaga (NP) 2009; Justice of the Peace Dewey Newton (NP) 2007; Sheriff Dave Glerup (NP) 2009; Surv. Chris T. Palmer (NP) 2009; Treas. Ellen "Nellie" Franklin (NP) 2007.

Hood River County

County Seat: 601 State St., Hood River 97031-2093
Phone: 541-386-3970 (General); 541-386-3535 (Court Administrator)
Fax: 541-386-9392
E-mail: boc@admin.co.hood-river.or.us
Web: www.co.hood-river.or.us
Established: June 23, 1908
Elev. at Hood River: 154'
Area: 533 sq. mi.
Average Temp.: January 33.6°, July 72°

Assessed Value: $1,289,640,193
Real Market Value: $2,434,873,797
Annual Precipitation: 30.85"
Economy: Agiculture, food processing, forest products and recreation.
Points of Interest: Bridge of the Gods, Cloud Cap Inn, Mt. Hood Recreation Area, Mt. Hood Meadows Ski Resort, Lost Lake, Panorama Point, Hood River Valley at blossom time.

The first white settlers in Hood River County filed a donation land claim in 1854. The first school was built in 1863 and a road from The Dalles was completed in 1867. By 1880 there were 17 families living in the valley. Hood River County was created in 1908 from Wasco County.

Agriculture, timber, lumber and recreation are the major sources of revenue and industry. Fruit grown in the fertile valley is of such exceptional quality the county leads the world in Anjou pear production. There are more than 14,000 acres of commercial orchards growing pears, apples, cherries and peaches. Hood River County also has two ports and two boat basins, with one serving local barge traffic, a steel boat manufacturing firm and Mid-Columbia yachting interests. Windsurfing on the Columbia River is a popular sport and attracts windsurfers from all over the world.

County Officials: Commissioners—Maui Meyers (NP) 2009, Les Perkins (NP) 2009, Rodger Schock, chair, (NP) 2009, Chuck Thomsen (NP) 2009, Carol York (NP) 2007; Dist. Atty. John Sewell (NP) 2009; Assess./Clerk Sandra Berry; Justice of the Peace Roberta K. Lee (NP) 2009; Sheriff Joe Wampler (NP) 2009; Surv. Randy Johnston; Treas. Sandra Borowy; Co. Admin. David Meriwether.

Jackson County

County Seat: 1101 W Main, Suite 201, Medford 97501
Phone: 1-800-452-5021 (General); 541-776-7171 (Court Administrator)
Fax: 541-774-6140
E-mail: becketks@jacksoncounty.org
Web: www.jacksoncounty.org
Established: Jan. 12, 1852
Elev. at Medford: 1,382'
Area: 2,801 sq. mi.
Average Temp.: January 37.6°, July 72.5°

Assessed Value: $12,332,932,674
Real Market Value: $20,017,569,271
Annual Precipitation: 19.84"
Economy: Medical, retail, tourism, agriculture, manufacturing and forest products.
Points of Interest: Mt. Ashland Ski Resort, Historic Jacksonville, Shakespearean Festival, Peter Britt Music Festival, Southern Oregon University, pear orchards, Howard Prairie Lake, Emigrant Lake, Hyatt Lake, Fish Lake, Rogue River, Lithia Park, Lost Creek Dam, Butte Creek Mill, Crater Lake Highway.

Named for President Andrew Jackson, Jackson County was formed in 1852 from Lane County and the unorganized area south of Douglas and Umpqua Counties. It included lands which now lie in Coos, Curry, Josephine, Klamath and Lake Counties. The discovery of gold near Jacksonville in 1852 and completion of a wagon road, which joined the county with California to the south and Douglas County to the north, brought many pioneers.

County Officials: Commissioners—Dave Gilmore (D) 2007, C.W. Smith (R) 2009, Jack Walker (R) 2007; Dist. Atty. Mark D. Huddleston (NP) 2009; Assess. Dan Ross (NP) 2009; Clerk Kathy Beckett (NP) 2007; Justices of the Peace Joe Charter (NP) 2011, Robert King Jr. (NP) 2009; Sheriff Michael Winters; Surv. Roger Roberts (NP) 2009; Treas. Gary Cadle; Co. Admin. Susan E. Slack.

❖ ❖ ❖   ❖ ❖ ❖

Jefferson County

County Seat: 66 SE "D" St., Madras 97741
Phone: 541-475-4451 (General); 541-475-3317 (Court Administrator)
Fax: 541-325-5018
E-mail: mike.morgan@co.jefferson.or.us
Established:
  Dec. 12, 1914
Elev. at Madras:
  2,242'
Area: 1,791 sq. mi.
Average Temp.:
  January 37.4°,
  July 70.1°

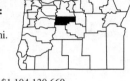

Assessed Value: $1,104,130,669
Real Market Value: $2,001,533,465
Annual Precipitation: 10.2"
Economy: Agriculture, forest products and recreation.
Points of Interest: Mt. Jefferson, Warm Springs Indian Reservation, Metolius River, Black Butte, Suttle Lake, Blue Lake, Santiam Summit, Lake Billy Chinook behind Round Butte Dam, Haystack Reservoir, Priday Agate Beds.

Jefferson County was established in 1914 from a portion of Crook County and named for Mount Jefferson on its western boundary. The county owes much of its agricultural prosperity to the railroad, which arrived in 1911, and to the development of irrigation projects in the late 1930s. The railroad, which links Madras with the Columbia River, was completed after constant feuds and battles between two lines working on opposite sides of the Deschutes River.

Vegetable, grass and flower seeds, garlic, mint and sugar beets are cultivated on some 60,000 irrigated acres. Jefferson County also has vast acreages of rangelands and a healthy industrial base related to forest products. The Warm Springs Forest Products Industry, a multi-million dollar complex owned by the Confederated Tribes of the Warm Springs Reservation—partially located in the northwestern corner of the county—is the single biggest industry. With 300 days of sunshine and a low yearly rainfall, fishing, hunting, camping, boating, water-skiing and rock hunting are popular recreations.

County Officials: Commissioners—Bill C. Bellamy (R) 2009, Walter Ponford (D) 2007, Mary Zenke (R) 2007; Dist. Atty. Peter L. Deuel (NP) 2009; Assess. Patsy Mault (R) 2007; Clerk Kathy Marston (D) 2007; Sheriff Jack Jones (NP) 2007; Surv. Gary L. DeJarnatt (R) 2009; Treas. Deena Goss (R) 2009; Co. Admin. Matthew Birney.

Josephine County

County Seat: Courthouse, 500 NW 6th St., Grants Pass 97526; Mailing Address: P.O. Box 69, Grants Pass 97528
Phone: 541-474-5243 (General); 541-476-2309 (Court Administrator)
Fax: 541-474-5246
E-mail: aharvey@co.josephine.or.us
Web: www.co.josephine.or.us
Established:
  Jan. 22, 1856
Elev. at Grants Pass: 948'
Area: 1,641 sq. mi.
Average Temp.:
  January 39.9°,
  July 71.6°

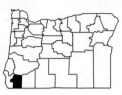

Assessed Value: $4,481,076,323
Real Market Value: $6,502,753,771
Annual Precipitation: 32.31"
Economy: Tourism, recreation, forest products, electronics and software.
Points of Interest: Oregon Caves National Monument, Wolf Creek Tavern, Sunny Valley Covered Bridge and Interpretive Center, Hellgate Canyon-Rogue River, Grants Pass Historic District, Growers Market, Kalmiopsis Wilderness, Rogue Community College, Barnstormers Theater, Rogue Music Theater.

Josephine County, named for Virginia "Josephine" Rollins, the first white woman to make this county her home, was established in 1856 out of the western portion of Jackson County. The county seat was originally located in Sailor Diggings (later Waldo), but in July of 1857 was relocated to Kerbyville, situated on the main route between the port of Crescent City, California and the gold fields.

The discovery of rich placers at Sailor Diggings in 1852 and the resulting gold rush brought the first settlers to this region. Several U.S. Army forts were maintained in the county and many engagements during the Rogue River Indian War (1855–1858) took place within its boundaries. In 1886, the county seat was finally relocated to Grants Pass, a new town on the railroad that was completed through Oregon that same year. Grants Pass is now the departure point for most Rogue River scenic waterway guided fishing and boat trips. The Illinois River, one of the Rogue's tributaries, has also been designated a scenic waterway.

County Officials: Commissioners—Dwight Ellis (NP) 2008, Jim Raffenburg (NP) 2008, Jim Riddle (NP) 2006; Dist. Atty. Stephen D. Campbell (NP) 2008; Assess. Mike Schneyder (NP) 2008; Clerk Georgette Brown (NP) 2008; Sheriff Dave Daniels (NP) 2006; Surv. Peter D. Allen (NP) 2008; Treas. John Harelson (NP) 2008.

❖❖❖

Klamath County

County Seat: 305 Main St., Klamath Falls 97601-6391
Phone: 541-883-5134 (General); 541-883-5503 (Court Administrator)
Fax: 541-885-6757
E-mail: lsmith@co.klamath.or.us
Web: www.co.klamath.or.us
Established:
Oct. 17, 1882
Elev. at Klamath Falls: 4,105'
Area: 6,135 sq. mi.
Average Temp.: January 29.8°, July 68.0°

Assessed Value: $3,681,892,959
Real Market Value: $5,575,104,787
Annual Precipitation: 14.31"
Economy: Forest products, agriculture, tourism and recreation.
Points of Interest: Crater Lake National Park, Collier Memorial State Park and Logging Museum, Klamath Lake (largest lake in Oregon), seven National Wildlife Refuges, Oregon Institute of Technology (OIT), Klamath County Museum, Favell Museum of Western Art, Ross Ragland Performing Arts Theatre.

The Klamath or "Clamitte" tribe of Indians, for which Klamath County was named, has had a presence for 10,000 years. White settlement began in 1846 along the Applegate Immigrant Trail, which precipitated clashes between the two cultures and led to the Modoc Indian War of 1872. The Oregon Legislature created Klamath County by dividing Lake County in 1882. Linkville was named county seat and its name was changed to Klamath Falls in 1893.

Klamath County's present-day position as a great lumber, agriculture and distribution center was assured in the early 1900s with the coming of the railroad and the start of one of the most successful of all federal reclamation projects—the Klamath Project, which drained much of the 128 square mile Lower Klamath Lake to provide 188,000 acres of irrigable land.

Natural geothermal hot wells provide heat for many homes, businesses and the OIT campus. The full potential of this energy resource continues to be studied. Klamath is recognized for its scenic beauty, outdoor recreation, abundant waterfowl and diverse landscape.

County Officials: Commissioners—Bill Brown (R) 2008, John Elliot (R) 2007, Al Switzer (R) 2008; Dist. Atty. Edwin I. Caleb (NP) 2007; Assess. Reg LeQuieu (R) 2007; Clerk Linda Smith (NP) 2007; Justice of the Peace Karen Oakes; Sheriff Tim Evinger (NP) 2008; Surv. Mike Markus; Treas. Michael R. Long (R) 2007.

Lake County

County Seat: Courthouse, 513 Center St., Lakeview 97630
Phone: 541-947-6006 (General); 541-947-6051 (Court Administrator)
Fax: 541-947-6015
Established:
October 24, 1874
Elev. at Lakeview: 4,800'
Area: 8,359 sq. mi.
Average Temp.: January 28.4°, July 67.0°
Assessed Value: $409,271,592
Real Market Value: $535,273,345
Annual Precipitation: 15.80"
Economy: Livestock, forest products, agriculture, recreation.
Points of Interest: Hart Mountain Antelope Refuge, Fort Rock and Fort Rock Homestead Village Museum, Abert Lake and Rim, Goose Lake, Hunter's Hot Springs, Old Perpetual Geyser, Schminck Memorial Museum and Lake County Museum, Lake County Round-Up Museum, Warner Canyon Ski Area, Gearhart Wilderness, Lost Forest, Crack-in-the-ground, Sheldon National Wildlife Refuge, Summer Lake Hot Springs, Hole-in-the-ground, sunstones (Oregon's state gemstone) near Plush, Warner Wetlands, Summer Lake Wildlife Area.

Lake County was created from Jackson and Wasco Counties by the 1874 Legislature. It then included the present Klamath County and all of the present Lake County except Warner Valley. In 1882 Klamath was removed and in 1885 the Warner area from Grant County was added.

Linkville, now Klamath Falls, was the first county seat. M. Bullard gave 20 acres as the Lakeview townsite. By the 1875 election a town had been started there and the county seat was moved to Lakeview. The Hart Mountain Antelope Refuge is a 270,000 acre wildlife haven for antelope, mule deer, bighorn sheep and upland birds. A number of migratory waterfowl flyways converge on Goose Lake, south of Lakeview, the Warner Wetlands near Plush, and the Summer Lake Wildlife area. Lakeview has been deemed the hang gliding capital of the West.

County Officials: Commissioners—Melvin Dick (R) 2007, J.R. Stewart (R) 2007, Brad Winters (D) 2008; Dist. Atty. David Schutt (NP) 2008; Assess. Phil Israel (NP) 2007; Clerk Stacie Geaney (NP) 2008; Sheriff Phil McDonald (NP) 2007; Surv. Rod Callaghan (I) 2007; Treas. Ann Turkle (NP) 2007.

Lane County

County Seat: Courthouse, 125 E 8th, Eugene 97401

Phone: 541-682-4203 (General); 541-682-4166 (Court Administrator)

Fax: 541-682-4616

E-mail: webmaster@co.lane.or.us

Web: www.lanecounty.org

Established:
Jan. 28, 1851

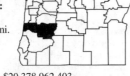

Elev. at Eugene:
422'

Area: 4,620 sq. mi.

Average Temp.:
January 40°,
July 70°

Assessed Value: $20,378,962,403

Real Market Value: $26,749,361,683

Annual Precipitation: 46"

Economy: Agriculture, higher education, high technology, forest products, recreation, RV manufacturing and tourism.

Points of Interest: Twenty historic covered bridges, Bohemia Mines, coastal sand dunes, Darlingtonia Botanical Wayside, Fern Ridge Reservoir, Heceta Head Lighthouse, Hendricks Park Rhododendron Garden, hot springs, Hult Center for the Performing Arts, Lane Community College, Lane ESD Planetarium, Martin Rapids whitewater, McKenzie Pass, Mt. Pisgah Arboretum, Old Town Florence, Pac-10 sports events, Proxy Falls, sea lion caves, University of Oregon, vineyards and wineries, Waldo Lake, Washburne State Park tide pools, Willamette Pass ski area.

Lane County was named for Gen. Joseph Lane, a rugged frontier hero who was Oregon's first territorial governor. Pioneers traveling the Oregon Trail in the late 1840s came to Lane County mainly to farm. The county's first district court met under a large oak tree until a clerk's office could be built in 1852. A few years later, the first courthouse opened in what is now downtown Eugene. With the building of the railroads, the market for timber opened in the 1880s. Today, wood products are still an important part of the economy in addition to high-tech manufacturing and tourism. Lane County government operates under a home rule charter approved by voters in 1962.

Although 90 percent of Lane County is forestland, Eugene and Springfield comprise the second largest urban area in Oregon.

County Officials: Commissioners—Bill Dwyer (NP) 2007, Bobby Green Sr. (NP) 2009, Anna Morrison (NP) 2007, Peter Sorenson (NP) 2009, Faye Stewart (NP) 2009; Dist. Atty. Doug Harcleroad 2009; Assess. Jim Gangle (NP) 2007; Clerk Annette Newingham; Justices of the Peace Cindy Cable (NP) 2009, Charles Navarro (NP) 2009, Cindy Sinclair (NP) 2009; Sheriff Russ Burger (NP) 2009; Surv. Bill Robinson; Co. Admin. Bill VanVactor.

Lincoln County

County Seat: Courthouse, 225 W Olive St., Rm. 201, Newport 97365

Phone: 541-265-6611 (General); 541-265-4236 (Court Administrator)

Fax: 541-265-4950

E-mail: rbovett@co.lincoln.or.us

Web: www.co.lincoln.or.us

Established:
Feb. 20, 1893

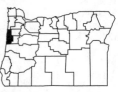

Elev. at Newport:
134'

Area: 992 sq. mi.

Average Temp.:
January 44.4°,
July 57.6°

Assessed Value: $4,920,505,462

Real Market Value: $6,558,372,977

Annual Precipitation: 71.93"

Economy: Tourism, government, services/retail, forest products and fishing.

Points of Interest: Agate Beach, Alsea Bay Interpretive Center, Beverly Beach State Park, Boiler Bay, Cape Perpetua Visitors' Center, Cascade Head, Connie Hansen Garden Conservancy, Devils Lake, Lincoln County Historical Museum, Newport Performing and Visual Arts Centers, OSU Hatfield Marine Science Center and Interpretive Center, Oregon Coast Aquarium, Otter Crest Viewpoint, Seal Rock Park, South Beach State Park, Yaquina Arts Center, Yaquina Bay State Park and Lighthouse, Yaquina Head Outstanding Natural Area.

With miles of beach and coastline, Lincoln County is one of the most popular visitor destinations on the Oregon Coast. Named for President Abraham Lincoln, Lincoln County was created by the Oregon Legislature in 1893. Lincoln County has a very temperate climate, and a short but productive growing season.

Depoe Bay is known as "the whale watching capital of the world." Lincoln City offers more than 2,000 hotel/motel/bed and breakfast rooms, and resorts as well as the Siletz Tribe's Chinook Winds Casino; Newport, known as Oregon's oceanography research center, features numerous interpretive centers and the Oregon Coast Aquarium, along with a large fishing fleet and working bay front; Siletz is the home of the Administration Center and reservation of the Confederated Tribes of Siletz Indians of Oregon; Toledo is known as Lincoln County's industrial center; Waldport features the Alsea Bay Interpretive Center; and Yachats is known as the "Gem of the Oregon Coast."

County Officials: Commissioners—Bill Hall (D) 2009, Don Lindly (D) 2007, Terry Thompson (D) 2007; Dist. Atty. Bernice Barnett (NP) 2009; Assess. Rob Thomas (NP) 2007; Clerk Dana Jenkins (NP) 2007; Sheriff Dennis Dotson 2009; Surv. Tom Hamilton (NP) 2009; Treas. Linda Pitzer (NP) 2009.

Linn County

County Seat: Courthouse, 300 4th Ave. SW, Albany 97321
Phone: 541-967-3825 (General); 541-967-3802 (Court Administrator)
Fax: 541-926-5109
Web: www.co.linn.or.us
Established:
Dec. 28, 1847
Elev. at Albany:
210'
Area: 2,297 sq. mi.
Average Temp.:
January 39.0°,
July 65.6°

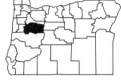

Assessed Value: $6,004,066,806
Real Market Value: $8,575,501,581
Annual Precipitation: 42.55"
Economy: Agriculture, forest products, rare metals, manufacturing and recreation.
Points of Interest: Willamette and Santiam Rivers; Foster, Green Peter and Detroit Reservoirs; Cascade Mountain range with Mt. Jefferson, Hoodoo Ski Bowl and the Pacific Crest Trail, covered bridges, Fair and Expo Center, Brownsville Museum and Albany historic districts.

Linn County was created in 1847 and named for U.S. Senator Lewis F. Linn of Missouri, who was the author of the Donation Land Act, which provided free land to settlers in the West. Linn County is in the center of the Willamette Valley, with the Willamette River as its western boundary and the crest of the Cascades as its eastern boundary. The climate and soil conditions provide one of Oregon's most diversified agriculture areas, allowing a wide variety of specialty crops and leading the nation in the production of common and perennial ryegrass. Linn County is also home to major producers of rare and primary metals, processed food, manufactured homes and motor homes as well as the traditional logging and wood products industries.

Recreational opportunities are extensive, and include hiking, climbing and skiing, picnicking and camping in county and state parks, boating, water skiing and fishing on lakes and rivers, petrified wood and agate beds, covered bridges and historic districts and events.

County Officials: Commissioners—John K. Lindsey (R) 2007, Roger Nyquist (R) 2009, Cliff Wooten (R) 2009; Dist. Atty. Jason Carlile (NP) 2005; Assess. Mark Noakes (NP) 2005; Clerk Steven Druckenmiller (NP) 2007; Justices of the Peace Jad Lemhouse (NP) 2009, Richard Triska (NP) 2009; Sheriff David K. Burright (NP) 2009; Surv. Charles Gibbs; Treas. Michelle Hawkins (NP) 2009; Co. Admin. Ralph Wyatt.

❖❖❖

Malheur County

County Seat: 251 B St. W, Vale 97918
Phone: 541-473-5151 (General); 541-473-5171 (Court Administrator)
Fax: 541-473-5523
E-mail: ddelong@malheur.co.org
Web: www.malheurco.org
Established:
Feb. 17, 1887
Elev. at Vale:
2,243'
Area: 9,926 sq. mi.
Average Temp.:
January 28.7°,
July 75.6°
Assessed Value: $1,299,216,979
Real Market Value: $1,905,394,520
Annual Precipitation: 9.64"
Economy: Agriculture, livestock, food processing and recreation.
Points of Interest: Oregon Trail, Keeney Pass, Owyhee Lake, Succor Creek State Park, Leslie Gulch Canyon, Jordan Craters, grave of trapper John Baptist Charbonneau, Nyssa Agricultural Museum, Vale Oregon Trail Murals, Jordan Valley Basque Pelota Court, the Four Rivers Cultural Center.

Malheur County was created in 1887 from Baker County. Malheur County derives its name from the "Riviere au Malheur" or "Unfortunate River" (later changed to "Malheur River"), named by French trappers whose property and furs were stolen from their river encampment.

Malheur County is a place filled with fascinating history, diverse landscape and friendly people. The landscape is enchanting and provides for a wide variety of excellent recreation such as hunting, fishing, hiking, rock climbing, rock hounding, boating and water skiing. The county is 94 percent rangeland. Basques, primarily shepherds, settled in Jordan Valley in the 1890s. Irrigated fields in the county's northeast corner, known as Western Treasure Valley, are the center of intensive and diversified farming.

County Officials: Commissioners—Judge Dan Joyce (R) 2010, Jim Nakano (R) 2006, Lewis Wettstein (R) 2009; Dist. Atty. Dan Norris (NP) 2009; Assess. Sharon Clark (NP) 2009; Clerk Deborah DeLong (NP) 2006; Justice of the Peace Terry Thompson (NP) 2009; Sheriff Andrew Bentz (NP) 2009; Surv. Jim Kimberling (NP); Treas. Jennifer Forsyth (NP) 2007; Co. Admin. Janice Belnap (NP).

❖❖❖

Marion County

County Seat: Courthouse, 555 Court St. NE, Salem 97309-5036
Phone: 503-588-5225 (General); 503-588-5368 (Court Administrator)
Fax: 503-373-4408
E-mail: tmiles@co.marion.or.us
Web: www.co.marion.or.us
Established:
  July 5, 1843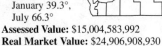
Elev. at Salem:
  154'
Area: 1,194 sq. mi.
Average Temp.:
  January 39.3°,
  July 66.3°
Assessed Value: $15,004,583,992
Real Market Value: $24,906,908,930
Annual Precipitation: 40.35"
Economy: Government, agriculture, food processing, forest products, manufacturing, education and tourism.
Points of Interest: State Capitol, Champoeg State Park, Silver Falls State Park, The Oregon Garden, Wheatland Ferry, Buena Vista Ferry, Detroit Dam and Santiam River, Breitenbush Hot Springs, Mt. Angel Abbey, food processing plants, Willamette University, Chemeketa Community College, Mission Mill Museum Village, Bush House, Deepwood House and the Gilbert House Children's Museum.

Marion County, then called Champooick, was created by the Provisional Government in 1843, 16 years before Oregon gained statehood. In 1849 the name was changed to Marion in honor of Gen. Francis Marion.

The county, located in the heart of the Willamette Valley, has the Willamette River as its western boundary and the Cascade Range on the east. Salem, the county seat, is one of the valley's oldest cities. Among its public buildings are the Marion County Courthouse, Courthouse Square county office building and Cherriots bus transit mall (opened in September 2000), State Capitol, Capitol Mall buildings and Salem Civic Center. The county was presided over by the Marion County Court until January 1, 1963, when the court was abolished and replaced by a Board of Commissioners.

County Officials: Commissioners—Sam Brentano (R) 2008, Janet Carlson (R) 2007, Patricia Milne (R) 2007; Dist. Atty. Walt Beglau (NP) 2009; Assess. Doug Ebner (NP) 2007; Clerk Bill Burgess (NP) 2008; Justices of the Peace Steven R. Summers (NP) 2009, Janice D. Zyryanoff (NP) 2007; Sheriff Raul Ramirez (NP) 2007; Surv. Mark Riggins; Treas. Laurie Steel (NP) 2007; Co. Admin. John Lattimer.

❖ ❖ ❖

Morrow County

County Seat: Courthouse, 100 Court St., Heppner 97836; or PO Box 788, Heppner 97836
Phone: 541-676-5603 (General); 541-676-5264 (Court Administrator)
Fax: 541-676-9902
E-mail: bchilders@co.morrow.or.us
Web: www.morrowcountyoregon.com
Established:
  Feb. 16, 1885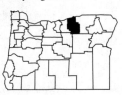
Elev. at Heppner:
  1,955'
Area: 2,049 sq. mi.
Average Temp.:
  January 33.1°,
  July 69.0°
Assessed Value: $1,029,029,550
Real Market Value: $1,169,946,290
Annual Precipitation: 12.5"
Economy: Agriculture, food processing, dairies, utilities, forest products, livestock and recreation.
Points of Interest: Columbia River, coal-fired generating plant, Blue Mountains, Umatilla National Forest, Oregon Trail, Blue Mountain Scenic Byway, Morrow County Museum, Port of Morrow and the Lewis and Clark Route.

Morrow County, created from Umatilla County in 1885, is located east of the Cascades in north-central Oregon. It was named for J.L. Morrow, an early resident. Morrow County contains more than one million acres of gently rolling plains and broad plateaus. This rich agricultural land can be roughly divided into three occupational zones—increasing amounts of irrigation farming in the north; vast fields of wheat yielding to cattle ranches in the center; and timber products in the south. With the advent of center pivot irrigation technology, Morrow County became one of Oregon's fastest growing areas in terms of population, personal income, and agricultural and industrial development. The Port of Morrow, second largest in the state in terms of tonnage, serves as a gateway to Pacific Northwest and Pacific Rim markets.

County Officials: Commissioners—Ray Grace (R) 2007, Judge Terry Tallman (R) 2007, John Wenholz (D) 2009; Dist. Atty. David Allen (NP) 2007; Assess. Greg Sweek (NP) 2009; Clerk Bobbi Childers (NP) 2009; Justice of the Peace Charlotte Gray (NP) 2011; Sheriff Kenneth Matlock (NP) 2009; Surv. Judd Coppick (R) 2009; Treas. Gayle Gutierrez (NP) 2009.

❖ ❖ ❖

Multnomah County

County Seat: 501 SE Hawthorne Blvd., Portland 97214
Phone: 503-823-4000 (General); 503-988-3957 (Court Administrator)
E-mail: countyinfo@co.multnomah.or.us
Web: www.co.multnomah.or.us
Established:
Dec. 22, 1854
Elev. at Portland:
77'
Area: 465 sq. mi.
Average Temp.:
January 38.9°,
July 67.7°

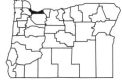

Assessed Value: $47,314,670,129
Real Market Value: $87,861,122,024
Annual Precipitation: 37.39"
Economy: Manufacturing, transportation, wholesale and retail trade, and tourism.
Points of Interest: Oregon Historical Center, Oregon Museum of Science and Industry, Portland Art Museum, Washington Park and Zoo, Rose Test Gardens, Japanese Gardens, Columbia River Gorge, Multnomah Falls, Blue Lake Park, Oxbow Park, Pittock Mansion, Port of Portland, Memorial Coliseum, Oregon Convention Center.

Lewis and Clark made note of the Indian village of Multnomah on Sauvie Island in 1805, and applied that name to all local Indians. The name is derived from nematlnomaq, probably meaning "downriver." Multnomah County was created from parts of Washington and Clackamas Counties by the Territorial Legislature in 1854, five years before Oregon became a state, because citizens found it inconvenient to travel to Hillsboro to conduct county business.

The county is both the smallest in size and largest in population in Oregon. Over 50 percent of its people live in Portland, a busy metropolis dominated by rivers and greenery. The remaining area includes picturesque rural land, from pastoral farms on Sauvie Island to the rugged Columbia River Gorge and the western slopes of Mt. Hood.

County Officials: Commissioners—Serena Cruz (NP) 2007; Maria Rojo Desteffey (NP) 2009, Diane Linn (NP) 2007, Lisa Naito (NP) 2008, Lonnie Roberts (NP) 2008; Dist. Atty. Michael D. Schrunk (NP) 2008; Assess. Robert Ellis; Recorder Cindy Swick; Sheriff Bernie Giusto (NP) 2007; Surv. Robert Hovden; Aud. Suzanne Flynn (NP) 2007; Co. Admin. Diane Linn (NP) 2007.

Polk County

County Seat: Courthouse, 850 Main St., Dallas 97338
Phone: 503-623-9217 (General); 503-623-3154 (Court Administrator)
Fax: 503-623-0717
E-mail: unger.valerie@co.polk.or.us
Web: www.co.polk.or.us
Established:
Dec. 22, 1845
Elev. at Dallas:
325'
Area: 745 sq. mi.
Average Temp.:
January 39.1°,
July 65.6°
Assessed Value: $3,297,143,255
Real Market Value: $4,871,835,926
Annual Precipitation: 51.66"
Economy: Agriculture, forest products, manufacturing, electronics and education.
Points of Interest: Western Oregon University, covered bridges, historic courthouse, Brunk House, Baskett Slough Wildlife Refuge, mountain scenery, wineries, National Historic Trail, Confederated Tribes of Grand Ronde Headquarters and Spirit Mountain Casino.

Polk County was created from the original Yamhill district in 1845, by the Provisional Legislature. It was named for then President James Knox Polk. The first county seat was at Cynthia Ann. City officials later changed its name to Dallas, after Vice-President George M. Dallas, and moved the community about a mile to improve its water supply.

The first courthouse was at Cynthia Ann. A second courthouse burned in 1898 and was replaced with the present building, built with sandstone quarried three miles west of Dallas. A three-story office annex was completed in 1966. Polk County Human Services was consolidated in the newly acquired Academy Building in 1989.

Traveling back roads in Polk County will reveal many attractions, from covered bridges and pleasant parks to vineyards, wineries, and bed and breakfast lodgings spotting the surrounding hills. Many roads meander through beautiful fertile valleys from the Willamette River to the timbered foothills of the Coast Range. Polk County was the primary destination of early wagon trains which took the southern route to Oregon. Cities located in Polk County include Dallas, Independence, Monmouth, Falls City and portions of Salem and Willamina.

County Officials: Commissioners—Ron Dodge (D) 2007, Mike Propes, (R) 2008, Tom Ritchey (R) 2007; Dist. Atty. John Fisher (NP) 2008; Assess. Dennis Day (R) 2009; Clerk Valerie Unger (NP) 2009; Sheriff Robert Wolfe (NP) 2007; Surv. John Nemecek; Treas. Linda Fox (NP) 2009; Co. Admin. Greg P. Hansen.

Sherman County

County Seat: Courthouse, 500 Court St., Moro 97039

Phone: 541-565-3606 (General); 541-565-3650 (Court Administrator)

Fax: 541-565-3312

E-mail: scclerk@sherman.k12.or.us

Web: www.sherman-county.com

Established:
Feb. 25, 1889

Elev. at Moro:
1,807'

Area: 831 sq. mi.

Average Temp.:
January 30.7°,
July 67.9°

Assessed Value: $211,685,559

Real Market Value: $293,534,956

Annual Precipitation: 9.15"

Economy: Tourism, wheat, barley and cattle.

Points of Interest: Historic county courthouse, Sherman County Museum, Gordon Ridge, John Day Dam, Sherar's Grade, Deschutes State Park, LePage Park, Giles French Park, Sherman County Fairgrounds and RV Park.

Sherman County, created in 1889 from the northeast corner of Wasco County, was named for Gen. William Tecumseh Sherman. It was separated from Wasco County as much for its unique geological setting as for the settlers' desire to have their own political process. The rolling hills are bordered by the deep canyons of the John Day River to the east, the Columbia River to the north and the Deschutes River and Buck Hollow to the west and south.

The county was settled in the 1870s by stockmen; by 1881 the homesteaders arrived, permanently changing the area by plowing and fencing the tall grass. Since then, the county has been a wheat-growing area with miles of waving grain on rolling hills of wind-blown glacial silt. The total absence of timber in the county exemplifies the true meaning of the "wide open spaces of the West." Its pastoral landscape has spectacular views of canyons and rivers with mountains silhouetted in the distance. Recreation abounds on the rivers, from the famous and scenic fly-fishing and whitewater rafting stream of the Deschutes to water-skiing, wind-surfing, boating, fishing and rafting on the John Day and Columbia Rivers. Sherman County is one of Oregon's leaders in soil and water conservation.

County Officials: Commissioners—Steve Burnet (R) 2007, Sherry Kaseberg (R) 2007, Judge Gary Thompson (R) 2007; Dist. Atty. Tara Lawrence (NP) 2007; Assess. Richard Stradley (R) 2009; Clerk Linda Cornie (NP) 2009; Justice of the Peace Ron McDermid (NP) 2009; Sheriff Brad Lohrey (NP) 2009; Surv. Daryl Ingebo; Treas. Marnene Benson (NP) 2007.

Tillamook County

County Seat: Courthouse, 201 Laurel Ave., Tillamook 97141

Phone: 503-842-3402 (General); 503-842-2596, ext. 124 (Court Administrator)

Fax: 503-842-2721

E-mail: toneil@co.tillamook.or.us

Web: www.co.tillamook.or.us

Established:
Dec. 15, 1853

Elev. at
Tillamook: 22'

Area: 1,125 sq. mi.

Average Temp.:
January 42.2°,
July 58.2°

Assessed Value: $2,849,424,305

Real Market Value: $3,582,116,191

Annual Precipitation: 90.90"

Economy: Agriculture, forest products, fishing and recreation.

Points of Interest: Neah-Kah-Nie Mountain; Tillamook, Nehalem, Netarts and Nestucca Bays; Oswald West State Park; Nehalem Bay State Park; Bob Straub State Park; Cape Lookout State Park; Pioneer Museum; Blue Heron Cheese Factory; Tillamook Cheese Factory; Naval Air Station Museum; Haystack Rock at Cape Kiwanda; Whalen Island State Park.

Tillamook County was formed in 1853 from Yamhill and Clatsop counties. The name Tillamook comes from the Tillamook (or Killamook) Indians.

Dairy farms dominate the county's fertile valley. It is the home of the world-famous Tillamook Cheese Factory. The reforested, 355,000 acre "Tillamook Burn" is rapidly maturing. Commercial thinning will become increasingly evident. With 75 miles of scenic coastline, four bays and nine rivers, Tillamook County offers the finest deep-sea and stream fishing, charter and dory boats, clamming, crabbing, beachcombing and hiking. Its forests also furnish excellent hunting.

County Officials: Commissioners—Charles Hurliman (R) 2009, Tim Josi (D) 2007, Mark Labhart (R) 2009; Dist. Atty. William Porter (NP) 2007; Assess. Tim Lutz (NP) 2009; Clerk Tassi O'Neil (NP) 2009; Justice of the Peace Neal Lemery (NP) 2007; Sheriff Todd Anderson (NP) 2009; Surv. Dan McNutt (NP) 2009; Treas. Karen Richards-Dye (NP) 2007.

Umatilla County

County Seat: Courthouse, 216 SE 4th St., Pendleton 97801
Phone: 541-276-7111 (General); 541-278-0341, ext. 224 (Court Administrator)
Fax: 541-278-5463
E-mail: dan@co.umatilla.or.us
Web: www.co.umatilla.or.us
Established: Sept. 27, 1862
Elev. at Pendleton: 1,068'
Area: 3,231 sq. mi.

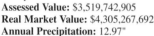

Average Temp.: January 31.9°, July 73.6°
Assessed Value: $3,519,742,905
Real Market Value: $4,305,267,692
Annual Precipitation: 12.97"
Economy: Agriculture, food processing, forest products, tourism, manufacturing, recreation, aggregate production and power generation.
Points of Interest: Pendleton Round-Up, Pendleton Woolen Mills, Old Town Pendleton, County Historical Society, Pendleton Underground, McNary Dam and Recreation Area, Echo Museum and Historic Area, Hat Rock, Battle Mountain and Emigrant Springs State Parks, Weston Historic District, Frazier Farmstead Museum in Milton-Freewater, N. Fork Umatilla Wilderness Area, Tollgate-Spout Springs Recreation Area, Courthouse Clock Tower, Confederated Tribes of the Umatilla Indian Reservation's Wildhorse Casino and Tamastslikt Cultural Center.

Umatilla County traces its creation in 1862 to the regional gold rushes, which spawned the riverport of Umatilla City and brought stockraisers to the lush grasslands.

Although Lewis and Clark and the Oregon Trail pioneers passed through Umatilla County, it did not bloom until the arrival of the railroad in 1881 and the development of dryland wheat farming.

Water in the form of irrigation has been key to economic diversification and growth, most recently in the Hermiston area, where the desert now yields lush watermelons and other products. Tourism is also increasingly important to Umatilla County where "Let-er-Buck" is heard by Pendleton Round-Up crowds.

County Officials: Commissioners—Dennis D. Doherty (NP) 2009, William S. Hansell (NP) 2007, Emile M. Holeman (NP) 2007; Dist. Atty. Christopher Brower (NP) 2009; Assess. Paul Chalmers; Sheriff John Trumbo (NP) 2009; Surv. Dave Krumbein; Financial Mgr. Robert Pahl; Co. Admin. Jim Barrow.

Union County

County Seat: Union County Commissioners, 1106 K St., La Grande 97850
Phone: 541-963-1006 (General); 541-962-9500, ext. 232 (Court Administrator)
Fax: 541-963-1079
E-mail: nhibbert@union-county.org
Web: www.union-county.org
Established: Oct. 14, 1864
Elev. at La Grande: 2,788'
Area: 2,038 sq. mi.
Average Temp.: January 30.9°, July 70.4°
Assessed Value: $1,140,900,882
Real Market Value: $1,956,244,580
Annual Precipitation: 18.79"
Economy: Agriculture, forest products, education and government
Points of Interest: Meacham and Tollgate winter sports areas, Grande Ronde Valley, Eastern Oregon University (La Grande).

Union County was created in 1864 and named for the town of Union, which had been established two years before and named by its founders for patriotic reasons during the Civil War. The county comprised a part of the northern portion of Baker County and in 1899 Union County gave up its eastern portion to Wallowa County.

The Grande Ronde Valley in Union County is nearly table flat and is covered with the rich silt of an old lake bed. Highly diversified, with a 160-day growing season and an annual rainfall of twenty inches, the valley boasts of never having had a general crop failure. The county's 1,092 farms average 473 acres a unit.

Union County's front door opens to the rugged Wallowa Mountains. Its back door faces the Blue Mountains, which attract hikers, skiers, and hunters.

County Officials: Commissioners—John Lamoreau (R) 2007, Colleen MacLeod (R) 2009, Steve McClure (R) 2007; Dist. Atty. Martin Birnbaum (NP) 2009; Assess. Linda Hill (R) 2009; Clerk R. Nellie Bogue Hibbert (R) 2009; Sheriff Steve Oliver (R) 2009; Surv. Greg Blackman (NP) 2006; Treas. Peggy Sutton (NP) 2009; Co. Admin. Marlene Perkins.

Wallowa County

County Seat: Courthouse, 101 S River St., Enterprise 97828
Phone: 541-426-4543, ext. 15 (General); 541-426-4991 (Court Administrator)
Fax: 541-426-0582
E-mail: wcboc@co.wallowa.or.us
Web: www.co.wallowa.or.us
Established: Feb. 11, 1887

Elev. at Enterprise: 3,757'
Area: 3,153 sq. mi.
Average Temp.: January 24.2°, July 63.0°
Assessed Value: $502,795,609
Real Market Value: $898,599,219
Annual Precipitation: 13.08"
Economy: Agriculture, art, livestock, forest products and recreation.
Points of Interest: Wallowa Lake, art galleries, Mt. Howard gondola, Eagle Cap Wilderness, Hells Canyon National Recreation Area, Minam, Wallowa and Grande Ronde Rivers.

This rather isolated area was claimed by the Chief Joseph band of the Nez Perce as its hunting and fishing grounds. The Nez Perce used the word "wallowa" to designate a tripod of poles used to support fish nets. In 1871, the first white settlers came to Wallowa County, crossing the mountains in search of livestock feed in the Wallowa Valley. The area had been part of Union County since 1864 but it was carved from that county in 1887 by a legislative act.

Wallowa County is a land of rugged mountains, gentle valleys and deep canyons. Peaks in the Wallowa Mountains soar to almost 10,000 feet in elevation and the Snake River dips to about 1,000 feet above sea level. Hells Canyon, carved by the Snake, is the nation's deepest gorge, averaging 5,500 feet from rim to river.

The scenery in the county is spectacular and serves as a magnet for tourists. Unrivaled opportunities for outdoor recreation create the county's reputation as a visitors' paradise. Permanent residents enjoy the same recreation opportunities, adding to a high quality of life supported by traditional farm and forest industries as well as art and tourism.

County Officials: Commissioners—Benjamin M. Boswell (R) 2009, Dan DeBoie (R) 2007, Mike Hayward, chair (R) 2009; Dist. Atty. Daniel Ousley (NP) 2009; Assess. Gay Fregulia (NP) 2009; Clerk Charlotte McIver (D) 2009; Sheriff Fred Steen (NP) 2009; Surv. Jack W. Burris (R) 2009; Treas. Ernestine Kilgore (D) 2009.

Wasco County

County Seat: Courthouse, 511 Washington St., The Dalles 97058
Phone: 541-506-2500 (General); 541-506-2700 (Court Administrator)
Fax: 541-506-2531
E-mail: KarenL@co.wasco.or.us
Web: www.co.wasco.or.us
Established: Jan. 11, 1854
Elev. at The Dalles: 98'
Area: 2,396 sq. mi.
Average Temp.: January 33.4°, July 73.1°
Assessed Value: $1,331,962,870
Real Market Value: $1,694,534,536
Annual Precipitation: 14.90"
Economy: Agriculture, forest products, manufacturing, electric power, aluminum and transportation.
Points of Interest: Columbia and Deschutes Rivers, Fort Dalles Museum, Pulpit Rock, The Dalles Dam, Celilo Converter Station, Confederated Tribes of the Warm Springs Reservation and Kah-Nee-Ta Resort, Mt. Hood, Sorosis Park, original Wasco County Courthouse, St. Peter's Landmark and the Columbia River Gorge Discovery Center.

When the Territorial Legislature created Wasco County in 1854 from parts of Clackamas, Lane, Linn and Marion counties, it embraced all of Oregon east of the Cascade Range, most of Idaho and parts of Montana and Wyoming. It was named for the Wasco (or Wascopam) Indian tribe.

Wasco's county seat is The Dalles. Now the trading hub of north-central Oregon, The Dalles gained earlier fame as the town at the end of the Oregon Trail. Thousands of years before that, humans scratched pictographs on rocks overlooking the Columbia River in this area. Later, Indian tribes gathered for generations near Celilo Falls to trade and fish. The county's Indian heritage continues in evidence today. Kah-Nee-Ta, a popular Oregon resort, is located on the Confederated Tribes of the Warm Springs Reservation in southern Wasco County.

County Officials: Commissioners—Dan Ericksen, chair, (R) 2007, Sherry Holliday (R) 2007, Scott McKay (D) 2007; Dist. Atty. Eric Nisley (NP) 2009; Assess. Tim Lynn; Clerk Karen LeBreton Coats (NP) 2009; Sheriff Ric Eiesland (NP) 2009; Surv. Dan Boldt (NP) 2007; Treas. Lynn Rasmussen.

Washington County

County Seat: Public Service Bldg., 155 N 1st Ave., Suite 300, Hillsboro 97124
Phone: 503-846-8685 (General); 503-846-8888 (Court Administrator)
Fax: 503-846-4545
E-mail: webmaster@co.washington.or.us
Web: www.co.washington.or.us
Established:
  July 5, 1843
Elev. at
  Hillsboro: 196'
Area: 727 sq. mi.
Average Temp.:
  January 39.9°,
  July 66.6°
Assessed Value: $35,792,982,193
Real Market Value: $52,640,588,947
Annual Precipitation: 37.71"
Economy: Agriculture, horticulture, forest products, food processing, electronics, sports equipment and apparel.
Points of Interest: Tualatin Valley orchards and vineyards, Pacific University, Wilson River and Sunset Highways, Hagg Lake, Old Scotch Church.

The original four counties created by the Provisional Government of Oregon were: Twality, Clackamas, Yamhill and Champoick. Twality was changed to Washington in honor of President George Washington by the Territorial Legislature on September 3, 1849. The actual organization of Washington County government came in 1854.

Now one of the state's fastest developing areas, the fertile Tualatin Valley was once filled with beaver and a favorite hunting ground for Hudson's Bay Company trappers. The first white settlers arrived around 1840, lured by rich soil. Despite its rapid urbanization, the valley still contains prime agricultural land. Many small towns rich in history dot the area. Pacific University, founded as Tualatin Academy in 1849, is one of the oldest colleges in the West. Washington County operates under a home rule charter approved by voters in 1962. The Northwest's largest enclosed shopping center, Washington Square, is located south of Beaverton.

County Officials: Commissioners—Tom Brian, chair (NP) 2006, Andy Duyck (NP) 2006, John Leeper (NP) 2006, Roy Rogers (NP) 2008, Dick Schouten (NP) 2008; Dist. Atty. Robert Hermann (NP) 2006; Assess./Clerk Jerry Hanson; Justice of the Peace James Shartel (NP) 2010; Sheriff R. Gordon Jr. (NP) 2009; Surv. James Elam; Aud. Alan Percell; Co. Admin. Charles D. Cameron.

Wheeler County

County Seat: Courthouse, 701 Adams St., Fossil 97830
Phone: 541-763-2400 (General); 541-763-3460 (Court Administrator)
Fax: 541-763-2026
E-mail: bsitton@ncesd.k12.or.us
Web: www.wheelerinfo.com
Established:
  Feb. 17, 1899
Elev. at Fossil:
  2,654'
Area: 1,713 sq. mi.
Average Temp.:
  January 35°,
  July 66°
Assessed Value: $81,663,238
Real Market Value: $329,389,423
Annual Precipitation: 14.66"
Economy: Livestock and tourism.
Points of Interest: Painted Hills, John Day Fossil Beds, John Day River.

Wheeler County was formed by the Oregon Legislature in 1899 from parts of Grant, Gilliam and Crook counties and was named for Henry H. Wheeler, who operated the first mail stage line from The Dalles to Canyon City. The new county consisted of 1,656 square miles with an estimated 46 townships, a population of 1,600 and taxable property worth one million dollars.

Wheeler County is as rugged and uneven as any Oregon county, with the terrain varying widely from sagebrush, juniper and rim rock to stands of pine and fir. Portions of two national forests lie within its boundaries with forest lands covering nearly one-third of the county. The area is probably best known as one of the most outstanding depositories of prehistoric fossils on the North American continent.

County Officials: Commissioners—H. John Asher (I) 2009, Ken Bond (D) 2007, Judge Jeanne E. Burch (R) 2007; Dist. Atty. Thomas W. Cutsforth (NP) 2007; Assess. Donald R. Cossitt (R) 2007; Clerk Barbara Sitton (NP) 2009; Justices of the Peace Linda Keys (NP) 2010, Theressa Ward (NP) 2009; Sheriff David Rouse (NP) 2009; Surv. Robert Bagett (NP) 2009; Treas. Nancy L. Misener (D) 2007.

Yamhill County

County Seat: Courthouse, 535 NE 5th St., Rm. 119, McMinnville 97128
Phone: 503-434-7518 (General); 503-434-7530 (Court Administrator)
Fax: 503-434-7520
Web: www.co.yamhill.or.us/clerk/
Established:
July 5, 1843
Elev. at McMinnville: 157'

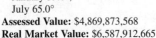

Area: 718 sq. mi.
Average Temp.:
January 39.0°,
July 65.0°
Assessed Value: $4,869,873,568
Real Market Value: $6,587,912,665
Annual Precipitation: 43.6"
Economy: Agriculture, wine production, steel manufacturing, forest products, dental instruments and aircraft servicing.
Points of Interest: Linfield College, George Fox University, Herbert Hoover House, military blockhouse, Yamhill County Historical Museum, Wheatland Ferry, Captain Michael Smith Evergreen Aviation Educational Center, Rogers Landing.

Yamhill County was created in 1843 as one of Oregon's original four districts. Its present boundaries were established in 1860. The county was named after the Yamhelas, members of the Kalapuya Indian family, who lived along the Yamhill River in the western Willamette Valley.

Today, agriculture is still the county's primary industry. Nursery and greenhouse crops; fruits, nuts, berries; and hay, silage, field and grass seeds are major agricultural products. Yamhill County ranks sixth out of Oregon's 36 counties in annual market value of its agricultural production. Yamhill County is also the heart of Oregon's wine industry. Thirty-six wineries represent the largest concentration of wineries in any county and produce the greatest number of award-winning wines in the state. A third of the county is covered with commercial timber. The mainstay of the western valley area is logging and timber products. Nonseasonal industries include a steel rolling mill, electronic and dental equipment manufacturing, an international airline and helicopter company, and a newsprint mill.

County Officials: Commissioners—Kathy George (R) 2007, Leslie Lewis (R) 2008, Mary Stern (D) 2007; Dist. Atty. Brad Berry (NP) 2008; Assess. David Lawson (NP) 2008; Clerk Jan Colman; Sheriff Jack Crabtree (NP) 2007; Surv. Dan Linscheid (NP) 2006; Treas. Nancy Reed (NP) 2008.

REGIONAL GOVERNMENTS

In January 1984, the 14 regional governments in Oregon came together to form the Oregon Regional Councils Association (ORCA) to promote greater cooperation between all levels of government.

The councils are multi-jurisdictional and multi-purpose organizations. They are voluntary associations of local governments cooperating on issues and problems which cross city, county, and in some cases state boundaries. The association provides a forum for information exchange and discussion of current issues of concern. For more information contact the executive director of any organization listed below.

Regional COGs in Oregon are formed under ORS 190.

Central Oregon Intergovernmental Council

Contact: Tom Moore, Executive Director
Address: 2363 SW Glacier Pl., Redmond 97756
Phone: 541-548-8163
Fax: 541-923-3416
Web: www.coic.org

Lane Council of Governments

Contact: George Kloeppel, Executive Director
Address: 99 E Broadway, Suite 400, Eugene 97401
Phone: 541-682-4283
Fax: 541-682-4099
Web: www.lcog.org

Mid-Columbia Council of Governments

Contact: John Arens, Executive Director
Address: 1113 Kelly Ave., The Dalles 97058
Phone: 541-298-4101
Fax: 541-298-2084
Web: www.mccog.com

Mid-Willamette Valley Council of Governments

Contact: David A. Galati, Executive Director
Address: 105 High St. SE, Salem 97301
Phone: 503-588-6177
Fax: 503-588-6094
E-mail: dgalati@mail.open.org
Web: www.mwvcog.org

Mid-Willamette Valley Senior Services Agency

Contact: Barry Donenfeld, Executive Director
Director's Phone: 503-304-3467
Address: 4670 E 3rd St., Tillamook 97141
Phone: 503-842-9700; Toll-free: 1-866-546-3731
Fax: 503-842-9701
Web: www.open.org/mwvssa/

Oregon Cascades West
Council of Governments

Contact: William Wagner, Executive Director
Address: 1400 Queen Ave. SE, Suite 201, Albany 97322
Phone: 541-967-8720
Fax: 541-967-6123
Web: www.ocwcog.org

Rogue Valley
Council of Governments

Contact: Michael Cavallaro, Executive Director
Address: PO Box 3275, Central Point 97502
Phone: 541-664-6674
Fax: 541-664-7927
Web: www.rvcog.org

Sage Community Development

Contact: Kathleen Simko, President
Address: 10624 W Executive Dr., Boise, ID 83713
Phone: 208-322-7033
Fax: 208 322 3569
E-mail: ksimko@sageidaho.com

Umpqua Regional
Council of Governments

Contact: Larry A. Layton, Executive Director
Address: 1036 SE Douglas Ave., Suite 8, Roseburg 97470
Phone: 541-440-4231
Fax: 541-440-6252
Web: www.ur-cog.cog.or.us

METRO

Contact: David Bragdon, President
Address: 600 NE Grand Ave., Portland 97232-2736
Phone: 503-797-1700
Fax: 503-797-1799
Web: www.metro-region.org/

District officials: President of Council, David Bragdon (2006); Councilors: Rod Park (1) 2006; Brian Newman (2) 2006; Carl Hosticka (3) 2008; Susan McLain (4) 2006; Rex Burkholder (5) 2008; Robert Liberty (6) 2008; Auditor Alexis Dow, 2006.

Metro covers approximately 460 square miles of the urban portions of Clackamas, Multnomah and Washington counties in northwestern Oregon. There are 25 cities in the Metro service area, including Beaverton, Gresham, Hillsboro, Lake Oswego, Milwaukie, Oregon City and Portland.

Metro has primary responsibility for regional land-use and transportation planning, and is further empowered to address any other issue of "metropolitan concern." This grant of authority clearly underscores the Portland metropolitan region's commitment to maintain and enhance the livability of the region.

In May of 1995, 62 percent of the citizens of the region voted to authorize $135.6 million in general obligation bonds to acquire and protect a system of regional open spaces, parks and streams.

History

Metro was formed in 1979, when voters approved the merger of a council of governments (Columbia Region Association of Governments—CRAG) that had land-use and transportation planning responsibilities with the Metropolitan Service District, which had been created to provide regional services that included the solid waste management plan and operation of a metropolitan zoo. The new Metropolitan Service District (MSD) was governed by an elected council and an elected executive officer. It had the combined authority of the two predecessor agencies and other potential additional powers.

In 1980, Metro became responsible for regional solid waste disposal when it took over operation of the one existing publicly owned regional landfill and began construction of a transfer station. In November 1986, voters approved general obligation bond funding for the Oregon Convention Center, built and operated by Metro. In January 1990, Metro assumed management responsibility for the Portland Center for the Performing Arts, Portland Civic Stadium and Portland Memorial Coliseum (though management of the coliseum was later returned to the city, which turned it over to the new Oregon Arena Corporation). Finally, in 1994, Metro assumed management responsibility for the Multnomah County parks system and Expo Center. Ownership of these facilities was transferred to Metro on July 1, 1996. In 2000, Portland Civic Stadium was turned over to Portland Family Entertainment for ownership and management.

Regional Planning Functions

Metro is the designated metropolitan planning organization responsible for the allocation of federal transportation funds to projects in the region. The region's success in attracting federal funding for highway and transit projects is due, in large part, to Metro's role in building and maintaining regional consensus on projects to be funded and ensuring that funding is allocated to high-priority projects.

Metro has developed a regional data center to forecast transportation and land-use needs. All local jurisdictions now rely on and contribute to this data center, eliminating duplication between governments and battles about "dueling data." This has allowed all jurisdictions in the region to focus on important policy choices rather than arguing about assumptions.

With the adoption of a state land-use planning law (SB 100), local governments were required to prepare comprehensive land-use plans. Metro (as CRAG) was the agency responsible for establishing and maintaining an urban growth boundary (UGB) for the Portland region. Through the enforcement of the UGB pursuant to Oregon's land-use laws, the region has maintained its unique character and is now a national model for urban growth management planning.

Metro's current role in regional land-use planning and growth management is an outgrowth of its role in establishing the urban growth boundary, transportation planning and data management. Local jurisdictions and the region's voters have recognized the value of a coordinated approach to land-use and livability issues, and have assigned that responsibility to Metro.

Charter Approval

Prior to 1992, Metro was organized under a grant of authority by the legislature and the Oregon Revised Statutes. Metro's powers were limited to those expressly granted by the legislature, and any extension of those powers had to first be approved by the legislature.

With the growth in the region, however, and Metro's increasingly important role, the region recognized that the power and authority of the regional government should be controlled directly by the voters of the region and not by the legislature. Accordingly, in 1990, the legislature referred a constitutional amendment to the voters to allow the creation of a home-rule regional government in the Portland metropolitan area. Voters approved that amendment, and a charter committee was formed shortly thereafter. In 1992, a charter for Metro was referred to voters, who approved it. Metro thereby achieved the distinction of not only being the nation's only elected regional government (as it had been since 1979), but also the only one organized under a home-rule charter approved by voters.

PORT DISTRICTS OF OREGON

Source: Oregon Public Ports Association
Address: 727 Center St. NE, Salem 97301
Phone: 503-585-1250
Fax: 503-585-8993

Port of Alsea, 1910

Address: PO Box 1060, Waldport 97394
Phone: 541-563-3872
Fax: 541-563-8538
E-mail: portofalsea@casco.net
Web: www.portofalsea.com
Commissioners: Suzanne Groshong, John Johnson, John Mare´, Ray Meehan, Mark Rowley; Port Mgr. Maggie Rivers. Meets 3rd Wed. of the month.

Port of Arlington, 1933

Address: PO Box 279, Arlington 97812
Phone: 541-454-2868
Fax: 541-454-2053
E-mail: portofarlington@hotmail.com
Commissioners: Brad Anderson, Julius Courtney, Jim Morris, Richard Rende, Timothy Weatherell; Exec. Sec. Alice Courtney. Meets 1st Tues. of the month.

Port of Astoria, 1914

Address: 1 Portway, Astoria 97103
Phone: 503-325-4521
Fax: 503-325-4525
E-mail: info@portofastoria.com
Web: www.portofastoria.com
Commissioners: Jim Bergeron, Dan Hess, Don McDaniel, Larry Pfund, Glenn Taggart; Exec. Dir. Peter Garin; Deputy Dir. Bill Cook. Meets 3rd Tues. of the month.

Port of Bandon, 1913

Address: PO Box 206, Bandon 97411
Phone: 541-347-3206
Fax: 541-347-4645
E-mail: port@portofbandon.com
Web: www.portofbandon.com
Commissioners: Ernest Amling, Donny Goddard, Steve Martizia, Robert S. Miller III, Reg Pullen; Port Mgr. Alex Linke. Meets 4th Thurs. of the month.

Port of Brookings Harbor, 1956

Address: PO Box 848, Brookings 97415
Phone: 541-469-2218
Fax: 541-469-0672
E-mail: info@port-brookings-harbor.org
Web: www.port-brookings-harbor.org
Commissioners: Ken Byrtus, Norma Fitzgerald, Ed Gray, Lloyd Whaley, John Zia; Exec. Dir. Russ Crabtree. Meets 3rd Tues. of the month.

Port of Cascade Locks, 1937

Address: PO Box 307, Cascade Locks 97014
Phone: 541-374-8619
Fax: 541-374-8428
E-mail: kmiller@portofcascadelocks.org
Web: www.portofcascadelocks.org
Commissioners: Joeinne Caldwell, Tim Lee, Jean McLean, Scot Sullenger, Kathy Woosley; Port Mgr. Chuck Daughtry. Meets 1st and 3rd Thurs. of the month.

Oregon International Port of Coos Bay, 1909

Address: PO Box 1215, Coos Bay 97420
Phone: 541-267-7678
Fax: 541-269-1475
E-mail: portcoos@portofcoosbay.com
Web: www.portofcoosbay.com
Commissioners: Jerry Hampel, David Kronsteiner, Catherine "Caddy" McKeown, R. Brady Scott, Daniel Smith, Gen. Mgr. Jeffrey Bishop. Meets 3rd Thurs. of the month.

Port of Garibaldi, 1906

Address: PO Box 10, Garibaldi 97118
Phone: 503-322-3292
Fax: 503-322-0029
E-mail: portofgaribaldi@oregoncoast.com

Commissioners: Valerie Folkema, Dave McGrath, Darus Peake, William Schreiber, Don Wustenberg; Mgr. Don Bacon. Meets 2nd Wed. of the month.

Port of Gold Beach, 1955

Address: PO Box 1126, Gold Beach 97444
Phone: 541-247-6269
Fax: 541-247-6268
E-mail: portgb@wave.net
Commissioners: Gloria Gates, Lawrence Johnson, Bill McNair, Bob VanLeer, Milt Walker; Mgr. Mike Nielson. Meets 3rd Thurs. of the month.

Port of Hood River, 1933

Address: PO Box 239, Hood River 97031
Phone: 541-386-1645
Fax: 541-386-1395
E-mail: porthr@gorge.net
Web: www.portofhoodriver.com
Commissioners: Sherry Bohn, Fred Duckwall, Don Hosford, Hoby Streich, Kathy Watson; Exec. Dir. Dave Harlan. Meets 1st and 3rd Tues. of the month.

Port of Morrow, 1958

Address: PO Box 200, Boardman 97818
Phone: 541-481-7678
Fax: 541-481-2679
Web: www.portofmorrow.com
Commissioners: Daniel Creamer, Jerry Healy, Larry Lindsay, Marv Padberg, Deane Seeger; Gen. Mgr. Gary Neal. Meets 2nd Wed. of the month.

Port of Nehalem, 1909

Address: 36155 9th St., Rm. 10, Nehalem; Mailing Address: PO Box 476, Nehalem 97131-0476
Phone: 503-368-7212
Fax: 503-368-7234
E-mail: portofnehalem@nehalemtel.net
Commissioners: Don Cameron, Charles B. Collin, Deslee Kahrs, Dale Stockton, Ken Upshaw; Adm. Sec. Betty L. Conrad. Meets 4th Wed. of the month; 3rd Wed. of the month Nov. and Dec.

Port of Newport, 1910

Address: 600 SE Bay Blvd., Newport 97365
Phone: 541-265-7758
Fax: 541-265-4235
Web: www.portofnewport.com
Commissioners: Mark Fisher, Ginny Goblirsch, Rob Halverson, David Jincks, Don Mathews; Gen. Mgr. Don Mann. Meets 4th Tues. of the month.

Port of Port Orford, 1919

Address: PO Box 490, Port Orford 97465
Phone: 541-332-7121
Fax: 541-332-7121
E-mail: portoffice@harborside.com
Web: www.portofportorford.com
Commissioners: Gifford Barnes, Ed Dowdy, David Knapp, Evan Kramer, George Welch; Port Mgr. Gary Anderson. Meets 3rd Tues. of the month.

Port of Portland, 1891

Address: PO Box 3529, Portland 97208
Phone: 503-944-7000; 1-800-547-8411
Fax: 503-944-7042
E-mail: webmaster@portptld.com
Web: www.portofportland.com
Commissioners: Steven H. Corey, Thomas J. Imeson, Judith Johansen, Mary F. Olson, Keith L. Thomson, William D. Thorndike Jr., Jay T. Waldron, Junki Yoshida, Grant C. Zadow; Exec. Dir. Bill Wyatt. Meets 2nd Wed. of the month.

Port of St. Helens, 1941

Address: 100 E St., Columbia City; Mailing Address: PO Box 598, St. Helens 97051
Phone: 503-397-2888
Fax: 503-397-6924
E-mail: williamson@portsh.org
Web: www.portsh.org
Commissioners: Mike Avent, Colleen DeShazer, Robert Keyser, Agnes Peterson, Pat Zimmerman; Exec. Dir. Peter Williamson. Meets 2nd and last Wed. of the month.

Port of Siuslaw, 1909

Address: PO Box 1220, Florence 97439
Phone: 541-997-3426
Fax: 541-997-9407
E-mail: port@portofsiuslaw.com
Web: www.portofsiuslaw.com
Commissioners: Joshua Green, David Jackson, Ken Miller, John Scott, Leonard VanCurlere; Port Mgr. Tom Kartrude. Meets 3rd Wed. of the month.

Port of The Dalles, 1933

Address: 3636 Klindt Dr., The Dalles 97058
Phone: 541-298-4148
Fax: 541-298-2136
E-mail: info@portofthedalles.com
Web: www.portofthedalles.com
Commissioners: Mike Courtney, Ken Farner, Bob McFadden, Scott Mengis, Rod Runyon; Exec. Dir. Scott Hege. Meets 2nd Wed. of the month.

Port of Tillamook Bay, 1953

Address: 4000 Blimp Blvd., Tillamook 97141
Phone: 503-842-2413
Fax: 503-842-3680
E-mail: info@potb.org
Web: www.potb.org
Commissioners: Ken Bell, Jerry Dove, Loten Hooley, Art Riedel; Mgr. Jack Crider. Meets 3rd Tues. of the month.

Port of Toledo, 1910

Address: 385 NW 1st, Unit #1, Toledo 97391-9720
Phone: 541-336-5207
Fax: 541-336-5160
E-mail: portoftoledo@newportnet.com
Web: www.portoftoledo.org
Commissioners: Jim Buzby, Cody Gray, Chuck Gerttula, Greg Harrison, Stu Strom; Port Mgr. Denny Heinen. Meets 3rd Tues. of the month.

Port of Umatilla, 1940

Address: PO Box 879, Umatilla 97882
Phone: 541-922-3224
Fax: 541-922-5609
Web: www.portofumatilla.com
Commissioners: Kurt Bendixsen, Bryan Brock, Tim Mabry, Marjorie Roff, Jerry Simpson; Gen. Mgr. Kim Puzey. Meets Tues. after 1st Wed. of the month.

Port of Umpqua, 1913

Address: PO Box 388, Reedsport 97467
Phone: 541-271-2232
Fax: 541-271-2747
E-mail: portofumpqua@charterinternet.com
Web: www.portofumpqua.org
Commissioners: Danny Campbell, Ken Corbett, Jim Mix, Cindy Sardina, Keith Tymchuk; Port Mgr. Penny Ryerson. Meets 3rd Wed. of the month.

SPECIAL SERVICE DISTRICTS

Contact: Greg Baker, Executive Director
Address: Special Districts Association of Oregon, PO Box 12613, Salem 97309-0613
Phone: 503-371-8667; Toll-free: 1-800-285-5461
Fax: 503-371-4781
E-mail: sdao@sdao.com
Web: www.sdao.com
ORS 198.010 and 198.335 provide for the creation of the following 28 types of districts: water control; irrigation; ports; regional air quality control authorities; fire; hospital; mass transit; sanitary districts and authorities; people's utility; domestic water supply districts and authorities; cemetery; park and recreation; metropolitan service; special road; road assessment; highway lighting; health; vector control; water improvement; weather modification; geothermal heating; transportation; county service; chemical control; weed control; emergency communications; diking; and soil and water conservation districts.

Special Districts are financed through property taxes or fees for services, or some combination thereof. The majority of special districts are directed by a governing body elected by the voters.

The Special Districts Association of Oregon was established in 1977. SDAO provides support services to member districts throughout the state in the areas of research and technical assistance, legislative representation, training programs, insurance services, information and reference materials, financing services, and employee benefits programs.

TRANSIT DISTRICTS

Basin Transit Service Transportation District

Contact: Ernest Palmer, General Manager
Address: 1130 Adams, Klamath Falls 97601
Phone: 541-883-2877
Fax: 541-884-6287

Grant County Transportation District

Contact: Donald L. Strong, Chair
Address: PO Box 126, John Day 97845
Phone: 541-575-2370
Fax: 541-575-2329

Hood River County Transportation District

Contact: Dan Schwanz, Executive Director
Address: 600 E Marina Way, Hood River 97031
Phone: 541-386-4202
Fax: 541-386-1228

Lane Transit District

Contact: Ken Hamm, General Manager
Address: PO Box 7070, Eugene 97401
Phone: 541-682-6100
Fax: 541-682-6111

Lincoln County Transportation District

Contact: Cynda Bruce, General Manager
Address: 410 NE Harney, Newport 97365
Phone: 541-265-4900
Fax: 541-574-1296

Rogue Valley Transportation District

Contact: Peter Jacobsen, General Manager
Address: 3200 Crater Lake Ave., Medford 97504
Phone: 541-779-5821
Fax: 541-773-2877

Salem Area Mass Transit District

Contact: Jeff Hamm, General Manager
Address: 555 Court St. NE, Suite 5230, Salem 97301-3736
Phone: 503-588-2424
Fax: 503-566-3933

South Clackamas Transportation District

Contact: Shirley Lyons, Manager
Address: PO Box 517, Molalla 97038
Phone: 503-632-7000
Fax: 503-632-5214

Sunset Empire Transportation District

Contact: Cindy Howe, Executive Director
Address: 465 NE Skipanon Dr., Warrenton 97146
Phone: 503-861-7433
Fax: 503-861-4299

Tri-County Metropolitan Transportation District of Oregon (TriMet)

Contact: Fred Hansen, General Manager
Address: 4012 SE 17th Ave., Portland 97202
Phone: 503-962-4915
Fax: 503-962-6451

Bridge at Coos Bay—Oregon State Archives Photograph, OHD-G477.5

The "Oregon System"—the initiative, referendum, and recall—gained Oregon national recognition for the degree of citizen involvement in the processes of self-government. Most recently, vote-by-mail has drawn national attention to Oregon. This detailed history of elections in Oregon illustrates the tangible results of participation in these processes.

VOTING AND VOTER REGISTRATION

Source: Secretary of State, Elections Division
Address: State Capitol Bldg., Suite 141, Salem 97310
Phone: 503-986-1518
Web: www.sos.state.or.us

Note: All information is subject to change by the legislature.

Elections in Oregon

All regular elections in Oregon are held on one of four days, except in case of emergency. The four elections are held in March, May, September and November of each year.

Elections are held on the:
- Second Tuesday in March;
- Third Tuesday in May;
- Third Tuesday in September; and
- First Tuesday after the first Monday in November.

Elections are generally conducted by mail. Voters registered as of the 21st day before an election are mailed a ballot to vote and return by election day. The use of vote-by-mail was first approved on a limited basis by the legislature in 1981 and was made a permanent feature of elections in 1987.

In 1998, Oregon voters amended state law to require that the primary and general elections in May and November of even-numbered years also be conducted vote-by-mail. Beginning in 2000 primary and general elections have been conducted by mail. At the primary election, voters registered in the major political parties, currently the Democratic and Republican parties, nominate candidates to run in the general election. All voters may vote on non-partisan contests, such as judicial elections, which are also held at the primary election. Most statewide ballot measures are on the general election ballot.

Registering to Vote

Registration by mail was authorized by the 1975 Legislature and is now the method most people use to register to vote in Oregon. Forms are located in most banks and public buildings, in every county elections office and in many state agencies. They also can be obtained from the Secretary of State, Elections Division.

Date of Election	Deadline to Register*
March 8, 2005	Feb. 15, 2005
May 17, 2005	Apr. 26, 2005
Sept. 20, 2005	Aug. 30, 2005
Nov. 8, 2005	Oct. 18, 2005

*A voter registration card received in an elections office after the deadline to register, but which contains a valid postmark, meets the registration deadline.

In October 2002 President Bush signed into law the "Help America Vote Act of 2002." The Act changes voter registration requirements nationwide for voting in federal elections.

To register to vote, a person must be a resident of Oregon and be able to answer yes to the following questions on the voter registration card:
- Are you a citizen of the United States of America? and
- Will you be 18 years of age on or before election day?

A person registering to vote is asked to provide identification only if they are a new registrant in the county in which they are registering, _and_ they are mailing the registration card via the U.S. Postal Service. Identification is _not required_ for updates within the same county, or for any new registrations delivered in person or by means other than mail via the U.S. Postal Service. Sufficient identification is: a copy of a current, valid photo identification (such as driver's license), or a copy of a paycheck stub, utility bill, bank statement or other government document showing the registrant's name and address. If identification is not provided at the time of registration, it will be requested by election officials in order for the person to vote at the next federal election.

Oregon residents who are not U.S. citizens by the deadline to register to vote, but who will be by election day, should contact their county elections office for information about how to register to vote.

Persons who become residents of Oregon after the deadline to register for a presidential election may be eligible to vote for U.S. president and vice-president. Contact your county elections office for more information.

Important! Persons registered to vote in other states may not transfer their voter registration to Oregon. To register to vote in Oregon, a person must complete either an Oregon voter registration card or a Federal Postcard Application, which is available in most states.

How to Maintain a Current Voter Registration

Registered voters must notify their county elections office in writing if:
- Their residence or mailing address changes;
- Their name changes; or
- They wish to change political party affiliation.

A voter may notify county elections officials of changes to the above by sending a new voter registration card to the appropriate county.

A voter may update voter registration information as late as election day and vote in that election.

If a voter has moved from one county in Oregon to another, the voter should fill out a voter registration card and send it to the new county elections office. If the voter registration card is sent after the 21st day before an election, the voter should call the county elections official to find out how to receive a ballot for that election.

Voting Absentee

Absentee ballots are mailed to overseas, military and out-of-state voters in advance of the regular mailing of ballots. Voters should contact their local elections office to obtain an absentee ballot.

Voters' Pamphlet

For each primary and general election and for most special elections, the Elections Division produces and distributes to every household a pamphlet containing information about candidates and measures that will appear on the ballot at the election. Most county elections offices also produce pamphlets that contain information about local candidates and measures.

2006 FILING DEADLINES

- The filing period for the 2006 primary election on May 16, 2006 begins on March 27, 2005 and ends on March 7, 2006. The deadline for filing voters' pamphlet material is March 9, 2006.
- The filing period for the 2006 general election on November 7, 2006 begins on September 18, 2005, and ends on August 29, 2006. The deadline for filing voters' pamphlet material is August 29, 2006.

RECENT ELECTION HISTORY

2004 Primary Election

Source: Official Abstract of Votes, available from the Elections Division, State Capitol Bldg., Suite 141, Salem 97310

Web: www.sos.state.or.us/elections/elechp.htm

Key: *Nominated; **Elected; WI = Write In

United States President

Democrat	Total
Kerry, John F.*	289,804
Kucinich, Dennis J.	60,019
LaRouche Jr., Lyndon H.	8,571
Miscellaneous	10,150
Republican	
Bush, George W.*	293,806
Miscellaneous	15,700

United States Senator

Democrat	Total
Wyden, Ron*	345,219
Miscellaneous	3,387
Republican	
Abshier, Thomas Lee	51,879
Bowerman, E.	18,779
Broussard, Bruce	53,084
Goberman, Pavel	12,230
King, Al*	85,035
Petrie, Philip	15,838
Miscellaneous	4,990

United States Representative

1st Congressional District

Democrat	Total
Wu, David*	62,001
Miscellaneous	631
Republican	
Ameri, Goli*	26,451
Meshell, Jason DC	14,495
Phillips, Tim	13,316
Miscellaneous	591

2nd Congressional District

Democrat	Total
McColgan, John C.*	45,521
Miscellaneous	997
Republican	
Walden, Greg*	79,686
Miscellaneous	549

3rd Congressional District

Democrat	Total
Blumenauer, Earl*	76,811
Sweeney, John	9,207
Miscellaneous	280
Republican	
Mars, Tami*	21,572
Miscellaneous	1,374

4th Congressional District

Democrat	Total
DeFazio, Peter A.*	78,414
Miscellaneous	610
Republican	
Feldcamp, Jim*	51,500
Miscellaneous	1,183

5th Congressional District

Democrat	Total
Hooley, Darlene*	59,407
Kaza, Andrew	10,027
Miscellaneous	366
Republican	
Winters, Jackie	29,529
Zupancic, Jim*	37,856
Miscellaneous	426

Secretary of State

Democrat	Total
Bradbury, Bill*	311,602
Wells, Paul Damian	41,196
Miscellaneous	1,839
Republican	
Close, Betsy L.*	144,001
Granum, Fred	124,072
Miscellaneous	2,748

State Treasurer

Democrat	Total
Edwards, Randall*	279,066
Miscellaneous	2,948

Republican

Caton, Jeff*	223,242
Miscellaneous	2,833

Attorney General

Democrat	**Total**
Myers, Hardy*	290,715
Miscellaneous	2,936
Republican	
Connolly, Paul*	222,127
Miscellaneous	2,806

Judge of the Supreme Court

Nonpartisan	**Total**

Position 4

Kistler, Rives**	382,348
Leuenberger, James E.	250,636
Miscellaneous	2,476

Position 5

Gillette, W. Michael (Mick)**	470,528
Miscellaneous	8,414

Position 7

Murgo, Rudy M.	217,206
Riggs, William**	397,239
Miscellaneous	2,400

Judge of the Court of Appeals

Nonpartisan	**Total**

Position 4

Linder, Virginia L.**	485,731
Miscellaneous	7,391

Position 7

Brockett, Phil	254,784
Wollheim, Robert**	350,294
Miscellaneous	2,438

Position 9

Deits, Mary J.**	468,262
Miscellaneous	7,376

Judge of the Circuit Court

Nonpartisan	**Total**

1st District—Position 2

Harris, Daniel L.**	27,587
Miscellaneous	314

1st District—Position 3

Arnold, G. Philip (Phil)**	28,166
Miscellaneous	351

1st District—Position 4

Crain, Patricia**	27,565
Miscellaneous	331

2nd District—Position 6

Merten, Maurice K.**	48,293
Miscellaneous	568

2nd District—Position 7

Bearden, Mary Ann**	48,870
Miscellaneous	491

2nd District—Position 11

Holland, Lauren S.**	48,697
Miscellaneous	523

3rd District—Position 4

Burton, Claudia M.**	40,031
Miscellaneous	517

3rd District—Position 6

James, Mary M.**	39,241
Miscellaneous	498

3rd District—Position 10

Wilson, John Bruce**	38,379
Miscellaneous	470

3rd District—Position 13

Hart, Tom**	38,636
Miscellaneous	497

4th District—Position 4

Galton, Sidney A.**	81,998
Miscellaneous	2,328

4th District—Position 37

Wyers, Jan**	82,093
Miscellaneous	2,442

5th District—Position 2

Miller, Eve L.**	41,545
Miscellaneous	514

5th District—Position 7

Herndon, Robert D.**	42,598
Miscellaneous	546

6th District—Position 2

Pahl, Ronald J.**	9,625
Miscellaneous	75

6th District—Position 3

Custer, Kittee	1,700
Hill, Daniel J.**	7,438
Jones, Bill	3,287
Miscellaneous	35

6th District—Position 4

Wallace, Jeff M.**	9,727
Miscellaneous	83

7th District—Position 1

Hull, Donald W.**	8,868
Miscellaneous	127

7th District—Position 2

Kelly, John V.**	8,899
Miscellaneous	110

7th District—Position 3

Crowley, Paul G.**	8,725
Miscellaneous	140

7th District—Position 4
Smith, Bernie**	8,233
Miscellaneous	169

11th District—Position 4
Adler, A. Michael**	23,743
Miscellaneous	349

11th District—Position 6
Perkins, Ed**	18,455
Spear Jr., Thomas M.	12,082
Miscellaneous	100

12th District—Position 3
Avera, Fred E.**	9,343
Miscellaneous	145

13th District—Position 2
Osborne, Roxanne Burgett**	13,047
Miscellaneous	207

13th District—Position 3
Adkisson, Marci Warner**	8,508
Bunch, Dan	5,182
Carter, Scott Orin	2,691
Miscellaneous	16

13th District—Position 4
Wogan, Cameron F.**	12,417
Miscellaneous	164

15th District—Position 1
Stone, Martin**	17,797
Miscellaneous	245

15th District—Position 2
Barron, Richard L.**	18,503
Miscellaneous	362

15th District—Position 3
Downer Jr., Hugh C.**	17,237
Miscellaneous	305

15th District—Position 4
Gillespie, Mike**	18,184
Miscellaneous	273

15th District—Position 6
Mickelson, Richard K.**	16,919
Miscellaneous	280

16th District—Position 2
Seitz, Joan G.**	18,654
Miscellaneous	141

16th District—Position 3
Ambrosini, George W.*	7,340
Garrison, Randy*	9,905
Lee, Charles	3,549
Madison, Kenneth W.	2,470
Miscellaneous	29

18th District—Position 2
Nelson, Phjlip L.**	6,921
Miscellaneous	98

19th District—Position 3
Smith, Berkeley**	8,434
Miscellaneous	231

20th District—Position 1
Kohl, Thomas W.**	46,150
Miscellaneous	722

20th District—Position 8
Nachtigal, Gayle A.**	47,928
Miscellaneous	806

20th District—Position 10
Upton, Suzanne M.**	46,527
Miscellaneous	757

21st District—Position 2
Holcomb, Janet Schoenhard**	12,582
Miscellaneous	209

23rd District—Position 1
Bispham, Carol R.**	12,621
Miscellaneous	250

25th District—Position 1
Collins, John L.**	12,983
Miscellaneous	214

27th District—Position 1
Roll, Rick W.**	4,926
Miscellaneous	66

27th District—Position 2
Hantke, David W.**	5,222
Miscellaneous	53

2004 General Election

Source: Official Abstract of Votes, available from the Elections Division, State Capitol Bldg., Suite 141, Salem 97310

Web: www.sos.state.or.us/elections/elechp.htm

*Elected

United States President
	Total
Badnarik, Michael—L	7,260
Bush, George W.—R	866,831
Cobb, David—P	5,315
Kerry, John F.—D*	943,163
Peroutka, Michael Anthony—C	5,257
Miscellaneous	8,956

United States Senator
	Total
Brownlow, David—C	12,397
Fitzgerald, Dan—L	29,582
Keane, Teresa—P	43,053
King, Al—R	565,254
Wyden, Ron—D*	1,128,728
Miscellaneous	1,536

United States Representative

1st Congressional District

	Total
Goli, Ameri—R	135,164
Wolf, Dean—C	13,882
Wu, David—D*	203,771
Miscellaneous	1,521

2nd Congressional District

	Total
Brown Jr., Jack Alan—C	4,060
Lindsay, Jim—L	4,792
McColgan, John C.—D	88,914
Walden, Greg—R*	248,461
Miscellaneous	638

3rd Congressional District

	Total
Blumenauer, Earl—D*	245,599
Brown, Walter F.—S	10,678
Mars, Tami—R	82,045
Winegarden, Dale—C	7,119
Miscellaneous	1,159

4th Congressional District

	Total
Boone, Jacob—L	3,190
DeFazio, Peter A.—D*	228,611
Feldkamp, Jim—R	140,882
Marsh, Michael Paul—C	1,799
Miscellaneous	427

5th Congressional District

	Total
Bitz, Joseph H.—C	2,971
Defoe, Jerry—L	6,463
Hooley, Darlene—D*	184,833
Zupancic, Jim—R	154,993
Miscellaneous	374

Secretary of State

	Total
Bradbury, Bill—D*	1,002,052
Close, Betsy L.—R	690,228
Morley, Richard—L	56,678
Miscellaneous	3,871

State Treasurer

	Total
Caton, Jeff—R	688,551
Edwards, Randall—D*	889,974
Shults, Mitch—L	52,819
Winegarden, Carole D.—C	49,875
Miscellaneous	2,284

Attorney General

	Total
Connolly, Paul—R	690,056
Hake, Richard D.—C	15,740
Myers, Hardy—D*	935,621
Smith Jr., Donald G.—L	64,581
Miscellaneous	2,000

Judge of the Court of Appeals

Nonpartisan

Position 3

	Total
Ortega, Darleen*	1,064,492
Miscellaneous	23,170

Judge of the Circuit Court

Nonpartisan

4th District—Position 15

	Total
Fuchs, Alicia A.*	188,905
Miscellaneous	6,055

4th District—Position 20

Bloch, Eric*	185,781
Miscellaneous	5,746

4th District—Position 25

Dailey, Kathleen*	186,361
Miscellaneous	5,550

5th District—Position 4

Huva, Susie L.	55,493
Van Dyk, Douglas V.*	71,049
Miscellaneous	697

5th District—Position 10

Rastetter, Thomas J.*	94,433
Miscellaneous	1,541

14th District—Position 3

Newman, Michael A.*	26,012
Miscellaneous	576

14th District—Position 4

Baker, Lindi*	26,594
Miscellaneous	587

16th District—Position 3

Ambrosini, George W.	22,415
Garrison, Randy*	25,576
Miscellaneous	116

21st District—Position 3

Connell, David B.*	20,902
Harding, Hal	11,803
Miscellaneous	216

25th District—Position 3

Hansen, Bernt (Al)	11,536
Jones, Carol E.*	21,178
Miscellaneous	175

C = Constitution
D = Democrat
I = Independent
L = Libertarian
P = Pacific Green
R = Republican
S = Socialist

Voter Participation 1974–2004

Primary Election

*Presidential election year

Year	Registered Voters	Voted	Percent
1974	1,248,596	593,172	47.5
1976*	1,310,248	798,986	61.0
1978	1,390,005	603,478	43.4
1980*	1,376,573	780,649	56.7
1982	1,437,693	669,529	46.6
1984*	1,457,067	767,565	52.7
1986	1,458,300	693,821	47.6
1988*	1,366,294	753,112	55.1
1990	1,437,462	660,990	46.0
1992*	1,543,353	758,459	49.1
1994	1,730,562	661,717	38.2
1996*	1,851,499	698,990	37.8
1998	1,906,677	665,340	34.9
2000*	1,808,080	927,351	51.3
2002	1,839,072	858,524	46.6
2004*	1,862,919	864,833	46.4

General Election

Year	Registered Voters	Voted	Percent
1974	1,143,073	792,557	69.3
1976*	1,420,146	1,048,561	73.8
1978	1,482,339	937,423	63.2
1980*	1,569,222	1,209,691	77.1
1982	1,516,589	1,063,913	70.2
1984*	1,608,693	1,265,824	78.7
1986	1,502,244	1,088,140	72.4
1988*	1,528,478	1,235,199	80.8
1990	1,476,500	1,133,125	76.7
1992*	1,775,416	1,498,959	84.4
1994	1,832,774	1,254,265	68.4
1996*	1,962,155	1,399,180	71.3
1998	1,965,981	1,160,400	59.0
2000*	1,954,006	1,559,215	79.8
2002	1,872,615	1,293,756	69.1
2004*	2,141,243	1,851,593	86.5

Voter Registration by County—November 2, 2004

County	Democrat	Republican	Non-affiliated*	Other	Total
Baker	3,279	5,061	2,061	165	10,566
Benton	20,368	17,244	12,903	1,269	51,784
Clackamas	84,625	88,017	49,675	7,186	229,503
Clatsop	9,413	7,072	5,211	819	22,515
Columbia	12,428	8,964	6,161	951	28,504
Coos	15,922	14,208	7,953	1,484	39,567
Crook	3,744	5,324	2,208	389	11,665
Curry	5,005	6,287	2,637	538	14,467
Deschutes	27,564	36,194	19,630	2,746	86,134
Douglas	22,085	30,267	12,890	2,311	67,553
Gilliam	439	571	257	28	1,295
Grant	1,383	2,394	878	115	4,770
Harney	1,174	2,258	706	29	4,167
Hood River	4,480	3,720	3,086	299	11,585
Jackson	41,498	51,614	26,474	3,713	123,299
Jefferson	3,356	4,171	1,918	299	9,744

County	Democrat	Republican	Non-affiliated*	Other	Total
Josephine	14,990	23,008	10,178	2,234	50,410
Klamath	10,713	18,252	6,961	914	36,840
Lake	1,264	2,569	614	122	4,569
Lane	87,504	64,113	46,229	8,548	206,394
Lincoln	12,005	8,832	7,021	617	28,475
Linn	20,716	24,358	12,136	1,647	58,857
Malheur	3,363	6,787	2,239	215	12,604
Marion	51,893	59,782	29,708	4,283	145,666
Morrow	1,720	1,991	1,176	145	5,032
Multnomah	212,723	94,251	20,151	103,568	430,693
Polk	14,138	18,017	9,428	730	42,313
Sherman	430	583	225	20	1,258
Tillamook	6,774	5,693	3,467	467	16,401
Umatilla	10,468	14,322	7,064	987	32,841
Union	5,250	7,229	3,240	488	16,207
Wallowa	1,528	2,593	794	81	4,996
Wasco	5,594	5,101	3,046	440	14,181
Washington	95,578	100,402	65,448	6,662	268,090
Wheeler	342	460	194	37	1,033
Yamhill	15,437	20,006	10,299	1,523	47,265
Totals	829,193	761,715	394,226	156,069	2,141,243

*A Non-affiliated voter is one who has chosen not to be a member of any political party and has indicated this on his/her voter registration card. Some counties refer to non-affiliated voters (NAV) as "Independents" or "IND."

OREGON ELECTION HISTORY

Voter Registration for General Elections 1950–2004

Year	Democrat	Republican	Other	Total
1950	378,357	361,158	11,755	751,270
1952	416,589	421,681	13,246	851,516
1954	402,283	404,694	12,562	819,539
1956	451,179	413,659	13,114	877,952
1958	447,198	395,089	12,759	855,046
1960	480,588	405,195	14,833	900,616
1962	473,561	395,351	14,778	883,690
1964	511,973	402,336	18,152	932,461
1966	518,228	412,586	19,011	949,825
1968	530,074	420,943	20,834	971,851
1970	521,662	410,693	23,104	955,459
1972	673,710	473,907	50,059	1,197,676
1974	652,414	439,667	50,992	1,143,073
1976	794,218	497,297	128,631	1,420,146
1978	808,182	511,621	163,536	1,482,339
1980	784,129	564,771	220,322	1,569,222
1982	751,100	551,718	213,771	1,516,589
1984	792,208	594,387	222,098	1,608,693
1986	728,177	587,154	186,913	1,502,244
1988	737,489	590,648	200,341	1,528,478
1990	692,100	570,933	213,467	1,476,500
1992	792,551	642,206	340,659	1,775,416
1994	786,990	665,956	379,828	1,832,774
1996	805,286	714,548	442,321	1,962,155
1998	791,970	704,593	469,418	1,965,981
2000	769,195	699,179	485,632	1,954,006
2002	729,460	680,444	462,711	1,872,615
2004	829,193	761,715	550,335	2,141,243

Votes Cast in Oregon for U.S. President 1860–2004

Key: *Elected; **Received highest vote in Oregon but lost election nationwide.

Year	Candidate	Party	Votes
1860	John Bell	Constitutional Union	212
	John C. Breckenridge	Democrat	5,074
	Stephen Douglas	Douglas Democrat	4,131
	Abraham Lincoln*	Republican	5,344
1864	Abraham Lincoln*	Republican	9,888
	George McClellan	Democrat	8,457
1868	U.S. Grant*	Republican	10,961
	Horatio Seymour**	Democrat	11,125
1872	U.S. Grant*	Republican	11,818
	Horace Greeley	Democrat-Liberal Republicans	7,742
	Charles O'Connor	National Labor Reformers	587
1876	Peter Cooper	Greenback	510
	Rutherford B. Hayes*	Republican	15,214
	Samuel Tilden	Democrat	14,157
1880	James A. Garfield*	Republican	20,619
	Winfield Hancock	Democrat	19,955
	James B. Weaver	Greenback Labor	249
1884	James G. Blaine**	Republican	26,860
	General B.F. Butler	Greenback Labor (Workingman)	726
	Grover Cleveland*	Democrat	24,604
	John P. St. John	Prohibition	492
1888	Grover Cleveland	Democrat	26,522
	Robert H. Cowdrey	United Labor	363
	Clinton B. Fisk	Prohibition	1,677
	Benjamin Harrison*	Republican	33,291
1892	John Bidwell	Prohibition	2,281
	Grover Cleveland*	Democrat	14,243
	Benjamin Harrison**	Republican	35,002
	James B. Weaver1	Populist	26,965
1896	William J. Bryan	Democrats, People's Party and Silver Republicans	46,739
	Joshua Levering	Prohibition	919
	William McKinley*	Republican	48,779
	John M. Palmer	National (Gold) Democrats	977
1900	Wharton Barker	Regular People's	275
	William J. Bryan	Democrat People's	33,385
	Eugene V. Debs	Social-Democrats	1,494
	William McKinley*	Republican	46,526
	John G. Woolley	Prohibition	2,536
1904	Eugene V. Debs	Socialist	7,619
	Alton Parker	Democrat	17,327
	Theodore Roosevelt*	Republican	60,455
	Silas C. Swallow	Prohibition	3,806
	Thomas E. Watson	People's	753
1908	William J. Bryan	Democrat	38,049
	Eugene W. Chafin	Prohibition	2,682
	Eugene V. Debs	Socialist	7,339
	Thomas L. Hisgen	Independence	289
	William H. Taft*	Republican	62,530
1912	Eugene W. Chafin	Prohibition	4,360
	Eugene V. Debs	Socialist	13,343
	Theodore Roosevelt	Progressive	37,600
	William H. Taft	Republican	34,673
	Woodrow Wilson*	Democrat	47,064
1916	Allan L. Benson	Socialist	9,711
	J. Frank Hanley	Prohibition	4,729
	Charles Evans Hughes**	Republican	126,813
	John M. Parker2	Progressive	310

Year	Candidate	Party	Votes
	Woodrow Wilson*	Democrat	120,087
1920	James M. Cox	Democrat	80,019
	William W. Cox	Industrial Labor	1,515
	Eugene V. Debs	Socialist	9,801
	Warren G. Harding*	Republican	143,592
	Aaron S. Watkins	Prohibition	3,595
1924	Calvin Coolidge*	Republican	142,579
	John W. Davis	Democrat	67,589
	Frank T. Johns	Socialist Labor	917
	Robert M. LaFollette	Independent	68,403
1928	William Z. Foster	Independent	1,094
	Herbert Hoover*	Republican	205,341
	Verne L. Reynolds	Socialist Labor	1,564
	Alfred E. Smith	Democrat	109,223
	Norman Thomas	Socialist Principles-Independent	2,720
1932	William Z. Foster	Communist	1,681
	Herbert Hoover	Republican	136,019
	Verne L. Reynolds	Socialist Labor	1,730
	Franklin D. Roosevelt*	Democrat	213,871
	Norman Thomas	Socialist	15,450
1936	John W. Aiken	Socialist Labor	500
	Alfred M. Landon	Republican	122,706
	William Lemke	Independent	21,831
	Franklin D. Roosevelt*	Democrat	266,733
	Norman Thomas	Independent	2,143
1940	John W. Aiken	Socialist Labor	2,487
	Franklin D. Roosevelt*	Democrat	258,415
	Wendell L. Willkie	Republican	219,555
1944	Thomas E. Dewey	Republican	225,365
	Franklin D. Roosevelt*	Democrat	248,635
	Norman Thomas	Independent	3,785
	Claude A. Watson	Independent	2,362
1948	Thomas E. Dewey**	Republican	260,904
	Norman Thomas	Independent	5,051
	Harry S. Truman*	Democrat	243,147
	Henry A. Wallace	Progressive	14,978
1952	Dwight D. Eisenhower*	Republican	420,815
	Vincent Hallinan	Independent	3,665
	Adlai Stevenson	Democrat	270,579
1956	Dwight D. Eisenhower*	Republican	406,393
	Adlai Stevenson	Democrat	329,204
1960	John F. Kennedy*	Democrat	367,402
	Richard M. Nixon**	Republican	408,060
1964	Barry M. Goldwater	Republican	282,779
	Lyndon B. Johnson*	Democrat	501,017
1968	Hubert H. Humphrey	Democrat	358,866
	Richard M. Nixon*	Republican	408,433
	George C. Wallace	Independent	49,683
1972	George S. McGovern	Democrat	392,760
	Richard M. Nixon*	Republican	486,686
	John G. Schmitz	Independent	46,211
1976	Jimmy Carter*	Democrat	490,407
	Gerald Ford**	Republican	492,120
	Eugene J. McCarthy	Independent	40,207
1980	John Anderson	Independent	112,389
	Jimmy Carter	Democrat	456,890
	Ed Clark	Libertarian	25,838
	Barry Commoner	Independent	13,642
	Ronald Reagan*	Republican	571,044
1984	Walter F. Mondale	Democrat	536,479
	Ronald Reagan*	Republican	685,700

Year	Candidate	Party	Votes
1988	George Bush*	Republican	560,126
	Michael S. Dukakis**	Democrat	616,206
	Lenora B. Fulani	Independent	6,487
	Ron Paul	Libertarian	14,811
1992	George Bush	Republican	475,757
	Bill Clinton*	Democrat	621,314
	Lenora Fulani	New Alliance Party	3,030
	Andre Marrou	Libertarian	4,277
	Ross Perot	Independent Initiative Party of Oregon	354,091
1996	Harry Browne	Libertarian	8,903
	Bill Clinton*	Democrat	649,641
	Bob Dole	Republican	538,152
	John Hagelin	Natural Law	2,798
	Mary Cal Hollis	Socialist	1,922
	Ralph Nader	Pacific	49,415
	Ross Perot	Reform	121,221
	Howard Phillips	US Taxpayers	3,379
2000	Harry Browne	Libertarian	7,447
	Patrick J. Buchanan	Independent	7,063
	George W. Bush*	Republican	713,577
	Al Gore**	Democrat	720,342
	John Hagelin	Reform	2,574
	Ralph Nader	Pacific Green	77,357
	Howard Phillips	Constitution	2,189
2004	Michael Badnarik	Libertarian	7,260
	George W. Bush*	Republican	866,831
	David Cobb	Pacific Green	5,315
	John F. Kerry**	Democrat	943,163
	Michael Anthony Peroutka	Constitution	5,257

[1]One Weaver elector was endorsed by the Democrats and elected as a Fusionist, receiving 35,811 votes.
[2]Vice-presidential candidate.

Initiative, Referendum and Recall

In 1902, the Oregon electorate overwhelmingly approved a ballot measure that created the initiative and referendum, a system of direct legislation by the people. In 1904, the electorate enacted the direct primary and, in 1908, the State Constitution was amended to include recall of public officials. These victories were the culmination of efforts by the Direct Legislation League, a group of political activists that progressive leader William S. U'Ren founded in 1898.

The initiative and referendum became known nationally as the "Oregon System," and adoption of these popular legislative tools put Oregon in the vanguard of progressive and enlightened politics, allowing the people to propose new laws or change the State Constitution through a general election ballot measure.

Since 1902, the people have passed 115 of the 330 initiative measures on the ballot and 21 of the 62 referenda on the ballot. During the same period, the legislature has referred 407 measures to the people, of which 233 have passed.

Both houses of the legislature must vote to refer a statute or constitutional amendment for a popular vote. Such referrals cannot be vetoed by the governor.

To place an initiative or referendum on the ballot, supporters must obtain a specified number of signatures from registered voters. The number required is determined by a fixed percentage of the votes cast for all candidates for governor at the general election preceding the filing of the petition. In the 2002 general election, 1,260,497 votes were cast for governor.

- Referendum petitions require four percent, or 50,420 signatures.
- Initiative petitions for statutory enactments require six percent, or 75,630 signatures.
- Initiative petitions for constitutional amendments require eight percent, or 100,840 signatures.

The constitutional amendment passed by the people in 1902 that created the initiative and referendum provided that a fixed percentage of the votes cast for justice of the Supreme Court would determine the number of signatures required to place an initiative or referendum on the ballot. Both a statutory enactment and a constitutional amendment required eight percent of the votes cast, while a referendum required five percent of the votes cast.

In 1954, the people amended the State Constitution to increase to 10 percent the number of signatures required for a constitutional amendment. The current requirements were established by a vote of the people in 1968.

Because measures were not assigned numbers until 1954, measures on the ballot at previous elections are listed in order of appearance on the ballot.

The 1993 legislature amended state law to require ballot measures to be numbered 1–99 before numbering begins again at 1.

The list on the next pages includes legislative referrals, referenda and statewide initiatives.

Key: *Adopted; L-Referred by the legislature; I-Submitted by initiative petition; R-Referendum by petition.

Election Date/Measure Number/Ballot Title	Yes	No
June 2, 1902		
1. Limits Uses Initiative and Referendum—L[1]	*62,024	5,668
June 6, 1904		
1. Office of State Printer—L[1]	*45,334	14,031
2. Direct Primary Nominating Convention Law—I[2]	*56,205	16,354
3. Local Option Liquor Law—I[2]	*43,316	40,198
June 4, 1906		
1. Shall act appropriating money maintaining Insane Asylum, Penitentiary, Deaf-Mute, Blind School, University, Agricultural College, and Normal Schools be approved—R	*43,918	26,758
2. Equal Suffrage Constitutional Amendment—I[1]	36,902	47,075
3. Amendment to local option law giving anti-prohibitionists and prohibitionists equal privileges—I[2]	35,297	45,144
4. Law to abolish tolls on the Mount Hood and Barlow Road and providing for its ownership by the State—I[2]	31,525	44,527
5. Constitutional amendment providing method of amending constitution and applying the referendum to all laws affecting constitutional conventions and amendments—I[1]	*47,661	18,751
6. Constitutional amendment giving cities and towns exclusive power to enact and amend their charters—I[1]	*52,567	19,852
7. Constitutional amendment to allow the state printing, binding, and Printers' compensation to be regulated by law at any time—I[1]	*63,749	9,571
8. Constitutional amendment for the initiative and referendum on local, special, and municipal laws and parts of laws—I[1]	*47,678	16,735
9. Bill for a law prohibiting free passes and discrimination by railroad companies and other public service corporations—I[2]	*57,281	16,779
10. An act requiring sleeping car companies, refrigerator car companies, and oil companies to pay an annual license upon gross earnings—I[2]	*69,635	6,441
11. An act requiring express companies, telegraph companies, and telephone companies to pay an annual license upon gross earnings—I[2]	*70,872	6,360
June 1, 1908		
1. To Increase Compensation of Legislators from $120 to $400 Per Session—L[1]	19,691	68,892
2. Permitting Location of State Institutions at Places Other than the State Capitol—L[1]	*41,975	40,868
3. Reorganization System of Courts and Increasing the Number of Supreme Judges from Three to Five—L[1]	30,243	50,591
4. Changing Date of General Elections from June to November—L[1]	*65,728	18,590
5. Giving Sheriffs Control of County Prisoners—R	*60,443	30,033
6. Requiring Railroads to Give Public Officials Free Passes—R	28,856	59,406
7. Appropriating $100,000 for Building Armories—R	33,507	54,848
8. Increasing Annual Appropriation for University of Oregon from $47,500 to $125,000—R	*44,115	40,535
9. Equal Suffrage—I[1]	36,858	58,670
10. Fishery Law Proposed by Fishwheel Operators—I[2]	*46,582	40,720
11. Giving Cities Control of Liquor Selling, Poolrooms, Theaters, etc., subject to local option law—I[1]	39,442	52,346
12. Modified Form of Single Tax Amendment—I[1]	32,066	60,871
13. Recall Power on Public Officials—I[1]	*58,381	31,002

Election Date/Measure Number/Ballot Title	Yes	No
14. Instructing Legislature to Vote for People Choice for United States Senator—I[2]	*69,668	21,162
15. Authorizing Proportional Representation Law—I[1]	*48,868	34,128
16. Corrupt Practices Act Governing Elections—I[2]	*54,042	31,301
17. Fishery Law Proposed by Gillnet Operators—I[2]	*56,130	30,280
18. Requiring Indictment To Be By Grand Jury—I[1]	*52,214	28,487
19. Creating Hood River County—I[2]	*43,948	26,778

November 8, 1910

	Yes	No
1. Permitting Female Taxpayers to Vote—I[1]	35,270	59,065
2. Establishing Branch Insane Asylum in Eastern Oregon—L[2]	*50,134	41,504
3. Calling Convention to Revise State Constitution—L[2]	23,143	59,974
4. Providing Separate Districts for Election of Each State Senator and Representative—L[1]	24,000	54,252
5. Repealing Requirements That All Taxes Shall Be Equal and Uniform—L[1]	37,619	40,172
6. Permitting Organized Districts to Vote Bonds for Construction of Railroads by Such Districts—L[1]	32,884	46,070
7. Authorizing Collection of State and County Taxes on Separate Classes of Property—L[1]	31,629	41,692
8. Requiring Baker County to Pay $1,000 a Year to Circuit Judge in Addition to His State Salary—R	13,161	71,503
9. Creating Nesmith County From Parts of Lane and Douglas—I[2]	22,866	60,951
10. To Establish a State Normal School at Monmouth—I[2]	*50,191	40,044
11. Creating Otis County From Parts of Harney, Malheur and Grant—I[2]	17,426	62,016
12. Annexing Part of Clackamas County to Multnomah—I[2]	16,250	69,002
13. Creating Williams County From Parts of Lane and Douglas—I[2]	14,508	64,090
14. Permitting People of Each County to Regulate Taxation for County Purposes and Abolishing Poll Taxes—I[1]	*44,171	42,127
15. Giving Cities and Towns Exclusive Power to Regulate Liquor Traffic Within Their Limits—I[1]	*53,321	50,779
16. For Protection of Laborers in Hazardous Employment, Fixing Employers' Liability, etc.—I[2]	*56,258	33,943
17. Creating Orchard County From Part of Umatilla—I[2]	15,664	62,712
18. Creating Clark County From Part of Grant—I[2]	15,613	61,704
19. To Establish State Normal School at Weston—I[2]	40,898	46,201
20. To Annex Part of Washington County to Multnomah—I[2]	14,047	68,221
21. To Establish State Normal School at Ashland—I[2]	38,473	48,655
22. Prohibiting Liquor Traffic—I[1]	43,540	61,221
23. Prohibiting the Sale of Liquors and Regulating Shipments of Same, and Providing for Search for Liquor—I[2]	42,651	63,564
24. Creating Board to Draft Employers' Liability Law for Submission to Legislature—I[2]	32,224	51,719
25. Prohibiting Taking of Fish in Rogue River Except With Hook and Line—I[2]	*49,712	33,397
26. Creating Deschutes County Out of Part of Crook—I[2]	17,592	60,486
27. Bill for General Law Under Which New Counties May Be Created or Boundaries Changed—I[2]	37,129	42,327
28. Permitting Counties to Vote Bonds for Permanent Road Improvement—I[1]	*51,275	32,906
29. Permitting Voters in Direct Primaries to Express Choice for President and Vice President, to Select Delegates to National Convention and Nominate Candidates for Presidential Electors—I[2]	*43,353	41,624
30. Creating Board of People's Inspectors of Government, Providing for Reports of Board in Official State Gazette to be Mailed to All Registered Voters Bi-monthly—I[2]	29,955	52,538
31. Extending Initiative and Referendum, Making Term of Members of Legislature Six Years, Increasing Salaries, Requiring Proportional Representation in Legislature, Election of President of Senate and Speaker of House Outside of Members, etc.—I[1]	37,031	44,366
32. Permitting Three-Fourths Verdict in Civil Cases—I[1]	*44,538	39,399

Election Date/Measure Number/Ballot Title	Yes	No
November 5, 1912		
1. Equal Suffrage Amendment—I[1]	*61,265	57,104
2. Creating Office of Lieutenant Governor—L[1]	50,562	61,644
3. Divorce of Local and State Taxation—L[1]	51,582	56,671
4. Permitting Different Tax Rates on Classes of Property—L[1]	52,045	54,483
5. Repeal of County Tax Option—L[1]	*63,881	47,150
6. Majority Rule on Constitutional Amendments—L[1]	32,934	70,325
7. Double Liability on Bank Stockholders—L[1]	*82,981	21,738
8. Statewide Public Utilities Regulation—R	*65,985	40,956
9. Creating Cascade County—I[2]	26,463	71,239
10. Millage Tax for University and Agricultural College—I[2]	48,701	57,279
11. Majority Rule on Initiated Laws—I[1]	35,721	68,861
12. County Bond and Road Construction Act—Grange Bill—I[2]	49,699	56,713
13. Creating State Highway Department—Grange Bill—I[2]	23,872	83,846
14. Changing Date State Printer Bill Becomes Effective—I[2]	34,793	69,542
15. Creating Office of Hotel Inspector—I[2]	16,910	91,995
16. Eight-hour Day on Public Works—I[2]	*64,508	48,078
17. Blue Sky Law—I[2]	48,765	57,293
18. Relating to Employment of State Prisoners—I[2]	*73,800	37,492
19. Relating to Employment of County and City Prisoners—I[2]	*71,367	37,731
20. State Road Bonding Act—I[2]	30,897	75,590
21. Limiting State Road Indebtedness—I[1]	*59,452	43,447
22. County Bonding Act—I[2]	43,611	60,210
23. Limiting County Road Indebtedness—I[1]	*57,258	43,858
24. Providing Method for Consolidating Cities and Creating New Counties—I[2]	40,199	56,992
25. Income Tax Amendment—I[1]	52,702	52,948
26. Tax Exemption on Household Effects—I[2]	*60,357	51,826
27. Tax Exemption on Moneys and Credits—I[2]	42,491	66,540
28. Revising Inheritance Tax Laws—I[2]	38,609	63,839
29. Freight Rates Act—I[2]	*58,306	45,534
30. County Road Bonding Act—I[1]	38,568	63,481
31. Abolishing Senate; Proxy Voting; U'Rren Constitution—I[1]	31,020	71,183
32. Statewide Single Tax with Graduated Tax Provision—I[1]	31,534	82,015
33. Abolishing Capital Punishment—I[2]	41,951	64,578
34. Prohibits Boycotts and Pickets—I[2]	49,826	60,560
35. Prohibits Use of Public Streets, Parks and Grounds in Cities over 5,000 Without Permit—I[2]	48,987	62,532
36. Appropriation for University of Oregon—R	29,437	78,985
37. Appropriation for University of Oregon—R	27,310	79,376
November 4, 1913 (Special Referendum Election)		
1. State University Building Repair Fund—R	*56,659	40,600
2. University of Oregon New Building Appropriation—R	*53,569	43,014
3. Sterilization Act—R	41,767	53,319
4. County Attorney Act—R	*54,179	38,159
5. Workmen's Compensation Act—R	*67,814	28,608
November 3, 1914		
1. Requiring Voters to be Citizens of the United States—L[1]	*164,879	39,847
2. Creating Office of Lieutenant Governor—L[1]	52,040	143,804
3. Permitting Certain City and County Boundaries to be Made Identical, and Governments Consolidated—L[1]	77,392	103,194
4. Permitting State to Create an Indebtedness Not to Exceed Two Percent of Assessed Valuation for Irrigation and Power Projects and Development of Untilled Lands—L[1]	49,759	135,550
5. Omitting Requirement that "All Taxation Shall Be Equal And Uniform"—L[1]	59,206	116,490
6. Changing Existing Rule of Uniformity and Equality of Taxation—Authorizing Classification of Property for Taxation Purposes—L[1]	52,362	122,704
7. To Establish State Normal School at Ashland—L[2]	84,041	109,643

Election Date/Measure Number/Ballot Title	Yes	No
8. Enabling Incorporated Municipalities to Surrender Charters and To Be Merged in Adjoining City or Town—L[1]	*96,116	77,671
9. To Establish State Normal School at Weston—L[2]	87,450	105,345
10. Providing Compensation for Members of Legislature at Five Dollars Per Day—L[1]	41,087	146,278
11. Universal Constitutional Eight Hour Day Amendment—I[1]	49,360	167,888
12. Eight-hour Day and Room-Ventilation Law for Female Workers—I[2]	88,480	120,296
13. Nonpartisan Judiciary Bill Prohibiting Party Nominations for Judicial Officers—I[2]	74,323	107,263
14. $1500 Tax Exemption Amendment—I[1]	65,495	136,193
15. Public Docks and Water Frontage Amendment—I[1]	67,128	114,564
16. Municipal Wharves and Docks Bill—I[2]	67,110	111,113
17. Prohibition Constitutional Amendment—I[1]	*136,842	100,362
18. Abolishing Death Penalty—I[1]	*100,552	100,395
19. Specific Personal Graduated Extra-tax Amendment of Article IX, Oregon Constitution—I[1]	59,186	124,943
20. Consolidating Corporation and Insurance Departments—I[2]	55,469	120,154
21. Dentistry Bill—I[2]	92,722	110,404
22. County Officers Term Amendment—I[1]	82,841	107,039
23. A Tax Code Commission Bill—I[2]	34,436	143,468
24. Abolishing Desert Land Board and Reorganizing Certain State Offices—I[2]	32,701	143,366
25. Proportional Representation Amendment to Oregon Constitution—I[1]	39,740	137,116
26. State Senate Constitutional Amendment—I[1]	62,376	123,429
27. Department of Industry and Public Works Amendment—I[1]	57,859	126,201
28. Primary Delegate Election Bill—I[2]	25,058	153,638
29. Equal Assessment and Taxation and $300 Exemption Amendment—I[1]	43,280	140,507
November 7, 1916		
1. Single Item Veto Amendment—L[1]	*141,773	53,207
2. Ship Tax Exemption Amendment—L[1]	*119,652	65,410
3. Negro and Mulatto Suffrage Amendment—L[1]	100,027	100,701
4. Full Rental Value Land Tax and Homemakers' Loan Fund Amendment—I[1]	43,390	154,980
5. For Pendleton Normal School and Ratifying Location Certain State Institutions—I[1]	96,829	109,523
6. Anti-compulsory Vaccination Bill—I[2]	99,745	100,119
7. Bill Repealing and Abolishing the Sunday Closing Law—I[2]	*125,836	93,076
8. Permitting Manufacture and Regulating Sale 4 Percent Malt Liquors—I[1]	85,973	140,599
9. Prohibition Amendment Forbidding Importation of Intoxicating Liquors for Beverage Purposes—I[1]	*114,932	109,671
10. Rural Credits Amendment—I[1]	*107,488	83,887
11. State-wide Tax and Indebtedness Limitation Amendment—I[1]	*99,536	84,031
June 4, 1917 (Special Election)		
1. Authorizing Ports to Create Limited Indebtedness to Encourage Water Transportation—L[1]	*67,445	54,864
2. Limiting Number of Bills Introduced and Increasing Pay of Legislators—L[1]	22,276	103,238
3. Declaration Against Implied Repeal of Constitutional Provisions by Amendments Thereto—L[1]	37,187	72,445
4. Uniform Tax Classification Amendment—L[1]	*62,118	53,245
5. Requiring Election City, Town and State Officers at Same Time—L[1]	*83,630	42,296
6. Four Hundred Thousand Dollar Tax Levy for a New Penitentiary—L[2]	46,666	86,165
7. Six Million Dollar State Road Bond Issue and Highway Bill—L[2]	*77,316	63,803
November 5, 1918		
1. Establishing and Maintaining Southern and Eastern Oregon Normal Schools—L[1]	49,935	66,070
2. Establishing Dependent, Delinquent and Defective Children's Home, Appropriating Money Therefor—L[2]	43,441	65,299
3. Prohibiting Seine and Setnet Fishing in Rogue River and Tributaries—R	45,511	50,227

Election Date/Measure Number/Ballot Title	Yes	No
4. Closing the Willamette River to Commercial Fishing South of Oswego—R	*55,555	40,908
5. Delinquent Tax Notice Bill—I[2]	*66,652	41,594
6. Fixing Compensation for Publication of Legal Notice—I[2]	*50,073	41,816
7. Authorizing Increase in Amount of Levy of State Taxes for Year 1919 (submitted by state tax commission under chapter 150, Laws 1917)	41,364	56,974

June 3, 1919 (Special Election)

	Yes	No
1. Six Percent County Indebtedness for Permanent Roads Amendment—L[1]	*49,728	33,561
2. Industrial and Reconstruction Hospital Amendment—L[1]	38,204	40,707
3. State Bond Payment of Irrigation and Drainage District Bond Interest—L[1]	*43,010	35,948
4. Five Million Dollar Reconstruction Bonding Amendment—L[1]	39,130	40,580
5. Lieutenant Governor Constitutional Amendment—L[1]	32,653	46,861
6. The Roosevelt Coast Military Highway Bill—L[2]	*56,966	29,159
7. Reconstruction Bonding Bill—L[2]	37,294	42,792
8. Soldiers', Sailors' and Marines' Educational Financial Aid Bill—L[2]	*49,158	33,513
9. Market Roads Tax Bill—L[2]	*53,191	28,039

May 21, 1920 (Special Election)

	Yes	No
1. Extending Eminent Domain Over Roads and Ways—L[1]	*100,256	35,655
2. Limitation of 4 Percent State Indebtedness for Permanent Roads—L[1]	*93,392	46,084
3. Restoring Capital Punishment—L[1]	*81,756	64,589
4. Crook and Curry Counties Bonding Amendment—L[1]	*72,378	36,699
5. Successor to Governor—L[1]	*78,241	56,946
6. Higher Educational Tax Act—L[2]	*102,722	46,577
7. Soldiers', Sailors' and Marines' Educational Aid Revenue Bill—L[2]	*91,294	50,482
8. State Elementary School Fund Tax—L[2]	*110,263	39,593
9. Blind School Tax Measure—L[2]	*115,337	30,739

November 2, 1920

	Yes	No
1. Compulsory Voting and Registration Amendment—L[1]	61,258	131,603
2. Constitutional Amendment Regulating Legislative Sessions and the Payment of Legislators—L[1]	80,342	85,524
3. Oleomargarine Bills—R	67,101	119,126
4. Single Tax Constitutional Amendment—I[1]	37,283	147,426
5. Fixing Term of Certain County Officers—I[1]	*97,854	80,983
6. Port of Portland Dock Commission Consolidation—I[2]	80,493	84,830
7. Anti-compulsory Vaccination Amendment—I[1]	63,018	127,570
8. Constitutional Amendment Fixing Legal Rate of Interest in Oregon—I[1]	28,976	158,673
9. Roosevelt Bird Refuge—I[2]	78,961	107,383
10. Divided Legislative Session Constitutional Amendment—I[1]	57,791	101,179
11. State Market Commission Act—I[2]	51,605	119,464

June 7, 1921 (Special Election)

	Yes	No
1. Legislative Regulation and Compensation Amendment—L[1]	42,924	72,596
2. World War Veterans' State Aid Fund, Constitutional Amendment—L[1]	*88,219	37,866
3. Emergency Clause Veto Constitutional Amendment—L[1]	*62,621	45,537
4. Hygiene Marriage Examination and License Bill—L[2]	56,858	65,793
5. Women Jurors and Revised Jury Law—L[2]	*59,882	59,265

November 7, 1922

	Yes	No
1. Amendment Permitting Linn County Tax Levy to Pay Outstanding Warrants—L	*89,177	57,049
2. Amendment Permitting Linn and Benton Counties to Pay Outstanding Warrants—L[1]	*86,547	53,844
3. Single Tax Amendment—I[1]	39,231	132,021
4. 1925 Exposition Tax Amendment—I[2]	82,837	95,587
5. Income Tax Amendment—I[2]	54,803	112,197
6. Compulsory Education Bill—I[2]	*115,506	103,685

November 6, 1923 (Special Election)

	Yes	No
1. Income Tax Act—L[2]	*58,647	58,131

November 4, 1924

	Yes	No
1. Voters' Literacy Amendment—L[1]	*184,031	48,645

Election Date/Measure Number/Ballot Title	Yes	No
2. Public Use and Welfare Amendment—L[1]	*134,071	65,133
3. Bonus Amendment—L[1]	*131,199	92,446
4. Oleomargarine Condensed Milk Bill—R	91,597	157,324
5. Naturopath Bill—I[2]	75,159	122,839
6. Workmen's Compulsory Compensation Law for Hazardous Occupations—I[1]	73,270	151,862
7. Income Tax Repeal—I[2]	*123,799	111,055
November 2, 1926		
1. Klamath County Bonding Amendment—L[1]	*81,954	68,128
2. Six Percent Limitation Amendment—L[1]	54,624	99,125
3. Repeal of Free Negro and Mulatto Section of the Constitution—L[1]	*108,332	64,954
4. Amendment Prohibiting Inheritance and Income Taxes—L[1]	59,442	121,973
5. The Seaside Normal School Act—L[2]	47,878	124,811
6. The Eastern Oregon State Normal School Act—L[2]	*101,327	80,084
7. The Recall Amendment—L[1]	*100,324	61,307
8 Curry County Bonding or Tax Levy Amendment—L[1]	*78,823	61,472
9. Amendment Relating to Elections to Fill Vacancies in Public Offices—L[1]	*100,397	54,474
10. Klamath and Clackamas County Bonding Amendment—L[1]	*75,229	61,718
11. The Eastern Oregon Tuberculosis Hospital Act—L[2]	*131,296	48,490
12. Cigarette and Tobacco Tax Bill—R	62,254	123,208
13. Motor Bus and Truck Bill—R	*99,746	78,685
14. Act Appropriating Ten Percent of Self-sustaining Boards' Receipts—R	46,389	97,460
15. Income Tax Bill With Property Tax Offset—I[2]	50,199	122,512
16. Bus and Truck Operating License Bill—I[2]	76,164	94,533
17. Fish Wheel, Trap, Seine and Gillnet Bill—I[2]	*102,119	73,086
18. Income Tax Bill—I[2]	83,991	93,997
19. Oregon Water and Power Board Development Measure—I[1]	35,313	147,092
20. Amendment Fixing Salaries of County Officers of Umatilla County—L[2]	1,988	2,646
21. To Provide Salaries for Certain Officials of Clackamas County—L[2]	2,826	6,199
June 28, 1927 (Special Election)		
1. Repeal of Negro, Chinaman and Mulatto Suffrage Section of Constitution—L[1]	*69,373	41,887
2. Portland School District Tax Levy Amendment—L[1]	46,784	55,817
3. Criminal Information Amendment—L[1]	*64,956	38,774
4. Legislators' Pay Amendment—L[1]	28,380	81,215
5. Voters' Registration Amendment—L[1]	*55,802	49,682
6. State and County Officers, Salary Amendment—L[1]	46,999	61,838
7. City and County Consolidation Amendment—L[1]	41,309	57,613
8. Veterans' Memorial and Armory Amendment—L[1]	25,180	80,476
9. State Tax Limitation Amendment—L[1]	19,393	84,697
10. Income Tax Bill—L[2]	48,745	67,039
11. Property Assessment and Taxation Enforcement Bill—L[2]	31,957	70,871
12. Nestucca Bay Fish Closing Bill—R	*53,684	47,552
November 6, 1928		
1. Five Cent Gasoline Tax Bill—I[1]	71,824	198,798
2. Bill for Reduction of Motor Vehicle License Fees—I[1]	98,248	174,219
3. Income Tax Bill—I[2]	118,696	132,961
4. Limiting Power of Legislature Over Laws Approved by the People—I[1]	108,230	124,200
5. Deschutes River Water and Fish Bill—I[2]	78,317	157,398
6. Rogue River Water and Fish Bill—I[2]	79,028	156,009
7. Umpqua River Water and Fish Bill—I[2]	76,108	154,345
8. McKenzie River Water and Fish Bill—I[2]	77,974	153,418
November 4, 1930		
1. Repeal of State Payment of Irrigation and Drainage District Interest—L[1]	*96,061	74,892
2. State Cabinet Form of Government Constitutional Amendment—L[1]	51,248	135,412
3. Bonus Loan Constitutional Amendment—L[1]	92,602	101,785
4. Motor Vehicle License Tax Constitutional Amendment—L[1]	71,557	115,480
5. Motor Vehicle License Tax Constitutional Amendment—L[1]	63,683	111,441
6. Constitutional Amendment for Filling Vacancies in the Legislature—L[1]	*85,836	76,455
7. Legislators' Compensation Constitutional Amendment—L[1]	70,937	108,070

Election Date/Measure Number/Ballot Title	Yes	No
8. Two Additional Circuit Judges Bill—R	39,770	137,549
9. Income Tax Bill—R	*105,189	95,207
10. Anti-cigarette Constitutional Amendment—I[1]	54,231	156,265
11. Rogue River Fishing Constitutional Amendment—I[1]	96,596	99,490
12. Lieutenant Governor Constitutional Amendment—I[1]	92,707	95,277
13. People's Water and Power Utility Districts Constitutional Amendment—I[1]	*117,776	84,778
November 8, 1932		
1. Taxpayer Voting Qualification Amendment—L[1]	*189,321	124,160
2. Amendment Authorizing Criminal Trials Without Juries by Consent of Accused—L[1]	*191,042	111,872
3. Six Percent Tax Limitation Amendment—L[1]	*149,833	121,852
4. Oleomargarine Tax Bill—R	131,273	200,496
5. Bill Prohibiting Commercial Fishing on the Rogue River—R	127,445	180,527
6. Higher Education Appropriation Bill—R	58,076	237,218
7. Bill to Repeal State Prohibition Law of Oregon—I[2]	*206,619	138,775
8. The Freight Truck and Bus Bill—I[2]	151,790	180,609
9. Bill Moving University, Normal and Law Schools, Establishing Junior Colleges—I[2]	47,275	292,486
10. Tax and Debt Control Constitutional Amendment—I[1]	99,171	162,552
11. Tax Supervising and Conservation Bill—I[2]	117,940	154,206
12. Personal Income Tax Law Amendment—I[2]	144,502	162,468
13. State Water Power and Hydroelectric Constitutional Amendment—I[1]	*168,937	130,494
July 21, 1933 (Special Election)		
1. An Amendment to the Constitution of the United States of America—L[0]	*136,713	72,854
2. Soldiers and Sailors Bonus Limitation Amendment—L[1]	*113,267	75,476
3. County Manager Form of Government Constitutional Amendment—L[1]	66,425	117,148
4. Prosecution by Information and Grand Jury Modification Amendment—L[1]	67,192	110,755
5. Debt and Taxation Limitations for Municipal Corporations Constitutional Amendment—L[1]	82,996	91,671
6. State Power Fund Bonds—L[2]	73,756	106,153
7. Sales Tax Bill—L[2]	45,603	167,512
8. Repeal of Oregon Prohibition Constitutional Amendment—L[1]	*143,044	72,745
9. Oleomargarine Tax Bill—R	66,880	144,542
May 18, 1934 (Special Election)		
1. County Indebtedness and Funding Bond Constitutional Amendment—L[1]	83,424	96,629
2. Criminal Trial Without Jury and Non-unanimous Verdict Constitutional Amendment—L[1]	*117,446	83,430
3. Bill Authorizing a State Tuberculosis Hospital in Multnomah County—L[2]	*104,459	98,815
4. Bill Authorizing a State Insane Hospital in Multnomah County—L[2]	92,575	108,816
5. School Relief Sales Tax Bill—R	64,677	156,182
November 6, 1934		
1. Grange Power Bill—R	124,518	139,283
2. Limitations of Taxes on Taxable Property Constitutional Amendment—I[1]	100,565	161,644
3. Healing Arts Constitutional Amendment—I[1]	70,626	191,836
January 31, 1936 (Special Election)		
1. Bill Changing Primary Elections to September With Other Resulting Changes—L[2]	61,270	155,922
2. Compensation of Members of the Legislature Constitutional Amendment—L[1]	28,661	184,332
3. Sales Tax Bill—L[2]	32,106	187,319
4. Bill Authorizing Student Activity Fees in State Higher Educational Institutions—R	50,971	163,191
November 3, 1936		
1. Bill Amending Old Age Assistance Act of 1935—R	174,293	179,236

Election Date/Measure Number/Ballot Title	Yes	No
2. Amendment Forbidding Prevention or Regulation of Certain Advertising If Truthful—I[1]	100,141	222,897
3. Tax Limitation Constitutional Amendment for School Districts Having 100,000 Population—I[1]	112,546	203,693
4. Noncompulsory Military Training Bill—I[2]	131,917	214,246
5. Amendment Limiting and Reducing Permissible Taxes on Tangible Property—I[1]	79,604	241,042
6. State Power Bill—I[2]	131,489	208,179
7. State Hydroelectric Temporary Administrative Board Constitutional Amendment—I[1]	100,356	208,741
8. State Bank Bill—I[2]	82,869	250,777

November 8, 1938

	Yes	No
1. Governor's 20-day Bill Consideration Amendment—L[1]	*233,384	93,752
2. Amendment Repealing the Double Liability of Stockholders in Banking Corporations—L[1]	133,525	165,797
3. Legislators Compensation Constitutional Amendments—L[1]	149,356	169,131
4. Bill Requiring Marriage License Applicants Medically Examined; Physically and Mentally—L[2]	*277,099	66,484
5. Slot Machines Seizure by Sheriffs and Destruction on Court Order—R	*204,561	126,580
6. Prohibiting Slot Machines, Pin-ball, Dart and Other Similar Games—R	*197,912	129,043
7. Townsend Plan Bill—I[3]	*183,781	149,711
8. Citizens' Retirement Annuity Bill; Levying Transactions Tax to Provide Fund—I[2]	112,172	219,557
9. Bill Regulating Picketing and Boycotting by Labor Groups and Organizations—I[2]	*197,771	148,460
10. Water Purification and Prevention of Pollution Bill—I[2]	*247,685	75,295
11. Bill Regulating Sale of Alcoholic Liquor for Beverage Purposes—I[2]	118,282	222,221
12. Constitutional Amendment Legalizing Certain Lotteries and Other Forms of Gambling—I[1]	141,792	180,329

November 5, 1940

	Yes	No
1. Amendment Removing Office Time Limit of State Secretary and Treasurer—L[1]	163,942	213,797
2. Amendment Making Three Years' Average People's Voted Levies, Tax Base—L[1]	129,699	183,488
3. Amendment Repealing the Double Liability of Stockholders of State Banks—L[1]	157,891	191,290
4. Legislators' Compensation Constitutional Amendment—L[1]	186,830	188,031
5. Bill Changing the Primary Nominating Elections from May to September—R	156,421	221,203
6. Bill to Further Regulate Sale and Use of Alcoholic Liquor—R	158,004	235,128
7. Bill Repealing Present Liquor Law; Authorizing Private Sale, Licensed, Taxed—I[2]	90,681	309,183
8. Amendment Legalizing Certain Gambling and Gaming Devices and Certain Lotteries—I[1]	150,157	258,010
9. Bill to Repeal the Oregon Milk Control Law—I[2]	201,983	213,838

November 3, 1942

	Yes	No
1. Legislators' Compensation Constitutional Amendment—L[1]	*129,318	109,898
2. Rural Credits Loan Fund Repeal Amendment—L[1]	*101,425	88,857
3. Amendment Specifying Exclusive Uses of Gasoline and Motor Vehicle Taxes—L[1]	*125,990	86,332
4. Amendment Authorizing Regulation by Law of Voting Privilege Forfeiture—L[1]	101,508	103,404
5. Cigarette Tax Bill—R	110,643	127,366
6. Bill Restricting and Prohibiting Net Fishing Coastal Streams and Bays—R	97,212	137,177
7. Bill Distributing Surplus Funds to School Districts, Reducing Taxes Therein—I[2]	*136,321	92,623

November 7, 1944

	Yes	No
1. Amendment To Provide Alternative Means for Securing Bank Deposits—L[1]	*228,744	115,745

Election Date/Measure Number/Ballot Title	Yes	No
2. Amendment Authorizing Change to Managerial Form of County Government—L[1]	*175,716	154,504
3. Amendment Authorizing "Oregon War Veterans' Fund," Providing Tax Therefor—L[1]	*190,520	178,581
4. Amendment to Authorize Legislative Regulation of Voting Privilege Forfeiture—L[1]	*183,855	156,219
5. Bill Providing Educational Aid to Certain Veterans World War II—L[2]	*238,350	135,317
6. Bill Imposing Tax on Retail Sales of Tangible Personal Property—L[2]	96,697	269,276
7. Burke Bill; Only State Selling Liquor over 14 Hundredths Alcohol—R	*228,853	180,158
8. Constitutional Amendment Increasing State Tax Fund for Public School Support—I[1]	177,153	186,976
9. Constitutional Amendment Providing Monthly Annuities From a Gross Income Tax—I[1]	180,691	219,981

June 22, 1945 (Special Election)

1. Bill Authorizing Tax Levy for State Building Fund—L[2]	*78,269	49,565
2. Bill Authorizing Cigarette Tax to Support Public Schools—L[2]	60,321	67,542

November 5, 1946

1. Constitutional Amendment Providing for Succession to Office of Governor—L[1]	*221,547	70,322
2. Bill Authorizing Tax for Construction and Equipment of State Armories—L[2]	75,693	219,006
3. Bill Establishing Rural School Districts and School Boards—L[2]	*155,733	134,673
4. Bill Authorizing Chinamen to Hold Real Estate and Mining Claims—L[1]	*161,865	133,111
5. Amendment Permitting Legislative Bills to be Read by Title Only—L[1]	*145,248	113,279
6. Constitutional Amendment Increasing Number of Senators to Thirty-one—L[1]	88,717	185,247
7. Bill Regulating Fishing in Coastal Streams and Inland Waters—R	*196,195	101,398
8. To Create State Old-age and Disability Pension Fund—I[2]	86,374	244,960
9. To Create Basic School Support Fund by Annual Tax Levy—I[2]	*157,904	151,765

October 7, 1947 (Special Election)

1. Bill Taxing Retail Sales for School, Welfare and Governmental Purposes—L[2]	67,514	180,333
2. Cigarette Tax Bill—R	103,794	140,876

November 2, 1948

1. Constitutional Six Percent Tax Limitation Amendment—L[1]	150,032	268,155
2. Constitutional Amendment Authorizing Indebtedness for State Forestation—L[1]	*211,912	209,317
3. Bill Authorizing State Boys' Camp Near Timber, Oregon—L[2]	*227,638	219,196
4. Bill Amending Licensing and Acquisition Provisions of Hydroelectric Commission Act—R	173,004	242,100
5. Constitutional Amendment Fixing Qualifications of Voters in School Elections—I[1]	*284,776	164,025
6. Oregon Old Age Pension Act—I[2]	*313,212	172,531
7. Bill Increasing Personal Income Tax Exemptions—I[2]	*405,842	63,373
8. Oregon Liquor Dispensing Licensing Act—I[2]	210,108	273,621
9. World War II Veterans' Bonus Amendment—I[1]	198,283	265,805
10. Prohibiting Salmon Fishing in Columbia River With Fixed Appliances—I[2]	*273,140	184,834
11. Question of Authorizing Additional State Tax, to be Offset by Income Tax Funds—R	143,856	256,167

November 7, 1950

1. Constitutional Amendment Fixing Legislators' Annual Compensation—L[1]	*243,518	205,361
2. Constitutional Amendment Lending State Tax Credit for Higher Education Buildings—L[1]	*256,895	192,573
3. Constitutional Amendment Augmenting "Oregon War Veterans' Fund"—L[1]	*268,171	183,724
4. Increasing Basic School Support Fund by Annual Tax Levy—L[2]	*234,394	231,856
5. Needy Aged Persons Public Assistance Act—R	*310,143	158,939

Election Date/Measure Number/Ballot Title	Yes	No
6. Providing Uniform Standard Time in Oregon—R	*277,633	195,319
7. World War II Veterans' Compensation Fund—I[1]	*239,553	216,958
8. Constitutional Amendment for Legislative Representation Reapportionment—I[1]	190,992	215,302
9. Making Sale of Promotively Advertised Alcoholic Beverage Unlawful—I[2]	113,524	378,732
November 4, 1952		
1. Amendment Making Superintendent of Public Instruction Appointive—L[1]	282,882	326,199
2. World War Veterans' State Aid Sinking Fund Repeal—L[1]	*454,898	147,128
3. Act Authorizing Domiciliary State Hospital for Aged Mentally Ill—L[2]	*480,479	153,402
4. Amendment Legal Voters of Taxing Unit Establish Tax Base—L[1]	*355,136	210,373
5. Amendment to Augment Oregon War Veterans' Fund—L[1]	*465,605	132,363
6. Amendment Creating Legislative Assembly Emergency Committee—L[1]	*364,539	194,492
7. Amendment Fixing Elective Terms of State Senators and Representatives—L[1]	*483,356	103,357
8. Amendatory Act Title Subject Amendment—L[1]	*315,071	191,087
9. Act Limiting State Property Tax—L[2]	*318,948	272,145
10. Motor Carrier Highway Transportation Tax Act—R	*409,588	230,241
11 School District Reorganization Act—R	295,700	301,974
12. Cigarette Stamp Tax Revenue Act—R	233,226	413,137
13. Establishing United States Standard Time in Oregon—I[2]	*399,981	256,981
14. Constitutional Amendment Prohibiting Lotteries, Bookmaking, Pari-mutuel Betting on Animal Racing—I[1]	230,097	411,884
15. Constitutional Amendment Authorizing Alcoholic Liquor Sale by Individual Glass—I[1]	*369,127	285,446
16. Constitutional Amendment Providing Equitable Taxing Method for Use of Highways—I[1]	135,468	484,730
17. Milk Production and Marketing Act Bill—I[2]	313,629	337,750
18. Constitutional Legislative Senator and Representative Apportionment Enforcement Amendment—I[1]	*357,550	194,292
November 2, 1954		
1. Salaries of State Legislators—L[1]	216,545	296,008
2. Subdividing Counties for Electing State Legislators—L[1]	*268,337	208,077
3. Mental Hospital In or Near Portland—L[2]	*397,625	128,685
4. Constitutional Amendments—How Proposed by People—L[1]	*251,078	230,770
5. State Property Tax—L[1]	208,419	264,569
6. Establishing Daylight Saving Time—I[2]	252,305	300,007
7. Prohibiting Certain Fishing in Coastal Streams—I[2]	232,775	278,805
8. Repealing Milk Control Law—I[2]	*293,745	247,591
November 6, 1956		
1. State Tax Laws—Immediate Effect Authorized—L[1]	175,932	487,550
2. Authorizing State Acceptance of Certain Gifts—L[1]	*498,633	153,033
3. Salaries of Certain State Officers—L[1]	*390,338	263,155
4. Qualifications for County Coroner and Surveyor—L[1]	*455,485	182,550
5. Salaries of State Legislators—L[1]	320,741	338,365
6. Cigarette Tax—R	280,055	414,613
7. Prohibiting Certain Fishing in Coastal Streams—I[2]	*401,882	259,309
November 4, 1958		
1. Fixing State Boundaries—L[1]	*399,396	114,318
2. Increasing Funds for War Veterans' Loans—L[1]	232,246	318,685
3. Salaries of State Legislators—L[1]	236,000	316,437
4. Capital Punishment Bill—L[1]	264,434	276,487
5. Financing Urban Redevelopment Projects—L[1]	221,330	268,716
6. Modifying County Debt Limitation—L[1]	*252,347	224,426
7. Special Grand Jury Bill—L[1]	*357,792	136,745
8. Authorizes Different Use of State Institution—L[1]	*303,282	193,177
9. Temporary Appointment and Assignment of Judges—L[1]	*373,466	125,898
10. State Power Development—L[1]	218,662	291,210
11. County Home Rule Amendment—L[1]	*311,516	157,023

Election Date/Measure Number/Ballot Title	Yes	No
12. Authorizing Discontinuing Certain State Tuberculosis Hospitals—L[1]	*319,790	195,945
13. Persons Eligible to Serve in Legislature—I[1]	*320,751	201,700
May 20, 1960		
1. Salaries of State Legislators—L[1]	250,456	281,542
November 8, 1960		
1. Fixing Commencement of Legislators' Term—L[1]	*579,022	92,187
2. Daylight Saving Time—L[2]	357,499	393,652
3. Financing Urban Redevelopment Projects—L[1]	*335,792	312,187
4. Permitting Prosecution by Information or Indictment—L[1]	306,190	340,197
5. Authorizing Legislature to Propose Revised Constitution—L[1]	*358,367	289,895
6. State Bonds for Higher Education Facilities—L[1]	*467,557	233,759
7. Voter Qualification Amendment—L[1]	*508,108	183,977
8. Authorizing Bonds for State Building Program—L[1]	232,250	433,515
9. Compulsory Retirement for Judges—L[1]	*578,471	123,283
10. Elective Offices: When to Become Vacant—L[1]	*486,019	169,865
11. Financing Improvements in Home Rule Counties—L[1]	*399,210	222,736
12. Continuity of Government in Enemy Attack—L[1]	*578,266	88,995
13. War Veterans' Bonding and Loan Amendment—L[1]	*415,931	266,630
14. Personal Income Tax Bill—R	115,610	570,025
15. Billboard Control Measure—I[2]	261,735	475,290
May 18, 1962		
1. Six Percent Limitation Amendment—L[1]	141,728	262,140
2. Salaries of State Legislators—L[1]	*241,171	178,749
November 6, 1962		
1. Reorganize State Militia—L[1]	*312,680	234,440
2. Forest Rehabilitation Debt Limit Amendment—L[1]	*323,799	199,174
3. Permanent Road Debt Limit Amendment—L[1]	*319,956	200,236
4. Power Development Debt Limit Amendment—L[1]	*298,255	208,755
5. State Courts Creation and Jurisdiction—L[1]	*307,855	193,487
6. Daylight Saving Time—L[2]	*388,154	229,661
7. Constitutional Six Percent Limitation Amendment—L[1]	*270,637	219,509
8. Legislative Apportionment Constitutional Amendment—I[1]	197,322	325,182
9. Repeals School District Reorganization Law—I[2]	206,540	320,917
October 15, 1963 (Special Election)		
1. Personal and Corporation Income Tax Bill—R	103,737	362,845
May 15, 1964		
1. Authorizing Bonds for Education Building Program—L[1]	*327,220	252,372
November 3, 1964		
1. Capital Punishment Bill—L[1]	*455,654	302,105
2. Leasing Property for State Use—L[1]	*477,031	238,241
3. Amending State Workmen's Compensation Law—I[2]	205,182	549,414
4. Prohibiting Commercial Fishing for Salmon, Steelhead—I[2]	221,797	534,731
May 24, 1966		
1. Cigarette Tax Bill—L[2]	*310,743	181,957
2. Superintendent of Public Instruction Constitutional Amendment—L[1]	197,096	267,319
November 8, 1966		
1. Public Transportation System Employes Constitutional Amendment—L[1]	*468,103	123,964
2. State Bonds for Educational Facilities—L[1]	237,282	332,983
May 28, 1968		
1. Common School Fund Constitutional Amendment—L[1]	*372,915	226,191
2. Constitutional Amendment Changing Initiative—Referendum Requirements—L[1]	*321,731	244,750
3. Higher Education and Community College Bonds—L[1]	*353,383	261,014
November 5, 1968		
1. Constitutional Amendment Broadening Veterans Loan Eligibility—L[1]	*651,250	96,065
2. Constitutional Amendment for Removal of Judges—L[1]	*690,989	56,973
3. Empowering Legislature to Extend Ocean Boundaries—L[1]	*588,166	143,768
4. Constitutional Amendment Broadening County Debt Limitation—L[1]	331,617	348,866

Election Date/Measure Number/Ballot Title	Yes	No
5. Government Consolidation City-County Over 300,000—L[1]	*393,789	278,483
6. Bond Issue to Acquire Ocean Beaches—I[1]	315,175	464,140
7. Constitutional Amendment Changing Property Tax Limitation—I[1]	276,451	503,443
June 3, 1969 (Special Election)		
1. Property Tax Relief and Sales Tax—L[1]	65,077	504,274
May 26, 1970		
1. Capital Construction Bonds for State Government—L[1]	190,257	300,126
2. Repeals "White Foreigner" Section of Constitution—L[1]	*326,374	168,464
3. Revised Constitution for Oregon—L[1]	182,074	322,682
4. Pollution Control Bonds—L[1]	*292,234	213,835
5. Lowers Oregon Voting Age to 19—L[1]	202,018	336,527
6. Local School Property Tax Equalization Measure—L[1]	180,602	323,189
November 3, 1970		
1. Constitutional Amendment Concerning Convening of Legislature—L[1]	261,428	340,104
2. Automatic Adoption, Federal Income Tax Amendments—L[1]	*342,138	269,467
3. Constitutional Amendment Concerning County Debt Limitation—L[1]	283,659	294,186
4. Investing Funds Donated to Higher Education—L[1]	*332,188	268,588
5. Veterans' Loan Amendment—L[1]	*481,031	133,564
6. Limits Term of Defeated Incumbents—L[1]	*436,897	158,409
7. Constitutional Amendment Authorizing Education Bonds—I[1]	269,372	318,651
8. Allows Penal Institutions Anywhere in Oregon—L[1]	*352,771	260,100
9. Scenic Waterways Bill—I[2]	*406,315	214,243
10. New Property Tax Bases for Schools—I[1]	223,735	405,437
11. Restricts Governmental Powers Over Rural Property—I[1]	272,765	342,503
January 18, 1972 (Special Election)		
1. Increases Cigarette Tax—R	*245,717	236,937
May 23, 1972		
1. Eliminates Literacy Requirement; Lowers Voting Age—L[1]	327,231	349,746
2. Repeals Requirement for Decennial State Census—L[1]	*420,568	206,436
3. Allows Legislators to Call Special Sessions—L[1]	241,371	391,698
4. Capital Construction Bonds for State Government—L[1]	232,391	364,323
5. Irrigation and Water Development Bonds—L[1]	233,175	374,295
6. Enabling County-City Vehicle Registration Tax—R	120,027	491,551
November 7, 1972		
1. Eliminates Location Requirements for State Institutions—L[1]	*594,080	232,948
2. Qualifications for Sheriff Set By Legislature—L[1]	*572,619	281,720
3. Amends County Purchase and Lease Limitations—L[1]	329,669	462,932
4. Changes State Constitution Provision Regarding Religion—L[1]	336,382	519,196
5. Minimum Jury Size of Six Members—L[1]	*591,191	265,636
6. Broadens Eligibility for Veterans' Loans—L[1]	*736,802	133,139
7. Repeals Governor's Retirement Act—I[2]	*571,959	292,561
8. Changes Succession to Office of Governor—I[1]	*697,297	151,174
9. Prohibits Property Tax for School Operations—I[1]	342,885	558,136
May 1, 1973 (Special Election)		
1. Property Tax Limitation; School Tax Revision—L[2]	253,682	358,219
May 28, 1974		
1. Income, Corporate Tax, School Support Increase—L[2]	136,851	410,733
2. Highway Fund Use for Mass Transit—L[1]	190,899	369,038
3. New School District Tax Base Limitation—L[1]	166,363	371,897
4. Authorizes Bonds for Water Development Fund—L[1]	198,563	328,221
5. Increases Veterans' Loan Bonding Authority—L[1]	*381,559	164,953
6. Permits Legislature to Call Special Session—L[1]	246,525	298,373
November 5, 1974		
1. Liquor Licenses for Public Passenger Carriers—L[1]	353,357	384,521
2. Opens All Legislative Deliberations to Public—L[1]	*546,255	165,778
3. Revises Constitutional Requirements for Grand Juries—L[1]	*437,557	246,902
4. Governor Vacancy Successor Age Requirement Eliminated—L[1]	*381,593	331,756
5. The measure designated as Number 5 by the 1973 Legislature was moved to the May 28, 1974 primary election by the 1974 special		

Elections and Records

Election Date/Measure Number/Ballot Title	Yes	No
session. On the advice of the Attorney General, this measure number was left blank.		
6. Permits Establishing Qualifications for County Assessors—L[1]	*552,737	146,364
7. Tax Base Includes Revenue Sharing Money—L[1]	322,023	329,858
8. Revises School District Election Voting Requirements—L[1]	337,565	378,071
9. Permits State Employes to be Legislators—L[1]	218,846	476,547
10. Revises Oregon Voter Qualification Requirements—L[1]	*362,731	355,506
11. Right to Jury in Civil Cases—L[1]	*480,631	216,853
12. Community Development Fund Bonds—L[1]	277,723	376,747
13. Obscenity and Sexual Conduct Bill—R	*393,743	352,958
14. Public Officials' Financial Ethics and Reporting. This measure was also referred to all 36 counties, with 30 voting yes and 6 voting no; and all cities with governing bodies, with 153 voting yes and 90 voting no.—L[2]	*498,002	177,946
15. Prohibits Purchase or Sale of Steelhead—I[2]	*458,417	274,182
May 25, 1976		
1. Expands Veterans' Home-Farm Loan Eligibility—L[1]	*549,553	158,997
2. Discipline of Judges—L[1]	*639,977	59,774
3. Housing Bonds—L[1]	*315,588	362,414
4. Authorizes Vehicle Tax Mass Transit Use—L[1]	170,331	531,219
November 2, 1976		
1. Validates Inadvertently Superseded Statutory Amendments—L[1]	*607,325	247,843
2. Allows Changing City, County Election Days—L[1]	376,489	536,967
3. Lowers Minimum Age for Legislative Service—L[1]	285,777	679,517
4. Repeals Emergency Succession Provision—L[1]	*507,308	368,646
5. Permits Legislature to Call Special Session—L[1]	*549,126	377,354
6. Allows Charitable, Fraternal, Religious Organizations Bingo—L[1]	*682,252	281,696
7. Partial Public Funding of Election Campaigns—L[2]	263,738	659,327
8. Increases Motor Fuel, Ton-Mile Taxes—R	465,143	505,124
9. Regulates Nuclear Power Plant Construction Approval—I[2]	423,008	584,845
10. Repeals Land Use Planning Coordination Statutes—I[2]	402,608	536,502
11. Prohibits Adding Fluorides to Water Systems—I[2]	419,567	555,981
12. Repeals Intergovernmental Cooperation, Planning District Statutes—I[2]	333,933	525,868
May 17, 1977 (Special Election)		
1. School Operating Levy Measure—L[1]	112,570	252,061
2. Authorizes Additional Veterans' Fund Uses—L[1]	*200,270	158,436
3. Increases Veterans' Loan Bonding Authority—L[1]	*250,783	106,953
November 8, 1977 (Special Election)		
1. Water Development Loan Fund Created—L[1]	*124,484	118,953
2. Development of Nonnuclear Energy Resources—L[1]	105,219	137,693
May 23, 1978		
1. Home Rule County Initiative-Referendum Requirements—L[1]	*306,506	156,623
2. Open Meetings Rules for Legislature—L[1]	*435,338	80,176
3. Housing for Low Income Elderly—L[1]	*291,778	250,810
4. Domestic Water Fund Created—L[1]	148,822	351,843
5. Highway Repair Priority, Gas Tax Increase—L[2]	190,301	365,170
6. Reorganizes Metropolitan Service District, Abolishes CRAG—L[2,4]	*110,600	91,090
November 7, 1978		
1. Appellate Judge Selection, Running on Record—L[1]	358,504	449,132
2. Authorizes Senate Confirmation of Governor's Appointments—L[1]	*468,458	349,604
3. Vehicle and Fee Increase Referendum—R	208,722	673,802
4. Shortens Formation Procedures for People's Utility Districts—I[2]	375,587	471,027
5. Authorizes, Regulates Practice of Denture Technology—I[2]	*704,480	201,463
6. Limitations on Ad Valorem Property Taxes—I[1]	424,029	453,741
7. Prohibits State Expenditures, Programs or Services for Abortion—I[1]	431,577	461,542
8. Requires Death Penalty for Murder under Specified Conditions—I[2]	*573,707	318,610
9. Limitations on Public Utility Rate Base—I[2]	*589,361	267,132
10. Land Use Planning, Zoning Constitutional Amendment—I[1]	334,523	515,138
11. Reduces Property Tax Payable by Homeowner and Renter—L[1]	383,532	467,765

Election Date/Measure Number/Ballot Title	Yes	No
12. Support of Constitutional Amendment (Federal) Require Balance Budget—L[5]	*641,862	134,758
May 20, 1980		
1. Constitutional Amendment Limits Uses of Gasoline and Highway User Taxes—L[1]	*451,695	257,230
2. Amends Liquor by the Drink Constitutional Provision—L[1]	325,030	384,346
3. State Bonds for Small Scale Local Energy Project Loan Fund—L[1]	*394,466	278,125
4. Veterans' Home and Farm Loan Eligibility Changes—L[1]	*574,148	130,452
5. Continues Tax Reduction Program—L[2]	*636,565	64,979
6. Definition of Multifamily Low Income Elderly Housing—L[1]	*536,002	138,675
November 4, 1980		
1. Repeal of Constitutional Provision Requiring Elected Superintendent of Public Instruction—L[1]	291,142	820,892
2. Guarantees Mentally Handicapped Voting Rights, Unless Adjudged Incompetent to Vote—L[1]	*678,573	455,020
3. Dedicates Oil, Natural Gas Taxes to Common School Fund—L[1]	*594,520	500,586
4. Increases Gas Tax from Seven to Nine Cents per Gallon—L[2]	298,421	849,745
5. Forbids Use, Sale of Snare, Leghold Traps for Most Purposes—I[2]	425,890	728,173
6. Constitutional Real Property Tax Limit Preserving 85% Districts' 1977 Revenue—I[1]	416,029	711,617
7. Nuclear Plant Licensing Requires Voter Approval, Waste Disposal Facility Existence—I[2]	*608,412	535,049
8. State Bonds for Fund to Finance Correctional Facilities—L[1]	523,955	551,383
May 18, 1982		
1. Use of State Bond Proceeds to Finance Municipal Water Projects—L[1]	*333,656	267,137
2. Multifamily Housing for Elderly and Disabled Persons—L[1]	*389,820	229,049
3. State Bonds for Fund to Finance Corrections Facilities—L[1]	281,548	333,476
4. Raises Taxes on Commercial Vehicles, Motor Vehicles Fuels for Roads—L[2]	308,574	323,268
5. Governor to Appoint Chief Justice of Oregon Supreme Court—L[2]	159,811	453,415
November 2, 1982		
1. Increases Tax Base When New Property Construction Increases District's Value—L[1]	219,034	768,150
2. Lengthens Governor's Time for Postsession Veto or Approval of Bills—L[1]	385,672	604,864
3. Constitutional Real Property Tax Limit Preserving 85% Districts' 1979 Revenue—I[1]	504,836	515,626
4. Permits Self-Service Dispensing of Motor Vehicle Fuel at Retail—I[2]	440,824	597,970
5. People of Oregon Urge Mutual Freeze on Nuclear Weapons Development—I[3]	*623,089	387,907
6. Ends State's Land Use Planning Powers, Retains Local Planning—I[2]	461,271	565,056
May 15, 1984		
1. State May Borrow and Lend Money for Public Works Projects—L[1]	332,175	365,571
2. Increases Fees for Licensing and Registration of Motor Vehicles—L[2]	234,060	487,457
November 6, 1984		
1. Changes Minimum Requirements for Recall of Public Officers—L[1]	*664,464	470,139
2. Constitutional Real Property Tax Limit—I[1]	599,424	616,252
3. Creates Citizens' Utility Board to Represent Interests of Utility Consumers—I[2]	*637,968	556,826
4. Constitutional Amendment Establishes State Lottery, Commission; Profits for Economic Development—I[1]	*794,441	412,341
5. Statutory Provisions for State Operated Lottery if Constitutionally Authorized—I[2]	*786,933	399,231
6. Exempts Death Sentences from Constitutional Guarantees Against Cruel, Vindictive Punishments—I[1]	*653,009	521,687
7. Requires by Statute Death or Mandatory Imprisonment for Aggravated Murder—I[2]	*893,818	295,988
8. Revises Numerous Criminal Laws Concerning Police Powers, Trials, Evidence, Sentencing—I[2]	552,410	597,964

Election Date/Measure Number/Ballot Title	Yes	No
9. Adds Requirements for Disposing Wastes Containing Naturally Occurring Radioactive Isotopes—I[2]	*655,973	524,214
September 17, 1985 (Special Election)		
1. Amends Constitution. Approves Limited 5% Sales Tax for Local Education—L[1]	189,733	664,365
May 20, 1986		
1. Constitutional Amendment: Bans Income Tax on Social Security Benefits—L[1]	*534,476	118,766
2. Constitutional Amendment: Effect on Merger of Taxing Units on Tax Base—L[1]	*333,277	230,886
3. Constitutional Amendment: Verification of Signatures on Initiative and Referendum Petitions—L[1]	*460,148	132,101
4. Requires Special Election for US Senator Vacancy, Removes Constitutional Provision—L[1]	*343,005	269,305
5. Constitutional Amendment: $96 Million Bonds for State-County Prison Buildings—L[1]	300,674	330,429
November 4, 1986		
1. Deletes Constitutional Requirement that Secretary of State Live in Salem—L[1]	*771,959	265,999
2. Constitutional Amendment Revising Legislative District Reapportionment Procedures After Federal Census—L[1]	*637,410	291,355
3. Constitutional Amendment Allows Charitable, Fraternal, Religious Organizations to Conduct Raffles—L[1]	*736,739	302,957
4. Replaces Public Utility Commissioner with Three Member Public Utility Commission—L[2]	*724,577	297,973
5. Legalizes Private Possession and Growing of Marijuana for Personal Use—I[2]	279,479	781,922
6. Constitutional Amendment Prohibits State Funding Abortions. Exception: Prevent Mother's Death—I[1]	477,920	580,163
7. Constitutional 5% Sales Tax, Funds Schools, Reduces Property Tax—I[1]	234,804	816,369
8. Prohibits Mandatory Local Measured Telephone Service Except Mobile Phone Service—I[2]	*802,099	201,918
9. Amends Constitution. Limits Property Tax Rates and Assessed Value Increases—I[1]	449,548	584,396
10. Revises Many Criminal Laws Concerning Victims' Rights, Evidence, Sentencing, Parole—I[2]	*774,766	251,509
11. Homeowner's, Renter's Property Tax Relief Program; Sales Tax Limitation Measure—I[1]	381,727	639,034
12. State Income Tax Changes, Increased Revenue to Property Tax Relief—I[2]	299,551	720,034
13. Constitutional Amendment: Twenty Day Pre-election Voter Registration Cutoff—I[1]	*693,460	343,450
14. Prohibits Nuclear Power Plant Operation Until Permanent Waste Site Licensed—I[2]	375,241	674,641
15. Supersedes "Radioactive Waste" Definition; Changes Energy Facility Payment Procedure—I[2]	424,099	558,741
16. Phases Out Nuclear Weapons Manufactured With Tax Credits, Civil Penalty—I[2]	400,119	590,971
May 19, 1987 (Special Election)		
1. State Role In Selection of High-Level Nuclear Waste Repository Site—L[2]	*299,581	100,854
2. Continues Existing Levies To Prevent School Closures: Tax Base Elections—L[1]	*223,417	178,839
May 17, 1988		
1. Authorizes Water Development Fund Loans for Fish Protection, Watershed Restoration—L[1]	*485,629	191,008
2. Protective Headgear for Motorcycle Operators and Passengers and Moped Riders—L[2]	*486,401	224,655

Election Date/Measure Number/Ballot Title	Yes	No
November 8, 1988		
1. Extends Governor's Veto Deadline After Legislature Adjourns; Requires Prior Announcement—L[1]	*615,012	520,939
2. Common School Fund Investments; Using Income for State Lands Management—L[1]	*621,894	510,694
3. Requires the Use of Safety Belts—L[2]	528,324	684,747
4. Requires Full Sentences Without Parole, Probation for Certain Repeat Felonies—I[2]	*947,805	252,985
5. Finances Intercollegiate Athletic Fund by Increasing Malt Beverage, Cigarette Taxes—I[2]	449,797	759,360
6. Indoor Clean Air Law Revisions Banning Public Smoking—I[2]	430,147	737,779
7. Oregon Scenic Waterway System—I[2]	*663,604	516,998
8. Revokes Ban on Sexual Orientation Discrimination in State Executive Branch—I[2]	*626,751	561,355
May 16, 1989 (Special Election)		
1. Establishes New Tax Base Limits on Schools—L[1]	183,818	263,283
June 27, 1989 (Special Election)		
1. Removes Constitutional Limitation on Use of Property Forfeited To State—L[1]	*340,506	141,649
2. Prohibits Selling/Exporting Timber from State Lands Unless Oregon Processed—L[1]	*446,151	48,558
May 15, 1990		
1. Permits Using Local Vehicle Taxes for Transit if Voters Approve—L[1]	294,099	324,458
2. Amends Constitution; Allows Pollution Control Bond Use for Related Activities—L[1]	*352,922	248,123
3. Amends State Constitution; Requires Annual Legislative Sessions of Limited Duration—L[1]	294,664	299,831
4. Amends Laws on Organization of International Port of Coos Bay—L[2]	4,234	4,745
5A. Advisory Vote: Changing the School Finance System—L[5]	*462,090	140,747
5B. Advisory Vote: Income Tax Increase Reducing Homeowner School Property Taxes—L[5]	177,964	408,842
5C. Advisory Vote: Income Tax Increase Eliminating Homeowner School Property Taxes—L[5]	128,642	449,725
5D. Advisory Vote: Sales Tax Reducing School Property Taxes—L[5]	202,367	385,820
5E. Advisory Vote: Sales Tax Eliminating School Property Taxes—L[5]	222,611	374,466
November 6, 1990		
1. Grants Metropolitan Service District Electors Right to Home Rule—L[1]	*510,947	491,170
2. Constitutional Amendment Allows Merged School Districts to Combine Tax Bases—L[1]	*680,463	354,288
3. Repeals Tax Exemption, Grants Additional Benefit Payments for PERS Retirees—R	406,372	617,586
4. Prohibits Trojan Operation Until Nuclear Waste, Cost, Earthquake Standards Met—I[2]	446,795	660,992
5. State Constitutional Limit on Property Taxes for Schools, Government Operations—I[1]	*574,833	522,022
6. Product Packaging Must Meet Recycling Standards or Receive Hardship Waiver—I[2]	467,418	636,804
7. Six-County Work in Lieu of Welfare Benefits Pilot Program—I[2]	*624,744	452,853
8. Amends Oregon Constitution to Prohibit Abortion With Three Exceptions—I[1]	355,963	747,599
9. Requires the Use of Safety Belts—I[2]	*598,460	512,872
10. Doctor Must Give Parent Notice Before Minor's Abortion—I[2]	530,851	577,806
11. School Choice System, Tax Credit for Education Outside Public Schools—I[1]	351,977	741,863
May 19, 1992		
1. Amends Constitution: Future Fuel Taxes May Go to Police—L[1]	244,173	451,715
November 3, 1992		
1. Bonds May be Issued for State Parks—L[1]	653,062	786,017
2. Future Fuel Taxes May Go to Parks—L[1]	399,259	1,039,322

Elections and Records

Election Date/Measure Number/Ballot Title	Yes	No
3. Limits Terms for Legislature, Statewide Offices, Congressional Offices—I[1]	*1,003,706	439,694
4. Bans Operation of Triple Truck-Trailer Combinations on Oregon Highways—I[2]	567,467	896,778
5. Closes Trojan Until Nuclear Waste, Cost, Earthquake, Health Conditions Met—I[2]	585,051	874,636
6. Bans Trojan Power Operation Unless Earthquake, Waste Storage Conditions Met—I[2]	619,329	830,850
7. Raises Tax Limit on Certain Property; Residential Renters' Tax Relief—I[1]	362,621	1,077,206
8. Restricts Lower Columbia Fish Harvests to Most Selective Means Available—I[2]	576,633	828,096
9. Government Cannot Facilitate, Must Discourage Homosexuality, Other "Behaviors"—I[1]	638,527	828,290
June 29, 1993 (Special Election)		
1. Allows Voter Approval of Urban Renewal Bond Repayment Outside Limit—L[1]	180,070	482,714
November 9, 1993 (Special Election)		
1. Should We Pass A 5% Sales Tax for Public Schools with these Restrictions?—L[1]	240,991	721,930
May 17, 1994[6]		
2. Allows New Motor Vehicle Fuel Revenues for Dedicated Purposes—L[1]	158,028	446,665
November 8, 1994[6]		
3. Amends Constitution: Changes Deadline for Filling Vacancies at General Election—L[1]	*776,197	382,126
4. Amends Constitution: Creates Vacancy if State Legislator Convicted of Felony—L[1]	*1,055,111	145,499
5. Amends Constitution: Bars New or Increased Taxes without Voter Approval—I[1]	543,302	671,025
6. Amends Constitution: Candidates May Use Only Contributions from District Residents—I[1]	*628,180	555,019
7. Amends Constitution: Guarantees Equal Protection: Lists Prohibited Grounds of Discrimination—I[1]	512,980	671,021
8. Amends Constitution: Public Employees Pay Part of Salary for Pension—I[1]	*611,760	610,776
9. Adopts Contribution and Spending Limits, Other Campaign Finance Law Changes—I[2]	*851,014	324,224
10. Amends Constitution: Legislature Cannot Reduce Voter-Approved Sentence Without 2/3 Vote—I[1]	*763,507	415,678
11. Mandatory Sentences for Listed Felonies; Covers Persons 15 and Up—I[2]	*788,695	412,816
12 Repeals Prevailing Rate Wage Requirement for Workers on Public Works—I[2]	450,553	731,146
13. Amends Constitution: Governments Cannot Approve, Create Classifications Based on, Homosexuality—I[1]	592,746	630,628
14. Amends Chemical Process Mining Laws: Adds Requirements, Prohibitions, Standards, Fees—I[1]	500,005	679,936
15. Amends Constitution: State Must Maintain Funding for Schools, Community Colleges—I[1]	438,018	760,853
16. Allows Terminally Ill Adults to Obtain Prescription for Lethal Drugs—I[2]	*627,980	596,018
17. Amends Constitution: Requires State Prison Inmates to Work Full Time—I[1]	*859,896	350,541
18. Bans Hunting Bears with Bait, Hunting Bears, Cougars with Dogs—I[2]	*629,527	586,026
19. Amends Constitution: No Free Speech Protection for Obscenity, Child Pornography—I[1]	549,754	652,139
20. Amends Constitution: "Equal Tax" on Trade Replaces Current Taxes—I[1]	284,195	898,416
May 16, 1995 (Special Election)		
21. Dedication of Lottery Funds to Education—L[1]	*671,027	99,728
22. Inhabitancy in State Legislative Districts—L[1]	*709,931	45,311

Election Date/Measure Number/Ballot Title	Yes	No
May 21, 1996		
23. Amends Constitution: Increases Minimum Value in Controversy Required to Obtain Jury Trial—L[1]	*466,580	177,218
24. Amends Constitution: Initiative Petition Signatures Must Be Collected From Each Congressional District—L[1]	279,399	360,592
25. Amends Constitution: Requires 3/5 Majority in Legislature to Pass Revenue-Raising Bills—L[1]	*349,918	289,930
November 5, 1996		
26. Amends Constitution: Changes the Principles that Govern Laws for Punishment of Crime—L[1]	*878,677	440,283
27. Amends Constitution: Grants Legislature New Power Over Both New, Existing Administrative Rules—L[1]	349,050	938,819
28. Amends Constitution: Repeals Certain Residency Requirements for State Veterans' Loans—L[1]	*708,341	593,136
29. Amends Constitution: Governor's Appointees Must Vacate Office If Successor Not Timely Confirmed—L[1]	335,057	958,947
30. Amends Constitution: State Must Pay Local Governments Costs of State-Mandated Programs—L[1]	*731,127	566,168
31. Amends Constitution: Obscenity May Receive No Greater Protection Than Under Federal Constitution—L[1]	630,980	706,974
32. Authorizes Bonds for Portland Region Light Rail, Transportation Projects Elsewhere—R[2]	622,764	704,970
33. Amends Constitution: Limits Legislative Change to Statutes Passed by Voters—I[1]	638,824	652,811
34. Wildlife Management Exclusive to Commission; Repeals 1994 Bear/Cougar Initiative—I[2]	570,803	762,979
35. Restricts Bases for Providers to Receive Pay for Health Care—I[2]	441,108	807,987
36. Increases Minimum Hourly Wage to $6.50 Over Three Years—I[2]	*769,725	584,303
37. Broadens Types of Beverage Containers Requiring Deposit and Refund Value—I[2]	540,645	818,336
38. Prohibits Livestock in Certain Polluted Waters or on Adjacent Lands—I[2]	479,921	852,661
39. Amends Constitution: Government, Private Entities Cannot Discriminate Among Health Care Provider Categories—I[1]	569,037	726,824
40. Amends Constitution: Gives Crime Victims Rights, Expands Admissible Evidence, Limits Pretrial Release—I[1]	*778,574	544,301
41. Amends Constitution: States How Public Employee Earnings Must Be Expressed—I[1]	446,115	838,088
42. Amends Constitution: Requires Testing of Public School Students; Public Report—I[1]	460,553	857,878
43. Amends Collective Bargaining Law for Public Safety Employees—I[2]	547,131	707,586
44. Increases, Adds Cigarette and Tobacco Taxes; Changes Tax Revenue Distribution—I[2]	*759,048	598,543
45. Amends Constitution: Raises Public Employees' Normal Retirement Age; Reduces Benefits—I[1]	458,238	866,461
46. Amends Constitution: Counts Non-Voters As "No" Votes on Tax Measures—I[1]	158,555	1,180,148
47. Amends Constitution: Reduces and Limits Property Taxes; Limits Local Revenues, Replacement Fees—I[1]	*704,554	642,613
48. Amends Constitution: Instructs State, Federal Legislators to Vote for Congressional Term Limits—I[1,3]	624,771	671,095
May 20, 1997 (Special Election)		
49. Amends Constitution: Restricts Inmate Lawsuits; Allows Interstate Shipment of Prison Made Products—L[1]	*699,813	70,940
50. Amends Constitution: Limits Assessed Value of Property for Tax Purposes; Limits Property Tax Rates—L[1]	*429,943	341,781
November 4, 1997 (Special Election)		
51. Repeals Law Allowing Terminally Ill Adults To Obtain Lethal Prescription—L[2]	445,830	666,275
52. Authorizes State Lottery Bond Program To Finance Public School Projects—L[2]	*805,742	293,425

Elections and Records

Elections and Records (side margin)

Election Date/Measure Number/Ballot Title	Yes	No
May 19, 1998		
53. Amends Constitution: Eliminates Voter Turnout Requirement For Passing Certain Property Tax Measures—L¹	303,539	319,871
November 3, 1998		
54. Amends Constitution: Authorizes State To Guarantee Bonded Indebtedness Of Certain Education Districts—L¹	*569,982	474,727
55. Amends Constitution: Permits State To Guarantee Earnings On Prepaid Tuition Trust Fund—L¹	456,464	579,251
56. Expands Notice To Landowners Regarding Changes To Land Use Laws—L²	*874,547	212,737
57. Makes Possession Of Limited Amount Of Marijuana Class C Misdemeanor—R²	371,967	736,968
58. Requires Issuing Copy Of Original Oregon Birth Certificate to Adoptees—I²	*621,832	462,084
59. Amends Constitution: Prohibits Using Public Resources To Collect Money For Political Purposes—I¹	539,757	561,952
60. Requires Vote By Mail In Biennial Primary, General Elections—I²	*757,204	334,021
61. Vote Not Tallied By Court Order		
62. Amends Constitution: Requires Campaign Finance Disclosures; Regulates Signature Gathering; Guarantees Contribution Methods—I¹	*721,448	347,112
63. Amends Constitution: Measures Proposing Supermajority Voting Requirements Require Same Supermajority For Passage—I¹	*566,064	457,762
64. Prohibits Many Present Timber Harvest Practices, Imposes More Restrictive Regulations—I²	215,491	897,535
65. Amends Constitution: Creates Process For Requiring Legislature To Review Administrative Rules—I¹	483,811	533,948
66. Amends Constitution: Dedicates Some Lottery Funding To Parks, Beaches; Habitat, Watershed Protection—I¹	*742,038	362,247
67. Allows Medical Use Of Marijuana Within Limits; Establishes Permit System—I²	*611,190	508,263
November 2, 1999 (Special Election)		
68. Amends Constitution: Allows Protecting Business, Certain Government Programs From Prison Work Programs—L¹	*406,526	289,407
69. Amends Constitution: Grants Victims Constitutional Rights In Criminal Prosecutions, Juvenile Court Delinquency Proceedings—L¹	*406,393	292,419
70. Amends Constitution: Gives Public, Through Prosecutor, Right To Demand Jury Trial In Criminal Cases—L¹	289,783	407,429
71. Amends Constitution: Limits Pretrial Release Of Accused Person To Protect Victims, Public—L¹	*404,404	292,696
72. Amends Constitution: Allows Murder Conviction By 11 To 1 Jury Verdict—L¹	316,351	382,685
73. Amends Constitution: Limits Immunity From Criminal Prosecution Of Person Ordered To Testify About His Or Her Conduct—L¹	320,160	369,843
74. Amends Constitution: Requires Terms Of Imprisonment Announced In Court Be Fully Served, With Exceptions—L¹	*368,899	325,078
75. Amends Constitution: Persons Convicted Of Certain Crimes Cannot Serve On Grand Juries, Criminal Trial Juries—L¹	*399,671	292,445
76. Amends Constitution: Requires Light, Heavy Motor Vehicle Classes Proportionately Share Highway Costs—L¹	*372,613	314,351
May 16, 2000		
77. Amends Constitution: Makes Certain Local Taxing Districts' Temporary Property Tax Authority Permanent—L¹	336,253	432,541
78. Amends Constitution: Lengthens Period For Verifying Signatures On Initiative And Referendum Petitions—L¹	*528,129	327,440
79. Amends Constitution: Increases Signatures Required To Place Initiative Amending Constitution On Ballot—L¹	356,912	505,081
80. Amends Constitution: Authorizes Using Fuel Tax, Vehicle Fees For Increasing Highway Policing—L¹	310,640	559,941
81. Amends Constitution: Allows Legislature To Limit Recovery Of Damages In Civil Actions—L¹	219,009	650,348

Election Date/Measure Number/Ballot Title	Yes	No
82. Repeals Truck Weight-Mile Tax; Establishes And Increases Fuel Taxes—R[2]	109,741	767,329
November 7, 2000		
83. Amends Constitution: Authorizes New Standards, Priorities For Veterans' Loans; Expands Qualified Recipients—L[1]	*1,084,870	365,203
84. Amends Constitution: State Must Continue Paying Local Governments For State-Mandated Programs—L[1]	*1,211,384	222,723
85. Amends Constitution: Modifies Population, Minimum Area Requirements For Formation Of New Counties—L[1]	634,307	767,366
86. Amends Constitution: Requires Refunding General Fund Revenues Exceeding State Estimates To Taxpayers—L[1]	*898,793	550,304
87. Amends Constitution: Allows Regulation Of Location Of Sexually Oriented Businesses Through Zoning—L[1]	694,410	771,901
88. Increases Maximum Deductible In Oregon For Federal Income Taxes Paid—L[2]	*739,270	724,097
89. Dedicates Tobacco Settlement Proceeds To Specified Health, Housing, Transportation Programs—L[2]	622,814	828,117
90. Authorizes Rates Giving Utilities Return On Investments In Retired Property—R[2]	158,810	1,208,545
91. Amends Constitution: Makes Federal Income Taxes Fully Deductible On Oregon Tax Returns—I[1]	661,342	814,885
92. Amends Constitution: Prohibits Payroll Deductions For Political Purposes Without Specific Written Authorization—I[1]	656,250	815,338
93. Amends Constitution: Voters Must Approve Most Taxes, Fees; Requires Certain Approval Percentage—I[1]	581,186	865,091
94. Repeals Mandatory Minimum Sentences For Certain Felonies, Requires Resentencing—I[2]	387,068	1,073,275
95. Amends Constitution: Student Learning Determines Teacher Pay; Qualifications, Not Seniority, Determine Retention—I[1]	514,926	962,250
96. Amends Constitution: Prohibits Making Initiative Process Harder, Except Through Initiative; Applies Retroactively—I[1]	527,613	866,588
97. Bans Body-Gripping Animal Traps, Some Poisons; Restricts Fur Commerce—I[2]	606,939	867,219
98. Amends Constitution: Prohibits Using Public Resources For Political Purposes; Limits Payroll Deductions—I[1]	678,024	776,489
99. Amends Constitution: Creates Commission Ensuring Quality Home Care Services For Elderly, Disabled—I[1]	*911,217	539,414
1. Amends Constitution: Legislature Must Fund School Quality Goals Adequately; Report; Establish Grants—I[1]	*940,223	477,461
2. Amends Constitution: Creates Process For Requiring Legislature To Review Administrative Rules—I[1]	605,575	779,190
3. Amends Constitution: Requires Conviction Before Forfeiture; Restricts Proceeds Usage; Requires Reporting, Penalty—I[1]	*952,792	465,081
4. Dedicates Tobacco-Settlement Proceeds; Earnings Fund Low-Income Health Care—I[2]	650,850	789,543
5. Expands Circumstances Requiring Background Checks Before Transfer Of Firearm—I[2]	*921,926	569,996
6. Provides Public Funding To Candidates Who Limit Spending, Private Contributions—I[2]	586,910	838,011
7. The Secretary of State has been enjoined from canvassing the votes for this measure—I[1]		
8. Amends Constitution: Limits State Appropriations To Percentage Of State's Prior Personal Income—I[1]	608,090	789,699
9. Prohibits Public School Instruction Encouraging, Promoting, Sanctioning Homosexual, Bisexual Behaviors—I[2]	702,572	788,691
May 21, 2002		
10. Amends Constitution: Allows Public Universities to Receive Equity in Private Companies as Compensation for Publicly Created Technology—L[1]	*608,640	177,004
11. Amends Constitution: Authorizes Less Expensive General Obligation Bond financing for OHSU Medical Research and other Capital Costs—L[1]	*589,869	190,226

Election Date/Measure Number/Ballot Title	Yes	No
12. Removed from Ballot		
13. Amends Constitution: Authorizes Using Education Fund Principal in Specified Circumstances; Transfers $220 Million to School Fund—L[1]	376,605	411,923

November 5, 2002

14. Amends Constitution: Removes Historical Racial References in Obsolete Sections of Constitution—L[1]	*867,901	352,027
15. Amends Constitution: Authorizes State to Issue General Obligation Bonds for Seismic Rehabilitation of Public Education Buildings—L[1]	*671,640	535,638
16. Amends Constitution: Authorizes State to Issue General Obligation Bonds for Seismic Rehabilitation of Emergency Services Buildings—L[1]	*669,451	530,587
17. Amends Constitution: Reduces Minimum Age Requirement to Serve as State Legislator from 21 Years to 18 Years—L[1]	341,717	910,331
18. Amends Constitution: Allows Certain Tax Districts to Establish Permanent Property Tax Rates and Divide into Tax Zones—L[1]	450,444	704,116

September 17, 2002 (Special Election)

19. Amends Constitution: Authorizes Using Education Stability Fund Principal in Specified Circumstances; Transfers $150 Million to State School Fund; Creates School Capital Matching Subaccount in Stability Fund—L[1]	*496,815	306,440
20. Increases Cigarette Tax; Uses Revenue for Health Plan, Other Programs—L[1]	*522,613	289,119

November 5, 2002

21. Amends Constitution: Revises Procedure for Filling Judicial Vacancies, Electing Judges; Allows Vote for "None of the Above"—I[1]	526,450	668,256
22. Amends Constitution: Requires Supreme Court Judges and Court of Appeals Judges to be Elected by District—I[1]	595,936	610,063
23. Creates Health Care Finance Plan for Medically Necessary Services; Creates Additional Income, Payroll Taxes—I[2]	265,310	969,537
24. Allows Licensed Denturists to Install Partial Dentures; Authorizes Cooperative Dentist-Denturist Business Ventures—I[2]	*907,979	286,492
25. Increases Minimum Wage to $6.90 in 2003; Increases for Inflation in Future Years—I[2]	*645,016	611,658
26. Amends Constitution: Prohibits Payment, Receipt of Payment Based on the Number of Initiative, Referendum Petition Signatures Obtained—I[1]	*921,606	301,415
27. Requires Labeling of Genetically-Engineered Foods Sold or Distributed in or from Oregon—I[2]	371,851	886,806

January 28, 2003 (Special Election)

28. Temporarily Increases Income Tax Rates—L[2]	575,846	676,312

September 16, 2003 (Special Election)

29. Amends Constitution: Authorizes State of Oregon to Incur General Obligation Debt for Savings on Pension Liabilities—L[1]	*360,209	291,778

February 3, 2004 (Special Election)

30. Enacts Temporary Personal Income Tax Surcharge; Increases, Changes Corporate, Other Taxes; Avoids Specific Budget Cuts—R[2]	481,315	691,462

November 2, 2004

31. Amends Constitution: Authorizes Law Permitting Postponement of Election for Particular Public Office When Nominee for Office Dies—L[1]	*1,122,852	588,502
32. Amends Constitution: Deletes Reference to Mobile Homes from Provision Dealing with Taxes and Fees on Motor Vehicles—L[1]	*1,048,090	661,576
33. Amends Medical Marijuana Act: Requires Marijuana Dispensaries for Supplying Patients/Caregivers; Raises Patients' Possession Limit—I[2]	764,015	1,021,814
34. Requires Balancing Timber Production, Resource Conservation/Preservation in Managing State Forests; Specifically Addresses Two Forests—I[2]	659,467	1,060,496
35. Amends Constitution: Limits Noneconomic Damages (Defined) Recoverable for Patient Injuries Caused by Healthcare Provider's Negligence or Recklessness—I[1]	869,054	896,857
36. Amends Constitution: Only Marriage Between One Man and One Woman Is Valid or Legally Recognized as Marriage—I[1]	*1,028,546	787,556
37. Governments Must Pay Owners, or Forgo Enforcement, when Certain Land Use Restrictions Reduce Property Value—I[2]	*1,054,589	685,079

Election Date/Measure Number/Ballot Title	Yes	No
38. Abolishes Saif; State Must Reinsure, Satisfy Saif's Obligations; Dedicates Proceeds, Potential Surplus to Public Purposes—I[2]	670,935	1,037,722

[0]Repeal of federal prohibition amendment.
[1]Constitutional amendment.
[2]Statutory enactment.
[3]Required communication to federal officials on behalf of people of Oregon.
[4]Tri-county measure voted on in Clackamas, Multnomah and Washington Counties.
[5]Advisory vote for legislators' information.

Earliest Authorities in Oregon

Pacific Fur Company*
Fort Astoria

Name	Term of Service	By What Authority/Remarks
McDougall, Duncan	Mar. 22, 1811–Feb. 15, 1812 Aug. 4, 1812–Aug. 20, 1813 Aug. 26, 1813–Oct. 16, 1813	Acting agent and partner; served in absence of Wilson Price Hunt by agreement with partners
Hunt, Wilson Price	Feb. 15, 1812–Aug. 4, 1812 Aug. 20, 1813–Aug. 26, 1813	Agent and partner by Articles of Agreement, June 23, 1810, Article 21

*Sold to John George McTavish and John Stuart, partners of the North West Company, Oct. 16, 1813; sale confirmed by Wilson Price Hunt, agent, March 10, 1814.

North West Company
Headquarters, Columbia District, Fort George (Astoria)

McTavish, John George	Oct. 16, 1813–Dec. 1, 1813	Acting governor and partner
McDonald, John (of Garth)	Dec. 1, 1813–Apr. 4, 1814	Governor and partner, Alexander Henry, trader
McTavish, Donald	Apr. 23, 1814–May 22, 1814	Governor and partner; with Alexander Henry, drowned in the Columbia River
Keith, James	May 22, 1814–June 7, 1816	Acting governor and partner

Chief of the Coast	Term of Service	Chief of the Interior
Keith, James	June 7, 1816–Mar. 21, 1821	McKenzie, Donald

Hudson's Bay Company*
Headquarters, Columbia District, Fort George (Astoria) 1821–1825; Fort Vancouver, 1825–1846

Chief Factor	Term of Service	Junior Chief Factor
McMillan, James	Spring, 1821–Fall, 1821	Cameron, John Dougald
Cameron, John Dougald	Fall, 1821–Spring, 1824	Kennedy, Alexander
Kennedy, Alexander	Spring, 1824–Mar. 18, 1825	McLoughlin, John
McLoughlin, John	Mar. 18, 1825–May 31, 1845	None appointed

*Appointments in 1821 by agreement with North West Company; and 1822–1825 by council of Northern Department, Sir George Simpson, Governor.

Oregon (WALAMET) Mission of the Methodist Episcopal Church
Mission Bottom 1834–1841; Chemeketa (Salem) 1841–1847

Name	Term of Service	Position
Lee, Jason	Oct. 6, 1834–Mar. 26, 1838	Appointed superintendent upon recommendation of the Board of Managers of the Missionary Society
Leslie, David	Mar. 26, 1838–May 27, 1840	Acting superintendent in absence of Lee
Lee, Jason	May 27, 1840–Dec. 25, 1843	Superintendent
Leslie, David	Dec. 25, 1843–June 1, 1844	Acting superintendent in absence of Lee

Elections and Records

Name	Term of Service	Position
Gary, George	June 1, 1844–July 18, 1847	Appointed superintendent; instructed to dissolve the mission properties

Provisional Government Executive Committee

Hill, David; Beers, Alanson; Gale, Joseph	July 5, 1843–May 25, 1844	Elected by meeting of inhabitants of the Oregon Territory
Stewart, P.G.; Russell Osborn; Bailey, W.J.	May 25, 1844–July 14, 1845	By vote of the people

Governors of Oregon

Under Provisional Government

Name/Political Party[1]	Term of Service	By What Authority/Remarks
Abernethy, George	July 14, 1845–Mar. 3, 1849	By people at 1845 general election; reelected 1848

Under Territorial Government

Lane, Joseph—D	Mar. 3, 1849–June 18, 1850	Appointed by President Polk; resigned
Prichette, Kintzing—D	June 18, 1850–Aug. 18, 1850	Acting governor, was secretary
Gaines, John P.—W	Aug. 18, 1850–May 16, 1853	Appointed by President Taylor
Lane, Joseph—D	May 16, 1853–May 19, 1853	Appointed by President Pierce; resigned
Curry, George L.—D	May 19, 1853–Dec. 2, 1853	Acting governor, was secretary
Davis, John W.—D	Dec. 2, 1853–Aug. 1, 1854	Appointed by President Pierce; resigned
Curry, George L.—D	Aug. 1, 1854–Mar. 3, 1859	Acting governor, was secretary; appointed by President Pierce, Nov. 1, 1854

Under State Government

Whiteaker, John—D	Mar. 3, 1859–Sept. 10, 1862	Elected 1858
Gibbs, A.C.—R	Sept. 10, 1862–Sept. 12, 1866	Elected 1862
Woods, George L.—R	Sept. 12, 1866–Sept. 14, 1870	Elected 1866
Grover, LaFayette—D	Sept. 14, 1870–Feb. 1, 1877	Elected 1870; reelected 1874; resigned
Chadwick, Stephen F.—D	Feb. 1, 1877–Sept. 11, 1878	Was secretary of state
Thayer, W.W.—D	Sept. 11, 1878–Sept. 13, 1882	Elected 1878
Moody, Z.F.—R	Sept. 13, 1882–Jan. 12, 1887	Elected 1882
Pennoyer, Sylvester—DP	Jan. 12, 1887–Jan. 14, 1895	Elected 1886; reelected 1890
Lord, William Paine—R	Jan. 14, 1895–Jan. 9, 1899	Elected 1894
Geer, T.T.—R	Jan. 9, 1899–Jan. 14, 1903	Elected 1898
Chamberlain, George E.—D	Jan. 15, 1903–Feb. 28, 1909	Elected 1902; reelected 1906; resigned
Benson, Frank W.—R	Mar. 1, 1909–June 17, 1910	Was secretary of state; resigned
Bowerman, Jay[2]—R	June 17, 1910–Jan. 8, 1911	Was president of Senate
West, Oswald—D	Jan. 11, 1911–Jan. 12, 1915	Elected 1910
Withycombe, James—R	Jan. 12, 1915–Mar. 3, 1919	Elected 1914; reelected 1918; died in office
Olcott, Ben W.—R	Mar. 3, 1919–Jan. 8, 1923	Was secretary of state
Pierce, Walter M.—D	Jan. 8, 1923–Jan. 10, 1927	Elected 1922
Patterson, I.L.—R	Jan. 10, 1927–Dec. 21, 1929	Elected 1926; died in office
Norblad, A.W.[3]—R	Dec. 22, 1929–Jan. 12, 1931	Was president of Senate
Meier, Julius L.—I	Jan. 12, 1931–Jan. 14, 1935	Elected 1930
Martin, Charles H.—D	Jan. 14, 1935–Jan. 9, 1939	Elected 1934
Sprague, Charles A.—R	Jan. 9, 1939–Jan. 11, 1943	Elected 1938
Snell, Earl—R	Jan. 11, 1943–Oct. 28, 1947	Elected 1942; reelected 1946; died in office
Hall, John H.[4]—R	Oct. 30, 1947–Jan. 10, 1949	Was speaker of House
McKay, Douglas—R	Jan. 10, 1949–Dec. 27, 1952	Elected 1948; reelected 1950; resigned

Name/Political Party	Term of Service	By What Authority/Remarks
Patterson, Paul L.—R	Dec. 27, 1952–Jan. 31, 1956	Was president of Senate; elected 1954; died in office
Smith, Elmo—R	Feb. 1, 1956–Jan. 14, 1957	Was president of Senate
Holmes, Robert D.—D	Jan. 14, 1957–Jan. 12, 1959	Elected 1956
Hatfield, Mark O.—R	Jan. 12, 1959–Jan. 9, 1967	Elected 1958; reelected 1962
McCall, Tom—R	Jan. 9, 1967–Jan 13, 1975	Elected 1966; reelected 1970
Straub, Robert W.—D	Jan. 13, 1975–Jan. 8, 1979	Elected 1974
Atiyeh, Victor G.—R	Jan. 8, 1979–Jan. 12, 1987	Elected 1978; reelected 1982
Goldschmidt, Neil—D	Jan. 12, 1987–Jan. 14, 1991	Elected 1986
Roberts, Barbara—D	Jan. 14, 1991–Jan. 9, 1995	Elected 1990
Kitzhaber, John—D	Jan. 9, 1995–Jan. 13, 2003	Elected 1994; reelected 1998
Kulongoski, Ted—D	Jan. 13, 2003–	Elected 2002

[1]D-Democrat; R-Republican; DP-Democrat People's; I-Independent; W-Whig.

[2]Jay Bowerman became governor when Frank Benson, who was serving as both governor and secretary of state, became incapacitated. Benson resigned as governor but continued as secretary of state until his death.

[3]In 1920, the Constitution was changed to allow the president of the Senate to succeed as governor.

[4]A plane crash on October 28, 1947 killed Governor Earl Snell, Secretary of State Robert S. Farrell Jr., President of the Senate Marshall E. Cornett and the pilot, Cliff Hogue. John Hall, speaker of the House and next in line of succession, automatically became governor. Earl Newbry was appointed by John Hall to the position of secretary of state.

Secretaries of State of Oregon

Under Provisional Government

Name/Political Party	Term of Service	By What Authority/Remarks
LeBreton, George W.	Feb. 18, 1841–Mar. 4, 1844	Elected by meeting of inhabitants of the Willamette Valley to office of clerk of courts and public recorder, thus served as first secretary; reelected 1843; died in office
Johnson, Overton	Mar. 4, 1844–May 25, 1844	Appointed clerk and recorder
Long, Dr. John E.	May 25, 1844–June 21, 1846	Elected clerk and recorder by people at first 1844 general election; reelected 1845 general election; reelected 1845 by Legislature; drowned
Prigg, Frederick	June 26, 1846–Sept. 16, 1848	Appointed secretary to succeed Long; elected 1846 by Legislature; resigned
Holderness, Samuel M.	Sept. 19, 1848–Mar. 10, 1849	Appointed to succeed Prigg; elected 1848 by Legislature

Under Territorial Government

Name/Political Party	Term of Service	By What Authority/Remarks
Magruder, Theophilus	Mar. 10, 1849–Apr. 9, 1849	Elected by Legislature
Prichette, Kintzing—D	Apr. 9, 1849–Sept. 18, 1850	Appointed by President Polk
Hamilton, Gen. E.D.—W	Sept. 18, 1850–May 14, 1853	Appointed by President Taylor
Curry, George L.—D	May 14, 1853–Jan. 27, 1855	Appointed by President Pierce
Harding, Benjamin—D	Jan. 27, 1855–Mar. 3, 1859	Appointed by President Pierce

Under State Government

Name/Political Party	Term of Service	By What Authority/Remarks
Heath, Lucien—D	Mar. 3, 1859–Sept. 8, 1862	Elected 1858
May, Samuel E.—R	Sept. 8, 1862–Sept. 10, 1870	Elected 1862; reelected 1866
Chadwick, Stephen F.[1]—D	Sept. 10, 1870–Sept. 2, 1878	Elected 1870; reelected 1874
Earhart, R.P.—R	Sept. 2, 1878–Jan. 10, 1887	Elected 1878; reelected 1882
McBride, George W.—R	Jan. 10, 1887–Jan. 14, 1895	Elected 1886; reelected 1890
Kincaid, Harrison R.—R	Jan. 14, 1895–Jan. 9, 1899	Elected 1894
Dunbar, Frank I.—R	Jan. 9, 1899–Jan. 14, 1907	Elected 1898; reelected 1902

Name/Political Party	Term of Service	By What Authority/Remarks
Benson, Frank W.[2]—R	Jan. 15, 1907–Apr. 14, 1911	Elected 1906; reelected 1910; died in office
Olcott, Ben W.[3]—R	Apr. 17, 1911–May 28, 1920	Appointed by Governor West; elected 1912; reelected 1916; resigned
Kozer, Sam A.—R	May 28, 1920–Sept. 24, 1928	Appointed by Governor Olcott; elected 1920; reelected 1924; resigned
Hoss, Hal E.—R	Sept. 24, 1928–Feb. 6, 1934	Appointed by Governor Patterson; elected 1928; reelected 1932; died in office
Stadelman, P.J.—R	Feb. 9, 1934–Jan. 7, 1935	Appointed by Governor Meier
Snell, Earl—R	Jan. 7, 1935–Jan. 4, 1943	Elected 1934; reelected 1938
Farrell, Robert S. Jr.—R	Jan. 4, 1943–Oct. 28, 1947	Elected 1942; reelected 1946; died in office
Newbry, Earl T.—R	Nov. 3, 1947–Jan. 7, 1957	Appointed by Governor Hall; elected 1948; reelected 1952
Hatfield, Mark—R	Jan. 7, 1957–Jan. 12, 1959	Elected 1956; resigned
Appling, Howell, Jr.—R	Jan. 12, 1959–Jan. 4, 1965	Appointed by Governor Hatfield; elected 1960
McCall, Tom L.—R	Jan. 4, 1965–Jan. 9, 1967	Elected 1964; resigned
Myers, Clay—R	Jan. 9, 1967–Jan. 3, 1977	Appointed by Governor McCall; elected 1968; reelected 1972
Paulus, Norma—R	Jan. 3, 1977–Jan. 7, 1985	Elected 1976; reelected 1980
Roberts, Barbara—D	Jan. 7, 1985–Jan. 14, 1991	Elected 1984, reelected 1988, resigned
Keisling, Phil—D	Jan. 14, 1991–Nov 8, 1999	Appointed by Governor Roberts; elected 1992; reelected 1996, resigned
Bradbury, Bill—D	Nov. 8, 1999–	Appointed by Governor Kitzhaber; elected 2000; reelected 2004

[1]When Stephen Chadwick succeeded L.F. Grover as governor in 1877, he did not resign as secretary of state. He signed documents and proclamations twice—as governor and as secretary of state—until September 1878.

[2]Frank Benson served as both secretary of state and governor; see Footnote 2 under Governors.

[3]When James Withycombe died in office on March 3, 1919, Ben W. Olcott succeeded him as governor. However, Governor Olcott did not resign or appoint a new secretary of state until May 28, 1920.

Treasurers of Oregon

Under Provisional Government

Name/Political Party	Term of Service	By What Authority/Remarks
Gray, W.H.	Mar. 1, 1843–July 5, 1843	Elected by meeting of citizens of the Willamette Valley
Willson, W.H.	July 5, 1843–May 14, 1844	Elected by meeting of the inhabitants of the Willamette settlements
Foster, Phillip	July 2, 1844–July 7, 1845	Elected by people at first 1844 general election
Ermatinger, Francis	July 7, 1845–Mar. 3, 1846	Elected by people at 1845 general election; reelected 1845 by Legislature; resigned
Couch, John H.	Mar. 4, 1846–Sept. 27, 1847	Appointed to succeed Ermatinger; elected by Legislature 1846; resigned
Kilbourn, William K.	Oct. 11, 1847–Sept. 28, 1849	Appointed to succeed Couch; elected by Legislature 1849

Under Territorial Government

Taylor, James	Sept. 28, 1849–Feb. 8, 1851	Elected by Legislature

Name/Political Party	Term of Service	By What Authority/Remarks
Rice, L.A.	Feb. 8, 1851–Sept. 22, 1851	Elected by Legislature; resigned
Buck, William W.	Sept. 27, 1851–Dec. 16, 1851	Appointed to succeed Rice
Boon, John D.—D	Dec. 16, 1851–Mar. 1, 1855	Elected by Legislature
Lane, Nat H.—D	Mar. 1, 1855–Jan. 10, 1856	Elected by Legislature
Boon, John D.—D	Jan. 10, 1856–Mar. 3, 1859	Elected by Legislature

Under State Government

Name/Political Party	Term of Service	By What Authority/Remarks
Boon, John D.—D	Mar. 3, 1859–Sept. 8, 1862	Elected 1858
Cooke, E.N.—R	Sept. 8, 1862–Sept. 12, 1870	Elected 1862; reelected 1866
Fleischner, L.—D	Sept. 12, 1870–Sept. 14, 1874	Elected 1870
Brown, A.H.—D	Sept. 14, 1874–Sept. 9, 1878	Elected 1874
Hirsch, E.—R	Sept. 9, 1878–Jan. 10, 1887	Elected 1878; reelected 1882
Webb, G.W.—D	Jan. 10, 1887–Jan. 12, 1891	Elected 1886
Metschan, Phil—R	Jan. 12, 1891–Jan. 9, 1899	Elected 1890; reelected 1894
Moore, Charles S.—R	Jan. 9, 1899–Jan. 14, 1907	Elected 1898; reelected 1902
Steel, George A.—R	Jan. 15, 1907–Jan. 3, 1911	Elected 1906
Kay, Thomas B.—R	Jan. 4, 1911–Jan. 6, 1919	Elected 1910; reelected 1914
Hoff, O.P.—R	Jan. 6, 1919–Mar. 18, 1924	Elected 1918; reelected 1922; died in office
Myers, Jefferson—D	Mar. 18, 1924–Jan. 4, 1925	Appointed by Governor Pierce
Kay, Thomas B.—R	Jan. 4, 1925–April 29, 1931	Elected 1924; reelected 1928; died in office
Holman, Rufus C.—R	May 1, 1931–Dec. 27, 1938	Appointed by Governor Meier; elected 1932; reelected 1936; resigned
Pearson, Walter E.—D	Dec. 27, 1938–Jan. 6, 1941	Appointed by Governor Martin
Scott, Leslie M.—R	Jan. 6, 1941–Jan. 3, 1949	Elected 1940; reelected 1944
Pearson, Walter J.—D	Jan. 3, 1949–Jan. 5, 1953	Elected 1948
Unander, Sig—R	Jan. 5, 1953–Dec. 31, 1959	Elected 1952; reelected 1956; resigned
Belton, Howard C.—R	Jan. 4, 1960–Jan. 4, 1965	Appointed by Governor Hatfield; elected 1960
Straub, Robert—D	Jan. 4, 1965–Jan. 1, 1973	Elected 1964; reelected 1968
Redden, James A.—D	Jan. 1, 1973–Jan. 3, 1977	Elected 1972
Myers, Clay—R	Jan. 3, 1977–Apr. 1, 1984	Elected 1976; reelected 1980; resigned
Rutherford, Bill—R	Apr. 1, 1984–July 9, 1987	Appointed by Governor Atiyeh; elected 1984; resigned
Meeker, Tony—R	July 9, 1987–Jan. 4, 1993	Appointed by Governor Goldschmidt; elected 1988
Hill, Jim—D	Jan. 4, 1993–Jan. 1, 2001	Elected 1992; reelected 1996
Edwards, Randall—D	Jan. 1, 2001–	Elected 2000; reelected 2004

Oregon Supreme Court Justices[1]

Under Provisional Government

Name	Term of Service	By What Authority/Remarks
Babcock, Dr. Ira L.	Feb. 18, 1841–May 1, 1843	Supreme judge with probate powers elected at meeting of inhabitants of the Willamette Valley
Wilson, W.E.	No record of service	Supreme judge with probate powers; elected at meeting of inhabitants of the Willamette Settlements, May 2, 1843
Russell, Osborn	Oct. 2, 1843–May 14, 1844	Supreme judge and probate judge; appointed by the Executive Committee
Babcock, Dr. Ira L.	June 27, 1844–Nov. 11, 1844	Presiding judge, Circuit Court; elected at first general election May 1844; resigned

Name	Term of Service	By What Authority/Remarks
Nesmith, James W.	Dec. 25, 1844–Aug. 9, 1845	Presiding judge, Circuit Court; appointed by Executive Committee; elected by people 1845
Ford, Nathaniel	Declined service	Supreme judge; elected by Legislature Aug. 9, 1845; declined to serve
Burnett, Peter H.	Sept. 6, 1845–Dec. 29, 1846	Supreme judge; elected by Legislature; declined appointment to Supreme Court 1848
Thornton, J. Quinn	Feb. 20, 1847–Nov. 9, 1847	Supreme judge; appointed by Governor Abernethy; resigned
Lancaster, Columbia	Nov. 30, 1847–Apr. 9, 1849	Supreme judge; appointed by Governor Abernethy
Lovejoy, A.L.	No record of service	Supreme judge; elected by Legislature Feb. 16, 1849

Under Territorial[2] and State Government[3]

Name	Term of Service	By What Authority/Remarks
Bryant, William P.	1848–1850	Appointed 1848; resigned 1850; chief justice 1848–1850
Pratt, Orville C.	1848–1852	Appointed 1848; term ended 1852
Nelson, Thomas	1850–1853	Appointed 1850 to succeed Bryant; term ended 1853; chief justice 1850–1853
Strong, William	1850–1853	Appointed 1850 to succeed Burnett; term ended 1853
Williams, George H.	1853–1858	Appointed 1853, 1857; resigned 1858; chief justice 1853–1858
Olney, Cyrus	1853–1858	Appointed 1853, 1857; resigned 1858
Deady, Matthew P.	1853–1859	Appointed 1853, 1857; elected 1858; resigned 1859
McFadden, Obadiah B.	1853–1854	Appointed 1853; term ended 1854
Boise, Reuben P.	1858–1870	Appointed 1858 to succeed Olney; elected 1859; 1876–1880 reelected 1864; term ended 1870; elected 1876; term ended 1878; appointed 1878; term ended 1880; chief justice 1862–1864, 1867–1870
Wait, Aaron E.	1859–1862	Elected 1858; resigned May 1, 1862; chief justice 1859–1862
Stratton, Riley E.	1859–1866	Elected 1858, 1864; died Dec. 26, 1866
Prim, Paine Page	1859–1880	Appointed 1859 to succeed Deady; elected 1860; reelected 1866, 1872; term ended 1878; appointed 1878; term ended 1880; chief justice 1864–1866, 1870–1872, 1876–1878
Page, William W.	1862	Appointed May 1862 to succeed Wait; term ended Sept. 1862
Shattuck, Erasmus D.	1862–1867	Elected 1862; resigned Dec. 1867; 1874–1878 elected 1874; term ended 1878; chief justice 1866–1867
Wilson, Joseph G.	1862–1870	New appointment Oct. 17, 1862; elected 1864; resigned May 1870
Skinner, Alonzo A.	1866–1867	Appointed 1866 to succeed Stratton; term ended 1867
Upton, William W.	1867–1874	Appointed Dec. 1867 to succeed Shattuck; elected 1868; term ended 1874; chief justice 1872–1874
Kelsay, John	1868–1870	Elected 1868 to succeed Stratton; term ended 1870
Whitten, Benoni	1870	Appointed May 1870 to succeed Wilson; term ended Sept. 1870
McArthur, Lewis L.	1870–1878	Elected 1870; reelected 1876; term ended 1878
Thayer, Andrew J.	1870–1873	Elected 1870; died Apr. 26, 1873
Bonham, Benjamin F.	1870–1876	Elected 1870; term ended 1876; chief justice 1874–1876

Name	Term of Service	By What Authority/Remarks
Moser, Lafayette F.	1873–1874	Appointed May 1873 to succeed A.J. Thayer; term ended 1874
Burnett, John	1874–1876	Elected 1874; term ended 1876
Watson, James F.	1876–1878	Elected 1876; term ended 1878
Kelly, James K.	1878–1880	Appointed 1878; term ended 1880; chief justice 1878–1880
Lord, William P.	1880–1894	Elected 1880; reelected 1882, 1888; term ended 1894; chief justice 1880–1882, 1886–1888, 1892–1894
Watson, Edward B.	1880–1884	Elected 1880; term ended 1884; chief justice 1882–1884
Waldo, John B.	1880–1886	Elected 1880; term ended 1886; chief justice 1884–1886
Thayer, William W.	1884–1890	Elected 1884; term ended 1890; chief justice 1888–1890
Strahan, Reuben S.	1886–1892	Elected 1886; term ended 1892; chief justice 1890–1892
Bean, Robert S.	1890–1909	Elected 1890; reelected 1896, 1902, 1908; resigned May 1, 1909; chief justice 1894–1896, 1900–1902, 1905–1909
Moore, Frank A.	1892–1918	Elected 1892; reelected 1898, 1904, 1910, 1916; died Sept. 25, 1918; chief justice 1896–1898, 1902–1905, 1909–1911, 1915–1917
Wolverton, Charles E.	1894–1905	Elected 1894, 1900; resigned Dec. 4, 1905; chief justice 1898–1900, 1905
Hailey, Thomas G.	1905–1907	Appointed Dec. 5, 1905 to succeed Wolverton; term ended Jan. 15, 1907
Eakin, Robert	1907–1917	Elected 1906, 1912; resigned Jan. 8, 1917; chief justice 1911–1913
King, William R.	1909–1911	Appointed Feb. 12, 1909; term ended Jan. 1, 1911
Slater, Woodson T.	1909–1911	Appointed Feb. 12, 1909; term ended Jan. 1, 1911
McBride, Thomas A.	1909–1930	Appointed May 1, 1909 to succeed Robert S. Bean; elected 1914; reelected 1920, 1926; died Sept. 9, 1930; chief justice 1913–1915, 1917–1921, 1923–1927
Bean, Henry J.	1911–1941	Elected 1910; reelected 1914, 1920, 1926, 1932, 1938; died May 8, 1941; chief justice 1931–1933, 1937–1939
Burnett, George H.	1911–1927	Elected 1910; reelected 1916, 1922; died Sept. 10, 1927; chief justice 1921–1923, 1927
McNary, Charles L.	1913–1915	Appointed June 3, 1913; term ended Jan. 4, 1915
Ramsey, William M.	1913–1915	Appointed June 3, 1913; term ended Jan. 4, 1915
Benson, Henry L.	1915–1921	Elected 1914; reelected 1920; died Oct. 16, 1921
Harris, Lawrence T.	1915–1924	Elected 1914; reelected 1920; resigned Jan. 15, 1924
McCamant, Wallace	1917–1918	Appointed Jan. 8, 1917 to succeed Eakin; resigned June 4, 1918
Johns, Charles A.	1918–1921	Appointed June 4, 1918 to succeed McCamant; elected 1918; resigned Oct. 7, 1921
Olson, Conrad P.	1918–1919	Appointed Sept. 27, 1918 to succeed Moore; term ended Jan. 7, 1919
Bennett, Alfred S.	1919–1920	Elected 1918; resigned Oct. 5, 1920
Brown, George M.	1920–1933	Appointed Oct. 14, 1920 to succeed Bennett; elected 1920; reelected 1926; term ended 1933
McCourt, John	1921–1924	Appointed Oct. 8, 1921 to succeed Johns; elected 1922; died Sept. 12, 1924
Rand, John L.	1921–1942	Appointed Oct. 18, 1921 to succeed Benson; elected 1922; reelected 1928, 1934, 1940;

Name	Term of Service	By What Authority/Remarks
		died Nov. 19, 1942; chief justice 1927–1929, 1933–1935, 1939–1941
Coshow, Oliver P.	1924–1931	Appointed Jan. 15, 1924 to succeed Harris; elected 1924; term ended 1931; chief justice 1929–1931
Pipes, Martin L.	1924	Appointed Sept. 1924 to succeed McCourt; term ended Dec. 31, 1924
Belt, Harry H.	1925–1950	Elected 1924; reelected 1930, 1936, 1942, 1948; died Aug. 6, 1950; chief justice 1945–1947
Rossman, George	1927–1965	Appointed Sept. 13, 1927 to succeed George H. Burnett; elected 1928; reelected 1934, 1940, 1946, 1952, 1958; term ended 1965; chief justice 1947–1949
Kelly, Percy R.	1930–1949	Appointed Sept. 24, 1930 to succeed McBride; elected 1930; reelected 1936, 1942, 1948; died June 14, 1949; chief justice 1941–1943
Campbell, James U.	1931–1937	Elected 1930; reelected 1936; died July 16, 1937; chief justice 1935–1937
Bailey, John O.	1933–1950	Elected 1932; reelected 1938, 1944; resigned Nov. 15, 1950; chief justice 1943–1945
Lusk, Hall S.	1937–1960	Appointed July 22, 1937 to succeed Campbell; elected 1938; reelected 1944, 1950, 1956; resigned Mar. 15, 1960; 1961–1968 recalled to temporary active service 1961 through 1968; chief justice 1949–1951
Brand, James T.	1941–1958	Appointed May 14, 1941 to succeed Henry J. Bean; elected 1942; reelected 1948, 1954; resigned June 30, 1958; chief justice 1951–1953
Hay, Arthur D.	1942–1952	Appointed Nov. 28, 1942 to succeed Rand; elected 1944; reelected 1950; died Dec. 19, 1952
Page, E.M.	1949–1950	Appointed July 8, 1949 to succeed Percy R. Kelly; resigned Jan. 18, 1950
Latourette, Earl C.	1950–1956	Appointed Jan. 19, 1950 to succeed E.M. Page; elected 1950; died Aug. 18, 1956; chief justice 1953–1955
Warner, Harold J.	1950–1963	Appointed Sept. 5, 1950 to succeed Belt; elected 1950; reelected 1956; term ended 1963; chief justice 1955–1957
Tooze, Walter L.	1950–1956	Appointed Nov. 16, 1950 to succeed Bailey; elected 1950; reelected 1956; died Dec. 21, 1956
Perry, William C.	1952–1970	Appointed Dec. 26, 1952 to succeed Hay; elected 1954; reelected 1960, 1966; resigned June 1, 1970; chief justice 1957–1959, 1967–1970
McAllister, William M.	1956–1976	Appointed Aug. 24, 1956 to succeed Latourette; elected 1956; reelected 1962, 1968, 1974; resigned Dec. 31, 1976; chief justice 1959–1967
Kester, Randall B.	1957–1958	Appointed Jan. 3, 1957 to succeed Tooze; resigned Mar. 1, 1958
Sloan, Gordon	1958–1970	Appointed Mar. 1, 1958 to succeed Kester; elected 1958; reelected 1964; resigned Oct. 1, 1970
O'Connell, Kenneth J.	1958–1977	Appointed July 1, 1958 to succeed Brand; elected 1958; reelected 1964, 1970; term ended 1977; chief justice 1970–1976
Goodwin, Alfred T.	1960–1969	Appointed Mar. 18, 1960 to succeed Lusk; elected 1960; reelected 1966; resigned Dec. 19, 1969
Denecke, Arno H.	1963–1982	Elected 1962; reelected 1968, 1974, 1980; resigned June 30, 1982; chief justice 1976–1982
Holman, Ralph M.	1965–1980	Elected 1964; reelected 1970, 1976; resigned Jan. 20, 1980

Name	Term of Service	By What Authority/Remarks
Tongue, Thomas H.	1969–1982	Appointed Dec. 29, 1969 to succeed Goodwin; elected 1970; reelected 1976; resigned Feb. 7, 1982
Howell, Edward H.	1970–1980	Appointed June 1, 1970 to succeed Perry; elected 1970; reelected 1976; resigned Nov. 30, 1980
Bryson, Dean F.	1970–1979	Elected 1970; appointed Oct. 23, 1970 (before elective term began) to succeed Sloan; reelected 1976; resigned April 1, 1979
Lent, Berkeley	1977–1988	Elected 1976; reelected 1982; resigned Sept. 30, 1988; chief justice 1982–1983
Linde, Hans	1977–1990	Appointed Jan. 3, 1977 to succeed McAllister; elected 1978; reelected 1984; resigned Jan. 31, 1990
Peterson, Edwin J.	1979 –1993	Appointed May 15, 1979 to succeed Bryson; elected 1980; reelected 1986, 1992; resigned Dec. 31, 1993; chief justice 1983 to 1991
Tanzer, Jacob	1980–1982	Appointed Jan. 21, 1980 to succeed Holman; elected 1980; resigned Dec. 31, 1982
Campbell, J.R.	1980–1988	Appointed Dec. 1, 1980 to succeed Howell; elected 1982; resigned Dec. 31, 1988
Roberts, Betty	1982–1986	Appointed Feb. 8, 1982 to succeed Tongue; elected 1982; resigned Feb. 7, 1986
Carson, Wallace P., Jr.	1982–	Appointed July 14, 1982 to succeed Denecke; elected 1982; reelected 1988, 1994, 2000; chief justice 1991 to date
Jones, Robert E.	1983–1990	Appointed Dec. 16, 1982 to succeed Tanzer; elected 1984; resigned April 30, 1990
Gillette, W. Michael	1986–	Appointed Feb. 10, 1986 to succeed Roberts; elected 1986; reelected 1992, 1998, 2004
Van Hoomissen, George	1988–2001	Elected May 17, 1988 to succeed Lent; reelected 1994; retired Dec. 31, 2000
Fadeley, Edward N.	1988–1998	Elected Nov. 8, 1988 to succeed Campbell; reelected 1994; resigned Jan. 31, 1998
Unis, Richard	1990–1996	Appointed Feb. 1, 1990 to succeed Linde; elected 1990; resigned June 30, 1996
Graber, Susan P.[4]	1990–1998	Appointed May 2, 1990 and Jan. 7, 1991 to succeed Jones; elected 1992; resigned April 1, 1998
Durham, Robert D.	1994–	Appointed Jan. 4, 1994 to succeed Peterson; elected 1994; reelected 2000
Kulongoski, Ted	1997–2001	Elected May, 1996; resigned June 14, 2001
Leeson, Susan M.	1998–2003	Appointed Feb. 26, 1998 to succeed Fadeley; elected 1998; resigned Jan. 31, 2003
Riggs, R. William	1998–	Appointed Sept. 8, 1998 to succeed Graber; elected 1998; reelected 2004
De Muniz, Paul J.	2001–	Elected Nov. 7, 2000 to succeed Van Hoomissen
Balmer, Thomas A.	2001–	Appointed Sept. 20, 2001 to succeed Kulongoski; elected 2002
Kistler, Rives	2003–	Appointed Aug. 15, 2003 to succeed Leeson; elected 2004

[1]Unless otherwise noted, justices took office in the year in which elected until 1905. Since then, terms have started on the first Monday in January and continued until the first Monday six years hence or until a successor has been sworn in, if later.

[2]Appointments under territorial government were made by the president of the United States.

[3]From 1859 to 1862, there were four Supreme Court justices. In 1862, a fifth justice was added. The justices at that time also rode circuit. In 1878, the Supreme Court and Circuit Court were separated; the Supreme Court then had three justices. In 1910, the number increased to five. The final increase to the present seven occurred in 1913.

[4]When Justice Jones resigned, he had already filed to run for another term and his name appeared on the ballot at the 1990 primary election. Because he was elected for another term, which began January 7, 1991, he had to resign from his new term, and Justice Graber was appointed again at that time.

Judges of the Court of Appeals

Oregon's Court of Appeals was established July 1, 1969 with five members; expanded to six members October 5, 1973; and to ten members September 1, 1977.

Name	Term of Service	By What Authority/Remarks
Langtry, Virgil	1969–1976	Appointed July 1, 1969; elected 1970; resigned Sept. 15, 1976
Foley, Robert H.	1969–1976	Appointed July 1, 1969; elected 1970; resigned Aug. 16, 1976
Schwab, Herbert M.	1969–1980	Appointed July 1, 1969; elected 1970; reelected 1976; resigned Dec. 31, 1980; chief judge 1969–1980
Fort, William S.	1969–1977	Appointed July 1, 1969; elected 1970; term ended 1977
Branchfield, Edward H.	1969–1971	Appointed July 1, 1969; term ended 1971
Thornton, Robert Y.	1971–1983	Elected 1970; reelected 1976; term ended 1983
Tanzer, Jacob	1973–1975 1976–1980	Appointed to new seat Oct. 5, 1973; term ended Jan. 6, 1975; elected 1976; appointed Aug. 16, 1976 (before elective term began) to succeed Foley; resigned Jan. 21, 1980
Lee, Jason	1975–1980	Elected 1974; died Feb. 19, 1980
Johnson, Lee	1977–1978	Elected 1976; resigned Dec. 18, 1978
Richardson, William L.	1976–1997	Elected 1976; appointed Oct. 15, 1976 (before elective term began) to succeed Langtry; reelected 1982, 1988, 1994; chief judge 1993–1997; resigned June 30, 1997
Buttler, John H.	1977–1992	Appointed to new seat Sept. 1, 1977; elected 1978; reelected 1984, 1990; resigned Dec. 31, 1992
Joseph, George M.	1977–1992	Appointed to new seat Sept. 1, 1977; elected 1978; reelected 1984, 1990; resigned Dec. 31, 1992; chief judge 1981–1992
Gillette, W. Michael	1977–1986	Appointed to new seat Sept. 1, 1977; elected 1978; reelected 1984; resigned Feb. 10, 1986
Roberts, Betty	1977–1982	Appointed to new seat Sept. 1, 1977; elected 1978; resigned Feb. 8, 1982
Campbell, J.R.	1979–1980	Appointed Mar. 19, 1979 to succeed Johnson; elected 1980; resigned Nov. 30, 1980
Warden, John C.	1980–1988	Appointed Feb. 19, 1980 to succeed Tanzer; term ended Jan. 5, 1981; appointed Jan. 6, 1981 to succeed Schwab; elected 1982; resigned Dec. 30, 1988
Warren, Edward H.	1980–1999	Appointed Mar. 10, 1980 to succeed Lee; elected 1980; reelected 1986, 1992, 1998; resigned 1999
Van Hoomissen, George A.	1981–1988	Elected 1980; reelected 1986; resigned Sept. 30, 1988
Young, Thomas F.	1981–1988	Appointed Jan. 5, 1981 to succeed Campbell; elected 1982; died Jan. 3, 1988
Rossman, Kurt C.	1982–1994	Appointed Mar. 2, 1982 to succeed Roberts; elected 1982; reelected 1988; resigned Dec. 31, 1994
Newman, Jonathan	1983–1991	Elected 1982; reelected 1988; resigned Aug. 31, 1991
Deits, Mary J.	1986–2004	Appointed Feb. 28, 1986 to succeed Gillette; elected 1986; reelected 1992, 1998; chief judge 1997–2004; resigned Oct. 31, 2004
Riggs, R. William	1988–1998	Appointed Oct. 24, 1988 to fill Van Hoomissen position; elected 1988 to succeed Warden; reelected 1994; resigned Sept. 8, 1998
Graber, Susan P.	1988–1990	Appointed Feb. 11, 1988 to succeed Young; elected 1988; resigned May 2, 1990
Edmonds, Walter I. Jr.	1989–	Appointed Jan. 1, 1989 to succeed Van Hoomissen; elected 1990; reelected 1996; reelected 2002

Name	Term of Service	By What Authority/Remarks
De Muniz, Paul J.	1990–2000	Appointed May 11, 1990 to succeed Graber; elected 1990; reelected 1996; resigned Dec. 29, 2000
Durham, Robert D.	1991–1994	Appointed Nov. 14, 1991 to succeed Newman; elected 1992; resigned Jan. 4, 1994
Landau, Jack L.	1993–	Appointed Dec. 15, 1992 to succeed Joseph; elected 1994; reelected 2000
Leeson, Susan M.	1993–1998	Appointed Dec. 15, 1992 to succeed Buttler; elected 1994; resigned Feb. 26, 1998
Haselton, Rick	1994–	Appointed Mar. 4, 1994 to succeed Durham; elected 1994; reelected 2000
Armstrong, Rex	1995–	Elected 1994; reelected 2000
Linder, Virginia L.	1997–	Appointed Sept. 24, 1997 to succeed Richardson; elected 1998; reelected 2004
Wollheim, Robert D.	1998–	Appointed Feb. 27, 1998 to succeed Leeson; elected 1998; reelected 2004
Brewer, David	1999–	Appointed Jan. 14, 1999 to succeed Warren; elected 2000; appointed chief judge, Nov. 1, 2004
Kistler, Rives	1999–2003	Appointed Jan. 14, 1999 to succeed Riggs; elected 2000; resigned Aug. 14, 2003
Schuman, David	2001–	Appointed March 19, 2001 to succeed De Muniz; elected 2002
Ortega, Darleen	2003–	Appointed Oct. 13, 2003 to succeed Kistler; elected 2004

Judges of the Oregon Tax Court

Oregon Tax Court was established January 1, 1962

Name	Term of Service	By What Authority/Remarks
Gunnar, Peter M.	1962–1965	Appointed by Governor Hatfield Jan. 1, 1962; elected 1962; resigned Feb. 18, 1965
Howell, Edward H.	1965–1970	Appointed by Governor Hatfield Feb. 19, 1965; elected 1966; resigned May 31, 1970
Roberts, Carlisle B.	1970–1983	Appointed by Governor McCall June 1, 1970; elected 1970; reelected 1976; term ended 1983
Stewart, Samuel B.	1983–1985	Elected 1982; died Feb. 25, 1985
Byers, Carl N.	1985–2001	Appointed by Governor Atiyeh Mar. 6, 1985; elected 1986; reelected 1992 & 1998; retired 2001
Breithaupt, Henry C.	2001–	Appointed by Governor Kitzhaber June 29, 2001 to succeed Byers; elected 2002

Attorneys General of Oregon

Name/Political Party	Term of Service	By What Authority/Remarks
Chamberlain, George E.—D	May 20, 1891–Jan. 14, 1895	Appointed by Governor Pennoyer; elected June 1892
Idleman, Cicero M.—R	Jan. 14, 1895–Jan. 9, 1899	Elected 1894
Blackburn, D.R.N.—R	Jan. 9, 1899–Jan. 12, 1903	Elected 1898
Crawford, Andrew M.—R	Jan. 13, 1903–Jan. 3, 1915	Elected 1902; reelected 1906, 1910
Brown, George M.—R	Jan. 4, 1915–Oct. 14, 1920	Elected 1914; reelected 1918; resigned
Van Winkle, Isaac H.—R	Oct. 14, 1920–Dec. 14, 1943	Appointed by Governor Olcott; elected 1920; reelected 1924, 1928, 1932, 1936, 1940; died in office
Neuner, George—R	Dec. 21, 1943–Jan. 5, 1953	Appointed by Governor Snell; elected 1944; reelected 1948
Thornton, Robert Y.—D	Jan. 5, 1953–May 20, 1969	Elected 1952; reelected 1956, 1960, 1964
Johnson, Lee—R	May 20, 1969–Jan. 3, 1977	Elected 1968; reelected 1972

Name/Political Party	Term of Service	By What Authority/Remarks
Redden, James—D	Jan. 3, 1977–Mar. 24, 1980	Elected 1976
Brown, James M.—D	Mar. 24, 1980–Jan. 4, 1981	Appointed by Governor Atiyeh
Frohnmayer, David B.—R	Jan. 5, 1981–Dec. 31, 1991	Elected 1980; reelected 1984, 1988; resigned 1991
Crookham, Charles S.—R	Jan 2, 1992–Jan. 3, 1993	Appointed by Governor Roberts
Kulongoski, Ted—D	Jan. 4, 1993–Jan. 4, 1997	Elected 1992
Myers, Hardy—D	Jan. 6, 1997–	Elected 1996; reelected 2000, 2004

Commissioners, Labor and Industries[1]

Name/Political Party	Term of Service	By What Authority/Remarks
Hoff, O.P.—R	June 2, 1903–Jan. 6, 1919	Appointed by Governor Chamberlain; elected 1906; reelected 1910, 1914
Gram, C.H.—R	Jan. 6, 1919–Jan. 4, 1943	Elected 1918; reelected 1922, 1926, 1930, 1934, 1938
Kimsey, W.E.—R	Jan. 4, 1943–Jan. 3, 1955	Elected 1942; reelected 1946, 1950
Nilsen, Norman O.—D	Jan. 3, 1955–Jan. 6, 1975	Elected 1954; reelected 1958, 1962, 1966, 1970
Stevenson, Bill—D	Jan. 6, 1975–Jan. 1, 1979	Elected 1974
Roberts, Mary Wendy—D.	Jan. 1, 1979–Jan 2, 1995	Elected 1978; reelected 1982, 1986, 1990
Roberts, Jack—R	Jan. 2, 1995–Jan. 6, 2003–	Elected 1994; reelected 1998
Gardner, Dan	Jan. 6, 2003–	Elected 2002

[1]This position, originally called Labor Commissioner, was changed to Commissioner of the Bureau of Labor Statistics and Inspector of Factories and Workshops in 1918. In 1930, the name changed to Commissioner of the Bureau of Labor. The 1979 Legislature changed the name to Commissioner of Labor and Industries.

The 1995 Legislature made this position nonpartisan, and the 1998 election was the first for this position after the change.

Superintendents of Public Instruction[1]

Name/Political Party	Term of Service	By What Authority/Remarks
Simpson, Sylvester C.—D	Jan. 29, 1873–Sept. 14, 1874	Appointed by Governor Grover
Rowland, L.L.—R	Sept. 14, 1874–Sept. 9, 1878	Elected 1874
Powell, J.L.—R	Sept. 9, 1878–Sept. 11, 1882	Elected 1878
McElroy, E.B.—R	Sept. 11, 1882–Jan. 14, 1895	Elected 1882; reelected 1886, 1890
Irwin, G.M.—R	Jan. 14, 1895–Jan. 9, 1899	Elected 1894
Ackerman, J.H.—R	Jan. 9, 1899–Jan. 3, 1911	Elected 1898; reelected 1902, 1906
Alderman, L.R.—R	Jan. 4, 1911–Jan. 28, 1913	Elected 1910; resigned
Churchill, J.A.—R	July 1, 1913–June 1, 1926	Appointed by Governor West; elected 914; reelected 1918, 1922; resigned
Turner, R.R.—D	June 1, 1926–Jan. 3, 1927	Appointed by Governor Pierce
Howard, Charles A.—R	Jan. 3, 1927–Sept. 1, 1937	Elected 1926; reelected 1930, 1934; resigned
Putnam, Rex—D	Sept. 1, 1937–Jan. 31, 1961	Appointed by Governor Martin; elected 1938; reelected 1942, 1946, 1950, 1954, 1958; resigned
Minear, Leon P.	Feb. 1, 1961–Mar. 31, 1968	Appointed by Governor Hatfield; elected 1966; resigned
Fasold, Jesse V.	Apr. 8, 1968–June 30, 1968	Appointed by Governor McCall; resigned
Parnell, Dale	July 1, 1968–Mar. 31, 1974	Appointed by Governor McCall; elected 1968; reelected 1970; resigned
Fasold, Jesse V.	Apr. 1, 1974–Jan. 6, 1975	Appointed by Governor McCall

Name/Political Party	Term of Service	By What Authority/Remarks
Duncan, Verne A.	Jan. 6, 1975–Nov. 15, 1989	Elected 1974; reelected 1978, 1982, 1986; resigned 1989
Erickson, John	Dec. 18, 1989–Sept. 30, 1990	Appointed by Governor Gold-schmidt; resigned
Paulus, Norma	Oct. 1, 1990–Jan. 4, 1999	Elected 1990; appointed by Governor Goldschmidt (before elective term began); reelected 1994
Bunn, Stan	Jan. 4, 1999–Jan. 6, 2003	Elected 1998
Castillo, Susan	Jan. 6, 2003–	Elected 2002

[1]From 1942 to 1961, this office was filled by election on nonpartisan ballot. In 1961, the state legislature passed a statute making the office appointive by the State Board of Education. The Supreme Court declared this unconstitutional in 1965, and a constitutional amendment to place the method of selection in the hands of the state legislature was defeated in 1966. Another attempt to repeal the constitutional provision requiring election was defeated in 1980.

Presidents of the Senate

Session	Name/Political Party	City	County
1860	Elkins, Luther—D		Linn
1862	Bowlby, Wilson—R		Washington
1864	Mitchell, J.H.—R	Portland	Multnomah
1865[1]	Mitchell, J.H.—R	Portland	Multnomah
1866	Cornelius, T.R.—R		Washington
1868	Burch, B.F.—D		Polk
1870	Fay, James D.—D		Jackson
1872	Fay, James D.—D		Jackson
1874	Cochran, R.B.—D		Lane
1876	Whiteaker, John—D		Lane
1878	Whiteaker, John—D		Lane
1880	Hirsch, Sol—R	Portland	Multnomah
1882	McConnell, W.J.—R		Yamhill
1885[2]	Waldo, William—R	Salem	Marion
1887	Carson, John C.—R	Portland	Multnomah
1889	Simon, Joseph—R	Portland	Multnomah
1891	Simon, Joseph—R	Portland	Multnomah
1893	Fulton, C.W.—R	Astoria	Clatsop
1895	Simon, Joseph—R	Portland	Multnomah
1897	Simon, Joseph—R	Portland	Multnomah
1898[1]	Simon, Joseph—R	Portland	Multnomah
1899	Taylor, T.C.—R	Pendleton	Umatilla
1901	Fulton, C.W.—R	Astoria	Clatsop
1903[2]	Brownell, George C.—R	Oregon City	Clackamas
1905	Kuykendall, W.—R	Eugene	Lane
1907	Haines, E.W.—R	Forest Grove	Washington
1909[2]	Bowerman, Jay—R	Condon	Gilliam
1911	Selling, Ben—R	Portland	Multnomah
1913	Malarkey, Dan J.—R	Portland	Multnomah
1915	Thompson, W. Lair—R	Lakeview	Lake
1917	Moser, Gus C.—R	Portland	Multnomah
1919	Vinton, W.T.—R	McMinnville	Yamhill
1920[1]	Vinton, W.T.—R	McMinnville	Yamhill
1921[2]	Ritner, Roy W.—R	Pendleton	Umatilla
1923	Upton, Jay—R	Prineville	Crook
1925	Moser, Gus C.—R	Portland	Multnomah
1927	Corbett, Henry L.—R	Portland	Multnomah
1929	Norblad, A.W.—R	Astoria	Clatsop
1931	Marks, Willard L.—R	Albany	Linn
1933[3]	Kiddle, Fred E.—R	Island City	Union
1935[2]	Corbett, Henry L.—R	Portland	Multnomah

Elections and Records

Session	Name/Political Party	City	County
1937	Franciscovich, F.M.—R	Astoria	Clatsop
1939	Duncan, Robert M.—R	Burns	Harney
1941	Walker, Dean H.—R	Independence	Polk
1943	Steiwer, W.H.—R	Fossil	Wheeler
1945	Belton, Howard C.—R	Canby	Clackamas
1947	Cornett, Marshall E.—R	Klamath Falls	Klamath
1949	Walsh, William E.—R	Coos Bay	Coos
1951	Patterson, Paul L.—R	Hillsboro	Washington
1953	Marsh, Eugene E.—R	McMinnville	Yamhill
1955	Smith, Elmo—R	John Day	Grant
1957[2]	Overhulse, Boyd R.—D	Madras	Jefferson
1959	Pearson, Walter J.—D	Portland	Multnomah
1961	Boivin, Harry D.—D	Klamath Falls	Klamath
1963[2]	Musa, Ben—D	The Dalles	Wasco
1965[2]	Boivin, Harry D.—D	Klamath Falls	Klamath
1967[2]	Potts, E.D.—D	Grants Pass	Josephine
1969	Potts, E.D.—D	Grants Pass	Josephine
1971[2]	Burns, John D.—D	Portland	Multnomah
1973	Boe, Jason—D	Reedsport	Douglas
1974[1]	Boe, Jason—D	Reedsport	Douglas
1975	Boe, Jason—D	Reedsport	Douglas
1977	Boe, Jason—D	Reedsport	Douglas
1978[1]	Boe, Jason—D	Reedsport	Douglas
1979	Boe, Jason—D	Reedsport	Douglas
1980[1]	Boe, Jason—D	Reedsport	Douglas
1981[4]	Heard, Fred W.—D	Klamath Falls	Klamath
1983[3]	Fadeley, Edward N.—D	Eugene	Lane
1985	Kitzhaber, M.D., John A.—D	Roseburg	Douglas
1987	Kitzhaber, M.D., John A.—D	Roseburg	Douglas
1989[2]	Kitzhaber, M.D., John A.—D	Roseburg	Douglas
1991	Kitzhaber, M.D., John A.—D	Roseburg	Douglas
1993	Bradbury, Bill—D	Bandon	Coos
1995[2]	Smith, Gordon H.—R	Pendleton	Umatilla
1997	Adams, Brady—R	Grants Pass	Josephine
1999	Adams, Brady—R	Grants Pass	Josephine
2001[5]	Derfler, Gene—R	Salem	Marion
2003	Courtney, Peter—D	Salem	Marion
2005	Courtney, Peter—D	Salem	Marion

[1]Special session
[2]Regular and special session
[3]Regular and two special sessions
[4]Regular and four special sessions
[5]Regular and five special sessions

Speakers of the House of Representatives

Session	Name/Political Party	City	County
1860	Harding, B.F.—D		Marion
1862	Palmer, Joel—R		Yamhill
1864	Moores, I.R.—R		Marion
1865[1]	Moores, I.R.—R		Marion
1866	Chenoweth, F.A.—R		Benton
1868	Whiteaker, John J.—D		Lane
1870	Hayden, Benjamin—D		Polk
1872	Mallory, Rufus—R		Marion
1874	Drain, J.C.—D		Douglas
1876	Weatherford, J.K.—D	Albany	Linn
1878	Thompson, J.M.—D		Lane
1880	Moody, Z.F.—R	The Dalles	Wasco

Session	Name/Political Party	City	County
1882	McBride, George W.—R		Columbia
1885[2]	Keady, W.P.—R	Corvallis	Benton
1887	Gregg, J.T.—R	Salem	Marion
1889	Smith, E.L.—R	Hood River	Hood River
1891	Geer, T.T.—R	Macleay	Marion
1893	Keady, W.P.—R	Portland	Multnomah
1895	Moores, C.B.—R	Salem	Marion
1897[4]	House failed to organize		
1898[1]	Carter, E.V.—R	Ashland	Jackson
1899	Carter, E.V.—R	Ashland	Jackson
1901	Reeder, L.B.—R	Pendleton	Umatilla
1903[2]	Harris, L.T.—R	Eugene	Lane
1905	Mills, A.L.—R	Portland	Multnomah
1907	Davey, Frank—R	Salem	Marion
1909[2]	McArthur, C.N.—R	Portland	Multnomah
1911	Rusk, John P.—R	Joseph	Wallowa
1913	McArthur, C.N.—R	Portland	Multnomah
1915	Selling, Ben—R	Portland	Multnomah
1917	Stanfield, R.N.—R	Stanfield	Umatilla
1919	Jones, Seymour—R	Salem	Marion
1920[1]	Jones, Seymour—R	Salem	Marion
1921[2]	Bean, Louis E.—R	Eugene	Lane
1923	Kubli, K.K.—R	Portland	Multnomah
1925	Burdick, Denton G.—R	Redmond	Deschutes
1927	Carkin, John H.—R	Medford	Jackson
1929	Hamilton, R.S.—R	Bend	Deschutes
1931	Lonergan, Frank J.—R	Portland	Multnomah
1933[3]	Snell, Earl W.—R	Arlington	Gilliam
1935	Cooter, John E.—D	Toledo	Lincoln
1935[1]	Latourette, Howard—D	Portland	Multnomah
1937	Boivin, Harry D.—D	Klamath Falls	Klamath
1939	Fatland, Ernest R.—R	Condon	Gilliam
1941	Farrell, Robert S. Jr.—R	Portland	Multnomah
1943	McAllister, William M.—R	Medford	Jackson
1945	Marsh, Eugene E.—R	McMinnville	Yamhill
1947	Hall, John H.—R	Portland	Multnomah
1949	Van Dyke, Frank J.—R	Medford	Jackson
1951	Steelhammer, John F.—R	Salem	Marion
1953	Wilhelm, Rudie Jr.—R	Portland	Multnomah
1955	Geary, Edward A.—R	Klamath Falls	Klamath
1957[2]	Dooley, Pat—D	Portland	Multnomah
1959	Duncan, Robert B.—D	Medford	Jackson
1961	Duncan, Robert B.—D	Medford	Jackson
1963[2]	Barton, Clarence—D	Coquille	Coos
1965[2]	Montgomery, F.F.—R	Eugene	Lane
1967[2]	Montgomery, F.F.—R	Eugene	Lane
1969	Smith, Robert F.—R	Burns	Harney
1971[2]	Smith, Robert F.—R	Burns	Harney
1973	Eymann, Richard O.—D	Springfield	Lane
1974[1]	Eymann, Richard O.—D	Springfield	Lane
1975	Lang, Philip D.—D	Portland	Multnomah
1977	Lang, Philip D.—D	Portland	Multnomah
1978[1]	Lang, Philip D.—D	Portland	Multnomah
1979	Myers, Hardy—D	Portland	Multnomah
1980[1]	Myers, Hardy—D	Portland	Multnomah
1981[5]	Myers, Hardy—D	Portland	Multnomah
1983[3]	Kerans, Grattan—D	Eugene	Lane
1985	Katz, Vera—D	Portland	Multnomah
1987	Katz, Vera—D	Portland	Multnomah

Session	Name/Political Party	City	County
1989[2]	Katz, Vera—D	Portland	Multnomah
1991	Campbell, Larry—R	Eugene	Lane
1993	Campbell, Larry—R	Eugene	Lane
1995[2]	Clarno, Bev—R	Bend	Deschutes
1997	Lundquist, Lynn—R	Powell Butte	Deschutes
1999	Snodgrass, Lynn—R	Boring	Clackamas
2001[6]	Simmons, Mark—R	Elgin	Union
2003	Minnis, Karen—R	Wood Village	Multnomah
2005	Minnis, Karen—R	Wood Village	Multnomah

[1]Special session
[2]Regular and special session
[3]Regular and two special sessions
[4]E.J. Davis was elected speaker by less than a quorum. Subsequently, Henry L. Benson was elected speaker by less than a quorum. The Supreme Court revised an 1871 decision and ordered the secretary of state to audit claims and draw warrants for all claims which the Legislature, through its enactments, permitted and directed, either expressly or by implication.
[5]Regular and four special sessions.
[6]Regular and five special sessions

U.S. Senators from Oregon

First Position[2]

Name/Political Party	Term of Service[1]	By What Authority/Remarks
Smith, Delazon[3]—D	Feb. 14–Mar. 3, 1859	Elected by Legislature 1858
Baker, Edward[4]—R	Dec. 5, 1860–Oct. 21, 1861	Elected by Legislature 1860; died in office
Stark, Benjamin—D	Oct. 29, 1861–Sept. 11, 1862	Appointed by Governor Whiteaker to succeed Baker
Harding, Benjamin F.—D	Sept. 11, 1862–1865	Elected by Legislature to succeed Baker
Williams, George H.—R	1865–1871	Elected by Legislature 1864
Kelly, James K.—D	1871–1877	Elected by Legislature 1870
Grover, LaFayette—D	1877–1883	Elected by Legislature 1876
Dolph, Joseph N.—R	1883–1895	Elected by Legislature 1882; reelected 1889
McBride, George W.—R	1895–1901	Elected by Legislature 1895
Mitchell, John H.—R	1901–1905	Elected by Legislature 1901; died in office Dec. 8, 1905
Gearin, John M.—D	Dec. 12, 1905–Jan. 23, 1907	Appointed by Governor Chamberlain to succeed Mitchell
Mulkey, Fred W.—R	Jan. 23–Mar. 2, 1907	Selected by general election 1906 for short term; elected by Legislature to serve remaining term of Mitchell and Gearin
Bourne, Jonathan Jr.—R	1907–1913	Selected by general election 1906; elected by Legislature 1907
Lane, Harry—D	1913–May 23, 1917	Selected by general election 1912; elected by Legislature 1913; died in office
McNary, Charles L.—R	May 29, 1917–Nov. 5, 1918	Appointed by Governor Withycombe to succeed Lane
Mulkey, Fred W.—R	Nov. 5–Dec. 17, 1918	Elected 1918 for short term; resigned to permit reappointment of McNary
McNary, Charles L.—R	Dec. 17, 1918–Feb. 24, 1944	Appointed 1918 for unexpired short term; elected 1918; reelected 1924, 1930, 1936, 1942; died in office

Name/Political Party	Term of Service[1]	By What Authority/Remarks
Cordon, Guy—R	Mar. 4, 1944–1955	Appointed by Governor Snell to succeed McNary; elected 1944; reelected 1948
Neuberger, Richard L.—D	1955–Mar. 9, 1960	Elected 1954; died in office
Lusk, Hall S.—D	Mar. 16, 1960–Nov. 8, 1960	Appointed by Governor Hatfield to succeed Neuberger
Neuberger, Maurine—D	Nov. 8, 1960–1967	Elected 1960 for short and full terms
Hatfield, Mark O.—R.	1967–1996	Elected 1966; reelected 1972, 1978, 1984, 1990
Smith, Gordon H.—R	1997–	Elected 1996; reelected 2002

Second Position[2]

Name/Political Party	Term of Service[1]	By What Authority/Remarks
Lane, Joseph—D	Feb. 14, 1859–1861	Elected by Legislature 1858
Nesmith, James W.—D	1861–1867	Elected by Legislature 1860
Corbett, Henry W.—R	1867–1873	Elected by Legislature 1866
Mitchell, John H.—R	1873–1879	Elected by Legislature 1872
Slater, James H.—D	1879–1885	Elected by Legislature 1878
Mitchell, John H.—R	1885–1897	Elected by Legislature 1885; reelected 1891
Corbett, Henry W.—R[5]	March, 1897	Appointed by Governor Lord, not seated
Simon, Joseph—R	Oct. 6, 1898–1903	Elected by Legislature to fill vacancy
Fulton, Charles W.—R	1903–1909	Elected by Legislature 1903
Chamberlain, George E.—D[6]	1909–1921	Selected by general election 1908; elected by Legislature; reelected by people 1914
Stanfield, Robert N.—R	1921–1927	Elected 1920
Steiwer, Frederick—R	1927–Feb. 1, 1938	Elected 1926; reelected 1932; resigned
Reames, Alfred Evan—D	Feb. 1–Nov. 9, 1938	Appointed by Governor Martin to succeed Steiwer
Barry, Alex G.—R	Nov. 9, 1938–1939	Elected 1938 for short term
Holman, Rufus C.—R	1939–1945	Elected 1938
Morse, Wayne[7]—D	1945–1969	Elected 1944; reelected 1950, 1956, 1962
Packwood, Robert—R	1969–1995	Elected 1968; reelected 1974, 1980, 1986, 1992; resigned 1995
Wyden, Ron[8]—D	1996–	Elected 1996, reelected 1998, 2004

[1]Unless otherwise noted, normal terms of office began on the fourth day of March and ended on the third day of March until 1933, when terms were changed to begin and end on the third day of January unless a different date was set by Congress.

[2]Delazon Smith and Joseph Lane drew lots in 1859 for the short and long term senate seats. Smith won the short term of only 17 days expiring March 3, 1859 (designated first position). Lane won the long term expiring March 3, 1861 (designated second position).

[3]When the Legislature first met after statehood in May 1859, Smith was defeated for reelection, and no successor was named. Consequently, Oregon had only one U.S. senator from March 3, 1859 until Baker was elected October 1, 1860.

[4]Senator Edward Baker was killed in the Battle of Balls Bluff, Va. while serving as a colonel in the Civil War, the only U.S. senator to serve in military action while a senator. His statue, cast of horatio stone and marble, stands 6 ft. 5 in. tall in the Capitol rotunda in Washington, D.C.

[5]When the Legislature failed to elect a successor to Mitchell, Governor Lord appointed Henry Corbett. After conflict, however, the U.S. Senate decided the governor did not have this authority and refused to seat Corbett. Therefore, Oregon was represented by only one U.S. senator from March 4, 1897 to October 6, 1898.

Elections and Records

[6]Direct election of U.S. senators resulted from Oregon's ratification of Article XVII of the U.S. Constitution January 23, 1913 (effective May 31, 1913). Oregon initiated a direct primary for selecting candidates in 1904.

[7]Wayne Morse was elected as a Republican in 1944 and reelected as a Republican in 1950. He changed to Independent in 1952 and to Democrat in 1955. He was reelected as a Democrat in 1956 and 1962.

[8]Elected to fill the unexpired term of Robert Packwood due to Senator Packwood's resignation. The elections, both primary and general, to fill Senator Packwood's seat were conducted by mail. The special primary and general elections were the first statewide vote-by-mail elections to fill a federal office in United States history.

U.S. Representatives from Oregon

Name/Political Party	Term of Service[1]	By What Authority/Remarks
Thurston, Samuel R.—D	June 6, 1849–Apr. 9, 1851	Territorial Delegate elected 1849; died at sea returning home from 1st session
Lane, Joseph—D	June 2, 1851–Feb. 14, 1859	Territorial Delegate elected 1851; reelected 1853, 1855, 1857
Grover, LaFayette—D	Feb. 15–Mar. 3, 1859	First Representative at large, elected 1858 for short term
Stout, Lansing—D	1859–1861	Elected 1858
Shiel, George K.—D	1861–1863	Elected 1860
McBride, John R.—R	1863–1865	Elected 1862
Henderson, J.H.D.—R	1865–1867	Elected 1864
Mallory, Rufus—R	1867–1869	Elected 1866
Smith, Joseph S.—D	1869–1871	Elected 1868
Slater, James H.—D	1871–1873	Elected 1870
Wilson, Joseph G.—R	1873	Elected 1872; died in July, 1873 before qualifying
Nesmith, James W.—D	1873–1875	Elected 1873
La Dow, George A.—D	1875	Elected 1874; died Mar. 4, 1875 before qualifying
Lane, Lafayette—D	Oct. 25, 1875–1877	Elected 1875
Williams, Richard—R	1877–1879	Elected 1876
Whiteaker, John—D	1879–1881	Elected 1878
George, Melvin C.—R	1881–1885	Elected 1880; reelected 1882
Hermann, Binger—R	1885–1893	Elected 1884; reelected 1886, 1888, 1890

1st District

Name/Political Party	Term of Service	By What Authority/Remarks
Hermann, Binger—R	1893–1897	Elected 1892; reelected 1894
Tongue, Thomas H.—R	1897–Jan. 11, 1903	Elected 1896; reelected 1898, 1900,1902; died in office
Hermann, Binger—R	June 1, 1903–1907	Elected 1903 to succeed Tongue; reelected 1904
Hawley, Willis C.—R	1907–1933	Elected 1906; reelected 1908, 1910, 1912, 1914, 1916, 1918, 1920, 1922, 1924, 1926, 1928, 1930
Mott, James W.—R	1933–Nov. 12, 1945	Elected 1932; reelected 1934, 1936,1938, 1940, 1942, 1944; died in office
Norblad, A. Walter Jr.—R	Jan. 11, 1946–Sept. 20, 1964	Elected 1945 to succeed Mott; reelected 1946, 1948, 1950, 1952, 1954,1956, 1958, 1960, 1962; died in office
Wyatt, Wendell—R	Nov. 3, 1964–1975	Elected 1964 to succeed Norblad; reelected 1966, 1968, 1970, 1972
AuCoin, Les—D	1975–1993	Elected 1974; reelected 1976, 1978, 1980, 1982, 1984, 1986, 1988, 1990
Furse, Elizabeth—D	1993–1999	Elected 1992; reelected 1994, 1996

Name/Political Party	Term of Service[1]	By What Authority/Remarks
Wu, David—D	1999–	Elected 1998; reelected 2000, 2002, 2004

2nd District

Name/Political Party	Term of Service[1]	By What Authority/Remarks
Ellis, William R.—R	1893–1899	Elected 1892; reelected 1894, 1896
Moody, Malcolm A.—R	1899–1903	Elected 1898; reelected 1900
Williamson, John N.—R	1903–1907	Elected 1902; reelected 1904
Ellis, William R.—R	1907–1911	Elected 1906; reelected 1908
Lafferty, Abraham W.—R.	1911–1913	Elected 1910
Sinnott, N.J.—R	1913–May 31, 1928	Elected 1912; reelected 1914, 1916,1918, 1920, 1922, 1924, 1926; resigned
Butler, Robert R.—R	Nov. 6, 1928–Jan. 7, 1933	Elected 1928 to succeed Sinnott; reelected 1930; died in office
Pierce, Walter M.—D	1933–1943	Elected 1932; reelected 1934, 1936, 1938, 1940
Stockman, Lowell—R	1943–1953	Elected 1942; reelected 1944, 1946, 1948, 1950
Coon, Samuel H.—R	1953–1957	Elected 1952; reelected 1954
Ullman, Albert C.—D	1957–1981	Elected 1956; reelected 1958, 1960, 1962,1964, 1966, 1968, 1970, 1972, 1974, 1976,1978
Smith, Denny—R	1981–1983	Elected 1980
Smith, Robert F.—R	1983–1995	Elected 1982; reelected 1984, 1986, 1988,1990, 1992
Cooley, Wes—R	1995–1997	Elected 1994
Smith, Robert F.—R	1997–1999	Elected 1996
Walden, Greg—R	1999–	Elected 1998; reelected 2000, 2002, 2004

3rd District

Name/Political Party	Term of Service[1]	By What Authority/Remarks
Lafferty, Abraham W.—R	1913–1915	Elected 1912
McArthur, Clifton N.—R	1915–1923	Elected 1914; reelected 1916, 1918, 1920
Watkins, Elton—D	1923–1925	Elected 1922
Crumpacker, Maurice E.—R	1925–July 25, 1927	Elected 1924; reelected 1926; died in office
Korell, Franklin F.—R	Oct. 18, 1927–1931	Elected 1927; reelected 1928
Martin, Charles H.—D	1931–1935	Elected 1930; reelected 1932
Ekwall, William A.—R	1935–1937	Elected 1934
Honeyman, Nan Wood—D	1937–1939	Elected 1936
Angell, Homer D.—R	1939–1955	Elected 1938; reelected 1940, 1942, 1944, 1946, 1948, 1950, 1952
Green, Edith S.—D	1955–1975	Elected 1954; reelected 1956, 1958, 1960, 1962, 1964, 1966, 1968, 1970, 1972
Duncan, Robert B.—D	1975–1981	Elected 1974; reelected 1976, 1978
Wyden, Ron—D	1981–1996	Elected 1980; reelected 1982, 1984, 1986, 1988, 1990, 1992, 1994
Blumenauer, Earl—D[2]	1997–	Elected 1996; reelected 1998, 2000, 2002, 2004

4th District

Name/Political Party	Term of Service[1]	By What Authority/Remarks
Ellsworth, Harris—R	1943–1957	Elected 1942; reelected 1944, 1946, 1948, 1950, 1952, 1954
Porter, Charles O.—D	1957–1961	Elected 1956; reelected 1958
Durno, Edwin R.—R	1961–1963	Elected 1960
Duncan, Robert B.—D	1963–1967	Elected 1962; reelected 1964

Name/Political Party	Term of Service[1]	By What Authority/Remarks
Dellenback, John—R	1967–1975	Elected 1966; reelected 1968, 1970, 1972
Weaver, James—D	1975–1987	Elected 1974; reelected 1976, 1978, 1980, 1982, 1984
DeFazio, Peter A.—D	1987–	Elected 1986; reelected 1988, 1990, 1992, 1994, 1996, 1998, 2000, 2002, 2004

5th District

Smith, Denny—R	1983–1991	Elected 1982; reelected 1984, 1986, 1988
Kopetski, Mike	1991–1995	Elected 1990; reelected 1992
Bunn, Jim—R	1995–1997	Elected 1994
Hooley, Darlene—D	1997–	Elected 1996; reelected 1998, 2000, 2002, 2004

[1]Unless otherwise noted, normal terms of office began on the fourth day of March and ended on the third day of March until 1933, when terms were changed to begin and end on the third day of January unless a different date was set by Congress.

[2]Elected to fill the unexpired term of Representative Ron Wyden. The term ended January 3, 1997. Reelected to a full term at the November 5, 1996 General Election.

Skier jumps snow cornice on Mt. Hood—Oregon State Archives Photograph, OHD-G391

The splendor of Oregon began well before it became a territory or a state. Historian Stephen Dow Beckham's finely executed history introduces the reader to the physical and geological changes that created the land we know as Oregon. He escorts us through the peaceful times when the Northwest was occupied by the native people, and the events that have occurred since Lewis and Clark spread word of the Columbia River to the rest of the nation.

OREGON HISTORY

Written by Stephen Dow Beckham
Pamplin Professor of History
Lewis and Clark College

An Inhabited Land

Nature marked time. Spring followed winter, passed into summer, merged into fall and, inevitably, gave birth to another winter. The progression was endless and predictable. Water was a consistent ingredient. The steady rain and mist fed the coast and western valleys, nourishing lush forests and grasslands. Salmon surged up the streams, filling the water from bank to bank in a cycle of birth and dying. The fish, exhausted after their journey and spawning, were dragged back downstream by the current. Bears and eagles watched and feasted, while the smolts stirred from the gravel to slip unnoticed down the rivers to the sea and renew the endless process.

Beyond the Cascade Mountains in the vast, arid stretches of central and eastern Oregon, the rainfall was less but life was nevertheless abundant. Aromatic sagebrush, hardy juniper, the sunny faces of balsam root, and tufts of lomatium gave form and color to the landscape. In the fall countless birds passed across the sky winging their way southward on their annual migration. Geese, ducks, pelicans, and sandhill cranes settled down to search for seeds, feed on brine shrimp in the alkaline lakes, or gain energy for their push to their winter rookeries. Nature constructed elaborate stage sets in the mountains, as tamarack, vine maple, big-leaf maple, and alder shed their chlorophyll and transformed from green to red, gold and brown. The turning of the leaves, like the migration of birds and of salmon, steelhead, sturgeon, and smelt, marked the change of seasons. Winter brought quiet. Life slowed and snow blanketed part of the land. Living things battened down and endured. And then, as always in nature, the process started over again.

The inevitable exceptions to these predictable events were dramatic and often inexplicable. From time to time the Cascade peaks shuddered and erupted with uncommon fury, releasing ash flows, watery floods of muddy debris, plumes of smoke, and slowly oozing lava. Occasionally a rupture appeared in the earth and, as in ancient times when the great basalt flows spread like taffy, layer upon layer, to form the Columbia Plateau, lavas poured out on the surface. They diverted rivers and formed a jumbled landscape, almost fortified in appearance, before ceasing their advance and cooling. Sometimes the earth simply shook and, with great drama, rose or fell. These massive quakes plunged forests surrounding wetlands into estuaries or the sea; they unleashed landslides that sometimes dammed rivers. The earthquakes, driven by the thrust of the Pacific Plate under the continent, changed the face of the land.

Humans witnessed these things.

For at least 10,000 years, and perhaps for another 5,000 to 10,000 years before that, they were in Oregon. Their names for themselves, their languages, and their lifeways are unknown, but they were here. Evidence of their presence is subtle but certain. In central and eastern Oregon, where discovery of prehistory is easier because the vegetation is sparse and artifacts are more likely to be preserved in dry rock shelters, archaeologists have found numerous traces. The record, while incomplete, is compelling.

Humans hunted the megafauna of the Late Pleistocene. Massive creatures, far larger than any alive today, lived during the Wisconsin Ice Age, which began to end about 15,000 years ago. Mammoths, mastodons, horses and camels lived contemporaneously with Oregon's first human inhabitants. Scattered in the sands of the High Desert are a mix of camel bones and pieces of fluted projectile points. Big game hunters using the atlatl—a spear-throwing device that gave them greater leverage and improved both distance and velocity—killed the big game animals that were yet in the land. Whether hunting hastened the animals' passing or whether environmental conditions drove them to extinction is not clear, but the animals and humans were neighbors in Oregon ten or more millennia ago.

The story of prehistory in Oregon has unfolded steadily since the advent of archaeological investigations mounted in the 1870s by Paul Schumacher and A.W. Chase along the coast. While the early researchers were primarily relic collectors, Dr. Luther S. Cressman of the University of Oregon helped in the 1930s to develop the discipline of systematic scientific research verifying the deep timeframe of an Indian presence in Oregon. Cressman's primary contributions unfolded at Fort Rock Cave, a deep rock shelter that, 10,000 years ago, was home to people living on an island in a vast inland lake in south-central Oregon. Cressman and his students investigated several sites, testing and excavating, but leaving portions of each location. How fortunate was that discipline, for following World War II and the development of radiocarbon dating, Cressman returned to Fort Rock to open new units of the site and established that more than 10,000 years ago the region had been occupied by humans.

Oregon's archaeological record grows fuller each year. It documents more than ten millennia of human habitation and successive adaptations to changing environmental conditions. At the end of the eighteenth century, Oregon possessed several distinctive lifeways. These, for the convenience of description, have been described in geographical terms as Coast, Plateau, and Great Basin. While this lumping violates some of the integrity of distinctive cultural practices, it helps clarify the complex human adaptations to distinctive biotic regions of the state.

Northwest Coast

The native peoples of the shoreline and western Oregon valleys, in general, shared lifeways common with Indians residing along the North Pacific from Cape Mendocino to southeast Alaska. From the Clatsop at the mouth of the Columbia to the Chetco at the California border and from the Clackamas near the falls of the Willamette to the Takelma and Shasta of the Rogue River Valley—these people shared a common setting: a wet, temperate region, heavily forested, connected by rivers running into the sea. Their environment provided the essentials of life: cedar to frame and cover their houses, materials for clothing and dugout canoes, salmon and other fish as primary subsistence, and a bounty of game, roots, and berries to supplement their diet

For these Indians life was predictable and generally easy. They had to work hard to secure and maintain supplies of firewood, repair their fishing traps, weirs, and nets, and engage in extensive gathering activities, but for them, nature was generous. Shoreline residents harvested vast quantities of mollusks and crustaceans from the intertidal zones. Valley Indians dug camas and wapato, gathered and processed acorns, hunted deer and elk, and worked a bit harder to survive. Annually they set fire to the meadows, opening and shaping the landscapes of the Willamette, Umpqua, and Rogue River valleys. Burning stimulated nutritious browse for deer, assisted women in the harvest of tarweed seeds, stimulated the regeneration of berries, and maintained an open understory, which undoubtedly enhanced the security of settlements.

Oregon natives of the western part of the state possessed sufficient time and wealth to develop special arts. The Chinookans of the Columbia River carved handsome, high-prowed canoes with animal effigies on their bows and erected remarkable wooden spirit figures at vigil and grave sites. The Tututni and Chetco of the south coast bartered for raw materials and made massive obsidian wealth-display blades; wove intricately decorated basketry with geometric designs of beargrass, maidenhair fern, and wild hazel bark; and sent their young people off on spirit quests to sacred sites atop mountain peaks or promontories overlooking the sea. The Coquille, Coos, Lower Umpqua, Siuslaw, Alsea, and Tillamook occupied estuaries that carry their names. A dozen bands from the Tualatin to the Santiam and Yoncalla lived in the Willamette Valley and northern Umpqua Valley. South of them resided the Upper Umpqua, Cow Creeks, Shasta Costa, Takelma, and Shasta. Western Oregon Indians had connections of trade and commerce reaching into northern California and to coastal Washington and British Columbia. They were involved in the flow of dentalium shells, elk hide armor, slaves, and surplus foods. Their lifeways echoed the strong traditions of art, ceremony, social class distinction, emphasis on wealth that ran for hundreds of miles along the North Pacific Coast.

Columbia Plateau

Living east of the Cascades, the Indians of Oregon's interior nevertheless had access to unparalleled riverine resources. The Columbia and its tributaries—Deschutes, John Day, Umatilla, Snake, Grande Ronde, and Owyhee—were filled with fish. For at least 10,000 years Celilo Falls, the place where the Columbia dropped over a series of basalt ledges and surged almost on its side through Five Mile Rapids, was their major fishery. So vast were the harvests of fish, the tribes that gathered at Celilo controlled one of the greatest, longest-operating trade centers in the American West. The commerce of Celilo was varied. Arriving from the coast were sleek dugout canoes, paddles, cattail matting, prized shells, and special foodstuffs such as smelt. From the south came war captives to be bartered into slavery, obsidian from more than twenty quarry sites destined for the hands of craftsmen in Washington and British Columbia (where none of this vital projectile material existed naturally), and, just prior to Euro-American contact, herds of horses. From the east came carefully preserved beargrass for basketry, buffalo hides and saddles and, again just before the arrival of American explorers, remarkable trade goods—glass beads, weapons, metal-tipped tools, and cotton and woolen cloth and clothing.

The Plateau people occupied a challenging environment. Summers were hot and windy; winters were cold and windy. The lodges to shelter human activities thus varied from pole-frame, mat-covered summer encampments to semisubterranean pit houses, framed with a cone of rafters covered with brush and earth to provide a refuge from the icy cold, snow, and darkness of winter. In spite of its harshness the region abounded in life. Following annual ceremonies, the women harvested the roots of wild celeries, balsams, and lomatiums. They picked huckleberries in the nearby mountains and gathered nutritious moss. The men ran down deer in the snow to secure not only meat but hides to tan for clothing and moccasins. They dipped, clubbed, netted, and speared salmon and wind-dried them in curing sheds along the river.

Oregon's Plateau Indians included the Wasco, Wishram, Warm Springs (or Tenino), John Day, Cayuse, Umatilla, and Nez Perce. They lived from the Cascade Mountains to the Wallowas, from the margins of the rivers to summer camps at high elevations. Their seasonal round responded to the rhythms of nature and took them from fishing

History

camps to berry-picking sites and hunting camps high in the mountains. With the onset of winter they returned to lower elevations and their permanent villages along the margins of the principal streams.

Great Basin

The high desert region is majestic and harsh. It is an unforgiving landscape where, at times, life is a scramble. For the Northern Paiute, Western Shoshoni, Bannock, Klamath, and Modoc, survival demanded unremitting labor and almost constant movement. While the Klamath and Modoc possessed staple foods such as suckers, trout, wocus (water-lily seed), and huckleberries, the tribes to the east had a more marginal existence. Their resilience in coping with high elevation, extreme temperatures, arid conditions, and isolation spoke to their time-tested survival skills in a challenging environment. The Klamath Basin peoples actually lived at a point of transition between Plateau, Basin, Coast and California lifeways, whereas the Northern Paiute, who held vast stretches of central and southeastern Oregon, were more closely tied to the basin environment.

Oregon's Great Basin peoples engaged in a seasonal round that often required 200 or more miles of travel per year. In winter they resided on the margins of lakes and rivers, seeking the lowest elevation and most moderate temperatures in harsh conditions. Their homes included rock shelters as well as lodges covered with brush and tule mats. In winters, confinement and the months of the long moons encouraged storytelling and necessitated tapping the food resources carefully stored in the previous seasons. When spring became summer, these people were on the move. They hunted waterfowl, antelope, and deer; gathered roots, berries, seeds, and nuts; fished; and traveled. They moved to higher and higher elevations, following food sources, until the aspen leaves turned to bright gold, telling them it was time to leave the high country and return to the winter encampments.

The peoples of the Great Basin traveled in extended family groups but sometimes gathered as bands for communal hunts. Women and children fanned out through the countryside and, moving slowly toward a ravine and making great noise, drove all creatures before them. Far down the trace, etched eons ago by erosion through basalt, the men stretched fiber nets. Here they clubbed frightened rabbits or, when lucky, killed deer and antelope with bow and arrow. Paddling carefully in the predawn cold onto the waters of the lakes in the middle of the High Desert, the men silently stretched nets between poles and, with a great noise, spooked the unsuspecting water birds. The birds rose to flee in the mist, only to become entangled in the mesh of netting, which the men then collapsed into the water, harvesting a bountiful supply of food for their families.

Great Basin residents practiced a mixed economy. They hunted, fished, trapped, dug, and picked food resources. They moved with the seasons in an almost continuous quest for subsistence. They covered a vast, open country, leaving their petroglyphs at sacred sites, caching foods, camping in rock shelters used by the ancient inhabitants of the region. Their finely developed survival skills enabled them to endure and prosper in a land that held them, at times, at the edge of existence.

The first inhabitants occupied three distinct biotic provinces or geographical areas. Their adaptation and mastery of the environment reached from the margins of the fog-shrouded and wet Pacific shoreline to the arid reaches of sagebrush and bunchgrass of the interior. Their subsistence activities took them from sea level to tree line in the Wallowas and on Steens Mountain. They were at home in the desert and in the grasslands of the Columbia Plateau. In the fall they set fire to the meadows to keep open the western Oregon valleys as well as to maintain the bald headlands along the Oregon coast. At the south-facing bases of the headlands they often erected their plank houses facing into the sun. They plied the rivers with dugout canoes; they hunted for ducks and geese on the lakes with balsa rafts made of dried tules.

The first inhabitants knew this land. They gave it names. They explained its features in their oral traditions, through experienced storytellers reciting the literature. They told of the myth age when only animals and no humans were in the land. They recounted tales of transition, when animals and humans interacted on a personal basis, a time when humans were not quite fully formed. They told of the historic past, of things remembered and partly remembered. They did this with gesture, eye contact, voice modulation, and sometimes by musical interlude wherein they or someone in the crowd sang a song relevant to the story. Their techniques varied. The Tillamook, for example, repeated stories line-by-line as they listened to the teller, thereby memorizing over a period of years the literature and history of their tribe. The challenge to the storyteller was thus to deliver with talent and stay true to the story elements, yet build the drama and unleash creativity.

The first inhabitants held a rich land. Its resources far exceeded their needs and their wants. They lived fully. While there is some evidence of migration and population dynamics, those tales of prehistory are lost in the mists of time. What is known is that Oregon was fully occupied by the eighteenth century. Indians of more than 30 different languages lived throughout the state. They knew and loved the land. It was their home.

Some Came By Sea

The first moment of contact was not recorded. Possibly it occurred when a Manilla Galleon made a landfall somewhere along the Oregon Coast. How the viewers must have wondered when, looking out to sea, they saw a great ship, propelled by billowing sails, not paddles, scudding to the wind and laboring through the waves. The prospect for such an encounter unfolded in 1565 when the Spanish, after several years of probing for a route, finally found a means to send a vessel northeast from the Philippines to catch the great Japanese Current for a sweeping circular transit of the North Pacific. While normally the galleons—one per year for 250 years—did not make a landfall until south of Cape Mendocino in northern California, some did so farther north.

The *San Francisco Xavier*, one of 30 vessels that failed to arrive in Acapulco or any of the other destination ports along the west coast of New Spain (Mexico), likely wrecked in 1707 on the Nehalem sand spit near the base of Neahkahnie Mountain. Tillamook Indian tales of strangers in their midst, discoveries of large chunks of beeswax and a lidded silver vase, and legends of buried treasure hint that a wayward galleon may have crashed into the shore. A thousand-ton vessel, it was probably laden with silk, porcelain, altar pieces reworked in Asia from gold and silver shipped from Central America, pepper, cloves, and other luxury items—each stored in cargo space allotted to the merchants who controlled the monopoly of the galleon trade.

Spanish voyages in the North Pacific were part of the nation's efforts to seek colonies, mission fields, and wealth. As early as 1543 Bartolome Ferrelo, a surviving captain of the ill-fated expedition under Juan Cabrillo, may have sailed as far north as the Oregon-California border. He and his shipmates sought the fabled Straits of Anian—a passage through the continent. Cape Ferrelo on the south coast bears his name. Some also believe that Francis Drake sojourned on the *Golden Hind* in 1579 in coastal Oregon. Having raided Spanish ports and stolen immense wealth in his voyage northward from Cape Horn, Drake was hiding out before crossing the Pacific and rounding the world to return to England. Although his anchorage is claimed at sites in California, heralded in a marker at Cape Arago, and said to have been at Whale Cove, no one has produced conclusive evidence of his visit to Oregon. Sebastian Vizcaino, sailing for Spain in 1603, possibly sighted and named Cape Sebastian north of the California border. The promontory marked his northernmost exploration along the Pacific shoreline.

Then came silence. As had been the case for thousands of years, Oregon was wholly an Indian land. The mid-1700s, however, unleashed forces that would forever change native dominion in the American West. The forces were in part intellectual. Europe had engaged in a renaissance, a rekindling of energies and rediscovery of classical learning. Emerging nation-states took pride in commerce, art, and education. The turning point, however, was the Enlightenment. By the early eighteenth century, several nations had philosophical societies whose members hungered for knowledge and who sought natural laws or evidence for what governed the universe. They became eager students of the world. Carl Linne, a Swede, developed systems to classify all living things as plants or animals, seeking to order the descriptions and terminologies. Luke Howard, an Englishman, developed a nomenclature for clouds. Isaac Newton provided mathematical evidence on the working of gravity and descriptions of optics. The quest for knowledge, developing collections of "curiosities," and, in time, exploring unknown lands took on national significance.

The reaching out of Russians to the Aleutians and into Alaska between 1728 and 1769 shocked the Spanish. Following the discoveries of Vitus Bering, Russian fur seekers swept into the region, destroying Aleut villages, enslaving the natives, and securing riches by shipping furs to the Asian and European markets. A cardinal principle of Spain, exercised since the 1520s, was to create protective borderlands to insulate her wealthiest colonies from foreign predators. By the 1760s, officials in New Spain were gravely worried that the Russians, somewhere to the north, might fall upon their outlying colonies in Baja California, Pimeria Alta (Arizona), or New Mexico. Viceroy Antonio de Bucareli in 1769 thus dispatched Gaspar de Portola by sea and Juan Batista de Anza by land with priests, soldiers, and families of workers to establish a new borderland—Alta California. Within two decades these Spanish colonists had a chain of missions, presidios, and pueblos extending from San Diego to San Francisco Bay.

When the Russians did not appear, the Spanish reached out again. In 1775 the viceroy ordered the first of a series of maritime expeditions to explore the coastline northward. The voyages of Juan Perez, Bruno Hezeta, and Bodega y Quadra gave more form to the European understanding of the coast. Working under wretched conditions, sailing against the current and suffering from ill health and spoiled water, the mariners nevertheless began an important era in exploration.

The British came next. In 1778 Captain James Cook, aboard *H.M.S. Resolution,* made a landfall on the central Oregon coast. He commemorated the day by naming the headland Cape Foulweather. A famed mariner who had twice before explored the Pacific, Cook was sent to find the Northwest Passage, a mythical sea route through the continent. He could not find what did not exist, but Cook sailed north to the Arctic Ocean and charted much of the outer coast. The Spanish responded immediately and dispatched Ignacio de Arteaga and Bodega y Quadra in 1779 to explore parts of coastal Alaska. In the 1780s the French expedition under Comte de Laperouse and the Spanish expedition under Alessandro Malaspina sailed the shore to chart, collect specimens of natural history and native culture, and assess the prospects of new colonies.

Significant in discerning the features of coastal Oregon were the labors of independent mariners, dispatched not by their governments but by investors who sought wealth through the fur trade. Cook's men discovered when they reached China in 1779 that a sea otter pelt purchased for a broken file or a few brass buttons brought a thousand-fold return when bartered to the merchants of the Pearl River delta. Captain John Meares of England and Captain Robert Gray of Boston both sailed the coast of Oregon in 1788–89 and traded with natives who paddled out to sea in their canoes or who, in Gray's trade at Tillamook Bay, dared to barter with the foreigners who sailed across the bar and dropped anchor near their villages.

On a second voyage to the coast in 1792, Gray decided to risk a perilous crossing, the unknown bar of the Columbia River. Although the river had been discerned by Hezeta and tentatively designated Rio San Roque, no mariner had entered it. Gray did. He and his men sailed through the breakers and over the shoals, passing the base of Cape Disappointment, named in frustration by Meares on a previous voyage, and dropped anchor in the broad estuary of the great river. Gray named it Columbia in honor of his ship, the *Columbia Rediviva*. A few weeks later Gray encountered the exploring party headed by Captain George Vancouver, another British expedition in search of the Northwest Passage. Gray told Vancouver of his "discovery" of the Columbia, a watershed known and occupied by thousands of people for at least 10,000 years. Vancouver could not resist. He brought the *Chatham* and the *Discovery* into the Columbia and dispatched Lieutenant William Broughton to chart its course. Broughton sailed as far east as the entrance to the Columbia Gorge, noting depths of the channel and Indian villages along the shore, persuaded, at last, that the river did not pass through the continent.

By the end of the 18th century an estimated 300 vessels from a dozen different countries had sailed to the Northwest Coast. Some of these had passed along the shores of Oregon. The logs of James Cook, John Meares, Robert Gray, John Boit, and Robert Haswell, as well as eight diaries of George Vancouver's shipmates recorded first impressions of the land and its people. "They were of a middling size with mild pleasing features & nowise sullen or distrustful in their behaviour," wrote Dr. Archibald Menzies in 1792 when describing the Quah-to-mah Indians near Cape Blanco.

The mariners named headlands, charted offshore rocks, explored some of the estuaries, notably the Columbia and Puget Sound, and obtained useful knowledge. The narratives of Cook and Vancouver were published shortly after their journeys. They whetted the appetite of others who wanted to know more about these lands. The collections of bows, arrows, baskets, and plants secured by Vancouver's expedition went into the holdings of the British Museum. What had been unknown was now better understood. The currents of the Enlightenment had swept halfway round the world and touched the Oregon country.

Land-based Fur Trade and Exploration

The mariners who sailed the coast or ran their vessels tentatively into the estuaries and harbors of Oregon initiated inexorable forces of change. They introduced trade goods that swept in swift current through the traditional cultures of the native peoples, altering forever their clothing, technology, and means of subsistence. They introduced diseases such as smallpox, measles, and fevers; in time these pathogens decimated the Indian population. However, an event that would have even greater consequence was the November, 1805, arrival at the mouth of the Columbia River of a weary but eager exploring party under the command of Meriwether Lewis and William Clark.

Dispatched in 1804 by President Thomas Jefferson, this military expedition, financed at public expense and underwritten in part by the American Philosophical Society, was the American nation's belated commitment to the Enlightenment. Ostensibly the party was to explore the newly acquired Louisiana Territory. Jefferson, however, wanted to find a water route, so far as practical, for the transit of commerce across North America. An avid student of nature and civilization, he laid out detailed instructions for the explorers to observe the flora, fauna, geology, climate, and Indian culture. They were to map the land, take temperatures of hot springs, note locations of major geographical features, record Indian vocabularies, and open diplomatic relations between the tribes and the United States.

The scripting of the expedition could not have been more perfect. The cast of characters included two stalwart leaders, young Army recruits, French-Canadian hunters, a Shoshoni woman— Sacagawea—and her infant son—Baptiste Charbonneau—York, an African-American slave of William Clark's, and a shaggy Newfoundland dog. The success of the Corps of Discovery in carrying out its multiple missions gave it luster while heightening interest in western lands and in government-financed exploration.

Lewis and Clark accomplished their mission with verve. They crossed the Rockies, entered the

Bitterroot Valley of Montana, followed the Nez Perce Trail west of Lolo Pass, and then embarked by dugouts to descend the Clearwater, Snake and Columbia rivers. They camped on the north and south banks of the Columbia, portaged at Celilo Falls, passed through the Gorge and established their winter quarters at Fort Clatsop on the Oregon shore near the river's mouth. During the rain-soaked winter of 1805–06, they wrote their journals, boiled salt from seawater on the nearby beach of the Pacific, recorded cultural information from the Clatsop and Chinook Indians, drew numerous maps, and hoped a trading vessel might carry some of their treasured notes safely to the president. None appeared. The following spring the party departed for home, paddling against the swift current until it reached the mouth of the Umatilla River. Having bartered for horses sufficient to carry the party and its supplies, the men set out overland to retrace their steps across the mountains and plains.

News of the Lewis and Clark Expedition enlivened interest in distant frontiers. Already fur seekers were pushing up the Missouri, Arkansas, and Red rivers. The descriptions of swift streams and ponds filled with beaver, mink, otter, and marten in the mountains persuaded several investors to send men with traps and trade goods to exploit those resources. John Colter, a member of the Corps of Discovery, turned around before reaching St. Louis and signed on with a fur trapping party headed for the Yellowstone country. The rush for furs had taken on a new life. This time Americans were major players.

Jefferson turned over the journals of the leaders to Nicholas Biddle, who edited them in an abridged two-volume edition, *The Journals of Lewis & Clark* (1814). So popular were their accounts of adventure that an eager public literally read the books to pieces.

Lewis and Clark had created a remarkable legacy. They had dramatically enhanced the geographical understanding of a far-flung part of North America. They collected 178 plant specimens—140 in the Oregon Country. They made notes upon or brought home specimens of 122 species and subspecies of animals—65 west of the Continental Divide. They expanded a nation's horizon and understanding in noteworthy ways.

The stirrings of change picked up momentum in 1808, when Simon Fraser and other employees of the North West Company, a fur-trading enterprise based in Montreal, crossed the Rockies and descended a mighty stream—the Fraser—to the Pacific Ocean. David Thompson, a skilled cartographer also in the employ of the North West Company, came next. He and his party crossed the Rockies and descended the Columbia. When he reached the ocean in 1811, he found an American fur trade post on the south shore. The Pacific Fur

Company had already established a toehold, the first permanent Euro-American settlement in the region, at Astoria.

The new post on the lower Columbia River fulfilled the speculative dream of John Jacob Astor. An emigrant from Germany who prospered as a middleman in the fur trade and investor in New York real estate, Astor had listened keenly to reports of the Lewis and Clark expedition. One of America's first millionaires, Astor thought big. His vision was to establish a post near the ocean shore in the Pacific Northwest. Land-based trappers and traders would secure furs for his rich trade in Canton. His warehouses on the lower Pearl River would exchange otter pelts for silks and porcelains for the American market. His sailing vessels would supply both his Columbia River post and the Russian American Company in Alaska. These ambitions led Astor to found the American Fur Company for the Rocky Mountain region in 1808, the Pacific Fur Company for the Columbia watershed in 1810, and the South West Company in 1811.

To attain his goals in Oregon, Astor planned a two-prong approach. He outfitted the *Tonquin*, a ship under Captain Jonathan Thorn, with trade goods, tools, and everything needed to sustain his new fort on the Columbia. Sailing in September, 1810, the *Tonquin* arrived in March 1811 at the Columbia River. Astor also ordered Wilson Price Hunt to lead an overland party, which departed from St. Louis in September 1810 for an arduous and nearly fatal winter crossing of the continent. Ultimately, in spite of drownings at the mouth of the Columbia and terrible privations for the overland party, the Astorians began clearing the dense spruce forest to erect their fort. "The buildings consisted of apartments for the proprietors and clerks, with a capacious dining-hall for both, extensive warehouses for the trading goods and furs, a provision store, a trading shop, smith's forge, carpenter's workshop," noted Ross Cox. All was enclosed by a log stockade with two bastions in which the Astorians mounted six-pound cannon.

Although the Pacific Fur Company's outpost appeared substantial when David Thompson arrived at its doorstep in 1812, its tenure proved fragile. The *Tonquin* was blown up and sank on a trading voyage north along the coast. Supplies were infrequent. The men at Astoria were driven by starvation to establish Willamette Post in the lower Willamette Valley to relieve some of the pressure on stores at the river's mouth. The connections with China were infrequent. When the partners-in-the-field at Astoria learned of the outbreak of the War of 1812, they rightly feared a British naval vessel might enter the river and seize their post. Thus, in 1813, they sold out to the North West Company. The sale ended Astor's dreams for the Pacific Fur

Company. His investment, however, proved highly consequential for the United States.

The Treaty of Ghent (1814) provided in the peace terms ending the war with Great Britain that all conditions would revert to "status ante bellum." The Americans subsequently interpreted this clause to mean that the American claim to the Oregon Country—enhanced by the construction of the fort at Astoria—remained unextinguished. To buttress this prospect the U.S. Navy dispatched Captain James Biddle on the *U.S. Ontario* to the Columbia River. In 1818 Biddle declared American possession of both shores of the estuary. John B. Prevost, an American special agent, arrived later that year and symbolically reasserted his nation's interest by raising the Stars and Stripes on the flagpole at Fort George, the post purchased and named by the North West Company for King George III of England.

During the 1810s the competition between the North West Company and the Hudson's Bay Company, the older, larger rival for control of the fur trade, erupted into bloodshed in the Red River Valley in Canada. Determined to end the conflict and to bring stability to the frontier, the British parliament in 1821 forcibly merged the companies. One firm survived—the Hudson's Bay Company, founded in 1670. This British corporation took over the interests of the North West Company in the Oregon Country. For the next 25 years the Hudson's Bay Company helped shape the destiny of the region.

The Hudson's Bay Company had a single concern: profit. To satisfy investors interested in return on their money, the directors in London named George Simpson to superintend the field operations. Simpson, in turn, named Dr. John McLoughlin, a former North West Company employee, to serve as Chief Factor in the watershed of the Columbia River. The directions of Simpson and steady hand of McLoughlin proved highly significant in the history of Oregon. Collectively they agreed on a simple, effective set of policies: peace with the Indian tribes, fair prices for furs secured through trade, and self-sufficiency for the posts in the region.

The Oregon Country was so distant that the company workers in the region had to provide for their own subsistence. Vessels could bring in tools and trade goods, but they could not provide food to sustain the nearly 600 men working for the company and their families. Simpson and McLoughlin thus developed the post system. Fort Vancouver, founded in 1822 near the confluence of the Willamette and Columbia rivers, was the hub. The spokes of connection reached to Fort George at the mouth of the Columbia, Fort Umpqua in southwestern Oregon, Fort Boise on the western Snake Plain in Idaho, and to Fort Nisqually, Fort Okanogan, and Fort Walla Walla in Washington. A series of more distant forts in British Columbia and southeast Alaska completed the system. Post traders were encouraged to plant vegetables, lay out orchards, and raise livestock. These stations tested the region's agricultural potentials. They found considerable promise in their ventures.

Simpson and McLoughlin also instituted the brigade system. In addition to the posts where nearby Indian tribes bartered furs for trade goods, the company outfitted brigades of 20 to 50 or more employees who, with their Indian wives and children, went into the field to trap and trade for months. Brigade leaders in Oregon included John Work, Michel LaFramboise, Alexander Roderick McLeod, and Peter Skene Ogden. The brigades penetrated the far reaches of the state. McLeod, for example, explored the Oregon coast south to the Rogue River in the 1820s. Work led brigades back and forth via the Willamette, Umpqua, and Rogue Valleys to the Sacramento Valley of California. Ogden mounted five brigades to the upper Snake River. His mission, defined by Simpson, was to eradicate the fur-bearing animals of the region. The plan of ecological disruption mounted by the company was to create an area so devoid of furs that Americans crossing the Rockies would become discouraged and turn back. The Hudson's Bay Company largely succeeded in all these objectives.

Simpson and McLoughlin also launched other initiatives. They established a coastal maritime trade. The *Beaver*, a steam-powered sidewheeler, brought manufactured items to native villages along the shore north to Alaska. They opened retail stores in San Francisco and Honolulu and offered lumber cut at the company mill on the north bank of the Columbia as well as salted salmon from Pillar Rock and Cascades fisheries on the river. They established the Puget Sound Agricultural Company with farms at Nisqually and Cowlitz Landing.

The legacies of the Hudson's Bay Company were many. Its employees fished for salmon, felled the towering firs, manufactured lumber, grew bountiful gardens, raised cereal crops, tended horses on the plateau and cows on the meadows west of the Cascades, and trapped and traded for furs. The brigade leaders mapped much of the land; their diaries, closely held by the company, contained valuable geographical information. The company had great impact on the Indian tribes. It spread manufactured goods, hastened cultural change, and introduced new diseases. Most of the firm's employees—including natives from Hawaii and Polynesia—married native women creating a mixed-blood population. Their children had connections with both local and foreign worlds and often grew up bilingual. The company spread the Chinook Jargon far and wide. This trade vocabulary of nearly 1,000 words was founded on the Chinookan language of the Columbia River. It became the primary means of communication across tribal lines and with Euro-Americans throughout the region.

The success of the Hudson's Bay Company in the Pacific Northwest did not pass unnoticed. In the 1820s Hall Jackson Kelley, an ardent, visionary schoolteacher in Massachusetts, began promoting American colonization of the region. Kelley printed circulars and pamphlets that raved about the region's potentials. He talked about the "spontaneous growth of the soil" and the "fruits of laborious industry," which would make Americans rich if they would settle in Oregon. Nathaniel Jarvis Wyeth, a wealthy Boston ice merchant, responded and, when Kelley's colony failed to develop, he formed the Pacific Trading Company, a joint-stock venture, to develop Oregon.

Wyeth's plans echoed those of John Jacob Astor. In 1832 he set out with uniformed associates to cross the continent and locate forts in the Oregon Country. His plan was to supply his land-based traders from western stations and ship furs and salmon to Asia. Desertions reduced his party to 11. John McLoughlin played the good host and extended the hospitality of Fort Vancouver to the American but did little to encourage his enterprise. In 1834 Wyeth returned to Oregon. He traveled with companions overland, driving wagons across the Great Plains and to South Pass, the subsequent route of the Oregon Trail. His party built Fort Hall on the upper Snake and erected Fort William on Sauvie Island at the mouth of the Willamette. Wyeth then set out to trap for furs in the Deschutes watershed. His diary documented his lonely, fruitless efforts to wrest a fortune from the fur-bearing animals of central Oregon. Wyeth's competitors were too powerful. The American Fur Company commanded the trade in the Rockies; the Hudson's Bay Company had a firm grip on the Pacific Northwest. Wyeth's supply ship arrived late and carried out a cargo of poorly preserved salmon. In 1836 he gave up. His business, which showed so much promise, had foundered on the realities of competition and demanding conditions in Oregon.

A fascinating legacy from the fur trade era was how its operators played host to wandering naturalists. David Douglas was singular among these. A Scotsman in the employ of the Royal Horticultural Society of London, Douglas came to Oregon in 1825–27 and 1830–32 to collect plants of potential uses in European landscapes as well as to obtain herbarium specimens to enlarge the understanding of botany. Douglas was ardent in his assignment. In 1826 he traveled alone into the South Umpqua watershed of southwestern Oregon in a quest for the sugar pine trees that produced the handsome seeds he had viewed at Fort Vancouver. His diaries documented his explorations; his name became popularly attached to *Pseudotsuga menziesii,* the famed Douglas Fir. In 1834 Thomas Nuttall, of Harvard University's Arnold Arboretum, and naturalist John Kirk Townsend accompanied Wyeth on his second overland journey. Townsend's *Narrative of Travels Beyond the Rocky Mountains* (1839) gave a positive account of the American West. The duplicates of his bird and mammal skins he sold to John James Audubon. These specimens added to scientific understanding and were rendered into lifelike images by the famed painter in his books on North American birds and the quadrupeds.

By the early 1840s the fur trade was in decline. Changes in fashion had significantly reduced the interest in men's top hats made of hair stripped from beaver pelts. Extermination of fur-bearing animals in vast parts of the American West was another factor. Furs were neither abundant nor cheap. The days of the fur trade were ending, but the legacy of the enterprise was large. The fur trade had opened primary routes of travel, altered Indian lifeways, filled in geographical information, and produced an important literature about Oregon. The Astorians—Ross Cox, Alexander Ross, Gabriel Franchere, Robert Stuart, and Peter Corney—all produced books in the nineteenth century describing Oregon. More significant, however, were the companion volumes penned by Washington Irving. His works, *Astoria or Anecdotes of an Enterprise Beyond the Rocky Mountains* (1836) and *Adventures of Captain Bonneville* (1837), were read by an eager public. Irving described the temperate climate and abundant resources of Oregon, portraying the land as a place of adventure and possible prosperity.

Federal Interests

The government of the United States maintained special interests in Oregon. It founded its claims on the "doctrine of the right of discovery." Although Robert Gray was a mariner for a private fur-trading company, he sailed under a sea letter issued by President George Washington. His crossing of the bar of the Columbia initiated the U.S. claim to having "discovered" Oregon. The Lewis and Clark Expedition was a military expedition financed and directed by the government. Fort Clatsop, though occupied less than five months in 1805–06, was deemed an American outpost. So, too, the Pacific Fur Company's Fort Astoria was an American venture, and the U.S. through the actions of Captain Biddle and John Prevost asserted national interests in 1818 pursuant to the terms of the Treaty of Ghent.

In 1818 the United States and Great Britain met in diplomatic conference to try to resolve their interests in the Oregon Country. The negotiators, at loggerheads over the extension of the 49th parallel to the Pacific, reached a compromise. In the Convention of 1818 they agreed to shared spheres of interest in the Columbia watershed, deferring the question of sovereignty for the time being.

History

The Americans were not idle. In the 1819 Adams-Onis Treaty, whereby Spain ceded Florida to the U.S., American negotiators secured all of the Spanish "discovery rights" north of the 42nd parallel—the northern boundary of California. In 1824 the United States negotiated an agreement permitting trade for ten years in Alaska and fixing Russia's southern boundary at 50° 40'. Slowly, steadily, the United States had narrowed the field among the nations vying for control of the Oregon Country. Great Britain, the United States, and the Indian tribes remained as competitors. In 1827 the two countries agreed to extend indefinitely their earlier agreement that each had a sphere of interest in the region. The new condition added to the convention was that either nation might give notice and demand a resolution of the issue within one year.

American "discovery rights" gained Supreme Court sanction when, in 1823, Chief Justice John Marshall ruled in a matter involving former Indian lands. Marshall opined in *Johnson v. McIntosh* that because natives were wanderers over the face of the earth, their rights were impaired and subordinate to the "discovery rights" of Europeans. While tribes retained an occupancy right, title was not vested in them. The Marshall ruling became a convenient justification to dispossess hundreds of tribes of their homelands.

President Andrew Jackson, an expansionist with interests in the West, attempted in 1835 to purchase the harbor of San Francisco for $500,000 from Mexico. The following year he dispatched the brig *Loriot* to the West Coast. Lieutenant William A. Slacum carried a presidential commission to examine Puget Sound, the Columbia estuary, and San Francisco Bay, assess those anchorages for strategic value, and examine the frontier economy of the region. Slacum's report, printed in the Congressional Serial Set, made a strong case for American acquisition of all three harbors.

Jackson next endorsed and Congress funded the multifaceted U.S. Exploring Expedition. Under the command of Lieutenant Charles Wilkes, this Navy party included five vessels, more than 300 seamen, and a corps of talented scientists, artists, and officers. After exploring the coasts of South America, Australia, and Hawaii, the expedition in 1841 sailed to Puget Sound and the Columbia River. Overland parties traveled south via the Cowlitz to Fort Vancouver, east through the Gorge to Fort Walla Walla, and south through the Willamette Valley to Sutter's Fort on the Sacramento River. James Dwight Dana collected fossils at Saddle Mountain at the mouth of the Columbia; Titian Ramsay Peale sketched the Umpqua Mountains; Horatio Hale compiled Indian vocabularies; and Charles Wilkes penned a fact-filled description of western Oregon.

In 1845 the narrative and scientific reports of the Wilkes Expedition, as it was popularly called, began to appear. Volumes four and five contained candid information about Oregon. Wilkes described the Willamette Valley and its "advantages for raising crops, pasturage of stock, and the facilities of settlers becoming rich." He wrote: "The salmon-fishery may be classed as one of the great sources of wealth, for it affords a large amount of food at a very low price, and of the very best quality . . . ." The sixth volume of reports, an atlas, included numerous charts of Puget Sound and the Columbia River useful for mariners. Over the next dozen years, specialists wrote scientific assessments of the flora and fauna collected by the expedition and published 14 oversized folios of hand-colored illustrations of the specimens. The knowledge about Oregon had increased dramatically and was based on sound authority.

While the Wilkes party was on the high seas headed to the Pacific Northwest, Robert Greenhow, librarian to the Department of State, compiled his *Memoir, Historical and Political, on the Northwest Coast of North America* (1840). Senator Lewis Linn of Missouri had the report printed for the Select Committee on Oregon Territory and requested the immediate publication of an additional 2,500 copies for the Senate to distribute. Greenhow presented a history of exploration, covered the diplomacy of sovereignty issues, discussed the fur trade, and argued that Oregon was a region *"lying entirely within the undisputed limits of the Republic."* Therein he revealed his agenda. Greenhow's memoir was a brief to make the case for American sovereignty over the Pacific Northwest.

Thomas Hart Benton, senator from Missouri and for more than 20 years a champion of American expansion, in 1842 secured congressional funding for his son-in-law, John Charles Fremont, to explore west to South Pass. The following year Fremont, a member of the U.S. Topographical Engineers, set out again, guided by Kit Carson, to follow overland emigrants across the Oregon Trail. Fremont kept a diary and collected minerals, plants, and zoological specimens. Charles Preuss, his cartographer, prepared eight detailed strip maps showing the route of the trail to Fort Walla Walla. In the map margins were notations on fords, grazing sites, camping locations, and the availability of firewood. Fremont's wife, Jessie, turned her husband's diaries into flowing prose. Published by the Government Printing Office in large numbers, the Fremont narratives and Preuss maps became a major publicity piece for Oregon and a virtual travelers' guide to the trail.

In early 1846 Lieutenant Neil M. Howison sailed to Oregon on the *Shark* to carry out another reconnaissance. Delayed by the wreck of the ship on the Columbia bar, Howison sojourned for five months and examined the land, interviewed residents, visited Indian villages, and reflected on what he saw.

He noted that the influence of Dr. John McLoughlin had "done more than any other man toward the rapid development of the resources of the country." Howison described wolves, grizzly bears, elk, and the thriving condition of cattle and sheep. "I can think of nothing vegetable in nature," he commented, "that Oregon will not produce." His report was ultimately issued in the Congressional Serial Set in 1848. It was another candid assessment of Oregon by an objective observer.

During the period 1792 to 1846, the U.S. government thus aided and abetted American interest in Oregon. The nation's leaders, both public and private, took actions to help buttress claims to Oregon through discovery, diplomacy, exercise of will, and the persuasive historical research of Robert Greenhow. The explorations of Lewis and Clark, Slacum, the Wilkes expedition, John Fremont, and Neil M. Howison generated maps, reports, and collections of specimens. These were analyzed and published. The evidence was growing about the prospects of the Pacific Northwest, and Oregon in particular.

Souls to Save

The first three decades of the nineteenth century were a time of intense religious fervor in America. The Second Great Awakening, kindled by the exhortations of Rev. Timothy Dwight, swept across the land. Camp meetings, revivals, sectarian controversies, the founding of home and foreign mission societies, building of seminaries to educate the ministry, and publication of books, tracts, hymns, and translations of the scriptures into Indian languages were all part of the religious commitment. Shakers gathered in celibate communities. Mormon converts followed the teachings of Joseph Smith Jr. Revivals sweeping over the country produced conversions and, in some, anticipation of the return of Christ to earth.

In 1832 the *Christian Advocate and Journal* carried a feature story about four Indians from the interior of the Pacific Northwest who had arrived in St. Louis. Although they may have come to confer with William Clark, the explorer and then superintendent of Indian affairs in the Louisiana Territory, the press interpreted their visit as a cry from heathens seeking the white man's book of God. This news proved electrifying to a population eager to promote evangelical Christianity. With the alleged request from the "savages of Oregon" for the word of God, mission societies were ready to send workers to the field to reap souls.

Rev. Jason Lee was first to respond. In 1833 the Methodist Episcopal Church authorized Lee, his nephew, Daniel Lee, and three lay assistants to go to Oregon. With mission board underwriting and a determination to preach to the Indians, this party embraced its calling and joined Nathaniel Wyeth in 1834 on his second overland trek to the Columbia estuary. Thus Nuttall and Townsend, with interests in natural history; Wyeth, who hoped to compete with the Hudson's Bay Company; and a cadre of missionaries joined forces to traverse the continent.

Although the initial request for missionaries had presumably come from the Nez Perces or Flatheads in the interior, Lee conferred with McLoughlin on a likely location for a mission west of the Cascades. He selected Mission Bottom on the southwest side of French Prairie in the northern Willamette Valley. Proximity to Fort Vancouver, the proven agricultural potential of the area, the nearby population of retired fur trappers, and the isolation of any site east of the mountains weighed heavily in Lee's decision.

The Methodists tried hard. They built a station, fenced and tilled fields, opened a school, and ministered to the Kalapuyans, whose villages had been ravaged by a horrendous fever starting in 1829. By the mid-1830s as many as 70 percent had perished. Lee and his associates thus coped with orphans, solitary survivors of families or entire villages, and the aged. To cope with the challenges, Lee ambitiously planned to increase his crew of workers. He sent back positive reports and in 1838 returned to the East to seek money and recruits. He raised an estimated $100,000 and brought 32 adults and 18 of their children to Oregon in 1839. The expanded staff opened a mission on the Clatsop Plains, another among the Clackamas Indians at Oregon City, a third at The Dalles, and yet another at the southern end of Puget Sound. In spite of their efforts, the Methodist laborers were not good linguists nor effective missionaries. The converts were few. Dr. Elijah White, a recruit, fired off criticisms to the mission board, which suspended Lee and closed the operations in 1843.

The Methodists, though converting few Indians, had tested the potentials of Oregon and succeeded in raising cereal crops, vegetables, and livestock. Their families prospered. They staked out land claims, including one which encroached on Dr. McLoughlin's milling site at Willamette Falls. Writing home about what they found, they gave good reports of Oregon. These Americans helped set the stage for overland emigration.

In the 1820s the American Board of Commissioners for Foreign Missions (ABCFM) had sent workers among the Cherokee, Creek, Choctaw, and other tribes. An ecumenical project drawing on the resources of the Congregational, Presbyterian, and Dutch Reformed denominations, the ABCFM also responded to the alleged request of Oregon Indians for missionaries. In 1835 Rev. Samuel Parker and Rev. Marcus Whitman traveled west to survey prospects. Although Whitman turned back at Green River in the Rocky Mountains, Parker continued to Oregon, explored widely and, after returning home by sea via Hawaii, published *Journal of an*

Exploring Tour Beyond the Rocky Mountains (1838). Whitman had seen enough to persuade him to devote his energies to the natives of the Pacific Northwest.

In 1836 Whitman, his new wife, Narcissa, Rev. Henry H. Spalding, and his wife, Eliza, set out for Oregon. Both women kept diaries, leaving a fascinating chronicle of the journey of the first white women across the continent. Jane Barnes, a barmaid from Portsmouth, England, had lived for a few months at Astoria during the tenure of the North West Company, but she had traveled by sea. The transit of two missionary women overland was duly noted by residents of the American frontier interested in lands in Oregon.

After visiting Fort Vancouver and obtaining supplies from the Hudson's Bay Company, the Whitmans settled at Waiilatpu, "the place of the rye grass," on the margins of the Walla Walla River near the base of the Blue Mountains. Their mission was to the Cayuse, Umatilla, and Nez Perce Indians. The Spaldings selected a site at Lapwai, Idaho, on the lower Clearwater River in Nez Perce country. For the next 11 years these missionaries and their associates who founded other stations on the Columbia Plateau wrestled with survival, mastering native languages, and trying to convert the Indians. An issue facing all was whether or not it was essential to transform Indians into sedentary farmers dressed like white people as a precondition to conversion to Christianity. The Indians found little attraction in the hard labor of farming, were reluctant to give up their traditional fisheries and hunting, and seemed generally disinterested in the whites' teachings. When Whitman whipped the Indians for disobedience, he fell in their esteem. Conversions were few; troubles accumulated.

In 1838 Fathers Francois N. Blanchet and Modest Demers set out with a Hudson's Bay Company brigade from Red River. They crossed overland through Canada and descended the Columbia to found Catholic missions in the region. The Anglican ministry of Rev. Herbert Beaver at Fort Vancouver in 1836–38 was short-lived and controversial. The fur trappers, many of them nominally Catholic or possessing Catholic ancestors, were receptive to Blanchet and Demers, who moved swiftly, marrying couples, baptizing Indian wives and children, and recording an impressive tally in their sacramental ledgers. They established missions at Fort Vancouver, Cowlitz Prairie, and French Prairie.

Where the protestants had only marginal success in gaining converts, the Catholics prospered. There were several reasons. They did not insist on a change in lifeways as a condition for baptism. They wore vestments, burned incense, rang handbells, recited a ritualistic mass, and generated a sense of mystery and interest in their services. They were single men governed by vows of chastity and steadfast purpose of ministry to their flock. They were bound by a commitment to poverty and not engaged in staking land claims or contesting McLoughlin for a mill site. They had a distant but consistent base of support through the Catholic Church. They had already established connections to the native peoples because Indian women from almost every tribe or band in the Pacific Northwest had married Catholic men. They were skilled linguists and were willing to undergo years of patient work to master the native languages.

In 1834 and 1835 a group of retired fur trappers, most of them French-Canadians living on French Prairie, had petitioned the Bishop of Red River in Canada for a priest. In 1836 they had built a log chapel. Blanchet and Demers thus found a receptive audience when they established the St. Paul Mission in October 1839. The parishioners erected a meeting hall and lodgings for the priest in 1841. The grandly named St. Joseph's College, a school funded in part by a bequest from a French philanthropist, opened in 1843 with 30 boys and three instructors. Nuns arrived in 1844 to establish Saint Marie de Willamette, a girls' school. Parishioners between 1844 and 1846 kilned bricks and erected the St. Paul Church.

Missions further accelerated changes in the lives of Oregon Indians. Many tribes, particularly in western Oregon, were imprinted by the itinerant priests and carried for generations a commitment to Catholicism. This was especially the case among the Kalapuyans and Upper Chinookans. Adrian Croquet, a Belgian priest, ministered to them on the Grand Ronde Reservation from 1860 to 1898. Catholic Oblate missions of St. Ann, St. Rose of the Cayuse, Walla Walla, St. Anthony, and Frenchtown likewise led to conversions among the Confederated Tribes of the Umatilla.

The protestants largely failed in their missionary efforts but left an impact in other ways. They proved that Euro-American families could thrive in the Oregon Country. They grew vegetables and fruit and raised livestock. They wrote reports and lectured in the East about the prospects of the region. They spoke of its mild climate, fertile soil, towering forests, abundant fish, and wild game. They helped set the stage for the opening of the Oregon Trail.

Overland to Oregon

Some said there was a contagion in the land and called it the "Oregon Fever." It caused dreams, persuaded men and women to give up all that was familiar, risk their lives and fortunes, and set out for the far shores of the Pacific. The overland emigrations of the mid-nineteenth century were one of the epochal events of human history. Seldom had so many people traveled so far by land to seek a new beginning.

The motives for moving to Oregon were clear. Tens of thousands of Americans residing along the frontier from Minnesota to Texas were land speculators. Many had moved before, to buy a new farm, erect a home and barn, clear and fence fields, and sell their "improvements." They were poised to do so again, particularly when senators Lewis Linn and Thomas Hart Benton of Missouri repeatedly introduced bills in Congress calling for grants of up to 1,000 free acres for those who would settle in Oregon. Land speculation ran in their veins. Even when the bills did not pass, thousands were ready to take the risk and hope, in time, Congress would reward their labors.

Oregon had a good press founded on careful observations and scientific authority. The reports of Lewis and Clark, the Astorians, the narratives of John B. Wyeth (1833), Samuel Parker (1838), William Slacum (1838), John Kirk Townsend (1839), Lieutenant John C. Fremont (1845), Lieutenant Charles Wilkes (1846), and Lieutenant Neil Howison (1848) described a rich land with attractive potentials. Letters from missionaries to newspapers and magazines, sermons and lectures delivered during fund-raising in the East, summary reports such as that by Robert Greenhow (1840)—all laid before the public the region's prospects. The pull factors attracting emigration to Oregon were land, timber, salmon, a climate favorable for agriculture, sites for water power, and a peaceful environment. Relations with natives had remained positive and stable throughout the fur-trade era.

On the other end, several push factors motivated frontier residents to consider relocating. The late 1830s and early 1840s were a period of calamitous flooding along the Missouri, Mississippi, and Ohio rivers. Many who had foolishly built on the floodplains watched their cabins, barns, and split-rail fences wash away in freshets and waited anxiously for weeks as floodwaters drowned their fields and ruined their crops. The Panic of 1837 plunged the country toward depression. Bank failures, currency problems, poor credit, and the inability to pay off loans beset millions. Many hungered for a chance to walk away from their losses and heartaches for a new beginning. Recurrent fevers, particularly malaria, beset many who lived on the frontier. Oregon had a good reputation for health; though thousands of Indians perished in the 1830s, most Euro-Americans remained well.

So the stage was set: Oregon's allure was strong, and the pressure to move out pushed many. A small emigration of about 100 people in 1842 followed Dr. Elijah White westward. The following spring, nearly a thousand emigrants gathered along the Missouri frontier to wait until the prairies were dry enough to permit travel. They had loaded their wagons with dried fruit and vegetables, flour, bran, cornmeal, beans, bacon, ham, and kegs of vinegar.

They brought weapons, clothing, tools, blankets and quilts, and a few treasured possessions. Most carried light tinware for eating, a reflector oven for baking biscuits, a spider for holding the coffee pot, and a frying pan. Musicians put in a violin, accordion, or Jew's harp. All else they sold or gave away to family and friends. Those who brought too much were compelled to abandon their possessions along the trail.

No one had ever seen anything like it before. The waves of emigrants grew. More than 3,000 traveled overland to Oregon in 1845; by 1850 an estimated 9,000 had crossed the trail to the Pacific Northwest. They knew their journey was a rite of passage. For the first time in their lives, and for many the only time, they penned daily entries in diaries. Their trip was epochal. They were part of history and wanted to record their participation in it.

The overland journey exacted many tolls. For some it was death on the trail. In many respects the Oregon Trail became one continuous, linear cemetery. Along its course lay the remains of men, women, and children who died of cholera, measles, dysentery, drownings, and accidents. Guns misfired; wagons overturned; cattle bolted; clothing caught on fire—the calamities that befell those on a four- to six-month camping trip were many. In spite of the hardships of 1,950 miles of trail between St. Joseph, Missouri, and Oregon City, Oregon, the trip was a great adventure. Vast herds of buffalo, visits of Indians wanting to trade, the distant Wind River Mountains, basalt flows and canyons along the Snake, and the succession of sunrises and sunsets were all part of the experience. Boys found swimming holes. Women and girls did their best to create a semblance of home by cooking creatively and maintaining norms of domesticity. The men went hunting and fishing, bartered with one another for horses and gear, and carved or marked their names in axle grease on prominent rocks near the trail.

The overland journey was often the migration of an extended family. Parents, children, and grandparents made up the parties. Sometimes several brothers, their families, their sisters and their families, and young hired hands from the neighborhood constituted the group. If one family migrated in 1846, three related families might migrate in 1847 to join them in Oregon. The Applegate family, immigrants of 1843 to Polk County and settlers by 1848 of the Umpqua Valley, were illustrative. Three brothers, their wives, and 39 children constituted this clan. The families took adjoining land claims near Yoncalla. The connections of kinship and friendship were part of the social fabric that knit frontier Oregon in the mid-nineteenth century.

The primary Oregon Trail ran from Fort Hall to Fort Boise in Idaho, then via Burnt River to the Grande Ronde Valley. It crossed the Blue Mountains and the Columbia Plateau, running up to 20 miles south of the river almost to The Dalles. Travelers then made a perilous trip by canoe, bateau, or log raft through the Columbia Gorge to western Oregon. By 1846 they had another option, transit of the Barlow Road, a rugged, rock-filled trace through the forests across the Cascade Mountains to Oregon City.

In 1845 Stephen H.L. Meek led nearly a thousand emigrants with their 200 wagons and livestock east from the Snake River onto Oregon's high desert. The shortcut he proposed over the Cascades proved a terrible trail. Eventually the wagon train had to work its way through the Deschutes River watershed to regain the old trail at The Dalles. That same year Samuel Barlow, Joel Palmer, William Rector, and others blazed a trace around the southern slopes of Mount Hood. They were compelled to abandon their wagons in the mountains, but the following year workmen opened the Barlow Road, a final overland segment of the Oregon Trail. Thousands traveled its course and paid the toll until 1919, when it passed to the State of Oregon. In 1846 explorers from the Willamette Valley opened the Applegate Trail. This route cut southwest from Fort Hall, crossed the deserts of northern Nevada, passed through the Klamath Basin and Rogue River Valley, and then entered the Willamette Valley from the south. Many who settled in southwestern Oregon in the 1850s and 1860s were emigrants on the Applegate Trail.

The Oregon Trail pioneers were creatures of habit. They carried their attitudes, prejudices, and ideas as part of their baggage. They were imitators rather than innovators. They attempted, as best they could remember, to recreate the governmental and social institutions they had left behind. They founded schools and academies and erected Federal, Greek Revival, and Gothic Revival buildings to house them—just like at home. Although they saw themselves as stalwart, brave, and independent, they were actually a highly dependent people, demanding righteously that the federal government give them land, survey their claims, guard them from Indians, erect lighthouses, establish postal routes, and construct wagon roads. They saw themselves as makers of history but seldom perceived they were locked into the historical fabric of which they were merely threads.

The "Oregon Question" and Provisional Government

Oregon was an Indian land but a prize lusted for by two partisans. In 1845 President James K. Polk informed Great Britain he wanted resolution of the issue of sovereignty in the Pacific Northwest. In the agreement reached in 1828, the nations had one year in which to resolve the long-simmering "Oregon Question." Polk was an avowed expansionist. A Democrat, he sought the presidency in 1844 on a simple platform: the annexation of Texas and the occupation of Oregon. The Tyler administration took care of acquiring Texas before Polk was sworn into office, but he persisted in an aggressive agenda of American expansion. Polk campaigned under the popular slogan "54-40 or fight," a contention that the southern boundary of Russian America was the northern boundary of Oregon. He pressed through diplomatic channels and used his inaugural address to assert American rights to all of Oregon. His ambitions far exceeded the area of American activity.

Resolution came on June 15, 1846, in the Oregon Treaty. Polk was already in pursuit of a greater prize—California—and had helped engineer a declaration of war against Mexico by massing troops along the Texas border until they were attacked by Mexican soldiers. Oregon became a sidebar in the unfolding story of the Mexican War. While Congress was willing to plunge the country into a war against its neighbor to the south, it was opposed to entering a conflict with Great Britain. That nation, beset with internal disputes over Corn Law reform, was likewise eager to reach a settlement. Thus in 1846 the two countries agreed to extend the boundary on the 49th parallel westward from the crest of the Rockies to the primary channel between Vancouver Island and the continent. British citizens and the Hudson's Bay Company retained trading and navigational rights in the Columbia River, though the United States subsequently terminated those privileges in 1859.

By 1846 the arguments of the United States to claim the Oregon Country were founded on more than "discovery rights." Several thousand Americans had settled in the region. Every year the arrival of new emigrants tipped the scale against the Hudson's Bay Company. The Americans had also established a Provisional Government. Its genesis came with the death in 1841 of Ewing Young. A former mountain man who had built up cattle herds in the Chehalem Valley and owned more than $3,000 in promissory notes from his neighbors, Young died without heirs. Residents gathered after his funeral to discuss what to do with his property. They agreed to name a committee to draft a civil code. Father Blanchet served as chair. When they assembled four months later, Blanchet reported his committee had not met. Disagreements between French-Canadians and Americans about the form of self-government and its powers had created an impasse.

The arrival of overland emigrants in 1842 and the increase of retired fur trappers who settled in the Willamette Valley with their mixed-blood families complicated matters. Old settlers and new arrivals worried about their land claims. They wondered what might happen if Congress passed Linn's bills granting lands to Americans who settled in Oregon. Wild animals brought to a head the decisions for a government. Grizzlies, black bears, cougars, and wolves ranged freely in the Willamette Valley. Their destruction of livestock gave cause in the spring of 1843 for a "Wolf Meeting." A second Wolf Meeting led to the decision to create a system of government. On May 2, 1843, at Champoeg, Joseph Meek posed the critical question: "Who's for a divide? All for the report of the committee and organization follow me," he shouted. By a close vote, perhaps 52 to 50, those wanting the government prevailed.

What was the significance of the Provisional Government? In spite of claims that the vote in the spring of 1843 on French Prairie sealed the fate of American sovereignty to the Oregon Country, there is no evidence that the Polk administration weighed the action. What was important and known to the decision-makers across the continent was that an American colony had developed on the shores of the far Pacific Ocean. The Provisional Government informed the Polk administration of its existence. It passed memorials in 1843 and 1845 seeking congressional attention to the needs of Americans in Oregon. The memorial of June 28, 1845, petitioned for naval yards, mail service, land grants, military protection, and territorial status. On December 8 Thomas Hart Benton presented the document to the Senate. These endorsements and his election were all the expansionist President Polk needed in an era when many felt it was America's manifest destiny to spread from sea to sea. Whitman's ride across the continent in 1838 and the events at Champoeg—the lore of Oregon history—did not tip the scales. The United States had embarked on a grand scheme of territorial growth. Oregon was only part of the plan.

The Oregon Provisional Government played an important role in creating order on a frontier. For more than two decades the Hudson's Bay Company held and exercised civil authority and control of the fur trade, while maintaining peace in dealing with Indian tribes. Its power did not extend to American settlers and ended in 1846 with the Oregon Treaty. The Provisional Government filled the void. It provided for laws governing land claims, instituted taxation, formed counties, created the offices of governor and legislators, and set up a court system. Popularly elected representatives hammered out these decisions between 1843 and 1845. The proposals were often revised, for newly arrived emigrants increased the electorate and brought their experience and men with political ambitions. The Provisional Government was in constant flux, but George Abernethy, a former lay worker for the Methodist Mission, continued as governor.

J. Henry Brown collected the correspondence and decisions made in Oregon City and published them as *Brown's Political History of Oregon* (1892). He dedicated his documentary volume to the "intrepid men and women" who helped lay the foundation of the Pacific states and "builded better than they knew." The legislature patterned many of its laws on those of the Iowa Territory, including weights and measures, criminal codes, and vagrancy. In 1843 the legislature put bounties on wolves, panthers, bears, and lynxes. Cash payments for the skin of the head with ears of these animals soon decimated their population and led to the extinction of several species in Oregon. The Law of Land Claims permitted individuals to file on as much as a square mile, but only one claim at a time, and restricted filings on key town sites or water-power locations.

The Provisional Legislature banned permanent residency of free African-Americans and mulattoes. Any reaching age 18 had two years to leave the Oregon Country, as did anyone held in slavery. The initial penalty for failure to leave was not less than 20 nor more than 39 lashes. In 1844 the legislature amended the law to put violators out to low bid for public labor and removal. The law, though never enforced, confirmed the racial prejudice of the frontier generation moving into the Willamette Valley.

Cayuse Indian War

Cold winds swept across the Columbia Plateau. In November 1847, they heralded the onset of the winter of discontent. Too long had the Cayuse Indians suffered from new diseases and the failed ministrations of Dr. Marcus Whitman. In their culture a shaman or curer who failed was subject to death. This doctor, a strapping, determined white man had come into their lands uninvited. The mission he and his wife established worked like a magnet to draw emigrants. Each year the wagon trains descended the Blue Mountains and, like the grasshoppers that swept across the countryside, they heralded discomforting changes. Smallpox, measles, fevers, death, and mourning came in their wake.

On November 29, 1847, a band of Cayuse men, fed by fear and resentment, fell upon the missionary station. In a matter of hours they murdered Marcus and Narcissa Whitman and a dozen others. Two more died subsequently of exposure and 47, many orphaned children of emigrants, were taken captive. The Spaldings fled Lapwai and skirted the Cayuse homeland in their dash to safety. Panic swept through the Willamette settlements. Initially the settlers thought the tribes of the Columbia Plateau might drive through the Gorge and attempt to murder them, too.

The Provisional Legislature faced its greatest test. While Peter Skene Ogden of the Hudson's Bay Company was rushing east with 16 men to try to ransom the hostages, Governor Abernethy called for "immediate and prompt action." The legislature authorized raising companies of volunteers to go to war against the Cayuse Tribe. It entrusted command to Colonel Cornelius Gilliam and named a committee to negotiate with the Hudson's Bay Company for loans of arms, ammunition, and supplies to mount the campaign. The government wrestled with two approaches: one, to send peace commissioners to try to persuade the Cayuse to turn over the perpetrators; and, two, to wage a war of retribution. In short order it did both. Governor Abernethy appointed a peace commission—Joel Palmer, Henry A.G. Lee, and Robert Newell. Gilliam, who did not approve of the commission, set out in January 1848 with more than 500 volunteers.

The Cayuse War became, at times, a war of nerves. The peace commissioners and friendly Indians tried to end hostilities and get the Cayuse to turn over the killers of those at the Whitman station. Gilliam and his forces, eager for action, provoked conflicts with both friendly and hostile Indians. In March, having persuaded the Cayuse to surrender five men, the military brought them to Oregon City. They were charged, tried, and hanged in 1850. The guilt of the five Indians and the jurisdiction of the court were not fully established. Controversy swirled for decades after this trial—the first culminating in capital punishment following legal proceedings in the Oregon Territory.

Territorial Government

The Oregon Country lay in limbo following the 1846 treaty with Great Britain. Congress had not acted and was diverted by both the Mexican War and the slavery question. The tragedy at the Whitman Mission demanded action. In December 1847, the Provisional Legislature drafted another memorial to lay again before Congress its "situation and wants." The petition discussed the deaths at Waiilatpu, lack of revenue laws, and uneasiness about land claims. Should Congress act, the memorial pointed out that "the present citizens of this country have strong claims upon the patronage of the General Government" for any appointments. Joseph Meek with nine compatriots carried the petition east in the early spring of 1848.

Much was at stake. If Congress created the Oregon Territory, the region would fall under the mantle of federal authority and funding. The residents of the region might expect, at last, action on the free land proposals and a host of benefits from the creation of a vital infrastructure to enhance security, improve commerce, and ease communication problems. On August 14, 1848, President Polk signed the Organic Act creating the Oregon Territory. Uncle Sam could now begin his labors in the Pacific Northwest in earnest.

Joseph Lane, a Mexican War hero and resident of Indiana, was appointed governor. He set out overland for Oregon City, where he was inaugurated on

March 3, 1849, proclaiming the sprawling region under the administration of the United States. The event was of singular consequence. Territorial status brought not only a governor but also three judges, an attorney, and a marshal—all federal appointees. Oregonians who were male, 21 years or older, and citizens of the United States had the franchise and could elect a territorial legislature. Its laws, however, were subject to veto by Congress and the legislature had limited power to incur debt. The residents could elect a delegate to speak for their interests before Congress. Samuel R. Thurston, the first named, lacked the power to vote, but he could advocate territorial interests.

The Organic Act extended the Northwest Ordinance of 1787 to the region. This legislation of the Continental Congress articulated the philosophy for development of new territories in the Ohio and upper Mississippi valleys. It prohibited slavery, provided land grants for support of public schools, and affirmed "utmost good faith" in dealing with Indian tribes. The ordinance and its inclusion in the Organic Act thus recognized aboriginal land title throughout the region. It voided the land laws of the Provisional Government, except for the claims to 640 acres of the various missions to the Indians. Oregon's act granted two square miles of land per township to fund schools.

Land remained foremost in the minds of the Oregonians. Thurston knew the anxiety and jockeying for claims. Thousands had risked their lives and futures on the prospect of getting land farms in Oregon. On September 29, 1850, Congress passed what became known as the Oregon Donation Land Act, establishing the system of land survey prior to deeding properties. By 1851 John P. Preston, surveyor-general, and his crews had established the Willamette Meridian running north and south between Canada and California and begun survey of the east and west Baseline. The coordinates met at Willamette Stone Park in the west hills above Portland. The system left an indelible imprint. From the beginning of time nature had etched the land in gentle contours. Henceforth straight lines, section corners, and a massive grid system—followed by roads, timber harvests, and fields—imprinted the landscape. The beauty of the system was that it was regular. It gave every parcel of land a unique address based on its distance from the primary coordinates.

Congress also established the General Land Office, the first of which opened in Oregon City and was followed, in time, by branches in The Dalles, La Grande, and Roseburg. Seekers of Donation Lands—ultimately 7,437 successful claimants in Oregon—could register their claims and await the surveys of the townships and their particular claims. Once the surveys were completed, they could obtain title, subdivide, and sell. Speculation was built into the fabric of the act, particularly because it permitted both men and women to acquire up to 320 acres—a square mile for married couples. This was far more land than any farmer might till or manage.

Territorial status brought highly significant investments in Oregon. The U.S. Coast Survey dispatched William Pope McArthur and the vessel *Ewing* to begin charting the coastline. Over the next several years the Coast Survey examined the shoreline and the estuaries. It produced charts with depth readings, noted dangerous rocks, and gave form to the shore. Its reports included handsome engravings of coastal headlands as mariners saw them from sea.

Dr. Elijah White had served since 1843 as Indian agent in Oregon. His appointment was strange in that he worked on federal salary when American sovereignty was not established. In 1849 Joseph Lane began duties both as governor and ex-officio superintendent of Indian affairs. He was succeeded by Anson Dart of Wisconsin and next by Joel Palmer, negotiator of several of the region's ratified treaties. The superintendents named Indian agents to serve at The Dalles, Clatsop Plains, Willamette Valley, Umpqua Valley, Rogue River Valley, and Port Orford.

Important federal services that came with territorial status included opening of postal routes and offices, federal courts, and customs houses. John Shively, an 1843 emigrant, was appointed as Oregon's first postmaster in 1847 in Astoria. Postal routes created vital communication links along a frontier. Congress established customs districts with agents at Port Orford, Umpqua River, and Astoria. In later years it opened offices for the Yaquina District and Portland. Federal officials were charged with collecting duties and recording statistical information on the ebb and flow of commerce. Their reports showed the rise of agriculture and industry, particularly the impact of the markets produced by the California Gold Rush for Oregon crops and lumber. Court officials had charge of dispute resolution. With three districts, they had a wide geographical reach and traveled a circuit to adjudicate complaints.

Using executive authority, U.S. presidents in the 1850s began withdrawing land from public entry to set aside sites for federal projects, including reservations for lighthouses, forts, and Indians. Several instances of the withdrawals proved unwise. In the case of lighthouses, some sites were too high above the sea or too remote from supplies to permit economical construction of stations. Most forts, though constructed, were of limited utility and were soon abandoned. The Coast (or Siletz) Reservation and the Grand Ronde Reservation, however, were two instances where presidential withdrawals helped shape both Indian history and settlement patterns. The large Siletz Reservation was dismembered in 1865 and 1875 and again after 1892. The Indian tenure, though diminishing, slowed pioneer settlement along much of the central coast.

Territorial status meant the arrival of the U.S. Army. Congress appropriated $76,500 in 1846 to establish garrisons along the Oregon Trail, but the project was diverted by the Mexican War. In 1849 the Mounted Riflemen finally headed west under the command of Major Osborne Cross. Their assignment was to build and staff forts to preclude further difficulties with the tribes. When the Riflemen's heavy wagons bogged down on the southern slopes of Mount Hood, the soldiers dug pits and cached many of their supplies at a place later known as Government Camp. They then pushed on to occupy temporary quarters at Oregon City and Astoria. During the 1850s the U.S. Army established Fort Orford (1851), Fort Dalles (1852), Fort Lane (1853), Fort Cascades (1855) on the north bank of the Columbia in the Gorge, Fort Umpqua, Fort Yamhill, and Fort Hoskins (all 1856). Construction created jobs for carpenters, brick masons, and laundresses. Soldiers brought payrolls flowing into the local economy as well as a sense of security from the Indians.

The Army provided another important service. Its engineers were authorized by Congress to survey and construct the Scottsburg-Myrtle Creek and Myrtle Creek-Camp Stuart military wagon roads. These routes connected in 1853–55 to carry freight and travelers from the head of tidewater on the Umpqua River to the mining districts in the Rogue River Valley and northern California. The Army also dispatched Lieutenant George Derby to survey a road over the Coast Range between Astoria and Salem. Although opened by axemen, the route drew only limited use. Derby in 1855 surveyed and supervised construction of the Fort Vancouver-Fort Cascades Military Portage Road into the Columbia Gorge. Uncle Sam's engineers, soldiers, and laborers helped create primary travel corridors to remote parts of the territory. As college graduates, the military officers also recorded weather data, collected fossils, pickled zoological specimens, wrote down Indian word lists, and sent interesting materials and communications to the Smithsonian Institution. These labors contributed to further understanding about the region.

While the federal government annually considered projects in the Oregon Territory, the legislature wrestled with local issues. These included frustration with the repeated appointment of nonresidents of the region to key positions, political fighting among Whigs, Democrats, and Know-Nothings, and the outbreak of warfare with the Indian tribes. Residents of Puget Sound and the Walla Walla district were especially restive with a government located in Oregon City or, after 1851, in Salem.

History

Congress addressed this matter and on March 2, 1853, President Millard Fillmore signed legislation creating the Washington Territory. This action gave final definition to Oregon's geography.

Another important consequence of territorial status was the extension of the Pacific Railroad Surveys into Oregon in 1855–56. Funded by Congress and staffed by the Topographical Engineers, this project sought five alternative routes across the continent to connect the Mississippi Valley with the Pacific Ocean. Additionally, the surveyors examined possibilities for north-south connections between the rail lines. Lieutenants Robert Stockton Williamson and Henry L. Abbot directed the surveys through the Willamette and Rogue River Valleys and along the eastern flank of the Cascade Mountains. Their handsome reports, accompanied by geological observations by Dr. John Strong Newberry, included hand-colored plates showing the countryside, botanical, zoological, and paleontological collections, and profiles of possible grades for railroad routes.

Territorial government catapulted the residents of Oregon into the nexus of federal authority. Although cheerfully independent, Oregonians embraced territorial status with expectation. They had frustration about political cronies named to top government posts, but they gained important services and facilities funded at national expense.

Spread of Settlement

Euro-American settlement in Oregon spread rapidly. Retired mountain men settled in French Prairie, Tualatin Plains, and the Chehalem Valley. By 1843 overland emigrants had crossed to the west bank of the Willamette to stake claims along Rickreall and Salt creeks. By 1845 they were at the lower reaches of the Santiam and Mary's Rivers. Settlers reached the southern end of the Willamette Valley in 1848 and within a year were pouring over the hills into the Umpqua Valley. Parties coming by sea settled in 1851 at the mouth of the Umpqua River and at Port Orford on the south coast. Others, restless with their sandy claims on the Clatsop Plains, braved the Indian trail across Neahkahnie Mountain to establish a colony on Tillamook Bay.

The field notes of the land surveyors and their township maps of the 1850s work like a time machine to reveal settlement patterns. Sometimes they noted Indian villages, often located at the confluences of stream courses or at the base of south-facing slopes to catch the rays of sunlight. They charted a network of trails transforming into wagon roads with ferries at river crossings. They showed house locations confirming that many settlers, savvy about flooding in mid-America, built their claim cabins far back from the riverbanks and often positioned them facing fields, the back door to the forest and its generous supplies of firewood. They

documented the prairie condition of the western Oregon valleys, the consequence of Indian fire ecology.

The Bureau of the Census in 1850 recorded 11,873 Oregonians: 4,671 females and 7,202 males—a gender disparity of 40 to 60 percent. In towns nearly 70 percent of the residents were men. "At Astoria, Milton City, and Portland," wrote demographer William Bowen, "they outnumbered women more than three to one." Bowen also found the imprint of kinship as an integrating force in frontier Oregon. "The neighborhood was one of the most basic associations of rural frontier life," he said, "a union of persons with similar backgrounds in small, fairly homogeneous communities, each slightly different from the rest." This meant that closely knit neighborhoods were quick to meet individual needs, prone to exclude outsiders (especially minorities, foreigners, and single men), but open to individuals who married into families and thereby joined the community. Bowen thus concluded that Oregon had two societies in the 1850s: a rural frontier dominated by extended families or clans and an urban frontier "drawing its members disproportionately from the ranks of unmarried men from the Northeast or abroad."

Urban development and farm improvements were driven by the California Gold Rush. A number of Oregonians headed south for the diggings in 1848 and many more did so in 1849. The men plowed and planted crops, departed for the mines, and left the women and children to weed, combat birds and varmints, water the vegetables, and mind the claim. Hundreds returned in the fall for harvest, their saddlebags heavy with leather pouches of gold dust and nuggets. Most discovered that the boom in California created a lucrative market for wheat, apples, vegetables, oysters, shingles, piling, and lumber. The influx of 100,000 new residents and statehood for California in 1850 became an important stimulus and force of stability in the Oregon economy.

Opportunities beckoned. Captain Asa Mead Simpson of Brunswick, Maine, grasped some. Six months in the Sierras convinced him in 1849 that there were better ways to find fortune in the West. He opened lumberyards in Stockton, Sacramento, and San Francisco. In the early 1850s he laid the foundations of a commercial empire stretching from Monterey Bay to Puget Sound. He shipped steam engines and saws for mills at Port Orford, Coos Bay, Umpqua River, Astoria, and Gray's Harbor in Washington Territory. With his partner, Captain George Flavel, he constructed and operated steam tugs to provide bar pilot service for his vessels and those of others. Simpson ran his enterprises for 64 years. His crews built more than 50 ships at his yards on the southern Oregon coast at North Bend.

Aaron Meier, a Jewish emigrant from Germany, worked his way north in the mid-1850s from the

Sierra gold fields to new mines in the Rogue River Valley. He carried needles, thread, buttons, and bolts of cloth in his traveling dry goods business. He worked hard, saved, and in 1857 opened a small retail store in Portland, then a town of 1,300 residents. The city's boom during the 1860s with opening of new mining fields in the interior and the flow of capital through the emerging city gave him the chance to expand his business. In time Sigmund Frank, his son-in-law, joined him. Meier & Frank Department Store was on its way to becoming one of the nation's largest retail outlets.

In 1852 Abigail Scott Duniway arrived in Oregon after her mother and a brother died during the overland crossing. Abigail married young and with her husband, Ben Duniway, selected a donation claim near Lafayette in Yamhill County. Then misfortune struck. Ben signed a note, using the farm as collateral. They lost the farm and Ben, injured in a farming accident, was an invalid for the rest of his life. Having a young family and no options, Abigail assumed full responsibilities. She taught school, made hats, ran a boarding house, and aspired to be somebody. By 1859 she had started to define her future. She wrote *Captain Gray's Company,* a novel based on her Oregon Trail diary. Having found her voice, in later years she became a nationally known suffrage advocate and for 16 years was editor and publisher of *The New Northwest,* a weekly newspaper.

Joel Palmer visited Oregon in 1845 and helped open the Barlow Road. He was much impressed with what he saw and described it in *Journal of Travels Over the Rocky Mountains* (1847). He emigrated with his family from Indiana in 1847 and platted Dayton on his farm at the falls of the Yamhill River. Palmer's opportunities came in public service. He served as commissary-general and a peace commissioner in the Cayuse War and in 1853 was appointed superintendent of Indian affairs. Over the next 24 months he negotiated ten treaties, eight of which were ratified. A humane man, he nevertheless implemented a program of dramatic reduction of the Indian domain but tried to provide reservations close to aboriginal areas and sought to preserve peace.

Matthew Paul Deady, a lawyer from Ohio, began teaching school in 1849 in Yamhill County. He soon returned to the practice of law, was elected to the Territorial Legislature, and in 1853 was named judge of the territorial supreme court. Deady served in the constitutional convention, as federal district judge, drafter of civil and criminal codes, compiler of Oregon laws, and a founder of the University of Oregon. His diary, published long after his death as *Pharisee Among Philistines* (1975), confirmed his biting intellect and close observations of society.

Simpson, Meier, Duniway, Palmer, and Deady were representative of the newcomers. Thousands aspired to make something of themselves. Oregon was a great platform for dreaming dreams and improving one's lot. A number rose to the surface early, finding their callings in business, public service, literature and social reform. Thousands of others engaged in hard work, some laboring in quiet desperation and others for a modest improvement in condition.

By the early 1860s settlement moved in new directions. Some overland emigrants had stopped at The Dalles. The community emerged by 1850 as a primary outfitting point on the western Columbia Plateau and grew steadily. By 1862 settlers were claiming lands in the Grande Ronde and Powder River valleys, along the John Day, in the Crooked River and Ochoco region of central Oregon, and in the Klamath Basin. The children of Oregon Trail pioneers were engaged in eastward migration. Precluded by high land prices or multiple heirs in large families from owning farms in western Oregon, they took surplus livestock and headed over the Cascades to the lush meadows along the margins of the region's streams and lakes. Members of the Riddle family, who settled in 1851 in the South Umpqua Valley, were pioneer settlers in the Harney Basin. James and Elizabeth Foster in 1872 moved their large family to Summer Lake. Foster's parents had emigrated through central Oregon in 1845 in the party led by Stephen H.L. Meek. Thousands of others followed this pattern.

Oregon remained a rural, small-town region in the 19th century. The Donation Land Act, by allowing claims from 160 to 320 acres per person, effectively dispersed the population. A number of townsites became ghost towns. Randolph, Waldo, Dardanelles, Elizabethtown, and Sailor's Diggings in the mines of southern Oregon vanished when the gold was gone. Cincinnati, Champoeg, Multnomah City, Peoria, and Lancaster were once thriving communities along the Willamette. Auburn, Greenhorn, Granite, and Bourne for a time served the mining populations of northeastern Oregon. Floods, fires, playing out of mineral deposits and changing travel patterns pushed them into oblivion.

Some communities naturally attracted growth. Ashland at the base of the Siskiyous in the Bear Creek Valley, Roseburg in the Umpqua Valley, Marshfield on upper Coos Bay, Prineville on the Crooked River, Pendleton at the base of the Blue Mountains and Baker City near the mines in the Blue Mountains became crossroads communities. For many towns the key to success was to capture county government. Promoters vied for such locations, for they guaranteed a flow of people recording deeds, appearing in court, securing contracts, or coping with society's needs. County government was as important as a good mill site, coal mine, or wagon road crossing in helping to anchor a community.

Indian Wars

Camas lilies bloomed in such profusion that meadows looked like lakes amid the forests. The tarweed seeds ripened and the women set the fires. Armed with beaters and funnel-shaped baskets, they began the annual cycle of gathering. Acorns ripened, matured, and fell from the oaks. Their flour, when leached of tannic acid, provided a nutritious gruel or bread when baked on flat stones near the fires. Salmon surged up the rivers. Eels clung to the rocks as they ascended the rapids. Deer and elk browsed on the nutritious plants in the foothills. Flecks of gold glistened in the crystal-clear water of the streambeds.

This was the setting when, during the winter of 1851–52, packers on the trail to California discovered the placer mines of southwestern Oregon. Within weeks a reckless population, most of them hardened miners from California, surged over the Siskiyous or stepped off the gangplanks of ships putting in at Crescent City, Port Orford, Umpqua City, or Scottsburg. The rush was on. It meant quick riches for those who found the right pothole in bedrock filled with nuggets or the fortunate miners whose riffle boxes captured the fine particles of gold that glistened in the black sand. For the Indians of the Rogue River country it meant that all they had known and their very lives were at stake.

The causes of conflict erupted everywhere. The Donation Land Act became law in 1850. Years passed before treaties, negotiated in 1853 and 1854, were ratified. Some, such as those of Anson Dart or the Willamette Valley Treaty Commission of 1851, never gained Senate approval. In spite of the promises of superintendents of Indian affairs Dart and Palmer, the white people poured in. Dispossession ruled. The miners drove the Takelma, Shasta, Chetco, Shasta Costa, Mikonotunne, Tututni, Galice Creeks and Cow Creeks from their villages. Located on old stream terraces, the Indian homes were prime locations for placer deposits.

The hungry newcomers hunted the game, decimating the deer and elk populations. The Territorial Legislature in 1854 prohibited sale of ammunition or guns to Indians, deepening their disadvantage. The miners and residents of Jacksonville, Canyonville, Kerbyville, and Gold Beach liked bacon and ham. They let hogs run wild, catching them in baited traps. The hogs ate the acorns, a primary subsistence food for the Indians.

Mining debris poured down the Illinois, Rogue, South Coquille and South Umpqua rivers. The salmon runs diminished; the eels died. Crayfish, fresh water mussels and trout choked on the flood of mud. Starvation threatened. The claimants of Donation Lands fenced their fields with split-rail fences and built log cabins. They worked with a will to stop Indian field burning. The Indian women found it impossible to harvest tarweed seeds and the blackberries that formerly regenerated with the annual fires did not grow back. The settlers turned under the fields of camas lilies, and their cattle and horses grazed off the blue-flowering plants.

The mining districts—whether in the Rogue River country or the Blue Mountains of northeastern Oregon—caused major ecological disruption. The rush for quick wealth through mineral exploitation unraveled nature's ways and long-established human subsistence activities. Then came the "exterminators"—unprincipled men who believed only dead Indians were good Indians. They formed volunteer companies and perpetrated massacres against the Chetco Indians in 1853, the Lower Coquille Indians in 1854, and in wanton aggression against Takelma Indians camped near the Table Rock Reservation in 1855.

Frederick M. Smith, sub-Indian agent at Port Orford, in 1854 addressed the attacks on the Indians in his district. They were ravaged by hunger, dispossession of their villages, onset of new and fatal diseases, and overt murders. Reporting the massacre of the Lower Coquille Indians, he wrote: *"Bold, brave, courageous men!* to attack a friendly and defenceless tribe of Indians; *to burn, roast, and shoot sixteen of their number, and all on suspicion* that they were about to rise and drive from their country *three hundred white men!"* Smith's lament, the mourning cries of the Indian women, the death rituals of rubbing the hair with pitch, and the inexorable course of hunger, attack, and death precipitated the conflicts known as the Rogue River Wars. The troubles seethed between 1852 and 1856. Finally the U.S. Army had sufficient forces to mount a campaign in 1855–56 to destroy the Indians' ability to resist.

Vanquished by the combined operations of the Oregon Volunteers and Army regulars, the Indians of the Rogue and Umpqua valleys and the southwestern Oregon coast were then removed to the Siletz and Grand Ronde reservations. Forced marches through winter snows or over the rocky headlands and through the sand dunes of coastal Oregon became trails of tears for hundreds driven to the distant reservations. Other survivors were herded aboard the *Columbia*, a sidewheel steamer, which removed them from Port Orford to the Columbia and lower Willamette River area. Then they had to walk the muddy trail to the reservations.

The myth of independence was shattered by the actions of Oregon's frontier residents. For their "services rendered" in the conflicts of 1853, the volunteers billed the federal government for $107,287, and they were the primary cause of the hostilities. When the conflicts ended in 1856, they worked for years to gain settlement. Finally in 1890 Congress passed the Oregon Indian Depredation Claims Act. Aged pioneers filed affidavits to claim reimbursement for lost pillows, ricks of hay, rail fences, and beans and bacon during the conflicts of the 1850s.

A dependent generation's elders once again tapped the federal treasury for support.

Troubles with the tribes erupted anew in the 1850s on the Columbia Plateau. In 1855 Superintendent Joel Palmer and Governor Isaac I. Stevens of Washington Territory summoned the Indians of the eastern plateau to the Walla Walla Treaty Council. In a matter of days they hammered out agreements, ceding lands but reserving others with the Nez Perce, Cayuse, Umatilla, and Yakima. Subsequently Palmer met the Wasco, Wishram, and Warm Springs (or Tenino) at The Dalles and entered into a treaty with them. All of these agreements were noteworthy for enumerating rights. The tribes, who had engaged in traditional subsistence activities from time immemorial, reserved rights to fish "at usual and accustomed grounds and stations," to erect fish-processing sheds for drying their catch, and to hunt, gather, and graze livestock on unenclosed lands.

While Congress was considering the treaties, the Bureau of Indian Affairs began urging the Indians to remove to their new reservations and take up an agrarian lifestyle. Few wanted to engage in such backbreaking labor or give up fishing, hunting, and gathering. The pressure was on. Emigrants arrived every fall and settlement spread east from The Dalles. Pioneer cabins lined the shores of the Gorge, threatening to disrupt the Indian fisheries. Then came gold discoveries on the Fraser and Thompson rivers in British Columbia and in the Colville district on the north-central plateau. The influx of miners led to an eruption of troubles and, in time, to the Yakima Indian War of 1855–58. The forces of the U.S. Army, supplemented by companies of Oregon Volunteers, defeated the hostile bands.

The 1850s were a wrenching time of transition. Steadily the Indian numbers diminished, their food sources destroyed and their lands appropriated. These were terrible times for the region's native peoples.

Statehood

Issues far from Oregon shaped affairs along the Pacific Coast in the 1850s. Sectional tensions heightened during the bumbling presidencies of Millard Fillmore, Franklin Pierce, and James Buchanan. The Compromise of 1850 gained a little time, but its concessions satisfied neither proslavery extremists in the South nor abolitionists in the North. The nation was on its course to the Civil War. Harriet Beecher Stowe's novel, *Uncle Tom's Cabin,* enraged slaveowners as it swept across the country in a powerful indictment of the "peculiar institution." Formation of the Republican Party in 1854, troubles in "Bleeding Kansas" in 1856, the Dred Scott decision in 1857, and John Brown's raid on the federal arsenal at Harper's Ferry in 1858 confirmed the divisions and tensions. The Republicans had drawn the line—no further expansion of slav-

ery. They nominated John C. Fremont, a popular western explorer, for the presidency. Although Fremont lost, within four years their candidate, Abraham Lincoln, was headed to Washington, D.C., as the 16th president. Passions were high. Then came secession and war.

Three parties vied for political control in Oregon. The Democrats were an odd lot, including northerners opposed to slavery and southern diehards who supported an institution barred by the Organic Act of 1848. The Whigs held political patronage in the early 1850s but watched their party disintegrate nationally. The Know-Nothings were opposed to the political clique that had managed territorial government in Salem. These divisions confirmed the heavy hold of old persuasions and attitudes—the intellectual baggage carried by emigrants.

Without enabling legislation from Congress, Oregonians voted in June 1857 to hold a constitutional convention. The delegates assembled in Salem during the summer and drafted a governing document. It was modeled on those of Iowa, Indiana, and Michigan. The constitution limited public debt and placed tight controls on banks and corporations. An agricultural people, the convention delegates argued, had little use for frivolous expenditures or unnecessary institutions. In the fall voters faced three questions. Did they approve the constitution? They voted yes. Did they want slavery? They voted 7,727 no and 2,645 yes. Did they want freed African-Americans to live in Oregon? They voted eight to one against permitting their residency.

The actions in 1857 were predictable. Oregonians hungered for control of their own government and an end to the patronage appointments produced by shifting administrations in Washington, D.C. They also affirmed they did not want slavery in Oregon. The question of driving free African-Americans from the new state revealed resoundingly racist attitudes. They did not see freed slaves, Indians, or women standing equally before the law. In this Oregonians differed little from Thomas Jefferson. Architect of the Declaration of Independence and its gracefully worded affirmations of natural rights, Jefferson was a slave-owner all his adult life. He could not rise to the noble philosophy of personal freedom he articulated in the 1770s. Oregonians in 1857 appeared to have drunk from the same well.

In June 1858, residents of the territory elected officials as defined by their new constitution. For months the fate of Oregon statehood floated on shifting political coalitions distrustful of changing the fragile balance of power in Congress. It was known Oregon would be a free state, yet its newly elected senators—Joseph Lane and Delazon Smith—were proslavery Democrats. Finally Congress acted and on February 14, 1859, President Buchanan signed the bill. Oregon joined the federal union.

Civil War in Oregon

The plunge to Civil War exploded on April 12, 1861, in the bombardment of Fort Sumter in Charleston Harbor. When it became apparent the conflict would not be short, the Army began removing regular soldiers from the District of Oregon. Because of the responsibility to guard the reservations and maintain a military presence, especially in central and eastern Oregon where gold discoveries generated a rapid influx of miners and settlers, federal and state officials scrambled to find replacement troops. The Department of the Pacific raised recruits and dispatched companies of California Volunteers to Fort Yamhill, Fort Hoskins, and Siletz Blockhouse. The Army abandoned Fort Umpqua in 1862. The First Oregon Volunteer Cavalry and the First Washington Territory Infantry went to central Oregon. During the Civil War, Oregon raised six companies of cavalry. Known officially as the First Oregon Cavalry, they served until June 1865.

Secessionist sympathizers surfaced in Oregon. The Knights of the Golden Circle, an anti-Union group, reportedly plotted the seizure of Fort Vancouver, military headquarters on the Columbia River. They did not act. When pro-Confederate partisans raised their flag in Jacksonville, they faced opposition and backed down. The Long Tom Rebellion was perhaps the most noteworthy outbreak of secessionist feeling. Emboldened by the assassination of President Lincoln, Philip Henry Mulkey walked the streets of Eugene on May 6, 1865, shouting: "Hurrah for Jeff Davis, and damn the man that won't!" The First Oregon Volunteer Infantry arrested Mulkey, who promptly grabbed a glass of water and toasted Jeff Davis, the Confederate president. A pro-Union mob, wanting to lynch Mulkey, broke down the jail door. Mulkey slashed one of the men with a hidden knife. Mulkey's supporters from the Long Tom district were ready to fight, but the infantry slipped Mulkey out of town under an armed guard, loaded him on a steamboat, and sent him off to three months in jail at Fort Vancouver. Mulkey sued for $10,000 for false arrest. After 14 court appearances over a two-year period, he settled for $200.

For many of the soldiers the Civil War in Oregon was a monotonous, numbing assignment. In their monthly post returns, officers recorded desertions, suicides, and bouts in the brig because of drunkenness and misbehavior. The Indians were quiet on the Siletz and Grand Ronde reservations. The rain was predictable and depressing. "Nothing transpired of importance," recorded Royal A. Bensell, a soldier at Fort Yamhill. Too many days brought that refrain in his Civil War diary.

East of the Cascades the troops had active engagement. Gold discoveries at Canyon City and other diggings on the headwaters of the John Day River and in the Powder River country on the eastern slopes of the Blue Mountains had drawn thousands of miners. The Northern Paiute, disrupted in their seasonal round and tempted by the easy pickings of clothing, food, and horses, embarked on raids and conflicts that demanded military intervention. The Oregon Volunteer Infantry and Cavalry established Camp Watson (1864) after placing troops at temporary stations: Dahlgren, Currey, Gibbs, Henderson, and Maury. The forces engaged in lengthy and often fruitless explorations searching for the elusive Indians.

Realizing that the problems east of the Cascades were of long duration, the U.S. Army established Fort Klamath (1863), Camp Warner (1866), and Fort Harney (1867). During the summer of 1864 Captains John M. Drake and George B. Curry and Lieutenant-Colonel Charles Drew led troops on sweeps through southeastern Oregon, northern Nevada, and southwestern Idaho. They had little success in finding the "enemy." "These tribes can be gathered upon a reservation, controlled, subsisted for a short time, and afterwards be made to subsist themselves," commented the superintendent of Indian affairs, "for one-tenth the cost of supporting military forces in pursuit of them." In time that happened. The Klamath Reservation and the short-lived Malheur Reservation included various bands of Northern Paiute. The Civil War in Oregon mostly involved guarding reservations or pursuing native peoples who were masters of escape in their own homelands.

Uncle Sam's Handiwork

Statehood meant that Oregonians had two senators and a representative to make their case in Congress. The congressional delegation delivered. Some argued it was critical to open communications across the new state. The Republican Party was not of a mind to continue projects wholly in the control and labor of federal employees. Its philosophy was to throw as much action as possible into the private sector. Thus between 1865 and 1869 Congress liberally awarded land grants to the state of Oregon to pass on to companies constructing "military wagon roads." Theoretically the routes were to link strategic locations suitable for use by troops during emergencies.

The new roads were the Oregon Central, Corvallis-Yaquina Bay, Willamette Valley and Cascade Mountain, The Dalles-Boise, and the Coos Bay. Two provided routes from Willamette Valley points in Albany and Springfield eastward to Boise. A third connected The Dalles via the John Day watershed to Boise. Two ran toward the coast: one from Albany to Yaquina City and another from Roseburg to Coos Bay. Under the terms of the grants, as soon as a company had completed a stretch of road, it could apply to the governor for certification of its success. The governor or his designated official would visit the route. If the road was deemed suitable for wagon use, the company then received three square miles of land for every mile of road. The tally for the five roads ran into millions of acres.

Land-grant wagon roads were founded on speculation and fraud. None of the companies had the experience, capital, or leadership to build satisfactory routes through such challenging terrain. They cleared and carved out traces, leaving many streams unbridged and routes subject to slides and frequent closures. The Oregon Central Military Wagon Road Company was unblushing in its scam. When its surveyors reached the Cascade summit, rather than heading east toward Boise, they swept south through the upper Deschutes and into the Klamath Reservation, cutting a swath of checkerboard lands out of the lush meadows along the Williamson and Sprague rivers. They moved on toward Goose Lake into Guano Valley, then over the southern slopes of Steens Mountain into the Pueblo Valley before turning northeasterly toward Boise. Their meandering route captured tens of thousands of acres of prime grazing land, dismembered the Klamath Reservation, and ensured a much larger grant than if they had surveyed a route directly toward Idaho.

Wagon road companies locked up land for years. The General Land Office held hundreds of thousands of acres of unclaimed grants. As long as the company or its successor purchasers did not take title, they did not have to pay taxes. The longer they waited, the greater the appreciation of value in timber, minerals, or grazing. By avoiding paying taxes and letting land values increase, the companies—or those who bought them to speculate in the grants—calculated a better return. Further, the companies did not maintain the roads yet dared to demand tolls from travelers. Lamentations of local residents who lived in the alternate sections along the routes finally compelled Congress to investigate and the courts to take back the remaining portions of the grants.

Among the loudest critics of the wagon road companies were land seekers. In the Homestead Act (1862), Congress gave the land-hungry an unparalleled opportunity. For a modest filing fee, five years of residency, and claim improvements, homesteaders could receive as much as 160 acres of the public domain for free. Congress became increasingly generous in giving away federal lands. It passed bounty land acts for veterans of wars, the Desert Land Act (1877), Enlarged Homestead Act (1909), and Stock Raising Homestead Act (1916). Shrewd speculators might accumulate hundreds of acres by working the system. Between 1850 and 1940, millions of acres in Oregon passed from public to private ownership through the land distribution acts promoted by developers of the American West.

Congressional action shaped Oregon in other areas. The coast was a dangerous place where strong winds buffeted the shore. Narrow channels led over fluctuating bars into the estuaries. The headlands were remote, hulking forms on the eastern landscape. Mariners desperately needed services. The bar of the Columbia gained a reputation as the "graveyard of the Pacific." Boats foundered, grounded, and smashed on rocky headlands, taking hundreds of lives. The U.S. Coast Survey continued to chart the estuaries and compile information in the *Coast Pilot,* an annual publication with data on landmarks, rocks, buoys, and anchorages. The U.S. Light-house Board was called upon to provide more assistance.

On a case-by-case basis Congress appropriated funds for design and construction of important facilities. These included lighthouses: Cape Arago (1866), Cape Blanco (1870), Yaquina Bay (1872), Cape Foulweather (1873), Point Adams (1875), Tillamook Rock (1881), Warrior Rock (1888) at the mouth of the Willamette River, Cape Meares (1890), Umpqua River, Heceta Head, Coquille River (all 1894), and Desdemona Sands (1905). The goal was to create a system of stations with interlocking lights. On a clear night at sea, a mariner might expect to sight at any point a distinctive beacon on shore to pinpoint the location. Fog signals powered by steam engines blasted warnings from a number of the stations to tell captains to drop anchor or beat a retreat until the mists cleared.

In 1892 an appropriation of $60,000 funded construction of *Columbia River Lightship No. 50.* Anchored off the treacherous bar of the Columbia, the lightship kept a lonely crew of eight who, for decades, kept watch, maintained kerosene lights, and fed coal into boilers to power a massive fog signal. Their wave-tossed perch with booming horn drew hardy men who, like those at remote lighthouses, endured modest pay and isolation.

Congress also funded construction of stations and staffing for the U.S. Life-Saving Service. The first station opened in 1878 at the Cape Arago Lighthouse near the entrance to Coos Bay. Numerous shipwrecks and loss of life associated with the export of coal and lumber from the harbor brought federal action. The small building had a surfboat and one oarsman. Launching the craft and rowing to a vessel in distress depended upon volunteers. By the end of the 19th century the U.S. Life-Saving Service had stations at Warrenton, Tillamook Bay, Yaquina Bay, Coos Bay, and the Umpqua and Coquille Rivers. Each had crew quarters, a boat house, and a practice mast for breeches-buoy drill. In the early 20th century the USLSS erected stations at Port Orford and Siuslaw River.

In the 1870s the U.S. Geological Survey began work in Oregon. John Evans, U.S. Geologist for Oregon Territory, had mounted initial surveys of mining areas in 1855–56. In the final three decades of the 19th century the agency inaugurated studies of mining districts to assess coal and gold deposits. Its skilled cartographers also commenced topographic mapping in conjunction with the U.S. Geodetic Survey. These maps, revised at 20-to-30 year intervals in the 20th century, gave form to the land. They provided vital information on roads, settlements, and terrain. In the 1890s the USGS performed a remarkable service. Its employees mounted the first comprehensive assessment of forests in the state. They estimated standing volumes of hardwoods and softwoods, mapped areas ravaged by forest fires, photographed the terrain, and published technical reports on forest conditions and grazing impacts.

The Bureau of Indian Affairs by 1856 had embarked on its mission to attempt to transform Indian tribes into the mainstream culture in one generation. It founded its work upon an agrarian economy regardless of the terrain, elevation, or traditional subsistence patterns of the tribes. Oregon's reservations were Siletz, Grand Ronde, Warm Springs, Umatilla, Klamath, and Malheur. The tribes retained but a fraction of their aboriginal lands. The Nez Perce, whose 1855 treaty reserved their aboriginal lands in northeastern Oregon, were beset by trespassers who, in 1877, provoked the Nez Perce War and the exodus of Chief Joseph's band. These Indians orchestrated a brilliant retreat through the Pacific Northwest, for months eluding the U.S. Army. When they finally surrendered, the government confined them first in Oklahoma and after 1885 on the Colville Reservation in Washington.

Indian agents, subagents, farmers, teachers, and doctors—all in the employ of the federal government—mounted the programs. They created farms and insisted, in spite of the weather, that Indians raise wheat in the boggy soil along the Oregon coast. Hundreds died in this ill-fated experiment. They also attempted to compel the Klamath and Warm Springs tribes to become farmers. The setting for their farms was amenable to gathering root crops or berries but not to cereal or vegetable crop production. Terrible hardship ensued.

The Bureau of Indian Affairs focused particular energy on younger Indians. It shuttled them into day schools and reservation boarding schools. The goal was to grab the brightest and nurture them in English and "civilized" lifeways so they might become a new generation of leaders. In 1879 Captain James Wilkinson of the U.S. Army opened the Indian Training School in Forest Grove. When local opposition mounted against the presence of "savages" in the town, the BIA moved the school to an onion field five miles from Salem. Chemawa Indian

School, founded in 1881, remains the oldest Indian boarding school in the United States. Its purpose was to insulate young people from the language, religion, and culture of their elders and compel them to adapt to a new lifeway. In many respects the federal program achieved its purpose.

In 1887 the General Allotment Act launched a major assault on tribalism. The law, extended over the next few years to Oregon reservations, provided for dividing up the tribal estate into individual allotments of 80 to 160 acres. The plan was for each Indian to receive a tract, farm it, transform in lifeways, master English and, after the passage of 25 years, gain certification as "competent." The Indian then became a citizen of the United States, received title to the allotment, and could pay taxes on the land! The program fostered a dramatic loss in Indian lands and created a nightmare of checkerboard ownerships within reservations.

The Army Corps of Engineers was also on duty in 19th century Oregon. Its employees mounted river navigability studies on the Columbia, Umpqua, and Willamette and planned dredging and jetty projects at several estuaries. These men charted the rivers, designed improvements and, with federal appropriations, oversaw blasting of rocks and reefs. Between 1878 and 1896 the Corps of Engineers supervised the region's most expensive "pork barrel" project—construction of the massive bypass canal and locks at the Cascades of the Columbia. The Corps also constructed the Yamhill River Locks (1900) and, starting in 1888, initiated jetty projects at Coquille River, Coos Bay, Siuslaw River, Yaquina Bay, and Columbia River. By 1920 the Corps of Engineers had spent $4.7 million on river and harbor projects; local contributions added nearly a fifth more when required by legislation. The flow of federal dollars was an immense benefit to Oregonians, for the state did not have the resources to fund such large-scale projects.

Uncle Sam delivered. Federal projects included land grants for wagon roads, homesteads, and war veterans. Congress paid for soldiers to fight Indians, personnel to manage reservations, funds to build and staff lighthouses and lifesaving stations, operation of postal routes, post offices, the federal court system, customs houses, the General Land Office, mapping and mineral assessments by the U.S. Geological Survey, and updating of navigational information by the U.S. Coast Survey. Uncle Sam was a key player in a state populated by farmers, stockraisers, fishers, miners, loggers and sawmill workers, and small-town business people.

Minorities

The welcome mat was not out. Oregon's early generations defined opportunity narrowly. The land and resources were the domain of men and women of Caucasian background; others need not apply. Even when the Donation Land Act provided that women qualified for claims, brothers and brothers-in-law tried to wrest claims away from widows. Entreaties of women for fairer treatment finally led to passage of the Married Women's Property Act in 1866, the right to vote in school elections in 1878, and admission to the bar in 1885. Women were a minority in Oregon. The frontier demography, especially in mining districts and rural areas, remained predominantly male for decades. Women's efforts to gain the general franchise were repeatedly rebuffed and not realized until the 20th century.

African-Americans were unequivocally not wanted. Some, nevertheless, persisted quietly and settled in the state. The Census of 1850 reported in the entire Pacific Northwest either 54 or 56. The Census of 1860 identified 124 blacks and mulattoes, a tiny fraction of the more than 52,000 residents enumerated. Those who settled in Oregon took risks, but they had known prejudice and discrimination far worse in other parts of the country. Sometimes, however, racial episodes erupted. These occurred sporadically in several parts of the state over a period of 70 years. By 1890, for example, the African-American population of Coos County was 36. Most worked for the local railroad or at the Beaver Hill and Libby coal mines. Recruited in West Virginia, they had emigrated across the country and walked through the Coast Range from Roseburg to the lower Coquille River, only to find that they and their families were expected to live in leaking boxcars. The men had to work in the deep shafts reaching below sea level for 90 cents per day. When they complained, they were accused of fomenting labor strife and compelled to leave.

Alonzo Tucker was an African-American who worked as a bootblack and operator of a gym in Marshfield. In 1906 dubious charges of rape were leveled against him by a white woman. When a mob of 200 armed men marched on the jail, the marshal freed Tucker, who hid beneath a dock. He was twice shot the next morning and then hanged from the Fourth Street Bridge by a mob that had grown to more than 300. The coroner's inquest found no fault; the victim, the report said, had died of asphyxiation. No indictments were brought. The local newspaper observed that the lynch mob was "quiet and orderly" and that the vigilante proceeding was no "unnecessary disturbance of the peace." In 1907 the Marshfield School Board instituted segregated education, alleging that the four African-American students "will materially retard the progress of the five hundred white children."

Not all African-Americans faced treatments like those in turn-of-the-century Coos County. Some found steady employment with the railroads, both on construction crews and on Pullman cars. Others opened restaurants, barber shops, beauty shops, and saloons. McCants Stewart in 1903 passed the Oregon bar exam and began legal practice. Dr. J.A. Merriam entered medical practice in Portland in that decade. A number entered the ministry and labored at the pulpit, in choirs, and in social halls to influence the spirituality of their families, friends, and neighbors. Outreach came in many forms. The Colored Benevolent Association of Portland, founded in 1867, fraternal lodges, baseball teams, and women's clubs were other means for African-Americans to help their communities.

Chinese-Americans

Poverty, warfare, overpopulation, and ambition racked the peoples of the Pearl River Delta in the mid-19th century. Foreigners carved out enclaves in Macao, Hong Kong, and Canton, bribed their way into the Chinese economy by importing opium, and siphoned off a rich trade in luxury items. Many Chinese aspired to a better life and Gum San—Gold Mountain—beckoned. Tales of gold discoveries along the Pacific Coast proved irresistible. Thousands of men responded. Their plan was simple—go to Gum San, work hard every day, store up gold, and return to purchase land and hold position in Chinese society.

As the gold rush drifted northward into Oregon, the Chinese followed the discoveries. They were relegated to the worked-over placers, barred from some districts altogether, and compelled to pay a head tax because of race. They worked, paid, and endured. By the 1870s, for example, Chinese males constituted nearly half the population of Grant County. They lived frugally and labored hard. They moved tons of rock to get to pay dirt in crevices and potholes in the upper John Day diggings. They ran restaurants, laundries, herbal pharmacies, and gambling dens.

Because of their distinctive dress, language, religion, and difference from the surrounding culture, the Chinese were treated brutally. The editor of the *Grant County News* on October 15, 1885, observed: "To every one it is apparent that the Chinese are a curse and a blight to this county, not only financially, but socially and morally . . . . What the Chinaman wears, he brings from China, and what he eats (except rats and lizards), he brings across the ocean, and thus American trade or production reaps no benefit from his presence." The presence of tongs—kinship and social organizations—and Chinese determination to carry wealth home fostered intense discrimination. Murders, assaults, segregation, intimidation, special taxation, and opposition confronted the Chinese at every turn.

What did they do? They persevered and many achieved their goals. They found employment in railroad construction. Chinese laborers provided much of the backbreaking toil to make the cuts for the Oregon & California Railroad as it inched southward through the Umpqua Mountains to the Rogue

River Valley or on the line of the Oregon Railway & Navigation Company as it stretched eastward in 1880–82 through the Columbia Gorge. Willing to endure cannery work, Chinese men by the 1870s had acquired a near monopoly of work in canneries from Astoria to The Dalles. They gutted the fish, operated the steam pressure cookers, fastened the labels, and prepared tons of cases for shipment to a world market. They labored at nearly 40 canneries lining the shores of the Columbia for low wages and compulsory residency in company dormitories.

The Chinese congregated in Chinatown in Portland or, when their seasonal work diminished, traveled to communities in San Francisco, Seattle, or Vancouver, British Columbia. Anti-Chinese bigotry grew in the 1880s. Chinese were driven out of several communities—Oregon City, Albina, and Mount Tabor. In 1887 vigilantes murdered ten or a dozen Chinese miners in Hells Canyon on the Oregon-Idaho border. The Chinese Exclusion Act then cut off immigration, leaving nearly 9,000 Chinese men in Oregon with little prospect of bringing a bride from home or paying for passage of family members. The downward spiral began. Each year Oregon had fewer residents of Chinese ancestry. Those who had resources returned home. Others, like Doc Hay and Lung On, remained, running an herbal drug store and car dealership in John Day. Bert Why operated a grocery store in North Bend. Most of the men who stayed remained single and lived lonely lives in Gum San.

Japanese-Americans

Jobs and land lured Japanese immigrants by the last decade of the 19th century. Overpopulation and limited opportunity at home, the favorable publicity of labor recruiters, and adventure drew Japanese to Oregon. They found places to work and live. Many men hired on as laborers to build railroads. Tadashichi Tanaka, Shinzaburo Ban, and Shintaro Takaki were all involved in 1891 in recruiting rail workers. The men helped build the Union Pacific, Southern Pacific, feeder lines, and logging railroads.

Japanese immigrant families settled in the Treasure Valley near Ontario, Hood River Valley, and at Gresham. The prospect of gaining a few acres, planting a garden, setting out an orchard, and producing high-quality vegetables and fruits drew husbands, wives, and children to work together to establish a substantial hold in a new land. Others settled on Second, Third, and Fourth streets in Northwest Portland, where they became shopkeepers. Some men worked in sawmills, but at risk. In 1925, for example, a woman in Toledo on Yaquina Bay sparked a nasty attack on Japanese families. Threats of violence and bricks thrown through windows drove 25 Japanese men, women, and children from the town, and earned Rosemary Shenk a court appearance.

Other Newcomers

Oregon by the end of the 19th century, in spite of exclusionist attitudes and wars fought against Indians by the pioneer generation, had a changing complexion. Jewish merchants operated mercantile stores, enriched cultural life through their love of music and literature, and founded synagogues. Japanese and Chinese workers took some of the worst but necessary jobs. They helped build the state's vital transportation links. They canned fish, raised fruit, and ran small businesses. African-Americans dominated the Pullman services, mined coal, and grew steadily in numbers. Oregon was not a comfortable place for minorities, but negative treatment was also dished out to "dumb Swedes," beer-drinking Germans, Irish and Italian Catholics. Many Oregonians wore their fears of those who were different on their shirtsleeves.

Emerging Economies

Natural resources drove economic development. A popular song said: "There'll be apples on each branch in Oregon; there'll be valleys filled with golden grain. There'll be cattle on each ranch in Oregon; and there'll be plenty of sun and rain." Farming, stockraising, mining, fishing, and logging became mainstays. Land became the target. The trick was to find, coax, extricate, and harvest everything useful the state had to offer, provided it was possible to get it to market.

Farmers took their oxen with plows and harrows into the prairies of the Rogue, Umpqua, and Willamette valleys to turn the sod and sow crops. They raised wheat, oats, barley, corn, and potatoes. Swampy lands at Cipole, Gaston, and Lake Labish produced fabulous onions. In time experimentation led to specialty crops: hops for making malt in the brewing business, flax for linen manufacturing, hemp for paper and rope, and grapes for wine. Oregon farmers by the 1880s went wild for prunes. Thousands of acres of hillside lands were opened and groomed as orchards. Investors erected prune dryers and flooded the world market with more prunes than could be consumed. Some directed their energies next into filberts, walnuts, turkey raising, and hog production. The agricultural potentials of western Oregon were varied.

Stockraising attracted a number of investors. Dairy farmers began their workday before sunrise and were still milking cows after sunset. Their cows grazed on the meadows surrounding Tillamook Bay, Nestucca, Salmon River, Coos Bay, Coquille River, and in the Willamette Valley. The sprawling hinterlands of Oregon—two-thirds of the state laying beyond the Cascades—became cattle, sheep, and horse country in the 19th century. The dramatic rise of livestock production occurred between 1862 and 1882. It responded to the presence of hungry men in the mines of the Blue Mountains, transcontinental railroad connections in Nevada with boxcars and refrigerator cars to haul meat to major cities, woolen mills demanding material for their spindles, and land amenable to pastoral labors. Pete French, Ben Snipes, David Shirk, John S. Devine, W.B. Todhunter, Dr. Bernard Daly, and others became barons of the ranges. By strategically gaining control of springs, streambanks, and lake margins, they were able to run their vast herds on the public domain without competition. David Shirk's herds ranged up and down Guano Valley. Devine and Todhunter ran the Whitehorse Ranch in the Pueblo Valley. Pete French, whose kingdom lay at the base of Steens Mountain, was gunned down by an angry homesteader in 1897. The jury trying the alleged murderer ruled that French had died of "natural causes"—a bullet in the head. There was no conviction.

Smaller producers also came into Trans-Cascadia. Some tended herds of sheep—as many as 5,000 in a flock—in lonely labor. The work entailed months driving the sheep to summer range at high elevation, backbreaking days of shearing and wrestling wool bales onto wagons, and marking and doctoring the critters. Sheep and cattle raisers did not mix. Angry words sometimes led to gunshots that felled livestock and nearly plunged Central Oregon partisans into a cycle of sheep and cattle wars. Basque and Mexican shepherds brought their skills to Jordan Valley, Catlow Valley, and Treasure Valley. Some filed on homesteads. Donato Uvernaga and Simon Acordagoitia, Basques who settled on the Owyhee, hand-dug canals and built a hulking waterwheel. The steady current lifted metal buckets of life-giving water from the river to nourish the fields these immigrants cleared of sagebrush deep in the canyons below the Mahogany Mountains.

Mining shifted rapidly from placer deposits to lode claims. In that transition, the mining moved from an individual to a corporate enterprise, for shared capital and risk were usually necessary to open adits, erect a shaft house, install a stamp mill or flotation table, and hire the crews necessary to operate a mine. Cooks and flunkies produced the grub served in the mess hall. Miners rode the ore buckets or climbed rickety ladders into the mine. The company engineer or mine manager directed the flow of ore through the processing plants. Oregon's 19th century ventures included gold mines in the Bohemia District of the Western Cascades, Siskiyous, and Blue Mountains. Much of the gold and silver produced in Oregon and farther east in Idaho flowed through Portland, stimulating the development of the state's largest city. Between 1864 and 1870, for example, $29.8 million in mineral wealth passed through Portland. Between 1852 and 1964, Oregon produced an estimated $136 million in gold and silver. Approximately 73

percent came from the mines of Baker and Grant counties.

Quicksilver mines tapped deposits in Lane and Douglas counties. Brave miners engaged in the risky business of smelting the ores to fill flasks of mercury at London, Nonpareil, Milltown Hill, and other small communities that grew up at the mine portals. In the 1880s Will Q. Brown opened nickel deposits at Riddle in the South Umpqua Valley. Over the next 90 years this mine produced more than $1 billion in nickel while generating an important payroll for Douglas County.

The need for fuel for steam engines drove Oregon's coal mining industry. Steam schooners, locomotives, donkey engines, and mill equipment depended on cheap, plentiful coal. The mines at Coos Bay opened in 1853 and for nearly a century the coal fields of the lower Coquille River and Coos Bay fired Oregon industry and helped heat San Francisco. The Beaver Hill Mine, one of the largest on the coast, had shafts reaching nearly 1,100 feet below sea level. The Coos Bay, Roseburg & Eastern Railroad moved coal from the mines to the bunkers at Coos Bay where it was loaded on steamers that would take it to distant markets.

Salmon annually filled the rivers. Some say the runs were so thick that it was possible to walk dryshod across the streams! Robert Deniston Hume grasped the potential. His brothers were pioneer cannery operators on the Sacramento and, starting in 1867, on the Columbia River. In 1876, Hume settled at the mouth of the Rogue River. By bravado and cunning, he carved out such an empire that, in time, he was referred to as a "pygmy monopolist." Hume gained ownership of both banks of the river from the Pacific upstream to the head of tidewater. This holding made it impossible for any competitor to land a boat or draw nets filled with fish without trespassing on his land. In time Hume constructed a company town—Wedderburn—where he ran a cannery, store, race track, and cold storage plant. His vessels, the *Alexander Duncan, Berwick,* and *Mary D. Hume,* transported his catch to markets. Hume became a pioneer in the hatchery business when in 1877 he began experimenting with raising fish on Indian Creek near the mouth of Rogue River.

Canneries at Coos Bay, Umpqua River, Kernville, and the Nestucca River processed the runs on the coastal streams. Canneries lined the banks of the Columbia between The Dalles and the sea. Samuel Elmore, Ben Young, Frank Warren, and Frank Seufert were major players in the salmon canning business. The trick was to move quickly when new technology gave advantage. Laborers caught the fish in traps, seine nets, set nets, and at fishwheels whose paddles scooping with the current pulled salmon, sturgeon, eels, and steelhead

History

from the river and dumped them into fish boxes headed for a cannery.

Transportation systems were central to the future of most investments and profits in Oregon enterprise. Packet service and schooners carried passengers and freight along the coast. Sternwheelers picked up and delivered milk on the estuaries and carried commerce and passengers on most of the larger streams. Steamboats plied the Willamette, transforming landings into sites for warehouses, grist mills, and small towns. Steamboats traversed Upper Klamath Lake and Goose Lake, taking children to school and tourists or shoppers to specific destinations. Investors constructed steamboats above the Cascades for water travel on the Columbia east to The Dalles and also on the upper river above Celilo Falls with connections to the mouth of the Snake and on to Lewiston, Idaho.

Packing companies and teamsters responded to the needs of mining communities and residents of distant communities. Outfitted with mules and horses, they carried the food, clothing, and tools demanded by the miners in Canyon City, Auburn, and Baker City or the farmers along Crooked River and Ochoco Creek. Teamsters like Henry H. Wheeler braved blizzards in winter and scorching heat in summer to carry mail, passengers, and freight across the Columbia Plateau and into the mountains of eastern Oregon.

Railroads heralded the most significant advances in transportation. Between 1855 and 1862 Joseph Ruckel and Harrison Olmstead laid the foundation. They hired men, secured a right-of-way, and constructed roadbed and trestles for a horse-drawn cart to travel their "railway" along the Oregon shore at the Cascade Rapids of the Columbia. They were locked in bitter competition with Bradford & Company, competitors on the north bank. Pressing against both firms was the Oregon Steam Navigation Company, which had developed in the 1850s a significant hold on steamboat service on the lower Willamette and Columbia rivers. In 1860 Jacob Kamm, John C. Ainsworth, and other investors in the OSN Company incorporated and in rapid steps bought out the Bradfords, Ruckel, and Olmstead. Holding the critical sea-level portages through the Columbia Gorge, they were ready to craft a major transportation system. Within months they accomplished their goal.

The OSN Company, one of the state's first large corporations, developed an intricate system of steamboats, portage railroads, and freight lines that gave it a hold on much of the commerce of the Pacific Northwest. It also built Oregon's first railroad. In 1862, as word of rich mines in the interior hit the front pages of newspapers, Ainsworth was in San Francisco purchasing rails and a small locomotive, the Oregon Pony, for shipment to the gorge. Within a few months, workers transformed the old cart-rail system of Ruckel and Olmstead into Oregon's first railroad line—a five-mile route from Tanner Creek to the head of the Cascades. Other crews had taken on the bigger task of building a railroad for 14 miles from The Dalles to Celilo. Although its investors sold a major interest to the Northern Pacific in 1872, they bought back the shares following the Panic of 1873. They finally sold out in 1880. Those who held stock in the OSN Company were worth millions. Their daring and commitment had played a major role in helping anchor Portland as a hub of commerce and trade in the Pacific Northwest.

Railroads provided critical links to Oregon towns. In many instances they created towns. In 1880 Henry Villard headed a group of investors who bought out the OSN Company. Their firm, the Oregon Railway & Navigation Company, built a railroad along the south bank of the Columbia east to the Umatilla River. In 1883, having gained control of the Northern Pacific, Villard created Oregon's first transcontinental link with the OR&N. His Oregon Short Line Railroad ran southeast over the Blue Mountains to Huntington and in 1884 joined a connection into Idaho to the Union Pacific. This provided a second transcontinental connection for the state.

Construction of the Oregon & California Railroad, a north-south line to run from Portland to the Sacramento Valley, was a long-desired goal but its completion proved frustrating. Driven by a fabulous land grant of nearly five million acres from Congress, rival companies vied for the right to construct the route. Ben Holladay, operator of the Overland Mail and the Pacific Mail Steamship Company, ultimately prevailed. He formed the Oregon & California Railroad Company, sold bonds, and began building. The line reached Roseburg in 1872 and then stopped. Bad times in national finances were part of the problem. Poor potentials for returns on exceedingly expensive construction into the Rogue River Valley and over the Siskiyou Mountains were another. Construction resumed in 1882 and ultimately linked the line into the Southern Pacific system in California.

The primary lines of the OR&N to the interior and the O&C through the western Oregon valleys encouraged logging, lumber manufacturing, export of wool and livestock, and sale of fruit, cereal crops, and other agricultural commodities to a vastly expanded market. The primary lines also encouraged two generations of smaller operators such as T. Egenton Hogg to dream of connecting units or even of new transcontinental linkages. Hogg managed in the 1880s to build a line from salt water at Yaquina City over the Coast Range and east via the Santiam as far as Detroit. The route of his Oregon Pacific Railroad appeared on maps in the 1890s but it never reached the Deschutes or the

Harney Basin, where speculators laid out towns in anticipation of its arrival.

The pieces were mostly in place by the latter 19th century for the state to sustain steady growth. Oregon had a resource-dependent economy driven by exploitation of fish, timber, minerals, and agricultural lands. The state had steamboats, stage lines, pack teams, and railroads to serve residents of small towns as well as emerging cities. Oregon's population grew steadily. At statehood in 1859 Oregon had 52,465 residents. The figure more than tripled to 174,768 in 1880, and reached 413,536 in 1900.

Troubled Times

Discontents stirred in the hearts and minds of Oregonians in the last three decades of the 19th century. Life left some feeling cheated. Hard work did not bring sufficient wages or sale of farm commodities to secure a decent living. Many jobs took place in the midst of danger in poorly lighted sawmills, dust-filled coal mines, slippery canneries, or woolen mills with whirling spindles. Loggers confronted falling trees, flying cables, surging freshets, and wretched living conditions in the camps where they lived. Clerks were underpaid and labored six days a week in monotonous jobs where they had neither health nor retirement plans and little prospect for advancement. Women attended academies, public schools, normal schools, colleges, and universities, but male Oregonians refused to grant them the right to vote. Too many, it seemed, coped with alcoholic husbands who plundered the egg and butter money for a few more coins to spend on "demon liquor."

The disenchanted found inspiration for reconstructing their world. Ideologies beckoned alluringly and became part of an interesting mix of forces that set the stage for significant changes in Oregon. They ranged from arguments for women's suffrage to the pleas of the Christian Women's Temperance Union to control, if not suspend, the manufacture and sale of alcoholic beverages. The ideologies ran from economic and social theories to racist and bigoted attacks on minorities and immigrants. Many suggested political action might solve a state's or a nation's problems in a time of increasing industrialization.

California journalist Henry George promoted a simple solution to destitution. He argued in *Progress and Poverty* (1879) that the United States could eradicate poverty by implementing a tax of 100 percent on the "unearned increment," the inflationary value of real estate. The redistribution of the "single tax," he said, could meet need and solve societal problems. Tens of thousands read his book and became "single taxers."

Edward Bellamy's *Looking Backward* (1887) intrigued others. Bellamy used a shallow plot line about a man who fell into a mesmeric trance in 1887—a time of labor strife, urban pollution, slums, and poverty—and who awakened in 2000. He found a reconstructed American society and economy with abundant prosperity and peace. All had changed through the miracle of "nationalism." In Bellamy's world the solution was government ownership of all means of production, transportation, housing, and basic utilities.

Hard rock miners listened to the speakers from the Knights of Labor and the Western Federation of Miners. Many were not happy with their lot. Coal miners on Oregon's southwest coast endured low wages, explosions, and horrendous working conditions. Men extracting quicksilver in Douglas County slowly poisoned themselves tending the furnaces to produce flasks of mercury. Gold miners labored hundreds of feet below ground in the quartz deposits of the Bohemia Mining District in the Western Cascades and in mine shafts in the Blue and Wallowa Mountains of eastern Oregon. They were inspired by the prospect of forming unions and joining with fellow miners to wrest better pay and safer working conditions from the companies for which they labored.

Thousands of farmers turned first to the Patrons of Husbandry, joining Granges, engaging in the rituals of the organization, and pressing the legislature to meet the needs of agrarians. Others joined the Northwestern Alliance, a nonpartisan organization of farmers who hoped for reform. Alliance members and Grangers lobbied for collection and publication of agricultural statistics, strengthening of education at Oregon Agricultural College in Corvallis, development of experimental farms to test crops, breeds of livestock, and the impact of fertilizer and chemical sprays. And not a few heard about Mary Elizabeth Lease of Kansas, who told farmers in America's heartland that they should "raise less corn and more hell!"

Many agrarians embraced the People's Party. In 1892 its platform attempted to create an agenda to meet their needs. The populists endorsed limits on immigration, government ownership of railroads, telegraph, and telephone, free coinage of silver to stimulate western mining, secret ballot, direct election of senators, and the subtreasury system whereby the government would buy unsold farm commodities, hold them, and then unload the products on the world market. Farmers would receive subtreasury notes—backed by the government—when they deposited potatoes, wheat, barley, or apples at the federal warehouse—and could pay off their loans. William Hope Harvey's *Coin's Financial School* (1892) made the case for expanding the amount of money in circulation. Professor Coin argued that if the federal government would purchase and coin all available silver, the nation's economy could be corrected, farmers could pay off the mortgages for steam tractors and combines, and prosperity would return.

As these ideas swept through the newspapers, out of the mouths of speakers, and through books, they found believers. In 1890 Oregon had 2,555 men employed in logging and log transportation, 1,962 working in sawmills, 2,756 engaged in fishing or the oyster harvest, 2,308 mining, and 17,316 working as agricultural laborers. Tens of thousands more Oregonians lived on family farms. Men rode the range to tend cattle, sheep, and horses, while women preserved food and cooked huge meals at roundup and shearing times. The farm population—owners and hired laborers—endured continuous work, dark nights, isolation, taxes on their lands, and uncertainty.

In 1889 many of the discontented met in Salem to form the Union Party. The meeting drew Prohibition advocates, members of the Knights of Labor, and the interest of Democrat Sylvester Pennoyer, seeking another term as governor. This was the atmosphere of social and political discontent that brought Oregonians to the People's Party. Hundreds turned out for rallies to meet General James B. Weaver, populist candidate for president. Abigail Scott Duniway, continuing her unrelenting campaign for women's suffrage, in 1892 introduced Mary Elizabeth Lease, the "Kansas Pythoness" and populist stump speaker, to an eager audience in Portland. Duniway's 1894 speech to an estimated 2,800 strikers inspired some to call her the "Patrick Henry of the Northwest" and led her brother, editor of *The Oregonian*, to refuse to print the text of her address.

While the Republicans and Democrats continued their hold on the majority of state offices, they found populists among their ranks in the legislature. Oregon Democrats got the reform message in the 1890s. Historian Dorothy O. Johansen quoted the saying "Scratch a Western Democrat and you find a Populist," an apt assessment of the Democrats' embrace of free silver, banking reform, income tax, and reform in government.

Oregon government needed change. Oregon Senator John Hipple Mitchell, a slippery man when it came to wives and influence peddling, reportedly said: "Ben Holladay's politics are my politics and what Ben Holladay wants I want." Holladay's hold on regional transportation systems and Mitchell's retainer as legal counsel for both the Oregon & California Railroad and the Northern Pacific left little doubt about the senator's loyalties. He may have been elected by the legislature, but he appeared to be in the pocket of special interests.

Frustrated Oregonians also turned to the pathetic performance of the builders of the state's military wagon roads. The grants locked up hundreds of thousands of acres in checkerboard sections on both margins of the traces and, by the 1890s, many of the holdings had passed to out-of-state owners. The grant for the Coos Bay Wagon Road—105,120 acres—passed quickly into the hands of speculators little interested in the road or its operation. For a time Californians Leland Stanford, Mark Hopkins, Charles Crocker, and Collis P. Huntington owned much of the grant. Other portions went to the Southern Oregon Improvement Company, a pool of investors in Boston and New Bedford, Massachusetts. Edward Martin of San Francisco formed the Eastern Oregon Land Company when he secured 450,000 acres of the land grant for The Dalles-Boise Military Wagon Road.

By not taking title to the grants, the owners avoided taxation yet no settler could homestead or purchase the land from the General Land Office. A few Oregonians perpetrated unblushing frauds in the scramble for properties under the Swamp Lands Act. Ostensibly the law encouraged reclamation and irrigation. It created, however, a situation where unscrupulous public officials conspired with speculators to gain ownership of tidelands, lush lake margins, and even dry ground. Plunderers also took advantage of the 1887 decision of the legislature to sell school lands, sections 16 and 36, in each township. Had the lands or revenues gone into a school fund, the endowment could have financed public education in Oregon in perpetuity.

In the 1890s neither the ideologues nor the political activists carried the day. Society, business, and political affairs continued much as usual. The times of discontent, however, set the stage for change. Ideas circulated that posed the prospect for deepseated reform. All that was needed was some principled leadership, public indignation with the corruption, and the will to try something new.

The Oregon System

William U'Ren was a quiet, contemplative man. Little in his countenance or demeanor betrayed the inner fire that drove his determination to change public participation in Oregon government. A single-tax advocate, U'Ren moved on to embrace the ideas of James W. Sullivan, author of *Direct Legislation by the Citizenship Through the Initiative and Referendum* (1892). If U'Ren could empower common citizens, he could wage war on vested interests, corruption, and the tensions that set classes against each other. U'Ren jettisoned the single tax, embraced Sullivan's philosophy, converted to populism, and in 1897 gained a seat in the legislature as a candidate of the People's Party. U'Ren was in a position to cut a deal because populists held 13 critical votes to swing power in the legislature.

The time for dealing was at hand. Senator John H. Mitchell, despised by many, came out firmly for the Republican platform and the gold standard. Jonathan Bourne, Jr., a Republican and silver mine owner, saw a chance to dump Mitchell, provided he could win populist votes. U'Ren set the price: initiative, referendum, voter registration, and an elections procedure law. Bourne bought the package but had to play a cat-and-mouse game in what was known as the "Holdup of '97." Bourne, U'Ren, and others forged a coalition and blocked the House from organizing. The Committee on Credentials declined to report, the anti-Mitchell representatives refused to take their oaths of office, and the Mitchell forces could not elect him, lacking a quorum in the House. U'Ren and Bourne pushed through each of the promised measures. By a cumbersome process, the legislature twice approved a constitutional amendment and, after ratification by a resounding public vote in 1902, Oregonians instituted the initiative and referendum, having amended the state constitution for the first time since 1859.

The combination of voter commitment to enact long-needed laws and the ability to do so with the initiative helped propel Oregon to national attention as a state leading in progressivism. The largely nonpartisan Oregon System, as it was heralded, addressed the accumulated social evils that had grown in numbers and complexity. The means were at hand to make government more efficient, honest, and responsive to human need.

Oregonians tallied important enactments: Direct Primary Law (1904), extension of initiative and referendum to local laws, city home rule, indictment by grand jury, taxes on telephone, telegraph, and railroad companies (all 1906), a recall amendment to the State Constitution, the Corrupt Practices Act (both 1908), three-fourths verdict in civil cases, employers' liability act (both 1910), women's suffrage, prohibition on private employment of convict labor, eight-hour day on public works (all 1912), presidential preference primary (1913), prohibition, and an eight-hour day and room ventilation for women workers (both 1914). Other laws abolished capital punishment, the infamous Oregon Boot, a heavy manacle attached to legs of prisoners, and required publication of the *Oregon Blue Book*.

The Oregon Land Fraud trials captured local and national interest. Francis Heney, special federal prosecutor, brought to justice 33 who had pillaged the federal lands, state school lands, and the timbered resources of the Siletz Indian Reservation. The kingpin of the Oregon Land Fraud Ring, Stephen A.D. Puter, penned in his prison cell *Looters of the Public Domain* (1908), a tell-all book with portraits of his co-conspirators and copies of documents confirming their criminal acts. Heney's prosecutions cleaned out many of the personnel of the General Land Office; twice indicted but failed to convict Binger Hermann, an Oregonian and former commissioner of the General Land Office in Washington, D.C.; and obtained prison sentences for

Senator John H. Mitchell and Congressman John N. Williamson.

Oregon governors George E. Chamberlain, who served from 1903 to 1909, and Oswald West, who served from 1911 to 1915, were in office during the era of progressivism and each, in a nonpartisan manner, helped facilitate the Oregon System. To persuade the legislature that he intended for progressive reform to prevail, in 1911 West vetoed 63 bills. When good legislation failed, he saw that it surfaced as initiative measures. As a consequence Oregonians gained a workers' compensation act, banking laws, and a Public Utility Commission. By executive order in 1913 West declared that Oregon beaches were public highways and set the precedent for the much-litigated but protected right of public access to the entire state shoreline. He gave full authority to his secretary, Fern Hobbs, and sent her with members of the National Guard to Copperfield, a notorious boom town on the railroad in Baker County. With a declaration of martial law on January 1, 1914, she closed all saloons and houses of prostitution. She left the guardsmen to monitor the situation. West never minced words. In his reminiscences he wrote about Oregon's land fraud ring: "These looters of the public domain—working with crooked federal and state officials—through rascality and fraud, gained title to thousands of acres of valuable, publicly-owned timber lands, and at minimum prices." West pounded them, even when penning his recollections in 1950.

Progressivism touched Oregon in another way. In 1907 Congress considered a crucial agricultural appropriations bill. Powerful lobbyists for timber companies persuaded Senator Charles Fulton from Astoria to attach to it an amendment rescinding presidential authority to create any more forest reserves in the Pacific Northwest under the Forest Reserve Act of 1891. In less than ten days Gifford Pinchot, new head of the U.S. Forest Service, and President Theodore Roosevelt poured over maps and identified millions of acres of critical forests. Roosevelt exercised the last hours of his executive authority and created the "Midnight Reserves." Oregon's national forests multiplied severalfold by the stroke of a pen and the willpower of two conservationists.

The Oregon System was the creative response to a mix of ideologies and discontents. It broke the power of many special interests and old political coalitions. It became a model for the rest of the country and was emulated in dozens of states and cities drawing inspiration from the power of a determined citizenry.

Mixed Blessings

Progressivism waned with the onset of World War I. Oregonians and other Americans began to tire of crusades. The entry into the Great War tested the resolution to continue problem-solving. Peace and commitment to its maintenance were casualties of both the war and the postwar world.

Industrial strife mounted when worker expectations remained unrealized as prosperity increased after 1900. Alienated, fearful, and distrustful of the establishment, some workers gravitated toward the Socialist Party and militant labor unions. The West Coast Shingle Weaver's Union as chartered by the American Federation of Labor and the International Union of Shingle Weavers, Sawmill Workers, and Woodsmen sought recruits. The Industrial Workers of the World grew by the thousands when disgruntled loggers and mill workers enlisted in its ranks. Known to most by its initials, IWW, the union was perceived by management as the "I Won't Work" contingent. Free speech fights, confrontations, strikes, and demands for better working conditions and higher wages became the tense legacy of workers and management on the eve of World War I.

Illustrative of the tensions were the vigilante actions of the businessmen of Bandon. In 1913, enraged by the publication of *Social Justice,* they seized its editor and publisher. Dr. Bailey K. Leach had used his newspaper to denounce vigilantism, the Boy Scouts of America as a paramilitary organization, and perceived thought control in the public library, which refused to accession Socialist literature. A mob grabbed Dr. Leach, placed a noose around his neck, and "deported" him from Bandon. Beaten and left barefoot on the North Spit at Coos Bay, having been compelled to kneel and kiss the American flag, he walked through the sand dunes and up the Umpqua River to the office of Governor Oswald West to complain of his treatment. An investigation mounted by the State Supreme Court led to the disbarment of an attorney in Marshfield. Leach was lucky. When IWW organizer Wesley Everest was deported in similar fashion from Coos Bay, he went to Centralia, Washington, to promote the union. In 1919 he was seized by a mob, castrated, and hanged from a railroad bridge. No one was charged with Everest's murder. To many, the rousing hymn of the IWW, "Hallelujah, I'm a Bum," justified violations of civil liberties and the law.

To counter the growth of labor unions and the Socialist Party, the federal government took control of spruce production in western Oregon and Washington. Deemed an essential material for airplane manufacturing, spruce became the assignment of the U.S. Army's Spruce Production Division. It assumed responsibilities for logging, lumbering, and filling orders. In 1917 General Brice P. Disque took command of troops who erected mills at Coquille and Toledo, Oregon, and Vancouver and Port Gamble, Washington. The Spruce Division produced 54 million board feet of airplane wing beams in Oregon and left a modern electrical sawmill and extensive railroad network in Lincoln County, which, in time, passed into private ownership.

The federal government also created the Loyal Legion of Loggers and Lumbermen. Ostensibly an employer-employee union, the 4-Ls recruited thousands of workers who pledged not to strike and to help the nation in its production of war materials. The Emergency Fleet Corporation, a federal agency, contracted with yards to turn out vessels for the war effort. Shipbuilders in Portland, Astoria, Tillamook, and Marshfield produced steel and wooden-hull vessels for the EFC. Fort Stevens at Warrenton took on new life since its primary construction during the Civil War and Spanish-American War. Troops drilled and trained on its parade grounds; some departed with other Oregonians for service on the battlefields of Europe.

World War I was a mixed blessing for Oregon. Initially it stimulated the economy with the production of war materials, foodstuffs, and ships, but it set the stage for the collapse of shipbuilding and the falloff of lumber production in the 1920s. Everywhere were signs of trouble: few housing starts, instability in banking, speculation in the stock market, and migration. More than 50,000 people left Oregon following World War I. Opportunities beckoned elsewhere.

In a sense, Oregon made their transit possible. Between 1911 and 1922 state, county, and local funds helped build the Columbia River Highway. The Columbia Gorge section, designed by Samuel Lancaster, an engineer brought in from Tennessee for the assignment, ran eastward with gentle grades and sensitive integration with the environment to open access to scenic waterfalls, hiking trails, and spectacular vistas between Portland and The Dalles. Modern construction techniques including steel-reinforced poured-concrete bridges created the region's first paved highway. In 1913 Oregon created the State Highway Commission. Four years later it expanded its membership and the legislature began steady appropriations to "Get Oregon Out of the Mud." The "good roads" campaign took on real life in 1919 when Oregon enacted a gasoline tax. The first state in the country to pay for roads through a gas tax, Oregon embraced the automobile age and began construction of the Pacific Highway. From its crossing at the Interstate Bridge across the Willamette, the route ran south via the Willamette, Umpqua, and Rogue valleys to California. Paved in concrete, its gentle course ran through productive farmlands, crossed rivers on major bridges, wended its way up the slopes of the Siskiyous, and confirmed Oregon's commitment to good roads.

Road construction led to legislation in 1921 promoted by Governor Ben Olcott to authorize the State Highway Commission to acquire rights-of-way for scenic conservation and roadside forest preserves. In 1922 the state accepted the gift of Sarah Helmick State Park in Polk County. These actions received legislative direction in 1925 with authorization to acquire lands for park purposes for waysides and natural areas. Governor I.L. Patterson in 1929 named the first State Park Commission, which worked closely with Samuel H. Boardman, the state parks engineer, for building a land base of state-owned park properties.

Although highway construction helped one sector of the economy, the advent of automobile traffic sounded the death knell for steamboats on the rivers and, in time, Oregon's electrical railroad system. The Oregon Electric Railway operated daily trains over 122 miles of track by 1912 between Portland and Eugene. A "No Soot-No Cinders" route, the commuter line also ran west to Forest Grove. The Southern Pacific's Red Electric began connections in 1914. It ran from Portland to Corvallis via Lake Oswego and Newberg. A branch line swung west to Hillsboro, Forest Grove, and McMinnville. For a time, travelers had the choice of ten departures from Portland and at least two from McMinnville. The efficiency of the electrics and the interurban lines was eclipsed by cars and buses. The 1920s were a time of transition. Smells of draft animals and the clacking sound of horseshoes mixed with the swift movement of electrical railroads and gasoline-driven cars and trucks. In time the familiar "Galloping Goose," the solitary passenger-mail car that ran on many of Oregon's short lines, disappeared. Residents of Friend, Shaniko, Prairie City, Cherry Grove, Bull Run, and other small towns would have to travel by road, not rail.

Wartime stress, emphasis on patriotism, distrust of German-Americans, eugenics campaigns championed by Dr. Bethenia Owens-Adair, and anti-Catholic bigotry created fertile ground in Oregon for the rise of the American Protective Association, Federation of Patriotic Societies, and the Ku Klux Klan. With a combined membership estimated at more than 64,000 Oregonians, these organizations fed on the fear and distrust of residents in a period of social flux and uncertainty. Although minorities were few in number, racism and bigotry were imported ideas. They came with newcomers from other parts of the country and grew in soil that already nurtured suspicion and tendencies to vigilante action. Chapters of the Ku Klux Klan formed in Tillamook, Medford, Eugene, and Portland, as well as many other towns. Robed Klansmen paraded in the streets, ignited crosses on hillsides, nailed American flags to the doors of Catholic schools, and intimidated African-Americans.

The Klan, FOPS, and Scottish Rite Masons sponsored a bill, passed in 1922 in the general election, to compel all children to attend public schools. The overtly anti-Catholic measure threatened to close all parochial schools and military academies. The state Supreme Court ruled the law unconstitutional in 1924 and the U.S. Supreme Court concurred in 1925. The Ku Klux Klan found a strange champion in the Oregon legislature. Kaspar K. Kubli, speaker of the House of Representatives, happened to possess winning initials and became a rallying point for efforts to drive through the Alien Property Act of 1923. The law prohibited Japanese from purchasing or leasing land in Oregon. The legislature also passed a law forbidding wearing of sectarian clothing, namely priestly vestments or nuns' habits, in classrooms.

A number of historians have written about the flaws of the 1920s and the nation's serious engagement with public-sanctioned bigotry. While some of the laws were overt, much more went on quietly but consistently. Oregon Indians, who became citizens of the United States in 1924, were forbidden to purchase alcohol, though some applied for a special card that certified their entitlement to drink. Oregon realtors declined to sell homes in certain areas to minorities. Oregon developers wrote into deeds restrictive covenants that prohibited holding ducks and geese and sale of the house and land to anyone of Chinese or Japanese ancestry. Large neighborhoods of Portland—Garthwick, Dunthorpe, Eastmoreland, Westmoreland—and Lake Oswego were kept "white" for decades by subtle but effective discrimination.

One of the hard-fought agendas of the 1920s was the encouragement of public power. In 1930 Oregonians approved the creation of public utility districts. The action shook some of the well-established utility companies, for they now faced the prospect that if their rates and actions were out of line with public interest, voters could set up their own company, and vie for hydropower rights on a stream or build a sawdust-fired electrical plant and offer service to consumers.

The 1920s were a period of rapid adjustment from wartime preparedness and boom to an uneven and deteriorating economy. Oregon moved from progressivism to the rise of selfish interests and secret societies that threatened liberties and promoted bigotry. Yet, in spite of following strange paths, the state laid the foundation of a fine highway system, state parks, and competitive rates for electrical power.

The Great Depression

On October 29, 1929, a calamity rocked the United States. Within hours the stock market, buoyed by speculation and unreasonable expectations, plunged into the abyss of "Black Tuesday." The onset of the Great Depression meant little to tens of thousands of Oregonians. They were already living in depressed circumstances, trying to make a go of arid homesteads, stump farms, or underpaid jobs in sawmills. Those who had savings, however, felt the debacle acutely. Banks went bankrupt. In spite of handsome buildings and facades of stability, white marble counters, brass grills at the teller cages, and hulking vaults, their resources were vulnerable and they fell by the droves, wiping out the accumulated resources of depositors. Bank failures led to foreclosures on homes, farms, and businesses and contributed to the general malaise that had seized the country.

In spite of his reputation as a humanitarian, President Herbert Hoover, a sometime Oregonian who had grown up in Newberg, wrestled unsuccessfully with checking the economic free-fall. Hoover was trapped both by his political philosophy and by problems so complex that no one really had a viable solution for them.

So in 1933 the nation turned to a pragmatist—Franklin Delano Roosevelt—who also did not have solutions but who had promised to try to remedy the Great Depression through bold actions. Roosevelt began deliberately in March. He declared a national "bank holiday," closing all financial institutions across the country so that federal inspectors could examine their books. If a bank reopened, it would do so because the government found it sound. It could be trusted. If a bank's affairs were beyond redemption, it remained closed. Roosevelt also spoke to all Americans—including hundreds of thousands of Oregonians who, since 1921, had purchased radios. In a series of "fireside chats" broadcast from the White House, he waged a campaign to build confidence. He promoted the reform, relief, and recovery agendas of the New Deal.

While few believe the Democrat programs of the 1930s effectively turned around the Great Depression, they were of immense consequence to Oregon. Through deficit spending and passing on payment obligations to succeeding generations, Congress authorized programs that helped change the face of Oregon. The Beer Act of March 1933 set the stage for repeal of Prohibition and permitted hop-raisers and brewers like Blitz-Weinhard to resume production. Far more significant, however, was creation that same month of the Civilian Conservation Corps. Intended to provide unemployment relief for several million young American males, the CCC developed projects in public land states like Oregon. The CCC established base camps and spike camps in most of the national forests and began a remarkable program of construction. The young men cut trail; built roads; constructed bridges; built campgrounds with handsome log facilities for cooking, eating, and public meetings; laid telephone wires; constructed drift fences to manage cattle; built log corrals; enclosed springs; dammed creeks to create small reservoirs; constructed guard stations and ranger stations; and carried the materials board-by-board to lofty peaks for fire lookouts. From Hells Canyon to the Chetco

River and from the Oriana Corral on the Fremont National Forest to the campground at Eagle Creek in the Columbia Gorge, the CCC made enduring, handsome improvements on federal lands.

Similarly the Works Projects Administration drew unemployed architects, stone masons, painters, weavers, metal workers, plumbers, and artisans into special Oregon projects. The WPA built Timberline Lodge, a dramatic recreation hotel, on the southern slopes of Mount Hood. WPA artisans created towering murals, iron gates, and furniture for the new library on the campus of the University of Oregon. WPA laborers erected post offices, customs buildings, and federal buildings from Burns to Tillamook. Not since Andrew Carnegie's matching-funds projects for public libraries in the 1910s had Oregon seen such a profusion of public structures.

The Public Works Administration and the Public Buildings Administration worked with the WPA in other ways to transform Oregon. Projects included a city hall in Canby, a dramatic capitol and state library in Salem, an armory in Klamath Falls, a high school in Corvallis, a dormitory at the State School for the Blind, a sewage disposal plant in Medford, and five stunning bridges spanning major estuaries on the Oregon coast. The bridges, completed in 1936, cost $5.4 million. In the midst of the Great Depression Oregon embarked on grading and paving Highway 101 to forge another important transportation link.

The WPA also employed teachers, lawyers, and architects. It mounted the Oregon Folklore Project, the Oregon Writers' Program, and the Inventory of the County Archives of Oregon. These workers published *Oregon: End of the Trail* (1940), *Mount Hood: A Guide* (1940), the annual *Oregon Almanac: A Handbook of Fact and Fancy, Oregon Oddities*—a magazine used in public schools—and 14 of a projected 35 descriptive guides to records in county courthouses. Each of the guides included an overview of county history based upon a review of the archives. In many instances these were the first historical assessments of Oregon counties. Working almost in tandem with the WPA were drafters, historians, and photographers engaged in the Historic American Buildings Survey. They compiled information, including measured drawings, on nearly a hundred significant structures in Oregon.

The New Deal had a grassroots impact in Oregon. This was most dramatically confirmed when, in 1935, Congress funded construction of a project that Roosevelt had promised during his 1932 campaign swing through the state. Bonneville Dam, one of the great engineering marvels of the early 20th century, was to span the Columbia River at the western end of the Gorge. Its massive reservoir would back up waters to The Dalles. Its locks would lift ships and barges for easy transit to the grain elevators of the western plateau. Its turbines would generate massive amounts of electricity to power industry and diversify the region's economy. Above all, construction of the dam would provide employment for 4,000 laborers and the multiplier effect would generate thousands more jobs to feed, house, and provide services to these workers and their families. Because navigation was a critical element with the building of the locks, the Army Corps of Engineers secured project supervision. Initial estimates for the dam, lock, powerhouse, and federal townsites for management personnel ran to $81 million.

As the dam neared completion, the Bonneville Power Administration in 1937 took over responsibility for construction of transmission lines and marketing of power to utility companies, public utility districts, and industrial users such as aluminum plants in Troutdale and The Dalles. In 1941 the BPA hired Woody Guthrie to compose and sing songs celebrating power development on the Columbia River. Guthrie's 17 songs included the popular "Roll On, Columbia." Its lyrics touted the New Deal achievements:

"At Bonneville now there are ships in the locks,
The waters have risen and cleared all the rocks,
Shiploads of plenty will steam past the docks,
So roll on, Columbia, roll on."

The New Deal touched the lives of Oregonians in other ways. The Taylor Grazing Act in 1934 changed the free-for-all of livestock using the public domain. Henry Gerber and local ranchers in the Langell Valley of Klamath County were acutely aware of the need to allocate grazing rights. The Bonanza Grazing Unit, headed by Gerber, was the first organized in the United States under the Taylor Act. In time the law brought 152 million acres under the U.S. Grazing Service and called for local boards of landowners to allocate the animal units per month allowed in national forests or on lands administered by the General Land Office. In 1946 Congress merged the land office and the grazing service to create the Bureau of Land Management.

The Soil Conservation Service, created in 1936, provided counsel and assistance to farmers faced with erosion by wind and water on the Columbia Plateau. The Production Credit Association worked with farmers to scale down mortgage payments by extending the length of their loans. The Federal Housing Administration, set up in 1934, provided low-interest loans to try to encourage home construction. The Bankhead-Jones Act of 1937 provided federal dollars to buy out impoverished homesteaders and transform the lands into federal holdings. The National Grasslands between Madras and Prineville was a product of the Bankhead-Jones Act. The Rural Electrification Administration worked with private utilities and public utility districts to extend lines to remote areas. By the late 1930s, thousands of rural Oregonians for the first time had electrical service and would be able to use a radio, refrigerator, vacuum cleaner, electric stove, washing machine and lights.

The Great Depression took a toll on Oregon but created a setting for massive improvement of infrastructure. Roads, bridges, buildings, dams, locks, powerhouses, electrical transmission lines, recreation facilities, and range management were an impressive tally of accomplishments. While many Oregonians were driven into a subsistence lifestyle of "making do" with homemade clothing, a garden, and austerity, the federal projects had infused confidence, generated payrolls, and laid the foundations for new industries and much wider use of public lands in the state.

World War II

The attack on Pearl Harbor on December 7, 1941, pulled the United States out of neutrality and plunged the nation again into world war. Because Oregon lay along the nation's Pacific Coast, it was considered in the war zone. The consequences were almost immediate. To create a wartime mentality as well as to prepare against attack, residents of coastal communities faced nightly blackouts. Block wardens monitored compliance. Shades and blankets covered windows and many painted over the upper half of their car headlamps. Volunteers joined the Ground Observer Corps to log the make and identity of airplanes. Soldiers maintained coastal patrols, supplementing Coast Guard personnel in their watch of the sea. Jeeps ran along the beaches to isolated dugouts where foot patrols with dogs stood duty.

War preparedness had begun in the late 1930s with scrap drives. Schoolchildren competed to see who could tally the heaviest pile of metal. The occasional school that located an old logging railroad locomotive surged to top honors. With the declaration of war, Oregonians confronted rationing of tires, gasoline, meat, sugar, and clothing. For those who lived far from town, rationing necessitated careful trip planning.

Executive Order 9066 of February 19, 1942, fell heavily on the Japanese-American population of Oregon. Although most were American citizens and many had sons, brothers, and fathers who had enlisted or were drafted into military service, the families of Japanese background living west of the Cascades in Oregon were placed under curfew and ordered to report to evacuation centers, preliminaries to removal to distant relocation camps. Over 120,000 Japanese-Americans from Oregon, Washington, and California endured relocation. Japanese-Americans in Hawaii—more fully in the war zone—were exempted from relocation. Those removed lost homes, crops, farm animals, property, bank accounts, and personal possessions.

History

The war gripped the United States and Oregonians. Dozens of towns erected permanent billboards that carried the names of citizens killed in defense of their country. Oregon had 2,826 wartime deaths and over 5,000 wounded. Tensions rose when a Japanese submarine surfaced off the mouth of the Columbia River and on June 21, 1942, fired 17 shells at Fort Stevens. Concern rose again on September 9 of the same year, when a small airplane, launched by a catapult from the deck of a Japanese submarine off Brookings, carried Nubuo Fujita and Shoji Okuda over the Siskiyou National Forest to drop incendiary bombs on Mount Emily. Oregon suffered civilian casualties on May 5, 1945, when participants in a church picnic near Bly poked an incendiary balloon that had floated across the Pacific. The device, intended to set forest fires, exploded and killed the minister's wife and five children.

A wartime economy helped pull Oregon out of the Great Depression. Federal expenditures mounted dramatically. The investment included facilities, construction salaries, and assembling of large numbers of personnel who needed housing, food, clothing, and other services. The U.S. Army built Camp Adair north of Corvallis and Camp Abbott on the upper Deschutes River south of Bend. These troop-training facilities served thousands of recruits. Camp Adair even included a fake Japanese village where soldiers practiced assaults should they reach the main islands of Japan. The Umatilla Army Depot near Hermiston became a sprawling repository for munitions in hundreds of semisubterranean silos. The Army also constructed hangars and airfields at Portland, Astoria, Newport, North Bend, and Floras Lake. The U.S. Navy built the Tongue Point naval station at Astoria and at the Tillamook Naval Air Station erected two of the largest woodframe buildings in the world. Blimps, stationed at Blimperon 33, moved out of these massive hangars and glided up and down the coast to patrol for enemy ships and submarines.

The electricity from Bonneville, dubbed by some in 1939 as the "dam of doubt," moved through the BPA grid to aluminum plants from Longview to Spokane. Inexpensive electricity heated the smelters to process bauxite into rolls of aluminum, which moved by rail to the Boeing manufacturing plants on Puget Sound. There was no doubt about the dramatic rise of employment where nearly 50,000 workers by 1944 were able to produce 16 airplanes every 24 hours. In Portland and nearby Vancouver, Henry J. Kaiser's shipyards employed an estimated 100,000 workers. Men and women worked side by side to build "Baby Flattops" and "Liberty Ships." By 1945 some 150,000 workers were engaged in 85 shipyards in Oregon and Washington.

Jobs in aluminum plants, shipyards, military bases, and lumber production for the war effort created a surge of migration. During World War II an estimated 194,000 people moved into the state. For the first time, Oregon's African-American population grew substantially—in Portland increasing from 2,565 in 1940 to 25,000 in 1944. Drawn by jobs, steady salaries, and the area's reputation as a decent place to live, newcomers coped with inflated rents, shantytowns, camps, and trailer parks. In 1942 Edgar Kaiser met some of the housing problem by building Vanport on the south bank of the Columbia. With 35,000 residents, the community became Oregon's second largest town until destroyed in May, 1948, by breaking levees during a major flood. Public housing projects, dubbed "cardboard palaces" by some, met short-term needs and, in some instances, were used for years or were transformed into student housing on college campuses.

When World War II ended, Oregon was a different place. The economy was good, even when labor disputes erupted with the West Coast Longshoremen's Union. The federal projects of the 1930s created an extensive infrastructure for the use and enjoyment of national forests and the public domain. Many Oregonians had disposable income and savings. The future beckoned far more brightly than during the drab years of the Great Depression or the uncertainties of World War II.

Rapid Developments

Postwar Oregon prospered. Although housing was short, residents made do. The GI Bill provided funding for a generation eager for higher education but blocked from the opportunity because of the Great Depression and World War II. College enrollments swelled as returning veterans and recent high school graduates settled down to earn degrees and pursue civilian careers. The state's college campuses grew in response to the increasing numbers of students. The legislature appropriated funds for new facilities at La Grande, Monmouth, Eugene, Klamath Falls, and Corvallis. From its beginnings at Vanport College, Portland State University emerged as a new urban campus in the state's largest city. In addition, the state's private colleges and universities likewise grew in enrollments and transformed from their sectarian origins to independent liberal arts institutions.

Savings that had accumulated during the war, low-interest FHA loans, and dramatic population growth in California fueled a booming logging and lumbering economy. Between 1945 and 1990 the state became a national leader in manufacture of forest products. For decades, Coos Bay held the title as the world's largest lumber shipping port. Oregon sawmills' wigwam burners belching smoke and sawdust cinders and heavily laden log trucks were icons for a thriving industry.

The infrastructure of roads, guard stations, and ranger stations—a legacy of labors by the CCC—

improved forest access. The shift from custodial care of the national forests to full-scale harvest of timber was the most dramatic factor in the growth of logging and lumber manufacturing. Court rulings to take back the O&C Railroad grant in 1915 brought 2.3 million acres and an estimated 50 billion board feet of timber to federal control. In 1919 recapture of the Coos Bay Wagon Road grant brought back another 96,000 acres of virgin forest and 2.5 billion board feet of timber. The Stanfield Act of 1926 set a formula for the revenues, later revised in 1937 and 1953 by Congress. The final distribution called for 50 percent of the timber receipts from O&C and Coos Bay Wagon Road lands to go to western Oregon counties, 25 percent to the federal treasury, and 25 percent to the U.S. Forest Service or the BLM for reforestation. The demand for lumber and the vested interest of Oregon counties in securing income from the sale of trees from federally managed forests helped drive the boom in this segment of Oregon's economy.

Logging and lumbering enterprises were highly competitive. Small operators, known as gyppos, struggled to hold together their businesses while they moved from contract to contract, cutting logs, running small mills, and seizing a share of the market. Some, like Kenneth Ford of Roseburg Lumber Company, persevered and became major figures in the industry. Many more ran small operations, employed several dozen workers, and, when fortunes changed, closed out their operations. Outside capital flowed into Oregon after 1945. Weyerhaeuser Corporation, Menasha Corporation, Evans Products, and Georgia-Pacific were among several firms with national connections that turned to old timber holdings or purchased unlogged forests from Oregon companies. These larger firms embraced new technologies and products, developing plywood and particleboard in addition to dimensional lumber. They created cost savings through greater efficiencies and research and development.

While some enterprises were thriving, others struggled. The salmon catch and pack in Oregon canneries peaked in the 1890s and headed steadily downward. Efforts to check the trend, especially in the Columbia River, led to construction of the state's Central Hatchery in 1909 at Bonneville and in 1926 to abolition of fishwheels. The hulking fishwheels, turned by the river's current, had scooped up tons of fish. While horse-drawn seine nets and mesh fishtraps at the river's mouth may have taken a greater toll on the salmon, the fishwheels were a visible symbol of overharvest. After 1950, Oregon's fish canneries steadily diminished; the last closed in 1979. The great silvery horde of fish no longer filled the streams. Conservation of remaining stocks dictated sharp restrictions on commercial and sport fishing.

Dam construction, an enduring commitment of federal investment in Oregon, moved steadily forward. It took a tremendous toll of anadromous fish, but so did logging, urbanization, and agricultural activities. During the 1950s and 1960s the Army Corps of Engineers had oversight of massive new projects—The Dalles, John Day, and McNary dams on the main stem of the Columbia, several more dams upstream, and Oxbow and Brownlee dams on the Snake River along Oregon's eastern border. Federal projects also checked the Willamette. Pre-1940 Corps projects had included Fern Ridge, Cottage Grove, and Dorena reservoirs. Postwar construction, financed by multimillion-dollar congressional appropriations, built Detroit, Big Cliff, Green Peter, and Foster dams on the Santiam forks; Lookout Point, Dexter, and Hills Creek dams on the Middle Fork of the Willamette; Cougar and Blue River dams in the McKenzie watershed; and Fall Creek dam near Eugene. By 1960 these facilities had largely tamed the Willamette River, checking flood waters and generating electricity.

Federal improvements touched Oregon in other significant ways. Beginning in the 1870s, renewing in the 1890s, and proceeding regularly through the 20th century, Congress made appropriations in the River and Harbor acts for major construction in Oregon. Projects included jetties at the mouths of the Columbia, Yaquina, Coquille, and Coos Bay. Congress also funded the Celilo Canal and Locks, 1906–16, a complicated transportation system blasted through basalt to provide ship passage around Five Mile Rapids and Celilo Falls into the upper Columbia River. Congress regularly renewed or funded start-up projects that dredged channels, removed rocks, and led to construction of new jetties on most of Oregon's coastal estuaries. Singularly significant in the postwar era was the Interstate Highway Act of 1956. Billions of federal dollars began flowing back to the states, allowing construction in Oregon of nonstop freeways—I-5 running north and south through western Oregon valleys between Washington and California and I-84 running east and west from Portland to Boise, Idaho. These projects created not only payrolls but significant contributions to the state's economy through efficient shipment of commodities.

Postwar changes swept through Oregon agriculture. While cattle-raising and wheat production remained mainstays in eastern Oregon, specialized crops of alfalfa, sugar beets, and potatoes drew a number of farmers to focus their energies on lands watered by turn-of-the-century reclamation projects. Farmers in the Treasure Valley near Ontario, the upper Deschutes watershed, and the Klamath Basin tapped irrigation water to embark on these ventures. On Oregon's southwestern coast cranberry production, founded in 1887, became important as Ocean Spray diversified its product line to include ruby-red juice fortified by Oregon cranberries. Walnuts, filberts, and turkeys created income for farmers in Yamhill and Washington counties. Pear, peach, apple, and cherry production prospered in the Hood River and Rogue River Valleys. Slowly but steadily, grass seed and nursery products grew in acreage in the Willamette Valley. Rose bushes, irises, grafted fruit trees, and ornamental shrubs grew in the valley's fertile soils. Workers dug, baled, and shipped these specialty products to national markets. Venturesome investors cleared old prune orchards and forested hillsides, planted vineyards, and constructed wineries. A new industry found a good market for Oregon wines.

Tourism emerged as a major industry. Oregon's scenic beauty of mountains, forests, deserts, and Pacific shoreline proved an irresistible attraction. Good roads, one of the largest state park systems in the country, restaurants, and hotels and motels facilitated the annual surge of visitors. Millions traveled Highway 101, exploring the cheese factory at Tillamook, gifts shops in Lincoln City, and the Sea Lion Caves. They toured sawmills at North Bend, rode a mail boat on the Rogue River, or purchased salt water taffy, carved myrtlewood, seashells, and cranberry candy. Others flocked to the Shakespearean plays in Ashland, marveled at Crater Lake, went bow-and-arrow hunting for deer at Hart Mountain, skied at Mount Bachelor, stayed overnight at Timberline Lodge, took a jetboat into Hells Canyon, or visited the John Day Fossil Beds National Monument. Those who came to visit bought meals, lodging, and keepsakes. They added to the state's prosperity.

Postwar Oregon was a troubled time for the state's Native Americans. Douglas O. McKay, former governor, had been appointed as secretary of the interior in the Eisenhower cabinet. Believing strongly in economy in government and seeing the Bureau of Indian Affairs as an anachronism of inefficiency, McKay joined others in pressing to sever ties with tribes. House Concurrent Resolution 108 in 1952 stated that it was the sense of Congress that the federal government should set free American Indians. Between 1954 and 1960, Congress terminated all government-to-government relationships with the Klamath and every tribe and band west of the Cascades in Oregon. The program required sale of reservation lands, issuance of deeds for individual trust lands, and curtailment of all BIA and Indian Health Service benefits. Then the momentum waned. Thousands of Oregon's native peoples had fallen into limbo as "terminated Indians." Finally in 1977 Senator Mark O. Hatfield introduced legislation to amend the situation for the Confederated Tribes of Siletz Indians. On a case-by-case basis the terminated tribes sought and won by 1989 the restoration of their federal relations. The road back was, for some, a frustrating journey of years of waiting, petitioning, and documenting their ongoing tribal life.

Elements of boom and bust coursed through Oregon in the years between 1945 and 1990. Booming conditions drove new construction and business prosperity in many small towns. Tens of thousands of new residents moved into the state. Yet not all was well in Oregon. The measures were visible: diminishing runs of fish, a vast checkerboard of clearcuts on the sides of mountains, a Willamette River so fetid that only the foolhardy dared to swim in it, spread of cheat grass, Russian olive, and other invading species like shad, bass, and squawfish. It was time to consider the consequences of rapid development.

Taking Stock

In 1962 Thomas Lawson McCall, a journalist, caught the state's attention with a television documentary, "Pollution in Paradise." In his clipped, forceful narration and with compelling photography, McCall showed what had happened to the Willamette River. Sewage, industrial wastes, garbage, abandoned docks and warehouses, tires, and hulks of automobiles befouled a once pristine, fish-filled stream. Between 1850 and 1920 the Willamette had served as western Oregon's artery of commerce and transportation. Use had bred abuse and, almost without seeing it, Oregonians had transformed the stream into an open sewer.

Tom McCall was elected governor in 1966. Stressing an eleventh commandment, "Thou shalt not pollute," McCall, a Republican, forged a broad-based coalition to address the consequences of rapid development, growing population, and ecological changes in the state. McCall's ideas were not always popular and his commentary sometimes appeared quirky. His approach, however, was earnest and, for a majority, compelling. During his eight years in office he and like-minded leaders—Stafford Hansell, a hogfarmer from Boardman, L.B. Day, a labor leader from Salem, and others—began a process of moving Oregonians from outright "ownership" of land to "stewardship."

The tally of accomplishments during the McCall years included creation of the Department of Environmental Quality (1969), extensive research and solution to Willamette Valley fieldburning, blocking of shipment of additional tons of nerve gas to the Umatilla Army Depot, creation of the Willamette Greenway—a 170-mile-long corridor of easements and park properties, the bottle bill (1971) requiring deposits on returnable beverage containers, and Senate Bill 100. This much-debated bill created the Land Conservation and Development Commission (1973). The LCDC moved every county and incorporated town into a system of statewide land-use planning. Hearings on draft goals and guidelines drew thousands of participants to meetings. Volunteers and staff hammered out a system for evaluating, in light of the statewide guidelines, comprehensive land-use plans required of all government entities. Repeatedly critics tried to overturn the LCDC. Each time a majority of voters sustained the system. Oregonians had started to come to terms with the realities of growth and the responsibilities inherent in sustaining livability.

The 1990s were a sobering decade for dozens of small towns and for the thousands involved in logging and lumbering. The boom ended in the forest products industry. Shrill voices decried the Endangered Species Act of 1973 and charged that spotted owls and marbled murrelets were not worth jobs and payrolls. The reality was that Oregon had not attained sustained yield in management of forests and that overharvest, similar to overfishing, forced adjustment. Sawmills closed. Towns like Powers, West Fir, Oakridge, Swiss Home, Hines, Valsetz, and Vernonia were shaken by the closures and departure of residents. Most communities adjusted. Some Oregonians, however, wrestled with difficulty when they discovered that the national forests and lands administered by the Bureau of Land Management—acreage on the other side of their fence—belonged to all the people of the United States, not the locals, and that interest groups thousands of miles away had a valid voice in crafting land policy and use of public resources.

The 1990s was also a decade of diversification in Oregon's economy. High-tech industries came of age. From modest beginnings in a garage in 1948, Howard Vollum and Jack Murdock built Tektronix, an electronics company, into one of the nation's largest companies by the mid-1980s. Oregon's reputation as a decent place to live with willing workers encouraged several corporations—among them Hewlett-Packard, Intel, and Wacker Siltronics—to construct fabrication plants and manufacture computer components. These billion-dollar facilities contributed to a thriving urban Oregon economy. While many rural Oregonians struggled with survival, many urban Oregonians found good jobs in new industries. Phil Knight and Bill Bowerman, longtime track coach at the University of Oregon, transformed the tennis shoe into a styled, engineered icon of the "fitness generation." Their Nike Corporation grew by the 1990s into a major manufacturer and retailer of sports and casual clothing. Its distinctive "swoosh" logo appeared on the outfits of professional athletes, amateurs, and even great-grandmothers who found ease and comfort wearing nonlacing tennis shoes or fleece jogging outfits.

In 1984 residents of the state approved a lottery. It grew rapidly in popularity as new games and promotions increased player options. Gambling profits proved irresistible to legislators who appropriated them to meet costs of basic social services and education. In 1992 the Cow Creek Band of Umpqua Tribe of Indians negotiated the first gaming compact with the governor under the Indian Gaming

Regulatory Act. Within five years the tribe was the second largest employer in Douglas County, operating a casino, restaurants, hotel, truck stop, and other businesses at Canyonville. Other tribes followed. In 1998 Spirit Mountain Casino, owned by the Confederated Tribes of the Grand Ronde community, surpassed Multnomah Falls as the most visited traveler destination in Oregon.

Oregon had not solved all its problems. Adequate financing for education at all levels eluded legislators, governors, teachers' unions, and students. Salmon recovery plans, at times, seemed more bundant than fish. Indian tribes, federal and state agencies, sport and commercial fishing organizations, and fish biologists all wrestled with finding ways to save remaining runs and rebuilding those that teetered on the edge of extinction. Poverty continued to grip Oregonians. Thousands of new residents—many of them Hispanics who had found hard jobs and tough living conditions in following the harvests and working in the state's nursery business—tried to make do.

A willingness to embrace new ventures has persisted in Oregon. In 1990 Measure 5 placed severe limitations on property taxes to support schools and government. In 1993 Oregonians were first in the nation to hold a vote-by-mail election. The following year they approved a Death With Dignity Act, permitting doctor-assisted suicide. In 1998 Oregon raised the minimum wage to the highest in the nation, easing for the hourly worker some of the struggle for existence but threatening enterprises operating on a shoestring. Oregonians refused to approve a sales tax, but continued to pay high property taxes and income taxes.

Such is the course of Oregon history. A majestic territory of immense potentials drew newcomers in the 1840s. In less than a decade they wrested control from the American Indians, changed the face of the land with surveys and property ownership, and engaged in ambitious exploitation of the state's resources. When it finally became evident that nature's plenty could not continue to yield in profusion, Oregonians embraced new models for doing things.

The state's history has stories of triumph and tragedy, hope and perseverance, and taking risks. The Oregon System became a national model for improving government in the twentieth century. Oregon has served as a great testing ground for federal projects which have provided a medley of benefits—electricity, navigation, irrigation, timber harvests, tourist facilities, and jobs. Oregon has led the nation in environmental legislation and commitment to working for quality of life for all of its citizens. For generations Oregonians have celebrated the special words in their state song: "Hail to thee, Land of Promise, My Oregon." Oregon's promise is strong and therein lies the state's future.

Chronological History of Oregon

Oregon's history contains many more significant dates than space will permit, but this list should prove helpful to those embarking on a study of the state.

Oregon Country 1543–1847

1543—Bartolome Ferrelo possibly reaches southwest coast

1565—Manilla Galleon trade opens across North Pacific

1579—Sir Francis Drake allegedly visits Oregon

1603—Sebastian Vizcaino possibly sights Cape Sebastian

1707—*San Francisco Xavier* probably wrecks at Nehalem

1765—First use of word "Ouragon" in Maj. Robert Rogers' petition to explore American West

1774—Capt. Juan Perez sails to Northwest Coast for Spain

1775—Capt. Bruno Hezeta sees mouth of Columbia and names it Rio San Roque

1778—Capt. James Cook makes landfall at Cape Foulweather and discovers fur wealth of Northwest Coast

1779—Jonathan Carver's book refers to the "River Oregon"

1788—Capt. Robert Gray trades with Indians in Tillamook Bay

Marius Lopius, African with Gray, probably murdered at Tillamook

1792—Capt. Robert Gray enters and names the Columbia River

Capt. George Vancouver expedition charts Columbia estuary

1803—Louisiana Purchase extends United States to Rocky Mountains

1804—President Thomas Jefferson dispatches Lewis and Clark Expedition

1805—Lewis and Clark Expedition explores lower Snake and Columbia rivers and establishes Fort Clatsop

1806—Lewis and Clark Expedition returns to the United States

1811—Pacific Fur Company establishes Fort Astoria

David Thompson descends Columbia River from Canada

1812—Overland Astorians discover South Pass in Wyoming, later route of Oregon Trail

1813—North West Company purchases Fort Astoria and names it Fort George

1814—Treaty of Ghent resolves the War of 1812

First English woman, Jane Barnes, visits Fort George

First domestic livestock imported by sea from California

1817—William Cullen Bryant refers to "Oregon" in poem *Thanatopsis*

1818—North West Company establishes Fort Nez Perces

James Biddle and John Prevost assert U.S. interests in Oregon

U.S. and Great Britain agree to "joint occupancy" of Oregon

1819—Adams-Onis Treaty cedes Spain's discovery rights north of 42 degrees to the U.S.

1821—Hudson's Bay Company subsumes North West Company

1824—U.S. and Russia agree to 50 degrees as southern boundary of Russian interests

Dr. John McLoughlin begins long tenure as Chief Factor for Hudson's Bay Company

1825—Workmen build Fort Vancouver on Columbia River

David Douglas begins botanical collecting

1827—U.S. and Great Britain agree to indefinite "joint occupancy"

First sawmill begins cutting lumber near Fort Vancouver

1828—Jedediah Smith's party travels overland from California but Indians murder 15 men on the Umpqua River

First grist mill starts making flour at Fort Vancouver

1829—Dr. John McLoughlin establishes claim at Willamette Falls, later Oregon City

1830—Fever pandemic begins calamitous death toll of Indians

1832—Newspapers report four Indians from Pacific Northwest in St. Louis seeking missionaries

Nathaniel Wyeth enters Oregon fur trade

Capt. B.L.E. Bonneville arrives overland to trap and trade for furs on Columbia Plateau

Hudson's Bay Company establishes Fort Umpqua at Elkton

1833—First school opens at Fort Vancouver

First lumber exports by Hudson's Bay Company to China

1834—Jason Lee's party establishes Methodist Mission near Wheatland

John K. Townsend and Thomas Nuttall collect natural history specimens

1836—First steamship *Beaver* begins service for Hudson's Bay Company on the Columbia River

Lt. William Slacum mounts reconnaissance of western Oregon

Whitman-Spalding mission party, including Narcissa Whitman and Eliza Spalding, arrives overland via Oregon Trail

Washington Irving publishes *Astoria*

1838—Willamette Cattle Company drives livestock overland from California

Priests Blanchet and Demers arrive overland from Canada

1839—Catholics establish mission at St. Paul

First book, a Nez Perce language primer, printed at Lapwai, Idaho

1841—Lt. Charles Wilkes mounts reconnaissance with U.S. Exploring Expedition

Ewing Young's death leads to public meetings

First Catholic boys' school founded at St. Paul

First ship, *Star of Oregon,* built by settlers

1842—Methodist missionaries found Indian school in Salem, an antecedent to Willamette University

First brick building, a house, erected by George Gay in Polk County

1843—First large migration of over 900 immigrants arrives via Oregon Trail

Lt. John C. Fremont mounts reconnaissance of Oregon Trail

"Wolf Meetings" lead to Provisional Government

Oregonians submit petition to Senate seeking U.S. jurisdiction

1844—First plat surveyed for a town at Oregon City

First Catholic girls' school founded at St. Paul

1845—Meek Cut-off opens as alleged short-cut to Oregon Trail

Estimated 3,000 overland immigrants arrive

Oregonians petition Congress for federal services

First Provisional governor, George Abernethy, elected

Francis Pettygrove and A.L. Lovejoy name Portland and commence plat of city

1846—Lt. Neil Howison mounts reconnaissance of western Oregon

Barlow Road opens as toll route

Applegate Trail opens as alternative to Oregon Trail

Oregon Treaty affirms U.S. sovereignty to Pacific Northwest

First newspaper, *Oregon Spectator,* founded in Oregon City

1847—Cayuse Indians attack Whitman Mission

Oregon Volunteers engage in Cayuse Indian War

First postmaster, John Shively, named at Astoria

First English book, a "Blue Back Speller," printed in Oregon City

The Oregon Territory 1848–58

1848—Joseph Meek carries petition east seeking federal "patronage"

Organic Act creates Oregon Territory

James Marshall discovers gold in California

First U.S. Customs Service office opens in Astoria

1849—First territorial governor, Joseph Lane, assumes duties

First Mounted Riflemen of U.S. Army arrive overland

First "Beaver" gold coins minted in Oregon City

1850—Congress passes Oregon Donation Land Act

First capital punishment—five Cayuse Indians hanged in Oregon City

Investors start printing *The Oregonian* in Portland

Census enumerates 11,873 Oregonians

1851—John Preston initiates cadastral land survey system

First General Land Office opens in Oregon City

Willamette Valley Treaty Commission negotiates treaties

Teamsters discover gold in Rogue River Valley

Anson Dart convenes Tansy Point Treaty Council at mouth of Columbia

First U.S. Army post, Fort Orford, built at Port Orford

U.S. Coast Survey begins charting shoreline

1852—U.S. Army establishes Fort Dalles on Oregon Trail

Congress names Salem capital of Oregon Territory

1853—Territorial legislature adopts Oregon law code

U.S. Army establishes Fort Lane in Rogue River Valley

Territorial legislature publishes *Oregon Archives*

Congress funds Scottsburg-Myrtle Creek Wagon Road

Cow Creeks and Rogue River Indians negotiate treaties with U.S.

Congress carves Washington Territory out of Oregon Territory

First coal exports begin on southwest Oregon coast

1854—Volunteers massacre Coquille Indians

Legislature prohibits sale of arms and ammunition to Indians

Legislature prohibits sale of ardent spirits to Indians

Legislature bars testimony of "Negroes, mulattoes, and Indians, or persons one half or more of Indian blood" in proceedings involving a white person

History

1855—Pacific Railroad Surveys examine potential routes

Umatilla and Nez Perce tribes sign treaties at Walla Walla Treaty Council, reserving land and rights to food resources

Warm Springs tribes sign treaty reserving land and rights to food resources

Rogue River Indian War commences

Yakima Indian War commences

President James Buchanan creates Siletz Reservation

Territorial capitol burns in Salem

1856—U.S. Army establishes Forts Umpqua, Hoskins, and Yamhill

President James Buchanan creates Grand Ronde Reservation

U.S. Army orders closure of settlement east of Cascades because of warfare with Indians

1857—Constitutional Convention meets in Salem

Draft constitution bars African-Americans from residency

Aaron Meier founds Meier & Frank Department Store

1858—First election selects state officials

State of Oregon 1859–Present

1859—Congress grants Oregon statehood on February 14

First bank established by Ladd & Tilton in Portland

First elected governor of state, John Whiteaker, inaugurated

1860—Census enumerates 52,465 residents

Oregon Steam Navigation Company commences service

First daily stage operates between Portland and Sacramento

1861—First Oregon State Fair held at Oregon City

1862—Congress passes Homestead Act

First Oregon Cavalry raises six companies

Gold rush commences to Blue Mountains

First portage railroad completed at Cascades

1863—U.S. Army establishes Fort Klamath

1864—Telegraph line connects Portland-Sacramento

U.S. Army establishes Camp Watson

Treaty creates Klamath Reservation

Popular vote approves Salem as state capital

1865—Long Tom Rebellion confirms pro-southern sympathies

Congress authorizes Oregon Central Military Wagon Road

1866—First lighthouse—Cape Arago—illuminates light signal

U.S. Army establishes Camp Warner

Married Women's Property Act protects women's rights

Congress authorizes Corvallis-Yaquina Bay Military Wagon Road

Congress authorizes Willamette Valley-Cascade Mountain Military Wagon Road

1867—U.S. Army establishes Fort Harney

Congress authorizes The Dalles-Boise Military Wagon Road

1868—Oregon State Agricultural College (OSU) opens

1869—Direct export of wheat to Europe begins

Congress authorizes Coos Bay Military Wagon Road

1870—Census enumerates 90,923 residents

Abigail Scott Duniway launches suffrage campaign

1872—Oregon & California Railroad completes line to Roseburg

Modoc Indian War commences

1873—Oregon Patrons of Husbandry (Grange) forms chapters

Modoc Indians face trial and execution at Fort Klamath

Oregon Pioneer Association forms

1875—First U.S. Life-Saving Service station opens near Coos Bay

1876—University of Oregon opens

Robert D. Hume builds salmon cannery on Rogue River

1877—Nez Perce Indian War involves Chief Joseph's band

Congress passes Desert Land Act

1878—High schools authorized for districts with 1,000 students

Bannock-Paiute Indian War sweeps into southeastern Oregon

Women gain right to vote in school elections

1879—BIA Indian Training School opens in Forest Grove

1880—Census enumerates 174,768 residents

O.R.& N. Company begins railroad through Gorge

1881—BIA Chemawa School opens near Salem

1882—Normal schools open in Monmouth, Ashland, and Drain to train teachers

1883—O.R.& N. Company railroad reaches Umatilla providing transcontinental links

1884—Oregon Short Line railroad extends to Huntington

1885—Women gain admittance to law practice

Chief Joseph's Nez Perce band locates on Colville Reservation

1887—Thugs murder ten Chinese miners in Hells Canyon

General Allotment Act assaults tribal lands on reservations
Cranberry harvests commence
1888—First Agricultural Experiment Station opens at Corvallis
1890—Congress passes Oregon Indian Depredation Claims Act
Census enumerates 313,767 residents
Chinese Consolidated Benevolent Association founded
1891—Congress passes Forest Reserve Act
1892—Congress authorizes Columbia River Lightship No. 50
Portland Art Association forms
1894—Mazama Club forms to promote outdoor adventure
1896—Workmen complete Cascade Locks
1897—Holdup of '97 blocks state legislature
1898—Oregon Historical Society receives charter
1900—Workmen complete Yamhill River Locks
Census enumerates 413,536 residents
1902—Crater Lake National Park opens
Congress passes Federal Reclamation Act
Voters amend Constitution for Initiative and Referendum
1903—Heppner Flood kills 225 people
First Voters' Pamphlet published
1904—Direct primary law passes
First African-American, George Hardin, named officer in Portland Police Bureau
1905—Lewis & Clark Centennial Exposition celebrates history
Klamath Irrigation Project commences
Oregon land fraud trials pursue wrongdoers
U.S. Forest Service begins work in national forests
1906—City home rule law approved
Indictment by grand jury law approved
Taxes begin on telephone, telegraph, and railroads
First meeting of Association of Oregon Counties
1907—President Theodore Roosevelt creates "Midnight Reserves" setting aside millions of acres of national forests
1908—Constitution amended for Recall provision
Corrupt Practices Act approved
First woman, Lola Baldwin, named head of Women's Division, Portland Police
1909—State's Central Fish Hatchery opens at Bonneville
Oregon Caves National Monument created
Pendleton Round-Up begins
Congress passes Enlarged Homestead Act
1910—Census enumerates 672,765 residents
Three-fourths verdict in civil cases approved

Employers' liability act approved
1911—Oregon Department of Forestry created
Columbia Gorge River Highway construction begins
Oregon Trunk Railroad completes line to Bend
1912—Women's suffrage approved
Prohibition of private convict labor approved
Eight-hour day on public works approved
1913—Oregon Highway Commission established
Presidential preference primary law approved
Gov. Oswald West declares beaches open to public
1914—Death penalty abolished
Prohibition approved
Eight-hour day approved for women
Congress revests O & C Railroad land grant
1916—Workmen complete Celilo Locks and Canal
Congress passes Stock-Raising Homestead Act
1917—U.S. Army Spruce Production Division begins logging
1918—Influenza pandemic kills hundreds
Emergency Fleet Corporation contracts for ships
Oregonians enlist to serve in World War I
1919—First gasoline tax in U.S. authorized to fund highways
Congress revests Coos Bay Wagon Road land grant
1920—Death penalty reinstated
Oregon League of Women Voters founded
Census enumerates 783,389 residents
1921—Ku Klux Klan organizes chapters
1922—First state park accepted by Oregon Highway Commission and named for Sarah Helmick
Compulsory School Act approved
First African-American woman, Beatrice Cannady, admitted to Oregon Bar
Japanese American Citizens' League founded
1923—Alien Land Law approved
Prohibition of sectarian garb in schools approved
Alien Business Restriction Law approved
1924—Compulsory School Act held unconstitutional
Congress extends citizenship to American Indians
Clarke-McNary Act aids federal-state forest fire protection
1925—State parks and waysides authorized
League of Oregon Cities founded
1926—Fishwheels abolished
Astor Column completed
Exclusion of African-Americans clause removed from constitution
1929—State Park Commission created
1930—Vale Irrigation Project begins water delivery

Census enumerates 953,786 residents

First woman, Mary Jane Spurlin, appointed judge in Oregon to Multnomah County District Court

1933—Tillamook Burn destroys 240,000 acres of forest

Civilian Conservation Corps and Works Projects Administration start projects

1934—First grazing district under Taylor Grazing Act forms at Bonanza

1935—Congress authorizes Bonneville Dam

Fire destroys State Capitol

1936—Bandon Fire destroys town and kills 11 residents

Workmen complete five major bridges on Highway 101

First woman, Nan Wood Honeyman, elected from Oregon to House of Representatives

1937—President F. D. Roosevelt dedicates Timberline Lodge

Gas chamber built for capital punishments

Oregon Shakespeare Festival forms in Ashland

Congress creates Bonneville Power Administration

Bankhead-Jones Act authorizes buy out of homesteaders

1938—544 Report for Willamette flood control approved

Bonneville Dam completed

1939—Tillamook Burn destroys 190,000 acres of forest

State capitol completed in Salem

1940—Census enumerates 1,089,684 residents

1941—Oregonians enlist to serve in World War II

1942—Executive Order 9066 authorizes removal of Japanese-Americans to internment camps

Japanese submarine shells Fort Stevens

Japanese airplane firebombs Siskiyou National Forest

U.S. Army builds Camp Adair and Camp Abbott

U.S. Navy builds Tillamook and Tongue Point naval air stations

Vanport founded to house wartime workers

1945—Six Oregonians die in explosion of Japanese incendiary balloon

Tillamook Burn destroys 180,000 acres of forest

Supplement to 1923 Alien Land Law passes

1946—Portland State University (PSU) founded

Rural School Law encourages consolidation of districts

1947—Plane crash kills governor Snell, secretary of state Farrell, and others

1948—Flood destroys Vanport in hours

Vollum and Murdock found Tektronix

1949—State Department of Forestry begins replanting Tillamook Burn

Fair Labor Practices Commission established

State Supreme Court invalidates 1923 and 1945 Alien Land acts

First woman, Dorothy McCullough Lee, elected Portland mayor

1950—Census enumerates 1,521,341 residents

1952—Constitution amended to provide for equal representation in state legislature

1954—Congress terminates Western Oregon Indian tribes

1956—Congress authorizes Interstate freeway system

Congress terminates Klamath Indian Tribe

1960—Census enumerates 1,768,687 residents

Congress passes Multiple Use-Sustained Yield Act for management of national forests

First woman Oregon senator, Maurine Neuberger, elected

1962—Columbus Day Storm causes major damage in Western Oregon

1964—Death penalty abolished

1966—Workmen complete Astoria-Megler Bridge spanning Columbia estuary

I-5 affords non-stop driving through Oregon

1969—Department of Environmental Quality created

Federal District Court in *Sohappy v. Smith* affirms Indian treaty fishing rights in Columbia River

1970—Census enumerates 2,091,000 residents

1971—Bottle Bill approved

Congress confirms Burns Paiute Reservation

1973—Land Conservation and Development Commission created

Public Meetings Law approved

Public Records Law approved

Tillamook State Forest created

Congress approves Endangered Species Act

1974—Congress creates John Day Fossil Beds National Monument

Oregon Health Sciences University forms out of mergers

Governor Tom McCall sets odd/even gasoline refueling days

1975—Congress creates Hells Canyon National Recreation Area

1976—First woman, Norma Paulus, elected secretary of state

1977—Aerosol sprays banned by law

Congress restores Confederated Tribes of Siletz

First woman, Betty Roberts, appointed to Oregon Court of Appeals

1978—Death penalty reinstated

1979—Federal District Court in *Kimball v. Callahan* affirms Klamath Indian hunting and fishing rights within former reservation

1980—Census enumerates 2,633,000 residents

Congress creates new Siletz Reservation

Mt. St. Helens eruption disrupts ship traffic on Columbia River

1981—Bhagwan Shree Rajneesh establishes Rajneeshpuram

1982—Congress restores Cow Creek Band of Umpqua Tribe of Indians

First woman, Betty Roberts, appointed justice of Oregon Supreme Court

1983—Congress restores Confederated Tribes of Grand Ronde Indian Community

1984—Congress restores Confederated Tribes of Coos, Lower Umpqua, and Siuslaw Indians

First Oregon lottery ratified by voters

1985—Bhagwan Shree Rajneesh deported and fined $400,000

First woman, Vera Katz, selected speaker of Oregon House

1986—Congress restores Klamath Tribe

Metropolitan Area Express (MAX) begins light-rail service in Portland

1988—Congress creates new Grand Ronde Reservation

Congress approves Civil Liberties Act paying $20,000 to each surviving interned Japanese-American

1989—Congress restores Coquille Indian Tribe

First Sports Action Lottery in U.S. sells tickets

1990—Census enumerates 2,842,000 residents

Ballot Measure 5 limits property taxes to support schools and government

U.S. Department of Fish and Wildlife lists Northern Spotted Owl as endangered

First woman, Barbara Roberts, elected governor

1992—First African-American, James A. Hill, Jr., elected to state office

First gaming compact signed with Cow Creek and Umpqua Tribe of Indians for casino

1993—First statewide vote-by-mail election held in U.S.

1994—First Death With Dignity Act approved permitting doctor-assisted suicide

1996—First vote-by-mail election for federal office held

1999—U.S. Department of Fish and Wildlife lists several salmon species from Columbia and Willamette rivers as endangered

2000—Census enumerates 3,421,399 residents

2002—Susan Castillo first Hispanic woman elected to statewide office

Near record forest fire season leaves 1,000,000 acres burned

ACT OF CONGRESS ADMITTING OREGON INTO THE UNION

Preamble

Whereas the people of Oregon have framed, ratified and adopted a constitution of state government which is republican in form, and in conformity with the Constitution of the United States and have applied for admission into the Union on an equal footing with the other states; therefore —

1. Admission of State—Boundaries

That Oregon be, and she is hereby, received into the Union on an equal footing with the other states in all respects whatever, with the following boundaries: In order that the boundaries of the state may be known and established, it is hereby ordained and declared that the State of Oregon shall be bounded as follows, to wit: Beginning one marine league at sea, due west from the point where the forty-second parallel of north latitude intersects the same, thence northerly, at the same distance from the line of the coast lying west and opposite the state, including all islands within the jurisdiction of the United States, to a point due west and opposite the middle of the north ship channel of the Columbia River; thence easterly, to and up the middle channel of said river, and, where it is divided by islands, up the middle and widest channel thereof, to a point near Fort Walla Walla, where the forty-sixth parallel of north latitude crosses said river, thence east, on said parallel, to the middle of the main channel of the Shoshone or Snake River; thence up the middle of the main channel of said river, to the mouth of the Owyhee River; thence due south, to the parallel of latitude forty-two degrees north; thence west, along said parallel, to the place of beginning, including jurisdiction in civil and criminal cases upon the Columbia River and Snake River, concurrently with states and territories of which those rivers form a boundary in common with this state.

2. Concurrent Jurisdiction on Columbia & Other Rivers— Navigable Waters to be Common Highways

The said State of Oregon shall have concurrent jurisdiction on the Columbia and all other rivers and waters bordering on the said State of Oregon, so far as the same shall form a common boundary to said state, and any other state or states now or hereafter to be formed or bounded by the same; and said rivers and waters, and all the navigable waters of said state, shall be common highways and forever free, as well as to the inhabitants of said state as to all other citizens of the United States, without any tax, duty & impost, or toll thereof.

3. Representation in Congress

Until the next census and apportionment of representatives, the State of Oregon shall be entitled to one representative in the Congress of the United States.

4. Propositions Submitted to People of State

The following propositions be and the same are hereby offered to the said people of Oregon for their free acceptance or rejection, which, if accepted, shall be obligatory on the United States and upon the said State of Oregon, to wit:

School Lands

First, that sections numbered sixteen and thirty-six in every township of public lands in said state, and where either of said sections, or any part thereof, has been sold or otherwise disposed of, other lands equivalent thereto, and as contiguous as may be, shall be granted to said state for the use of schools.

University Lands

Second, the seventy-two sections of land shall be set apart and reserved for the use and support of a state university, to be selected by the Governor of said state, subject to the approval of the Commissioner of the General Land Office, and to be appropriated and applied in such manner as the legislature of said state may prescribe for the purpose aforesaid, but for no other purpose.

Lands For Public Buildings

Third, that ten entire sections of land, to be selected by the Governor of said state, in legal subdivisions, shall be granted to said state for the purpose of completing the public buildings, or for the erection of others at the seat of government, under the direction of the legislature thereof.

Salt Springs & Contiguous Lands

Fourth, that all salt springs within said state, not exceeding twelve in number, with six sections of land adjoining, or as contiguous as may be to each, shall be granted to said state for its use, the same to be selected by the Governor thereof within one year

after the admission of said state, and when so selected, to be used or disposed of on such terms, conditions and regulations as the legislature shall direct; provided, that no salt spring or land, the right whereof is now vested in any individual or individuals, or which may be hereafter confirmed or adjudged to any individual or individuals, shall by this article be granted to said state.

Percentage on Land Sales

Fifth, that 5 per centum of the net proceeds of sales of all public lands lying within said state which shall be sold by Congress after the admission of said state into the Union, after deducting all the expenses incident to the same, shall be paid to said state, for the purpose of making public roads and internal improvements, as the legislature shall direct; provided, that the foregoing propositions, hereinbefore offered, are on the condition that the people of Oregon shall provide by an ordinance, irrevocable without the consent of the United States, that said state shall never interfere with the primary disposal of the soil within the same by the United States, or with any regulations Congress may find necessary for securing the title in said soil to bona fide purchasers thereof; and that in no case shall nonresident proprietors be taxed higher than residents.

Conditions on Which Propositions Are Offered

Sixth, and that the state shall never tax the lands or the property of the United States in said state; provided, however, that in case any of the lands herein granted to the State of Oregon have heretofore been confirmed to the Territory of Oregon for the purposes specified in this act, the amount so confirmed shall be deducted from the quantity specified in this act.

5. Residue of Territory

Until Congress shall otherwise direct, the residue of the Territory of Oregon shall be and is hereby incorporated into and made a part of the Territory of Washington.

Approved February 14, 1859.

Proposition of Congress accepted by the Legislative Assembly of the State of Oregon on June 3, 1859.

Sailboating on Tenmile Lake—Oregon State Archives Photograph, OHD-G233

The Oregon Constitution has been the foundation of government in Oregon since 1859. Oregonians have amended it repeatedly, and, since 1902, citizens have been able to place amendments on the statewide ballot by means of the initiative process. This section contains the Oregon Constitution with amendments from the November 2003 election.

CONSTITUTION OF OREGON
2003 EDITION

The Oregon Constitution was framed by a convention of 60 delegates chosen by the people. The convention met on the third Monday in August 1857 and adjourned on September 18 of the same year. On November 9, 1857, the Constitution was approved by the vote of the people of Oregon Territory. The Act of Congress admitting Oregon into the Union was approved February 14, 1859, and on that date the Constitution went into effect.

The Constitution is here published as it is in effect following the approval of an amendment on September 16, 2003. The text of the original signed copy of the Constitution filed in the office of the Secretary of State is retained unless it has been repealed or superseded by amendment. Where the original text has been amended or where a new provision has been added to the original Constitution, the source of the amendment or addition is indicated in the source note immediately following the text of the amended or new section. Notations also have been made setting out the history of repealed sections.

Unless otherwise specifically noted, the leadlines for the sections have been supplied by the Legislative Counsel.

PREAMBLE

We the people of the State of Oregon to the end that Justice be established, order maintained, and liberty perpetuated, do ordain this Constitution. —

ARTICLE I
BILL OF RIGHTS

Section 1. Natural rights inherent in people. We declare that all men, when they form a social compact are equal in right: that all power is inherent in the people, and all free governments are founded on their authority, and instituted for their peace, safety, and happiness; and they have at all times a right to alter, reform, or abolish the government in such manner as they may think proper.—

Section 2. Freedom of worship. All men shall be secure in the Natural right, to worship Almighty God according to the dictates of their own consciences.—

Section 3. Freedom of religious opinion. No law shall in any case whatever control the free exercise, and enjoyment of religeous (sic) opinions, or interfere with the rights of conscience.—

Section 4. No religious qualification for office. No religious test shall be required as a qualification for any office of trust or profit.—

Section 5. No money to be appropriated for religion. No money shall be drawn from the Treasury for the benefit of any religeous (sic), or theological institution, nor shall any money be appropriated for the payment of any religeous (sic) services in either house of the Legislative Assembly.—

Section 6. No religious test for witnesses or jurors. No person shall be rendered incompetent as a witness, or juror in consequence of his opinions on matters of religeon (sic); nor be questioned in any Court of Justice touching his religeous (sic) belief to affect the weight of his testimony.—

Section 7. Manner of administering oath or affirmation. The mode of administering an oath, or affirmation shall be such as may be most consistent with, and binding upon the conscience of the person to whom such oath or affirmation may be administered.—

Section 8. Freedom of speech and press. No law shall be passed restraining the free expression of opinion, or restricting the right to speak, write, or print freely on any subject whatever; but every person shall be responsible for the abuse of this right.—

Section 9. Unreasonable searches or seizures. No law shall violate the right of the people to be secure in their persons, houses, papers, and effects, against unreasonable search, or seizure; and no warrant shall issue but upon probable cause, supported by oath, or affirmation, and particularly describing the place to be searched, and the person or thing to be seized.—

Section 10. Administration of justice. No court shall be secret, but justice shall be administered, openly and without purchase, completely and without delay, and every man shall have remedy by due course of law for injury done him in his person, property, or reputation.—

Section 11. Rights of Accused in Criminal Prosecution. In all criminal prosecutions, the accused shall have the right to public trial by an impartial jury in the county in which the offense shall have been committed; to be heard by himself and counsel; to demand the nature and cause of the accusation against him, and to have a copy thereof; to meet the witnesses face to face, and to have compulsory process for obtaining witnesses in his favor; provided, however, that any accused person, in other than capital cases, and with the consent of the trial judge, may elect to waive trial by jury and consent to be tried by the judge of the court alone, such election to be in writing; provided, however, that in the circuit court ten members of the jury may render a verdict of guilty or not guilty, save and except a verdict of guilty of first degree murder, which shall be found only by a unanimous verdict, and not otherwise; provided further, that the existing laws and constitutional provisions relative to criminal prosecutions shall be continued and remain in effect as to all prosecutions for crimes committed before the taking effect of this amendment. [Constitution of 1859; Amendment proposed by S.J.R. 4, 1931, and adopted by the people Nov. 8, 1932; Amendment proposed by S.J.R. 4, 1931 (2d s.s.), and adopted by the people May 18, 1934]

Note: The leadline to section 11 was a part of the measure submitted to the people by S.J.R. 4, 1931.

Section 12. Double jeopardy; compulsory self-incrimination. No person shall be put in jeopardy twice for the same offence (sic), nor be compelled in any criminal prosecution to testify against himself.—

Section 13. Treatment of arrested or confined persons. No person arrested, or confined in jail, shall be treated with unnecessary rigor.—

Constitution

Section 14. Bailable offenses. Offences (sic), except murder, and treason, shall be bailable by sufficient sureties. Murder or treason, shall not be bailable, when the proof is evident, or the presumption strong.—

Section 15. Foundation principles of criminal law. Laws for the punishment of crime shall be founded on these principles: protection of society, personal responsibility, accountability for one's actions and reformation. [Constitution of 1859; Amendment proposed by S.J.R. 32, 1995, and adopted by the people Nov. 5, 1996]

Section 16. Excessive bail and fines; cruel and unusual punishments; power of jury in criminal case. Excessive bail shall not be required, nor excessive fines imposed. Cruel and unusual punishments shall not be inflicted, but all penalties shall be proportioned to the offense.—In all criminal cases whatever, the jury shall have the right to determine the law, and the facts under the direction of the Court as to the law, and the right of new trial, as in civil cases.

Section 17. Jury trial in civil cases. In all civil cases the right of Trial by Jury shall remain inviolate.—

Section 18. Private property or services taken for public use. Private property shall not be taken for public use, nor the particular services of any man be demanded, without just compensation; nor except in the case of the state, without such compensation first assessed and tendered; provided, that the use of all roads, ways and waterways necessary to promote the transportation of the raw products of mine or farm or forest or water for beneficial use or drainage is necessary to the development and welfare of the state and is declared a public use. [Constitution of 1859; Amendment proposed by S.J.R. 17, 1919, and adopted by the people May 21, 1920; Amendment proposed by S.J.R. 8, 1923, and adopted by the people Nov. 4, 1924]

Section 19. Imprisonment for debt. There shall be no imprisonment for debt, except in case of fraud or absconding debtors.—

Section 20. Equality of privileges and immunities of citizens. No law shall be passed granting to any citizen or class of citizens privileges, or immunities, which, upon the same terms, shall not equally belong to all citizens.—

Section 21. Ex-post facto laws; laws impairing contracts; laws depending on authorization in order to take effect; laws submitted to electors. No *ex-post facto* law, or law impairing the obligation of contracts shall ever be passed, nor shall any law be passed, the taking effect of which shall be made to depend upon any authority, except as provided in this Constitution; provided, that laws locating the Capitol of the State, locating County Seats, and submitting town, and corporate acts, and other local, and Special laws may take effect, or not, upon a vote of the electors interested.—

Section 22. Suspension of operation of laws. The operation of the laws shall never be suspended, except by the Authority of the Legislative Assembly.

Section 23. Habeas corpus. The privilege of the writ of *habeas corpus* shall not be suspended unless in case of rebellion, or invasion the public safety require it.—

Section 24. Treason. Treason against the State shall consist only in levying war against it, or adhering to its enemies, giving them aid or comfort.—No person shall be convicted of treason unless on the testimony of two witnesses to the same overt act, or confession in open Court.—

Section 25. Corruption of blood or forfeiture of estate. No conviction shall work corruption of blood, or forfeiture of estate.—

Section 26. Assemblages of people; instruction of representatives; application to legislature. No law shall be passed restraining any of the inhabitants of the State from assembling together in a peaceable manner to consult for their common good; nor from instructing their Representatives; nor from applying to the Legislature for redress of greviances (sic).—

Section 27. Right to bear arms; military subordinate to civil power. The people shall have the right to bear arms for the defence (sic) of themselves, and the State, but the Military shall be kept in strict subordination to the civil power[.]

Section 28. Quartering soldiers. No soldier shall, in time of peace, be quartered in any house, without the consent of the owner, nor in time of war, except in the manner prescribed by law.

Section 29. Titles of nobility; hereditary distinctions. No law shall be passed granting any title of Nobility, or conferring hereditary distinctions.—

Section 30. Emigration. No law shall be passed prohibiting emigration from the State.—

Section 31. Rights of aliens; immigration to state. [Constitution of 1859; repeal proposed by H.J.R. 16, 1969, and adopted the people May 26, 1970]

Section 32. Taxes and duties; uniformity of taxation. No tax or duty shall be imposed without the consent of the people or their representatives in the Legislative Assembly; and all taxation shall be uniform on the same class of subjects within the territorial limits of the authority levying the tax. [Constitution of 1859; Amendment proposed by H.J.R. 16, 1917, and adopted by the people June 4, 1917]

Section 33. Enumeration of rights not exclusive. This enumeration of rights, and privileges shall not be construed to impair or deny others retained by the people.—

Section 34. Slavery or involuntary servitude. There shall be neither slavery, nor involuntary servitude in the State, otherwise than as a punishment for crime, whereof the party shall have been duly convicted.— [Added to Bill of Rights as unnumbered section by vote of the people at time of adoption of the Oregon Constitution in accordance with section 4 of Article XVIII thereof]

Section 35. Restrictions on rights of certain persons. [Added to Bill of Rights as unnumbered section by vote of the people at time of adoption of the Oregon Constitution in accordance with Section 4 of Article XVIII thereof; Repeal proposed by H.J.R. 8, 1925, and adopted by the people Nov. 2, 1926]

Section 36. Liquor prohibition. [Created through initiative petition filed July 1, 1914, and adopted by the people Nov. 3, 1914; Repeal proposed by initiative petition filed March 20, 1933, and adopted by the people July 21, 1933]

Section 36. Capital punishment abolished. [Created through initiative petition filed July 2, 1914, and adopted by the people Nov. 3, 1914; Repeal proposed by S.J.R. 8, 1920 (s.s.), and adopted by the people May 21, 1920, as Const. Art. I, :S.38]

Note: At the general election in 1914 two sections, each designated as section 36, were created and added to the Constitution by separate initiative petitions. One of these sections was the prohibition section and the other abolished capital punishment.

Section 36a. Prohibition of importation of liquors. [Created through initiative petition filed July 6, 1916, and adopted by the people Nov. 7, 1916; Repeal proposed by initiative petition filed March 20, 1933, and adopted by the people July 21, 1933]

Section 37. Penalty for murder in first degree. [Created through S.J.R. 8, 1920, and adopted by the people May 21, 1920;

Repeal proposed by S.J.R. 3, 1963, and adopted by the people Nov. 3, 1964]

Section 38. Laws abrogated by amendment abolishing death penalty revived. [Created through S.J.R. 8, 1920, and adopted by the people May 21, 1920; Repeal proposed by S.J.R. 3, 1963, and adopted by the people Nov. 3, 1964]

Section 39. Sale of liquor by individual glass. The State shall have power to license private clubs, fraternal organizations, veterans' organizations, railroad corporations operating interstate trains and commercial establishments where food is cooked and served, for the purpose of selling alcoholic liquor by the individual glass at retail, for consumption on the premises, including mixed drinks and cocktails, compounded or mixed on the premises only. The Legislative Assembly shall provide in such detail as it shall deem advisable for carrying out and administering the provisions of this amendment and shall provide adequate safeguards to carry out the original intent and purpose of the Oregon Liquor Control Act, including the promotion of temperance in the use and consumption of alcoholic beverages, encourage the use and consumption of lighter beverages and aid in the establishment of Oregon industry. This power is subject to the following:

(1) The provisions of this amendment shall take effect and be in operation sixty (60) days after the approval and adoption by the people of Oregon; provided, however, the right of a local option election exists in the counties and in any incorporated city or town having a population of at least five hundred (500). The Legislative Assembly shall prescribe a means and a procedure by which the voters of any county or incorporated city or town as limited above in any county, may through a local option election determine whether to prohibit or permit such power, and such procedure shall specifically include that whenever fifteen per cent (15%) of the registered voters of any county in the state or of any incorporated city or town as limited above, in any county in the state, shall file a petition requesting an election in this matter, the question shall be voted upon at the next regular November biennial election, provided said petition is filed not less than sixty (60) days before the day of election.

(2) Legislation relating to this matter shall operate uniformly throughout the state and all individuals shall be treated equally; and all provisions shall be liberally construed for the accomplishment of these purposes. [Created through initiative petition filed July 2, 1952, and adopted by the people Nov. 4, 1952]

Section 40. Penalty for aggravated murder. Notwithstanding sections 15 and 16 of this Article, the penalty for aggravated murder as defined by law shall be death upon unanimous affirmative jury findings as provided by law and otherwise shall be life imprisonment with minimum sentence as provided by law. [Created through initiative petition filed July 6, 1983, and adopted by the people Nov. 6, 1984]

Section 41. Work and training for corrections institution inmates; work programs; limitations; duties of corrections director. (1) Whereas the people of the state of Oregon find and declare that inmates who are confined in corrections institutions should work as hard as the taxpayers who provide for their upkeep; and whereas the people also find and declare that inmates confined within corrections institutions must be fully engaged in productive activity if they are to successfully re-enter society with practical skills and a viable work ethic; now, therefore, the people declare:

(2) All inmates of state corrections institutions shall be actively engaged full-time in work or on-the-job training. The work or on-the-job training programs shall be established and overseen by the corrections director, who shall ensure that such programs are cost-effective and are designed to develop inmate motivation, work capabilities and cooperation. Such programs may include boot camp prison programs. Education may be provided to inmates as part of work or on-the-job training so long as each inmate is engaged at least half-time in hands-on training or work activity.

(3) Each inmate shall begin full-time work or on-the-job training immediately upon admission to a corrections institution, allowing for a short time for administrative intake and processing. The specific quantity of hours per day to be spent in work or on-the-job training shall be determined by the corrections director, but the overall time spent in work or training shall be full-time. However, no inmate has a legally enforceable right to a job or to otherwise participate in work, on-the-job training or educational programs or to compensation for work or labor performed while an inmate of any state, county or city corrections facility or institution. The corrections director may reduce or exempt participation in work or training programs by those inmates deemed by corrections officials as physically or mentally disabled, or as too dangerous to society to engage in such programs.

(4) There shall be sufficient work and training programs to ensure that every eligible inmate is productively involved in one or more programs. Where an inmate is drug and alcohol addicted so as to prevent the inmate from effectively participating in work or training programs, corrections officials shall provide appropriate drug or alcohol treatment.

(5) The intent of the people is that taxpayer-supported institutions and programs shall be free to benefit from inmate work. Prison work programs shall be designed and carried out so as to achieve savings in government operations, so as to achieve a net profit in private sector activities or so as to benefit the community.

(6) The provisions of this section are mandatory for all state corrections institutions. The provisions of this section are permissive for county or city corrections facilities. No law, ordinance or charter shall prevent or restrict a county or city governing body from implementing all or part of the provisions of this section. Compensation, if any, shall be determined and established by the governing body of the county or city which chooses to engage in prison work programs, and the governing body may choose to adopt any power or exemption allowed in this section.

(7) The corrections director shall contact public and private enterprises in this state and seek proposals to use inmate work. The corrections director may: (a) install and equip plants in any state corrections institution, or any other location, for the employment or training of any of the inmates therein; or (b) purchase, acquire, install, maintain and operate materials, machinery and appliances necessary to the conduct and operation of such plants. The corrections director shall use every effort to enter into contracts or agreements with private business concerns or government agencies to accomplish the production or marketing of products or services produced or performed by inmates. The corrections director may carry out the director's powers and duties under this section by delegation to others.

(8) Compensation, if any, for inmates who engage in prison work programs shall be determined and established by the corrections director. Such compensation shall not be subject to existing public or private sector minimum or prevailing wage laws, except where required to comply with federal law. Inmate compensation from enterprises entering into agreements with the state shall be exempt from unemployment compensation taxes to the extent allowed under federal law. Inmate injury or disease attributable to any inmate work shall be covered by a corrections system inmate injury fund rather than the workers compensation law. Except as otherwise required by federal law to permit transportation in interstate commerce of goods, wares or merchandise manufactured, produced or mined, wholly or in part by inmates or except as otherwise required by state law, any compensation earned through prison work programs shall only be used for the following purposes: (a) reimbursement for all or a portion of the costs of the inmate's rehabilitation, housing, health care, and living costs; (b) restitution or compensation to the victims of the particular inmate's crime; (c) restitution or compensation to the victims of crime generally through a fund designed for that purpose; (d) financial support for immediate family of the inmate outside the corrections institution; and (e) payment of fines, court costs, and applicable taxes.

(9) All income generated from prison work programs shall be kept separate from general fund accounts and shall only be used for implementing, maintaining and developing prison work programs. Prison industry work programs shall be exempt from statutory competitive bid and purchase requirements. Expenditures for prison work programs shall be exempt from the legislative appropriations process to the extent the programs rely on income sources other than state taxes and fees. Where state taxes or fees are the source of capital or operating expenditures, the appropriations shall be made by the legislative assembly. The state programs shall be run in a businesslike fashion and shall be subject to regulation by the corrections director. Expenditures from income generated by state prison work programs must be approved by the corrections director. Agreements with private enterprise as to state prison work programs must be approved by the corrections director. The corrections director shall make all state records available for public scrutiny and the records shall be subject to audit by the Secretary of State.

(10) Prison work products or services shall be available to any public agency and to any private enterprise of any state, any nation or any American Indian or Alaskan Native tribe without restriction imposed by any state or local law, ordinance or regulation as to competition with other public or private sector enterprises. The products and services of corrections work programs shall be provided on such terms as are set by the corrections director. To the extent determined possible by the corrections director, the corrections director shall avoid establishing or expanding for-profit prison work programs that produce goods or services offered for sale in the private sector if the establishment or expansion would displace or significantly reduce preexisting private enterprise. To the extent determined possible by the corrections director, the corrections director shall avoid establishing or expanding prison work programs if the establishment or expansion would displace or significantly reduce government or nonprofit programs that employ persons with developmental disabilities. However, the decision to

establish, maintain, expand, reduce or terminate any prison work program remains in the sole discretion of the corrections director.

(11) Inmate work shall be used as much as possible to help operate the corrections institutions themselves, to support other government operations and to support community charitable organizations. This work includes, but is not limited to, institutional food production; maintenance and repair of buildings, grounds, and equipment; office support services, including printing; prison clothing production and maintenance; prison medical services; training other inmates; agricultural and forestry work, especially in parks and public forest lands; and environmental clean-up projects. Every state agency shall cooperate with the corrections director in establishing inmate work programs.

(12) As used throughout this section, unless the context requires otherwise: "full-time" means the equivalent of at least forty hours per seven day week, specifically including time spent by inmates as required by the Department of Corrections, while the inmate is participating in work or on-the-job training, to provide for the safety and security of the public, correctional staff and inmates; "corrections director" means the person in charge of the state corrections system.

(13) This section is self-implementing and supersedes all existing inconsistent statutes. This section shall become effective April 1, 1995. If any part of this section or its application to any person or circumstance is held to be invalid for any reason, then the remaining parts or applications to any persons or circumstances shall not be affected but shall remain in full force and effect. [Created through initiative petition filed Jan. 12, 1994, and adopted by the people Nov. 8, 1994; Amendment proposed by H.J.R. 2, 1997, and adopted by the people May 20, 1997; Amendment proposed by H.J.R. 82, 1999, and adopted by the people Nov. 2, 1999]

Note: Added to Article I as unnumbered section by initiative petition (Measure No. 17, 1994) adopted by the people Nov. 8, 1994.

Note: An initiative petition (Measure No. 40, 1996) proposed adding a new section relating to crime victims' rights to the Oregon Constitution. That section, appearing as section 42 of Article I in previous editions of this Constitution, was declared void for not being enacted in compliance with section 1, Article XVII of this Constitution. See *Armatta v. Kitzhaber,* 327 Or. 250, 959 P.2d 49 (1998).

Section 42. Rights of victim in criminal prosecutions and juvenile court delinquency proceedings. (1) To preserve and protect the right of crime victims to justice, to ensure crime victims a meaningful role in the criminal and juvenile justice systems, to accord crime victims due dignity and respect and to ensure that criminal and juvenile court delinquency proceedings are conducted to seek the truth as to the defendant's innocence or guilt, and also to ensure that a fair balance is struck between the rights of crime victims and the rights of criminal defendants in the course and conduct of criminal and juvenile court delinquency proceedings, the following rights are hereby granted to victims in all prosecutions for crimes and in juvenile court delinquency proceedings:

(a) The right to be present at and, upon specific request, to be informed in advance of any critical stage of the proceedings held in open court when the defendant will be present, and to be heard at the pretrial release hearing and the sentencing or juvenile court delinquency disposition;

(b) The right, upon request, to obtain information about the conviction, sentence, imprisonment, criminal history and future release from physical custody of the criminal defendant or convicted criminal and equivalent information regarding the alleged youth offender or youth offender;

(c) The right to refuse an interview, deposition or other discovery request by the criminal defendant or other person acting on behalf of the criminal defendant provided, however, that nothing in this paragraph shall restrict any other constitutional right of the defendant to discovery against the state;

(d) The right to receive prompt restitution from the convicted criminal who caused the victim's loss or injury;

(e) The right to have a copy of a transcript of any court proceeding in open court, if one is otherwise prepared;

(f) The right to be consulted, upon request, regarding plea negotiations involving any violent felony; and

(g) The right to be informed of these rights as soon as practicable.

(2) This section applies to all criminal and juvenile court delinquency proceedings pending or commenced on or after the effective date of this section. Nothing in this section reduces a criminal defendant's rights under the Constitution of the United States. Except as otherwise specifically provided, this section supersedes any conflicting section of this Constitution. Nothing in this section is intended to create any cause of action for compensation or damages nor may this section be used to invalidate an accusatory instrument, ruling of a court, conviction or adjudication or otherwise suspend or terminate any criminal or juvenile delinquency proceedings at any point after the case is commenced or on appeal.

(3) As used in this section:

(a) "Convicted criminal" includes a youth offender in juvenile court delinquency proceedings.

(b) "Criminal defendant" includes an alleged youth offender in juvenile court delinquency proceedings.

(c) "Victim" means any person determined by the prosecuting attorney to have suffered direct financial, psychological or physical harm as a result of a crime and, in the case of a victim who is a minor, the legal guardian of the minor. In the event that no person has been determined to be a victim of the crime, the people of Oregon, represented by the prosecuting attorney, are considered to be the victims. In no event is it intended that the criminal defendant be considered the victim.

(d) "Violent felony" means a felony in which there was actual or threatened serious physical injury to a victim or a felony sexual offense. [Created through H.J.R. 87, 1999, and adopted by the people Nov. 2, 1999]

Note: The effective date of House Joint Resolutions 87, 89, 90 and 94, compiled as sections 42, 43, 44 and 45, Article I, is Dec. 2, 1999.

Note: Sections 42, 43, 44 and 45, were added to Article I as unnumbered sections by the amendments proposed by House Joint Resolutions 87, 89, 90 and 94, 1999, and adopted by the people Nov. 2, 1999.

Section 43. Rights of victim and public to protection from accused person during criminal proceedings; denial of pretrial release. (1) To ensure that a fair balance is struck between the rights of crime victims and the rights of criminal defendants in the course and conduct of criminal proceedings, the following rights are hereby granted to victims in all prosecutions for crimes:

(a) The right to be reasonably protected from the criminal defendant or the convicted criminal throughout the criminal justice process and from the alleged youth offender or youth offender throughout the juvenile delinquency proceedings.

(b) The right to have decisions by the court regarding the pretrial release of a criminal defendant based upon the principle of reasonable protection of the victim and the public, as well as the likelihood that the criminal defendant will appear for trial. Murder, aggravated murder and treason shall not be bailable when the proof is evident or the presumption strong that the person is guilty. Other violent felonies shall not be bailable when a court has determined there is probable cause to believe the criminal defendant committed the crime, and the court finds, by clear and convincing evidence, that there is danger of physical injury or sexual victimization to the victim or members of the public by the criminal defendant while on release.

(2) This section applies to proceedings pending or commenced on or after the effective date of this section. Nothing in this section abridges any right of the criminal defendant guaranteed by the Constitution of the United States, including the rights to be represented by counsel, have counsel appointed if indigent, testify, present witnesses, cross-examine witnesses or present information at the release hearing. Nothing in this section creates any cause of action for compensation or damages nor may this section be used to invalidate an accusatory instrument, ruling of a court, conviction or adjudication or otherwise suspend or terminate any criminal or juvenile delinquency proceeding at any point after the case is commenced or on appeal. Except as otherwise specifically provided, this section supersedes any conflicting section of this Constitution.

(3) As used in this section:

(a) "Victim" means any person determined by the prosecuting attorney to have suffered direct financial, psychological or physical harm as a result of a crime and, in the case of a victim who is a minor, the legal guardian of the minor. In the event no person has been determined to be a victim of the crime, the people of Oregon, represented by the prosecuting attorney, are considered to be the victims. In no event is it intended that the criminal defendant be considered the victim.

(b) "Violent felony" means a felony in which there was actual or threatened serious physical injury to a victim or a felony sexual offense.

(4) The prosecuting attorney is the party authorized to assert the rights of the victim and the public established by this section. [Created through H.J.R. 90, 1999, and adopted by the people Nov. 2, 1999]

Note: See notes under section 42 of this Article.

Section 44. Term of imprisonment imposed by court to be fully served; exceptions. (1)(a) A term of imprisonment imposed by a judge in open court may not be set aside or otherwise not carried out, except as authorized by the sentencing court or through the subsequent exercise of:

(A) The power of the Governor to grant reprieves, commutations and pardons; or

(B) Judicial authority to grant appellate or post-conviction relief.

(b) No law shall limit a court's authority to sentence a criminal defendant consecutively for crimes against different victims.

(2) This section applies to all offenses committed on or after the effective date of this section. Nothing in this section reduces a criminal defendant's rights under the Constitution of the United States. Except as otherwise specifically provided, this section supersedes any conflicting section of this Constitution. Nothing in this section creates any cause of action for compensation or damages nor may this section be used to invalidate an accusatory instrument, ruling of a court, conviction or adjudication or otherwise suspend or terminate any criminal or juvenile delinquency proceedings at any point after the case is commenced or on appeal.

(3) As used in this section, "victim" means any person determined by the prosecuting attorney to have suffered direct financial, psychological or physical harm as a result of a crime and, in the case of a victim who is a minor, the legal guardian of the minor. In the event no person has been determined to be a victim of the crime, the people of Oregon, represented by the prosecuting attorney, are considered to be the victims. In no event is it intended that the criminal defendant be considered the victim. [Created through H.J.R. 94, 1999, and adopted by the people Nov. 2, 1999]

Note: See notes under section 42 of this Article.

Section 45. Person convicted of certain crimes not eligible to serve as juror on grand jury or trial jury in criminal case. (1) In all grand juries and in all prosecutions for crimes tried to a jury, the jury shall be composed of persons who have not been convicted:

(a) Of a felony or served a felony sentence within the 15 years immediately preceding the date the persons are required to report for jury duty; or

(b) Of a misdemeanor involving violence or dishonesty or served a sentence for a misdemeanor involving violence or dishonesty within the five years immediately preceding the date the persons are required to report for jury duty.

(2) This section applies to all criminal proceedings pending or commenced on or after the effective date of this section, except a criminal proceeding in which a jury has been impaneled and sworn on the effective date of this section. Nothing in this section reduces a criminal defendant's rights under the Constitution of the United States. Except as otherwise specifically provided, this section supersedes any conflicting section of this Constitution. Nothing in this section is intended to create any cause of action for compensation or damages nor may this section be used to disqualify a jury, invalidate an accusatory instrument, ruling of a court, conviction or adjudication or otherwise suspend or terminate any criminal proceeding at any point after a jury is impaneled and sworn or on appeal. [Created through H.J.R. 89, 1999, and adopted by the people Nov. 2, 1999]

Note: See notes under section 42 of this Article.

ARTICLE II
SUFFRAGE AND ELECTIONS

Section 1. Elections free. All elections shall be free and equal.—

Section 2. Qualifications of electors. (1) Every citizen of the United States is entitled to vote in all elections not otherwise provided for by this Constitution if such citizen:

(a) Is 18 years of age or older;

(b) Has resided in this state during the six months immediately preceding the election, except that provision may be made by law to permit a person who has resided in this state less than 30 days immediately preceding the election, but who is otherwise qualified under this subsection, to vote in the election for candidates for nomination or election for President or Vice President of the United States or elector of President and Vice President of the United States; and

(c) Is registered not less than 20 calendar days immediately preceding any election in the manner provided by law.

(2) Except as otherwise provided in section 6, Article VIII of this Constitution with respect to the qualifications of voters in all school district elections, provision may be made by law to require that persons who vote upon questions of levying special taxes or issuing public bonds shall be taxpayers. [Constitution of 1859; Amendment proposed by initiative petition filed Dec. 20, 1910, and adopted by the people Nov. 5, 1912; Amendment proposed by S.J.R. 6, 1913, and adopted by the people Nov. 3, 1914; Amendment proposed by S.J.R. 6, 1923, and adopted by the people Nov. 4, 1924; Amendment proposed by H.J.R. 7, 1927, and adopted by the people June 28, 1927; Amendment proposed by H.J.R. 5, 1931, and adopted by the people Nov. 8, 1932; Amendment proposed by H.J.R. 26, 1959, and adopted by the people Nov. 8, 1960; Amendment proposed by H.J.R. 41, 1973, and adopted by the people Nov. 5, 1974; Amendment proposed by initiative petition filed July 20, 1986, and adopted by the people Nov. 4, 1986]

Note: The leadline to section 2 was a part of the measure submitted to the people by initiative petition (Measure No. 13, 1986) and adopted by the people Nov. 4, 1986.

Section 3. Rights of certain electors. A person suffering from a mental handicap is entitled to the full rights of an elector, if otherwise qualified, unless the person has been adjudicated incompetent to vote as provided by law. The privilege of an elector, upon conviction of any crime which is punishable by imprisonment in the penitentiary, shall be forfeited, unless otherwise provided by law. [Constitution of 1859; Amendment proposed by S.J.R. 9, 1943, and adopted by the people Nov. 7, 1944; Amendment proposed by S.J.R. 26, 1979, and adopted by the people Nov. 4, 1980]

Section 4. Residence. For the purpose of voting, no person shall be deemed to have gained, or lost a residence, by reason of his presence, or absence while employed in the service of the United States, or of this State; nor while engaged in the navigation of the waters of this State, or of the United States, or of the high seas; nor while a student of any Seminary of Learning; nor while kept at any alms house, or other assylum (sic), at public expence (sic); nor while confined in any public prison.—

Section 5. Soldiers, seamen and marines; residence; right to vote. No soldier, seaman, or marine in the Army, or Navy of the United States, or of their allies, shall be deemed to have acquired a residence in the state, in consequence of having been stationed within the same; nor shall any such soldier, seaman, or marine have the right to vote.—

Section 6. Right of suffrage for certain persons. [Constitution of 1859; Repeal proposed by H.J.R. 4, 1927, and adopted by the people June 28, 1927]

Section 7. Bribery at elections. Every person shall be disqualified from holding office, during the term for which he may have been elected, who shall have given, or offered a bribe, threat, or reward to procure his election.

Section 8. Regulation of elections. The Legislative Assembly shall enact laws to support the privilege of free suffrage, prescribing the manner of regulating, and conducting elections, and prohibiting under adequate penalties, all undue influence therein, from power, bribery, tumult, and other improper conduct.—

Section 9. Penalty for dueling. Every person who shall give, or accept a challenge to fight a duel, or who shall knowingly carry to another person such challenge, or who shall agree to go out of the State to fight a duel, shall be ineligible to any office of trust, or profit.—

Section 10. Lucrative offices; holding other offices forbidden. No person holding a lucrative office, or appointment under the United States, or under this State, shall be eligible to a seat in the Legislative Assembly; nor shall any person hold more than one lucrative office at the same time, except as in this Constition (sic) expressly permitted; Provided, that Officers in the Militia, to which there is attached no annual salary, and the Office of Post Master, where the compensation does not exceed One Hundred Dollars per annum, shall not be deemed lucrative.—

Section 11. When collector or holder of public moneys ineligible to office. No person who may hereafter be a collector, or holder of public moneys, shall be eligible to any office of trust or profit, until he shall have accounted for, and paid over according to law, all sums for which he may be liable.—

Section 12. Temporary appointments to office. In all cases, in which it is provided that an office shall not be filled by the same person, more than a certain number of years continuously, an appointment *pro tempore* shall not be reckoned a part of that term.—

Section 13. Privileges of electors. In all cases, except treason, felony, and breach of the peace, electors shall be free from arrest in going to elections, during their attendance there, and in returning from the same; and no elector shall be obliged to do duty in the Militia on any day of election, except in time of war, or public danger.—

Section 14. Time of holding elections and assuming duties of office. The regular general biennial election in Oregon for the year A. D. 1910 and thereafter shall be held on the first Tuesday after the first Monday in November. All officers except the Governor, elected for a six year term in 1904 or for a four year term in 1906 or for a two year term in 1908 shall continue to hold their respective offices until the first Monday in January, 1911; and all officers, except the Governor elected at any regular general biennial election after the adoption of this amendment shall assume the duties of their respective offices on the first Monday in January following such election. All laws pertaining to the nomination of candidates, registration of voters and all other things incident to the holding of the regular biennial election shall be enforced and be effected the same number of days before the first Tuesday after the first Monday in November that they have heretofore been before the first Monday in June biennially, except as may hereafter be provided by law. [Constitution of 1859; Amendment proposed by H.J.R. 7, 1907, and adopted by the people June 1, 1908]

Section 14a. Time of holding elections in incorporated cities and towns. Incorporated cities and towns shall hold their nominating and regular elections for their several elective officers at the same time that the primary and general biennial elections for State and county officers are held, and the election precincts and officers shall be the same for all elections held at the same time. All provisions of the charters and ordinances of incorporated cities and towns pertaining to the holding of elections shall continue in full force and effect except so far as they relate to the time of holding such elections. Every officer who, at the time of the adoption of this amendment, is the duly qualified incumbent of an elective office of an incorporated city or town shall hold his office for the term for which he was elected and until his successor is elected and qualified. The Legislature, and cities and towns, shall enact such supplementary legislation as may be necessary to carry the provisions of this amendment into effect. [Created through H.J.R. 22, 1917, and adopted by the people June 4, 1917]

Section 15. Method of voting in legislature. In all elections by the Legislative Assembly, or by either branch thereof, votes shall be given openly or viva voce, and not by ballot, forever; and in all elections by the people, votes shall be given openly, or viva voce, until the Legislative Assembly shall otherwise direct.—

Section 16. Election by plurality; proportional representation. In all elections authorized by this constitution until otherwise provided by law, the person or persons receiving the highest number of votes shall be declared elected, but provision may be made by law for elections by equal proportional representation of all the voters for every office which is filled by the election of two or more persons whose official duties, rights and powers are equal and concurrent. Every qualified elector resident in his precinct and registered as may be required by law, may vote for one person under the title for each office. Provision may be made by law for the voter's direct or indirect expression of his first, second or additional choices among the candidates for any office. For an office which is filled by the election of one person it may be required by law that the person elected shall be the final choice of a majority of the electors voting for candidates for that office. These principles may be applied by law to nominations by political parties and organizations. [Constitution of 1859; Amendment proposed by initiative petition filed Jan. 29, 1908, and adopted by the people June 1, 1908]

Section 17. Place of voting. All qualified electors shall vote in the election precinct in the County where they may reside, for County Officers, and in any County in the State for State Officers, or in any County of a Congressional District in which such electors may reside, for Members of Congress.—

Section 18. Recall; meaning of words "the legislative assembly shall provide." (1) Every public officer in Oregon is subject, as herein provided, to recall by the electors of the state or of the electoral district from which the public officer is elected.

(2) Fifteen per cent, but not more, of the number of electors who voted for Governor in the officer's electoral district at the most recent election at which a candidate for Governor was elected to a full term, may be required to file their petition demanding the officer's recall by the people.

(3) They shall set forth in the petition the reasons for the demand.

(4) If the public officer offers to resign, the resignation shall be accepted and take effect on the day it is offered, and the vacancy shall be filled as may be provided by law. If the public officer does not resign within five days after the petition is filed, a special election shall be ordered to be held within 35 days in the electoral district to determine whether the people will recall the officer.

(5) On the ballot at the election shall be printed in not more than 200 words the reasons for demanding the recall of the officer as set forth in the recall petition, and, in not more than 200 words, the officer's justification of the officer's course in office. The officer shall continue to perform the duties of office until the result of the special election is officially declared. If an officer is recalled from any public office the vacancy shall be filled immediately in the manner provided by law for filling a vacancy in that office arising from any other cause.

(6) The recall petition shall be filed with the officer with whom a petition for nomination to such office should be filed, and the same officer shall order the special election when it is required. No such petition shall be circulated against any officer until the officer has actually held the office six months, save and except that it may be filed against a senator or representative in the legislative assembly at any time after five days from the beginning of the first session after the election of the senator or representative.

(7) After one such petition and special election, no further recall petition shall be filed against the same officer during the term for which the officer was elected unless such further petitioners first pay into the public treasury which has paid such special election expenses, the whole amount of its expenses for the preceding special election.

(8) Such additional legislation as may aid the operation of this section shall be provided by the legislative assembly, including provision for payment by the public treasury of the reasonable special election campaign expenses of such officer. But the words, "the legislative assembly shall provide," or any similar or equivalent words in this constitution or any amendment thereto, shall not be construed to grant to the legislative assembly any exclusive power of lawmaking nor in any way to limit the initiative and referendum powers reserved by the people. [Created through initiative petition filed Jan. 29, 1908, and adopted by the people June 1, 1908; Amendment proposed by S.J.R. 16, 1925, and adopted by the people Nov. 2, 1926;

Amendment proposed by H.J.R. 1, 1983, and adopted by the people Nov. 6, 1984]

Note: The word "Recall" constituted the headline to section 18 and was a part of the measure submitted to the people by S.J.R. 16, 1925.

Note: An initiative petition (Measure No. 3, 1992) proposed adding new sections relating to term limits to the Oregon Constitution. Those sections, appearing as sections 19, 20 and 21 of Article II in previous editions of this Constitution, were declared void for not being enacted in compliance with section 1, Article XVII of this Constitution. See *Lehman v. Bradbury*, 333 Or. 231, 37 P.3d 989 (2002).

Section 22. Political campaign contribution limitations. Section (1) For purposes of campaigning for an elected public office, a candidate may use or direct only contributions which originate from individuals who at the time of their donation were residents of the electoral district of the public office sought by the candidate, unless the contribution consists of volunteer time, information provided to the candidate, or funding provided by federal, state, or local government for purposes of campaigning for an elected public office.

Section (2) Where more than ten percent (10%) of a candidate's total campaign funding is in violation of Section (1), and the candidate is subsequently elected, the elected official shall forfeit the office and shall not hold a subsequent elected public office for a period equal to twice the tenure of the office sought. Where more than ten percent (10%) of a candidate's total campaign funding is in violation of Section (1) and the candidate is not elected, the unelected candidate shall not hold a subsequent elected public office for a period equal to twice the tenure of the office sought.

Section (3) A qualified donor (an individual who is a resident within the electoral district of the office sought by the candidate) shall not contribute to a candidate's campaign any restricted contributions of Section (1) received from an unqualified donor for the purpose of contributing to a candidate's campaign for elected public office. An unqualified donor (an entity which is not an individual and who is not a resident of the electoral district of the office sought by the candidate) shall not give any restricted contributions of Section (1) to a qualified donor for the purpose of contributing to a candidate's campaign for elected public office.

Section (4) A violation of Section (3) shall be an unclassified felony. [Created through initiative petition filed Jan. 25, 1993, and adopted by the people Nov. 8, 1994]

Note: An initiative petition (Measure No. 6, 1994) adopted by the people Nov. 8, 1994, proposed a constitutional amendment as an unnumbered section. Section 22 sections (1), (2), (3) and (4) were designated in the proposed amendment as "SECTION 1.," "SECTION 2.," "SECTION 3." and "SECTION 4.," respectively.

Section 23. Approval by more than majority required for certain measures submitted to people. (1) Any measure that includes any proposed requirement for more than a majority of votes cast by the electorate to approve any change in law or government action shall become effective only if approved by at least the same percentage of voters specified in the proposed voting requirement.

(2) For the purposes of this section, "measure" includes all initiatives and all measures referred to the voters by the Legislative Assembly.

(3) The requirements of this section apply to all measures presented to the voters at the November 3, 1998 election and thereafter.

(4) The purpose of this section is to prevent greater-than-majority voting requirements from being imposed by only a majority of the voters. [Created through initiative petition filed Jan. 15, 1998, and adopted by the people Nov. 3, 1998]

Note: Added as unnumbered section to the Constitution but not to any Article therein by initiative petition (Measure No. 63, 1998) adopted by the people Nov. 3, 1998.

Note: An initiative petition (Measure No. 62, 1998) proposed adding new sections and a subsection relating to political campaigns to the Oregon Constitution. Those sections, appearing as sections 24 to 32 of Article II and sections 1 (6), 1b and 1c of Article IV in previous editions of this Constitution, were declared void for not being enacted in compliance with section 1, Article XVII of this Constitution. See *Swett v. Bradbury*, 333 Or. 597, 43 P.3d 1094 (2002).

ARTICLE III
DISTRIBUTION OF POWERS

Section 1. Separation of powers. The powers of the Government shall be divided into three seperate (sic) departments, the Legislative, the Executive, including the administrative, and the Judicial; and no person charged with official duties under one of these departments, shall exercise any of the functions of another, except as in this Constitution expressly provided.—

Section 2. Budgetary control over executive and administrative officers and agencies. The Legislative Assembly shall have power to establish an agency to exercise budgetary control over all executive and administrative state officers, departments, boards, commissions and agencies of the State Government. [Created through S.J.R. 24, 1951, and adopted by the people Nov. 4, 1952.

Note: Section 2 was designated as "Sec. 1" by S.J.R. 24, 1951, and adopted by the people Nov. 4, 1952.

Section 3. Joint legislative committee to allocate emergency fund appropriations and to authorize expenditures beyond budgetary limits. (1) The Legislative Assembly is authorized to establish by law a joint committee composed of members of both houses of the Legislative Assembly, the membership to be as fixed by law, which committee may exercise, during the interim between sessions of the Legislative Assembly, such of the following powers as may be conferred upon it by law:

(a) Where an emergency exists, to allocate to any state agency, out of any emergency fund that may be appropriated to the committee for that purpose, additional funds beyond the amount appropriated to the agency by the Legislative Assembly, or funds to carry on an activity required by law for which an appropriation was not made.

(b) Where an emergency exists, to authorize any state agency to expend, from funds dedicated or continuously appropriated for the uses and purposes of the agency, sums in excess of the amount of the budget of the agency as approved in accordance with law.

(c) In the case of a new activity coming into existence at such a time as to preclude the possibility of submitting a budget to the Legislative Assembly for approval, to approve, or revise and approve, a budget of the money appropriated for such new activity.

(d) Where an emergency exists, to revise or amend the budgets of state agencies to the extent of authorizing transfers between expenditure classifications within the budget of an agency.

(2) The Legislative Assembly shall prescribe by law what shall constitute an emergency for the purposes of this section.

(3) As used in this section, "state agency" means any elected or appointed officer, board, commission, department, institution, branch or other agency of the state government.

(4) The term of members of the joint committee established pursuant to this section shall run from the adjournment of one regular session to the organization of the next regular session. No member of a committee shall cease to be such member solely by reason of the expiration of his term of office as a member of the Legislative Assembly. [Created through S.J.R. 24, 1951, and adopted by the people Nov. 4, 1952]

Note: Section 3 was designated as "Sec. 2" by S.J.R. 24, 1951, and adopted by the people Nov. 4, 1952.

Section 4. Senate confirmation of executive appointments. (1) The Legislative Assembly in the manner provided by law may require that all appointments and reappointments to state public office made by the Governor shall be subject to confirmation by the Senate.

(2) The appointee shall not be eligible to serve until confirmed in the manner required by law and if not confirmed in that manner, shall not be eligible to serve in the public office.

(3) In addition to appointive offices, the provisions of this section shall apply to any state elective office when the Governor is authorized by law or this Constitution to fill any vacancy therein, except the office of judge of any court, United States Senator or Representative and a district, county or precinct office. [Created through S.J.R. 20, 1977, and adopted by the people Nov. 7, 1978]

ARTICLE IV
LEGISLATIVE DEPARTMENT

Constitution

23. Certain local and special laws prohibited
24. Suit against state
25. Majority necessary to pass bills and resolutions; special requirements for bills raising revenue; signatures of presiding officers required
26. Protest by member
27. All statutes public laws; exceptions
28. When Act takes effect
29. Compensation of members
30. Members not eligible to other offices
31. Oath of members
32. Income tax defined by federal law; review of tax laws required
33. Reduction of criminal sentences approved by initiative or referendum process

Section 1. Legislative power; initiative and referendum. (1) The legislative power of the state, except for the initiative and referendum powers reserved to the people, is vested in a Legislative Assembly, consisting of a Senate and a House of Representatives.

(2)(a) The people reserve to themselves the initiative power, which is to propose laws and amendments to the Constitution and enact or reject them at an election independently of the Legislative Assembly.

(b) An initiative law may be proposed only by a petition signed by a number of qualified voters equal to six percent of the total number of votes cast for all candidates for Governor at the election at which a Governor was elected for a term of four years next preceding the filing of the petition.

(c) An initiative amendment to the Constitution may be proposed only by a petition signed by a number of qualified voters equal to eight percent of the total number of votes cast for all candidates for Governor at the election at which a Governor was elected for a term of four years next preceding the filing of the petition.

(d) An initiative petition shall include the full text of the proposed law or amendment to the Constitution. A proposed law or amendment to the Constitution shall embrace one subject only and matters properly connected therewith.

(e) An initiative petition shall be filed not less than four months before the election at which the proposed law or amendment to the Constitution is to be voted upon.

(3)(a) The people reserve to themselves the referendum power, which is to approve or reject at an election any Act, or part thereof, of the Legislative Assembly that does not become effective earlier than 90 days after the end of the session at which the Act is passed.

(b) A referendum on an Act or part thereof may be ordered by a petition signed by a number of qualified voters equal to four percent of the total number of votes cast for all candidates for Governor at the election at which a Governor was elected for a term of four years next preceding the filing of the petition. A referendum petition shall be filed not more than 90 days after the end of the session at which the Act is passed.

(c) A referendum on an Act may be ordered by the Legislative Assembly by law. Notwithstanding section 15b, Article V of this Constitution, bills ordering a referendum and bills on which a referendum is ordered are not subject to veto by the Governor.

(4)(a) Petitions or orders for the initiative or referendum shall be filed with the Secretary of State. The Legislative Assembly shall provide by law for the manner in which the Secretary of State shall determine whether a petition contains the required number of signatures of qualified voters. The Secretary of State shall complete the verification process within the 30-day period after the last day on which the petition may be filed as provided in paragraph (e) of subsection (2) or paragraph (b) of subsection (3) of this section.

(b) Initiative and referendum measures shall be submitted to the people as provided in this section and by law not inconsistent therewith.

(c) All elections on initiative and referendum measures shall be held at the regular general elections, unless otherwise ordered by the Legislative Assembly.

(d) Notwithstanding section 1, Article XVII of this Constitution, an initiative or referendum measure becomes effective 30 days after the day on which it is enacted or approved by a majority of the votes cast thereon. A referendum ordered by petition on a part of an Act does not delay the remainder of the Act from becoming effective.

(5) The initiative and referendum powers reserved to the people by subsections (2) and (3) of this section are further reserved to the qualified voters of each municipality and district as to all local, special and municipal legislation of every character in or for their municipality or district. The manner of exercising those powers shall be provided by general laws, but cities may provide the manner of exercising those powers as to their municipal legislation. In a city, not more than 15 percent of the qualified voters may be required to propose legislation by the initiative, and not more than 10 percent of the qualified voters may be required to order a referendum on legislation. [Created through H.J.R. 16, 1967, and adopted by the people May 28, 1968 (this section adopted in lieu of former sections 1 and 1a of this Article); Amendment proposed by S.J.R. 27, 1985, and adopted by the people May 20, 1986; Amendment proposed by S.J.R. 3, 1999, and adopted by the people May 16, 2000]

Note: An initiative petition (Measure No. 62, 1998) proposed adding new sections and a subsection relating to political campaigns to the Oregon Constitution. Those sections, appearing as sections 24 to 32 of Article II and sections 1 (6), 1b and 1c of Article IV in previous editions of this Constitution, were declared void for not being enacted in compliance with section 1, Article XVII of this Constitution. See *Swett v. Bradbury*, 333 Or. 597, 43 P.3d 1094 (2002).

Section 1. Legislative authority vested in assembly; initiative and referendum; style of bills. [Constitution of 1859; Amendment proposed by H.J.R. 1, 1901, and adopted by the people June 2, 1902; Amendment proposed by S.J.R. 6, 1953, and adopted by the people Nov. 2, 1954; Repeal proposed by H.J.R. 16, 1967, and adopted by the people May 28, 1968 (present section 1 of this Article adopted in lieu of this section)]

Section 1a. Initiative and referendum on parts of laws and on local, special and municipal laws. [Created through initiative petition filed Feb. 3, 1906, and adopted by the people June 4, 1906; Repeal proposed by H.J.R. 16, 1967, and adopted by the people May 28, 1968 (present section 1 of this Article adopted in lieu of this section)]

Note: Section 1b as submitted to the people was preceded by the following: To protect the integrity of initiative and referendum petitions, the People of Oregon add the following provisions to the Constitution of the State of Oregon:

Section 1b. Payment for signatures. It shall be unlawful to pay or receive money or other thing of value based on the number of signatures obtained on an initiative or referendum petition. Nothing herein prohibits payment for signature gathering which is not based, either directly or indirectly, on the number of signatures obtained. [Created through initiative petition filed Nov. 7, 2001, and adopted by the people Nov. 5, 2002]

Note: Added as unnumbered section to the Constitution but not to any Article therein by initiative petition (Measure No. 26, 2002) adopted by the people Nov. 5, 2002.

Section 1d. Effective date of amendment to section 1, Article IV, by S.J.R. 3, 1999. [Created through S.J.R. 3, 1999, and adopted by the people May 16, 2000; Repealed Dec. 31, 2002, as specified in text of section adopted by the people May 16, 2000]

Section 2. Number of Senators and Representatives. The Senate shall consist of sixteen, and the House of Representatives of thirty four members, which number shall not be increased until the year Eighteen Hundred and Sixty, after which time the Legislative Assembly may increase the number of Senators and Representatives, always keeping as near as may be the same ratio as to the number of Senators, and Representatives: Provided that the Senate shall never exceed thirty and the House of Representatives sixty members.—

Section 3. How Senators and Representatives chosen; filling vacancies; qualifications. (1) The senators and representatives shall be chosen by the electors of the respective counties or districts or subdistricts within a county or district into which the state may from time to time be divided by law.

(2) If a vacancy in the office of senator or representative from any county or district or subdistrict shall occur, such vacancy shall be filled as may be provided by law. A person who is appointed to fill a vacancy in the office of senator or representative shall have been an inhabitant of the district the person is appointed to represent for at least one year next preceding the date of the appointment. However, for purposes of an appointment occurring during the period beginning on January 1 of the year next following the operative date of an apportionment under section 6 of this Article, the person must have been an inhabitant of the district for one year next preceding the date of the appointment or from January 1 of the year following the reapportionment to the date of the appointment, whichever is less. [Constitution of 1859; Amendment proposed by S.J.R. 20, 1929, and adopted by the people Nov. 4, 1930; Amendment proposed by H.J.R. 20, 1953, and adopted by the people Nov. 2, 1954; Amendment proposed by S.J.R. 14, 1995, and adopted by the people May 16, 1995]

Section 3a. Applicability of qualifications for appointment to legislative vacancy. [Section 3a was designated section 1b, which was created by S.J.R. 14, 1995, and adopted by the people May 16, 1995; Repealed Dec. 31, 1999, as specified in text of section adopted by the people May 16, 1995]

Section 4. Term of office of legislators; classification of Senators. (1) The Senators shall be elected for the term of four years, and Representatives for the term of two years. The term of each Senator and Representative shall commence on the second Monday in January following his election, and shall continue for the full period of four years or two years, as the case may be, unless a different commencing day for such terms shall have been appointed by law.

(2) The Senators shall continue to be divided into two classes, in accordance with the division by lot provided for under the former provisions of this Constitution, so that one-half, as nearly as possible, of the number of Senators shall be elected biennially.

(3) Any Senator or Representative whose term, under the former provisions of this section, would have expired on the first Monday in January 1961, shall continue in office until the second Monday in January 1961. [Constitution of 1859; Amendment proposed by S.J.R. 23, 1951,

and adopted by the people Nov. 4, 1952; Amendment proposed by S.J.R. 28, 1959, and adopted by the people Nov. 8, 1960]

Section 5. Census. [Constitution of 1859; Repeal proposed by H.J.R. 16, 1971, and adopted by the people May 23, 1972]

Section 6. Apportionment of Senators and Representatives. [Constitution of 1859; Amendment proposed by initiative petition filed July 3, 1952, and adopted by the people Nov. 4, 1952; Repeal proposed by H.J.R. 6, 1985, and adopted by the people Nov. 4, 1986 (present section 6 of this Article adopted in lieu of this section)]

Section 6. Apportionment of Senators and Representatives. (1) At the regular session of the Legislative Assembly next following an enumeration of the inhabitants by the United States Government, the number of Senators and Representatives shall be fixed by law and apportioned among legislative districts according to population. A senatorial district shall consist of two representative districts. Any Senator whose term continues through the next regular legislative session after the effective date of the reapportionment shall be specifically assigned to a senatorial district. The ratio of Senators and Representatives, respectively, to population shall be determined by dividing the total population of the state by the number of Senators and by the number of Representatives. A reapportionment by the Legislative Assembly shall become operative no sooner than September 1 of the year of reapportionment.

(2) This subsection governs judicial review and correction of a reapportionment enacted by the Legislative Assembly.

(a) Original jurisdiction is vested in the Supreme Court, upon the petition of any elector of the state filed with the Supreme Court on or before August 1 of the year in which the Legislative Assembly enacts a reapportionment, to review any reapportionment so enacted.

(b) If the Supreme Court determines that the reapportionment thus reviewed complies with subsection (1) of this section and all law applicable thereto, it shall dismiss the petition by written opinion on or before September 1 of the same year and the reapportionment shall become operative on September 1.

(c) If the Supreme Court determines that the reapportionment does not comply with subsection (1) of this section and all law applicable thereto, the reapportionment shall be void. In its written opinion, the Supreme Court shall specify with particularity wherein the reapportionment fails to comply. The opinion shall further direct the Secretary of State to draft a reapportionment of the Senators and Representatives in accordance with the provisions of subsection (1) of this section and all law applicable thereto. The Supreme Court shall file its order with the Secretary of State on or before September 15. The Secretary of State shall conduct a hearing on the reapportionment at which the public may submit evidence, views and argument. The Secretary of State shall cause a transcription of the hearing to be prepared which, with the evidence, shall become part of the record. The Secretary of State shall file the corrected reapportionment with the Supreme Court on or before November 1 of the same year.

(d) On or before November 15, the Supreme Court shall review the corrected reapportionment to assure its compliance with subsection (1) of this section and all law applicable thereto and may further correct the reapportionment if the court considers correction to be necessary.

(e) The corrected reapportionment shall become operative upon November 15.

Constitution

(3) This subsection governs enactment, judicial review and correction of a reapportionment if the Legislative Assembly fails to enact any reapportionment by July 1 of the year of the regular session of the Legislative Assembly next following an enumeration of the inhabitants by the United States Government.

(a) The Secretary of State shall make a reapportionment of the Senators and Representatives in accordance with the provisions of subsection (1) of this section and all law applicable thereto. The Secretary of State shall conduct a hearing on the reapportionment at which the public may submit evidence, views and argument. The Secretary of State shall cause a transcription of the hearing to be prepared which, with the evidence, shall become part of the record. The reapportionment so made shall be filed with the Supreme Court by August 15 of the same year. It shall become operative on September 15.

(b) Original jurisdiction is vested in the Supreme Court upon the petition of any elector of the state filed with the Supreme Court on or before September 15 of the same year to review any reapportionment and the record made by the Secretary of State.

(c) If the Supreme Court determines that the reapportionment thus reviewed complies with subsection (1) of this section and all law applicable thereto, it shall dismiss the petition by written opinion on or before October 15 of the same year and the reapportionment shall become operative on October 15.

(d) If the Supreme Court determines that the reapportionment does not comply with subsection (1) of this section and all law applicable thereto, the reapportionment shall be void. The Supreme Court shall return the reapportionment by November 1 to the Secretary of State accompanied by a written opinion specifying with particularity wherein the reapportionment fails to comply. The opinion shall further direct the Secretary of State to correct the reapportionment in those particulars, and in no others, and file the corrected reapportionment with the Supreme Court on or before December 1 of the same year.

(e) On or before December 15, the Supreme Court shall review the corrected reapportionment to assure its compliance with subsection (1) of this section and all law applicable thereto and may further correct the reapportionment if the court considers correction to be necessary.

(f) The reapportionment shall become operative on December 15.

(4) Any reapportionment that becomes operative as provided in this section is a law of the state except for purposes of initiative and referendum. A reapportionment shall not be operative before the date on which an appeal may be taken therefrom or before the date specified in this section, whichever is later.

(5) Notwithstanding section 18, Article II of this Constitution, after the convening of the next regular legislative session following the reapportionment, a Senator whose term continues through that legislative session is subject to recall by the electors of the district to which the Senator is assigned and not by the electors of the district existing before the latest reapportionment. The number of signatures required on the recall petition is 15 percent of the total votes cast for all candidates for Governor at the most recent election at which a candidate for Governor was elected to a full term in the two representative districts comprising the senatorial district to which the Senator was assigned. [Created through H.J.R. 6, 1985,

and adopted by the people Nov. 4, 1986 (this section adopted in lieu of former section 6 of this Article)]

Section 7. Senatorial districts; senatorial and representative subdistricts. A senatorial district, when more than one county shall constitute the same, shall be composed of contiguous counties, and no county shall be divided in creating such senatorial districts. Senatorial or representative districts comprising not more than one county may be divided into subdistricts from time to time by law. Subdistricts shall be composed of contiguous territory within the district; and the ratios to population of senators or representatives, as the case may be, elected from the subdistricts, shall be substantially equal within the district. [Constitution of 1859; Amendment proposed by H.J.R. 20, 1953, and adopted by the people Nov. 2, 1954]

Section 8. Qualification of Senators and Representatives; effect of felony conviction. (1) No person shall be a Senator or Representative who at the time of election is not a citizen of the United States; nor anyone who has not been for one year next preceding the election an inhabitant of the district from which the Senator or Representative may be chosen. However, for purposes of the general election next following the operative date of an apportionment under section 6 of this Article, the person must have been an inhabitant of the district from January 1 of the year following the reapportionment to the date of the election.

(2) Senators and Representatives shall be at least twenty one years of age.

(3) No person shall be a Senator or Representative who has been convicted of a felony during:

(a) The term of office of the person as a Senator or Representative; or

(b) The period beginning on the date of the election at which the person was elected to the office of Senator or Representative and ending on the first day of the term of office to which the person was elected.

(4) No person is eligible to be elected as a Senator or Representative if that person has been convicted of a felony and has not completed the sentence received for the conviction prior to the date that person would take office if elected. As used in this subsection, "sentence received for the conviction" includes a term of imprisonment, any period of probation or post-prison supervision and payment of a monetary obligation imposed as all or part of a sentence.

(5) Notwithstanding sections 11 and 15, Article IV of this Constitution:

(a) The office of a Senator or Representative convicted of a felony during the term to which the Senator or Representative was elected or appointed shall become vacant on the date the Senator or Representative is convicted.

(b) A person elected to the office of Senator or Representative and convicted of a felony during the period beginning on the date of the election and ending on the first day of the term of office to which the person was elected shall be ineligible to take office and the office shall become vacant on the first day of the next term of office.

(6) Subject to subsection (4) of this section, a person who is ineligible to be a Senator or Representative under subsection (3) of this section may:

(a) Be a Senator or Representative after the expiration of the term of office during which the person is ineligible; and

(b) Be a candidate for the office of Senator or Representative prior to the expiration of the term of office during which the person is ineligible.

(7) No person shall be a Senator or Representative who at all times during the term of office of the person as a Senator or Representative is not an inhabitant of the district from which the Senator or Representative may be chosen or has been appointed to represent. A person shall not lose status as an inhabitant of a district if the person is absent from the district for purposes of business of the Legislative Assembly. Following the operative date of an apportionment under section 6 of this Article, until the expiration of the term of office of the person, a person may be an inhabitant of any district. [Constitution of 1859; Amendment proposed by H.J.R. 6, 1985, and adopted by the people Nov. 4, 1986; Amendment proposed by S.J.R. 33, 1993, and adopted by the people Nov. 8, 1994; Amendment proposed by S.J.R. 14, 1995, and adopted by the people May 16, 1995]

Section 8a. Applicability of qualification for legislative office. [Created by S.J.R. 14, 1995, and adopted by the people May 16, 1995; Repealed Dec. 31, 1999, as specified in text of section adopted by the people May 16, 1995]

Section 9. Legislators free from arrest and not subject to civil process in certain cases; words uttered in debate. Senators and Representatives in all cases, except for treason, felony, or breaches of the peace, shall be privileged from arrest during the session of the Legislative Assembly, and in going to and returning from the same; and shall not be subject to any civil process during the session of the Legislative Assembly, nor during the fifteen days next before the commencement thereof: Nor shall a member for words uttered in debate in either house, be questioned in any other place.—

Section 10. Regular sessions of the Legislative Assembly. The sessions of the Legislative Assembly shall be held biennially at the Capitol of the State commencing on the second Monday of September, in the year eighteen hundred and fifty eight, and on the same day of every second year thereafter, unless a different day shall have been appointed by law.—

Section 10a. Emergency sessions of the Legislative Assembly. In the event of an emergency the Legislative Assembly shall be convened by the presiding officers of both Houses at the Capitol of the State at times other than required by section 10 of this Article upon the written request of the majority of the members of each House to commence within five days after receipt of the minimum requisite number of requests. [Created through H.J.R. 28, 1975, and adopted by the people Nov. 2, 1976]

Section 11. Legislative officers; rules of proceedings; adjournments. Each house when assembled, shall choose its own officers, judge of the election, qualifications, and returns of its own members; determine its own rules of proceeding, and sit upon its own adjournments; but neither house shall without the concurrence of the other, adjourn for more than three days, nor to any other place than that in which it may be sitting.—

Section 12. Quorum; failure to effect organization. Two thirds of each house shall constitute a quorum to do business, but a smaller number may meet; adjourn from day to day, and compel the attendance of absent members. A quorum being in attendance, if either house fail to effect an organization within the first five days thereafter, the members of the house so failing shall be entitled to no compensation from the end of the said five days until an organization shall have been effected.—

Section 13. Journal; when yeas and nays to be entered. Each house shall keep a journal of its proceedings.—The yeas and nays on any question, shall at the request of any two members, be entered, together with the names of the members demanding the same, on the journal; provided that on a motion to adjourn it shall require one tenth of the members present to order the yeas, and nays.

Section 14. Deliberations to be open; rules to implement requirement. The deliberations of each house, of committees of each house or joint committees and of committees of the whole, shall be open. Each house shall adopt rules to implement the requirement of this section and the houses jointly shall adopt rules to implement the requirements of this section in any joint activity that the two houses may undertake. [Constitution of 1859; Amendment proposed by S.J.R. 36, 1973, and adopted by the people Nov. 5, 1974; Amendment proposed by H.J.R. 29, 1977, and adopted by the people May 23, 1978]

Section 15. Punishment and expulsion of members. Either house may punish its members for disorderly behavior, and may with the concurrence of two thirds, expel a member; but not a second time for the same cause.—

Section 16. Punishment of nonmembers. Either house, during its session, may punish by imprisonment, any person, not a member, who shall have been guilty of disrespect to the house by disorderly or contemptious (sic) behavior in its presence, but such imprisonment shall not at any time, exceed twenty (sic) twenty four hours.—

Section 17. General powers of Legislative Assembly. Each house shall have all powers necessary for a branch of the Legislative Department, of a free, and independant (sic) State.—

Section 18. Where bills to originate. Bills may originate in either house, but may be amended, or rejected in the other; except that bills for raising revenue shall originate in the House of Representatives.—

Section 19. Reading of bills; vote on final passage. Every bill shall be read by title only on three several days, in each house, unless in case of emergency two-thirds of the house where such bill may be pending shall, by a vote of yeas and nays, deem it expedient to dispense with this rule; provided, however, on its final passage such bill shall be read section by section unless such requirement be suspended by a vote of two-thirds of the house where such bill may be pending, and the vote on the final passage of every bill or joint resolution shall be taken by yeas and nays. [Constitution of 1859; Amendment proposed by S.J.R. 15, 1945, and adopted by the people Nov. 5, 1946]

Section 20. Subject and title of Act. Every Act shall embrace but one subject, and matters properly connected therewith, which subject shall be expressed in the title. But if any subject shall be embraced in an Act which shall not be expressed in the title, such Act shall be void only as to so much thereof as shall not be expressed in the title.

This section shall not be construed to prevent the inclusion in an amendatory Act, under a proper title, of matters otherwise germane to the same general subject, although the title or titles of the original Act or Acts may not have been sufficiently broad to have permitted such matter to have been so included in such original Act or

Acts, or any of them. [Constitution of 1859; Amendment proposed by S.J.R. 41, 1951, and adopted by the people Nov. 4, 1952]

Section 21. Acts to be plainly worded. Every act, and joint resolution shall be plainly worded, avoiding as far as practicable the use of technical terms.—

Section 22. Mode of revision and amendment. No act shall ever be revised, or amended by mere reference to its title, but the act revised, or section amended shall be set forth, and published at full length. However, if, at any session of the Legislative Assembly, there are enacted two or more acts amending the same section, each of the acts shall be given effect to the extent that the amendments do not conflict in purpose. If the amendments conflict in purpose, the act last signed by the Governor shall control. [Constitution of 1859; Amendment proposed by S.J.R. 28, 1975, and adopted by the people Nov. 2, 1976]

Section 23. Certain local and special laws prohibited. The Legislative Assembly, shall not pass special or local laws, in any of the following enumerated cases, that is to say:—

Regulating the jurisdiction, and duties of justices of the peace, and of constables;

For the punishment of Crimes, and Misdemeanors;

Regulating the practice in Courts of Justice;

Providing for changing the venue in civil, and Criminal cases;

Granting divorces;

Changing the names of persons;

For laying, opening, and working on highways, and for the election, or appointment of supervisors;

Vacating roads, Town plats, Streets, Alleys, and Public squares;

Summoning and empanneling (sic) grand, and petit jurors;

For the assessment and collection of Taxes, for State, County, Township, or road purposes;

Providing for supporting Common schools, and for the preservation of school funds;

In relation to interest on money;

Providing for opening, and conducting the elections of State, County, and Township officers, and designating the places of voting;

Providing for the sale of real estate, belonging to minors, or other persons laboring under legal disabilities, by executors, administrators, guardians, or trustees.—

Section 24. Suit against state. Provision may be made by general law, for bringing suit against the State, as to all liabilities originating after, or existing at the time of the adoption of this Constitution; but no special act authorizeing (sic) such suit to be brought, or making compensation to any person claiming damages against the State, shall ever be passed.—

Section 25. Majority necessary to pass bills and resolutions; special requirements for bills raising revenue; signatures of presiding officers required. (1) Except as otherwise provided in subsection (2) of this section, a majority of all the members elected to each House shall be necessary to pass every bill or Joint resolution.

(2) Three-fifths of all members elected to each House shall be necessary to pass bills for raising revenue.

(3) All bills, and Joint resolutions passed, shall be signed by the presiding officers of the respective houses.

[Constitution of 1859; Amendment proposed by H.J.R. 14, 1995, and adopted by the people May 21, 1996]

Section 26. Protest by member. Any member of either house, shall have the right to protest, and have his protest, with his reasons for dissent, entered on the journal.—

Section 27. All statutes public laws; exceptions. Every Statute shall be a public law, unless otherwise declared in the Statute itself.—

Section 28. When Act takes effect. No act shall take effect, until ninety days from the end of the session at which the same shall have been passed, except in case of emergency; which emergency shall be declared in the preamble, or in the body of the law.

Section 29. Compensation of members. The members of the Legislative Assembly shall receive for their services a salary to be established and paid in the same manner as the salaries of other elected state officers and employes. [Constitution of 1859; Amendment proposed by S.J.R. 3, 1941, and adopted by the people Nov. 3, 1942; Amendment proposed by H.J.R. 5, 1949, and adopted by the people Nov. 7, 1950; Amendment proposed by H.J.R. 8, 1961, and adopted by the people May 18, 1962]

Section 30. Members not eligible to other offices. No Senator or Representative shall, during the time for which he may have been elected, be eligible to any office the election to which is vested in the Legislative Assembly; nor shall be appointed to any civil office of profit which shall have been created, or the emoluments of which shall have been increased during such term; but this latter provision shall not be construed to apply to any officer elective by the people.—

Section 31. Oath of members. The members of the Legislative Assembly shall before they enter on the duties of their respective offices, take and subscribe the following oath or affirmation;—I do solemnly swear (or affirm as the case may be) that I will support the Constitution of the United States, and the Constitution of the State of Oregon, and that I will faithfully discharge the duties of Senator (or Representative as the case may be) according to the best of my Ability, And such oath may be administered by the Govenor (sic), Secretary of State, or a judge of the Supreme Court.—

Section 32. Income tax defined by federal law; review of tax laws required. Notwithstanding any other provision of this Constitution, the Legislative Assembly, in any law imposing a tax or taxes on, in respect to or measured by income, may define the income on, in respect to or by which such tax or taxes are imposed or measured, by reference to any provision of the laws of the United States as the same may be or become effective at any time or from time to time, and may prescribe exceptions or modifications to any such provisions. At each regular session the Legislative Assembly shall, and at any special session may, provide for a review of the Oregon laws imposing a tax upon or measured by income, but no such laws shall be amended or repealed except by a legislative Act. [Created through H.J.R. 3, 1969, and adopted by the people Nov. 3, 1970]

Section 33. Reduction of criminal sentences approved by initiative or referendum process. Notwithstanding the provisions of section 25 of this Article, a two-thirds vote of all the members elected to each house shall be necessary to pass a bill that reduces a criminal sentence approved by the people under section

1 of this Article. [Created through initiative petition filed Nov. 16, 1993, and adopted by the people Nov. 8, 1994]

ARTICLE V
EXECUTIVE DEPARTMENT

Section 1. Governor as chief executive; term of office; period of eligibility. The cheif (sic) executive power of the State, shall be vested in a Governor, who shall hold his office for the term of four years; and no person shall be eligible to such office more than Eight, in any period of twelve years.—

Section 2. Qualifications of Governor. No person except a citizen of the United States, shall be eligible to the Office of Governor, nor shall any person be eligible to that office who shall not have attained the age of thirty years, and who shall not have been three years next preceding his election, a resident within this State. The minimum age requirement of this section does not apply to a person who succeeds to the office of Governor under section 8a of this Article. [Constitution of 1859; Amendment proposed by H.J.R. 52, 1973, and adopted by the people Nov. 5, 1974]

Section 3. Who not eligible. No member of Congress, or person holding any office under the United States, or under this State, or under any other power, shall fill the Office of Governor, except as may be otherwise provided in this Constitution.—

Section 4. Election of Governor. The Governor shall be elected by the qualified Electors of the State at the times, and places of choosing members of the Legislative Assembly; and the returns of every Election for Governor, shall be sealed up, and transmitted to the Secretary of State; directed to the Speaker of the House of Representatives, who shall open, and publish them in the presence of both houses of the Legislative Assembly.—

Section 5. Greatest number of votes decisive; election by legislature in case of tie. The person having the highest number of votes for Governor, shall be elected; but in case two or more persons shall have an equal and the highest number of votes for Governor, the two houses of the Legislative Assembly at the next regular session

thereof, shall forthwith by joint vote, proceed to elect one of the said persons Governor.—

Section 6. Contested elections. Contested Elections for Governor shall be determined by the Legislative Assembly in such manner as may be prescribed by law.—

Section 7. Term of office. The official term of the Governor shall be four years; and shall commence at such times as may be prescribed by this constitution, or prescribed by law.—

Section 8. Vacancy in office of Governor. [Constitution of 1859; Amendment proposed by S.J.R. 10, 1920 (s.s.), and adopted by the people May 21, 1920; Amendment proposed by S.J.R. 8, 1945, and adopted by the people Nov. 5, 1946; Repeal proposed by initiative petition filed July 7, 1972, and adopted by the people Nov. 7, 1972 (present section 8a of this Article adopted in lieu of this section)]

Section 8a. Vacancy in office of Governor. In case of the removal from office of the Governor, or of his death, resignation, or disability to discharge the duties of his office as prescribed by law, the Secretary of State; or if there be none, or in case of his removal from office, death, resignation, or disability to discharge the duties of his office as prescribed by law, then the State Treasurer; or if there be none, or in case of his removal from office, death, resignation, or disability to discharge the duties of his office as prescribed by law, then the President of the Senate; or if there be none, or in case of his removal from office, death, resignation, or disability to discharge the duties of his office as prescribed by law, then the Speaker of the House of Representatives, shall become Governor until the disability be removed, or a Governor be elected at the next general biennial election. The Governor elected to fill the vacancy shall hold office for the unexpired term of the outgoing Governor. The Secretary of State or the State Treasurer shall appoint a person to fill his office until the election of a Governor, at which time the office so filled by appointment shall be filled by election; or, in the event of a disability of the Governor, to be Acting Secretary of State or Acting State Treasurer until the disability be removed. The person so appointed shall not be eligible to succeed to the office of Governor by automatic succession under this section during the term of his appointment. [Created through initiative petition filed July 7, 1972, and adopted by the people Nov. 7, 1972 (this section adopted in lieu of former section 8 of this Article)]

Section 9. Governor as commander in chief of state military forces. The Governor shall be commander in cheif (sic) of the military, and naval forces of this State, and may call out such forces to execute the laws, to suppress insurrection (sic), or to repel invasion.—

Section 10. Governor to see laws executed. He shall take care that the Laws be faithfully executed.—

Section 11. Recommendations to legislature. He shall from time to time give to the Legislative Assembly information touching the condition of the State, and recommend (sic) such measures as he shall judge to be expedient[.]

Section 12. Governor may convene legislature. He may on extraordinary occasions convene the Legislative Assembly by proclamation, and shall state to both houses when assembled, the purpose for which they shall have been convened.—

Section 13. Transaction of governmental business. He shall transact all necessary business with the officers of government, and may require information in writing from the offices of the Administrative, and Military

Constitution

385

Departments upon any subject relating to the duties of their respective offices.—

Section 14. Reprieves, commutations and pardons; remission of fines and forfeitures. He shall have power to grant reprieves, commutations, and pardons, after conviction, for all offences (sic) except treason, subject to such regulations as may be provided by law. Upon conviction for treason he shall have power to suspend the execution of the sentence until the case shall be reported to the Legislative Assembly, at its next meeting, when the Legislative Assembly shall either grant a pardon, commute the sentence, direct the execution of the sentence, or grant a farther (sic) reprieve.—

He shall have power to remit fines, and forfeitures, under such regulations as may be prescribed by law; and shall report to the Legislative Assembly at its next meeting each case of reprieve, commutation, or pardon granted, and the reasons for granting the same; and also the names of all persons in whose favor remission of fines, and forfeitures shall have been made, and the several amounts remitted[.]

Section 15. [This section of the Constitution of 1859 was redesignated as section 15b by the amendment proposed by S.J.R. 12, 1915, and adopted by the people Nov. 7, 1916]

Section 15a. Single item and emergency clause veto. The Governor shall have power to veto single items in appropriation bills, and any provision in new bills declaring an emergency, without thereby affecting any other provision of such bill. [Created through S.J.R. 12, 1915, and adopted by the people Nov. 7, 1916; Amendment proposed by S.J.R. 13, 1921, and adopted by the people June 7, 1921]

Section 15b. Legislative enactments; approval by Governor; notice of intention to disapprove; disapproval and reconsideration by legislature; failure of Governor to return bill. (1) Every bill which shall have passed the Legislative Assembly shall, before it becomes a law, be presented to the Governor; if the Governor approve, the Governor shall sign it; but if not, the Governor shall return it with written objections to that house in which it shall have originated, which house shall enter the objections at large upon the journal and proceed to reconsider it.

(2) If, after such reconsideration, two-thirds of the members present shall agree to pass the bill, it shall be sent, together with the objections, to the other house, by which it shall likewise be reconsidered, and, if approved by two-thirds of the members present, it shall become a law. But in all such cases, the votes of both houses shall be determined by yeas and nays, and the names of the members voting for or against the bill shall be entered on the journal of each house respectively.

(3) If any bill shall not be returned by the Governor within five days (Saturdays and Sundays excepted) after it shall have been presented to the Governor, it shall be a law without signature, unless the general adjournment shall prevent its return, in which case it shall be a law, unless the Governor within thirty days next after the adjournment (Saturdays and Sundays excepted) shall file such bill, with written objections thereto, in the office of the Secretary of State, who shall lay the same before the Legislative Assembly at its next session in like manner as if it had been returned by the Governor.

(4) Before filing a bill after adjournment with written objections, the Governor must announce publicly the possible intention to do so at least five days before filing the bill with written objections. However, nothing in this subsection requires the Governor to file any bill with objections because of the announcement. [Created through S.J.R. 12, 1915, and adopted by the people Nov. 7, 1916; Amendment proposed by H.J.R. 9, 1937, and adopted by the people Nov. 8, 1938; Amendment proposed by S.J.R. 4, 1987, and adopted by the people Nov. 8, 1988]

Note: See note under section 15, Article V.

Section 16. Governor to Fill Vacancies by Appointment. When during a recess of the legislative assembly a vacancy occurs in any office, the appointment to which is vested in the legislative assembly, or when at any time a vacancy occurs in any other state office, or in the office of judge of any court, the governor shall fill such vacancy by appointment, which shall expire when a successor has been elected and qualified. When any vacancy occurs in any elective office of the state or of any district or county thereof, the vacancy shall be filled at the next general election, provided such vacancy occurs more than sixty-one (61) days prior to such general election. [Constitution of 1859; Amendment proposed by H.J.R. 5, 1925, and adopted by the people Nov. 2, 1926; Amendment proposed by H.J.R. 30, 1985, and adopted by the people May 20, 1986; Amendment proposed by S.J.R. 4, 1993, and adopted by the people Nov. 8, 1994]

Note: The leadline to section 16 was a part of the measure submitted to the people by H.J.R. 5, 1925.

Section 17. Governor to issue writs of election to fill vacancies in legislature. He shall issue writs of Election to fill such vacancies as may have occured (sic) in the Legislative Assembly.

Section 18. Commissions. All commissions shall issue in the name of the State; shall be signed by the Govenor (sic), sealed with the seal of the State, and attested by the Secretary of State.—

ARTICLE VI
ADMINISTRATIVE DEPARTMENT

Section 1. Election of Secretary and Treasurer of state; terms of office; period of eligibility. There shall be elected by the qualified electors of the State, at the times and places of choosing Members of the Legislative Assembly, a Secretary, and Treasurer of State, who shall severally hold their offices for the term of four years; but no person shall be eligible to either of said offices more than Eight in any period of Twelve years.—

Section 2. Duties of Secretary of State. The Secretary of State shall keep a fair record of the official acts of the Legislative Assembly, and Executive Department of the State; and shall when required lay the same, and all matters relative thereto before either branch of the Legislative Assembly. He shall be by virtue of his office, Auditor of public Accounts, and shall perform such other duties as shall be assigned him by law.

Section 3. Seal of state. There shall be a seal of State, kept by the Secretary of State for official purposes, which shall be called "The seal of the State of Oregon."—

Section 4. Powers and duties of Treasurer. The powers, and duties of the Treasurer of State shall be such as may be prescribed by law.—

Section 5. Offices and records of executive officers. The Governor, Secretary of State, and Treasurer of State shall severally keep the public records, books and papers at the seat of government in any manner relating to their respective offices. [Constitution of 1859; Amendment proposed by S.J.R. 13, 1985, and adopted by the people Nov. 4, 1986]

Section 6. County Officers: There shall be elected in each county by the qualified electors thereof at the time of holding general elections, a county clerk, treasurer and sheriff who shall severally hold their offices for the term of four years. [Constitution of 1859; Amendment proposed by initiative petition filed June 9, 1920, and adopted by the people Nov. 2, 1920; Amendment proposed by H.J.R. 7, 1955, and adopted by the people Nov. 6, 1956]

Note: The leadline to section 6 was a part of the measure proposed by initiative petition filed June 9, 1920, and adopted by the people Nov. 2, 1920.

Section 7. Other officers. Such other county, township, precinct, and City officers as may be necessary, shall be elected, or appointed in such manner as may be prescribed by law.—

Section 8. County officers' qualifications; location of offices of county and city officers; duties of such officers. Every county officer shall be an elector of the county, and the county assessor, county sheriff, county coroner and county surveyor shall possess such other qualifications as may be prescribed by law. All county and city officers shall keep their respective offices at such places therein, and perform such duties, as may be prescribed by law. [Constitution of 1859; Amendment proposed by H.J.R. 7, 1955, and adopted by the people Nov. 6, 1956; Amendment proposed by H.J.R. 42, 1971, and adopted by the people Nov. 7, 1972; Amendment proposed by H.J.R. 22, 1973, and adopted by the people Nov. 5, 1974]

Section 9. Vacancies in county, township, precinct and city offices. Vacancies in County, Township, precinct and City offices shall be filled in such manner as may be prescribed by law.—

Section 9a. County manager form of government. [Created through H.J.R. 3, 1943, and adopted by the people Nov. 7, 1944; Repeal proposed by H.J.R. 22, 1957, and adopted by the people Nov. 4, 1958]

Section 10. County home rule under county charter. The Legislative Assembly shall provide by law a method whereby the legal voters of any county, by majority vote of such voters voting thereon at any legally called election, may adopt, amend, revise or repeal a county charter. A county charter may provide for the exercise by the county of authority over matters of county concern. Local improvements shall be financed only by taxes, assessments or charges imposed on benefited property, unless otherwise provided by law or charter. A county charter shall prescribe the organization of the county government and shall provide directly, or by its authority, for the number, election or appointment, qualifications, tenure, compensation, powers and duties of such officers as the county deems necessary. Such officers shall among them exercise all the powers and perform all the duties, as distributed by the county charter or by its authority, now or hereafter, by the Constitution or laws of this state, granted to or imposed upon any coun-

ty officer. Except as expressly provided by general law, a county charter shall not affect the selection, tenure, compensation, powers or duties prescribed by law for judges in their judicial capacity, for justices of the peace or for district attorneys. The initiative and referendum powers reserved to the people by this Constitution hereby are further reserved to the legal voters of every county relative to the adoption, amendment, revision or repeal of a county charter and to legislation passed by counties which have adopted such a charter; and no county shall require that referendum petitions be filed less than 90 days after the provisions of the charter or the legislation proposed for referral is adopted by the county governing body. To be circulated, referendum or initiative petitions shall set forth in full the charter or legislative provisions proposed for adoption or referral. Referendum petitions shall not be required to include a ballot title to be circulated. In a county a number of signatures of qualified voters equal to but not greater than four percent of the total number of all votes cast in the county for all candidates for Governor at the election at which a Governor was elected for a term of four years next preceding the filing of the petition shall be required for a petition to order a referendum on county legislation or a part thereof. A number of signatures equal to but not greater than six percent of the total number of votes cast in the county for all candidates for Governor at the election at which a Governor was elected for a term of four years next preceding the filing of the petition shall be required for a petition to propose an initiative ordinance. A number of signatures equal to but not greater than eight percent of the total number of votes cast in the county for all candidates for Governor at the election at which a Governor was elected for a term of four years next preceding the filing of the petition shall be required for a petition to propose a charter amendment. [Created through H.J.R. 22, 1957, and adopted by the people Nov. 4, 1958; Amendment proposed by S.J.R. 48, 1959, and adopted by the people Nov. 8, 1960; Amendment proposed by H.J.R. 21, 1977, and adopted by the people May 23, 1978]

ARTICLE VII (Amended)
JUDICIAL DEPARTMENT

Sec. 1. Courts; election of judges; term of office; compensation
1a. Retirement of judges; recall to temporary active service
2. Amendment's effect on courts, jurisdiction and judicial system; Supreme Court's original jurisdiction
2a. Temporary appointment and assignment of judges
2b. Inferior courts may be affected in certain respects by special or local laws
3. Jury trial; re-examination of issues by appellate court; record on appeal to Supreme Court; affirmance notwithstanding error; determination of case by Supreme Court
4. Supreme Court; terms; statements of decisions of court
5. Juries; indictment; information; verdict in civil cases
6. Incompetency or malfeasance of public officer
7. Oath of office of Judges of Supreme Court
8. Removal, suspension or censure of judges
9. Juries of less than 12 jurors

Section 1. Courts; election of judges; term of office; compensation. The judicial power of the state shall be vested in one supreme court and in such other courts as may from time to time be created by law. The judges of the supreme and other courts shall be elected by the legal voters of the state or of their respective districts for a

Constitution

term of six years, and shall receive such compensation as may be provided by law, which compensation shall not be diminished during the term for which they are elected. [Created through initiative petition filed July 7, 1910, and adopted by the people Nov. 8, 1910]

Section 1a. Retirement of judges; recall to temporary active service.
Notwithstanding the provisions of section 1, Article VII (Amended) of this Constitution, a judge of any court shall retire from judicial office at the end of the calendar year in which he attains the age of 75 years. The Legislative Assembly or the people may by law:

(1) Fix a lesser age for mandatory retirement not earlier than the end of the calendar year in which the judge attains the age of 70 years;

(2) Provide for recalling retired judges to temporary active service on the court from which they are retired; and

(3) Authorize or require the retirement of judges for physical or mental disability or any other cause rendering judges incapable of performing their judicial duties.

This section shall not affect the term to which any judge shall have been elected or appointed prior to or at the time of approval and ratification of this section. [Created through S.J.R. 3, 1959, and adopted by the people Nov. 8, 1960]

Section 2. Amendment's effect on courts, jurisdiction and judicial system; Supreme Court's original jurisdiction.
The courts, jurisdiction, and judicial system of Oregon, except so far as expressly changed by this amendment, shall remain as at present constituted until otherwise provided by law. But the supreme court may, in its own discretion, take original jurisdiction in mandamus, quo warranto and habeas corpus proceedings. [Created through initiative petition filed July 7, 1910, and adopted by the people Nov. 8, 1910]

Section 2a. Temporary appointment and assignment of judges.
The Legislative Assembly or the people may by law empower the Supreme Court to:

(1) Appoint retired judges of the Supreme Court or judges of courts inferior to the Supreme Court as temporary members of the Supreme Court.

(2) Appoint members of the bar as judges pro tempore of courts inferior to the Supreme Court.

(3) Assign judges of courts inferior to the Supreme Court to serve temporarily outside the district for which they were elected.

A judge or member of the bar so appointed or assigned shall while serving have all the judicial powers and duties of a regularly elected judge of the court to which he is assigned or appointed. [Created through S.J.R. 30, 1957, and adopted by the people Nov. 4, 1958]

Section 2b. Inferior courts may be affected in certain respects by special or local laws.
Notwithstanding the provisions of section 23, Article IV of this Constitution, laws creating courts inferior to the Supreme Court or prescribing and defining the jurisdiction of such courts or the manner in which such jurisdiction may be exercised, may be made applicable:

(1) To all judicial districts or other subdivisions of this state; or

(2) To designated classes of judicial districts or other subdivisions; or

(3) To particular judicial districts or other subdivisions. [Created through S.J.R. 34, 1961, and adopted by the people Nov. 6, 1962]

Section 3. Jury trial; re-examination of issues by appellate court; record on appeal to Supreme Court; affirmance notwithstanding error; determination of case by Supreme Court.
In actions at law, where the value in controversy shall exceed $750, the right of trial by jury shall be preserved, and no fact tried by a jury shall be otherwise re-examined in any court of this state, unless the court can affirmatively say there is no evidence to support the verdict. Until otherwise provided by law, upon appeal of any case to the supreme court, either party may have attached to the bill of exceptions the whole testimony, the instructions of the court to the jury, and any other matter material to the decision of the appeal. If the supreme court shall be of opinion, after consideration of all the matters thus submitted, that the judgment of the court appealed from was such as should have been rendered in the case, such judgment shall be affirmed, notwithstanding any error committed during the trial; or if, in any respect, the judgment appealed from should be changed, and the supreme court shall be of opinion that it can determine what judgment should have been entered in the court below, it shall direct such judgment to be entered in the same manner and with like effect as decrees are now entered in equity cases on appeal to the supreme court. Provided, that nothing in this section shall be construed to authorize the supreme court to find the defendant in a criminal case guilty of an offense for which a greater penalty is provided than that of which the accused was convicted in the lower court. [Created through initiative petition filed July 7, 1910, and adopted by the people Nov. 8, 1910; Amendment proposed by H.J.R. 71, 1973, and adopted by the people Nov. 5, 1974; Amendment proposed by H.J.R. 47, 1995, and adopted by the people May 21, 1996]

Section 4. Supreme Court; terms; statements of decisions of court.
The terms of the supreme court shall be appointed by law; but there shall be one term at the seat of government annually. At the close of each term the judges shall file with the secretary of state concise written statements of the decisions made at that term. [Created through initiative petition filed July 7, 1910, and adopted by the people Nov. 8, 1910]

Section 5. Juries; indictment; information.
[Created through initiative petition filed July 7, 1910, and adopted by the people Nov. 8, 1910; Amendment proposed by S.J.R. 23, 1957, and adopted by the people Nov. 4, 1958; Repeal proposed by S.J.R. 1, 1973, and adopted by the people Nov. 5, 1974 (present section 5 of this Article adopted in lieu of this section)]

Section 5. Juries; indictment; information; verdict in civil cases.
(1) The Legislative Assembly shall provide by law for:

(a) Selecting juries and qualifications of jurors;

(b) Drawing and summoning grand jurors from the regular jury list at any time, separate from the panel of petit jurors;

(c) Empaneling more than one grand jury in a county; and

(d) The sitting of a grand jury during vacation as well as session of the court.

(2) A grand jury shall consist of seven jurors chosen by lot from the whole number of jurors in attendance at the court, five of whom must concur to find an indictment.

(3) Except as provided in subsections (4) and (5) of this section, a person shall be charged in a circuit court with the commission of any crime punishable as a felony only on indictment by a grand jury.

(4) The district attorney may charge a person on an information filed in circuit court of a crime punishable as a felony if the person appears before the judge of the circuit court and knowingly waives indictment.

(5) The district attorney may charge a person on an information filed in circuit court if, after a preliminary hearing before a magistrate, the person has been held to answer upon a showing of probable cause that a crime punishable as a felony has been committed and that the person has committed it, or if the person knowingly waives preliminary hearing.

(6) An information shall be substantially in the form provided by law for an indictment. The district attorney may file an amended indictment or information whenever, by ruling of the court, an indictment or information is held to be defective in form.

(7) In civil cases three-fourths of the jury may render a verdict. [Created through S.J.R. 1, 1973, and adopted by the people Nov. 5, 1974 (this section adopted in lieu of former section 5 of this Article)]

Section 6. Incompetency or malfeasance of public officer. Public officers shall not be impeached; but incompetency, corruption, malfeasance or delinquency in office may be tried in the same manner as criminal offenses, and judgment may be given of dismissal from office, and such further punishment as may have been prescribed by law. [Created through initiative petition filed July 7, 1910, and adopted by the people Nov. 8, 1910]

Section 7. Oath of office of Judges of Supreme Court. Every judge of the supreme court, before entering upon the duties of his office, shall take and subscribe, and transmit to the secretary of state, the following oath:

"I, _____, do solemnly swear (or affirm) that I will support the constitution of the United States, and the constitution of the State of Oregon, and that I will faithfully and impartially discharge the duties of a judge of the supreme court of this state, according to the best of my ability, and that I will not accept any other office, except judicial offices, during the term for which I have been elected." [Created through initiative petition filed July 7, 1910, and adopted by the people Nov. 8, 1910]

Section 8. Removal, suspension or censure of judges. (1) In the manner provided by law, and notwithstanding section 1 of this Article, a judge of any court may be removed or suspended from his judicial office by the Supreme Court, or censured by the Supreme Court, for:

(a) Conviction in a court of this or any other state, or of the United States, of a crime punishable as a felony or a crime involving moral turpitude; or

(b) Wilful misconduct in a judicial office where such misconduct bears a demonstrable relationship to the effective performance of judicial duties; or

(c) Wilful or persistent failure to perform judicial duties; or

(d) Generally incompetent performance of judicial duties; or

(e) Wilful violation of any rule of judicial conduct as shall be established by the Supreme Court; or

(f) Habitual drunkenness or illegal use of narcotic or dangerous drugs.

(2) Notwithstanding section 6 of this Article, the methods provided in this section, section 1a of this Article and in section 18, Article II of this Constitution, are the exclusive methods of the removal, suspension, or censure of a judge. [Created through S.J.R. 9, 1967, and adopted by the people Nov. 5, 1968; Amendment proposed by S.J.R. 48, 1975, and adopted by the people May 25, 1976]

Section 9. Juries of less than 12 jurors. Provision may be made by law for juries consisting of less than 12 but not less than six jurors. [Created through S.J.R. 17, 1971, and adopted by the people Nov. 7, 1972]

ARTICLE VII (Original)
THE JUDICIAL DEPARTMENT

Note: Original Article VII, compiled below, has been supplanted in part by amended Article VII and in part by statutes enacted by the Legislative Assembly. The provisions of original Article VII relating to courts, jurisdiction and the judicial system, by the terms of section 2 of amended Article VII, are given the status of a statute and are subject to change by statutes enacted by the Legislative Assembly, except so far as changed by amended Article VII.

Section 1. Courts in which judicial power vested. The Judicial power of the State shall be vested in a Suprume (sic) Court, Circuits (sic) Courts, and County Courts, which shall be Courts of Record having general jurisdiction, to be defined, limited, and regulated by law in accordance with this Constitution.—Justices of the Peace may also be invested with limited Judicial powers, and Municipal Courts may be created to administer the regulations of incorporated towns, and cities.—

Section 2. Supreme Court. The Supreme Court shall consist of Four Justices to be chosen in districts by the electors thereof, who shall be citizens of the United States, and who shall have resided in the State at least three years next preceding their election, and after their election to reside in their respective districts: The number of Justices, the Districts may be increased, but shall never exceed seven; and the boundaries of districts may be changed, but no Change of Districts, shall have the effect to remove a Judge from office, or require him to change his residence without his consent. [Constitution of 1859; Amendment proposed by S.J.R. 7, 2001, and adopted by the people Nov. 5, 2002]

Section 3. Terms of office of Judges. The Judges first chosen under this Constitution shall allot among themselves, their terms of office, so that the term of one of

Constitution

389

them shall expire in Two years, one in Four years, and Two in Six years, and thereafter, one or more shall be chosen every Two years to serve for the term of Six years.—

Section 4. Vacancy. Every vacancy in the office of Judge of the Supreme Court shall be filled by election for the remainder of the vacant term, unless it would expire at the next election, and until so filled, or when it would so expire, the Governor shall fill the vacancy by appointment.

Section 5. Chief Justice. The Judge who has the shortest term to serve, or the oldest of several having such shortest term, and not holding by appointment shall be the Cheif (sic) Justice.—

Section 6. Jurisdiction. The Supreme Court shall have jurisdiction only to revise the final decisions of the Circuit Courts, and every cause shall be tried, and every decision shall be made by those Judges only, or a majority of them, who did not try the cause, or make the decision in the Circuit Court.—

Section 7. Term of Supreme Court; statements of decisions of court. The terms of the Supreme Court shall be appointed by Law; but there shall be one term at the seat of Government annually:—

And at the close of each term the Judges shall file with the Secretary of State, Concise written Statements of the decisions made at that term.—

Note: Section 7 is in substance the same as section 4 of amended Article VII.

Section 8. Circuit court. The Circuits (sic) Courts shall be held twice at least in each year in each County organized for judicial purposes, by one of the Justices of the Supreme Court at times to be appointed by law; and at such other times as may be appointed by the Judges severally in pursuance of law.

Section 9. Jurisdiction of circuit courts. All judicial power, authority, and jurisdiction not vested by this Constitution, or by laws consistent therewith, exclusively in some other Court shall belong to the Circuit Courts, and they shall have appellate jurisdiction, and supervisory control over the County Courts, and all other inferior Courts, Officers, and tribunals.—

Section 10. Supreme and circuit judges; election in classes. The Legislative Assembly, may provide for the election of Supreme, and Circuit Judges, in distinct classes, one of which classes shall consist of three Justices of the Supreme Court, who shall not perform Circuit duty, and the other class shall consist of the necessary number of Circuit Judges, who shall hold full terms without allotment, and who shall take the same oath as the Supreme Judges. [Constitution of 1859; Amendment proposed by S.J.R. 7, 2001, and adopted by the people Nov. 5, 2002]

Section 11. County judges and terms of county courts. There shall be elected in each County for the term of Four years a County Judge, who shall hold the County Court at times to be regulated by law.—

Section 12. Jurisdiction of county courts; county commissioners. The County Court shall have the jurisdiction pertaining to Probate Courts, and boards of County Commissioners, and such other powers, and duties, and such civil Jurisdiction, not exceeding the amount or value of five hundred dollars, and such criminal jurisdiction not extending to death or imprisonment in the penitentiary, as may be prescribed by law.—But the Legislative Assembly may provide for the election of Two Commissioners to sit with the County Judge whilst transacting County business, in any, or all of the Counties, or may provide a seperate (sic) board for transacting such business.—

Section 13. Writs granted by county judge; habeas corpus proceedings. The County Judge may grant preliminary injuctions (sic), and such other writs as the Legislative Assembly may authorize him to grant, returnable to the Circuit Court, or otherwise as may be provided by law; and may hear, and decide questions arising upon habeas corpus; provided such decision be not against the authority, or proceedings of a Court, or Judge of equal, or higher jurisdiction.—

Section 14. Expenses of court in certain counties. The Counties having less than ten thousand inhabitants, shall be reimbursed wholly or in part for the salary, and expenses of the County Court by fees, percentage, & other equitable taxation, of the business done in said Court & in the office of the County Clerk. [Constitution of 1859; Amendment proposed by S.J.R. 7, 2001, and adopted by the people Nov. 5, 2002]

Section 15. County clerk; recorder. A County Clerk shall be elected in each County for the term of Two years, who shall keep all the public records, books, and papers of the County; record conveyances, and perform the duties of Clerk of the Circuit, and County Courts, and such other duties as may be prescribed by law:—But whenever the number of voters in any County shall exceed Twelve Hundred, the Legislative Assembly may authorize the election of one person as Clerk of the Circuit Court, one person as Clerk of the County Court, and one person Recorder of conveyances.—

Section 16. Sheriff. A sheriff shall be elected in each County for the term of Two years, who shall be the ministerial officer of the Circuit, and County Courts, and shall perform such other duties as may be prescribed by law.—

Section 17. Prosecuting attorneys. There shall be elected by districts comprised of one, or more counties, a sufficient number of prosecuting Attorneys, who shall be the law officers of the State, and of the counties within their respective districts, and shall perform such duties pertaining to the administration of Law, and general police as the Legislative Assembly may direct.—

Section 18. Verdict by Three-fourths Jury in Civil Cases; Jurors; Grand Jurors; Indictment May Be Amended, When. [Constitution of 1859; Amendment proposed by initiative petition filed Jan. 30, 1908, and adopted by the people June 1, 1908; Amendment proposed by H.J.R. 14, 1927, and adopted by the people June 28, 1927; Repeal proposed by S.J.R. 23, 1957, and adopted by the people Nov. 4, 1958]

Section 19. Official delinquencies. Public Officers shall not be impeached, but incompetency, corruption, malfeasance, or delinquency in office may be tried in the same manner as criminal offences (sic), and judgment may be given of dismissal from Office, and such further punishment as may here be prescribed by law.—

Note: Section 19 is the same as section 6 of amended Article VII.

Section 20. Removal of Judges of Supreme Court and prosecuting attorneys from office. The Govenor (sic) may remove from Office a Judge of the Supreme Court, or Prosecuting Attorney upon the Joint resolution of the Legislative Assembly, in which Two Thirds of the members elected to each house shall concur, for incompetency, Corruption, malfeasance, or delinquency in office, or other sufficient cause stated in such resolution.—

Section 21. Oath of office of Supreme Court Judges. Every judge of the Supreme Court before entering upon the duties of his office shall take, subscribe, and transmit to the Secretary of State the following oath.—I _____ do solemnly swear (or affirm) that I will support the Constitution of the United States, and the constitution of the State of Oregon, and that I will faithfully, and impartially discharge the duties of a Judge of the Supreme, and Circuits (sic) Courts of said State according to the best of my ability, and that I will not accept any other office, except Judicial offices during the term for which I have been elected.—

ARTICLE VIII
EDUCATION AND SCHOOL LANDS

Sec. 1. Superintendent of Public Instruction
    2. Common School Fund
    3. System of common schools
    4. Distribution of school fund income
    5. State Land Board; land management
    6. Qualifications of electors at school elections
    7. Prohibition of sale of state timber processed in Oregon
    8. Adequate and Equitable Funding

Section 1. Superintendent of Public Instruction
The Governor shall be superintendent of public instruction, and his powers, and duties in that capacity shall be such as may be prescribed by law; but after the term of five years from the adoption of this Constitution, it shall be competent for the Legislative Assembly to provide by law for the election of a superintendent, to provide for his compensation, and prescribe his powers and duties.

Section 2. Common School Fund. (1) The sources of the Common School Fund are:

(a) The proceeds of all lands granted to this state for educational purposes, except the lands granted to aid in the establishment of institutions of higher education under the Acts of February 14, 1859 (11 Stat. 383) and July 2, 1862 (12 Stat. 503).

(b) All the moneys and clear proceeds of all property which may accrue to the state by escheat.

(c) The proceeds of all gifts, devises and bequests, made by any person to the state for common school purposes.

(d) The proceeds of all property granted to the state, when the purposes of such grant shall not be stated.

(e) The proceeds of the five hundred thousand acres of land to which this state is entitled under the Act of September 4, 1841 (5 Stat. 455).

(f) The five percent of the net proceeds of the sales of public lands to which this state became entitled on her admission into the union.

(g) After providing for the cost of administration and any refunds or credits authorized by law, the proceeds from any tax or excise levied on, with respect to or measured by the extraction, production, storage, use, sale, distribution or receipt of oil or natural gas and the proceeds from any tax or excise levied on the ownership of oil or natural gas. However, the rate of such taxes shall not be greater than six percent of the market value of all oil and natural gas produced or salvaged from the earth or waters of this state as and when owned or produced. This paragraph does not include proceeds from any tax or excise as described in section 3, Article IX of this Constitution.

(2) All revenues derived from the sources mentioned in subsection (1) of this section shall become a part of the Common School Fund. The State Land Board may expend moneys in the Common School Fund to carry out its powers and duties under subsection (2) of section 5 of this Article. Unexpended moneys in the Common School Fund shall be invested as the Legislative Assembly shall provide by law and shall not be subject to the limitations of section 6, Article XI of this Constitution. The State Land Board may apply, as it considers appropriate, income derived from the investment of the Common School Fund to the operating expenses of the State Land Board in exercising its powers and duties under subsection (2) of section 5 of this Article. The remainder of the income derived from the investment of the Common School Fund shall be applied to the support of primary and secondary education as prescribed by law. [Constitution of 1859; Amendment proposed by H.J.R. 7, 1967, and adopted by the people May 28, 1968; Amendment proposed by H.J.R. 6, 1979, and adopted by the people Nov. 4, 1980; Amendment to subsection (2) proposed by S.J.R. 1, 1987, and adopted by the people Nov. 8, 1988; Amendment to paragraph (b) of subsection (1) proposed by H.J.R. 3, 1989, and adopted by the people June 27, 1989]

Section 3. System of common schools. The Legislative Assembly shall provide by law for the establishment of a uniform, and general system of Common schools.

Section 4. Distribution of school fund income. Provision shall be made by law for the distribution of the income of the common school fund among the several Counties of this state in proportion to the number of children resident therein between the ages, four and twenty years.—

Section 5. State Land Board; land management. (1) The Governor, Secretary of State and State Treasurer shall constitute a State Land Board for the disposition and management of lands described in section 2 of this Article, and other lands owned by this state that are placed under their jurisdiction by law. Their powers and duties shall be prescribed by law.

(2) The board shall manage lands under its jurisdiction with the object of obtaining the greatest benefit for the people of this state, consistent with the conservation of this resource under sound techniques of land management. [Constitution of 1859; Amendment proposed by H.J.R. 7, 1967, and adopted by the people May 28, 1968]

Section 6. Qualifications of electors at school elections. In all school district elections every citizen of the United States of the age of twenty-one years and upward who shall have resided in the school district during the six months immediately preceding such election, and who shall be duly registered prior to such election in the manner provided by law, shall be entitled to vote, provided such citizen is able to read and write the English language. [Created through initiative petition filed June 25, 1948, and adopted by the people Nov. 2, 1948]

Note: The leadline to section 6 was a part of the measure proposed by initiative petition filed June 25, 1948, and adopted by the people Nov. 2, 1948.

Section 7. Prohibition of sale of state timber unless timber processed in Oregon. (1) Notwithstanding subsection (2) of section 5 of this Article or any other provision of this Constitution, the State Land Board shall not authorize the sale or export of timber from lands described in section 2 of this Article unless such timber will be processed in Oregon. The limitation on sale or export in this subsection shall not apply to species, grades or quantities of timber which may be found by the State Land Board to be surplus to domestic needs.

(2) Notwithstanding any prior agreements or other provisions of law or this Constitution, the Legislative Assembly shall not authorize the sale or export of timber from state lands other than those described in section 2 of this Article unless such timber will be processed in Oregon. The limitation on sale or export in this subsection shall not apply to species, grades or quantities of timber which may be found by the State Forester to be surplus to domestic needs.

(3) This section first becomes operative when federal law is enacted allowing this state to exercise such authority or when a court or the Attorney General of this state determines that such authority lawfully may be exercised. [Created through S.J.R. 8, 1989, and adopted by the people June 27, 1989]

Section 8. Adequate and Equitable Funding. (1) The Legislative Assembly shall appropriate in each biennium a sum of money sufficient to ensure that the state's system of public education meets quality goals established by law, and publish a report that either demonstrates the appropriation is sufficient, or identifies the reasons for the insufficiency, its extent, and its impact on the ability of the state's system of public education to meet those goals.

(2) Consistent with such legal obligation as it may have to maintain substantial equity in state funding, the Legislative Assembly shall establish a system of Equalization Grants to eligible districts for each year in which the voters of such districts approve local option taxes as described in Article XI, section 11 (4)(a)(B) of this Constitution. The amount of such Grants and eligibility criteria shall be determined by the Legislative Assembly. [Created through initiative petition filed Oct. 22, 1999, and adopted by the people Nov. 7, 2000]

Note: Added to Article VIII as unnumbered section by initiative petition (Measure No. 1, 2000) adopted by the people Nov. 7, 2000.

Note: The leadline to section 8 was a part of the measure submitted to the people by Measure No. 1, 2000.

ARTICLE IX
FINANCE

Sec. 1. Assessment and taxation; uniform rules; uniformity of operation of laws
1a. Poll or head tax; declaration of emergency in tax laws
1b. Ships exempt from taxation until 1935
1c. Financing redevelopment and urban renewal projects
2. Legislature to provide revenue to pay current state expenses and interest
3. Tax imposed only by law; statement of purpose
3a. Use of revenue from taxes on motor vehicle use and fuel; legislative review of allocation of taxes between vehicle classes
3b. Rate of levy on oil or natural gas; exception
4. Appropriation necessary for withdrawal from treasury
5. Publication of accounts
6. Deficiency of funds; tax levy to pay
7. Appropriation laws not to contain provisions on other subjects
8. Stationery for use of state
9. Taxation of certain benefits prohibited
10. Retirement plan contributions by governmental employees
11. Retirement plan rate of return contract guarantee prohibited
12. Retirement not to be increased by unused sick leave
13. Retirement plan restriction severability

14. Revenue estimate; return of excess revenue to taxpayers; legislative increase in estimate

Section 1. Assessment and taxation; uniform rules; uniformity of operation of laws. The Legislative Assembly shall, and the people through the initiative may, provide by law uniform rules of assessment and taxation. All taxes shall be levied and collected under general laws operating uniformly throughout the State. [Constitution of 1859; Amendment proposed by H.J.R. 16, 1917, and adopted by the people June 4, 1917]

Section 1a. Poll or head tax; declaration of emergency in tax laws. No poll or head tax shall be levied or collected in Oregon. The Legislative Assembly shall not declare an emergency in any act regulating taxation or exemption. [Created through initiative petition filed June 23, 1910, and adopted by the people Nov. 8, 1910; Amendment proposed by S.J.R. 10, 1911, and adopted by the people Nov. 5, 1912]

Section 1b. Ships exempt from taxation until 1935. All ships and vessels of fifty tons or more capacity engaged in either passenger or freight coasting or foreign trade, whose home ports of registration are in the State of Oregon, shall be and are hereby exempted from all taxes of every kind whatsoever, excepting taxes for State purposes, until the first day of January, 1935. [Created through S.J.R. 18, 1915, and adopted by the people Nov. 7, 1916]

Section 1c. Financing redevelopment and urban renewal projects. The Legislative Assembly may provide that the ad valorem taxes levied by any taxing unit, in which is located all or part of an area included in a redevelopment or urban renewal project, may be divided so that the taxes levied against any increase in the assessed value, as defined by law, of property in such area obtaining after the effective date of the ordinance or resolution approving the redevelopment or urban renewal plan for such area, shall be used to pay any indebtedness incurred for the redevelopment or urban renewal project. The legislature may enact such laws as may be necessary to carry out the purposes of this section. [Created through S.J.R. 32, 1959, and adopted by the people Nov. 8, 1960; Amendment proposed by H.J.R. 85, 1997, and adopted by the people May 20, 1997]

Section 2. Legislature to provide revenue to pay current state expenses and interest. The Legislative Assembly shall provide for raising revenue sufficiently to defray the expenses of the State for each fiscal year, and also a sufficient sum to pay the interest on the State debt, if there be any.—

Section 3. Laws imposing taxes; gasoline and motor vehicle taxes. [Constitution of 1859; Amendment proposed by S.J.R. 11, 1941, and adopted by the people Nov. 3, 1942; Repeal proposed by S.J.R. 7, 1979, and adopted by the people May 20, 1980]

Section 3. Tax imposed only by law; statement of purpose. No tax shall be levied except in accordance with law. Every law imposing a tax shall state distinctly the purpose to which the revenue shall be applied. [Created through S.J.R. 7, 1979, and adopted by the people May 20, 1980 (this section and section 3a adopted in lieu of former section 3 of this Article)]

Section 3a. Use of revenue from taxes on motor vehicle use and fuel; legislative review of allocation of taxes between vehicle classes. (1) Except as provided in subsection (2) of this section, revenue from the following shall be used exclusively for the construction, reconstruction, improvement, repair, maintenance, operation and use of public highways, roads, streets and roadside rest areas in this state:

(a) Any tax levied on, with respect to, or measured by the storage, withdrawal, use, sale, distribution, importation or receipt of motor vehicle fuel or any other product used for the propulsion of motor vehicles; and

(b) Any tax or excise levied on the ownership, operation or use of motor vehicles.

(2) Revenues described in subsection (1) of this section:

(a) May also be used for the cost of administration and any refunds or credits authorized by law.

(b) May also be used for the retirement of bonds for which such revenues have been pledged.

(c) If from levies under paragraph (b) of subsection (1) of this section on campers, mobile homes, motor homes, travel trailers, snowmobiles, or like vehicles, may also be used for the acquisition, development, maintenance or care of parks or recreation areas.

(d) If from levies under paragraph (b) of subsection (1) of this section on vehicles used or held out for use for commercial purposes, may also be used for enforcement of commercial vehicle weight, size, load, conformation and equipment regulation.

(3) Revenues described in subsection (1) of this section that are generated by taxes or excises imposed by the state shall be generated in a manner that ensures that the share of revenues paid for the use of light vehicles, including cars, and the share of revenues paid for the use of heavy vehicles, including trucks, is fair and proportionate to the costs incurred for the highway system because of each class of vehicle. The Legislative Assembly shall provide for a biennial review and, if necessary, adjustment, of revenue sources to ensure fairness and proportionality. [Created through S.J.R. 7, 1979, and adopted by the people May 20, 1980 (this section and section 3 adopted in lieu of former section 3 of this Article); Amendment proposed by S.J.R. 44, 1999, and adopted by the people Nov. 2, 1999]

Section 3b. Rate of levy on oil or natural gas; exception. Any tax or excise levied on, with respect to or measured by the extraction, production, storage, use, sale, distribution or receipt of oil or natural gas, or the ownership thereof, shall not be levied at a rate that is greater than six percent of the market value of all oil and natural gas produced or salvaged from the earth or waters of this state as and when owned or produced. This section does not apply to any tax or excise the proceeds of which are dedicated as described in sections 3 and 3a of this Article. [Created through H.J.R. 6, 1979, and adopted by the people Nov. 4, 1980]

Note: Section 3b was designated as "Section 3a" by H.J.R. 6, 1979, and adopted by the people Nov. 4, 1980.

Section 4. Appropriation necessary for withdrawal from treasury. No money shall be drawn from the treasury, but in pursuance of appropriations made by law.—

Section 5. Publication of accounts. An accurate statement of the receipts, and expenditures of the public money shall be published with the laws of each regular session of the Legislative Assembly.—

Section 6. Deficiency of funds; tax levy to pay. Whenever the expenses, of any fiscal year, shall exceed the income, the Legislative Assembly shall provide for levying a tax, for the ensuing fiscal year, sufficient, with other sources of income, to pay the deficiency, as well as the estimated expense of the ensuing fiscal year.—

Section 7. Appropriation laws not to contain provisions on other subjects. Laws making appropriations, for the salaries of public officers, and other current expenses of the State, shall contain provisions upon no other subject.—

Section 8. Stationery for use of state. All stationary (sic) required for the use of the State shall be furnished by the lowest responsible bidder, under such regulations as may be prescribed by law. But no State Officer, or member of the Legislative Assembly shall be interested in any bid, or contract for furnishing such stationery.—

Section 9. Taxation of certain benefits prohibited. Benefits payable under the federal old age and survivors insurance program or benefits under section 3(a), 4(a) or 4(f) of the federal Railroad Retirement Act of 1974, as amended, or their successors, shall not be considered income for the purposes of any tax levied by the state or by a local government in this state. Such benefits shall not be used in computing the tax liability of any person under any such tax. Nothing in this section is intended to affect any benefits to which the beneficiary would otherwise be entitled. This section applies to tax periods beginning on or after January 1, 1986. [Created through H.J.R. 26, 1985, and adopted by the people May 20, 1986]

Section 10. Retirement plan contributions by governmental employees. (1) Notwithstanding any existing State or Federal laws, an employee of the State of Oregon or any political subdivision of the state who is a member of a retirement system or plan established by law, charter or ordinance, or who will receive a retirement benefit from a system or plan offered by the state or a political subdivision of the state, must contribute to the system or plan an amount equal to six percent of their salary or gross wage.

(2) On and after January 1, 1995, the state and political subdivisions of the state shall not thereafter contract or otherwise agree to make any payment or contribution to a retirement system or plan that would have the effect of relieving an employee, regardless of when that employee was employed, of the obligation imposed by subsection (1) of this section.

(3) On and after January 1, 1995, the state and political subdivisions of the state shall not thereafter contract or otherwise agree to increase any salary, benefit or other compensation payable to an employee for the purpose of offsetting or compensating an employee for the obligation imposed by subsection (1) of this section. [Created through initiative petition filed May 10, 1993, and adopted by the people Nov. 8, 1994]

Section 11. Retirement plan rate of return contract guarantee prohibited. (1) Neither the state nor any political subdivision of the state shall contract to guarantee any rate of interest or return on the funds in a retirement system or plan established by law, charter or ordinance for the benefit of an employee of the state or a political subdivision of the state. [Created through initiative petition filed May 10, 1993, and adopted by the people Nov. 8, 1994]

Section 12. Retirement not to be increased by unused sick leave. (1) Notwithstanding any existing Federal or State law, the retirement benefits of an employee of the state or any political subdivision of the state retiring on or after January 1, 1995, shall not in any way be increased as a result of or due to unused sick leave. [Created through initiative petition filed May 10, 1993, and adopted by the people Nov. 8, 1994]

Section 13. Retirement plan restriction severability. If any part of Sections 10, 11 or 12 of this Article is held to be unconstitutional under the Federal or State

Constitution, the remaining parts shall not be affected and shall remain in full force and effect. [Created through initiative petition filed May 10, 1993, and adopted by the people Nov. 8, 1994]

Section 14. Revenue estimate; return of excess revenue to taxpayers; legislative increase in estimate. (1) As soon as is practicable after adjournment sine die of a regular session of the Legislative Assembly, the Governor shall cause an estimate to be prepared of revenues that will be received by the General Fund for the biennium beginning July 1. The estimated revenues from corporate income and excise taxes shall be separately stated from the estimated revenues from other General Fund sources.

(2) As soon as is practicable after the end of the biennium, the Governor shall cause actual collections of revenues received by the General Fund for that biennium to be determined. The revenues received from corporate income and excise taxes shall be determined separately from the revenues received from other General Fund sources.

(3) If the revenues received by the General Fund from corporate income and excise taxes during the biennium exceed the amount estimated to be received from corporate income and excise taxes for the biennium, by two percent or more, the total amount of the excess shall be returned to corporate income and excise taxpayers.

(4) If the revenues received from General Fund revenue sources, exclusive of those described in subsection (3) of this section, during the biennium exceed the amount estimated to be received from such sources for the biennium, by two percent or more, the total amount of the excess shall be returned to personal income taxpayers.

(5) The Legislative Assembly may enact laws:

(a) Establishing a tax credit, refund payment or other mechanism by which the excess revenues are returned to taxpayers, and establishing administrative procedures connected therewith.

(b) Allowing the excess revenues to be reduced by administrative costs associated with returning the excess revenues.

(c) Permitting a taxpayer's share of the excess revenues not to be returned to the taxpayer if the taxpayer's share is less than a de minimis amount identified by the Legislative Assembly.

(d) Permitting a taxpayer's share of excess revenues to be offset by any liability of the taxpayer for which the state is authorized to undertake collection efforts.

(6)(a) Prior to the close of a biennium for which an estimate described in subsection (1) of this section has been made, the Legislative Assembly, by a two-thirds majority vote of all members elected to each House, may enact legislation declaring an emergency and increasing the amount of the estimate prepared pursuant to subsection (1) of this section.

(b) The prohibition against declaring an emergency in an act regulating taxation or exemption in section 1a, Article IX of this Constitution, does not apply to legislation enacted pursuant to this subsection.

(7) This section does not apply:

(a) If, for a biennium or any portion of a biennium, a state tax is not imposed on or measured by the income of individuals.

(b) To revenues derived from any minimum tax imposed on corporations for the privilege of carrying on or doing business in this state that is imposed as a fixed amount and that is nonapportioned (except for changes of accounting periods).

(c) To biennia beginning before July 1, 2001. [Created through H.J.R. 17, 1999, and adopted by the people Nov. 7, 2000]

ARTICLE X
THE MILITIA

Sec. 1. State militia
2. Persons exempt
3. Officers

Section 1. State militia. The Legislative Assembly shall provide by law for the organization, maintenance and discipline of a state militia for the defense and protection of the State. [Constitution of 1859; Amendment proposed by H.J.R. 5, 1961, and adopted by the people Nov. 6, 1962]

Section 2. Persons exempt. Persons whose religious tenets, or conscientious scruples forbid them to bear arms shall not be compelled to do so. [Constitution of 1859; Amendment proposed by H.J.R. 5, 1961, and adopted by the people Nov. 6, 1962]

Section 3. Officers. The Governor, in his capacity as Commander-in-Chief of the military forces of the State, shall appoint and commission an Adjutant General. All other officers of the militia of the State shall be appointed and commissioned by the Governor upon the recommendation of the Adjutant General. [Constitution of 1859; Amendment proposed by H.J.R. 5, 1961, and adopted by the people Nov. 6, 1962]

Section 4. Staff officers; commissions. [Constitution of 1859; Repeal proposed by H.J.R. 5, 1961, and adopted by the people Nov. 6, 1962]

Section 5. Legislature to make regulations for militia. [Constitution of 1859; Repeal proposed by H.J.R. 5, 1961, and adopted by the people Nov. 6, 1962]

Section 6. Continuity of government in event of enemy attack. [Created through H.J.R. 9, 1959, and adopted by the people Nov. 8, 1960; Repeal proposed by H.J.R. 24, 1975, and adopted by the people Nov. 2, 1976]

ARTICLE XI
CORPORATIONS AND INTERNAL
IMPROVEMENTS

Sec. 1. Prohibition of state banks
2. Formation of corporations; municipal charters; intoxicating liquor regulation
2a. Merger of adjoining municipalities; county-city consolidation
3. Liability of stockholders
4. Compensation for property taken by corporation
5. Restriction of municipal powers in Acts of incorporation
6. State not to be stockholder in company; exceptions
7. Credit of State Not to Be Loaned; Limitation Upon Power of Contracting Debts
8. State not to assume debts of counties, towns or other corporations
9. Limitations on powers of county or city to assist corporations
10. County debt limitation
11. Property tax limitations on assessed value and rate of tax; exceptions
11b. Property tax categories; limitation on categories; exceptions
11c. Limits in addition to other tax limits
11d. Effect of section 11b on exemptions and assessments
11e. Severability of sections 11b, 11c and 11d

12. Peoples' utility districts
13. Interests of employes when operation of transportation system assumed by public body
14. Metropolitan service district charter
15. Funding of programs imposed upon local governments; exceptions

Section 1. Prohibition of state banks. The Legislative Assembly shall not have the power to establish, or incorporate any bank or banking company, or monied (sic) institution whatever; nor shall any bank company, or instition (sic) exist in the State, with the privilege of making, issuing, or putting in circulation, any bill, check, certificate, prommisory (sic) note, or other paper, or the paper of any bank company, or person, to circulate as money.—

Note: The semicolon appearing in the signed Constitution after the word "whatever" in section 1, was not in the original draft reported to, and adopted by the convention and is not part of the Constitution. State v. H.S. & L.A., (1880) 8 Or. 396, 401.

Section 2. Formation of corporations; municipal charters; intoxicating liquor regulation. Corporations may be formed under general laws, but shall not be created by the Legislative Assembly by special laws. The Legislative Assembly shall not enact, amend or repeal any charter or act of incorporation for any municipality, city or town. The legal voters of every city and town are hereby granted power to enact and amend their municipal charter, subject to the Constitution and criminal laws of the State of Oregon, and the exclusive power to license, regulate, control, or to suppress or prohibit, the sale of intoxicating liquors therein is vested in such municipality; but such municipality shall within its limits be subject to the provisions of the local option law of the State of Oregon. [Constitution of 1859; Amendment proposed by initiative petition filed Dec.13, 1905, and adopted by the people June 4, 1906; Amendment proposed by initiative petition filed June 23, 1910, and adopted by the people Nov. 8, 1910]

Section 2a. Merger of adjoining municipalities; county-city consolidation. (1) The Legislative Assembly, or the people by the Initiative, may enact a general law providing a method whereby an incorporated city or town or municipal corporation may surrender its charter and be merged into an adjoining city or town, provided a majority of the electors of each of the incorporated cities or towns or municipal corporations affected authorize the surrender or merger, as the case may be.

(2) In all counties having a city therein containing over 300,000 inhabitants, the county and city government thereof may be consolidated in such manner as may be provided by law with one set of officers. The consolidated county and city may be incorporated under general laws providing for incorporation for municipal purposes. The provisions of this Constitution applicable to cities, and also those applicable to counties, so far as not inconsistent or prohibited to cities, shall be applicable to such consolidated government. [Created through H.J.R. 10, 1913, and adopted by the people Nov. 3, 1914; Amendment proposed by S.J.R. 29, 1967, and adopted by the people Nov. 5, 1968]

Section 3. Liability of stockholders. The stockholders of all corporations and joint stock companies shall be liable for the indebtedness of said corporation to the amount of their stock subscribed and unpaid and no more, excepting that the stockholders of corporations or joint stock companies conducting the business of banking shall be individually liable equally and ratably and not one for another, for the benefit of the depositors of said bank, to the amount of their stock, at the par value thereof, in addition to the par value of such shares, unless such banking corporation shall have provided security through membership in the federal deposit insurance corporation or other instrumentality of the United States or otherwise for the benefit of the depositors of said bank equivalent in amount to such double liability of said stockholders. [Constitution of 1859; Amendment proposed by S.J.R. 13, 1911, and adopted by the people Nov. 5, 1912; Amendment proposed by H.J.R. 2, 1943, and adopted by the people Nov. 7, 1944]

Section 4. Compensation for property taken by corporation. No person's property shall be taken by any corporation under authority of law, without compensation being first made, or secured in such manner as may be prescribed by law.

Section 5. Restriction of municipal powers in Acts of incorporation. Acts of the Legislative Assembly, incorporating towns, and cities, shall restrict their powers of taxation, borrowing money, contracting debts, and loaning their credit.—

Section 6. State not to be stockholder in company; exceptions. (1) The state shall not subscribe to, or be interested in the stock of any company, association or corporation. However, as provided by law the state may hold and dispose of stock, including stock already received, that is donated or bequeathed; and may invest, in the stock of any company, association or corporation, any funds or moneys that:

(a) Are donated or bequeathed for higher education purposes;

(b) Are the proceeds from the disposition of stock that is donated or bequeathed for higher education purposes, including stock already received; or

(c) Are dividends paid with respect to stock that is donated or bequeathed for higher education purposes, including stock already received.

(2) Notwithstanding the limits contained in subsection (1) of this section, the state may hold and dispose of stock:

(a) Received in exchange for technology created in whole or in part by a public institution of post-secondary education; or

(b) Received prior to December 5, 2002, as a state asset invested in the creation or development of technology or resources within Oregon. [Constitution of 1859; Amendment proposed by H.J.R. 11, 1955, and adopted by the people Nov. 6, 1956; Amendment proposed by H.J.R. 27, 1969, and adopted by the people Nov. 3, 1970; Amendment proposed by S.J.R. 17, 2001, and adopted by the people May 21, 2002]

Section 7. Credit of State Not to Be Loaned; Limitation Upon Power of Contracting Debts. The Legislative Assembly shall not lend the credit of the state nor in any manner create any debt or liabilities which shall singly or in the aggregate with previous debts or liabilities exceed the sum of fifty thousand dollars, except in case of war or to repel invasion or suppress insurrection or to build and maintain permanent roads; and the Legislative Assembly shall not lend the credit of the state nor in any manner create any debts or liabilities to build and maintain permanent roads which shall singly or in the aggregate with previous debts or liabilities incurred for that purpose exceed one percent of the true cash value of all the property of the state taxed on an ad valorem basis; and every contract of indebtedness entered into or assumed by or on behalf of the state in violation of the provisions of this section shall be void and of no effect. This section does not apply to any agreement entered into pursuant to law by the state or any agency thereof for the lease of real property to the state or agency for any period not exceeding 20 years and for a public purpose. [Constitution of 1859; Amendment proposed by initiative petition filed July 2, 1912, and adopted by the people Nov. 5, 1912; Amendment proposed by H.J.R. 11, 1920 (s.s.), and adopted by the people May 21, 1920; Amendment proposed by S.J.R. 4, 1961, and adopted by the people Nov. 6, 1962; Amendment proposed by S.J.R. 19, 1963, and adopted by the people Nov. 3, 1964]

Note: The headline to section 7 was a part of the measure submitted to the people by H.J.R. 11, 1920 (s.s.).

Section 8. State not to assume debts of counties, towns or other corporations. The State shall never assume the debts of any county, town, or other corporation whatever, unless such debts, shall have been created to repel invasion, suppress insurrection, or defend the State in war.—

Section 9. Limitations on powers of county or city to assist corporations. No county, city, town or other municipal corporation, by vote of its citizens, or otherwise, shall become a stockholder in any joint company, corporation or association, whatever, or raise money for, or loan its credit to, or in aid of, any such company, corporation or association. Provided, that any municipal corporation designated as a port under any general or special law of the state of Oregon, may be empowered by statute to raise money and expend the same in the form of a bonus to aid in establishing water transportation lines between such port and any other domestic or foreign port or ports, and to aid in establishing water transportation lines on the interior rivers of this state, or on the rivers between Washington and Oregon, or on the rivers of Washington and Idaho reached by navigation from Oregon's rivers; any debts of a municipality to raise money created for the aforesaid purpose shall be incurred only on approval of a majority of those voting on the question, and shall not, either singly or in the aggregate, with previous debts and liabilities incurred for that purpose, exceed one per cent of the assessed valuation of all property in the municipality. [Constitution of 1859; Amendment proposed by S.J.R. 13, 1917, and adopted by the people June 4, 1917]

Section 10. County debt limitation. No county shall create any debt or liabilities which shall singly or in the aggregate, with previous debts or liabilities, exceed the sum of $5,000; provided, however, counties may incur bonded indebtedness in excess of such $5,000 limitation to carry out purposes authorized by statute, such bonded indebtedness not to exceed limits fixed by statute. [Constitution of 1859; Amendment proposed by initiative petition filed July 7, 1910, and adopted by the people Nov. 8, 1910; Amendment proposed by initiative petition filed July 2, 1912, and adopted by the people Nov. 5, 1912; Amendment proposed by S.J.R. 11, 1919, and adopted by the people June 3, 1919; Amendment proposed by H.J.R. 7, 1920 (s.s.), and adopted by the people May 21, 1920; Amendment proposed by S.J.R. 1, 1921 (s.s.), and adopted by the people Nov. 7, 1922; Amendment proposed by S.J.R. 5, 1921 (s.s.), and adopted by the people Nov. 7, 1922; Amendment proposed by H.J.R. 3, 1925, and adopted by the people Nov. 2, 1926; Amendment proposed by S.J.R. 18, 1925, and adopted by the people Nov. 2, 1926; Amendment proposed by H.J.R. 19, 1925, and adopted by the people Nov. 2, 1926; Amendment proposed by H.J.R. 21, 1957, and adopted by the people Nov. 4, 1958]

Section 11. Tax and indebtedness limitation. [Created through initiative petition filed July 6, 1916, and adopted by the people Nov. 7, 1916; Amendment proposed by H.J.R. 9, 1931, and adopted by the people Nov. 8, 1932; Amendment proposed by H.J.R. 9, 1951, and adopted by the people Nov. 4, 1952; Repeal proposed by S.J.R. 33, 1961, and adopted by the people Nov. 6, 1962 (second section 11 of this Article adopted in lieu of this section)]

Section 11. Tax base limitation. [Created through S.J.R. 33, 1961, and adopted by the people Nov. 6, 1962 (this section adopted in lieu of first section 11 of this Article); Amendment proposed by H.J.R. 28, 1985, and adopted by the people May 20, 1986; Repeal proposed by H.J.R. 85, 1997, and adopted by the people May 20, 1997 (present section 11 of this Article adopted in lieu of this section and sections 11a, 11f, 11g, 11h, 11i and 11j of this Article)]

Section 11. Property tax limitations on assessed value and rate of tax; exceptions. (1)(a) For the tax year beginning July 1, 1997, each unit of property in this state shall have a maximum assessed value for ad valorem property tax purposes that does not exceed the property's real market value for the tax year beginning July 1, 1995, reduced by 10 percent.

(b) For tax years beginning after July 1, 1997, the property's maximum assessed value shall not increase by more than three percent from the previous tax year.

(c) Notwithstanding paragraph (a) or (b) of this subsection, property shall be valued at the ratio of average maximum assessed value to average real market value of property located in the area in which the property is located that is within the same property class, if on or after July 1, 1995:

(A) The property is new property or new improvements to property;

(B) The property is partitioned or subdivided;

(C) The property is rezoned and used consistently with the rezoning;

(D) The property is first taken into account as omitted property;

(E) The property becomes disqualified from exemption, partial exemption or special assessment; or

(F) A lot line adjustment is made with respect to the property, except that the total assessed value of all property affected by a lot line adjustment shall not exceed the total maximum assessed value of the affected property under paragraph (a) or (b) of this subsection.

(d) Property shall be valued under paragraph (c) of this subsection only for the first tax year in which the changes described in paragraph (c) of this subsection are taken into account following the effective date of this section. For each tax year thereafter, the limits described in paragraph (b) of this subsection apply.

(e) The Legislative Assembly shall enact laws that establish property classes and areas sufficient to make a determination under paragraph (c) of this subsection.

(f) Each property's assessed value shall not exceed the property's real market value.

(g) There shall not be a reappraisal of the real market value used in the tax year beginning July 1, 1995, for purposes of determining the property's maximum assessed value under paragraph (a) of this subsection.

(2) The maximum assessed value of property that is assessed under a partial exemption or special assessment law shall be determined by applying the percentage reduction of paragraph (a) and the limit of paragraph (b) of subsection (1) of this section, or if newly eligible for partial exemption or special assessment, using a ratio developed in a manner consistent with paragraph (c) of subsection (1) of this section to the property's partially exempt or specially assessed value in the manner provided by law. After disqualification from partial

exemption or special assessment, any additional taxes authorized by law may be imposed, but in the aggregate may not exceed the amount that would have been imposed under this section had the property not been partially exempt or specially assessed for the years for which the additional taxes are being collected.

(3)(a)(A) The Legislative Assembly shall enact laws to reduce the amount of ad valorem property taxes imposed by local taxing districts in this state so that the total of all ad valorem property taxes imposed in this state for the tax year beginning July 1, 1997, is reduced by 17 percent from the total of all ad valorem property taxes that would have been imposed under repealed sections 11 and 11a of this Article (1995 Edition) and section 11b of this Article but not taking into account Ballot Measure 47 (1996), for the tax year beginning July 1, 1997.

(B) The ad valorem property taxes to be reduced under subparagraph (A) of this paragraph are those taxes that would have been imposed under repealed sections 11 or 11a of this Article (1995 Edition) or section 11b of this Article, as modified by subsection (11) of this section, other than taxes described in subsection (4), (5), (6) or (7) of this section, taxes imposed to pay bonded indebtedness described in section 11b of this Article, as modified by paragraph (d) of subsection (11) of this section, or taxes described in section 1c, Article IX of this Constitution.

(C) It shall be the policy of this state to distribute the reductions caused by this paragraph so as to reflect:

(i) The lesser of ad valorem property taxes imposed for the tax year beginning July 1, 1995, reduced by 10 percent, or ad valorem property taxes imposed for the tax year beginning July 1, 1994;

(ii) Growth in new value under subparagraph (A), (B), (C), (D) or (E) of paragraph (c) of subsection (1) of this section, as added to the assessment and tax rolls for the tax year beginning July 1, 1996, or July 1, 1997 (or, if applicable, for the tax year beginning July 1, 1995); and

(iii) Ad valorem property taxes authorized by voters to be imposed in tax years beginning on or after July 1, 1996, and imposed according to that authority for the tax year beginning July 1, 1997.

(D) It shall be the policy of this state and the local taxing districts of this state to prioritize public safety and public education in responding to the reductions caused by this paragraph while minimizing the loss of decision-making control of local taxing districts.

(E) If the total value for the tax year beginning July 1, 1997, of additions of value described in subparagraph (A), (B), (C), (D) or (E) of paragraph (c) of subsection (1) of this section that are added to the assessment and tax rolls for the tax year beginning July 1, 1996, or July 1, 1997, exceeds four percent of the total assessed value of property statewide for the tax year beginning July 1, 1997 (before taking into account the additions of value described in subparagraph (A), (B), (C), (D) or (E) of paragraph (c) of subsection (1) of this section), then any ad valorem property taxes attributable to the excess above four percent shall reduce the dollar amount of the reduction described in subparagraph (A) of this paragraph.

(b) For the tax year beginning July 1, 1997, the ad valorem property taxes that were reduced under paragraph (a) of this subsection shall be imposed on the assessed value of property in a local taxing district as provided by

law, and the rate of the ad valorem property taxes imposed under this paragraph shall be the local taxing district's permanent limit on the rate of ad valorem property taxes imposed by the district for tax years beginning after July 1, 1997, except as provided in subsection (5) of this section.

(c)(A) A local taxing district that has not previously imposed ad valorem property taxes and that seeks to impose ad valorem property taxes shall establish a limit on the rate of ad valorem property tax to be imposed by the district. The rate limit established under this subparagraph shall be approved by a majority of voters voting on the question. The rate limit approved under this subparagraph shall serve as the district's permanent rate limit under paragraph (b) of this subsection.

(B) The voter participation requirements described in subsection (8) of this section apply to an election under this paragraph.

(d) If two or more local taxing districts seek to consolidate or merge, the limit on the rate of ad valorem property tax to be imposed by the consolidated or merged district shall be the rate that would produce the same tax revenue as the local taxing districts would have cumulatively produced in the year of consolidation or merger, if the consolidation or merger had not occurred.

(e)(A) If a local taxing district divides, the limit on the rate of ad valorem property tax to be imposed by each local taxing district after division shall be the same as the local taxing district's rate limit under paragraph (b) of this subsection prior to division.

(B) Notwithstanding subparagraph (A) of this paragraph, the limit determined under this paragraph shall not be greater than the rate that would have produced the same amount of ad valorem property tax revenue in the year of division, had the division not occurred.

(f) Rates of ad valorem property tax established under this subsection may be carried to a number of decimal places provided by law and rounded as provided by law.

(g) Urban renewal levies described in this subsection shall be imposed as provided in subsections (15) and (16) of this section and may not be imposed under this subsection.

(h) Ad valorem property taxes described in this subsection shall be subject to the limitations described in section 11b of this Article, as modified by subsection (11) of this section.

(4)(a)(A) A local taxing district other than a school district may impose a local option ad valorem property tax that exceeds the limitations imposed under this section by submitting the question of the levy to voters in the local taxing district and obtaining the approval of a majority of the voters voting on the question.

(B) The Legislative Assembly may enact laws permitting a school district to impose a local option ad valorem property tax as otherwise provided under this subsection.

(b) A levy imposed pursuant to legislation enacted under this subsection may be imposed for no more than five years, except that a levy for a capital project may be imposed for no more than the lesser of the expected useful life of the capital project or 10 years.

(c) The voter participation requirements described in subsection (8) of this section apply to an election held under this subsection.

(5)(a) Any portion of a local taxing district levy shall not be subject to reduction and limitation under paragraphs (a) and (b) of subsection (3) of this section if that portion of the levy is used to repay:

(A) Principal and interest for any bond issued before December 5, 1996, and secured by a pledge or explicit commitment of ad valorem property taxes or a covenant to levy or collect ad valorem property taxes;

(B) Principal and interest for any other formal, written borrowing of moneys executed before December 5, 1996, for which ad valorem property tax revenues have been pledged or explicitly committed, or that are secured by a covenant to levy or collect ad valorem property taxes;

(C) Principal and interest for any bond issued to refund an obligation described in subparagraph (A) or (B) of this paragraph; or

(D) Local government pension and disability plan obligations that commit ad valorem property taxes and to ad valorem property taxes imposed to fulfill those obligations.

(b)(A) A levy described in this subsection shall be imposed on assessed value as otherwise provided by law in an amount sufficient to repay the debt described in this subsection. Ad valorem property taxes may not be imposed under this subsection that repay the debt at an earlier date or on a different schedule than established in the agreement creating the debt.

(B) A levy described in this subsection shall be subject to the limitations imposed under section 11b of this Article, as modified by subsection (11) of this section.

(c)(A) As used in this subsection, "local government pension and disability plan obligations that commit ad valorem property taxes" is limited to contractual obligations for which the levy of ad valorem property taxes has been committed by a local government charter provision that was in effect on December 5, 1996, and, if in effect on December 5, 1996, as amended thereafter.

(B) The rates of ad valorem property taxes described in this paragraph may be adjusted so that the maximum allowable rate is capable of raising the revenue that the levy would have been authorized to raise if applied to property valued at real market value.

(C) Notwithstanding subparagraph (B) of this paragraph, ad valorem property taxes described in this paragraph shall be taken into account for purposes of the limitations in section 11b of this Article, as modified by subsection (11) of this section.

(D) If any proposed amendment to a charter described in subparagraph (A) of this paragraph permits the ad valorem property tax levy for local government pension and disability plan obligations to be increased, the amendment must be approved by voters in an election. The voter participation requirements described in subsection (8) of this section apply to an election under this subparagraph. No amendment to any charter described in this paragraph may cause ad valorem property taxes to exceed the limitations of section 11b of this Article, as amended by subsection (11) of this section.

(d) If the levy described in this subsection was a tax base or other permanent continuing levy, other than a levy imposed for the purpose described in subparagraph (D) of paragraph (a) of this subsection, prior to the effective date of this section, for the tax year following the repayment of debt described in this subsection the local taxing district's rate of ad valorem property tax established under paragraph (b) of subsection (3) of this section shall be increased to the rate that would have been in effect had the levy not been excepted from the reduction described in subsection (3) of this section. No adjustment shall be made to the rate of ad valorem property tax of local taxing districts other than the district imposing a levy under this subsection.

(e) If this subsection would apply to a levy described in paragraph (d) of this subsection, the local taxing district imposing the levy may elect out of the provisions of this subsection. The levy of a local taxing district making the election shall be included in the reduction and ad valorem property tax rate determination described in subsection (3) of this section.

(6)(a) The ad valorem property tax of a local taxing district, other than a city, county or school district, that is used to support a hospital facility shall not be subject to the reduction described in paragraph (a) of subsection (3) of this section. The entire ad valorem property tax imposed under this subsection for the tax year beginning July 1, 1997, shall be the local taxing district's permanent limit on the rate of ad valorem property taxes imposed by the district under paragraph (b) of subsection (3) of this section.

(b) Ad valorem property taxes described in this subsection shall be subject to the limitations imposed under section 11b of this Article, as modified by subsection (11) of this section.

(7) Notwithstanding any other existing or former provision of this Constitution, the following are validated, ratified, approved and confirmed:

(a) Any levy of ad valorem property taxes approved by a majority of voters voting on the question in an election held before December 5, 1996, if the election met the voter participation requirements described in subsection (8) of this section and the ad valorem property taxes were first imposed for the tax year beginning July 1, 1996, or July 1, 1997. A levy described in this paragraph shall not be subject to reduction under paragraph (a) of subsection (3) of this section but shall be taken into account in determining the local taxing district's permanent rate of ad valorem property tax under paragraph (b) of subsection (3) this section. This paragraph does not apply to levies described in subsection (5) of this section or to levies to pay bonded indebtedness described in section 11b of this Article, as modified by subsection (11) of this section.

(b) Any serial or one-year levy to replace an existing serial or one-year levy approved by a majority of the voters voting on the question at an election held after December 4, 1996, and to be first imposed for the tax year beginning July 1, 1997, if the rate or the amount of the levy approved is not greater than the rate or the amount of the levy replaced.

(c) Any levy of ad valorem property taxes approved by a majority of voters voting on the question in an election held on or after December 5, 1996, and before the effective date of this section if the election met the voter participation requirements described in subsection (8) of this section and the ad valorem property taxes were first imposed for the tax year beginning July 1, 1997. A levy described in this paragraph shall be treated as a local option ad valorem property tax under subsection (4) of this section. This paragraph does not apply to levies described in subsection (5) of this section or to levies to pay bonded indebtedness described in section 11b of this Article, as modified by subsection (11) of this section.

(8) An election described in subsection (3), (4), (5)(c)(D), (7)(a) or (c) or (11) of this section shall authorize the matter upon which the election is being held only if:

(a) At least 50 percent of registered voters eligible to vote in the election cast a ballot; or

(b) The election is a general election in an even-numbered year.

(9) The Legislative Assembly shall replace, from the state's General Fund, revenue lost by the public school system because of the limitations of this section. The amount of the replacement revenue shall not be less than the total replaced in fiscal year 1997-1998.

(10)(a) As used in this section:

(A) "Improvements" includes new construction, reconstruction, major additions, remodeling, renovation and rehabilitation, including installation, but does not include minor construction or ongoing maintenance and repair.

(B) "Ad valorem property tax" does not include taxes imposed to pay principal and interest on bonded indebtedness described in paragraph (d) of subsection (11) of this section.

(b) In calculating the addition to value for new property and improvements, the amount added shall be net of the value of retired property.

(11) For purposes of this section and for purposes of implementing the limits in section 11b of this Article in tax years beginning on or after July 1, 1997:

(a)(A) The real market value of property shall be the amount in cash that could reasonably be expected to be paid by an informed buyer to an informed seller, each acting without compulsion in an arm's length transaction occurring as of the assessment date for the tax year, as established by law.

(B) The Legislative Assembly shall enact laws to adjust the real market value of property to reflect a substantial casualty loss of value after the assessment date.

(b) The $5 (public school system) and $10 (other government) limits on property taxes per $1,000 of real market value described in subsection (1) of section 11b of this Article shall be determined on the basis of property taxes imposed in each geographic area taxed by the same local taxing districts.

(c)(A) All property taxes described in this section are subject to the limits described in paragraph (b) of this subsection, except for taxes described in paragraph (d) of this subsection.

(B) If property taxes exceed the limitations imposed under either category of local taxing district under paragraph (b) of this subsection:

(i) Any local option ad valorem property taxes imposed under this subsection shall be proportionally reduced by those local taxing districts within the category that is imposing local option ad valorem property taxes; and

(ii) After local option ad valorem property taxes have been eliminated, all other ad valorem property taxes shall be proportionally reduced by those taxing districts within the category, until the limits are no longer exceeded.

(C) The percentages used to make the proportional reductions under subparagraph (B) of this paragraph shall be calculated separately for each category.

(d) Bonded indebtedness, the taxes of which are not subject to limitation under this section or section 11b of this Article, consists of:

(A) Bonded indebtedness authorized by a provision of this Constitution;

(B) Bonded indebtedness issued on or before November 6, 1990; or

(C) Bonded indebtedness:

(i) Incurred for capital construction or capital improvements; and

(ii)(I) If issued after November 6, 1990, and approved prior to December 5, 1996, the issuance of which has been approved by a majority of voters voting on the question; or

(II) If approved by voters after December 5, 1996, the issuance of which has been approved by a majority of voters voting on the question in an election that is in compliance with the voter participation requirements in subsection (8) of this section.

(12) Bonded indebtedness described in subsection (11) of this section includes bonded indebtedness issued to refund bonded indebtedness described in subsection (11) of this section.

(13) As used in subsection (11) of this section, with respect to bonded indebtedness issued on or after December 5, 1996, "capital construction" and "capital improvements":

(a) Include public safety and law enforcement vehicles with a projected useful life of five years or more; and

(b) Do not include:

(A) Maintenance and repairs, the need for which could reasonably be anticipated.

(B) Supplies and equipment that are not intrinsic to the structure.

(14) Ad valorem property taxes imposed to pay principal and interest on bonded indebtedness described in section 11b of this Article, as modified by subsection (11) of this section, shall be imposed on the assessed value of the property determined under this section or, in the case of specially assessed property, as otherwise provided by law or as limited by this section, whichever is applicable.

(15) If ad valorem property taxes are divided as provided in section 1c, Article IX of this Constitution, in order to fund a redevelopment or urban renewal project, then notwithstanding subsection (1) of this section, the ad valorem property taxes levied against the increase shall be used exclusively to pay any indebtedness incurred for the redevelopment or urban renewal project.

(16) The Legislative Assembly shall enact laws that allow collection of ad valorem property taxes sufficient to pay, when due, indebtedness incurred to carry out urban renewal plans existing on December 5, 1996. These collections shall cease when the indebtedness is paid. Unless excepted from limitation under section 11b of this Article, as modified by subsection (11) of this section, nothing in this subsection shall be construed to remove ad valorem property taxes levied against the increase from the dollar limits in paragraph (b) of subsection (11) of this section.

(17)(a) If, in an election on November 5, 1996, voters approved a new tax base for a local taxing district under repealed section 11 of this Article (1995 Edition) that was not to go into effect until the tax year beginning July 1, 1998, the local taxing district's permanent rate limit under subsection (3) of this section shall be recalculated for the tax year beginning on July 1, 1998, to reflect:

(A) Ad valorem property taxes that would have been imposed had repealed section 11 of this Article (1995 Edition) remained in effect; and

(B) Any other permanent continuing levies that would have been imposed under repealed section 11 of this Article (1995 Edition), as reduced by subsection (3) of this section.

(b) The rate limit determined under this subsection shall be the local taxing district's permanent rate limit for tax years beginning on or after July 1, 1999.

(18) Section 32, Article I, and section 1, Article IX of this Constitution, shall not apply to this section.

(19)(a) The Legislative Assembly shall by statute limit the ability of local taxing districts to impose new or additional fees, taxes, assessments or other charges for the purpose of using the proceeds as alternative sources of funding to make up for ad valorem property tax revenue reductions caused by the initial implementation of this section, unless the new or additional fee, tax, assessment or other charge is approved by voters.

(b) This subsection shall not apply to new or additional fees, taxes, assessments or other charges for a government product or service that a person:

(A) May legally obtain from a source other than government; and

(B) Is reasonably able to obtain from a source other than government.

(c) As used in this subsection, "new or additional fees, taxes, assessments or other charges" does not include moneys received by a local taxing district as:

(A) Rent or lease payments;

(B) Interest, dividends, royalties or other investment earnings;

(C) Fines, penalties and unitary assessments;

(D) Amounts charged to and paid by another unit of government for products, services or property; or

(E) Payments derived from a contract entered into by the local taxing district as a proprietary function of the local taxing district.

(d) This subsection does not apply to a local taxing district that derived less than 10 percent of the local taxing district's operating revenues from ad valorem property taxes, other than ad valorem property taxes imposed to pay bonded indebtedness, during the fiscal year ending June 30, 1996.

(e) An election under this subsection need not comply with the voter participation requirements described in subsection (8) of this section.

(20) If any provision of this section is determined to be unconstitutional or otherwise invalid, the remaining provisions shall continue in full force and effect. [Created through H.J.R. 85, 1997, and adopted by the people May 20, 1997 (this section adopted in lieu of former sections 11, 11a, 11f, 11g, 11h, 11i and 11j of this Article)]

Note: The effective date of House Joint Resolution 85, 1997, is June 19, 1997.

Section 11a. School district tax levy. [Created through S.J.R. 3, 1987, and adopted by the people May 19, 1987; Repeal proposed by H.J.R. 85, 1997, and adopted by the people May 20, 1997 (present section 11 adopted in lieu of this section and sections 11, 11f, 11g, 11h, 11i and 11j of this Article)]

Section 11b. Property tax categories; limitation on categories; exceptions. (1) During and after the fiscal year 1991-92, taxes imposed upon any property shall be separated into two categories: One which dedicates revenues raised specifically to fund the public school system and one which dedicates revenues raised to fund government operations other than the public school system. The taxes in each category shall be limited as set forth in the table which follows and these limits shall apply whether the taxes imposed on property are calculated on the basis of the value of that property or on some other basis:

MAXIMUM ALLOWABLE TAXES
For Each $1000.00 of
Property's Real Market Value

Fiscal Year	School System	Other than Schools
1991-1992	$15.00	$10.00
1992-1993	$12.50	$10.00
1993-1994	$10.00	$10.00
1994-1995	$ 7.50	$10.00
1995-1996	$ 5.00	$10.00
and thereafter		

Property tax revenues are deemed to be dedicated to funding the public school system if the revenues are to be used exclusively for educational services, including support services, provided by some unit of government, at any level from pre-kindergarten through post-graduate training.

(2) The following definitions shall apply to this section:

(a) "Real market value" is the minimum amount in cash which could reasonably be expected by an informed seller acting without compulsion, from an informed buyer acting without compulsion, in an "arms-length" transaction during the period for which the property is taxed.

(b) A "tax" is any charge imposed by a governmental unit upon property or upon a property owner as a direct consequence of ownership of that property except incurred charges and assessments for local improvements.

(c) "Incurred charges" include and are specifically limited to those charges by government which can be controlled or avoided by the property owner.

(i) because the charges are based on the quantity of the goods or services used and the owner has direct control over the quantity; or

(ii) because the goods or services are provided only on the specific request of the property owner; or

(iii) because the goods or services are provided by the governmental unit only after the individual property owner has failed to meet routine obligations of ownership and such action is deemed necessary to enforce regulations pertaining to health or safety.

Incurred charges shall not exceed the actual costs of providing the goods or services.

(d) A "local improvement" is a capital construction project undertaken by a governmental unit

(i) which provides a special benefit only to specific properties or rectifies a problem caused by specific properties, and

(ii) the costs of which are assessed against those properties in a single assessment upon the completion of the project, and

(iii) for which the payment of the assessment plus appropriate interest may be spread over a period of at least ten years.

The total of all assessments for a local improvement shall not exceed the actual costs incurred by the governmental unit in designing, constructing and financing the project.

(3) The limitations of subsection (1) of this section apply to all taxes imposed on property or property ownership except

(a) Taxes imposed to pay the principal and interest on bonded indebtedness authorized by a specific provision of this Constitution.

(b) Taxes imposed to pay the principal and interest on bonded indebtedness incurred or to be incurred for capital construction or improvements, provided the bonds are offered as general obligations of the issuing governmental unit and provided further that either the bonds were issued not later than November 6, 1990, or the question of the issuance of the specific bonds has been approved by the electors of the issuing governmental unit.

(4) In the event that taxes authorized by any provision of this Constitution to be imposed upon any property should exceed the limitation imposed on either category of taxing units defined in subsection (1) of this section, then, notwithstanding any other provision of this Constitution, the taxes imposed upon such property by the taxing units in that category shall be reduced evenly by the percentage necessary to meet the limitation for that category. The percentages used to reduce the taxes imposed shall be calculated separately for each category and may vary from property to property within the same taxing unit. The limitation imposed by this section shall not affect the tax base of a taxing unit.

(5) The Legislative Assembly shall replace from the State's general fund any revenue lost by the public school system because of the limitations of this section. The Legislative Assembly is authorized, however, to adopt laws which would limit the total of such replacement revenue plus the taxes imposed within the limitations of this section in any year to the corresponding total for the previous year plus 6 percent. This subsection applies only during fiscal years 1991-92 through 1995-96, inclusive. [Created through initiative petition filed May 8, 1990, and adopted by the people Nov. 6, 1990]

Section 11c. Limits in addition to other tax limits. The limits in section 11b of this Article are in addition to any limits imposed on individual taxing units by this Constitution. [Created through initiative petition filed May 8, 1990, and adopted by the people Nov. 6, 1990]

Section 11d. Effect of section 11b on exemptions and assessments. Nothing in sections 11b to 11e of this Article is intended to require or to prohibit the amendment of any current statute which partially or totally exempts certain classes of property or which prescribes special rules for assessing certain classes of property, unless such amendment is required or prohibited by the implementation of the limitations imposed by section 11b of this Article. [Created through initiative petition filed May 8, 1990, and adopted by the people Nov. 6, 1990]

Section 11e. Severability of sections 11b, 11c and 11d. If any portion, clause or phrase of sections 11b to 11e of this Article is for any reason held to be invalid or unconstitutional by a court of competent jurisdiction, the remaining portions, clauses and phrases shall not be affected but shall remain in full force and effect. [Created through initiative petition filed May 8, 1990, and adopted by the people Nov. 6, 1990]

Section 11f. School district tax levy following merger. [Created through H.J.R. 14, 1989, and adopted by the people Nov. 6, 1990; Repeal proposed by H.J.R. 85, 1997, and adopted by the people May 20, 1997 (present section 11 adopted in lieu of this section and sections 11, 11a, 11g, 11h, 11i and 11j of this Article)] **Note:** Section 11f was designated as "Section 11b" by H.J.R. 14, 1989, and adopted by the people Nov. 6, 1990.

Section 11g. Tax increase limitation; exceptions. [Created through initiative petition filed Dec. 8, 1995, and adopted by the people Nov. 5, 1996; Repeal proposed by H.J.R. 85, 1997, and adopted by the people May 20, 1997 (present section 11 adopted in lieu of this section and sections 11, 11a, 11f, 11h, 11i and 11j of this Article)]

Section 11h. Voluntary contributions for support of schools or other public entities. [Created through initiative petition filed Dec. 8, 1995, and adopted by the people Nov. 5, 1996; Repeal proposed by H.J.R. 85, 1997, and adopted by the people May 20, 1997 (present section 11 adopted in lieu of this section and sections 11, 11a, 11f, 11g, 11i and 11j of this Article)]

Section 11i. Legislation to implement limitation and contribution provisions. [Created through initiative petition filed Dec. 8, 1995, and adopted by the people Nov. 5, 1996; Repeal proposed by H.J.R. 85, 1997, and adopted by the people May 20, 1997 (present section 11 adopted in lieu of this section and sections 11, 11a, 11f, 11g, 11h and 11j of this Article)]

Section 11j. Severability of sections 11g, 11h and 11i. [Created through initiative petition filed Dec. 8, 1995, and adopted by the people Nov. 5, 1996; Repeal proposed by H.J.R. 85, 1997, and adopted by the people May 20, 1997 (present section 11 adopted in lieu of this section and sections 11, 11a, 11f, 11g, 11h and 11i of this Article)]

Section 12. Peoples' utility districts. Peoples' Utility Districts may be created of territory, contiguous or otherwise, within one or more counties, and may consist of an incorporated municipality, or municipalities, with or without unincorporated territory, for the purpose of supplying water for domestic and municipal purposes; for the development of water power and/or electric energy; and for the distribution, disposal and sale of water, water power and electric energy. Such districts shall be managed by boards of directors, consisting of five members, who shall be residents of such districts. Such districts shall have power:

(a) To call and hold elections within their respective districts.

(b) To levy taxes upon the taxable property of such districts.

(c) To issue, sell and assume evidences of indebtedness.

(d) To enter into contracts.

(e) To exercise the power of eminent domain.

(f) To acquire and hold real and other property necessary or incident to the business of such districts.

(g) To acquire, develop, and/or otherwise provide for a supply of water, water power and electric energy.

Such districts may sell, distribute and/or otherwise dispose of water, water power and electric energy within or without the territory of such districts.

The legislative assembly shall and the people may provide any legislation, that may be necessary, in addition to existing laws, to carry out the provisions of this section. [Created through initiative petition filed July 3, 1930, and adopted by the people Nov. 4, 1930]

Section 13. Interests of employes when operation of transportation system assumed by public body. Notwithstanding the provisions of section 20, Article I, section 10, Article VI, and sections 2 and 9, Article XI, of this Constitution, when any city, county, political subdivision, public agency or municipal corporation assumes

Constitution

responsibility for the operation of a public transportation system, the city, county, political subdivision, public agency or municipal corporation shall make fair and equitable arrangements to protect the interests of employes and retired employes affected. Such protective arrangements may include, without being limited to, such provisions as may be necessary for the preservation of rights, privileges and benefits (including continuation of pension rights and payment of benefits) under existing collective bargaining agreements, or otherwise. [Created through H.J.R. 13, 1965, and adopted by the people Nov. 8, 1966]

Section 14. Metropolitan service district charter. (1) The Legislative Assembly shall provide by law a method whereby the legal electors of any metropolitan service district organized under the laws of this state, by majority vote of such electors voting thereon at any legally called election, may adopt, amend, revise or repeal a district charter.

(2) A district charter shall prescribe the organization of the district government and shall provide directly, or by its authority, for the number, election or appointment, qualifications, tenure, compensation, powers and duties of such officers as the district considers necessary. Such officers shall among them exercise all the powers and perform all the duties, as granted to, imposed upon or distributed among district officers by the Constitution or laws of this state, by the district charter or by its authority.

(3) A district charter may provide for the exercise by ordinance of powers granted to the district by the Constitution or laws of this state.

(4) A metropolitan service district shall have jurisdiction over matters of metropolitan concern as set forth in the charter of the district.

(5) The initiative and referendum powers reserved to the people by this Constitution hereby are further reserved to the legal electors of a metropolitan service district relative to the adoption, amendment, revision or repeal of a district charter and district legislation enacted thereunder. Such powers shall be exercised in the manner provided for county measures under section 10, Article VI of this Constitution. [Created by S.J.R. 2, 1989, and adopted by the people Nov. 6, 1990]

Section 15. Funding of programs imposed upon local governments; exceptions. (1) Except as provided in subsection (7) of this section, when the Legislative Assembly or any state agency requires any local government to establish a new program or provide an increased level of service for an existing program, the State of Oregon shall appropriate and allocate to the local government moneys sufficient to pay the ongoing, usual and reasonable costs of performing the mandated service or activity.

(2) As used in this section:

(a) "Enterprise activity" means a program under which a local government sells products or services in competition with a nongovernment entity.

(b) "Local government" means a city, county, municipal corporation or municipal utility operated by a board or commission.

(c) "Program" means a program or project imposed by enactment of the Legislative Assembly or by rule or order of a state agency under which a local government must provide administrative, financial, social, health or other specified services to persons, government agencies or to the public generally.

(d) "Usual and reasonable costs" means those costs incurred by the affected local governments for a specific program using generally accepted methods of service delivery and administrative practice.

(3) A local government is not required to comply with any state law or administrative rule or order enacted or adopted after January 1, 1997, that requires the expenditure of money by the local government for a new program or increased level of service for an existing program until the state appropriates and allocates to the local government reimbursement for any costs incurred to carry out the law, rule or order and unless the Legislative Assembly provides, by appropriation, reimbursement in each succeeding year for such costs. However, a local government may refuse to comply with a state law or administrative rule or order under this subsection only if the amount appropriated and allocated to the local government by the Legislative Assembly for a program in a fiscal year:

(a) Is less than 95 percent of the usual and reasonable costs incurred by the local government in conducting the program at the same level of service in the preceding fiscal year; or

(b) Requires the local government to spend for the program, in addition to the amount appropriated and allocated by the Legislative Assembly, an amount that exceeds one-hundredth of one percent of the annual budget adopted by the governing body of the local government for that fiscal year.

(4) When a local government determines that a program is a program for which moneys are required to be appropriated and allocated under subsection (1) of this section, if the local government expended moneys to conduct the program and was not reimbursed under this section for the usual and reasonable costs of the program, the local government may submit the issue of reimbursement to nonbinding arbitration by a panel of three arbitrators. The panel shall consist of one representative from the Oregon Department of Administrative Services, the League of Oregon Cities and the Association of Oregon Counties. The panel shall determine whether the costs incurred by the local government are required to be reimbursed under this section and the amount of reimbursement. The decision of the arbitration panel is not binding upon the parties and may not be enforced by any court in this state.

(5) In any legal proceeding or arbitration proceeding under this section, the local government shall bear the burden of proving by a preponderance of the evidence that moneys appropriated by the Legislative Assembly are not sufficient to reimburse the local government for the usual and reasonable costs of a program.

(6) Except upon approval by three-fifths of the membership of each house of the Legislative Assembly, the Legislative Assembly shall not enact, amend or repeal any law if the anticipated effect of the action is to reduce the amount of state revenues derived from a specific state tax and distributed to local governments as an aggregate during the distribution period for such revenues immediately preceding January 1, 1997.

(7) This section shall not apply to:

(a) Any law that is approved by three-fifths of the membership of each house of the Legislative Assembly.

(b) Any costs resulting from a law creating or changing the definition of a crime or a law establishing sentences for conviction of a crime.

(c) An existing program as enacted by legislation prior to January 1, 1997, except for legislation withdrawing state funds for programs required prior to January 1, 1997, unless the program is made optional.

(d) A new program or an increased level of program services established pursuant to action of the Federal Government so long as the program or increased level of program services imposes costs on local governments that are no greater than the usual and reasonable costs to local governments resulting from compliance with the minimum program standards required under federal law or regulations.

(e) Any requirement imposed by the judicial branch of government.

(f) Legislation enacted or approved by electors in this state under the initiative and referendum powers reserved to the people under section 1, Article IV of this Constitution.

(g) Programs that are intended to inform citizens about the activities of local governments.

(8) When a local government is not required under subsection (3) of this section to comply with a state law or administrative rule or order relating to an enterprise activity, if a nongovernment entity competes with the local government by selling products or services that are similar to the products and services sold under the enterprise activity, the nongovernment entity is not required to comply with the state law or administrative rule or order relating to that enterprise activity.

(9) Nothing in this section shall give rise to a claim by a private person against the State of Oregon based on the establishment of a new program or an increased level of service for an existing program without sufficient appropriation and allocation of funds to pay the ongoing, usual and reasonable costs of performing the mandated service or activity.

(10) Subsection (4) of this section does not apply to a local government when the local government is voluntarily providing a program four years after the effective date of the enactment, rule or order that imposed the program.

(11) In lieu of appropriating and allocating funds under this section, the Legislative Assembly may identify and direct the imposition of a fee or charge to be used by a local government to recover the actual cost of the program. [Created through H.J.R. 2, 1995, and adopted by the people Nov. 5, 1996]

Section 15a. Subsequent vote for reaffirmation of section 15. [Created through H.J.R. 2, 1995, and adopted by the people Nov. 5, 1996; Repeal proposed by S.J.R. 39, 1999, and adopted by the people Nov. 7, 2000]

ARTICLE XI-A
RURAL CREDITS

[Created through initiative petition filed July 6, 1916, and adopted by the people Nov. 7, 1916; Repeal proposed by S.J.R. 1, 1941, and adopted by the people Nov. 3, 1942]

ARTICLE XI-A
FARM AND HOME LOANS TO VETERANS

Section 1. State empowered to make farm and home loans to veterans; standards and priorities for loans. (1) Notwithstanding the limits contained in section 7, Article XI of this Constitution, the credit of the State of Oregon may be loaned and indebtedness incurred in an amount not to exceed eight percent of the true cash value of all the property in the state, for the purpose of creating a fund, to be known as the "Oregon War Veterans' Fund," to be advanced for the acquisition of farms and homes for the benefit of male and female residents of the State of Oregon who served in the Armed Forces of the United States. Secured repayment thereof shall be and is a prerequisite to the advancement of money from such fund, except that moneys in the Oregon War Veterans' Fund may also be appropriated to the Director of Veterans' Affairs to be expended, without security, for the following purposes:

(a) Aiding war veterans' organizations in connection with their programs of service to war veterans;

(b) Training service officers appointed by the counties to give aid as provided by law to veterans and their dependents;

(c) Aiding the counties in connection with programs of service to war veterans;

(d) The duties of the Director of Veterans' Affairs as conservator of the estates of beneficiaries of the United States Veterans' Administration; and

(e) The duties of the Director of Veterans' Affairs in providing services to war veterans, their dependents and survivors.

(2) The Director of Veterans' Affairs may establish standards and priorities with respect to the granting of loans from the Oregon War Veterans' Fund that, as determined by the director, best accomplish the purposes and promote the financial sustainability of the Oregon War Veterans' Fund, including, but not limited to, standards and priorities necessary to maintain the tax-exempt status of earnings from bonds issued under authority of this section and section 2 of this Article. [Created through H.J.R. 7, 1943, and adopted by the people Nov. 7, 1944; Amendment proposed by H.J.R. 1, 1949, and adopted by the people Nov. 7, 1950; Amendment proposed by H.J.R. 14, 1951, and adopted by the people Nov. 4, 1952; Amendment proposed by S.J.R. 14, 1959, and adopted by the people Nov. 8, 1960; Amendment proposed by H.J.R. 9, 1967, and adopted by the people Nov. 5, 1968; Amendment proposed by H.J.R. 33, 1969, and adopted by the people Nov. 3, 1970; Amendment proposed by H.J.R. 12, 1973, and adopted by the people May 28, 1974; Amendment proposed by H.J.R. 10, 1977, and adopted by the people May 17, 1977; Amendment proposed by S.J.R. 53, 1977, and adopted by the people May 17, 1977; Amendment proposed by S.J.R. 2, 1999, and adopted by the people Nov. 7, 2000]

Section 2. Bonds. Bonds of the state of Oregon containing a direct promise on behalf of the state to pay the face value thereof, with the interest therein provided for, may be issued to an amount authorized by section 1 hereof for the purpose of creating said "Oregon War Veterans' Fund." Said bonds shall be a direct obligation of the state and shall be in such form and shall run for such periods of time and bear such rates of interest as provided by statute. [Created through H.J.R. 7, 1943, and adopted by the people Nov. 7, 1944; Amendment proposed by H.J.R. 1, 1949, and adopted by the people Nov. 7, 1950]

Section 3. Eligibility to receive loans. No person shall receive money from the Oregon War Veterans' Fund except the following:

Constitution

(1) A person who:

(a) Resides in the State of Oregon at the time of applying for a loan from the fund;

(b) Served honorably in active duty, other than active duty for training, in the Armed Forces of the United States:

(A) For a period of not less than 210 days or who was, prior to completion of such period of service, discharged or released from active duty on account of service-connected injury or illness; or

(B) In a theater of operations for which a campaign or expeditionary ribbon or medal is authorized by the United States;

(c) Has been honorably separated or discharged from the Armed Forces of the United States or has been furloughed to a reserve; and

(d) Makes application for a loan within the 30-year period immediately following the date on which the person was released from active duty in the Armed Forces of the United States.

(2)(a) The spouse of a person who is qualified to receive a loan under subsection (1) of this section but who has either been missing in action or a prisoner of war while on active duty in the Armed Forces of the United States even though the status of missing or being a prisoner occurred prior to completion of the minimum length of service or residence set forth in subsection (1) of this section, provided the spouse resides in this state at the time of application for the loan.

(b) The surviving spouse of a person who was qualified to receive a loan under subsection (1) of this section but who died while on active duty in the Armed Forces of the United States even though the death occurred prior to completion of the minimum length of service or residence set forth in subsection (1) of this section, provided the surviving spouse resides in this state at the time of application for the loan.

(c) The eligibility of a surviving spouse under this subsection shall terminate on his or her remarriage. [Created through H.J.R. 7, 1943, and adopted by the people Nov. 7, 1944; Amendment proposed by H.J.R. 1, 1949, and adopted by the people Nov. 7, 1950; Amendment proposed by H.J.R. 14, 1951, and adopted by the people Nov. 4, 1952; Amendment proposed by S.J.R. 14, 1959, and adopted by the people Nov. 8, 1960; Amendment proposed by H.J.R. 9, 1967, and adopted by the people Nov. 5, 1968; Amendment proposed by S.J.R. 23, 1971, and adopted by the people Nov. 7, 1972; Amendment proposed by H.J.R. 23, 1975, and adopted by the people May 25, 1976; Amendment proposed by H.J.R. 23, 1979, and adopted by the people May 20, 1980; Amendment proposed by S.J.R. 3, 1995, and adopted by the people Nov. 5, 1996; Amendment proposed by S.J.R. 2, 1999, and adopted by the people Nov. 7, 2000]

Section 4. Tax levy. There shall be levied each year, at the same time and in the same manner that other taxes are levied, a tax upon all property in the state of Oregon not exempt from taxation, not to exceed two (2) mills on each dollar valuation, to provide for the payment of principal and interest of the bonds authorized to be issued by this article. The two (2) mills additional tax herein provided for hereby is specifically authorized and said tax levy hereby authorized shall be in addition to all other taxes which may be levied according to law. [Created through H.J.R. 7, 1943, and adopted by the people Nov. 7, 1944; Amendment proposed by H.J.R. 85, 1997, and adopted by the people May 20, 1997]

Section 5. Repeal of conflicting constitutional provisions. The provisions of the constitution in conflict with this amendment hereby are repealed so far as they conflict herewith. [Created through H.J.R. 7, 1943, and adopted by the people Nov. 7, 1944]

Section 6. Refunding bonds. Refunding bonds may be issued and sold to refund any bonds issued under authority of sections 1 and 2 of this article. There may be issued and outstanding at any one time bonds aggregating the amount authorized by section 1 hereof, but at no time shall the total of all bonds outstanding, including refunding bonds, exceed the amount so authorized. [Created through H.J.R. 7, 1943, and adopted by the people Nov. 7, 1944]

ARTICLE XI-B
STATE PAYMENT OF IRRIGATION AND DRAINAGE DISTRICT INTEREST

[Created through H.J.R. 32, 1919, and adopted by the people June 3, 1919; Repeal proposed by H.J.R. 1, 1929, and adopted by the people Nov. 4, 1930]

ARTICLE XI-C
WORLD WAR VETERANS' STATE AID SINKING FUND

[Created through H.J.R. 12, 1921, and adopted by the people June 7, 1921; Amendment proposed by H.J.R. 7, 1923, and adopted by the people Nov. 4, 1924; Repeal proposed by S.J.R. 12, 1951, and adopted by the people Nov. 4, 1952]

ARTICLE XI-D
STATE POWER DEVELOPMENT

Sec. 1. State's rights, title and interest to water and water-power sites to be held in perpetuity
  2. State's powers enumerated
  3. Legislation to effectuate article
  4. Construction of article

Section 1. State's rights, title and interest to water and water-power sites to be held in perpetuity. The rights, title and interest in and to all water for the development of water power and to water power sites, which the state of Oregon now owns or may hereafter acquire, shall be held by it in perpetuity. [Created through initiative petition filed July 7, 1932, and adopted by the people Nov. 8, 1932]

Section 2. State's powers enumerated. The state of Oregon is authorized and empowered:

1. To control and/or develop the water power within the state;

2. To lease water and water power sites for the development of water power;

3. To control, use, transmit, distribute, sell and/or dispose of electric energy;

4. To develop, separately or in conjunction with the United States, or in conjunction with the political subdivisions of this state, any water power within the state, and to acquire, construct, maintain and/or operate hydroelectric power plants, transmission and distribution lines;

5. To develop, separately or in conjunction with the United States, with any state or states, or political subdivisions thereof, or with any political subdivision of this state, any water power in any interstate stream and to acquire, construct, maintain and/or operate hydroelectric power plants, transmission and distribution lines;

6. To contract with the United States, with any state or states, or political subdivisions thereof, or with any political subdivision of this state, for the purchase or acquisition of water, water power and/or electric energy for use, transmission, distribution, sale and/or disposal thereof;

7. To fix rates and charges for the use of water in the development of water power and for the sale and/or disposal of water power and/or electric energy;

8. To loan the credit of the state, and to incur indebtedness to an amount not exceeding one and one-half percent of the true cash value of all the property in the state taxed on an ad valorem basis, for the purpose of providing funds with which to carry out the provisions of this article, notwithstanding any limitations elsewhere contained in this constitution;

9. To do any and all things necessary or convenient to carry out the provisions of this article. [Created through initiative petition filed July 7, 1932, and adopted by the people Nov. 8, 1932; Amendment proposed by S.J.R. 6, 1961, and adopted by the people Nov. 6, 1962]

Section 3. Legislation to effectuate article. The legislative assembly shall, and the people may, provide any legislation that may be necessary in addition to existing laws, to carry out the provisions of this article; Provided, that any board or commission created, or empowered to administer the laws enacted to carry out the purposes of this article shall consist of three members and be elected without party affiliation or designation. [Created through initiative petition filed July 7, 1932, and adopted by the people Nov. 8, 1932]

Section 4. Construction of article. Nothing in this article shall be construed to affect in any way the laws, and the administration thereof, now existing or hereafter enacted, relating to the appropriation and use of water for beneficial purposes, other than for the development of water power. [Created through initiative petition filed July 7, 1932, and adopted by the people Nov. 8, 1932]

ARTICLE XI-E
STATE REFORESTATION

Section 1. State empowered to lend credit for forest rehabilitation and reforestation; bonds; taxation. The credit of the state may be loaned and indebtedness incurred in an amount which shall not exceed at any one time 3/16 of 1 percent of the true cash value of all the property in the state taxed on an ad valorem basis, to provide funds for forest rehabilitation and reforestation and for the acquisition, management, and development of lands for such purposes. So long as any such indebtedness shall remain outstanding, the funds derived from the sale, exchange, or use of said lands, and from the disposal of products therefrom, shall be applied only in the liquidation of such indebtedness. Bonds or other obligations issued pursuant hereto may be renewed or refunded. An ad valorem tax shall be levied annually upon all the property in the state of Oregon taxed on an ad valorem basis, in sufficient amount to provide for the payment of such indebtedness and the interest thereon. The legislative assembly may provide other revenues to supplement or replace the said tax levies. The legislature shall enact legislation to carry out the provisions hereof. This amendment shall supersede all constitutional provisions in conflict herewith. [Created through H.J.R. 24, 1947, and adopted by the people Nov. 2, 1948; Amendment proposed by S.J.R. 7, 1961, and adopted by the people Nov. 6, 1962;

Amendment proposed by H.J.R. 85, 1997, and adopted by the people May 20, 1997]

ARTICLE XI-F(1)
HIGHER EDUCATION BUILDING PROJECTS

Sec. 1. State empowered to lend credit for higher education building projects
2. Only self-liquidating projects authorized
3. Sources of revenue
4. Bonds
5. Legislation to effectuate Article

Section 1. State empowered to lend credit for higher education building projects. The credit of the state may be loaned and indebtedness incurred in an amount which shall not exceed at any one time three-fourths of one percent of the true cash value of all the taxable property in the state, as determined by law to provide funds with which to redeem and refund outstanding revenue bonds issued to finance the cost of buildings and other projects for higher education, and to construct, improve, repair, equip, and furnish buildings and other structures for such purpose, and to purchase or improve sites therefor. [Created through H.J.R. 26, 1949, and adopted by the people Nov. 7, 1950; Amendment proposed by H.J.R. 12, 1959, and adopted by the people Nov. 8, 1960]

Section 2. Only self-liquidating projects authorized. The buildings and structures hereafter constructed for higher education pursuant to this amendment shall be such only as conservatively shall appear to the constructing authority to be wholly self-liquidating and self-supporting from revenues, gifts, grants, or building fees. All unpledged net revenues of buildings and other projects may be pooled with the net revenues of new buildings or projects in order to render the new buildings or projects self-liquidating and self-supporting. [Created through H.J.R. 26, 1949, and adopted by the people Nov. 7, 1950]

Section 3. Sources of revenue. Ad valorem taxes shall be levied annually upon all the taxable property in the state of Oregon in sufficient amount, with the aforesaid revenues, gifts, grants, or building fees, to provide for the payment of such indebtedness and the interest thereon. The legislative assembly may provide other revenues to supplement or replace such tax levies. [Created through H.J.R. 26, 1949, and adopted by the people Nov. 7, 1950]

Section 4. Bonds. Bonds issued pursuant to this article shall be the direct general obligations of the state, and be in such form, run for such periods of time, and bear such rates of interest, as shall be provided by statute. Such bonds may be refunded with bonds of like obligation. Unless provided by statute, no bonds shall be issued pursuant to this article for the construction of buildings or other structures for higher education until after all of the aforesaid outstanding revenue bonds shall have been redeemed or refunded. [Created through H.J.R. 26, 1949, and adopted by the people Nov. 7, 1950]

Section 5. Legislation to effectuate Article. The legislative assembly shall enact legislation to carry out the provisions hereof. This article shall supersede all conflicting constitutional provisions. [Created through H.J.R. 26, 1949, and adopted by the people Nov. 7, 1950]

ARTICLE XI-F(2)
VETERANS' BONUS

Sec. 1. State empowered to lend credit to pay veterans' bonus; issuance of bonds

2. Definitions
3. Amount of bonus
4. Survivors of certain deceased veterans entitled to maximum amount
5. Certain persons not eligible
6. Order of distribution among survivors
7. Bonus not saleable or assignable; bonus free from creditors' claims and state taxes
8. Administration of Article; rules and regulations
9. Applications
10. Furnishing forms; printing, office supplies and equipment; employes; payment of expenses

Section 1. State empowered to lend credit to pay veterans' bonus; issuance of bonds. Notwithstanding the limitations contained in Section 7 of Article XI of the constitution, the credit of the State of Oregon may be loaned and indebtedness incurred in an amount not exceeding 5 percent of the assessed valuation of all the property in the state, for the purpose of creating a fund to be paid to residents of the State of Oregon who served in the armed forces of the United States between September 16, 1940, and June 30, 1946, and were honorably discharged from such service, which fund shall be known as the "World War II Veterans' Compensation Fund."

Bonds of the State of Oregon, containing a direct promise on behalf of the state to pay the face value thereof with the interest thereon provided for may be issued to an amount authorized in Section 1 hereof for the purpose of creating said World War II Veterans' Compensation Fund. Refunding bonds may be issued and sold to refund any bonds issued under authority of Section 1 hereof. There may be issued and outstanding at any one time bonds aggregating the amount authorized by Section 1, but at no time shall the total of all bonds outstanding, including refunding bonds, exceed the amount so authorized. Said bonds shall be a direct obligation of the State and shall be in such form and shall run for such periods of time and bear such rates of interest as shall be provided by statute. No person shall be eligible to receive money from said fund except the veterans as defined in Section 3 of this act [sic]. The legislature shall and the people may provide any additional legislation that may be necessary, in addition to existing laws, to carry out the provisions of this section. [Created through initiative petition filed June 30, 1950, and adopted by the people Nov. 7, 1950]

Section 2. Definitions. The following words, terms, and phrases, as used in this act [sic] shall have the following meaning unless the text otherwise requires:

1. "Domestic service" means service within the continental limits of the United States, excluding Alaska, Hawaii, Canal Zone and Puerto Rico.

2. "Foreign Service" means service in all other places, including sea duty.

3. "Husband" means the unremarried husband, and "wife" means the unremarried wife.

4. "Child or Children" means child or children of issue, child or children by adoption or child or children to whom the deceased person has stood in loco parentis for one year or more immediately preceding his death.

5. "Parent or Parents" means natural parent or parents; parent or parents by adoption; or, person or persons, including stepparent or stepparents, who have stood in loco parentis to the deceased person for a period of one year or more immediately prior to entrance into the armed service of the United States.

6. "Veterans" means any person who shall have served in active duty in the armed forces of the United States at

any time between September 16, 1940, and June 30, 1946, both dates inclusive, and who, at the time of commencing such service, was and had been a bona fide resident of the State of Oregon for at least one year immediately preceding the commencement of such service, and who shall have been separated from such service under honorable conditions, or who is still in such service, or who has been retired. [Created through initiative petition filed June 30, 1950, and adopted by the people Nov. 7, 1950]

Section 3. Amount of bonus. Every veteran who was in such service for a period of at least 90 days shall be entitled to receive compensation at the rate of Ten Dollars ($10.00) for each full month during which such veteran was in active domestic service and Fifteen Dollars ($15.00) for each full month during which such veteran was in active foreign service within said period of time. Any veteran who was serving on active duty in the armed forces between September 16, 1940, and June 30, 1946, whose services were terminated by reason of service-connected disabilities, and who, upon filing a claim for disabilities with the United States Veterans' Administration within three months after separation from the armed service, was rated not less than 50% disabled as a result of such claim, shall be deemed to have served sufficient time to entitle him or her to the maximum payment under this act [sic] and shall be so entitled. The maximum amount of compensation payable under this act [sic] shall be six hundred dollars ($600.00) and no such compensation shall be paid to any veteran who shall have received from another state a bonus or compensation because of such military service. [Created through initiative petition filed June 30, 1950, and adopted by the people Nov. 7, 1950]

Section 4. Survivors of certain deceased veterans entitled to maximum amount. The survivor or survivors, of the deceased veteran whose death was caused or contributed to by a service-connected disease or disability incurred in service under conditions other than dishonorable, shall be entitled, in the order of survivorship provided in this act [sic], to receive the maximum amount of said compensation irrespective of the amount such deceased would have been entitled to receive if living. [Created through initiative petition filed June 30, 1950, and adopted by the people Nov. 7, 1950]

Section 5. Certain persons not eligible. No compensation shall be paid under this act [sic] to any veteran who, during the period of service refused on conscientious, political or other grounds to subject himself to full military discipline and unqualified service, or to any veteran for any periods of time spent under penal confinement during the period of active duty, or for service in the merchant marine: Provided, however, that for the purposes of this act [sic], active service in the chaplain corps, or medical corps shall be deemed unqualified service under full military discipline. [Created through initiative petition filed June 30, 1950, and adopted by the people Nov. 7, 1950]

Section 6. Order of distribution among survivors. The survivor or survivors of any deceased veteran who would have been entitled to compensation under this act [sic], other than those mentioned in Section 4 of this act [sic], shall be entitled to receive the same amount of compensation as said deceased veteran would have received, if living, which shall be distributed as follows:

1. To the husband or wife, as the case may be, the whole amount.

2. If there be no husband or wife, to the child or children, equally; and

3. If there be no husband or wife or child or children, to the parent or parents, equally.

[Created through initiative petition filed June 30, 1950, and adopted by the people Nov. 7, 1950]

Section 7. Bonus not saleable or assignable; bonus free from creditors' claims and state taxes. No sale or assignment of any right or claim to compensation under this act [sic] shall be valid, no claims of creditors shall be enforcible against rights or claims to or payments of such compensation, and such compensation shall be exempt from all taxes imposed by the laws of this state. [Created through initiative petition filed June 30, 1950, and adopted by the people Nov. 7, 1950]

Section 8. Administration of article; rules and regulations. The director of Veterans' Affairs, State of Oregon, referred to herein as the "director" hereby is authorized and empowered, and it shall be his duty, to administer the provisions of this act [sic], and with the approval of the veterans advisory committee may make such rules and regulations as are deemed necessary to accomplish the purpose hereof. [Created through initiative petition filed June 30, 1950, and adopted by the people Nov. 7, 1950]

Section 9. Applications. All applications for certificates under this act [sic] shall be made within two years from the effective date hereof and upon forms to be supplied by the director. Said applications shall be duly verified by the claimant before a notary public or other person authorized to take acknowledgments, and shall set forth applicant's name, residence at the time of entry into the service, date and place of enlistment, induction or entry upon active federal service, beginning and ending dates of foreign service, date of discharge, retirement or release from active federal service, statement of time lost by reason of penal confinement during the period of active duty; together with the applicant's original discharge, or certificate in lieu of lost discharge, or certificate of service, or if the applicant has not been released at the time of application, a statement by competent military authority that the applicant during the period for which compensation is claimed did not refuse to subject himself to full military discipline and unqualified service, and that the applicant has not been separated from service under circumstances other than honorable. The director may require such further information to be included in such application as deemed necessary to enable him to determine the eligibility of the applicant. Such applications, together with satisfactory evidence of honorable service, shall be filed with the director. The director shall make such reasonable requirements for applicants as may be necessary to prevent fraud or the payment of compensation to persons not entitled thereto. [Created through initiative petition filed June 30, 1950, and adopted by the people Nov. 7, 1950]

Section 10. Furnishing forms; printing, office supplies and equipment; employes; payment of expenses. The director shall furnish free of charge, upon request, the necessary forms upon which applications may be made and may authorize the county clerks, Veterans organizations and other organizations, and notaries public willing to assist veterans without charge, to act for him in receiving application under this act [sic], and shall furnish such clerks, organizations and notaries public, with the proper forms for such purpose. The director

hereby is authorized and directed with the approval of the veterans' advisory committee, to procure such printing, office supplies and equipment and to employ such persons as may be necessary in order to properly carry out the provisions of this act [sic], and all expense incurred by him in the administration thereof shall be paid out of the World War II Veterans' Compensation Fund, in the manner provided by law for payment of claims from other state funds. [Created through initiative petition filed June 30, 1950, and adopted by the people Nov. 7, 1950]

ARTICLE XI-G
HIGHER EDUCATION INSTITUTIONS AND ACTIVITIES; COMMUNITY COLLEGES

Sec. 1. State empowered to lend credit for financing higher education institutions and activities, and community colleges
2. Bonds
3. Sources of revenue

Section 1. State empowered to lend credit for financing higher education institutions and activities, and community colleges. (1) Notwithstanding the limitations contained in section 7, Article XI of this Constitution, and in addition to other exceptions from the limitations of such section, the credit of the state may be loaned and indebtedness incurred in an amount not to exceed at any time three-fourths of one percent of the true cash value of all taxable property in the state, as determined by law.

(2) Proceeds from any loan authorized or indebtedness incurred under this section shall be used to provide funds with which to construct, improve, repair, equip and furnish those buildings, structures and projects, or parts thereof, and to purchase or improve sites therefor, designated by the Legislative Assembly for higher education institutions and activities and for community colleges authorized by law to receive state aid.

(3) The amount of any loan authorized or indebtedness incurred under this section by means of bonds to be issued in any biennium shall not exceed the dollar amount appropriated from the General Fund for the same or similar purposes. Any dollar amounts appropriated to meet the requirements of this subsection shall be specifically designated therefor by the Legislative Assembly.

(4) Nothing in this section prevents the financing of buildings, structures and projects, or parts thereof, by a combination of the moneys available under this section, under Article XI-F(1) of this Constitution, and from other lawful sources. However, moneys available under this section shall not be expended on or for any buildings, structures or projects, or parts thereof, that are wholly self-liquidating and self-supporting. [Created through H.J.R. 8, 1963 (s.s.), and adopted by the people May 15, 1964; Amendment proposed by H.J.R. 2, 1967 (s.s.), and adopted by the people May 28, 1968]

Section 2. Bonds. Bonds issued pursuant to this Article shall be the direct general obligations of the state and shall be in such form, run for such periods of time, and bear such rates of interest as the Legislative Assembly provides. Such bonds may be refunded with bonds of like obligation. [Created through H.J.R. 8, 1963 (s.s.), and adopted by the people May 15, 1964]

Section 3. Sources of revenue. Ad valorem taxes shall be levied annually upon the taxable property within the State of Oregon in sufficient amount to provide for the prompt payment of bonds issued pursuant to this Article and the interest thereon. The Legislative Assembly may provide other revenues to supplement or replace, in whole or in part, such tax levies. [Created through H.J.R. 8, 1963 (s.s.), and adopted by the people May 15, 1964]

ARTICLE XI-H
POLLUTION CONTROL

Sec. 1. State empowered to lend credit for financing pollution control facilities or related activities
2. Only facilities seventy percent self-supporting and self-liquidating authorized; exceptions
3. Authority of public bodies to receive funds
4. Sources of revenue
5. Bonds
6. Legislation to effectuate Article

Section 1. State empowered to lend credit for financing pollution control facilities or related activities. In the manner provided by law and notwithstanding the limitations contained in sections 7 and 8, Article XI, of this Constitution, the credit of the State of Oregon may be loaned and indebtedness incurred in an amount not to exceed, at any one time, one percent of the true cash value of all taxable property in the state:

(1) To provide funds to be advanced, by contract, grant, loan or otherwise, to any municipal corporation, city, county or agency of the State of Oregon, or combinations thereof, for the purpose of planning, acquisition, construction, alteration or improvement of facilities for or activities related to, the collection, treatment, dilution and disposal of all forms of waste in or upon the air, water and lands of this state; and

(2) To provide funds for the acquisition, by purchase, loan or otherwise, of bonds, notes or other obligations of any municipal corporation, city, county or agency of the State of Oregon, or combinations thereof, issued or made for the purposes of subsection (1) of this section. [Created through H.J.R. 14, 1969, and adopted by the people May 26, 1970; Amendment proposed by S.J.R. 41, 1989, and adopted by the people May 22, 1990]

Section 2. Only facilities seventy percent self-supporting and self-liquidating authorized; exceptions. The facilities for which funds are advanced and for which bonds, notes or other obligations are issued or made and acquired pursuant to this Article shall be only such facilities as conservatively appear to the agency designated by law to make the determination to be not less than 70 percent self-supporting and self-liquidating from revenues, gifts, grants from the Federal Government, user charges, assessments and other fees. This section shall not apply to any activities for which funds are advanced and shall not apply to facilities for the collection, treatment, dilution, removal and disposal of hazardous substances. [Created through H.J.R. 14, 1969, and adopted by the people May 26, 1970; Amendment proposed by S.J.R. 41, 1989, and adopted by the people May 22, 1990]

Section 3. Authority of public bodies to receive funds. Notwithstanding the limitations contained in section 10, Article XI of this Constitution, municipal corporations, cities, counties, and agencies of the State of Oregon, or combinations thereof, may receive funds referred to in section 1 of this Article, by contract, grant, loan or otherwise and may also receive such funds through disposition to the state, by sale, loan or otherwise, of bonds, notes or other obligations issued or made for the purposes set forth in section 1 of this Article.

[Created through H.J.R. 14, 1969, and adopted by the people May 26, 1970]

Section 4. Sources of revenue. Ad valorem taxes shall be levied annually upon all taxable property within the State of Oregon in sufficient amount to provide, together with the revenues, gifts, grants from the Federal Government, user charges, assessments and other fees referred to in section 2 of this Article for the payment of indebtedness incurred by the state and the interest thereon. The Legislative Assembly may provide other revenues to supplement or replace such tax levies. [Created through H.J.R. 14, 1969, and adopted by the people May 26, 1970]

Section 5. Bonds. Bonds issued pursuant to section 1 of this Article shall be the direct obligations of the state and shall be in such form, run for such periods of time, and bear such rates of interest, as shall be provided by law. Such bonds may be refunded with bonds of like obligation. [Created through H.J.R. 14, 1969, and adopted by the people May 26, 1970]

Section 6. Legislation to effectuate Article. The Legislative Assembly shall enact legislation to carry out the provisions of this Article. This Article shall supersede all conflicting constitutional provisions and shall supersede any conflicting provision of a county or city charter or act of incorporation. [Created through H.J.R. 14, 1969, and adopted by the people May 26, 1970]

ARTICLE XI-I(1)
WATER DEVELOPMENT PROJECTS

Sec. 1. State empowered to lend credit to established Water Development Fund; eligibility; use
2. Bonds
3. Refunding bonds
4. Sources of revenue
5. Legislation to effectuate Article

Section 1. State empowered to lend credit to establish Water Development Fund; eligibility; use. Notwithstanding the limits contained in sections 7 and 8, Article XI of this Constitution, the credit of the State of Oregon may be loaned and indebtedness incurred in an amount not to exceed one and one-half percent of the true cash value of all the property in the state for the purpose of creating a fund to be known as the Water Development Fund. The fund shall be used to provide financing for loans for residents of this state for construction of water development projects for irrigation, drainage, fish protection, watershed restoration and municipal uses and for the acquisition of easements and rights of way for water development projects authorized by law. Secured repayment thereof shall be and is a prerequisite to the advancement of money from such fund. As used in this section, "resident" includes both natural persons and any corporation or cooperative, either for profit or nonprofit, whose principal income is from farming in Oregon or municipal or quasi-municipal or other body subject to the laws of the State of Oregon. Not less than 50 percent of the potential amount available from the fund will be reserved for irrigation and drainage projects. For municipal use, only municipalities and communities with populations less than 30,000 are eligible for loans from the fund. [Created through S.J.R. 1, 1977, and adopted by the people Nov. 8, 1977; Amendment proposed by S.J.R. 6, 1981, and adopted by the people May 18, 1982; Amendment proposed by H.J.R. 45, 1987, and adopted by the people May 17, 1988]

Section 2. Bonds. Bonds of the State of Oregon containing a direct promise on behalf of the state to pay the face value thereof, with the interest therein provided for, may be issued to an amount authorized by section 1 of this Article for the purpose of creating such fund. The bonds shall be a direct obligation of the state and shall be in such form and shall run for such periods of time and bear such rates of interest as provided by statute. [Created through S.J.R. 1, 1977, and adopted by the people Nov. 8, 1977]

Section 3. Refunding bonds. Refunding bonds may be issued and sold to refund any bonds issued under authority of sections 1 and 2 of this Article. There may be issued and outstanding at any time bonds aggregating the amount authorized by section 1 of this Article but at no time shall the total of all bonds outstanding, including refunding bonds, exceed the amount so authorized. [Created through S.J.R. 1, 1977, and adopted by the people Nov. 8, 1977]

Section 4. Sources of revenue. Ad valorem taxes shall be levied annually upon all the taxable property in the State of Oregon in sufficient amount to provide for the payment of principal and interest of the bonds issued pursuant to this Article. The Legislative Assembly may provide other revenues to supplement or replace, in whole or in part, such tax levies. [Created through S.J.R. 1, 1977, and adopted by the people Nov. 8, 1977]

Section 5. Legislation to effectuate Article. The Legislative Assembly shall enact legislation to carry out the provisions of this Article. This Article supersedes any conflicting provision of a county or city charter or act of incorporation. [Created through S.J.R. 1, 1977, and adopted by the people Nov. 8, 1977]

ARTICLE XI-I(2)
MULTIFAMILY HOUSING FOR ELDERLY AND DISABLED

Sec. 1. State empowered to lend credit for multifamily housing for elderly and disabled persons
2. Sources of revenue
3. Bonds
4. Legislation to effectuate Article

Section 1. State empowered to lend credit for multifamily housing for elderly and disabled persons. In the manner provided by law and notwithstanding the limitations contained in section 7, Article XI of this Constitution, the credit of the State of Oregon may be loaned and indebtedness incurred in an amount not to exceed, at any one time, one-half of one percent of the true cash value of all taxable property in the state to provide funds to be advanced, by contract, grant, loan or otherwise, for the purpose of providing additional financing for multifamily housing for the elderly and for disabled persons. Multifamily housing means a structure or facility designed to contain more than one living unit. Additional financing may be provided to the elderly to purchase ownership interest in the structure or facility. [Created through H.J.R. 61, 1977, and adopted by the people May 23, 1978; Amendment proposed by S.J.R. 34, 1979, and adopted by the people May 20, 1980; Amendment proposed by H.J.R. 1, 1981, and adopted by the people May 18, 1982]

Section 2. Sources of revenue. The bonds shall be payable from contract or loan proceeds; bond reserves; other funds available for these purposes; and, if necessary, state ad valorem taxes. [Created through H.J.R. 61, 1977, and adopted by the people May 23, 1978]

Section 3. Bonds. Bonds issued pursuant to section 1 of this Article shall be the direct obligations of the state and shall be in such form, run for such periods of time

and bear such rates of interest as shall be provided by law. The bonds may be refunded with bonds of like obligation. [Created through H.J.R. 61, 1977, and adopted by the people May 23, 1978]

Section 4. Legislation to effectuate Article. The Legislative Assembly shall enact legislation to carry out the provisions of this Article. This Article shall supersede all conflicting constitutional provisions. [Created through H.J.R. 61, 1977, and adopted by the people May 23, 1978]

ARTICLE XI-J
SMALL SCALE LOCAL ENERGY LOANS

Sec. 1. State empowered to loan credit for small scale local energy loans; eligibility; use
2. Bonds
3. Refunding bonds
4. Sources of revenue
5. Legislation to effectuate Article

Section 1. State empowered to loan credit for small scale local energy loans; eligibility; use. Notwithstanding the limits contained in sections 7 and 8, Article XI of this Constitution, the credit of the State of Oregon may be loaned and indebtedness incurred in an amount not to exceed one-half of one percent of the true cash value of all the property in the state for the purpose of creating a fund to be known as the Small Scale Local Energy Project Loan Fund. The fund shall be used to provide financing for the development of small scale local energy projects. Secured repayment thereof shall be and is a prerequisite to the advancement of money from such fund. [Created through S.J.R. 24, 1979, and adopted by the people May 20, 1980]

Section 2. Bonds. Bonds of the State of Oregon containing a direct promise on behalf of the state to pay the face value thereof, with the interest therein provided for, may be issued to an amount authorized by section 1 of this Article for the purpose of creating such fund. The bonds shall be a direct obligation of the state and shall be in such form and shall run for such periods of time and bear such rates of interest as provided by statute. [Created through S.J.R. 24, 1979, and adopted by the people May 20, 1980]

Section 3. Refunding bonds. Refunding bonds may be issued and sold to refund any bonds issued under authority of sections 1 and 2 of this Article. There may be issued and outstanding at any time bonds aggregating the amount authorized by section 1 of this Article but at no time shall the total of all bonds outstanding including refunding bonds, exceed the amount so authorized. [Created through S.J.R. 24, 1979, and adopted by the people May 20, 1980]

Section 4. Sources of revenue. Ad valorem taxes shall be levied annually upon all the taxable property in the State of Oregon in sufficient amount to provide for the payment of principal and interest of the bonds issued pursuant to this Article. The Legislative Assembly may provide other revenues to supplement or replace, in whole or in part, such tax levies. [Created through S.J.R. 24, 1979, and adopted by the people May 20, 1980]

Section 5. Legislation to effectuate Article. The Legislative Assembly shall enact legislation to carry out the provisions of this Article. This Article supersedes any conflicting provision of a county or city charter or act of incorporation. [Created through S.J.R. 24, 1979, and adopted by the people May 20, 1980]

Constitution

ARTICLE XI-K
GUARANTEE OF
BONDED INDEBTEDNESS OF
EDUCATION DISTRICTS

Sec. 1. State empowered to guarantee bonded indebtedness of education districts
2. State empowered to lend credit for state guarantee of bonded indebtedness of education districts
3. Repayment by education districts
4. Sources of revenue
5. Bonds
6. Legislation to effectuate Article

Section 1. State empowered to guarantee bonded indebtedness of education districts. To secure lower interest costs on the general obligation bonds of school districts, education service districts and community college districts, the State of Oregon may guarantee the general obligation bonded indebtedness of those districts as provided in sections 2 to 6 of this Article and laws enacted pursuant to this Article. [Created through H.J.R. 71, 1997, and adopted by the people Nov. 3, 1998]

Section 2. State empowered to lend credit for state guarantee of bonded indebtedness of education districts. In the manner provided by law and notwithstanding the limitations contained in sections 7 and 8, Article XI of this Constitution, the credit of the State of Oregon may be loaned and indebtedness incurred, in an amount not to exceed, at any one time, one-half of one percent of the true cash value of all taxable property in the state, to provide funds as necessary to satisfy the state guaranty of the bonded general obligation indebtedness of school districts, education service districts and community college districts that qualify, under procedures that shall be established by law, to issue general obligation bonds that are guaranteed by the full faith and credit of this state. The state may guarantee the general obligation debt of qualified school districts, education service districts and community college districts and may guarantee general obligation bonded indebtedness incurred to refund the school district, education service district or community college district general obligation bonded indebtedness. [Created through H.J.R. 71, 1997, and adopted by the people Nov. 3, 1998]

Section 3. Repayment by education districts. The Legislative Assembly may provide that reimbursement to the state shall be obtained from, but shall not be limited to, moneys that otherwise would be used for the support of the educational programs of the school district, the education service district or the community college district that incurred the bonded indebtedness with respect to which any payment under the state's guaranty is made. [Created through H.J.R. 71, 1997, and adopted by the people Nov. 3, 1998]

Section 4. Sources of revenue. The State of Oregon may issue bonds if and as necessary to provide funding to satisfy the state's guaranty obligations undertaken pursuant to this Article. In addition, notwithstanding anything to the contrary in Article VIII of this Constitution, the state may borrow available moneys from the Common School Fund if such borrowing is reasonably necessary to satisfy the state's guaranty obligations undertaken pursuant to this Article. The State of Oregon also may issue bonds if and as necessary to provide funding to repay the borrowed moneys, and any interest thereon, to the Common School Fund. The bonds shall be payable from any moneys reimbursed to the state under section 3 of this Article, from any moneys recoverable

from the school district, the education service district or the community college district that incurred the bonded indebtedness with respect to which any payment under the state's guaranty is made, any other funds available for these purposes and, if necessary, from state ad valorem taxes. [Created through H.J.R. 71, 1997, and adopted by the people Nov. 3, 1998]

Section 5. Bonds. Bonds of the state issued pursuant to this Article shall be the direct obligations of the state and shall be in such form, run for such periods of time and bear such rates of interest as shall be provided by law. The bonds may be refunded with bonds of like obligation. [Created through H.J.R. 71, 1997, and adopted by the people Nov. 3, 1998]

Section 6. Legislation to effectuate Article. The Legislative Assembly shall enact legislation to carry out the provisions of this Article, including provisions that authorize the state's recovery, from any school district, education service district or community college district that incurred the bonded indebtedness with respect to which any payment under the state's guaranty is made, any amounts necessary to make the state whole. This Article shall supersede all conflicting constitutional provisions and shall supersede any conflicting provision of any law, ordinance or charter pertaining to any school district, education service district or community college district. [Created through H.J.R. 71, 1997, and adopted by the people Nov. 3, 1998]

ARTICLE XI-L
OREGON HEALTH AND SCIENCE
UNIVERSITY

Sec. 1. State empowered to lend credit for financing capital costs of Oregon Health and Science University; bonds
2. Sources of repayment
3. Refunding bonds
4. Legislation to effectuate Article
5. Relationship to conflicting provisions of Constitution

Section 1. State empowered to lend credit for financing capital costs of Oregon Health and Science University; bonds. (1) In the manner provided by law and notwithstanding the limitations contained in section 7, Article XI of this Constitution, the credit of the State of Oregon may be loaned and indebtedness incurred, in an aggregate outstanding principal amount not to exceed, at any one time, one-half of one percent of the real market value of all property in the state, to provide funds to finance capital costs of Oregon Health and Science University. Bonds issued under this section may not be paid from ad valorem property taxes.

(2) Any indebtedness incurred under this section shall be in the form of general obligation bonds of the State of Oregon containing a direct promise on behalf of the State of Oregon to pay the principal, premium, if any, and interest on such bonds, in an aggregate outstanding principal amount not to exceed the amount authorized in subsection (1) of this section. The bonds shall be the direct obligation of the State of Oregon and shall be in such form, run for such period of time, have such terms and bear such rates of interest as may be provided by statute. The full faith and credit and taxing power of the State of Oregon shall be pledged to the payment of the principal, premium, if any, and interest on such bonds provided, however, that the ad valorem taxing power of the State of Oregon may not be pledged to the payment of such bonds.

(3) The proceeds from bonds issued under this section shall be used to finance capital costs of Oregon Health and Science University and costs of issuing bonds pursuant to this Article. Bonds issued under this section to finance capital costs of Oregon Health and Science University shall be issued in an aggregate principal amount that produces net proceeds for the university in an amount that does not exceed $200 million.

(4) The proceeds from bonds issued under this section may not be used to finance operating costs of Oregon Health and Science University.

(5) As used in this Article, "bonds" means bonds, notes or other financial obligations of the State of Oregon issued under this section. [Created through H.J.R. 19, 2001, and adopted by the people May 21, 2002]

Section 2. Sources of repayment. The principal, premium, if any, interest and any other amounts payable with respect to bonds issued under section 1 of this Article shall be repaid as determined by the Legislative Assembly from the following sources:

(1) Amounts appropriated for such purpose by the Legislative Assembly from the General Fund, including any taxes levied to pay the bonds other than ad valorem property taxes;

(2) Amounts allocated for such purpose by the Legislative Assembly from the proceeds of the State Lottery or from the Master Settlement Agreement entered into on November 23, 1998, by the State of Oregon and leading United States tobacco product manufacturers; and

(3) Amounts appropriated or allocated for such purpose by the Legislative Assembly from other sources of revenue. [Created through H.J.R. 19, 2001, and adopted by the people May 21, 2002]

Section 3. Refunding bonds. Bonds issued under section 1 of this Article may be refunded with bonds of like obligation. [Created through H.J.R. 19, 2001, and adopted by the people May 21, 2002]

Section 4. Legislation to effectuate Article. The Legislative Assembly may enact legislation to carry out the provisions of this Article. [Created through H.J.R. 19, 2001, and adopted by the people May 21, 2002]

Section 5. Relationship to conflicting provision of Constitution. This Article shall supersede all conflicting provisions of this constitution. [Created through H.J.R. 19, 2001, and adopted by the people May 21, 2002]

ARTICLE XI-M
SEISMIC REHABILITATION OF
PUBLIC EDUCATION BUILDINGS

Note: Article XI-M was designated as "Article XI-L" by S.J.R. 21, 2001, and adopted by the people Nov. 5, 2002.

Section 1. State empowered to lend credit for seismic rehabilitation of public education buildings; bonds. (1) In the manner provided by law and notwithstanding the limitations contained in section 7, Article XI of this Constitution, the credit of the State of Oregon may be loaned and indebtedness incurred, in an aggregate outstanding principal amount not to exceed, at any one time,

one-fifth of one percent of the real market value of all property in the state, to provide funds for the planning and implementation of seismic rehabilitation of public education buildings, including surveying and conducting engineering evaluations of the need for seismic rehabilitation.

(2) Any indebtedness incurred under this section must be in the form of general obligation bonds of the State of Oregon containing a direct promise on behalf of the State of Oregon to pay the principal, premium, if any, interest and other amounts payable with respect to the bonds, in an aggregate outstanding principal amount not to exceed the amount authorized in subsection (1) of this section. The bonds are the direct obligation of the State of Oregon and must be in a form, run for a period of time, have terms and bear rates of interest as may be provided by statute. The full faith and credit and taxing power of the State of Oregon must be pledged to the payment of the principal, premium, if any, and interest on the general obligation bonds; however, the ad valorem taxing power of the State of Oregon may not be pledged to the payment of the bonds issued under this section.

(3) As used in this section, "public education building" means a building owned by the State Board of Higher Education, a school district, an education service district, a community college district or a community college service district. [Created through S.J.R. 21, 2001, and adopted by the people Nov. 5, 2002]

Section 2. Sources of repayment. The principal, premium, if any, interest and other amounts payable with respect to the general obligation bonds issued under section 1 of this Article must be repaid as determined by the Legislative Assembly from the following sources:

(1) Amounts appropriated for the purpose by the Legislative Assembly from the General Fund, including taxes, other than ad valorem property taxes, levied to pay the bonds;

(2) Amounts allocated for the purpose by the Legislative Assembly from the proceeds of the State Lottery or from the Master Settlement Agreement entered into on November 23, 1998, by the State of Oregon and leading United States tobacco product manufacturers; and

(3) Amounts appropriated or allocated for the purpose by the Legislative Assembly from other sources of revenue. [Created through S.J.R. 21, 2001, and adopted by the people Nov. 5, 2002]

Section 3. Refunding bonds. General obligation bonds issued under section 1 of this Article may be refunded with bonds of like obligation. [Created through S.J.R. 21, 2001, and adopted by the people Nov. 5, 2002]

Section 4. Legislation to effectuate Article. The Legislative Assembly may enact legislation to carry out the provisions of this Article. [Created through S.J.R. 21, 2001, and adopted by the people Nov. 5, 2002]

Section 5. Relationship to conflicting provisions of Constitution. This Article supersedes conflicting provisions of this Constitution. [Created through S.J.R. 21, 2001, and adopted by the people Nov. 5, 2002]

ARTICLE XI-N
SEISMIC REHABILITATION OF
EMERGENCY SERVICES BUILDINGS

Note: Article XI-N was designated as "Article XI-L" by S.J.R. 22, 2001, and adopted by the people Nov. 5, 2002.

Section 1. State empowered to lend credit for seismic rehabilitation of emergency services buildings; bonds. (1) In the manner provided by law and notwithstanding the limitations contained in section 7, Article XI of this Constitution, the credit of the State of Oregon may be loaned and indebtedness incurred, in an aggregate outstanding principal amount not to exceed, at any one time, one-fifth of one percent of the real market value of all property in the state, to provide funds for the planning and implementation of seismic rehabilitation of emergency services buildings, including surveying and conducting engineering evaluations of the need for seismic rehabilitation.

(2) Any indebtedness incurred under this section must be in the form of general obligation bonds of the State of Oregon containing a direct promise on behalf of the State of Oregon to pay the principal, premium, if any, interest and other amounts payable with respect to the bonds, in an aggregate outstanding principal amount not to exceed the amount authorized in subsection (1) of this section. The bonds are the direct obligation of the State of Oregon and must be in a form, run for a period of time, have terms and bear rates of interest as may be provided by statute. The full faith and credit and taxing power of the State of Oregon must be pledged to the payment of the principal, premium, if any, and interest on the general obligation bonds; however, the ad valorem taxing power of the State of Oregon may not be pledged to the payment of the bonds issued under this section.

(3) As used in this section:

(a) "Acute inpatient care facility" means a licensed hospital with an organized medical staff, with permanent facilities that include inpatient beds, and with comprehensive medical services, including physician services and continuous nursing services under the supervision of registered nurses, to provide diagnosis and medical or surgical treatment primarily for but not limited to acutely ill patients and accident victims. "Acute inpatient care facility" includes the Oregon Health and Science University.

(b) "Emergency services building" means a public building used for fire protection services, a hospital building that contains an acute inpatient care facility, a police station, a sheriff's office or a similar facility used by a state, county, district or municipal law enforcement agency. [Created through S.J.R. 22, 2001, and adopted by the people Nov. 5, 2002]

Section 2. Sources of repayment. The principal, premium, if any, interest and other amounts payable with respect to the general obligation bonds issued under section 1 of this Article must be repaid as determined by the Legislative Assembly from the following sources:

(1) Amounts appropriated for the purpose by the Legislative Assembly from the General Fund, including taxes, other than ad valorem property taxes, levied to pay the bonds;

(2) Amounts allocated for the purpose by the Legislative Assembly from the proceeds of the State Lottery or from the Master Settlement Agreement entered into on November 23, 1998, by the State of Oregon and leading United States tobacco product manufacturers; and

(3) Amounts appropriated or allocated for the purpose by the Legislative Assembly from other sources of revenue. [Created through S.J.R. 22, 2001, and adopted by the people Nov. 5, 2002]

Section 3. Refunding bonds. General obligation bonds issued under section 1 of this Article may be refunded with bonds of like obligation. [Created through S.J.R. 22, 2001, and adopted by the people Nov. 5, 2002]

Section 4. Legislation to effectuate Article. The Legislative Assembly may enact legislation to carry out the provisions of this Article. [Created through S.J.R. 22, 2001, and adopted by the people Nov. 5, 2002]

Section 5. Relationship to conflicting provisions of Constitution. This Article supersedes conflicting provisions of this Constitution. [Created through S.J.R. 22, 2001, and adopted by the people Nov. 5, 2002]

ARTICLE XI-O
PENSION LIABILITIES

Section 1. State empowered to lend credit for pension liabilities. (1) In the manner provided by law and notwithstanding the limitations contained in section 7, Article XI of this Constitution, the credit of the State of Oregon may be loaned and indebtedness incurred to finance the State of Oregon's pension liabilities. Indebtedness authorized by this section also may be used to pay costs of issuing or incurring indebtedness under this section.

(2) Indebtedness incurred under this section is a general obligation of the State of Oregon and must contain a direct promise on behalf of the State of Oregon to pay the principal, premium, if any, and interest on that indebtedness. The State of Oregon shall pledge its full faith and credit and taxing power to pay that indebtedness; however, the ad valorem taxing power of the State of Oregon may not be pledged to pay that indebtedness. The amount of indebtedness authorized by this section and outstanding at any time may not exceed one percent of the real market value of all property in the state. [Created through H.J.R. 18, 2003, and adopted by the people Sept. 16, 2003]

Section 2. Refunding obligation. Indebtedness incurred under section 1 of this Article may be refunded with like obligations. [Created through H.J.R. 18, 2003, and adopted by the people Sept. 16, 2003]

Section 3. Legislation to effectuate Article. The Legislative Assembly may enact legislation to carry out the provisions of this Article. [Created through H.J.R. 18, 2003, and adopted by the people Sept. 16, 2003]

Section 4. Relationship to conflicting provisions of Constitution. This Article supersedes all conflicting provisions of this Constitution. [Created through H.J.R. 18, 2003, and adopted by the people Sept. 16, 2003]

ARTICLE XII
STATE PRINTING

Section 1. State printing; State Printer. Laws may be enacted providing for the state printing and binding, and for the election or appointment of a state printer, who shall have had not less than ten years' experience in the art of printing. The state printer shall receive such compensation as may from time to time be provided by law. Until such laws shall be enacted the state printer shall be elected, and the printing done as heretofore provided by this constitution and the general laws. [Constitution of 1859; Amendment proposed by S.J.R. 1, 1901, and adopted by the people June 6, 1904; Amendment proposed by initiative petition filed Feb. 3, 1906, and adopted by the people June 4, 1906]

ARTICLE XIII
SALARIES

Section 1. Salaries or other compensation of state officers. [Constitution of 1859; Repeal proposed by S.J.R. 12, 1955, and adopted by the people Nov. 6, 1956]

ARTICLE XIV
SEAT OF GOVERNMENT

Sec. 1. Seat of government
2. Erection of state house prior to 1865

Section 1. Seat of government. [Constitution of 1859; Repeal proposed by S.J.R. 41, 1957, and adopted by the people Nov. 4, 1958 (present section 1 and former 1958 section 3 of this Article adopted in lieu of this section and former original section 3 of this Article)]

Section 1. Seat of government. The permanent seat of government for the state shall be Marion County. [Created through S.J.R. 41, 1957, and adopted by the people Nov. 4, 1958 (this section and former 1958 section 3 of this Article adopted in lieu of former original sections 1 and 3 of this Article)]

Section 2. Erection of state house prior to 1865. No tax shall be levied, or money of the State expended, or debt contracted for the erection of a State House prior to the year eighteen hundred and sixty five.—

Section 3. Limitation on removal of seat of government; location of state institutions. [Constitution of 1859; Amendment proposed by S.J.R. 1, 1907, and adopted by the people June 1, 1908; Repeal proposed by S.J.R. 41, 1957, and adopted by the people Nov. 4, 1958 (present section 1 and former 1958 section 3 of this Article adopted in lieu of this section and former section 1 of this Article)]

Section 3. Location and use of state institutions. [Created through S.J.R. 41, 1957, and adopted by the people Nov. 4, 1958 (this section, designated as "Section 2" by S.J.R. 41, 1957, and present section 1 of this Article in lieu of former original sections 1 and 3 of this Article); Repeal proposed by S.J.R. 9, 1971, and adopted by the people Nov. 7, 1972]

ARTICLE XV
MISCELLANEOUS

Sec. 1. Officers to hold office until successors elected; exceptions; effect on defeated incumbent
2. Tenure of office; how fixed; maximum tenure
3. Oaths of office
4. Regulation of lotteries; state lottery; use of net proceeds from state lottery
4a. Use of net proceeds from state lottery for parks and recreation areas
4b. Use of net proceeds from state lottery for salmon restoration and watershed and wildlife habitat protection
4c. Audit of agency receiving certain net proceeds from state lottery
4d. Subsequent vote for reaffirmation of sections 4a, 4b and 4c and amendment to section 4
5. Property of married women not subject to debts of husband; registration of separate property
6. Minimum area and population of counties
7. Officers not to receive fees from or represent claimants against state

8. Persons eligible to serve in legislature
9. When elective office becomes vacant
10. The Oregon Property Protection Act of 2000
11. Home Care Commission

Section 1. Officers to hold office until successors elected; exceptions; effect on defeated incumbent. (1) All officers, except members of the Legislative Assembly and incumbents who seek reelection and are defeated, shall hold their offices until their successors are elected, and qualified.

(2) If an incumbent seeks reelection and is defeated, he shall hold office only until the end of his term; and if an election contest is pending in the courts regarding that office when the term of such an incumbent ends and a successor to the office has not been elected or if elected, has not qualified because of such election contest, the person appointed to fill the vacancy thus created shall serve only until the contest and any appeal is finally determined notwithstanding any other provision of this constitution. [Constitution of 1859; Amendment proposed by H.J.R. 51, 1969, and adopted by the people Nov. 3, 1970]

Section 2. Tenure of office; how fixed; maximum tenure. When the duration of any office is not provided for by this Constitution, it may be declared by law; and if not so declared, such office shall be held during the pleasure of the authority making the appointment. But the Legislative Assembly shall not create any office, the tenure of which shall be longer than four years.

Section 3. Oaths of office. Every person elected or appointed to any office under this Constitution, shall, before entering on the duties thereof, take an oath or affirmation to support the Constitution of the United States, and of this State, and also an oath of office.

Section 4. Regulation of lotteries; state lottery; use of net proceeds from state lottery. (1) Except as provided in subsections (2), (3), (4), (10) and (11) of this section, lotteries and the sale of lottery tickets, for any purpose whatever, are prohibited, and the Legislative Assembly shall prevent the same by penal laws.

(2) The Legislative Assembly may provide for the establishment, operation, and regulation of raffles and the lottery commonly known as bingo or lotto by charitable, fraternal, or religious organizations. As used in this section, charitable, fraternal or religious organization means such organizations or foundations as defined by law because of their charitable, fraternal, or religious purposes. The regulations shall define eligible organizations or foundations, and may prescribe the frequency of raffles, bingo or lotto, set a maximum monetary limit for prizes and require a statement of the odds on winning a prize. The Legislative Assembly shall vest the regulatory authority in any appropriate state agency.

(3) There is hereby created the State Lottery Commission which shall establish and operate a State Lottery. All proceeds from the State Lottery, including interest, but excluding costs of administration and payment of prizes, shall be used for any of the following purposes: creating jobs, furthering economic development, financing public education in Oregon or restoring and protecting Oregon's parks, beaches, watersheds and critical fish and wildlife habitats.

(4)(a) The State Lottery Commission shall be comprised of five members appointed by the Governor and confirmed by the Senate who shall serve at the pleasure of the Governor. At least one of the Commissioners shall have a minimum of five years experience in law enforcement and at least one of the Commissioners shall be a certified public accountant. The Commission is empowered to promulgate rules related to the procedures of the Commission and the operation of the State Lottery. Such rules and any statutes enacted to further implement this article shall insure the integrity, security, honesty, and fairness of the Lottery. The Commission shall have such additional powers and duties as may be provided by law.

(b) The Governor shall appoint a Director subject to confirmation by the Senate who shall serve at the pleasure of the Governor. The Director shall be qualified by training and experience to direct the operations of a state-operated lottery. The Director shall be responsible for managing the affairs of the Commission. The Director may appoint and prescribe the duties of no more than four Assistant Directors as the Director deems necessary. One of the Assistant Directors shall be responsible for a security division to assure security, integrity, honesty, and fairness in the operations and administration of the State Lottery. To fulfill these responsibilities, the Assistant Director for security shall be qualified by training and experience, including at least five years of law enforcement experience, and knowledge and experience in computer security.

(c) The Director shall implement and operate a State Lottery pursuant to the rules, and under the guidance, of the Commission. The State Lottery may operate any game procedure authorized by the commission, except parimutuel racing, social games, and the games commonly known in Oregon as bingo or lotto, whereby prizes are distributed using any existing or future methods among adult persons who have paid for tickets or shares in that game; provided that, in lottery games utilizing computer terminals or other devices, no coins or currency shall ever be dispensed directly to players from such computer terminals or devices.

(d) There is hereby created within the General Fund the Oregon State Lottery Fund which is continuously appropriated for the purpose of administering and operating the Commission and the State Lottery. The State Lottery shall operate as a self-supporting revenue-raising agency of state government and no appropriations, loans, or other transfers of state funds shall be made to it. The State Lottery shall pay all prizes and all of its expenses out of the revenues it receives from the sale of tickets or shares to the public and turnover the net proceeds therefrom to a fund to be established by the Legislative Assembly from which the Legislative Assembly shall make appropriations for the benefit of any of the following public purposes: creating jobs, furthering economic development, financing public education in Oregon or restoring and protecting Oregon's parks, beaches, watersheds and critical fish and wildlife habitats. Effective July 1, 1997, 15% of the net proceeds from the State Lottery shall be deposited, from the fund created by the Legislative Assembly under this paragraph, in an education stability fund. Effective July 1, 2003, 18% of the net proceeds from the State Lottery shall be deposited, from the fund created by the Legislative Assembly under this paragraph, in an education stability fund. Earnings on moneys in the education stability fund shall be retained in the fund or expended for the public purpose of financing public education in Oregon as provided by law. Except as provided in subsections (6) and (8) of this section, moneys in the education stability fund shall be invested as provided by law and shall not be subject to the limitations of section 6,

Article XI of this Constitution. The Legislative Assembly may appropriate other moneys or revenue to the education stability fund. The Legislative Assembly shall appropriate amounts sufficient to pay lottery bonds before appropriating the net proceeds from the State Lottery for any other purpose. At least 84% of the total annual revenues from the sale of all lottery tickets or shares shall be returned to the public in the form of prizes and net revenues benefiting the public purpose.

(5) Notwithstanding paragraph (d) of subsection (4) of this section, the amount in the education stability fund created under paragraph (d) of subsection (4) of this section may not exceed an amount that is equal to five percent of the amount that was accrued as revenues in the state's General Fund during the prior biennium. If the amount in the education stability fund exceeds five percent of the amount that was accrued as revenues in the state's General Fund during the prior biennium:

(a) Additional net proceeds from the State Lottery may not be deposited in the education stability fund until the amount in the education stability fund is reduced to less than five percent of the amount that was accrued as revenues in the state's General Fund during the prior biennium; and

(b) Fifteen percent of the net proceeds from the State Lottery shall be deposited into the school capital matching subaccount created under subsection (8) of this section.

(6) The Legislative Assembly may by law appropriate, allocate or transfer any portion of the principal of the education stability fund created under paragraph (d) of subsection (4) of this section for expenditure on public education if:

(a) The proposed appropriation, allocation or transfer is approved by three-fifths of the members serving in each house of the Legislative Assembly and the Legislative Assembly finds one of the following:

(A) That the last quarterly economic and revenue forecast for a biennium indicates that moneys available to the state's General Fund for the next biennium will be at least three percent less than appropriations from the state's General Fund for the current biennium;

(B) That there has been a decline for two or more consecutive quarters in the last 12 months in seasonally adjusted nonfarm payroll employment; or

(C) That a quarterly economic and revenue forecast projects that revenues in the state's General Fund in the current biennium will be at least two percent below what the revenues were projected to be in the revenue forecast on which the legislatively adopted budget for the current biennium was based; or

(b) If the proposed appropriation, allocation or transfer is approved by three-fifths of the members serving in each house of the Legislative Assembly and the Governor declares an emergency.

(7) The Legislative Assembly may by law prescribe the procedures to be used and identify the persons required to make the forecasts described in subsection (6) of this section.

(8)(a) There is created a school capital matching subaccount within the education stability fund created under paragraph (d) of subsection (4) of this section.

(b) The Legislative Assembly may by law appropriate, allocate or transfer moneys or revenue to the school capital matching subaccount.

(c) To the extent funds are available, the Legislative Assembly may appropriate, allocate or transfer moneys in the school capital matching subaccount and earnings on moneys in the subaccount for the purpose of providing state matching funds to school districts for capital costs incurred by the school districts.

(9) Notwithstanding paragraph (d) of subsection (4) of this section, on May 1, 2003, the State Treasurer shall transfer $150 million from the education stability fund created under paragraph (d) of subsection (4) of this section to a fund created by law and known as the State School Fund. Moneys transferred under this subsection may be used in the manner provided by law for moneys in the State School Fund.

(10) Effective July 1, 1999, 15% of the net proceeds from the State Lottery shall be deposited in a parks and natural resources fund created by the Legislative Assembly. Of the moneys in the parks and natural resources fund, 50% shall be distributed for the public purpose of financing the protection, repair, operation, and creation of state parks, ocean shore and public beach access areas, historic sites and recreation areas, and 50% shall be distributed for the public purpose of financing the restoration and protection of native salmonid populations, watersheds, fish and wildlife habitats and water quality in Oregon. The Legislative Assembly shall not limit expenditures from the parks and natural resources fund. The Legislative Assembly may appropriate other moneys or revenue to the parks and natural resources fund.

(11) Only one State Lottery operation shall be permitted in the State.

(12) The Legislative Assembly has no power to authorize, and shall prohibit, casinos from operation in the State of Oregon. [Constitution of 1859; Amendment proposed by H.J.R. 14, 1975, and adopted by the people Nov. 2, 1976; Amendment proposed by initiative petition filed April 3, 1984, and adopted by the people Nov. 6, 1984 (paragraph designations in subsection (4) were not included in the petition); Amendment proposed by H.J.R. 20, 1985, and adopted by the people Nov. 4, 1986; Amendment proposed by H.J.R. 15, 1995, and adopted by the people May 16, 1995; Amendment proposed by initiative petition filed March 11, 1998, and adopted by the people Nov. 3, 1998; Amendment proposed by H.J.R. 80, 2002 (3rd s.s.), and adopted by the people Sept. 17, 2002]

Note: The amendments to section 4, as adopted by the people in Measure No. 66, 1998, incorrectly set forth the text of section 4 as it existed at the time the measure was submitted to the people. The text of the measure, as approved by the voters, was printed here.

Section 4a. Use of net proceeds from state lottery for parks and recreation areas. Any state agency that receives moneys from the parks and natural resources fund established under section 4 of this Article for the public purpose of financing the protection, repair, operation, creation and development of state parks, ocean shores and public beach access areas, historic sites and recreation areas shall have the authority to use the moneys for the following purposes:

(1) Maintain, construct, improve, develop, manage and operate state park and recreation facilities, programs and areas.

(2) Acquire real property, or interest therein, deemed necessary for the creation and operation of state parks, ocean shores public beach access areas, recreation and historic sites or because of natural, scenic, cultural, historic and recreational values.

(3) Operate grant programs for local government entities deemed necessary to accomplish the public purposes of the parks and natural resources fund established under section 4 of this Article. [Created through initiative petition filed March 11, 1998, and adopted by the people Nov. 3, 1998]

Section 4b. Use of net proceeds from state lottery for salmon restoration and watershed and wildlife habitat protection. Moneys disbursed for the public purpose of financing the restoration and protection of wild salmonid populations, watersheds, fish and wildlife habitats and water quality from the fund established under Section 4 of this Article shall be administered by one state agency. At least 65% of the moneys will be used for capital expenditures. These moneys, including grants, shall be used for all of the following purposes:

(1) Watershed, fish and wildlife, and riparian and other native species, habitat conservation activities, including but not limited to planning, coordination, assessment, implementation, restoration, inventory, information management and monitoring activities.

(2) Watershed and riparian education efforts.

(3) The development and implementation of watershed and water quality enhancement plans.

(4) Entering into agreements to obtain from willing owners determinate interests in lands and waters that protect watershed resources, including but not limited to fee simple interests in land, leases of land or conservation easements.

(5) Enforcement of fish and wildlife and habitat protection laws and regulations. [Created through initiative petition filed March 11, 1998, and adopted by the people Nov. 3, 1998]

Section 4c. Audit of agency receiving certain net proceeds from state lottery. Any state agency that receives moneys from the parks and natural resources fund established under section 4 of this Article shall secure an independent audit, pursuant to section 2, Article VI of this Constitution, to measure the financial integrity, effectiveness and performance of the agency receiving such moneys. Each agency shall submit the audit to the Legislative Assembly as part of a biennial report to the Legislative Assembly. [Created through initiative petition filed March 11, 1998, and adopted by the people Nov. 3, 1998]

Note: Added as section 4c to the Constitution but not to any Article therein by initiative petition (Measure No. 66, 1998) adopted by the people Nov. 3, 1998.

Section 4d. Subsequent vote for reaffirmation of sections 4a, 4b and 4c and amendment to section 4. The Legislative Assembly shall submit to a vote of the people at the November 2014 general elections the question of continuation of this amendment. This Section is repealed on January 1, 2015. [Created through initiative petition filed March 11, 1998, and adopted by the people Nov. 3, 1998]

Note: Added to the Constitution but not to any Article therein by initiative petition (Measure No. 66, 1998) adopted by the people Nov. 3, 1998. Section 4d was designated as "Section 5a" by Measure No. 66, 1998.

Note: "This amendment" in section 4d refers to the amendment to section 4 of this Article and the creation of sections 4a, 4b, 4c and 4d of this Article by Measure No. 66, 1998.

Section 5. Property of married women not subject to debts of husband; registration of separate property. The property and pecuniary rights of every married woman, at the time of marriage or afterwards, acquired by gift, devise, or inheritance shall not be subject to the debts, or contracts of the husband; and laws shall be passed providing for the registration of the wife's seperate (sic) property.

Section 6. Minimum area and population of counties. No county shall be reduced to an area of less than four hundred square miles; nor shall any new county be established in this State containing a less area, nor unless such new county shall contain a population of at least twelve hundred inhabitants.

Section 7. Officers not to receive fees from or represent claimants against state. No State officers, or members of the Legislative Assembly, shall directly or indirectly receive a fee, or be engaged as counsel, agent, or Attorney in the prosecution of any claim against this State.—

Section 8. Certain persons not to hold real estate or mining claims; working mining claims. [Constitution of 1859; Repeal proposed by S.J.R. 14, 1945, and adopted by the people Nov. 5, 1946]

Section 8. Persons eligible to serve in legislature. Notwithstanding the provisions of section 1 article III and section 10 article II of the Constitution of the State of Oregon, a person employed by the State Board of Higher Education, a member of any school board or employee thereof, shall be eligible to a seat in the Legislative Assembly and such membership in the Legislative Assembly shall not prevent such person from being employed by the State Board of Higher Education or from being a member or employee of a school board. [Created through initiative petition filed June 13, 1958, and adopted by the people Nov. 4, 1958]

Section 9. When elective office becomes vacant. The Legislative Assembly may provide that any elective public office becomes vacant, under such conditions or circumstances as the Legislative Assembly may specify, whenever a person holding the office is elected to another public office more than 90 days prior to the expiration of the term of the office he is holding. For the purposes of this section, a person elected is considered to be elected as of the date the election is held. [Created through S.J.R. 41, 1959, and adopted by the people Nov. 8, 1960]

Section 10. The Oregon Property Protection Act of 2000. (1) This section may be known and shall be cited as the "Oregon Property Protection Act of 2000."

(2) Statement of principles. The People, in the exercise of the power reserved to them under the Constitution of the State of Oregon, declare that:

(a) A basic tenet of a democratic society is that a person is presumed innocent and should not be punished until proven guilty;

(b) The property of a person should not be forfeited in a forfeiture proceeding by government unless and until that person is convicted of a crime involving the property;

(c) The value of property forfeited should be proportional to the specific conduct for which the owner of the property has been convicted; and

(d) Proceeds from forfeited property should be used for treatment of drug abuse unless otherwise specified by law for another purpose.

(3) Forfeitures prohibited without conviction. No judgment of forfeiture of property in a civil forfeiture proceeding by the State or any of its political subdivisions shall be allowed or entered until and unless the owner of the property is convicted of a crime in Oregon or another jurisdiction and the property is found by clear and convincing evidence to have been instrumental in committing or facilitating the crime or to be proceeds of that crime. The value of the property forfeited under the provisions of this subsection shall not be excessive and shall be substantially proportional to the specific conduct for which the owner of the property has been convicted. For purposes of this section, "property" means any interest in anything of value, including the whole of any lot or tract of land and tangible and intangible personal property, including currency, instruments or securities or any other kind of privilege, interest, claim or right whether due or to become due. Nothing in this section shall prohibit a person from voluntarily giving a judgment of forfeiture.

(4) Protection of innocent property owners. In a civil forfeiture proceeding if a financial institution claiming an interest in the property demonstrates that it holds an interest, its interest shall not be subject to forfeiture.

In a civil forfeiture proceeding if a person claiming an interest in the property, other than a financial institution or a defendant who has been charged with or convicted of a crime involving that property, demonstrates that the person has an interest in the property, that person's interest shall not be subject to forfeiture unless:

(a) The forfeiting agency proves by clear and convincing evidence that the person took the property or the interest with the intent to defeat the forfeiture; or

(b) A conviction under subsection (3) is later obtained against the person.

(5) Exception for unclaimed property and contraband. Notwithstanding the provisions of subsection (3) of this section, if, following notice to all persons known to have an interest or who may have an interest, no person claims an interest in the seized property or if the property is contraband, a judgment of forfeiture may be allowed and entered without a criminal conviction. For purposes of this subsection, "contraband" means personal property, articles or things, including but not limited to controlled substances or drug paraphernalia, that a person is prohibited by Oregon statute or local ordinance from producing, obtaining or possessing.

(6) Law enforcement seizures unaffected. Nothing in this section shall be construed to affect the temporary seizure of property for evidentiary, forfeiture, or protective purposes, or to alter the power of the Governor to remit fines or forfeitures under Article V, Section 14, of this Constitution.

(7) Disposition of property and proceeds to drug treatment. Any sale of forfeited property shall be conducted in a commercially reasonable manner. Property or proceeds forfeited under subsections (3), (5), or (8) of this section shall not be used for law enforcement purposes but shall be distributed or applied in the following order:

(a) To the satisfaction of any foreclosed liens, security interests and contracts in the order of their priority;

(b) To the State or any of its political subdivisions for actual and reasonable expenses related to the costs of the forfeiture proceeding, including attorney fees, storage, maintenance, management, and disposition of the property incurred in connection with the sale of any forfeited property in an amount not to exceed twenty-five percent of the total proceeds in any single forfeiture;

(c) To the State or any of its political subdivisions to be used exclusively for drug treatment, unless another disposition is specially provided by law.

(8) State and federal sharing. The State of Oregon or any of its political subdivisions shall take all necessary steps to obtain shared property or proceeds from the United States Department of Justice resulting from a forfeiture. Any property or proceeds received from the United States Department of Justice by the State of Oregon or any of its political subdivisions shall be applied as provided in subsection (7) of this section.

(9) Restrictions on State transfers. Neither the State of Oregon, its political subdivisions, nor any forfeiting agency shall transfer forfeiture proceedings to the federal government unless a state court has affirmatively found that:

(a) The activity giving rise to the forfeiture is interstate in nature and sufficiently complex to justify the transfer;

(b) The seized property may only be forfeited under federal law; or

(c) Pursuing forfeiture under state law would unduly burden the state forfeiting agencies.

(10) Penalty for violations. Any person acting under color of law, official title or position who takes any action intending to conceal, transfer, withhold, retain, divert or otherwise prevent any proceeds, conveyances, real property, or any things of value forfeited under the law of this State or the United States from being applied, deposited or used in accordance with subsections (7), (8) or (9) of this section shall be subject to a civil penalty in an amount treble the value of the forfeited property concealed, transferred, withheld, retained or diverted. Nothing in this subsection shall be construed to impair judicial immunity if otherwise applicable.

(11) Reporting requirement. All forfeiting agencies shall report the nature and disposition of all property and proceeds seized for forfeiture or forfeited to a State asset forfeiture oversight committee that is independent of any forfeiting agency. The asset forfeiture oversight committee shall generate and make available to the public an annual report of the information collected. The asset forfeiture oversight committee shall also make recommendations to ensure that asset forfeiture proceedings are handled in a manner that is fair to innocent property owners and interest holders.

(12) Severability. If any part of this section or its application to any person or circumstance is held to be invalid for any reason, then the remaining parts or applications to any persons or circumstances shall not be affected but shall remain in full force and effect. [Created through initiative petition filed Jan. 5, 2000, and adopted by the people Nov. 7, 2000]

Note: The leadlines to section 10 and subsections (2) to (12) of section 10 were a part of the measure submitted by initiative petition (Measure No. 3, 2000) adopted by the people Nov. 7, 2000.

Note: The text of section 11 (sections 1 to 3, Measure No. 99, 2000) as submitted to the people was preceded by a preamble that reads as follows:

WHEREAS, thousands of Oregon seniors and persons with disabilities live independently in their own homes, which they prefer and is less costly than institutional care (i.e. nursing homes), because over 10,000 home care workers, (also known as client employed providers), paid by the State of Oregon provide in-home support services;

WHEREAS, home care workers provide services that range from housekeeping, shopping, meal preparation, money management and personal care to medical care and treatment, but receive little, if any, training in those areas resulting in a detrimental impact on quality of care;

WHEREAS, the quality of care provided to seniors and people with disabilities is diminished when there is a lack of stability in the workforce which is the result of home care workers receiving low wages, minimal training and benefits;

WHEREAS, both home care workers and clients receiving home care services would benefit from creating an entity which has the authority to provide, and is held accountable for the quality of services provided in Oregon's in-home system of long-term care.

Section 11. Home Care Commission. (1) Ensuring High Quality Home Care Services: Creation and Duties of the Quality Home Care Commission. (a) The Home Care Commission is created as an independent public commission consisting of nine members appointed by the Governor.

(b) The duties and functions of the Home Care Commission include, but are not limited to:

(A) Ensuring that high quality, comprehensive home care services are provided to the elderly and people with disabilities who receive personal care services in their homes by home care workers hired directly by the client and financed by payments from the State or by payments from a county or other public agency which receives money for that purpose from the State;

(B) Providing routine, emergency and respite referrals of qualified home care providers to the elderly and people with disabilities who receive personal care services by home care workers hired directly by the client and financed in whole or in part by the State, or by payment from a county or other public agency which receives money for that purpose from the State;

(C) Provide training opportunities for home care workers, seniors and people with disabilities as consumers of personal care services;

(D) Establish qualifications for home care workers;

(E) Establish and maintain a registry of qualified home care workers;

(F) Cooperate with area agencies on aging and disability services and other local agencies to provide the services described and set forth in this section.

(2) Home Care Commission Operation/Selection. (a) The Home Care Commission shall be comprised of nine members. Five members of the Commission shall be current or former consumers of home care services for the elderly or people with disabilities. One member shall be a representative of the Oregon Disabilities Commission, (or a successor entity, for as long as a comparable entity exists). One member shall be a representative of the Governor's Commission on Senior Services, (or a successor entity, for as long as a comparable entity exists). One member shall be a representative of the Oregon Association of Area Agencies on Aging and Disabilities, (or a successor entity, for as long as a comparable entity exists). One member shall be a representative of the Senior and Disabled Services Division, (or a successor entity, for as long as a comparable entity exists).

(b) The term of office of each member is three years, subject to confirmation by the Senate. If there is a vacancy for any cause, the Governor shall make an appointment to become immediately effective for the unexpired term. A member is eligible for reappointment and may serve no more than three consecutive terms. In making appointments to the Commission, the Governor may take into consideration any nominations or recommendations made by the representative groups or agencies.

(3) Other Provisions — Legal Duties and Responsibilities of the Commission. (a) The Home Care Commission shall, in its own name, for the purpose of carrying into effect and promoting its functions, have authority to contract, lease, acquire, hold, own, encumber, insure, sell, replace, deal in and with and dispose of real and personal property.

(b) When conducting any activities in this Section or in subsection (1) of this section, and in making decisions relating to those activities, the Home Care Commission shall first consider the effect of its activities and its decisions on improving the quality of service delivery and ensuring adequate hours of service are provided to clients who are served by home care workers.

(c) Clients of home care services retain their right to select the providers of their choice, including family members.

(d) Employees of the Commission are not employees of the State of Oregon for any purpose.

(e) Notwithstanding the provisions in paragraph (d) of this subsection, the State of Oregon shall be held responsible for unemployment insurance payments for home care workers.

(f) For purposes of collective bargaining, the Commission shall be the employer of record of home care workers hired directly by the client and paid by the State, or by a county or other public agency which receives money for that purpose from the State. Home care workers have the right to form, join and participate in the activities of labor organizations of their own choosing for the purpose of representation and collective bargaining with the Commission on matters concerning employment relations. These rights shall be exercised in accordance with the rights granted to public employees with mediation and interest arbitration as the method of concluding the collective bargaining process. Home care workers shall not have the right to strike.

(g) The Commission may adopt rules to carry out its functions. [Created through initiative petition filed Nov. 10, 1999, and adopted by the people Nov. 7, 2000]

Note: The leadlines to subsections (1), (2) and (3) of section 11, except the periods in subsections (2) and (3), were a part of the measure submitted to the people by initiative petition (Measure No. 99, 2000) and adopted by the people Nov. 7, 2000.

Note: Section 11 was submitted to the voters as sections 1, 2 and 3 and added to the Constitution but not to any Article therein by Measure No. 99, 2000.

Note: In Measure No. 99, 2000, subsection (1)(a) and (b)(A) to (F) were designated as section 1 (A) and (B)(1) to (6); subsection (2)(a) and (b) as section 2 (A) and (B); and subsection (3)(a) to (g) as section 3 (A) to (G). The reference to subsection (1) of this section was a reference to Section 1 above, and the reference to paragraph (d) of this subsection was a reference to subsection (D) of this section.

Note: In Measure No. 99, 2000, the period in subsection (1)(b)(F) appeared as a semicolon, and there was no period in subsection (3)(e).

ARTICLE XVI
BOUNDARIES

Section 1. State boundaries. The State of Oregon shall be bounded as provided by section 1 of the Act of Congress of February 1859, admitting the State of Oregon into the Union of the United States, until:

(1) Such boundaries are modified by appropriate interstate compact or compacts heretofore or hereafter approved by the Congress of the United States; or

(2) The Legislative Assembly by law extends the boundaries or jurisdiction of this state an additional distance seaward under authority of a law heretofore or hereafter enacted by the Congress of the United States. [Constitution of 1859; Amendment proposed by S.J.R. 4, 1957, and adopted by the people Nov. 4, 1958; Amendment proposed by H.J.R. 24, 1967, and adopted by the people Nov. 5, 1968]

ARTICLE XVII
AMENDMENTS AND REVISIONS

Sec. 1. Method of amending Constitution
     2. Method of revising Constitution

Section 1. Method of amending Constitution. Any amendment or amendments to this Constitution may be proposed in either branch of the legislative assembly, and if the same shall be agreed to by a majority of all the members elected to each of the two houses, such proposed amendment or amendments shall, with the yeas and nays thereon, be entered in their journals and referred by the secretary of state to the people for their approval or rejection, at the next regular general election, except when the legislative assembly shall order a special election for that purpose. If a majority of the electors voting on any such amendment shall vote in favor thereof, it shall thereby become a part of this Constitution. The votes for and against such amendment, or amendments, severally, whether proposed by the legislative assembly or by initiative petition, shall be canvassed by the secretary of state in the presence of the governor, and if it shall appear to the governor that the majority of the votes cast at said election on said amendment, or amendments, severally, are cast in favor thereof, it shall be his duty forthwith after such canvass, by his proclamation, to declare the said amendment, or amendments, severally, having received said majority of votes to have been adopted by the people of Oregon as part of the Constitution thereof, and the same shall be in effect as a part of the Constitution from the date of such proclamation. When two or more amendments shall be submitted in the manner aforesaid to the voters of this state at the same election, they shall be so submitted that each amendment shall be voted on separately. No convention shall be called to amend or propose amendments to this Constitution, or to propose a new Constitution, unless the law providing for such convention shall first be approved by the people on a referendum vote at a regular general election. This article shall not be construed to impair the right of the people to amend this Constitution by vote upon an initiative petition therefor. [Created through initiative petition filed Feb. 3, 1906, and adopted by the people June 4, 1906]

Note: The above section replaces sections 1 and 2 of Article XVII of the original Constitution.

Section 2. Method of revising Constitution. (1) In addition to the power to amend this Constitution granted by section 1, Article IV, and section 1 of this Article, a revision of all or part of this Constitution may be proposed in either house of the Legislative Assembly and, if the proposed revision is agreed to by at least two-thirds of all the members of each house, the proposed revision shall, with the yeas and nays thereon, be entered in their journals and referred by the Secretary of State to the people for their approval or rejection, notwithstanding section 1, Article IV of this Constitution, at the next regular state-wide primary election, except when the Legislative Assembly orders a special election for that purpose. A proposed revision may deal with more than one subject and shall be voted upon as one question. The votes for and against the proposed revision shall be canvassed by the Secretary of State in the presence of the Governor and, if it appears to the Governor that the majority of the votes cast in the election on the proposed revision are in favor of the proposed revision, he shall, promptly following the canvass, declare, by his proclamation, that the proposed revision has received a majority of votes and has been adopted by the people as the Constitution of the State of Oregon or as a part of the Constitution of the State of Oregon, as the case may be. The revision shall be in effect as the Constitution or as a part of this Constitution from the date of such proclamation.

(2) Subject to subsection (3) of this section, an amendment proposed to the Constitution under section 1, Article IV, or under section 1 of this Article may be submitted to the people in the form of alternative provisions so that one provision will become a part of the Constitution if a proposed revision is adopted by the people and the other provision will become a part of the Constitution if a proposed revision is rejected by the people. A proposed amendment submitted in the form of alternative provisions as authorized by this subsection shall be voted upon as one question.

(3) Subsection (2) of this section applies only when:

(a) The Legislative Assembly proposes and refers to the people a revision under subsection (1) of this section; and

(b) An amendment is proposed under section 1, Article IV, or under section 1 of this Article; and

(c) The proposed amendment will be submitted to the people at an election held during the period between the adjournment of the legislative session at which the proposed revision is referred to the people and the next regular legislative session. [Created through H.J.R. 5, 1959, and adopted by the people Nov. 8, 1960]

ARTICLE XVIII
SCHEDULE

Section 1. Election to accept or reject Constitution. For the purpose of taking the vote of the electors of the State, for the acceptance or rejection of this Constitution, an election shall be held on the second Monday of November, in the year 1857, to be conducted according to existing laws regulating the election of Delegates in Congress, so far as applicable, except as herein otherwise provided.

Section 2. Questions submitted to voters. Each elector who offers to vote upon this Constitution, shall be asked by the judges of election this question:

Do you vote for the Constitution? Yes, or No.

And also this question:

Do you vote for Slavery in Oregon? Yes, or No.

And in the poll books shall be columns headed respectively.

"Constitution, Yes."   "Constitution, No."

"Slavery, Yes."   "Slavery, No." —

And the names of the electors shall be entered in the poll books, together with their answers to the said questions, under their appropriate heads. The abstracts of the votes transmitted to the Secretary of the Territory, shall be publicly opened, and canvassed by the Governor and Secretary, or by either of them in the absence of the other; and the Governor, or in his absence the Secretary, shall forthwith issue his proclamation, and publish the same in the several newspapers printed in this State, declaring the result of the said election upon each of said questions. [Constitution of 1859; Amendment proposed by S.J.R. 7, 2001, and adopted by the people Nov. 5, 2002]

Section 3. Majority of votes required to accept or reject Constitution. If a majority of all the votes given for, and against the Constitution, shall be given for the Constitution, then this Constitution shall be deemed to be approved, and accepted by the electors of the State, and shall take effect accordingly; and if a majority of such votes shall be given against the Constitution, then this Constitution shall be deemed to be rejected by the electors of the State, and shall be void.—

Section 4. Vote on certain sections of Constitution. If this Constitution shall be accepted by the electors, and a majority of all the votes given for, and against slavery, shall be given for slavery, then the following section shall be added to the Bill of Rights, and shall be part of this Constitution:

"Sec. ___Persons lawfully held as slaves in any State, Territory, or District of the United States, under the laws thereof, may be brought into this State, and such Slaves, and their descendants may be held as slaves within this State, and shall not be emancipated without the consent of their owners."

And if a majority of such votes shall be given against slavery, then the foregoing section shall not, but the following sections shall be added to the Bill of Rights, and shall be a part of this Constitution.

"Sec. ___There shall be neither slavery, nor involuntary servitude in the State, otherwise than as a punishment for crime, whereof the party shall have been duly convicted."— [Constitution of 1859; Amendment proposed by S.J.R. 7, 2001, and adopted by the people Nov. 5, 2002]

Note: See sections 34 and 35 of Article I, Oregon Constitution.

Section 5. Apportionment of Senators and Representatives. Until an enumeration of the inhabitants of the State shall be made, and the senators and representatives apportioned as directed in the Constitution, the County of Marion shall have two senators, and four representatives.

Linn two senators, and four representatives.

Lane two senators, and three representatives.

Clackamas and Wasco, one senator jointly, and Clackamas three representatives, and Wasco one representative.

Yamhill one senator, and two representatives.

Polk one senator, and two representatives.

Benton one senator, and two representatives.

Multnomah, one senator, and two representatives.

Washington, Columbia, Clatsop, and Tillamook one senator jointly, and Washington one representative, and Washington and Columbia one representative jointly, and Clatsop and Tillamook one representative jointly.

Douglas, one senator, and two representatives.

Jackson one senator, and three representatives.

Josephine one senator, and one representative.

Umpqua, Coos and Curry, one senator jointly, and Umpqua one representative, and Coos and Curry one representative jointly. [Constitution of 1859; Amendment proposed by S.J.R. 7, 2001, and adopted by the people Nov. 5, 2002]

Section 6. Election under Constitution; organization of state. If this Constitution shall be ratified, an election shall be held on the first Monday of June 1858, for the election of members of the Legislative Assembly, a Representative in Congress, and State and County officers, and the Legislative Assembly shall convene at the Capital on the first Monday of July 1858, and proceed to elect two senators in Congress, and make such further provision as may be necessary to the complete organization of a State government.—

Section 7. Former laws continued in force. All laws in force in the Territory of Oregon when this Constitution takes effect, and consistent therewith, shall continue in force until altered, or repealed.—

Section 8. Officers to continue in office. All officers of the Territory of Oregon, or under its laws, when this Constitution takes effect, shall continue in office, until superseded by the State authorities.—

Section 9. Crimes against territory. Crimes and misdemeanors committed against the Territory of Oregon shall be punished by the State, as they might have been punished by the Territory, if the change of government had not been made.—

Section 10. Saving existing rights and liabilities. All property and rights of the Territory, and of the several counties, subdivisions, and political bodies corporate, of, or in the Territory, including fines, penalties, forfeitures, debts and claims, of whatsoever nature, and recognizances, obligations, and undertakings to, or for the use of the Territory, or any county, political corporation, office, or otherwise, to or for the public, shall inure to the State, or remain to the county, local division, corporation, officer, or public, as if the change of government had not been made. And private rights shall not be affected by such change.—

Section 11. Judicial districts. Until otherwise provided by law, the judicial districts of the State, shall be constituted as follows: The counties of Jackson, Josephine, and Douglas, shall constitute the first district. The counties of Umpqua, Coos, Curry, Lane, and Benton, shall constitute the second district.—The counties of Linn, Marion, Polk, Yamhill and Washington, shall constitute the third district.—The counties of Clackamas, Multnomah, Wasco, Columbia, Clatsop, and Tillamook, shall constitute the fourth district—and the County of Tillamook shall be attached to the county of Clatsop for judicial purposes.

OREGON GEOLOGY

JOHN DAY FOSSIL BEDS

THIS FORMATION TAKES ITS NAME FROM THE RIVER NAMED FOR JOHN DAY OF THE ASTOR OVERLAND PARTY OF 1811.

FAMOUS THE WORLD OVER FOR THEIR WEALTH OF FOSSIL BONES, THE COLORFUL JOHN DAY BEDS WERE LAID DOWN IN LATE OLIGOCENE TIMES WHEN VOLCANIC ASH CHOKED STREAMS AND FILLED LAKE BASINS. ANIMALS OF BOTH FORESTS AND PLAINS WERE ENTOMBED. IT WAS A VARIED FAUNA INCLUDING BEAR DOGS AND GIANT CATS. RHINOS LIVED ON RIVER BANKS. TINY CAMELS AND THREE-TOED HORSES WERE ABUNDANT. THEIR BONES ARE BURIED HERE, AND WHEN BROUGHT TO LIGHT BY EROSION ILLUSTRATE ONE CHAPTER OF THE STORY OF OREGON'S ANCIENT PAST.

John Day Fossil Beds—Oregon State Archives Photograph, OHD-5061

Index

Alphabetization is word-by-word (e.g., "Child Support" precedes "Childbirth").

A

Abandoned funds (Department of State Lands), 84

Abbreviation, postal, 2

Absentee voting, 273

Abuse. See Child abuse; Domestic violence

Access and Habitat Board (Department of Fish and Wildlife), 57

Accidents, workplace, 42–43

Accountancy Board, 28

Accountants and tax preparers
Accountancy Board, 28
Tax Practitioners, Board of, 86

ACLB (Appraiser Certification and Licensure Board), 36–37

Acupuncturists (Board of Medical Examiners for the State of Oregon), 71

Administration Division (Student Assistance Commission), 85

Administrative Hearings Office (Employment Department), 54

Administrative rules, 19
Office of Legislative Counsel's role, 153
Regulatory Streamlining, Office of (Department of Consumer and Business Services), 42

Administrative Services, Department of, 28–32

Administrative Services (Department of Human Services), 65

Administrative Services Division (Department of Fish and Wildlife), 57

Advisory Commission on Prison Terms and Parole Standards (State Board of Parole and Post-Prison Supervision), 76

Advisory Committee on Prevailing Wage, Wage and Hour Division (Bureau of Labor and Industries), 27

Advisory Committee to the Director of Veterans' Affairs, 90

Advisory Councils
Consumer, Civil Enforcement Division (Justice Department), 24
Disability Services (Department of Human Services), 66
Electrologists, Permanent Color Technicians and Tattoo Artists (Health Licensing Office), 62
Employment Department, 53
Hearing Aids (Health Licensing Office), 61

Historic Trails (State Parks and Recreation Department), 75, 183
Mental Health Planning and Management (Department of Human Services), 66
Natural Heritage, 84
9-1-1 Advisory Council, 79
Passenger Rail (Department of Transportation), 89
Recreation Trails (State Parks and Recreation Department), 75

Advocate's Office for Minority, Women and Emerging Small Businesses, 18

Aeronautics. See Airplanes and airports

Affirmative Action Office (Office of the Governor), 18

Affordable housing, 63

African-Americans
Black History Museum, 38
Commission on Black Affairs, 37
history of, in Oregon, 347

Aged persons. See Elderly persons

Agricultural Commodity Commissions, 35–36

Agricultural Commodity Inspection Division, 32

Agricultural Development and Marketing Division (Department of Agriculture), 32

Agriculture
Department of State Lands, 84
economy, 348–349, 359–360
irrigation, 408–409
laborer regulation, 27
Minor Crops Advisory Committee, 35
New Crops Development Board, 34
veterans, farm loans to (Constitution of Oregon), 403–404

Agriculture, State Board of, 32, 34

Agriculture, State Department of, 32–36

Air National Guard, Oregon, 72

Air Quality Division (Department of Environmental Quality), 55

Airplanes and airports, 2
Department of Aviation, 37

Albacore Commission, 35

Alcohol abuse, 189
Governor's Advisory Committee on DUII, 89
Governor's Council on Alcohol and Drug Abuse (Department of Human Services), 66

Alcohol servers (Liquor Control Commission), 70

Alcoholic beverages
  Bill of Rights of Oregon, 373
  Constitution of Oregon, 373, 395
  Liquor Control Commission, 70
Alfalfa Seed Commission, 35
Alternative Trade Adjustment Assistance
  (ATAA), 188
Altitude, 2
Amendments to Constitution of Oregon,
  418–419
American beaver (state animal), 2
American Indians. See Indian tribes
Animal Health and Identification Division
  (Department of Agriculture), 32
Animals. See also Livestock
  hunting regulation, 56–57
  Oregon Zoo, 185–186
  state animal, 2
  Veterinary Medical Examining Board,
  Oregon State, 91
Antitrust, 24
Appeals
  Appellate Division (Justice Department), 24
  civil cases (Constitution of Oregon), 388
  crime victim assistance, 43
  Fair Dismissal Appeals Board (Education
  Department), 28
  forestland classification, 58
  Land Use Board of Appeals, 69
  Oregon Court of Appeals, 96, 312–313
  Oregon Supreme Court. See Supreme
  Court, Oregon
  workers' compensation, 43
Appellate Division (Justice Department), 24
Applegate Trail, 336
Appraiser Certification and Licensure Board,
  36–37
Apprenticeship and Training Division (Bureau of
  Labor and Industries), 25–26
Aquariums
  Hatfield Marine Science Center (HMSC),
  185
  Oregon Coast Aquarium, Inc., 184
Architect Examiners, State Board of, 37
Archives Division (Secretary of State), 19, 181
Armories (Military Construction Program), 72
Army Corps of Engineers' projects, 346
Army National Guard, Oregon, 72
Arrest and Return, 18
Arrest warrants (Law Enforcement Data System
  (LEDS)), 78
Arson (Criminal Investigation Services
  Division), 77
Art Institute of Portland, 173
The Art Ranch, 179

Arts, 176–180
  Education program, 176
  local and regional arts agencies, 178–180
  Oregon Cultural Trust, 52
  regional arts councils, 177–178
Arts Action Alliance of Clackamas County, 180
Arts Alliance of Yamhill County, 179
Arts Builds Communities initiative, 176
Arts Central, 177
Arts Commission (Economic and Community
  Development Department), 52
Arts Commission (Economic Development
  Department), 176
Arts Council of Morrow County, 179
Arts Council of Pendleton, 180
Arts Council of Southern Oregon, 177
Arts in Oregon Council, 180
Asbestos (Air Quality Division), 55
Asians. See Minorities
Asset and Property Management Division
  (Housing and Community Services
  Department), 63
Assisted living facilities (Office of the Long-
  Term Care Ombudsman), 70
Assisted suicide, 361
Astor, John Jacob, 329–330
Astor Street Opry Company, 178
ATAA (Alternative Trade Adjustment
  Assistance), 188
Athletic Trainers Board (Health Licensing
  Office), 61
Attorney General, 15, 23–24
  list of, by date, 313–314
Attorneys
  admission to practice, 96, 124
  Board of Bar Examiners, 124
  discipline of, 96
  Oregon State Bar, 124–125
Audiology, State Board of Examiners for
  Speech-Language Pathology and, 83
Audit Committee, Joint Legislative, 152
Auditor of public accounts, 19
Auditors (Accountancy Board), 28
Audits Division (Secretary of State), 19–20
Autopsies (State Medical Examiner), 80
Aviation Department, 37

B

Baccalaureate Bond Program, Debt Management
  Division (State Treasury), 21
Bail (Oregon Bill of Rights), 371–386
Ballistics (Forensic Services Division), 78
Ballot initiatives. See Initiative, referendum and
  recall

Banks and banking
Constitution of Oregon, 395
Division of Finance and Corporate Securities (Department of Consumer and Business Services), 41
Bar Examiners, Board of, 124
Barbers (Board of Cosmetology), 61–62
Bartlett Pear Commission, 35
Beaches. See Coastline
Beauticians
Advisory Council for Electrologists, Permanent Color Technicians and Tattoo Artists, 61
Board of Cosmetology, 61–62
Beaver State, 2
Beaverton Arts Commission, 178
Beef Council, 35
Beer
Liquor Control Commission, 70
Oregon Hop Commission, 36
Benefits Counseling and Education Aid Programs, Veterans' Services Division (Department of Veterans' Affairs), 90
Benton, Thomas Hart, 332
Beverage, state (milk), 2
Bicycle and Pedestrian Advisory Committee (Department of Transportation), 88
Bill of Rights (Constitution of Oregon), 371–390
Bingo, 24
Birds. See also headings starting with "Wildlife"
hunting regulation, 56–57
state bird, 2
Birth
Board of Direct Entry Midwifery, 62
statistics, 2
Black Affairs, Commission on, 37
Black History Museum, 37
Blackberry Commission, Oregon Raspberry and, 36
Blind persons
Commission for the Blind, 38
Oregon School for the Blind, 27, 164
Blue Mountain Community College, 166
Blue Mountains, 4
Blueberry Commission, 35
Blumenauer, Earl (U.S. Representative), 212
Board of Accountancy, 28
Board of Agriculture, 32, 34
Board of Architect Examiners, 37
Board of Bar Examiners, 124
Board of Boiler Rules (Department of Consumer and Business Services), 40
Board of Chiropractic Examiners, 39
Board of Clinical Social Workers, 39

Board of Cosmetology (Health Licensing Office), 61–62
Board of Denture Technology (Health Licensing Office), 62
Board of Direct Entry Midwifery (Health Licensing Office), 62
Board of Education, 27–28
Board of Examiners for Engineering and Land Surveying, 55
Board of Examiners for Speech-Language Pathology and Audiology, 83
Board of Examiners of Licensed Dietitians, 50
Board of Examiners of Nursing Home Administrators, 73
Board of Forestry, 58
Board of Geologist Examiners, 59–60
Board of Higher Education, 167–168
Board of Massage Therapists, 71
Board of Medical Examiners for the State of Oregon, 71
Board of Naturopathic Examiners, 73
Board of Parole and Post-Prison Supervision, 76
Board of Pharmacy, 76
Board of Psychologist Examiners, 81
Board of Radiologic Technology, 82–83
Board on Public Safety Standards and Training (Department of Public Safety Standards and Training), 82
Boats and boating
Fish and Wildlife Division (Department of State Police), 77
history of steamboats, 350
State Marine Board, 71
Body Piercing Licensing Program, 62
Boiler Rules, Board of (Department of Consumer and Business Services), 40
Bonds, government
education district bonds (Constitution of Oregon), 410
ORBAC Bonds (Baccalaureate Bond Program), 21
Oregon Facilities Authority (OFA) bonds, 23
State Treasury's duties and responsibilities, 21
Borders and boundaries, 2, 338
congressional act of statehood, 367–368
Constitution of Oregon, 418
Bottle refunds (Liquor Control Commission), 70
Boxing (Gaming Enforcement Division), 78
Bradbury, Bill (Secretary of State), 13, 19
Brands (Animal Health and Identification Division), 32
British settlement, 327–328, 336

Index

Consumer Advisory Council, Civil Enforcement Division (Justice Department), 24
Consumer and Business Services, Department of (DCBS), 40–44
Consumer protection, 24
  agricultural products, 32
  Department of Consumer and Business Services, 40–44
  Measurement Standards Division (Department of Agriculture), 33
Consumer Week, 24
Continuing Care Retirement Community Advisory Council (Department of Human Services), 67
Contractors. See specific type
Controller's Division (Department of Administrative Services), 31
Cook, James (Captain), 327–328
Coquille Valley Art Association, 178
Corban College, 174
Cornucopia Arts Council, 178
Corporate excise tax, 159
Corporate income tax, 189
Corporate names, registration of, 19
Corporation Division (Secretary of State), 20
Correctional institutions, 3, 47–50. See also Prisons and prisoners
  juveniles. See Juvenile corrections
Corrections, Department of, 44–50
Corrections Education Advisory Board (Department of Corrections), 46–47
Corrections Enterprises (Department of Corrections), 45–46
Council for the Humanities, 182
Council on Civil and Human Rights (Bureau of Labor and Industries), 26
Council on Court Procedures, 125
Council on Developmental Disabilities (Department of Human Services), 67
Counseling Program, Veterans' Services Division (Department of Veterans' Affairs), 90
Counselors and Therapists, Oregon Board of Licensed Professional, 51
Counter Drug and Drug Demand Reduction Programs (CD) (DDR) (Oregon Military Department), 72
Counties, 247–266. See also Local government
  Commission on Children and Families, 38
  Constitution of Oregon, 395, 396, 416
  corrections activities, 44
  finance, 159. See also Taxation
  Forestland Classification Committees, 58
  government (Constitution of Oregon), 387
  largest, 2
  map, 10

number of, 2
population, 247
smallest, 2
County Courts, 126
  Constitution of Oregon, 388
County Forestland Classification Committees, 58
Court Appointed Special Advocates (CASA) (State Commission on Children and Families), 38
Court of Appeals, Oregon, 96, 312–313
Court Procedures, Council on, 125
Courtney, Peter (President of State Senate), 128, 134
Courts, 95–126. See also Judges
  case loads, 100
  Circuit Courts, 98–123, 388
  Constitution of Oregon, 387–389
  Council on Court Procedures, 125
  County Courts, 126, 388
  Court of Appeals, 96, 312–313
  Justice Court, 126
  list of judges, by date, 307–313
  Municipal Courts, 126
  Oregon Tax Court, 98, 313
  publication of decisions, 124
  State Court Administrator, 124
  Supreme Court, 96, 97, 307–308
CPAs (Accountancy Board), 28
Crabs, Dungeness Crab Commission, 36
Crafts. See Arts
Credit unions (Division of Finance and Corporate Securities), 41
Crime reporting (Oregon Uniform Crime Reporting Program), 79
Crimes, victims of
  Crime Victims' Compensation Program, 24
  rights of (Oregon Bill of Rights), 374–375
Criminal Investigation Services Division (Department of State Police), 77
Criminal Justice Commission, Oregon, 50
Criminal Justice Division (Justice Department), 24–25
Criminal Justice Services Division (Department of State Police), 77
Criminal prosecution
  forfeiture of property upon conviction (Oregon Property Protection Act of 2000), 416–417
  rights guaranteed by Oregon Bill of Rights, 371
Crisis/Relief Nurseries (State Commission on Children and Families), 38
Crops. See Agriculture and headings starting with "Agricultural"
Cross country skiing, 6

Crossroads Center for the Creative and Performing Arts, 178

Cruel and unusual punishment (Oregon Bill of Rights), 372

CTFO (Children's Trust Fund), 38–39

Cultural Trust (Economic and Community Development Department), 52

Culture, 176–180. See also headings starting with "Arts"; Museums

D

Dairy Products Commission, 35

Dams, 3
    energy generation, 404–405
    history of, 358

Dance, state, 2

Day care (Child Care Division), 53–54

Daylight time, 6

DCBS (Department of Consumer and Business Services), 40–44

Deaf, Oregon School for the, 27, 163–164

Deaf and Hard of Hearing Access Program, 51

Death
    investigations to determine cause of (State Medical Examiner), 80
    statistics, 2

Death penalty (Oregon Bill of Rights), 373

Death With Dignity Act, 361

Debt collection or consolidating agencies (Division of Finance and Corporate Securities), 41

Debt Management Division (State Treasury), 21

Debt Policy Advisory Commission, Debt Management Division (State Treasury), 21

DeFazio, Peter (U.S. Representative), 212

Delinquency. See headings starting with "Juvenile"

Democratic Party, 215

Demographic trends, Economic Analysis Office (Department of Administrative Services), 30

Dentistry, Oregon Board of, 50

Denture Technology, Board of, 62

Department of Administrative Services, 28–32

Department of Agriculture, 32–36

Department of Aviation, 37

Department of Community Colleges and Workforce Development, 165

Department of Consumer and Business Services (DCBS), 40–44

Department of Corrections, 44–50

Department of Education. See Education Department

Department of Energy, 54–55

Department of Environmental Quality (DEQ), 55–56

Department of Fish and Wildlife (ODFW), 56–57

Department of Forestry, 57–59

Department of Geology and Mineral Industries, 60

Department of Human Services (DHS), 65–67

Department of Land Conservation and Development (LCDC), 68–69

Department of Public Safety Standards and Training (DPSST), 81–82

Department of Revenue, 83

Department of State Lands, 84–85

Department of State Police, 76–80

Department of Transportation (ODOT), 87–89

Department of Veterans' Affairs, 90–91

Depression, state history during, 355–357

Deputy Secretary of State, 19

DEQ (Department of Environmental Quality), 55–56

Developmental disabilities. See also Mental health
    Council on Developmental Disabilities, 67
    special education, 163–165

DHS (Department of Human Services), 65–67

Dietitians, Board of Examiners of Licensed, 50

Director's Office (Department of Administrative Services), 28–29

Director's Office (Department of Human Services), 65

Director's Office (Department of Transportation), 87

Director's Office (Housing and Community Services Department), 63

Disabilities Commission, Oregon, 51

Disabled persons. See also Developmental disabilities
    Disability Services Advisory Council (Department of Human Services), 66
    early intervention services for preschool children with disabilities, 164
    Home Care Commission, 417–418
    housing for (Constitution of Oregon), 409
    Seniors and People with Disabilities (Department of Human Services), 67

Disasters. See also Earthquakes
    Department of Geology and Mineral Industries, 60
    Office of Emergency Management (Department of State Police), 79

Discipline of attorneys, 96

Discipline of judges, 96, 125

Discrimination. See also Minorities
    Affirmative Action Office, 18

Bill of Rights, Oregon, 371
Civil Rights Division (Bureau of Labor and Industries), 26
Council on Civil and Human Rights (Bureau of Labor and Industries), 26
history of, 346–348, 355
Diseases, animal, 32
Diseases, occupational, 43
Diseases, plant, 34
Diseases, tree, 58
District Attorney Assistance Program, 24
District Attorneys Association, 24
District Courts. See now Circuit Courts
Divorce statistics, 3
DMV (Driver and Motor Vehicle Services), 88
DNA analysis (Forensic Services Division), 78
Doctor-assisted suicide, 361
Doctors (Board of Medical Examiners), 71
Domestic Preparedness and Citizen Corps Program (Office of Emergency Management, State Police), 79
Domestic violence
Governor's Council on Domestic Violence, 77
Law Enforcement Data System (LEDS) (restraining orders), 79
Double jeopardy (Oregon Bill of Rights), 371
Double majority vote to increase property tax rate, 159
Douglas, David, 331
Douglas-fir (state tree), 7, 331
Downhill skiing, 6
DPSST (Department of Public Safety Standards and Training), 81–82
Driver and Motor Vehicle Services (DMV) (Department of Transportation), 88
Driver's licenses, 88
Driving under the influence, Governor's Advisory Committee on, 89
Drug abuse, 189
Counter Drug and Drug Demand Reduction Programs (Oregon Military Department), 72
Criminal Investigation Services Division (Department of State Police), 77
Criminal Justice Services Division (Department of State Police), 77
Governor's Council on Alcohol and Drug Abuse (Department of Human Services), 66
Governor's Drug and Violent Crime Advisory Board, 77
Drunk driving, Governor's Advisory Committee on DUII, 89
Dueling penalty (Constitution of Oregon), 377
Dungeness Crab Commission, 35
Duniway, Abigail Scott, 341, 352

E

Early Intervention Services, Statewide Interagency Coordinating Council for, 164–165
Earthquakes
Department of Geology and Mineral Industries, 60
seismic rehabilitation of emergency services buildings (Constitution of Oregon), 411–412
seismic rehabilitation of public education buildings (Constitution of Oregon), 411
Seismic Safety Policy Advisory Committee (Department of State Police), 79
Eastern Oregon Correctional Institution, 47
Eastern Oregon Regional Arts Council, 177
Eastern Oregon University (EOU), 168
Eastern Oregon Youth Correctional Facility, 94
Economic Analysis Office (Department of Administrative Services), 30
Economic and Community Development Department, 51–53, 189
Economic Revitalization Team (Governor's Office), 18
Economy, 187–190. See also specific industries and sectors (e.g., Agriculture)
employment. See Employment and labor
high tech sector. See High tech industry
historic development, 348–351
impact of growth, 188–189
income, 189
land ownership and management, 189
performance, 188–189
rural, 188
state finances. See Government finance
tourism, 360
unemployment. See Unemployment
Web sites related to, 190
Ecosystem management. See Environment
Education, 161–174. See also Colleges and universities; Schools
Constitution of Oregon, 391–392
Corrections Education Advisory Board (Department of Corrections), 46–47
district bonds (Constitution of Oregon), 410
early childhood education, 163
Great Start (State Commission on Children and Families), 38
Head Start program, 163
Information and Education Division (Department of Fish and Wildlife), 57
juvenile corrections education programs, 164
Oregon Educational Act for the 21st Century, 162

Index

Family Support Council (Department of Human Services), 67

Healthy Start Family Support Services (State Commission on Children and Families), 38

Oregon Commission on Children and Families, 38

Safe and Stable Families (State Commission on Children and Families), 38

Together for Children (State Commission on Children and Families), 38

Family Health Insurance Assistance Program (FHIAP) (Insurance Pool Governing Board), 68

Family Law Section (Justice Department), 24

Family Resource Centers (State Commission on Children and Families), 38

Farms. See Agriculture

Father of Oregon, 3

FBI's National Crime Information Center (NCIC), 78

Federal government, 210–215. See also Congress, U.S.
contact information in Oregon, 215
funds from, 157
officials, 214–215
presidential elections (voting history), 279–281

Feedlots (Natural Resources Division), 33

Fertilizer (Pesticides Division), 33

Fescue
Fine Fescue Commission, 35
Tall Fescue Commission, 36
Tall Fescue Commission (Department of Agriculture), 36

FHIAP (Family Health Insurance Assistance Program), 68

Field burning, 33
Natural Resources Division (Department of Agriculture), 33

Film and Video Office, Oregon (Economic and Community Development Department), 52

Finance, government. See Government finance

Finance and Corporate Securities, Division of (Department of Consumer and Business Services), 41

Finance and Policy Analysis (Department of Human Services), 66

Finance Division (State Treasury), 22

Financial and Recovery Services Section (Office of Emergency Management), 79

Financial Fraud/Consumer Protection Section (Justice Department), 24

Financial Management Division (Housing and Community Services Department), 64

Fingerprints (Forensic Services Division), 78

Fire
Emergency Fire Cost Committee (State Forestry Department), 58
Fire Marshall, State (Department of State Police), 80
forest fires (State Forestry Department), 58
seismic rehabilitation of firefighters' buildings (Constitution of Oregon), 411–412

Fish and fishing. See also specific type of fish (e.g., Salmon)
Albacore Commission, 35
hatcheries, 5, 57, 359
Pacific States Marine Fisheries Commission, 74
Salmon Commission, 36
state fish, 3

Fish and Wildlife, Department of (ODFW), 56–57

Fish and Wildlife Commission (Department of Fish and Wildlife), 56

Fish and Wildlife Division (Department of State Police), 77

Fish Division (Department of Fish and Wildlife), 57

Five River Gallery, 180

529 College Savings Board, 23

529 College Savings Network, 23

Flag, state, 3

Floods. See also Disasters
Department of Geology and Mineral Industries, 60

Florence Arts & Crafts Association, 178

Florence Performing Arts Association, 178

Flower, state, 3

Food and food safety
food processing industry, 349–350
Food Safety Division (Department of Agriculture), 33
Laboratory Services Division (Department of Agriculture), 33
Measurement Standards Division (Department of Agriculture), 33

Foreign trade. See International trade

Forensic Services Division (Department of State Police), 78

Forensics
Forensic Services Division (Department of State Police), 78
State Medical Examiner (Department of State Police), 80

Forest fires, Emergency Fire Cost Committee (State Forestry Department), 58

Forest Resource Trust Advisory Committee (State Forestry Department), 59

Forest Resources Institute, 59

Senate confirmation of, 129, 131, 379

Governor's Arts Awards, 176

Governor's Commission on Senior Services (Department of Human Services), 67

Governor's Council of Economic Advisors (Department of Administrative Services), 30

Governor's Council on Alcohol and Drug Abuse (Department of Human Services), 66

Governor's Council on Domestic Violence, 77

Governor's Drug and Violent Crime Advisory Board, 77

Governor's Natural Resource Office, 18

Governor's Office of Education and Workforce Policy, 19

Grading (Commodity Inspection Division), 32

Grain elevators (Commodity Inspection Division), 32

Grains Commission (Department of Agriculture), 35

Grand jury service, disqualification from (Oregon Bill of Rights), 376

Granges, 351

Grants. See also Educational assistance
Grants and Scholarships Division (Student Assistance Commission), 85
Housing and Community Services Department, 62
Watershed Enhancement Board (OWEB), 92–93

Grants Pass Museum of Art, 178

Grape (state flower), 3

Grass seeds. See Seeds

Gray, Robert (Captain), 328, 331

Great Depression, 355–357

Great Start (State Commission on Children and Families), 38

Greater Condon Arts Association, 178

Gresham Art Advisory Committee, 178

Ground water. See headings starting with "Water"

Ground Water Advisory Committee (Water Resources Department), 92

Growth Account Board, Oregon (State Treasury), 23

GSPC (Government Standards and Practices Commission), 60–61

Guarantee Services/Default Prevention Division (Student Assistance Commission), 85–86

"Guilty except for insanity," oversight of persons found to be (Psychiatric Security Review Board), 81

Gun regulation (Law Enforcement Data System (LEDS)), 79

H

Habeas corpus, 388
Oregon Bill of Rights, 372

Habitat Division (Department of Fish and Wildlife), 57

Hairdressers
Advisory Council for Electrologists, Permanent Color Technicians and Tattoo Artists, 61
Board of Cosmetology, 61–62

Hairy triton (state seashell), 6

Handgun licenses (Law Enforcement Data System (LEDS)), 79

Handicapped persons. See Disabled persons

Hanford Cleanup Board (Department of Energy), 55

Harney County Arts & Crafts, 178

Hatcheries, fish, 5, 57, 359

Hatfield Marine Science Center (HMSC), 185

Hazardous waste (Land Quality Division, Department of Environmental Quality), 56

Hazelnut (state nut), 5

Hazelnut Commission (Department of Agriculture), 35

Head Start program, 163

Heald College, 173

Health care
Conference of Local Health Officials (Department of Human Services), 66
Department of Human Resources, 65–67
Family Health Insurance Assistance Program (Insurance Pool Governing Board), 67
Insurance Pool Governing Board (IPGB), 67
Occupational Safety and Health Division (Department of Consumer and Business Services), 42
Oregon Health and Science University (OHSU), 168–169, 410
Oregon Medical Insurance Pool (OMIP) (Department of Consumer and Business Services), 42
Public Health Advisory Board, 67

Health, Housing, Educational and Cultural Facilities Authority (HHECFA). See now Oregon Facilities Authority

Health insurance
portability, Oregon Medical Insurance Pool (OMIP) (Department of Consumer and Business Services), 42
uninsured population, 189

Health Licensing Office, 61–62

Health Policy and Research Office (Department of Administrative Services), 30

Health Policy Commission, Office for Oregon Health Plan Policy and Research (Department of Administrative Services), 30

Health Resources Commission, Office for Oregon Health Policy and Research (Department of Administrative Services), 30

Health Services (Department of Human Services), 66

Health Services Commission, Office for Oregon Health Policy and Research (Department of Administrative Services), 30

Healthy Start Family Support Services (State Commission on Children and Families), 38

Hearing Aids, Advisory Council on, 61

Hearings Division, Workers' Compensation Board, 43

Hearings Unit, Commissioner's Office and Program Services Division, 25

Heating fuel. See Energy

Hell's Canyon (deepest gorge), 3

Help America Vote Act of 2002, 272

Heritage Commission (State Parks and Recreation Department), 75

Heritage organizations, 180–183
　Natural Heritage Advisory Council, 84
　Oregon Heritage Commission (State Parks and Recreation Department), 75

HHECFA (Health, Housing, Educational and Cultural Facilities Authority). See now Oregon Facilities Authority

High Desert Museum, 183

High schools. See Schools

High tech industry, 188, 189, 361

Higher education. See Colleges and universities

Highland Bentgrass Commission (Department of Agriculture), 36

Highway Cost Allocation Study, 30

Highway Division (Department of Transportation), 88

Highways and roads
　development, 354–355, 359
　Historic Columbia River Highway Advisory Committee (Department of Transportation), 88
　Motor Carrier Transportation Division (Department of Transportation), 88–89
　Pacific Highway, 354
　Patrol Services Division (Department of State Police), 80

Hillcrest Youth Correctional Facility, 94

Hillsboro Community Arts, 179

Historian Laureate, 3

Historic Cemeteries, Commission on, 182

Historic Columbia River Highway Advisory Committee (Department of Transportation), 88

Historic markers (Travel Information Council), 90

Historic preservation
　Oregon Cultural Trust, 52
　Oregon Heritage Commission (State Parks and Recreation Department), 75
　State Advisory Committee on Historic Preservation (State Parks and Recreation Department), 75
　State Historic Preservation Office (State Parks and Recreation Department), 75

Historic Trails Advisory Council (State Parks and Recreation Department), 75, 183

Historical Records Advisory Board, Archives Division (Secretary of State), 19

Historical Society, 182–183

History, 323–368
　agriculture, 348–349, 359–360
　automobiles, effect of, 355
　British settlement, 327–328
　cattle and sheep business, 348–349
　chronological history by year, 362–367
　Civil War, 344
　Depression era, 355–357
　discovery of Columbia River, 328–329
　discrimination, 346–348, 355
　earliest authorities governing state, 303–304
　economy, 358–359
　environmental concerns, 360–361
　European explorers, 327–328
　evangelical movement and missionaries, 333–334
　federal action in 1800s, 344–3456
　federal action post-World War II, 359
　first natives, 324–326
　fur trade, 328–331
　geologic formation of Oregon, 324
　gold strikes in Oregon, 342, 344
　Indian wars, 337–338, 342–343
　lumber industry, 359, 361
　minorities, 346–348, 355, 357
　Oregon System, 352–353, 361
　organizations, 180–183
　political parties, 352
　post-WWII development, 358–360
　progressivism, 351–354
　Provisional Government, 336–337
　railroads, 350–351
　salmon fishing, 349, 359
　settlement of state, 330–333
　settlements, spread of, 340–341
　statehood, 343, 367–368
　territorial status, 338–340, 363–364
　tourism, 360

transportation systems, 350–351
World Wars, effect of, 354, 357–358
HMSC (Hatfield Marine Science Center), 185
Holidays, legal, 3–4
Home Care Commission, 417–418
Home rule
    Charter (Metro), 268
    Constitution of Oregon, 387
Homeland security (Office of Emergency
    Management, State Police), 79
Homicide
    aggravated murder penalty (Oregon Bill of
        Rights), 373
    Criminal Investigation Services Division
        (Department of State Police), 77
Hooley, Darlene (U.S. Representative), 213
Hop Commission (Department of Agriculture),
    36
Horse racing (Oregon Racing Commission), 82
Horses (Animal Health and Identification
    Division), 32
Hospitals and seismic rehabilitation (Constitution
    of Oregon), 411–412
Hot springs, 3
Hotlines (Technical Assistance for Employers
    Program), 25
Hours of work (Wage and Hour Division), 27
House of Representatives, State. See Legislative
    Assembly
House of Representatives, U.S. See Congress,
    U.S.
Housing
    disabled and elderly (Constitution of
        Oregon), 409
    Housing and Community Services
        Department (OHCSD), 62–65
    Manufactured Dwelling Park Community
        Relations, 63
    Manufactured Structures and Parks
        Advisory Board (Department of Consumer
        and Business Services), 41
    prices, 189
    Residential Structures Board (Department
        of Consumer and Business Services), 41
    State Housing Council, 63
    veterans. See Veterans
Housing and Community Services Department
    (OHCSD), 62–65
Housing Division (Housing and Community
    Services Department), 64
Hudson's Bay Company, 303, 330, 331, 336
Human Resource Services Division (Department
    of Administrative Services), 29
Human Resource Services Division (Department
    of State Police), 78

Human Resources Division (Department of
    Corrections), 44–45
Human Resources Division (Department of Fish
    and Wildlife), 57
Human Resources Division (Secretary of State),
    20
Human Services, Department of (DHS), 65–67
Hunting regulation, Department of Fish and
    Wildlife, 56–57
Husband and wife
    divorce statistics, 3
    separate property (Constitution of Oregon),
        415–416
Hydropower. See Electricity

I

Income, per capita, 189
Income tax, 159, 189, 384
    kicker, tax refunds, 158–159
Independent Living Council, Statewide
    (Department of Human Services), 66
Indian tribes, 5, 216–217
    Bureau of Indian Affairs, 346, 360
    Columbia River Intertribal Fish
        Commission, 216–217
    first natives of state, 324–326
    Legislative Commission on Indian Services,
        152, 217
    missionaries and, 333–334
    reservations, 216, 360
    Tribal Gaming Centers, 78, 217, 361
    wars, 337–338, 342–343
Indictment (Constitution of Oregon), 388
Indigent defendants, defense of, 126
Industry. See Economy
Information and Education Division (Department
    of Fish and Wildlife), 57
Information Management and Technology, Joint
    Committee on (Legislative Assembly), 152
Information Management Division (Department
    of State Police), 78–79
Information Resource Management Division
    (Department of Administrative Services),
    29–30
Information Services Division (Housing and
    Community Services Department), 64–65
Information Services Division (State Treasury),
    22
Information Systems Division (Department of
    Fish and Wildlife), 57
Information Systems Division (Secretary of
    State), 20
Information Systems Unit (Department of
    Corrections), 44

Information Technology Division (Student Assistance Commission), 86
Information Technology Office (Department of Administrative Services), 31
Initiative, referendum and recall, 20, 272, 281–303
 Constitution of Oregon, 378, 380
 history of, 281–282, 352–353, 361
 list of (with ballot title), 282–303
 taxes, 159
Injuries, occupational, 42–43
Inmates. See Prisons and prisoners
Insects
 Plant Division (Department of Agriculture), 34
 State Forestry Department, 58
 state insect, 3
Inspections
 Commodity Inspection Division (Department of Agriculture), 32
 motor vehicles inspection (Air Quality Division), 55
Inspections Division (Department of Corrections), 45
Insurance Division (Department of Consumer and Business Services), 41–42
Insurance Pool Governing Board (IPGB), 67
International trade
 agricultural products, 32
 Commodity Inspection Division (Department of Agriculture), 32
 consuls, 217–218
 Economic and Community Development Department, 51–53
 economic impact, 188
 Laboratory Services Division, Export Service Center (Department of Agriculture), 33
Interstate agencies and compacts
 Klamath River Basin Compact, 92
 Western Interstate Commission for Higher Education, 168
 Western States Water Council, 92
Intestate succession when no known heirs (Department of State Lands), 84
Invasive species
 Invasive Species Council (Department of Agriculture), 34
 Plant Division (Department of Agriculture), 34
Investment advisors (Division of Finance and Corporate Securities), 41
Investment Council (State Treasury), 23
Investment Division (State Treasury), 22–23
Investment of state funds, 21–23

IPGB (Insurance Pool Governing Board), 67
Irrigation, 408–409
 Constitution of Oregon, 408–409
 Water Development Loan Program (Water Resources Department), 92
IRT (Innovative Readiness Training Program), 72
ITT Technical Institute, 173

J

Jails, 3
Japanese-Americans, 348, 355
Jefferson County Arts Association, 179
Jewish merchants, 340–341, 348
Judges. See also Courts
 Circuit Judges Association, 123
 Commission on Judicial Fitness and Disability, 96, 125
 Constitution of Oregon, 387–389
 county judge, 126
 discipline of, 96, 125, 389
 Judicial Conference, 123–124
 list of, by date, 307–313
 photographs, 97–119
 retirement of, 388
 senior judges, 100
 Supreme Court Justices, 96
 temporary assignment of, 388
Judicial branch of government, 95–126. See also Courts; Judges
 Constitution of Oregon, 387–389
 districts, 3
Judicial Conference, 123–124
Judicial districts, 3
Judicial Fitness and Disability, Commission on, 96, 125
Juneteenth Celebration, 37
Juniper Arts Council, 179
Jurisdiction of courts. See specific court
Jury trials
 civil cases (Constitution of Oregon), 388
 disqualification from jury service (Constitution of Oregon), 376
 number of jurors (Constitution of Oregon), 389
 Oregon Bill of Rights, 371, 372
 selection of jurors (Constitution of Oregon), 389
Justice Department, 23–25
Justice of the peace, 126
Justices. See Supreme Court, Oregon
Juvenile corrections
 correctional facilities, 94, 164
 education programs, 164

transition programs, 94
  Youth Authority, 93–94
Juvenile delinquents
  victim's rights in court proceedings,
    374–375
  Youth Investment, 38
Juveniles. See Children

K

Keizer Art Association, 179
Kicker, income tax refunds, 158–159
Klamath Art Association, 179
Klamath Arts Council, 179
Klamath Community College, 166
Klamath Mountains, 4
Klamath River Basin Compact, 92
Ku Klux Klan, 355
Kulongoski, Ted (Governor), 12, 18
Kwanza Celebration, 37

L

Labeling
  Animal Health and Identification Division
    (Department of Agriculture), 32
  Commodity Inspection Division
    (Department of Agriculture), 32
  Food Safety Division (Department of
    Agriculture), 33
Labor. See Employment and labor
Labor and Industries Bureau, 25–27
Labor and Industries Commissioner, 16, 25
  list of, by date, 314
Laboratories
  Forensic Services Division (Department of
    State Police), 78
  Laboratory Services (Department of
    Agriculture), 33
Lake Oswego Arts Commission, 179
Lake Oswego Crafts & Art League, 179
Lakes
  deepest, 3
  largest natural bodies, 7
  total number of, 3
Land Board. See State Land Board
Land Conservation and Development,
  Department of (LCDC), 68–69, 360–361
Land Fraud trials, 353
Land Quality Division (Department of
  Environmental Quality), 56
Land Surveying, State Board of Examiners for
  Engineering and, 55
Land Use Board of Appeals (LUBA), 69

Land use planning
  congressional act of statehood, 368
  Metro, 267–268
Land use regulation and just compensation, 189
Lands, state. See State buildings and lands
Landscape Architect Board, State, 69
Landscape Contractors Board, State, 69
Landslides (Department of Geology and Mineral
  Industries), 60
Lane Arts Council, 177
Lane Community College, 166
Lane Council of Governments, 266
Lane County Local Government Boundary
  Commission, 69
Law Commission, 153
Law Enforcement Data System (LEDS) Division
  (Department of State Police), 79
Law enforcement officers. See Police
Laws. See also Legislative Assembly
  effective date, 129
  ex post facto laws (Oregon Bill of Rights),
    372
  Office of Legislative Counsel's role,
    152–153
  Oregon Law Commission's role, 153
  process of passing laws, 129, 383–384
  publication of session laws, 152–153
  veto of legislation, 18, 129, 386
Lawsuits against state, 24–25
  Constitution of Oregon, 384
  Risk Management Division (Department of
    Administrative Services), 31
Lawyers. See Attorneys
LCDC (Department of Land Conservation and
  Development), 68–69, 360–361
Learn & Serve America, 163
LEDS Advisory Committee (Department of State
  Police), 79
Legal holidays, 3–4
Legislative Assembly, 127–153
  apportionment of members, 381–382
  Audit Committee, Joint Legislative, 152
  Caucus Offices, 129
  Chief Clerk of the House of
    Representatives, 128
  chronology of sessions (chart), 130
  Committee on Executive Appointments, 151
  Committee Records, 150
  Committee Services, 149–150
  Constitution of Oregon, 379–385
  contacting legislator, 130–131
  effective date of laws, 129, 384
  Emergency Board, 151
  emergency sessions, 383

Index

Public Employees Retirement System (PERS), 81

retirement benefits and plans, tax status (Constitution of Oregon), 393

Local Officials Advisory Committee (Department of Land Conservation and Development), 68

Logging industry. See Lumber industry

Long-term care

Continuing Care Retirement Community Advisory Council (Department of Human Services), 67

Long Term Care Ombudsman, Office of the, 70

Medicaid Long-Term Care Quality and Reimbursement Advisory Council (Department of Human Services), 67

Lottery, Oregon State, 70–71, 361

Constitution of Oregon, 413–415

Gaming Enforcement Division (Department of State Police), 78

Lottery Fund, 156–157

Low-income housing (Housing and Community Services Department), 63

LUBA (Land Use Board of Appeals), 69

Lumber industry, 359, 361, 391–392. See also Forests

M

MacLaren Youth Correctional Facility, 94

Magazines, 198–200

Magistrate Division, Oregon Tax Court, 98

Malheur Field Station, 183–184

Manufactured Dwelling Park Community Relations, 63

Manufactured Structures and Parks Advisory Board (Department of Consumer and Business Services), 41

Manufacturing, 188. See also Economy

Maps

Congressional Districts for U.S. House of Representatives, 213

Oregon, cities and counties, 10

State Representative Districts, 133

State Senate Districts, 132

Marine Board, State, 71

Maritime Pilots, Oregon Board of, 87

Markers, historic (Travel Information Council), 90

Marriage

counselors (Oregon Board of Licensed Professional Counselors and Therapists), 50

divorce statistics, 3

separate property of wife (Constitution of Oregon), 415–416

statistics, 4

Martin Luther King Jr. Holiday Recognition, 37

Marylhurst University, 173

Mass transit, 267, 270

Public Transit Division (Department of Transportation), 89

Massage Therapists, Board of, 71

McGuire, Paddy (Deputy Secretary of State), 19

McLoughlin, John (Dr.), 3, 330, 331, 333

Measure 5 (1990), 160, 361

Measure 37 (2004), 189

Measure 50 (1997), 160

Measurement Standards Division (Department of Agriculture), 33

Mechanical Board (Department of Consumer and Business Services), 41

Medford Parks and Recreation Department, 179

Media, 191–208

freedom of press (Oregon Bill of Rights), 371

Mediation in workers' compensation, 43

Medicaid Advisory Committee (Department of Human Services), 66

Medicaid Fraud Unit (Justice Department), 24

Medicaid Long-Term Care Quality and Reimbursement Advisory Council (Department of Human Services), 67

Medical assistance

Medicaid Advisory Committee, 66

Medicaid Fraud Unit (Justice Department), 24

Medicaid Long-Term Care Quality and Reimbursement Advisory Council, 67

Medical examiners

Board of Medical Examiners for the State of Oregon, 71

State Medical Examiner (Department of State Police), 80

State Medical Examiner Advisory Board (Department of State Police), 80

Medical Insurance Pool (OMIP) (Department of Consumer and Business Services), 42

Medical Insurance Pool Board (Department of Consumer and Business Services), 42

Memorials and monuments, national, 5

Mental health, 189. See also Developmental disabilities

Mental Health Planning and Management Advisory Council (Department of Human Services), 66

Psychiatric Security Review Board, 80–81

Metals industry, 188

Metro, 267–268

Metropolitan service districts, 402

Mid-Columbia Council of Governments, 266

Mid-Willamette Valley Council of Governments, 266

Mid-Willamette Valley Senior Services Agency, 266

Mileage distances from Portland, 4

Military Construction Program (Oregon Military Department), 72

Military Council (Oregon Military Department), 72

Military Department, Oregon, 72
governor as commander in chief, 385

Military power (Oregon Bill of Rights), 372

Militia (Constitution of Oregon), 394

Milk (state beverage), 2

Mill Creek Correctional Institution, 47–48

Mineral Land Regulation and Reclamation Program (Department of Geology and Mineral Industries), 60

Minerals
Department of State Lands, 84
history of mining, 349
reclamation, 60

Minimum wage, 27, 189, 361

Mining. See Gold strikes; Minerals

Minnis, Karen (Speaker of the House), 128, 139

Minor Crops Advisory Committee, 34

Minorities
Advocate's Office for Minority, Women and Emerging Small Businesses, 18
African-Americans. See African-Americans
Chinese-Americans, 347–348, 355
history of, 346–348, 355, 357
Japanese-Americans, 348, 355
Office of Minority, Women and Emerging Small Business (Department of Consumer and Business Services), 42

Minors. See Children

Mint Commission (Department of Agriculture), 36

Missing Children Clearinghouse (Criminal Investigation Services Division), 77

Missionaries, 333–334

Modoc. See Indian tribes

Monmouth/Independence Community Arts Association, 179

Morrow County, Arts Council of, 179

Mortgage bankers and brokers (Division of Finance and Corporate Securities), 41

Mortuary and Cemetery Board, State, 72–73

Mother of Oregon, 4

Motor Carrier Transportation Division (Department of Transportation), 88–89

Motor home parks (Manufactured Structures and Parks Advisory Board), 41

Motor vehicles
effect of, 355
inspection (Air Quality Division), 55
taxes (Constitution of Oregon), 392–393

Motorcycle Safety, Governor's Advisory Committee on, 89

Motto, state, 4

Mount Angel Seminary, 173

Mt. Hood, 2

Mt. Hood Community College, 166

Mountain time zone, 7

Mountains, 4

Multnomah Bible College, 173

Municipal Courts, 126

Municipal Debt Advisory Commission, Debt Management Division (State Treasury), 21

Municipalities. See Cities

Murder. See Homicide

Museums
Black History Museum, 37
High Desert Museum, 183
Museum at Warm Springs, 181
Oregon Historical Society Museum, 183
Oregon Museum of Science and Industry (OMSI), 184–185
Portland Art Museum, 176
University of Oregon Museum of Natural History, 186

Myers, Hardy (Attorney General), 15, 23

N

NAFTA (North American Free Trade Agreement), 188

NAFTA-TAA, 188

Nail technology regulation, Board of Cosmetology, 61–62

Name of Oregon, 5

National cemeteries, 5

National College of Naturopathic Medicine, 173

National Crime Information Center (NCIC), 78

National fish hatcheries, 5

National forests. See Forests

National Guard, 72

National Historic Oregon Trail Interpretive Center, 181–182

National Indian Gaming Regulatory Act (NIGRA), 217, 361

National Law Enforcement Telecommunications System (NLETS), 78

National memorials and monuments, 5

National parks, 5

National recreation areas, 5

National scenic areas, 5
Columbia River Gorge Commission, 39

National trail, historic, 5
National wildlife refuges, 5
Native Americans. See Indian tribes
Natural disasters. See Disasters
Natural gas taxation (Constitution of Oregon), 393
Natural Heritage Advisory Council, 84
Natural History, University of Oregon Museum of, 186
Natural resources. See also Environment
    Department of Fish and Wildlife, 56–57
    fish. See Fish and fishing; headings starting with "Fish and Wildlife"
    forests. See Forests
    Governor's Natural Resource Office, 18
    history of economic development, 348–351
    Laboratory Services (Department of Agriculture), 33
    Land Conservation and Development, Department of, 68–69
    museums, aquariums, etc., 183–186
    Natural Resources Division (Department of Agriculture), 33
    Nature of the Northwest Information Center (Department of Geology and Mineral Industries), 60
    scenic areas. See National scenic areas
    Soil and Water Conservation Commission, 34–35
    wildlife. See Wildlife
Natural Resources Division (Department of Agriculture), 33
Natural sciences, 183–186
Nature of the Northwest Information Center (Department of Geology and Mineral Industries), 60
Naturopathic medicine, Board of Naturopathic Examiners, 73
NCIC (National Crime Information Center), 78
New Crops Development Board, 34
New Deal, 356–357
Newspapers, 192–198
    freedom of press (Oregon Bill of Rights), 371
Nez Perce. See Indian tribes
NIGRA (National Indian Gaming Regulatory Act), 217, 361
Nike Corporation, 361
9-1-1 Advisory Council (Department of State Police), 79
NLETS (National Law Enforcement Telecommunications System), 78
Nobel prize winners from Oregon, 2
North American Free Trade Agreement (NAFTA), 188

North Clackamas Art Guild, 179
North Coast Youth Correctional Facility, 94
North West Company, 303, 329, 330
Northwest Christian College, 173
Northwest Film Center, 173
Northwest Ordinance of 1787, 338
Notaries public, commissioning of, 20
Noxious weeds (State Weed Board), 35
Nuclear energy/waste
    Department of Energy, 55
    Hanford Cleanup Board (Department of Energy), 55
Nurseries, plant. See Plants
Nursery Research and Regulatory Committee, 34
Nursing
    Oregon State Board of Nursing, 73
    Walla Walla College School of Nursing, 174
Nursing homes
    Board of Examiners of Nursing Home Administrators, 73
    Continuing Care Retirement Community Advisory Council (Department of Human Services), 67
    Office of the Long-Term Care Ombudsman, 70
Nuts
    Hazelnut Commission, 36
    state nut, 5

O

Oaths
    Bill of Rights of Oregon, 371
    Constitution of Oregon, 384, 389, 391, 413
OBAE (Board of Architect Examiners), 37
OBCE (State Board of Chiropractic Examiners), 39
OCCF (Oregon Commission on Children and Families), 38
Occupational Safety and Health Division (Department of Consumer and Business Services), 42–43
Occupational Therapy Licensing Board, 73
Ocean/Coastal Division (Department of Land Conservation and Development), 68
OCH (Oregon Council for the Humanities), 182
OCTA (Oregon Cable Telecommunications Association), 208
ODFW (Department of Fish and Wildlife), 56–57
ODOT (Department of Transportation), 87–89
OERS (Oregon Emergency Response System), 79
Office for Oregon Health Policy and Research (Department of Administrative Services), 30

Roads. See Highways and roads
Rock, state, 6
Rogers, Robert (Major), 5
Rogue Community College, 166
Rogue Gallery & Arts Center, 179
Rogue Valley Council of Governments, 267
Rogue Valley Youth Correctional Facility, 94
Ross Ragland Theater, 179
Rules of administrative agencies, 19
    Office of Legislative Counsel's role,
      152–153
Rural Policy Office (Governor's Office), 19
Ryegrass Growers Seed Commission
    (Department of Agriculture), 36

S

Safe and Stable Families (State Commission on
    Children and Families), 38
Safety
    Board on Public Safety Standards and
      Training, 82
    Department of Public Safety Standards and
      Training, 81–82
    Occupational Safety and Health Division
      (Department of Consumer and Business
      Services), 42–43
    police. See Police
    State Fire Marshall, 80
    Transportation Safety Committee
      (Department of Transportation), 89
    Transportation Safety Division (Department
      of Transportation), 89
Sage Community Development, 267
Salaries. See Wages
Salem (capitol of state), 220–221, 413
Salem Art Association, 180
Salem Bible College, 174
Salmon
    Chinook salmon (state fish), 3
    history of commercial fishing, 349, 359
    lottery proceeds for restoration and protec-
      tion, 415
    Salmon Commission (Department of
      Agriculture), 6
Santiam Correctional Institution, 48–49
SAT results (chart), 162
Savings and loan associations (Division of
    Finance and Corporate Securities), 41
Savings for college tuition. See Educational
    assistance
Savings Growth Plan Advisory Committee
    (Public Employees Retirement System), 81
SBDCs (Small Business Development Centers),
    165

Scenic areas, national. See National scenic areas
Schools, 162–165
    Certificate of Advanced Mastery, 162
    Certificate of Initial Mastery, 162
    Common School Fund, 84, 391
    Constitution of Oregon, 391–392
    Counter Drug and Drug Demand Reduction
      Programs (Oregon Military Department), 72
    curriculum, 162
    districts, 6, 27
    education district bonds (Constitution of
      Oregon), 410
    Fair Dismissal Appeals Board (Education
      Department), 28
    funding, 84, 156, 159, 189, 414–415
    Oregon Educational Act for the 21st
      Century, 162
    Oregon Scholars, 85
    professional technical education, 163
    SAT results (chart), 162
    seismic rehabilitation of buildings
      (Constitution of Oregon), 411
    special education, 163–165
    Starbase program (Oregon Air National
      Guard), 72
    State Board of Education, 27–28
    student statistics, 6
    Superintendent of Public Instruction, 17, 27,
      314–315, 391
    Teacher Standards and Practices
      Commission, 86–87
Seal, state, 6, 387
Search and Rescue Program (Office of
    Emergency Management), 79
Search and seizure (Oregon Bill of Rights), 371
Seashell, state, 6
Secondary schools. See Schools
Secretary of State, 13, 19–20
    Constitution of Oregon, 386
    list of, by date, 305–306
Secretary of the Senate, 128
Securities, Division of Finance and Corporate
    (Department of Consumer and Business
    Services), 41
Seeds
    Alfalfa Seed Commission, 35
    Commodity Inspection Division
      (Department of Agriculture), 32
    Natural Resources Division (Department of
      Agriculture), 33
    Orchardgrass Seed Producers Commission,
      36
    Plant Division (Department of Agriculture),
      34
    Ryegrass Growers Seed Commission, 36

Index

Victims of crime
Crime Victims' Compensation Program, 24
rights of (Oregon Bill of Rights), 374–375
Violence. See also Child abuse; Domestic violence
Communities in Partnership to Stop
Violence Against Women and Children, 93
Governor's Drug and Violent Crime
Advisory Board, 77
Voting. See Elections

W

Wage and Hour Commission (Bureau of Labor and Industries), 27
Wage and Hour Division (Bureau of Labor and Industries), 27
Wages, 188, 189
high technology industry, 189
minimum wage, 27, 189, 361
Prevailing Wage Advisory Committee (Bureau of Labor and Industries), 27
Wage and Hour Commission (Bureau of Labor and Industries), 27
Wage and Hour Division (Bureau of Labor and Industries), 27
Wagon road companies, 344–345
Wagon trains, 334–336
Walden, Greg (U.S. Representative), 211
Walla Walla College School of Nursing, 174
Wallowa Valley Arts Council, 178, 179
Warner Pacific College, 174
Water. See also Lakes; Rivers; following headings starting with "Water"
Constitution of Oregon, 408–409
Department of Environmental Quality (DEQ), 55
Natural Resources Division (Department of Agriculture), 33
rainfall, 6
Soil and Water Conservation Commission, 34–35
Water Quality Division (Department of Environmental Quality), 56
Water Development Loan Program (Water Resources Department), 92
Water power. See Electricity
Water Quality Division (Department of Environmental Quality), 56
Water Resources Commission, 91
Water Resources Department, 91–92
Water resources development
Constitution of Oregon, 408–409
Western States Water Council, 92
Waterfalls, 7

Watershed Enhancement Board (OWEB), 92–93
Watershed management. See also Natural resources
Constitution of Oregon, 408–409
Natural Resources Division (Department of Agriculture), 33
Watershed Enhancement Board, Oregon (OWEB), 92–93
Waterways. See also Rivers
Constitution of Oregon, 408–409
Department of State Lands, 84
Ways and Means, Joint Committee on, 151–152
Web sites
URLs are given as part of addresses for state departments, agencies, officers, etc., in Executive and Legislative sections.
budget and taxes, 160
colleges and universities information, 173
federal government in Oregon, 215
state departments and agencies related to economy, 190
Weed Board (Department of Agriculture), 35
Weeds
Plant Division (Department of Agriculture), 34
State Weed Board (Department of Agriculture), 35
Welfare. See also Medical assistance
Child Welfare Advisory Committee (Department of Human Services), 66
Department of Human Services (DHS), 65–67
West Linn Arts Commission, 180
Western Baptist College, 174
Western Business College, 174
Western Interstate Commission for Higher Education, 168
Western meadowlark (state bird), 2
Western Oregon Onion Commission (Department of Agriculture), 36
Western Oregon University (WOU), 171–172
Western Seminary, 174
Western States Chiropractic College, 174
Western States Water Council, 92
Wetlands (Department of State Lands), 84
Wheat Commission (Department of Agriculture), 36
Wildlife. See also Natural resources
Department of Fish and Wildlife, 56–57
Fish and Wildlife Division (Department of State Police), 77
High Desert Museum, 183
hunting regulation, 56–57
Malheur Field Station, 183–184
State Fish and Wildlife Commission, 56

Wildlife Diversity Program, 57
Wildlife Division (Department of Fish and
Wildlife), 57
Wildlife refuges, national, 5
Wilkes Expedition, 332
Willamette University, 172, 174
Williams, Mary (Solicitor General), 24
Wilsonville Arts and Cultural Council, 180
Wine
    Liquor Control Commission, 70
    Wine Advisory Board, 35, 36, 70
    wineries, 360
Winter Recreation Advisory Committee
(Department of Transportation), 88
Women
    Advocate's Office for Minority, Women and
    Emerging Small Businesses, 18
    Commission for Women, 93
    Corvallis House Young Women's Transition
    Program, 94
    Office of Minority, Women and Emerging
    Small Business (Department of Consumer
    and Business Services), 42
    property rights of (Constitution of Oregon),
    415–416
Wood. See Lumber industry
Woodburn Art Center, 180
Woodlands. See Forests
Worker Benefit Fund, 43
Workers' Compensation Board, 43
Workers' Compensation Division (Department of
Consumer and Business Services), 43–44
Workers' Compensation Management-Labor
Advisory Committee, 44
Workers' Compensation Ombudsman
(Department of Consumer and Business
Services), 43

Working conditions, regulation
    Bureau of Labor and Industries, 27
    Occupational Safety and Health Division
    (Department of Consumer and Business
    Services), 42–43
Works Projects Administration (WPA), 356
World Forestry Center, 186
World War I, 354
World War II, 357–358
WOU (Western Oregon University), 171–172
WPA (Works Projects Administration), 356
Wrestling (Gaming Enforcement Division), 78
Wu, David (U.S. Representative), 211
Wy' East Artisans Guild, 180
Wyden, Ron (U.S. Senator), 210
Wyeth, Nathaniel Jarvis, 331

X

X-ray technicians (Board of Radiologic
Technology), 82–83

Y

Yakima Indian War, 343
Youth. See Children; Juvenile corrections
Youth Authority, Oregon, 93–94, 164
Youth Challenge Program (Oregon Military
Department), 72
Youth Investment (State Commission on
Children and Families), 38

Z

Zoo, Oregon, 185–186